# HISTORY OF THE KING'S WORKS
## VOLUME V

*Frontispiece:* Somerset House: interior of the Courtyard looking west, *circa* 1800
(Sir John Soane's Museum, Drawer xvii, set 6).

# THE HISTORY OF
# THE KING'S WORKS

GENERAL EDITOR: H. M. COLVIN

## *Volume V*
## 1660–1782

### H. M. COLVIN
*Fellow of St. John's College, Oxford*

### J. MORDAUNT CROOK
*Reader in Architectural History, Bedford College, London*

### KERRY DOWNES
*Reader in Fine Art, University of Reading*

### JOHN NEWMAN
*Lecturer at the Courtauld Institute of Art, London*

LONDON: HER MAJESTY'S STATIONERY OFFICE
1976

720·6142

ISBN 011 670571 X*

DEDICATED
*by gracious permission*
*to Her Majesty*
QUEEN ELIZABETH II

# Foreword

BY THE SECRETARY OF STATE
FOR THE ENVIRONMENT

I WELCOME this penultimate volume of the *History of the King's Works* as a worthy successor to its forerunners. It describes a period when the King's Works widened its field of activities. It ceased to be preoccupied with the Sovereign and the Court or with fortifications and became increasingly concerned with government building in the modern sense—culminating (in the present volume) in the construction of Somerset House, the first 'purpose-built' public offices; where incidentally the main rooms have recently been restored and will soon be opened to the public. Since then, successive Government Departments concerned with public works have, under different titles, steadily broadened this field of activity, so that most government building has become, directly or indirectly, their responsibility. Today this responsibility is part of a much larger Department of State, which nevertheless remains conscious of its great traditions. We are again grateful to Mr Colvin and his contributors.

PETER SHORE

# Editor's Preface

THE FIFTH volume of this *History* covers a clearly-defined period in the history of the Office of Works—the period between the restoration of the monarchy in 1660 and the reforms of 1782 described in Volume VI. For 49 of those 122 years the Surveyor-General of the Royal Works was Sir Christopher Wren, and it is Wren's surveyorship that forms the dominant theme of this volume. Though the architectural fruits of his long tenure of office are for the most part well enough known, this is the first attempt to write a coherent account of the department over which he presided for nearly half a century.

After Wren there ensued sixty years during which his post was treated as a political sinecure. Reprehensible though the system may have been, the Office of Works itself continued to fulfil its functions in a competent enough manner right up to the day in 1782 when its useless superstructure of placemen was demolished, not without some damage to the sound structure beneath. Although these were years during which the architectural initiative passed largely from the Crown to the aristocracy, the Georgian Office of Works still retained its importance as the heart of English architectural practice. Between 1718 and 1782 almost every English architect of importance held a post in the Royal Works, and for many years their Office was as much the stronghold of Palladianism as it had formerly been of Wren's empirical baroque. It was the royal palaces described in Part II to which Wren and his colleagues devoted most of their official labours: under the Georges it was the public buildings described in Part III which took up much of their successors' time. Of these the most notable was Somerset House, but the unfulfilled project for a new Parliament House is no less interesting to the architectural historian.

The four contributors wish to repeat the acknowledgements expressed in previous volumes to those who have assisted their researches. Without frequent and some-times privileged access to documents in the Public Record Office, the British Museum and the Royal Archives at Windsor this volume could not have been written. Valuable help has also been given by the Lord Great Chamberlain's Department, the Lord Chamberlain's Office, the House of Lords Record Office, the National Register of Archives, the Secretary of the Duchy of Cornwall and the Curator of Sir John Soane's Museum.

For permission to consult documents in private ownership we are grateful to the late Duke of Norfolk, the Duke of Portland, the late Duke of Marlborough, the late Marquess of Cholmondeley, Earl Spencer, Lord St. Oswald, the late Lord Monson, Sir Marcus Worsley, Bart., and the Trustees of the Chatsworth Settlement. Others to whom we are indebted for help in various ways include Mr. P. G. M.

Dickson, Mr. John Harris, Mr. R. J. Hill, C.V.O., Mr. R. C. Mackworth-Young, C.V.O., the Revd. Canon James Mansel, M.V.O., Mr. A. H. Pasmore, Miss Dorothy Stroud and Mr. K. V. Thomas.

Her Majesty the Queen has graciously given permission for the reproduction of several drawings and paintings in the Royal Collection. Other illustrations are reproduced by kind permission of the Librarian of All Souls College, Oxford, the Trustees of the 8th Earl of Berkeley, deceased, the Curators of the Bodleian Library, the Trustees of the British Museum, the Trustees of the London Museum, the Librarian of Magdalene College, Cambridge, the National Portrait Gallery, London, the Royal Commission on Historical Monuments, the Royal Institute of British Architects, the Trustees of Sir John Soane's Museum, the Society of Antiquaries of London and Westminster City Library.

All the plans and drawings have been prepared for publication in the Drawing Office of the Ancient Monuments Branch of the Department of the Environment, and the index has been compiled by Mr. R. Tatton-Brown, formerly of the same Department.

H. M. C.

THE HISTORY OF THE KING'S WORKS VOL V 1660-1782

## CORRECTION

Page 35   Line 2

For   'Carlisle' *read* 'Godolphin (who had
       succeeded Carlisle as Treasurer on
       8 May )'

*Department of the Environment.*
*December 1977.*

LONDON: HER MAJESTY'S STATIONERY OFFICE.

# Contents

## PART III

## PUBLIC BUILDINGS

### by H. M. Colvin

# List of Plates

H K W—B

# List of Figures

## PLANS

(in separate case issued with Vols. I–II)

Further plans to be issued with Vol. IV will
include Hampton Court, Kensington and Whitehall Palaces

# ABBREVIATIONS USED IN REFERENCES

| | |
|---|---|
| B.M. | British Museum. |
| *Cal. S.P. Dom.* | *Calendar of State Papers Domestic.* |
| Colvin, *Dictionary* | H. M. Colvin, *A Biographical Dictionary of English Architects 1660–1840*, 1954. |
| *D.N.B.* | *The Dictionary of National Biography.* |
| *E.H.R.* | *The English Historical Review.* |
| Farington | The Diaries of Joseph Farington, complete typescript in the Royal Library, Windsor Castle, and Print Room, British Museum. |
| *Gent's Mag.* | *The Gentleman's Magazine.* |
| Hist. MSS. Comm. | Historical Manuscripts Commission. |
| Hist. Mon. Comm. | Historical Monuments Commission. |
| Hope | W. H. St. John Hope, *Windsor Castle, An Architectural History*, 2 vols. 1913. |
| Luttrell | Narcissus Luttrell, *A Brief Historical Relation of State Affairs from 1678 to 1714*, 6 vols., 1857. |
| *Parl. Pap.* | *Parliamentary Papers* (House of Commons). |
| P.C.C. | Probate Registers of the Provincial Court of Canterbury (now in P.R.O.). |
| P.R.O. | Public Record Office. |
| RA | The Royal Archives, Windsor Castle. |
| R.I.B.A. | The Royal Institute of British Architects. |
| *V.C.H.* | *The Victoria County History.* |

## REFERENCES TO THE PUBLIC RECORDS

| | |
|---|---|
| Adm. | Admiralty. |
| AO 1 | Exchequer and Audit Department, Declared Accounts. |
| C 66 | Chancery, Patent Rolls. |
| Crest | Crown Estate Commissioners. |
| E 36 | Exchequer, Treasury of the Receipt, Miscellaneous Books. |
| E101 | ,, King's Remembrancer, Accounts Various. |
| E351 | ,, Pipe Office, Declared Accounts. |
| LC | Lord Chamberlain's Department. |
| LR 5 | Office of the Auditors of Land Revenue, Accounts (Vouchers). |
| LR 6 | ,, ,, ,, ,, ,, ,, ,, Receivers' Accounts. |
| MPC, MR, etc. | Maps and Plans. |
| PC | Privy Council Office. |

| SP | 29 and 30 | State Papers, Charles II. |
| | 44 | ,,       ,,      Entry Books of Letters. |
| T | 1 | Treasury Board Papers. |
| | 4 | ,,       Reference Books. |
| | 27 | ,,       General Letter Books. |
| | 29 | ,,       Minute Books. |
| | 52 | ,,       King's Warrants. |
| | 54 | ,,       Warrants not relating to Money. |
| | 56 | ,,       Warrants Various. |
| | 98 | ,,       Board Papers, Supplementary. |
| WO | 30 | War Office, Miscellanea. |
| WO | 47 | Board of Ordnance Minutes. |
| | 51 | Ordnance Office, Bill Books. |
| Works | | See Appendix A. |

# PART I

# The Office of Works, 1660–1782

*Chapter I*

# THE KING'S WORKS, 1660–1669

THE RESTORATION of the monarchy in 1660 meant the reconstitution of the former departments of the Royal Household, among them the Office of His Majesty's Works. The Office was re-established on exactly the same basis as before the Inter-regnum, and several of Charles I's officials survived to reclaim their posts. Inigo Jones had been dead for nearly ten years, but Francis Wethered successfully claimed the comptrollership to which he had been appointed in 1641.[1] He had been in the royal service since the 1620s, and must by now have been in his sixties. Richard Gammon, reappointed Clerk of Works at the Tower of London, was another survivor from Inigo Jones's day. The appointment of Simon Basill as Clerk of the Works at Hampton Court recalled an even earlier age, for he was the son of Simon Basill, Jones's predecessor in the surveyorship, and had himself been Clerk of the Works at Greenwich and Eltham in the previous reign. Among the Patent Artisans, John Davenport, Master Carpenter, Thomas Bagley, Master Glazier, and Michael Bastian, Chief Smith, were the only ones whose employment in the Works went back to the reign of Charles I. Bastian claimed to have 'undergone many hardshipps and imprisonments for his loyalty and good affection to His Majesty's service', including the loss of his post to 'one Drew, late Smith to the Usurper Oliver Cromwell',[2] but Davenport appears to have served throughout the Commonwealth and Protectorate.[3] John Embree, the former Sergeant Plumber, was still alive, but 'having served the usurping powers, not only as plumber, but as Surveyor of their Workes, and having purchased part of his Majestie's lands belonging to his Pallace of Whitehall, and sold and demolished the Cloysters, and divers Chappells belonginge to the Cathedrall Church of Excester', he was suspended from his office, which was given instead to Peter Brent.[4] For the post of Master Mason, vacant since the death of Nicholas Stone in 1647, there were two rival claimants, John Stone, Nicholas's son, and Edward Marshall, a leading London mason. Stone had gone over to Breda just before the Restoration to press his case in person. He claimed that his father had 'for his loyalty' been 'sequestred, plundered and imprisoned', and that he himself had 'lately horsed and armed a man for your Majesties service

---

[1] On 14 May 1660 the House of Lords ordered that he should 'be put into the Execution of his Office of Comptroller of the King's Works, until the Pleasure of the King be further known' (*Lords' Journals* xi, p. 27).
[2] SP 29/6, f. 247. George Drew was in fact employed for some months in 1660 before Bastian made good his claim: see a warrant from the Lord Chamberlain to the Treasurer of the Chamber to pay him for work performed (LC 5/137, p. 37). [3] See vol. iii of this *History*. [4] SP 29/40, f. 53; *Cal. S.P. Dom. 1660–1*, p. 586.

under Sir George Booth, and endeavoured to endeare as many of his friends to hazard in the same service'. Marshall, on the other hand, was 'a Pretender . . . who in no kind served your Majestie'.[1] Marshall, however, claimed to have been granted the post by Charles I (presumably in reversion after Nicholas Stone's death), and maintained that he had 'made it his constant endeavour to promote anything that might conduce to the service of your Majesty . . . in the late Common Council'.[2] In fact, Nicholas Stone had held two distinct offices, that of Master Mason to the Office of Works and Master Mason at Windsor Castle, and the Secretary of State (to whom the rival petitions were referred by the king), sensibly settled the matter by recommending Marshall for the former, and Stone for the latter office. Stone was lucky to get it, for at Breda he had had a stroke which incapacitated him from exercising his office in person.[3]

Hugh May, the new Paymaster, probably owed his appointment to the influence of the Duke of Buckingham. For in 1669 he told Samuel Pepys that he had served the Duke 'for twenty years together, in all his wants and dangers', and there is evidence that in 1650–1 he had been engaged in effecting the transfer of works of art from York House to Holland, where they were to be sold for the duke's benefit. In 1656 he had joined the duke abroad and, like his cousin Baptist May, later keeper of the Privy Purse, he must have been well known in Royalist circles.[4] As Paymaster he needed financial rather than architectural expertise, but he may have received some training in draughtsmanship from Peter Lely (in whose house he had been living in the 1650s), and after the Restoration he emerged as one of the leading English architects. In appointing May as Paymaster the king not only rejected a petition from a certain John Markham, who claimed that he was 'very capable' of serving the king in that capacity, but also revoked a reversionary grant of the office to Ninian Cuningham made by Charles I in 1639.[5]

Only two of the appointments made to the Office of Works in 1660–1 introduced men whose recommendation for office was loyalty or favour unaccompanied by any technical qualification. One was Sir Robert Howard, sixth son of Thomas Howard, Earl of Berkshire, a self-seeking Cavalier for whom the office of Sergeant Painter was merely a welcome addition to an income already large and soon to be larger still as he moved into the lucrative field of government finance.[6] Although this 'universal pretender' (as Evelyn called him) did in fact account for the painting of palaces and the gilding of state barges,[7] there is no evidence that he touched a paint-brush himself, and in 1663 his comfortable financial circumstances enabled him to relinquish a post that scarcely became the son of an earl and a Knight of the Bath.[8] His successor was Robert Streater, a professional painter of some ability who retained the post until his death in 1679.[9]

[1] SP 29/3, No. 112, printed in *The Note-Book of Nicholas Stone*, ed. Spiers (Walpole Soc. 1919), p. 28.
[2] SP 29/1, f. 199.          [3] *The Note-Book of Nicholas Stone*, pp. 28–30.
[4] H. M. Colvin, *Biographical Dictionary of English Architects 1660–1840* (1954), p. 382.
[5] SP 29/1, f. 197; E 351/3274 (reciting the terms of May's appointment).
[6] For his career see H. J. Oliver, *Sir Robert Howard* (Duke University Press, 1963).
[7] E 351/3420 (an account for 'painted workes' at Whitehall rendered by Howard in his own name); *Cal. S.P. Dom. 1661–2*, pp. 236, 270, 277.
[8] *Cal. S.P. Dom. 1663–4*, p. 58. Did Howard sell the Office to Streater?
[9] For assessments of Streater as an artist see T. Borenius, 'Robert Streater', *Burlington Mag.* lxxxiv (1944), and E. Croft-Murray, *Decorative Painting in England* i (1962), pp. 43–5.

The other man whose appointment can only be explained in terms of personal favour to a deserving Royalist was the Surveyor himself. John Denham had given many proofs of his loyalty since the day in 1642 when, as sheriff of Surrey, he had rashly but gallantly attempted to hold Farnham Castle against Waller. Defeated in battle, he had subsequently fought a more effective war on paper, ridiculing his parliamentary enemies in a series of squibs and satires which helped to maintain the morale of his royalist friends. When peace was discussed in 1646, Denham was one of the persons on whose removal from the royal counsels the parliament insisted. When negotiations broke down, Denham continued to serve the royal cause in secret, and in 1648 he played some part in arranging the escape of the Dukes of York and Gloucester to Holland. He had subsequently been active in various ways on behalf of the exiled Court, and after the Restoration he was clearly entitled to expect some acknowledgement of his services. According to his own account, it was in September 1649 that Charles II, 'departing from St. Germayns to Jersey was pleased freely (without my asking) to confer upon me that place wherein I now have the honour to serve', but it was at Breda in April or May 1660 that he made good his claim to the office. On 13 June 1660 Denham's patent passed the Great Seal, and early in the following year he was made a Knight of the Bath at Charles II's coronation.[1]

Though Denham was a man of taste, his abilities were literary rather than practical. As Evelyn put it, he was 'a better poet than architect',[2] and it would not have been difficult to find half a dozen other men who were at least as well qualified as he to direct the king's works. One obvious candidate was John Webb, for many years the assistant of Inigo Jones, and as such by far the most able and experienced architect then to be found in England. It was Webb's misfortune that, despite his close association with the royal works, he had held no office under the Crown which he might now reclaim. The fact that in 1642–3 he had remained in effective control of the Works while Jones was away with the king gave him no right to the succession, though he did his best to represent it in that light. Nor did it avail him that he had recently been employed by the Convention Parliament to survey the king's houses in preparation for his return. It was, therefore, in vain that Webb recalled that he 'was by the especiall comand of your Majesties Royall Father of ever blessed memory, brought up by Inigo Jones Esq[r], Your Majesties late Surveyor of the Works in the study of Architecture, for enabling him to do your Royall Father and your Majestie service in the said office', and pointed out that 'Mr. Denham may possibly, as most gentry in England at this day have, some knowledge in the Theory of Architecture; but nothing of the practique, soe that he must of necessity have another at his Majestie's charge to doe his businesse; whereas Mr. Webb himselfe designes, orders, and directs whatever given in command, without any other man's assistance.' Denham's claims on the king's generosity were

---

[1] For Denham's career see John Aubrey, *Brief Lives*, ed. A. Clark, i (1898), pp. 216–21, *D.N.B.*, and *The Poetical Work of Sir John Denham*, ed. T. H. Banks (Yale, 1928). His account of his appointment forms part of the dedication of his *Poems and Translations* (1668). The fact that the place was 'disposed of at Bredagh' is mentioned in a letter from John Webb's son-in-law John Westley to the Duke of Ormonde dated 19 March 1661/2 (Bodleian, Carte MS. 31, ff. 440–1—a reference for which I am indebted to Dr. Rolf Loeber).
[2] *The Diary of John Evelyn*, ed. E. S. de Beer (1959), p. 430 (19 October 1661).

too great to be set aside, and Webb had to be content with a promise of the reversion of the surveyorship, for which he obtained a warrant in June 1660. But even this was opposed by Denham who, according to Webb, 'stopped it at the Great Seale, under pretence only that your Petitioner was elder than himselfe, adding withal that if I had his reversion hee could not sell it'. For a time he went into retirement at Butleigh in Somerset, where he had bought an estate in 1653.[1] But without him the Office of Works was sadly lacking in architectural expertise. The only one of its senior officers who had any ability as an architectural designer was Hugh May, yet his was a post that was concerned, not with plans and elevations, but with bills and accounts. Inevitably, a Surveyor who could not himself survey was obliged to seek outside assistance. In 1661, when a new building was contemplated at Greenwich, it was William de Keyser, a former assistant of Nicholas Stone, who was employed to draw the 'uprights', and in 1667 Edward Jerman, a leading City architect, was asked to survey Windsor Castle on behalf of the Office.[2] The employment of William Samwell to design the king's house at Newmarket was another proof of the Surveyor's lack of architectural skill.[3] In these circumstances Webb's experience was too valuable to be dispensed with altogether, and in 1663 he was recalled in order to design the king's new palace at Greenwich, to superintend the fortification of Woolwich Dockyard, and to initiate others into the art of creating those theatrical settings for Court Masques of which Jones had been so accomplished a master. But, although Denham was no architect, there is sufficient evidence that he was not altogether ineffective as the administrative head of the Royal Works. He played his part in the regulation of building in accordance with the proclamation of 16 August 1661,[4] he was an active member of the Commission for the repair of St. Paul's Cathedral before the Great Fire of 1666,[5] and the Gresham Trustees found his assistance so valuable in connection with the rebuilding of the Royal Exchange that they acknowledged it by a dinner and a gift of 30 guineas.[6] For Denham the Surveyorship of the Works was far from being a sinecure: but Evelyn, politely dedicating his translation of Fréart's *Parallel of the Antient Architecture with the Modern* to 'the Superintendant and Surveyor of his Majestie's Buildings and Works', was obliged to praise him more for his efforts in paving London streets than for any architectural achievement, and when Denham died in 1669 not even the panegyrist who wrote his elegy could find anything sufficiently meritorious in his tenure of office to justify a complimentary couplet.[7] As for posterity, Denham's surveyorship, at a distance of three centuries, can only be regarded as a somewhat undistinguished prelude to that of Sir Christopher Wren.

The regulations by which Denham and his colleagues were to conduct the

---

[1] For Webb's petitions see *Wren Soc.* xviii, pp. 155–6 and SP 29/5, ff. 118–19. The abortive warrant is calendered in *Cal. S. P. Dom. 1660–1*, p. 76, and Webb's reversionary patent, complete but for the Seal, remains among the Butleigh deeds in the Somerset Record Office (DD/S/BT, Box 21).

[2] Works 5/2 (under Whitehall); 5/10.

[3] Below, pp. 214–6.

[4] R. Steele, *Tudor and Stuart Proclamations* (1910), pp. 399–400, No. 3322; *Cal. S.P. Dom. 1663–4*, pp. 86, 114, 401–2, 580–1, 612.

[5] *Wren Soc.* xiii, pp. 13–14.

[6] T. F. Reddaway, *The Rebuilding of London after the Great Fire* (1940), p. 269, n. 3.

[7] This poem by Christopher Wase will be found in SP 29/270, ff. 329–30.

business of their office were dated 4 February 1662/3, and bore the royal sign manual and the signature of the Treasurer, the Earl of Southampton.[1] They were copied word for word from those (dating from 1609) that had been in force before the Civil War. In 1660, as in 1609, the conduct of the Works was entrusted to a board consisting of the Surveyor, Comptroller, Master Mason and Master Carpenter. The chief responsibility of this board was to pass the accounts kept by the clerks of works at the several royal houses, for which purpose it was to meet once a month in the office at Scotland Yard. Payments were to be made twice a week by the Paymaster in the presence of all or some of the officers, and it was of course he who received the money from the Exchequer and who had ultimately to account personally for its expenditure. The Board's discretion in the matter of works was limited to routine maintenance, and on this not more than £40 a year was supposed to be spent at Whitehall, Hampton Court or Greenwich without warrant from the Treasury. Elsewhere the limit was £20 a year. All materials were to be obtained through the Purveyor at the most favourable rates, and neither the officers nor the principal artisans attached to the Works might act as suppliers. The Treasury had power to alter or add to the regulations, and the Surveyor was bound by the terms of his patent to 'follow and obey such good orders as are already made or shalbe thought meete heereafter to be established by us or by our Treasurer of England or by the Commissioners of the Treasury'.[2] Though the Office was a part of the Royal Household, it was thus the Lord Treasurer, not the Lord Chamberlain, to whom it was effectively subordinate. The latter might, indeed, call for repairs under his warrant, but such warrants had to be submitted regularly to scrutiny by the Treasury, and were subject to the financial limits laid down by that body.

Only in the matter of salaries was there any modification of the code established by Salisbury in 1609. Recognising that the prices of materials and labour had almost doubled since the time of James I, the Treasury agreed that some increase in the officers' salaries was called for, 'they having no Augmentation since the first making of the orders, nor doe there allowances bare any proportion with the rest of our servants of the like quality, they not having any profitts whatsoever save by our allowance only, & being bound to a daily attendance which most of our other servants are not'. It was accordingly agreed to increase the officers' salaries by one third.[3] The increment amounted in the case of the Surveyor to £97 9s. 10d., bringing his total salary up to £382 5s. 8d. This was now made up as follows:

*Paid by Exchequer*
  Fee of 2s. per day with 6d. for a clerk                                      £ 45  12s.  6d.

*Paid by Great Wardrobe*
  In lieu of livery                                                           £ 12  13s.  4d.

---

[1] The Office copy is now Works 6/368/2. For others see *Cal. Treas. Papers* i, p. 5 and *Cal. S.P. Dom. 1663–4*, p. 36.
[2] Patent Roll Charles II, pt. 36, no. 29.
[3] SP 44/13, p. 198.

*Paid by Paymaster of the Works*

| | | | |
|---|---|---|---|
| Diet, boathire and riding charges at 4s. per day | £ 73 | 0s. | 0d. |
| Allowance in lieu of Dead Pays, plus 8d. for a clerk | £ 73 | 0s. | 0d. |
| Additional allowance of 5s. 2d. per day | £ 94 | 5s. | 10d. |
| Compensation for Fees and Avails from surplus materials | £ 80 | 0s. | 0d. |
| Christmas Reward | £ 3 | 14s. | 0d. |
| | £382 | 5s. | 8d.[1] |

The allowances of the other officers were increased proportionately, making their emoluments as follows:[2]

| | | | |
|---|---|---|---|
| Comptroller | £197 | 14s. | 2d. |
| Paymaster | £189 | 2s. | 10d. |
| Clerk Ingrosser | £120 | 7s. | 6d. |
| Clerk of Works at Whitehall, Westminster & St. James's | £ 87 | 3s. | 4d. |
| Clerk of Works at Tower of London & Somerset House | £ 42 | 1s. | 3d. |
| Clerk of Works at Greenwich | £ 42 | 1s. | 3d. |
| Clerk of Works at Hampton Court | £ 42 | 1s. | 3d. |
| Master Mason | £139 | 4s. | 0d. |
| Master Carpenter | £153 | 9s. | 11d. |
| Master Joiner | £ 80 | 0s. | 0d. |
| Master Bricklayer | £ 59 | 18s. | 4d. |
| Master Plasterer | £ 59 | 18s. | 4d. |
| Master Smith | £ 45 | 12s. | 6d.[3] |
| Master Carver | £ 35 | 7s. | 6d. |
| Master Glazier | £ 19 | 9s. | 6d. |
| Master Matlayer | £ 26 | 16s. | 10d. |
| Sergeant Painter | £ 10 | 0s. | 0d.[4] |
| Sergeant Plumber | £ 20 | 5s. | 0d. |
| Purveyor | £ 77 | 11s. | 3d. |

In addition the Officers of the Works were allowed to claim 'riding charges', or travelling expenses, at fixed rates. For this purpose the Surveyor was for some reason entitled to charge less than several of his colleagues. His rate was only 4s. 10d. a day, whereas the Comptroller could charge 6s. 10d., the Paymaster 5s. 8d., and the Master Mason and the Master Carpenter 5s. 4d.

These were, by seventeenth-century standards, fairly modest incomes. Only the Surveyor could easily sustain the status of a gentleman on his official salary, and

---

[1] The first three items make up the 13s. 2d. per day which appears in the Paymaster's Accounts. The third sub-total of £94 5s. 10d. exceeds the sum of 5s. 2d. a day for 365 days by £2 14s. 0d. The difference was apparently made up by a nominal allowance for riding charges.     [2] SP 29/58, ff. 212–13.

[3] This total included £18 5s. 0d. which the Master Smith received from the Treasurer of the Chamber for the office of Master Locksmith of the Household. The two offices were often, but not invariably, held by the same person. There was also a Joiner of the Privy Lodgings, who was chiefly employed in making or repairing furniture and picture-frames, but this office was not held by the Master Joiner to the Works.

[4] The Sergeant Painter's fee was charged neither to the Exchequer nor to the Paymaster, but to the Small Customs of London.

with less than £200 each the Comptroller and the Paymaster were far from hand-somely remunerated. Other royal servants, moreover, could count on those fees and perquisites from which the Officers of the Works had been officially debarred since the reforms of 1609, which deprived them of 'fees and avails' in the form of 'waste' materials, and gave them increased allowances instead. But it is difficult to believe that these unofficial pickings were wholly unknown in the venal reign of Charles II, and for the Surveyor at least, there were subsidiary employments, such as the com-mission for repairing St. Paul's Cathedral, which brought in a supplementary salary that was perfectly legitimate.[1] In addition the four members of the Board enjoyed the use of rent-free houses, not only in Scotland Yard, but also at Hampton Court.[2] The purpose of these houses was to enable them to observe that 'daily attendance' to which they were officially bound. But there was nothing to prevent them letting the whole or a part of any house which they enjoyed, and this was undoubtedly done.[3] When one recollects that Denham was also allowed to use a vacant plot adjoining his official residence in Whitehall to erect a highly profitable range of chambers, it is less surprising to find John Aubrey reporting that he 'gott seaven thousand pounds' by his office, 'as Sir Christopher Wren told me, to his own knowledge'.[4]

The Clerks of the Works were five in number, one for each of the principal palaces and one to prepare the consolidated account for the whole Office. This last, known as the Chief Clerk, or Clerk Ingrosser, was nominated by the Treasurer, 'so that he have not dependence upon any one officer', but the others were appointed by the Surveyor. Denham inherited two of his Clerks (Simon Basill and Richard Gammon) from the regime of Inigo Jones, but presumably exercised his prerogative in favour of Thomas Rotherham (Whitehall) and Richard Gammon's son Leonard (Greenwich).[5] When Basill died in March 1663 Denham took the opportunity to give his post at Hampton Court to a personal servant named Henry Cooper for whom he also obtained the place of harbinger to the queen.[6] The Clerks, like the members of the Board, were entitled to free lodgings in their respective palaces, and

---

[1] Denham's fees as surveyor for the repair of St. Paul's are mentioned in his will (P.C.C. 57 PENN). Hugh May was in receipt of a separate salary of £30 a year as Comptroller of Works to the Queen Mother (*Cal. S.P. Dom. 1671*, pp. 561–2).

[2] After the acquisition of Kensington Palace the Surveyor and Comptroller also had houses there. The Surveyor's house at Kensington, since demolished, is marked on a plan of 1754 (Works 34/118). For survey plans showing the official houses on the Green at Hampton Court, see P.R.O., MPE 500 (1783) and 329 (1799).

[3] Evidence of this in the seventeenth century is difficult to find, but when Vanbrugh was dismissed from the Comptrollership in 1713, he was found to have let all three of his official houses, the one in Scotland Yard to Auditor Godolphin, that at Hampton Court to Lady Thomas, and that at Kensington to Mr. Addison (Works 4/1, p. 93, Works, 6/5, pp. 205, 262). He himself was living in the new house that he had built elsewhere in Whitehall. In March 1676 Hooke noted that 'Sir Christopher Wren let his house for £32 per annum for one year' (*Diary*, ed. Robinson and Adams, p. 220), but this may not necessarily have been an official house, though it is likely that it was. By the Regulation of 1705 an Officer might not let his lodgings 'without the concurrence of a majority of the other Officers'.

[4] J. Aubrey, *Brief Lives*, ed. A. Clark, i (1898), p. 219. In March 1661 he and two others (the Marquis of Ormonde and Daniel O'Neill) were authorised to prosecute those who had despoiled the royal houses during the Interregnum. They were to enjoy three-quarters of the proceeds, the king taking the remainder (B.M., Egerton MS. 2551, f. 137). For Denham's building activities in Scotland Yard, see below, p. 445.

[5] Leonard Gammon was later promoted to the Clerkship of the Works at Whitehall, Westminster and St. James's, a position in which (if Vanbrugh is to be believed) he did not prove a credit to the Office (*The Complete Works of Sir John Vanbrugh*, vol. 4, p. 12).

[6] These acts of patronage are referred to in Denham's will (P.C.C. 57 PENN).

HKW—C

must have enjoyed a good deal of leisure at times when there was no building activity to supervise. Besides his official stipend Thomas Rotherham for many years received an additional £45 a year for acting as Clerk of the Works to Queen Catherine of Braganza at Somerset House and Hammersmith,[1] and some of his colleagues no doubt supplemented their incomes by other employments.

In the case of the Master Craftsmen it was, of course, accepted that the Office of Works commanded only a portion of their time. As working members of the Board the Master Mason and the Master Carpenter received substantially larger emoluments than any of the other Patent Artisans, but both of them were leading members of their respective trades with flourishing businesses of their own. For them, as for their colleagues the Master Bricklayer, the Master Joiner, the Master Plasterer, the Master Carver, the Master Glazier, the Master Smith, the Sergeant Plumber and the Sergeant Painter, the royal service was not only a welcome addition to their income, but also an advertisement. To be one of the king's craftsmen was to be visibly at the top of one's trade, and to enjoy almost automatically the patronage of the great who saw one's handiwork in Presence Chamber or Drawing Room. When Lord Sandwich planned to refurbish the interior of his country house, it was natural that he should apply to the Surveyor of the Works 'to get a man to go with him to Hinchinbroke, to contrive with him about some alterations', and equally natural that the man the Surveyor should recommend was Thomas Kinward the Master Joiner.[2] Pepys's diary preserves the record of what must have been a typical incident, as advantageous to the client as it was profitable to the craftsman. As the only central building organisation in the kingdom, the Office of His Majesty's Works was the place where the best architectural advice was to be found, and the title of 'Master Mason' or 'Sergeant Painter' was as coveted a designation in Stuart England as 'By Appointment' has been in more recent times.

The Paymaster was in a different category. His salary was modest enough,[3] but large sums of money passed through his hands, and a seventeenth-century paymaster, like a modern banker, did not let money lie idle in his hands. He used it for his own profit, and provided he could make the payments demanded of his office, no one thought any the worse of him for enriching himself in the process. Great fortunes were made in this way, notably by Paymasters of the Army, but in the case of the Works the chronic shortage of money must severely have restricted the opportunities for profitable speculation, and there is certainly no evidence that Hugh May made his fortune as Paymaster from 1660 to 1668. He was, however, practising privately as an architect; he was involved in the commission for the repair of Old St. Paul's, and after the Great Fire he was one of the three surveyors nominated by the king to supervise the rebuilding of the City in conjunction with three representatives chosen by the Lord Mayor and Corporation.[4] For a time he also acted as Deputy Surveyor during Denham's temporary incapacity.[5] These— and perhaps other, more confidential, duties—took up so much of his time that in

---

[1] Below, p. 254, n. 4.     [2] *The Diary of Samuel Pepys*, ed. Wheatley, i, p. 303.

[3] It was supplemented by a 'poundage' of 10s. on every £100 that he handled. This 'poundage' was intended to pay the Exchequer fees for which he was liable, and does not appear to have been more than adequate for that purpose (*Cal. Treas. Books* xi, pp. 315–16, xxiii, pp. 132–3).

[4] Colvin, *Biographical Dictionary*, pp. 383–4.     [5] Below, p. 15.

March 1667 he was allowed to have a paid deputy at the Office of Works on account of his 'extraordinary business'.[1] When, in July 1668, he succeeded Wethered as Comptroller, his deputy Philip Packer took his place as Paymaster.[2] Packer was the third son of John Packer, a former Clerk of the Privy Seal, and had inherited his estate at Groombridge in Kent. In 1682 he succeeded another member of his family in the lucrative office of Usher of the Exchequer which in due course he was to hand over to his son John.[3] Even without this substantial addition to his income he had been able to build at Groombridge a handsome new house where in 1674 he entertained his friend John Evelyn.[4]

From 1660 until 1715 virtually the only administrative records of the Office of Works are its accounts and its correspondence with the Treasury. There was no Pepys to chronicle its jealousies and tribulations, nor were its activities such as to attract more than the rarest mention in contemporary journals and newsletters. Some indication of its routine in the reign of Charles II is, however, given by two documents dating from the 1660s. One is an agreement drawn up by the officers of the Works shortly after the old Regulations of 1609 had been formally confirmed by the Treasurer.[5] The other is a critique of the Office and its organisation submitted to the Treasury by an unknown person in July 1667.[6] The former document was the result of a conference held at Scotland Yard on 27 March 1663 at which the officers of the Works considered how they were to conduct their daily business. They resolved that they would 'constantly meet in the Office every morning between 8 and 9 to consider of business which is incident that day', and that 'the Clerks of the Works, Purveyor, and all the Master Artizans, do give their attendance at the same hours, if not otherwise employ'd by the Office'. No work was to be carried out without specific direction by the officers, and all current business was to be entered in a day book and crossed out when it had been done. As soon as an order was given by the officers it was to be carried out 'with all convenient expedition, especially such as immediately concern the Royal Family'. All labourers were to present themselves at the ringing of the office's bell, and were not to depart until it was rung again. Their hours of work are not specified, but they were to be allowed half an hour for breakfast, 'and no more, upon pain of losing half a day for the first time, and a whole days wages for the 2nd time'. When work was over, all timber, boards and other materials that remained unused were to be returned to the Store to be checked by the Clerk, and the Master Bricklayer and the Master Plasterer were to be responsible for the safe keeping of the 'scaffolding-stuff, tubbs, etc.', 'and give an account to the Clerk for the same upon pain of making good what is lost'. The Clerk of the Works was to make out warrants for all new materials

[1] *Cal. S.P. Dom. 1666–7*, p. 548. In May 1664 £4000 were entrusted to him 'for secret service' (*Cal. S.P. Dom. 1663–4*, p. 594).

[2] *Cal. Treas. Books* ii, pp. 362, 366.

[3] *Cal. S.P. Dom. 1664–5*, p. 339; *Cal. Treas. Books* vii, p. 436, xiii, p. 209.

[4] *The Diary of John Evelyn*, ed. de Beer (1959), p. 601. Packer's portrait remains in the house, which is described and illustrated in *Country Life*, December 1955 and in Oliver Hill and J. Cornforth, *English Country Houses: Caroline* (1966), pp. 123–30.

[5] The text was transcribed at the end of Harley's copy of the Regulations, now among the Duke of Portland's papers on loan to the B.M. (Loan 29/217, ff. 635–6).

[6] P.R.O. Shaftesbury Papers 30/24/7/601.

taken into the Store, and a duplicate of each warrant was to be left with the Surveyor or Comptroller for production at the next 'sitting day' of the Board.

The second document is entitled 'Severall proposalls humbly offered for regulating the Office of his Majesties Works', and bears the date July 1667. It is preserved among the papers of Anthony, Lord Ashley, afterwards Earl of Shaftesbury, and was evidently submitted to the Treasury, of which he was then a Lord. It is unsigned, but it displays too intimate a knowledge of Works procedure to have been written by anyone outside the Office, and recollections of the conduct of the Works under Inigo Jones point to a senior member who had held office before the Civil War. Wethered, the Comptroller, is perhaps the most likely person to have been its author. Its purpose is to show how the Office of Works, once notable 'both for able officers, good conduct, frugality of expence, and sure payment', may be 'reduced to the same order againe'. There is in fact evidence that in the summer of 1667 financial stringency induced the Treasury to scrutinise the administration of the Office with economy in view,[1] and this document is both a defence of the existing establishment and a plea for a stricter standard of conduct on the part of its officers. Accordingly it begins by rebutting the view that the 'multiplicity of officers retardeth his Majesties works, and causeth them to be long in hand', and that 'it draws a great charge upon his Majesty likewise', not only in salaries, but because, however vigilant the Surveyor may be, every officer 'will endeavour to gaine friends by doing work for them' at the king's expense. Then it goes on to discuss the proper function of each officer from the Surveyor downwards. Much of what it advocates is too obvious to be worth repeating, and some of its assumptions must, in 1667, have been somewhat unrealistic. Thus, it takes it for granted that the essential function of the Surveyor is to act as a royal architect, although the author must have been well aware that Denham was incapable of giving directions for new buildings 'by draught' as well as 'in writing'. His account of the Comptroller's duties is, however, valuable as the only formal statement of that officer's functions that has come down to us. The Comptroller is responsible for fixing the rates at which work is carried out, and for examining the bills to see that they agree exactly with the rates ('to which purpose hee is to read the bills himselfe, & not permitt the Clearke to do it'). It is his responsibility to see that no job is done by day work that might more economically be done by task, and that 'in all bargaines bee expressly incerted in what manner the work is to be done, what scantlings the Timbers shalbee of, what thickness the walls, withall particular circumstances incident to the respective trade, and in what time it is to bee finished'. The rates of pay for day-work are also fixed by him in conjunction with the other officers, 'one rate to be allowed from Lady day to Michaelmas, another from thence to Lady day againe'.[2] He is to 'peruse the check books once or twice a week at least, and be often present himselfe to see the workmen called, when the Clerk thinks least of it', and is also to 'take care that not any workman or laborer bee longer kept in work then occasion serves'. Finally he is to 'have a frequent inspection into the store'.

---

[1] *Cal. Treas. Books* ii, pp. 32, 50, 87, 131.
[2] Except at Whitehall, where, in view of the fact that 'severall are necessarily to be kept constantly in work', it may be advisable 'to allow them one moderate rate throughout the whole year'.

The functions of the Master Mason and Master Carpenter were to 'bee always present at passing the monthly books and give their opinions to the best of their knowledg for the rates of work'. In addition they were to 'cast upp by the plotts and bargaine the iust value' of work let out to task, 'the better to informe the Surveyour what monyes upon occasion may bee safely imprested upon such work'. The Surveyor with the consent of the Comptroller was then 'to give order to the Paymaster to pay the same'. Only the Paymaster was entitled to receive money from the Exchequer, and in paying it out he was to take care that it was received by 'the Party himselfe upon whose head the entry is made', and not by any intermediary. If necessary, the payee could be required to produce a witness to vouch to his identity, 'this being a speciall means to prevent false entries, & dead pays'. The author might have added that when money was short (as so often it was) what actually happened was that the Paymaster gave the workmen and labourers promises to pay known as 'tickets'.

All four of the officers were, in accordance with the Regulations of 1663, to meet once a month to pass the accounts submitted by the respective Clerks of the Works, who were to 'bee at the Office by eight of the Clock in the morning, and deliver in their books fairely written to the Comptroller, with their bills and Check books also, and then attend below [until] occasion require them to be called'. Upstairs the Clerk Ingrosser went slowly through the books, reading out the entries, while the Comptroller examined the corresponding bills to see that they tallied. Once the accounts were passed they were to be locked up by themselves in a press, of which the Surveyor, Comptroller and Clerk Ingrosser were each to have a key. Once every six months the accumulated books were to be signed by all four officers for submission to the auditor and an abstract was to be made for transmission to the Treasury.[1] No other records are referred to except a ledger for entering contracts,[2] and it is evident that no minutes were kept of the Board's proceedings. The 'day book' mentioned in the officers' agreement was of course of an ephemeral character, and at this period even the all-important Treasury warrants do not seem to have been entered in a book for reference.[3]

From these two surviving documents, together with the Regulations of 1663, a fairly clear picture therefore emerges of the routine at Scotland Yard. Some of the dishonest or inefficient practices which it was designed to prevent can also be discerned. 'False entries and dead pays' were one. The embezzlement of materials was another. The author of the 'Proposalls' insisted that even 'old decayed timber' was not to be burned by the Clerks of the Works, but was 'to be preserved for the use of the Plummer & Plaisterer, & for the officers at their monthly meetings, & for the Surveyour himselfe'. As much work as possible was to be done by task, because day work was apt to bring 'an exceeding charge upon the King'. But on no account was any taskwork to be let to any of the officers, 'because they are the vouchers of work done by other men, not of what they shall doe themselves'. Nor was any officer to buy up the workmen's 'tickets' at a discount, for having done

---

[1] Many of these abstracts survive among the Treasury Papers, though not all of them are for six-monthly periods.

[2] The ledger commencing in 1668 survives as Works 5/145.

[3] The surviving series of registers of Treasury Warrants begins in 1685 (Works 6/2).

so he would take advantage of his position to press for early payment, thus jumping the queue to his own profit and their disadvantage. Finally, the officers were neither to 'take upon them other employments', nor 'to create works to keep themselves in action'. How widely any of these abuses were practised it is not easy to say: the record that was designed to deceive the seventeenth-century auditor conceals the truth equally effectively from the modern historian. But in the matter of tickets the anonymous reformer had a specific allegation to make: the Paymaster's clerk was in the habit of buying 'divers bills at 2s. 6d. & 3s. [discount] per pound', and 'although hee ought, in regard of so faire an allowance, to expect his time, & bee paid in course, hee is nevertheless reimbursed out of the first monyes that come in, & the materials & workmen in their due course left unpaid thereby'.

Of the practical problems of architectural maintenance the documents discussed above say little. The author of the 'Proposalls' recommended 'that every year at the beginning of March, the underhowsekeepers of every his Majesties howses in charge, bee sent unto to bring in a particular bill of what defects they have observed the winter before, takeing with him the Cleark of the Works, & then about the later end of the same month, the whole body of the Office goe to view them, and make a general survey of all needfull reparations to bee done the year following in the said howses, and sett a valuation, both upon the charge of the workemanship and the materials to bee used therein, which being cast upp, and the whole fairely engrossed, shalbe presented [to] the Lord Treasurer, & Chancelor of the Exchequer, and they to signe the said survey for the warrant of the office that year'. He also urged 'that after every raine the Cleark with the underhowsekeeper goe about the howse for which he serves, and see what dripps there bee and whether any gutters bee stopped, that such defects may be forthwith mended, & not lett run to farther ruine'. This has its counterpart in the officers' agreement in 1663, where it is laid down that 'immediately after any great rain or snow the Bricklayer and Plummer do search the Gutters, Leads & Tilings, and give notice therof to the Clerk and he to the Officers of the Works'. But no record of any spring survey survives among the records of either Works or Treasury, and in practice the initiative in asking for repairs or alterations appears more often to have come from the occupants of the buildings than from the Officers of the Works themselves. The absence of any system of routine inspection was, indeed, one of the most obvious weaknesses of seventeenth-century Works organisation, and it was not until the eighteenth century, and the surveyorship of Sir William Chambers, that it appears to have been remedied.

The author of the 'Proposalls' concludes by reminding the Treasury that the basic necessity of an efficient Works organisation is a regular supply of money. The year in which he wrote was in fact one in which the conduct of the Works was acutely embarrassed by shortage of money. Hitherto the annual allowance for the maintenance of the royal palaces had been £10,000 a year.[1] This had not proved sufficient, and by May 1667 the Paymaster had spent (or owed) £8155 more than he had received.[2] In 1664 work had started on the king's new palace

[1] *Cal. S.P. Dom. 1663–4*, p. 106.
[2] E 351/3280. See also the financial statement calendared in *S.P. Dom. 1667*, p. 433.

at Greenwich, for which money had been raised from various sources, but much more was needed to continue it, and on 10 July 1667 Denham and May came to the Treasury and submitted a paper asking for supplies. Three weeks later they were recalled and authorised to borrow £5000 at a rate of interest not exceeding 10 per cent.[1] Further meetings and discussions followed in the course of which the whole establishment and organisation of the Office were reviewed by the Treasury in the hope of achieving some economies.[2] It was evidently as a contribution to these discussions that the anonymous 'Proposalls' were submitted in July. No significant change in establishment or routine appears to have resulted, but on 28 November the Officers of the Works were again summoned to the Treasury and told that from 24 March 1668 onwards £8000 a year was all that could be spared for their Office. This was part of a general policy of retrenchment forced on the king by parliamentary parsimony in the matter of supply, and also affected the Ordnance, Chamber, Jewel House, Privy Purse and other Household departments.[3] However, expenditure continued to remain at a figure well above £10,000 a year, and when May handed over the paymastership to Packer in August 1668 his account showed a 'superplusage', that is an excess of expenditure over income, of some £10,000.[4]

Denham's surveyorship lasted for eight and a half years. His first wife having died, he married again in 1665 at the age of 50. His second wife, Margaret Brooke, was young, beautiful and flirtatious. Soon the Duke of York was deeply in love with her, and although it was believed that she never became his mistress, the shame and scandal proved too much for her husband's sanity. Aubrey noted that the first symptoms of madness appeared when he set out from London to inspect the Portland Stone quarries in Dorset, but unaccountably turned back when he was within a mile of his destination. Then 'he went to Hounslowe, and demanded rents of lands he had sold many yeares before; went to the King, and told him he was the Holy Ghost'.[5] Hugh May had hurriedly to be authorised to execute the office of Surveyor.[6] By the following year Denham had recovered his sanity, and was able both to resume his official functions and to write some 'excellent verses'. But early in 1669 he was taken ill, and himself took steps to appoint a deputy, as he was entitled to do by his patent. The person whom he nominated on 6 March 1669 as his 'sole lawful and sufficient deputy' was not the Comptroller but Dr. Christopher Wren. According to his own letter to the Secretary of State his choice of Wren was 'by the King's desire intimated to me by my Lord Duke of Buckingham', and this is confirmed by the terms of the confirmatory royal warrant, in which

[1] *Cal. Treas. Books* ii, pp. 32, 44, 50.

[2] *Cal. Treas. Books* ii, pp. 87 (Officers of the Works to send their regulations to the Treasury), 237–8 (Officers of the Works 'called in about their establishment and orders'). The establishment list calendared in *S.P. Dom. 1661–2*, p. 473 can be dated by internal evidence to 1667–8, and was part of the papers submitted to the Treasury by Denham and his colleagues.

[3] *Cal. Treas. Books* ii, pp. 565, 572, vii, pp. 1647, 1651.

[4] E 351/3282–3. By 1670 payments, chiefly from the proceeds of the Hearth Tax, had reduced the 'superplusage' on May's account to £1177, and it was then transferred by agreement to Packer's account so that May's might be cleared. The agreement between May and Packer is P.R.O., E 101/683/123. For the Hearth Tax money see Privy Council Register 61, p. 276.

[5] J. Aubrey, *Brief Lives*, ed. A. Clark i (1898), p. 219.

[6] *Cal. S.P. Dom. 1665–6*, p. 354 (16 April 1666).

Wren's appointment is stated to be 'according to our particular direction & recommendation'.[1] When Denham died two weeks later, it was obvious that Wren was destined to be his successor, and on 29 March 1669 the great seal was duly affixed to his patent as Surveyor of the King's Works.[2]

Since 1661 Christopher Wren had occupied the Savilian Chair of Astronomy at Oxford, where he had previously been a Fellow of All Souls. In academic circles he was well known as a man of unusual ability in more than one field of scientific inquiry. As a member of the group of scientific scholars who later formed the nucleus of the Royal Society he had taken a leading part in the new, experimental learning of which they were the pioneers. It was as an experimental scientist that Wren was outstanding, and in devising models and other apparatus with which to test his own and his friends' theories he developed those faculties that were later to give him his facility in architectural design. At Court Wren was known not only as a brilliant don who had become a member of the king's new Royal Society, but as a member of a distinguished clerical family whose loyalty to Church and King had been proved by persecution during the Interregnum. Such a man appealed both to the king's intellect and to his generosity, and soon after the acquisition of Tangier in 1661 Charles II had tried to attract him to the royal service by offering him the reversion of Denham's Surveyorship of the Works if he would go out there to supervise the fortifications.[3] This offer Wren wisely declined on grounds of health, but it shows that works—whether military or architectural— were already regarded as a suitable field in which Wren might employ his talents. He was, in fact, beginning to take up architecture on his own account, designing a chapel at Pembroke College, Cambridge (1663) and a 'theatre' or assembly-hall for Oxford (1664). In 1663 he was consulted by the commissioners for repairing St. Paul's Cathedral, and found himself discussing the difficult problems involved on equal terms with Hugh May, Roger Pratt, Sir John Denham and John Evelyn. In 1665 he went to Paris to widen his architectural experience by seeing 'the most esteem'd Fabricks' there. Back in England he was applying himself once more to the restoration of St. Paul's when the Great Fire of London not only placed the old cathedral beyond hope of redemption, but gave Wren a unique opportunity of demonstrating his ability as an architect. Neglecting his academic duties, he was soon immersed in the task of replanning the devastated city and of designing a new cathedral whose architectural language would be 'true Latin'. When, in March 1669, Denham's illness made it clear that the Surveyorship of the Works would soon be at the king's disposal, there could be no doubt that Wren was the man to whose abilities the post would give the greatest scope. His appointment, first as Denham's deputy, and

---

[1] SP 29/257, f. 59; SP 44/30, f. 118. In his letter Denham revokes 'any verball deputations (although I know of none) if Mr. May or any else pretend; it was without my knowledge or consent in the time of my sickness or absence'.

[2] Patent Roll 21 Charles II, Part 3, m. 19. Denham had held office for life, but Wren's appointment, in accordance with a policy initiated in 1668 to discontinue life appointments to government offices, was 'during pleasure' only (cf. J. C. Sainty, 'A Reform in the Tenure of Offices during the Reign of Charles II', *Bulletin of the Institute of Historical Research* xli, Nov. 1968).

[3] S. Wren, *Parentalia* (1750), p. 260n. The exact date of the offer is uncertain, as it is associated in *Parentalia* with a letter stated by the editor to have been written in 1663, but in fact dated to 1661–2 by a reference to Dr. Baylie as Vice-Chancellor of Oxford University.

then as his successor, has already been described. In 1673 he resigned his professorship at Oxford, and on 14 November of the same year he received the honour of knighthood, two days after the establishment of a Royal Commission to rebuild St. Paul's in accordance with his designs.

Wren stepped into the Surveyor's office over the heads of two men who had good claims to the post—John Webb, who had been promised the reversion in 1660, and Hugh May, upon whom much of the burden of administration had fallen during Denham's last years. Webb's bitter disappointment is plain from the petition which he promptly addressed to the king. He reminded Charles of his past services, of his promised reversion of the surveyorship, and of the slow payment of his inadequate remuneration for his services at Greenwich. He had, he said, 'acted under Sir John Denham, a person of honour', but he 'conceives it much beneath him, to doe the like under one, who in whatever respects is his inferiour by farr. May your Majestie please if not to confirm your petitioner's grant as in the honor of a King you appear to be obliged, then to joyne him in patent with Mr. Wren, and hee shalbe ready to instruct him in the course of the Office of your Works, whereof hee professeth to bee wholy ignorant, and your petitioner, if you vouchsafe, may take care of your Majesties works at Greenwich, or elsewhere as hitherto hee hath done'.[1] But once more Webb's claims were ignored. His career had been broken by the Civil War, and expertise alone was not enough to assure him of royal favour from a king as fickle as Charles II. Abandoning a Court where his talents were so little appreciated, he retired to Somerset, where in October 1672 he died. In his will he left to his son the precious collection of books and drawings that in different circumstances he might have been glad to pass on to the new Surveyor.[2] Forty years later their rediscovery was to play a part in the change of taste which facilitated, if it did not inspire, the dismissal of Sir Christopher Wren by a Hanoverian king.

Hugh May's position was quite different. He was well known at Court, and was relying on the Duke of Buckingham, to whom he had rendered such valuable services during the Interregnum. But (as he told Pepys on 21 March) the duke had been 'so ungrateful as to put him by', and had 'brought in Dr. Wren'.[3] May was not, however, forgotten. 'He tells me [Pepys noted] that the King is kind to him, and hath promised him a pension of £300 a year out of the Works'—an increment which was in fact granted to him three days later as a mark of the king's 'gracious acceptance' of his 'loyal and faithfull service'.[4] This, he told Pepys, 'will be of more content to him' than a place rendered irksome by 'their present wants of money'. With a total salary of nearly £500 May might well think that after all he had not been too badly treated. Nor was this the end of royal favour. For in the following year he succeeded his brother Adrian both as Clerk of the Recognizances in the Courts of Common Pleas and King's Bench and as inspector of French and English gardeners at Whitehall, St. James's, Greenwich and Hampton Court.[5] The latter

---

[1] SP 29/251, f. 186 (printed in *Wren Soc.* xviii, p. 156).
[2] Wren had had access to them at some time, for in one of his architectural tracts he refers to a notebook of Pirro Ligorio which he had seen 'among the Collections of Inigo Jones' (*Wren Soc.*, xix, pp. 124, 128).
[3] *The Diary of Samuel Pepys*, ed. Wheatley, vol. 8, pp. 268–9.
[4] SP 44/30, f. 122.           [5] *Cal. S.P. Dom. 1670*, pp. 195, 294.

post was worth £200 a year, while the former entitled him to a fee of 3s. 4d. for each recognizance. In addition he was in 1673 to be appointed Comptroller of the Works at Windsor, and to receive from 1675 onwards the handsome fee of £500 a year for his services in repairing and remodelling that castle.[1] During the years from 1670 onwards Hugh May must therefore have been very comfortably off. Although still the subordinate of a man younger—and for the moment less experienced in architectural matters—than himself, he had not come so badly out of the contest for office of which Christopher Wren was the victor.

[1] *Cal. Treas. Books* v, pp. 82, 361, 1036, 1459; vi, pp. 111, 503.

*Chapter II*

# THE SURVEYORSHIP OF SIR CHRISTOPHER WREN

THE SURVEYORSHIP of Sir Christopher Wren was the longest in the whole history of the Office of Works. For all but fifty years he presided over the Board which regulated its affairs. The octogenarian who was ungraciously dismissed in April 1718 had served six crowned heads and acknowledged the authority of twenty-four successive Lord Treasurers. In a country which went through as many political vicissitudes as England did between 1669 and 1718 so long a tenure of office was in itself something of an achievement. It is true that Wren's post was not among those that were politically significant, but his patent had duly to be renewed at the commencement of each new reign, and, as the history of the Comptrollership will show, renewal was not necessarily automatic. But Wren did more than hang on to an office of profit for 49 years. For most of that time he was the undisputed arbiter of English architectural taste. Like Inigo Jones before him, he was essentially a Court architect, but under the later Stuarts the architectural patronage of the Court extended beyond the narrow limits of Whitehall to which Jones's superlative talents had been so largely confined, and during his tenure of office Wren designed and supervised in person the erection of one of the largest cathedrals in Europe, devised more than fifty churches to serve the specific needs of Anglican worship, planned two large hospitals, one for soldiers, the other, more monumental, for sailors, built a customs house, a theatre, an observatory, an academic library, and several other university buildings. All this was outside his routine duties, which included the maintenance of Windsor Castle, half-a-dozen palaces, the Tower of London, the Houses of Parliament and several subsidiary buildings.

Wren was therefore not only an architect of unusual distinction: he was also an able administrator who could cope with the many practical problems inherent in large-scale building operations. Creative genius and executive ability are not always united in the same head: but Wren had a measure of both, and the combination does much to explain why the protégé of Buckingham and Charles II proved equally acceptable to James II, to William and Mary, and to Anne. A Court architect for 49 years must necessarily be something of a courtier himself, and Wren no doubt knew his way about Whitehall in more than an architectural sense. But his interests were too intellectual for him ever to become an habitué of Charles II's 'sad, vicious, negligent Court', and this detachment may have been another quality that served him in good stead. For once his early connection—such as it was—with Buckingham was severed, he had no known patron, and could not be identified with any particular faction, in or out of office. It cannot be said that he was not politically involved. On three occasions—in 1685, 1689 and 1701—he stood for parliament as a Tory, and in 1715 he supported his son's candidature for Windsor in a manner that was unashamedly partisan.[1] But Wren's genius was not political, and he appears to have made little mark in the Commons. He was therefore not among those whose prominence in the political scene marked them out for deprivation of office either in 1688 or in 1714. The Revolution of 1688 must, nevertheless, have given Wren some anxious moments. 'You are happy', he told a country gentleman, 'who can enjoy your Quiet in a Garden undisturbed, with wealth & plenty about you, wee are bound to our good behaviour uncertain which way the next wind may tosse us, ... and therfore watch as those who travell in suspected places'.[2] This was written while James II was still on the throne. When William III took his place there was a new danger—that the king would dismiss Wren to make way for some favourite architect from France or Holland, or that he would be prevailed upon to confer the surveyorship upon some aspiring Whig. Fortunately St. Paul's had the queen's whole-hearted support, and if Wren's dismissal was ever discussed, her solicitude for the cathedral may well have been decisive in keeping him in office.[3] And so, competent, courteous and generally respected, Wren retained his post long enough to become an established figure whose security of tenure seemed almost unquestioned. When he succeeded Denham in 1669 he was 37. At 50 he was designing Winchester Palace for Charles II. At 60 he was busy building for William and Mary at Whitehall and Hampton Court. When Queen Anne came to the throne he was 70, when she died he was 82. It was time to retire, but by now office had doubtless become too much of a habit for Wren to relinquish it voluntarily, and in the end he outlived not only his own usefulness as a servant of the Crown, but also the architectural fashions that he had helped to create. Then, a Tory in a world that regarded him as a relic of an aesthetically outmoded past, he was dismissed to make way for a place-seeking Whig armed with a portfolio of 'Palladian' drawings.

Although Wren's personality as an architect emerges clearly enough from his buildings, our understanding of the way in which he conducted the affairs of his office is limited. At Scotland Yard no minutes were kept until 1715, and the accounts rarely reveal anything beyond the names of the craftsmen employed and the amounts due to them. Wren himself wrote no memoirs, kept no diary, did not even correspond regularly with anyone about his public or private affairs. From the journal of his colleague Robert Hooke much can be learned about their joint responsibility for the rebuilding of the City Churches, but Hooke was never an official of the Works, and he tells us little about the affairs of that Office.[4] So far as the monthly meetings

---

[1] Below, pp. 120–1.
[2] *Wren Soc.* xii, p. 23. The letter is merely dated 'May 14th', but the year is probably 1687 (see Margaret Whinney in *Archaeological Jnl.* cx, 1953, p. 210).
[3] Jane Lang, *Rebuilding St. Paul's* (1956), p. 137.
[4] When May was ill in 1673 Hooke notes that 'Dr. Wren told me of Mays sickness and place', which

of the Board were concerned, Wren no doubt maintained the routine laid down in the regulations of 1663.[1] But unlike his predecessor, Wren was a practising architect, and much more of his time must have been devoted to drawing, estimating, and discussing practical details with the Master Workmen. His functions as a creative designer did in fact correspond closely to those envisaged by the anonymous author of the 'Proposalls' of 1667:[2]

> When the Surveyour hath made a designe for any work commanded and his Majesty hath approved thereof, then to make an estimate of the charge, and communicate the same with his Majesties Intentions to the rest of the officers, that every one of them may know what is to bee done. . . . And that when the Estimate is perfected hee present it to his Majesty; that hee may know the charge before the work begin.
>
> When the work is of any considerable importance, hee cause a modell thereof to bee made, whereby every particular part being exactly discovered, all manner of alterations may bee avoided. Lett the modell nevertheless bee of no great cost, if of pastboord it sufficeth. And when it is done hee is to shew it to his Majesty for his more full satisfaction.
>
> Hee [must] have all his designes and moulds ready before hee enters upon bargaining with the workmen; which at first will submit to reasonable rates rather then miss the work, but whatever is to be agreed for afterwards they will exact extreamly.

The personal contact with his royal master implied in this account was in fact a common occurrence in Wren's life. The informality with which Charles II conversed with men like Evelyn and Pepys must certainly have extended to his Surveyor, and many of Wren's designs must at one time or another have been laid out in the king's closet for his inspection. Once, in conversation with Evelyn, Charles called for crayon and paper, 'and then laying it on the window stoole, he with his owne hands, designed to me the plot for the future building of White-hall.'[3] Had Wren kept a diary, it would undoubtedly have contained some similar instances of the king's interest in matters architectural.[4] As it is, the written evidence of Wren's contacts with Charles II is meagre. But we know that in December 1687 James II personally inspected the Royal Mews with Wren with a view to rebuilding them, and that in March 1694 William III 'went to Winchester, and took with him Sir Christopher Wren to survey the house there, in order to goe on with building that which was begun by King Charles the 2d.'[5] Queen Mary, too, 'pleased herself from time to time, in examining and surveying the Drawings, Contrivances, and whole progress of the Works' at Hampton Court, thus giving Wren 'many Opportunities of a free Conversation with her Majesty, not only on the Subject of Architecture,

---

may suggest that Wren thought of Hooke as a possible successor to May as Comptroller (*The Diary of Robert Hooke*, ed. H. W. Robinson and W. Adams, 1935, p. 38).

[1] Payments at the rate of 40s. a month for the 'dyett of the Officers of the Works at their monthly meetings about his Majesty's service' are a regular item in the Paymaster's accounts.

[2] Above, p. 12.

[3] *The Diary of John Evelyn*, ed. E. S. de Beer (1959), p. 466.

[4] For 'a new method of fortification invented by the king', and commemorated by a medal, see *Cal. S.P. Dom. 1668–9*, p. 653.

[5] Hist. MSS. Comm., *Downshire* I (i), p. 282; N. Luttrell, *Brief Historical Relation* iii, p. 280.

but other Branches of Mathematicks, and useful Learning',[1] while the Works records preserve the terms of a summons which he received from Queen Anne in 1714 to go to speak with her about alterations at Kensington.[2]

These conferences between sovereign and surveyor might result in a formal warrant for the work in question from the Lord Chamberlain.[3] But sometimes the Lord Chamberlain was ignored and the Surveyor received the royal directions by word of mouth. This informal mode of communication might be flattering to the Surveyor, but was deprecated by the Treasury. In 1667 it was by 'verbal order' that Charles II directed Denham 'to give to Captain Lanier a part of the old house at Greenwich'. Shocked at this casual alienation of part of a royal palace, the Treasury resolved to move the king 'that such things pass not but by regular way of examination, so that His Majesty be not taken by surprise'.[4] There was nothing in the Orders of 1663 to guide the Surveyor in situations of this kind, but his conduct on receipt of the king's verbal order was laid down in those of 1705. He was to submit an estimate to the Treasury, and either the Clerk Ingrosser or the Paymaster was then to solicit for a warrant to proceed. In this way the Treasury was kept informed of prospective expenditure on building, and could, if necessary, restrain any undue extravagance. One such instance is revealed by a letter which Wren wrote to the Secretary of State in 1699. Before leaving the country in June, William III had (he wrote)

> [given] me two thinges in command: one was the alteration of some Roomes for his convenience at Kensington, and this is in hand and will be speedily brought to a conclusion; the other was an alteration of his own Lodgings at Newmercat to be don by October, when he thought he might be there. I layd before the Lords of the Treasury the Estimates of both, and . . . spared noe attendance, but without effect; for I was told at the board that His Majestie had noe great valew for Newmercat; that they had taken care for soe many thinges relating to Workes & Gardens, that they could not comply with more expence; I submitted, and humbly prayed they would interpose between His Majesties displeasure, if this seem'd a Neglect in me, which they promised they would doe. . . . The sollicitude I am in least this should be misrepresented makes me presume upon your Favor to lay this before His Majestie.[5]

King and Treasury were, however, rarely at variance: indeed, the Stuart kings and queens frequently attended meetings of the Treasury, and were often present when matters relating to the Works were under discussion. The laconic entries in the Treasury Minutes rarely reveal more than the final decision, but Roger North gives the substance of one architectural dialogue that took place in the Treasury Chamber. Charles II, anxious to see Winchester Palace completed in his lifetime,

[1] S. Wren, *Parentalia* (1750), p. 326.
[2] Works 6/5, p. 301.
[3] Such warrants were entered by the Lord Chamberlain's clerks in his Warrant Books (P.R.O. LC 5), and by the Surveyor's clerk in one of the Office Books, e.g. Works 6/3, which contains copies of the warrants received from the Lord Chamberlain between 1701 and 1709.
[4] *Cal. Treas. Books* ii, p. 91.
[5] Bodleian Library, MS. Facs. d. 121, f. 129. For another letter from Wren, this time addressed to the king in person, see *Wren Soc.* iv, pp. 58–9.

caused Sᵣ. Christopher Wren the Surveyor General of his buildings to attend at the Treasury when the King was there, and pressed him to say how soon it might be done. He answered in two years. The King urged him to say if it might possibly be done in one year. Yes, said the Surveyor General, but not so well, nor without great confusion, charge and inconvenience, and however diligent they were, he feared disappointments would happen. Well, said the King, if it be possible to be done in one year, I will have it so, for a year is a great deal in my life.[1]

In April 1688, when James II contemplated restoring the 'pallace' at Berwick-on-Tweed, it was likewise at the Treasury that Wren was 'directed to attend the king'. He brought with him a detailed report on the building that he had obtained from a surveyor at York. Having read this out to the king, he 'explained it to him & told him whom I had imployed . . . but when I asked His Mᵃᵗⁱᵉ what he had to command in this businesse, his answer was he thought he should repair the Chapell, & he would consider of it'.[2]

This basic relationship between king, Treasury and Surveyor was altered only once between 1660 and 1718, when for two years—1700–2—the Earl of Ranelagh had the status of a minister of works to William III, giving directions and issuing warrants without reference to the Treasury.[3] With this exception it can be said that it was in the Treasury that most of the effective decisions about the conduct of the King's Works were made. As servants of the Crown the officers of the Works were not subject to any regular form of parliamentary control. If Lords or Commons desired alterations to their respective Chambers, or to some other public building, they might indeed summon the king's Surveyor to the bar of one of their Houses to give information or advice, but the outcome was either a 'humble address' which in due course came before the Treasury Board for approval, or a warrant from the Lord Great Chamberlain which the Surveyor was expected to submit to the Treasury for approval in the usual way.[4] Only in the urgent circumstances of a coronation or a royal funeral was Treasury control tacitly relaxed. At other times failure to submit estimates and to await warrants was by no means unknown, but retribution was apt to follow. In 1709 Lord Treasurer Godolphin was so enraged by the discovery of works carried out without proper authority that, 'knowing no better way to put a stop to this evil than to forbear the paying for them', he temporarily forbad all supplies to the Paymaster, and ordered the relevant regulation to be engrossed on parchment and hung up in all the offices of Her Majesty's Works.[5]

One of the most persistent causes of unauthorised work was the repair and embellishment of private lodgings in the royal palaces. The author of the 'Proposalls' of 1667 was evidently speaking from experience when he wrote of the tendency of every Works official 'to gain friends [at Court] by doing work for them'; and Hugh May had the same compulsion in mind when he told Pepys that the Surveyorship was an awkward position to hold, because 'under their present wants of money' it meant disobliging so many people who could not be allowed 'to do what they desire to their lodgings'.[6] There were of course always private individuals close to the king

[1] Roger North, *Lives of the Norths*, ed. Jessopp, ii (1890), p. 207.
[2] *Wren Soc.* xviii, p. 68: letter to John Etty at York.   [3] Below, p. 35.
[4] Below, pp. 392, 401.   [5] Below, p. 49.   [6] *The Diary of Samuel Pepys*, ed. Wheatley, i (1896), pp. 268–9.

who could count on well-fitted apartments maintained at royal expense, and the records of the Office testify to the favour shown in this way to the Duke of Buckingham, the Countess of Castlemaine, the Earl of Albemarle, and others. But for members of the royal household and those who enjoyed lodgings 'by grace and favour' the king's generosity was limited to keeping the structure 'wind and water tight', and all alterations, internal repairs and decorations were supposed to be paid for by the occupant. An order to this effect was formally made by the Treasury in 1667,[1] and it was subsequently reiterated on many occasions. But the distinction between essential and non-essential repairs was not always clear, and the frequency with which the Treasury found it necessary to draw attention to the rule shows that Clerks of the Works were not always inflexible in their interpretation of their duty. Steps also had to be taken to prevent private persons altering or enlarging their lodgings in such a way as to weaken them structurally or make it impossible at some future date 'to reform, beautify or new build any part of the palaces' in question.[2] In 1684 the Surveyor was instructed to inform the Treasury whenever any person 'sues for or obtains any permission or warrant to you for such building', and not to permit it until the king's pleasure had been ascertained.[3] The principle was thus established that 'no building ought to be made within his Majesty's palace(s) but what is supervised by the Surveyor of his Majesty's Works',[4] but this too had to be reaffirmed in 1715, when for the first time clauses dealing with the repair of private lodgings were included in the regulations of the Office. Article 17 laid down that 'no work shall be ordered by the Board to be done' in any lodgings 'but such as are necessary for keeping out the weather & preserve the Building unless by his Majesty's especial command to be signified by his Chamberlain of the Household to the Commissioners of the Treasury', while an additional order dated 22 July (and subsequently incorporated as Article 28) strengthened the Office's hand in dealing with work carried out at private expense. It insisted that no lodging might be altered or enlarged without the approval of the king and the knowledge of the Surveyor.[5] These two orders were due to the Comptroller, Sir John Vanbrugh, who persuaded his friend the Earl of Carlisle to get them signed by the king 'purely to enable the Board to withstand the importunities of Persons they could not else have refus'd, without bringing more enemys upon them, than they were able to contend with'.[6] In 1716 both the Secretary of State and the Comptroller of the Household were politely reminded of Article 28 and obliged to apply to the Lord Chamberlain before being allowed to proceed.[7] In 1718, soon after Wren's dismissal, a new and stricter order was issued declaring that the king would be at no further charge in repairing or furnishing lodgings inhabited by persons 'of his grace and favour only, without their having any legal estate or interest therein'.[8] On receiving this order the Board instructed Clerks of the Works to stop all works in the royal palaces forthwith, 'except such as are now in hand for His Majesty's immediate service in the Royal Apartments', but pointed out to the Treasury that among those affected were

---

[1] *Cal. Treas. Books* ii, p. 50.     [2] *Cal. Treas. Books* iv, p. 553; vii, p. 1080.
[3] *Cal. Treas. Books* vii, p. 1080. It was in the spirit of this ruling that in 1686 the king refused to rebuild the Lord Chamberlain's office in Whitehall (*Cal. Treas. Books* viii, pp. 807, 875, 891).
[4] *Cal. Treas. Books* viii, p. 679.     [5] *Cal. Treas. Books* xxix, p. 648; Works 6/11, pp. 7, 13.
[6] T1/220, f. 145.     [7] Works 6/6, pp. 152–5.     [8] Works 6/11, f. 110.

'the Dutchess of Munster, Countess of Pigbourg, Madam Kilmansack, the Grand Mareschall, Mr. Robethon' and several other members of the king's German household, none of whom had any 'legal estate or interest' in their lodgings. A total prohibition on work for these favoured individuals would, they said, 'unavoidably be attended with inconveniences too obvious to mention'.[1] The Treasury declined to be helpful, but the 'inconveniences' were avoided by a verbal order from the king followed by a series of warrants from the Lord Chamberlain sanctioning various works for the benefit of the Germans.[2]

The Treasury not only circumscribed the Office of Works by regulation and warrant: it imposed a considerable burden on the Surveyor by frequent demands for information or advice on matters quite outside the Office's normal responsibility. Hundreds of these requests reached Wren's desk in the course of his surveyorship, and for many years he kept a private register of them.[3] This register was begun to record cases which he was called upon to deal with under the royal proclamation of August 1661 restraining building in the neighbourhood of London and Wesminster.[4] This was a continuation of the policy initiated by Queen Elizabeth and once enforced with the help of the Court of Star Chamber. After the Restoration an attempt was made to reimpose it by the authority of the Privy Council, but without the Star Chamber it lacked effective sanction, and in many cases more emphasis was placed on proper planning and the use of brick and stone than on the total prohibition of all new building within two miles of London and Westminster. Even in this form it was short-lived. For it became a casualty of the Court's failure to control the House of Commons. In 1675 a Bill was introduced to restrain building in the vicinity of London, and might eventually have passed into law, but for the fact that in 1678 it re-emerged as a proposal to raise supplies by taxing all new buildings erected since 1656.[5] Once the principle of restraint was linked with the contentious matter of supply it was doomed, and the Privy Council evidently lost confidence in its ability to impose by prerogative a policy that was not endorsed by parliament. So the attempt to control building did not outlast the reign of Charles II. But so long as it persisted the Surveyor and his subordinates at the Office of Works

[1] Works 6/7, f. 84.      [2] Works 6/7, ff. 124–5; Works 4/1, 6 November 1718.
[3] Now in Sir John Soane's Museum, and printed in full in *Wren Soc.*, vol. xviii.
[4] R. Steele, *Tudor and Stuart Proclamations* i (1910), pp. 399–400, No. 3322.
[5] *Commons' Journals* 9, pp. 319, 339, 442, 452, 505; A. Grey, *Debates in the House of Commons* (1763) iii, pp. 9–10, v, pp. 179–189; B.M., Add. MS. 32471, ff. 65–72. Attempts to reintroduce the same combination of measures in 1685 and 1689 came to nothing (*Commons' Journals* 9, p. 739; 10, pp. 112, 127, 153, 321, 324) In February 1709 a new Bill to restrain building in London and Westminster was introduced, much to the alarm of the building trades, who petitioned against it, but it was eventually dropped (*Commons' Journals* 16, pp. 123, 136, 148, 209, 284, 288, 294, 300, 313, 315, 324, 333, 345, 347, 357, 374). In April 1709 the Officers of the Works received instructions from the Lords to propose a bill 'for the better regulating the manner of Building in the Cities of London and Westminster, in relation to the beautifying the streets, etc.' This was eventually introduced in April 1711 but suffered the same fate as its predecessors (*Lords' Journals* 18, p. 706; 19, pp. 263, 273, 275). The draft is printed in Hist. MSS. Comm. *House of Lords* N.S. ix, pp. 128–30. The measures advocated were similar to those embodied in the Acts of 1707 and 1709 'for the better preventing Mischiefs that may happen by fire', whose provisions included important architectural regulations affecting all new buildings erected in London and Westminster (*Statutes at Large*, 4, pp. 325–7, 365–7) and the bill may have been abandoned on the ground that it was redundant. For general accounts of the measures taken to restrain building in London after the Restoration see N. G. Brett-James, *The Growth of Stuart London* (1935), chap. xii, and Carolyn A. Edie, 'New Buildings, New Taxes, and old Interests' in *Journal of British Studies* vi(2) (1967), pp. 35–63.

were the 'Police Architectonical' upon whose judgement the Privy Council relied.[1] It was to Wren that particular cases were referred for investigation and report, and if the amenities of a palace were threatened, it was his responsibility to take the initiative in bringing the matter to the Council's attention. Thus in 1671 it was at Wren's instance that the Privy Council put a stop to some unlicensed building in Soho which he considered to be undesirable on both social and architectural grounds, and because the Sergeant Plumber reported that it was interfering with the supply of water to Whitehall, which depended on springs rising in this area.[2]

The last case of this kind in Wren's register occurred in 1676. After this it is Treasury 'references' which provide the bulk of the entries. The matters referred to the Surveyor General by the Treasury ranged from the state of the public records to the military value of Greek Fire.[3] Any petition for remuneration by a workman, for the payment of arrears, for the reversion of an artisan's patent, for the repair of private lodgings or of public offices was liable to be referred to Wren and had to be looked into and reported on. Sometimes this involved consultation with the Surveyor of Crown Lands, as in 1681, when Nicholas Barbon offered to rebuild the Mews in return for a lease of their existing site.[4] Sometimes it meant searching the Office Books, as in 1716, when someone claimed that it was the king's responsibility to repair Glastonbury Abbey.[5] When Evelyn's house at Deptford was half wrecked by the Czar of Russia's unruly entourage, it was Wren who had to go and assess the damage;[6] when Vanbrugh was building Blenheim Palace it was Wren who was expected to scrutinise the contracts on behalf of the Treasury and 'view the works in order to estimate the charge of the whole'.[7] Often it meant examining bills submitted to the Treasury by another department which employed its own workmen: the Exchequer, the Mint, the Customs, the Horse Guards, the Lottery Office or the Mews. In the case of the Mews this became a regular routine until in 1716 the Office of Works assumed full responsibility for their maintenance. However much of this bureaucratic business Wren may have succeeded in delegating to his subordinates, it is evident from his answers that he felt bound to investigate many of them in person. For none of these surveys and reports was Wren entitled to any official remuneration other than the riding charges involved, nor is it likely that he was open to unofficial presents from the parties involved, though they would certainly have been proffered.

The Treasury lords who made so many demands on the Surveyor's time also largely controlled the appointment of his staff. All the officers except the Clerks of the Works were appointed by patent, and no patent could pass without Treasury approval. When a post fell vacant it was, however, the Treasury's normal practice to consult the Board about the fitness of any applicants, and to accept its recommendation. Occasionally an influential person would intervene on behalf of an individual candidate. When Maurice Emmett, Master Bricklayer, died in 1694,

---

[1] Hawksmoor laments the failure to support 'the Police Architectonical' in his *Remarks on the Founding and Carrying on the Buildings of the Royal Hospital at Greenwich* (1728), reprinted in *Wren. Soc.* vi, p. 18.
[2] *Wren Soc.*, xviii, pp. 18–19.
[3] For the records, see below, pp. 382–3. For Greek Fire see *Cal. Treas. Books* xxi, pp. 402, 423.
[4] Below, p. 209.　　[5] Works 6/6, p. 160.
[6] *Cal. Treas. Papers 1697–1702*, pp. 158–9.　　[7] *Cal. Treas. Books* xx, p. 356.

Thomas Hughes applied for the post and 'Sir Christopher Wren made a report of his being very well qualified for that employment, but Her late Majesty dying before anything could be perfected for him, the late Earl of Portland interpos'd in favour of Mr. Richard Stacey', who was accordingly appointed early in 1695.[1] When Stacey died in 1714, it was, however, Hughes who succeeded him to enjoy the post for over ten years. The appointment of John Smallwell as Master Joiner in 1718 was due to the recommendation of the Duke of Newcastle, for whom he had been working at Claremont and elsewhere.[2] In 1708 one candidate for the post of Sergeant Plumber had the support of Vanbrugh and Hawksmoor, who certified that he was 'now employed as Plumber at Blenheim House, . . . where he hath performed the severall works, in very good and workmanlike manner', but the successful applicant was Joseph Roberts, who was recommended by Wren as 'a very able and honest man' to whom large sums of money were owing by the Crown, and who nevertheless 'continued with great cheerfulness' to give credit to the Office.[3] It was not often that royalty concerned itself in the appointment of mere artisans, but when it did so its intervention was decisive. The appointment of the courtier Sir Robert Howard as Sergeant Painter has already been mentioned as an instance of favour on the part of Charles II.[4] In 1678 Alexander Fort obtained the reversion of the post of Master Joiner, which he claimed on Thomas Kinward's death in 1682. But, 'for reasons best known to himself', Charles II refused to allow his patent to take effect. James II declined to lift the suspension, owing (so Fort claimed) to the unlucky circumstance of his being employed on the Duke of Monmouth's house in Soho at the time of the latter's rebellion ('although he was no otherwise concerned than in doing his work at the said house'), and it was not until the accession of William and Mary that he was at last allowed to enjoy the benefits of his office.[5] All the appointments made immediately after the Restoration were for life, but in 1668 the Treasury began to make new appointments to government offices tenable only 'during pleasure'. This policy was relaxed under Danby in the 1670s, with the result that several Works posts were granted for life, including those of Master Mason (1673 and 1678), Sergeant Plumber (1676) and Master Bricklayer (1677). But from 1679 onwards all Works appointments held by letters patent were 'during pleasure' only.[6]

At a time when the building trades were to a large extent in the hands of closely-knit families, it was inevitable that there should be a strong hereditary element among the master craftsmen retained for the king's service. If the business was flourishing and the son competent, an application for a reversionary grant of the office would receive favourable consideration. In this way Joshua Marshall was permitted to succeed his father Edward as Master Mason, John Grove junior to step into his father's place as Master Plasterer, Charles Atherton to take over as Master Plumber from his father-in-law Peter Brent.[7] Three generations of Irelands served the king

[1] *Cal. Treas. Books* x, pp. 835, 928; Works 6/5, pp. 266–7.

[2] Works 4/1, 10 and 17 June 1718. Smallwell's accounts for his work for the duke are B.M., Add. MS. 33442.    [3] T 98/1, f. 312; *Cal. Treas. Papers 1708–14*, p. 187.    [4] Above, p. 4.

[5] Works 6/14, f. 59; *Cal. Treas. Books* viii, pp. 1652–3.

[6] J. C. Sainty, 'A Reform in the Tenure of Offices during the Reign of Charles II'. *Bulletin of the Institute of Historical Research* xli (November 1968).

[7] *Cal. Treas. Books* iv, p. 421; *Wren. Soc.* xviii, pp. 40, 41. In the same way John Churchill succeeded his father-in-law Matthew Banckes in 1706, having acted as his deputy during the last year of his life (*Cal. Treas. Books* xx, pp. 285, 295, 646).

as Master Glazier from 1677 to 1725, while the two Streaters, father and son, successively occupied the post of Sergeant Painter from 1663 until 1703, when, for reasons unknown, the younger Streater was suspended from office.[1] Thomas Highmore, who took Streater's place, was the uncle of his successor James Thornhill, whose descendants continued to hold the position until the reign of George III.[2]

But hereditary competence alone was not a sufficient recommendation for office. As Wren once explained to the Treasury, 'there is another ability requisite, which is a good stock to carry on the workes of the Crown, where the business required is suddain, & the time short, and seldom ready money'.[3] In these circumstances Joseph Roberts's cheerful willingness to give further credit to an Office already deeply in his debt was a valuable asset. In 1706 it was Charles Hopson's substantial capital as well as his proved ability in his 'art' that led the Board to recommend him for the office of Master Joiner in preference to Thomas Fort, whose father had just died in penury.[4] The majority of the Master Artisans were in fact leading members of their respective trades. Many of them held office as Wardens or Masters of their respective companies, and Hopson the joiner went on to become Sheriff of London and Middlesex and Sir Charles Hopson before his death in 1710.

Although the Master Craftsmen had a prescriptive right to employment on the royal works, they did not enjoy a monopoly of the tasks that the Officers of the Works had to offer. When major works were in progress, outside craftsmen had to be engaged alongside the regular Works contractors, and individual artists of excellence might always be brought in for specific tasks. Thus at Hampton Court Hopson was employed in preference to Alexander Fort, 'as being the man that had the best materials and such numbers of men, as might finish [the king's new apartment] by the time his Majestie had appointed', and the decorative ironwork was entrusted to the brilliant French smith, Jean Tijou, instead of to William Bache, the Master Smith.[5] This freedom in the choice of workmen had, as Wren pointed out to the Treasury in 1704, always been the Office's practice, 'as by a great many examples in their Books, ever since the Restauration and in all times before, will appear. The Officers having ever asserted a power over the Patentees to employ whom they please when necessity requires (which they are judges of, as they are of the prices) without which power they could not be responsible for the performance in tyme, and the Patentees would be too apt to impose upon the Office by enhauncing the price of worke'.[6]

Occasionally means were found to pay a retaining fee to a favoured artist for whom there was no vacancy in the Office of Works. Thus in 1684 the post of Chief Painter, previously held by Sir Peter Lely, was revived for the benefit of Antonio Verrio, then employed as a decorative painter at Windsor Castle. The salary of £200 a year was paid by the Treasurer of the Chamber, not by the Paymaster of

---

[1] T1/86, ff. 478–9. For the works and career of the two Streaters see E. Croft-Murray, *Decorative Painting in England* i, pp. 226–8. The statement that Robert Streater jr. shared the office with Robert Highmore from 1703 until his death in 1711 is not, however, correct, and the petition cited above makes it clear that Streater was dismissed against his will.

[2] Sir James Thornhill was succeeded by his son John Thornhill, who in 1757 resigned in favour of his brother-in-law William Hogarth (d. 1764).     [3] Works 6/14, f. 115.

[4] There was 'not money to inter the deceased' (Works 6/14, f. 115).

[5] For Hopson see Works 6/14, f. 59, for Tijou, below, p. 170–4.     [6] Works 6/14, f.59.

the Works.[1] The post of 'Sculptor in Ordinary to the King' was another Court appointment independent of the Works establishment. It was worth £50 a year, and the duties included the custody of the royal collection of 'Moulds, Statues and Modells'. It went back to the reign of Charles I, when it had been held by the French sculptor Isaac Besnier. In 1660 the post was reclaimed by Isaac's brother Peter, upon whose death in 1693 it went to Caius Gabriel Cibber, a sculptor of Danish origin long resident in England. When he died in 1700 no further appointment was made.[2] Daniel Marot, the French Huguenot architect whose work for William III included the staircase at Het Loo and the parterre at Hampton Court, held no formal position in England, but for some years he was in receipt of an annual fee of £75 out of the Privy Purse.[3]

One outstanding English craftsman had to wait for many years for an established post in the Works. This was Grinling Gibbons, whose incomparable virtuosity as a wood-carver had been brought to the king's notice in 1671 by John Evelyn. Evelyn also introduced him to Wren, who 'faithfully promised to employ him for the future', and to Hugh May, who soon made good use of his talents at Windsor.[4] Here Gibbons was allowed £100 a year to keep his own workmanship in repair.[5] It was not, however, until the reign of William and Mary that he could be formally installed as Master Sculptor and Carver in Wood. This post had been created in 1661 on the ground that 'the Art of Sculpture or Carving in Wood is an Art peculiar of itself' which was not catered for by 'any other Art of manuall workmanshipp whereof Our Services are already furnished'.[6] Its first holder had been Henry Phillips, a carver of whose abilities little is known. Towards the end of his life he retired from active participation in the Works, and his place (though not, it seems, his office) was taken by his cousin William Emmett, brother of Maurice, the Master Bricklayer.[7] As soon as Phillips died in 1693 the post was given to Gibbons, who later on was to become Master Carpenter and as such a member of the Board. Much of Gibbons's most accomplished woodcarving was done for the embellishment of the royal palaces, and in later years he was to be associated with Wren in grandiose designs for monuments to William and Mary.[8]

In the appointment of Clerks of the Works, Wren, like Denham, was governed

[1] *Cal. S.P. Dom. 1684–5*, p. 83; *Cal. Treas. Papers 1702–7*, p. 93; *Cal. Treas. Books* viii, pp 1012, 1702, 1845, 1969, 2118. In 1688 Verrio lost his post. According to Vertue he 'was so angry with the government that he refus'd to work for King W[m].'. His place was given jointly to the portrait-painters, John Ryley and Godfrey Kneller. For his works in the royal service see E. Croft-Murray, *Decorative Painting in England* i, pp. 53–7.

[2] SP 29/2, f. 83; H. Faber, *C. G. Cibber* (1926), pp. 12–15. In 1698 Cibber claimed that he had 'performed the Duty of the said Place & Office at White-Hall, Hampton-Court, Windsor, Kensington, & elsewhere for His Majestie's service' (*ibid.*, p. 13).

[3] *Cal. Treas. Books* xv, p. 373, xvi, p. 402, xvii, p. 1050; below, p. 171.

[4] David Green, *Grinling Gibbons* (1964), pp. 33–5; below, pp. 320 *et seq.*

[5] *Cal. Treas. Books* viii, pp. 1463–4, 1490, 1829. He continued to receive this fee up to the death of Queen Anne, after which it was discontinued (Works 6/7, p. 142). The office of 'Surveyor and Repairer of the Carved Work at Windsor' was, however, revived in 1724 and given to James Richards, but at a reduced fee of only £50 per annum.

[6] Works 6/2, f. 12.

[7] According to George Vertue William Emmett was 'Sculptor to the Crown before Gibons' (Walpole Soc. *Vertue Notebooks* i, p. 129), and payments in which he is referred to as 'Carver of the Works' were indeed made in 1688–92 (*Cal. Treas. Books* x, p. 1). But Phillips continued to receive his fee as Master Carver until his death in 1693, and he is referred to as Gibbons's immediate predecessor in the warrant for the latter's patent (*Cal. Treas. Books* x, pp. 387, 716, 1138). Evidently Emmett was no more than his acting deputy. Phillips refers to William Emmett as his 'cousin' in his will (P.C.C. 193 COKER).     [8] Below, p. 456.

by the Orders of 1663, which reserved the nomination of the Clerk Ingrosser to the Treasury, but left him free to choose the remaining clerks himself. In doing so he was expected to obtain the approval of the other officers of the Board.[1] These arrangements were confirmed by the Orders of 1705, which laid down that 'a Clerk of the Works (when a place is void) shall be as formerly nominated by the Surveyor and his Qualification for the Employment approved by the other three Officers or any two of them and when a Clerk is once admitted and sworn he shall not be displaced but by Order of the Lord High Treasurer or Commissioners of the Treasury'. The Surveyor had sometimes to defend his prerogative. In 1678 he successfully resisted an attempt by Sir Robert Howard, the predatory Auditor of the Exchequer, to obtain a reversionary grant of the clerkship of the works at Whitehall for a relation of his named Thomas Nevill, but two years later Nevill was admitted (perhaps by agreement) to the lesser post of Clerk of Works at Greenwich.[2] It was in exceptional circumstances (to be described later) that in 1715 the Treasury temporarily deprived Wren of what he described in a letter to Lowndes as 'the Antient Right and Privilege of my Office, in the Nomination of my Clerks, a Right that has been Granted me in every Reign for these Fifty Years'.[3]

The number of Clerks fluctuated with the number of houses maintained by the Office. Before the Civil War there had been seven, but immediately after the Restoration there were only four, one for Whitehall, Westminster and St. James's, one for the Tower and Somerset House, one for Hampton Court and one for Greenwich. In 1670 the recent acquisition of Audley End by Charles II necessitated a fifth, who in 1675 also took charge of the king's new house at Newmarket. A sixth was appointed in 1687 to take care of the half-completed palace at Winchester, and a seventh in 1689 to superintend the works at Kensington House, just purchased by William III from the Earl of Nottingham. Another Clerk was added in 1716, when the Mews and the Savoy were placed under the Office's care. Windsor was under separate management until 1715, but thereafter its Clerk was on the same footing as the others. Each Clerk was assisted by a Labourer in Trust, who looked after the stores and acted as foreman of the 'daymen', that is the labourers employed directly by the Office. According to the Orders of 1705 Labourers in Trust were to be approved by the Surveyor and were each to have 'his Lodging and a Dogg in the Storeyard'. They were paid up to 6d. a day more than other labourers.[4]

The names of Wren's Clerks will be found in Appendix D. Many of them passed their entire working lives in the service of the Office, and made little mark outside it. Among them, however, were some able men who could do more than merely keep accounts and carry out instructions from Scotland Yard. The outstanding case was that of Nicholas Hawksmoor. Appointed Clerk of the Works at Kensington in 1689, he had been Wren's personal clerk since the age of eighteen, and was for many years his principal draughtsman and assistant. By the age of 30 he was beginning to practise on his own, and soon became not only an important figure in the Office of Works

---

[1] This was not normally recorded in writing in the Office's books, but in January 1703/4, the Master Mason and Master Carpenter, as members of the Board, signed a formal declaration that they were 'satisfied that Ralph Buckle is qualified to be Clerk of Her Majesty's Works at Newmarket' (Works 6/14, f. 55).
[2] *Cal. S.P. Dom. 1678*, pp. 549, 580, 599; *Cal. Treas. Books* v, pp. 1077, 1464; vi, pp. 292, 704.
[3] T1/187, f. 22.    [4] Works 6/368/3, art. 14.

but also one of the leading English architects. His greatest architectural opportunities were provided by private patrons like Lord Leominster and by the Commissioners appointed in 1711 to build churches in the London suburbs, but it was in the Surveyor's office that he served his apprenticeship, and it was the Office of Works that remained his base and provided him with regular employment.[1] William Dickinson was another of Wren's clerks who could and did assist him at the drawing board. He was probably a son of the William Dickinson who was Clerk Ingrosser from 1660 to 1702. The elder Dickinson seems to have been a 'writing clerk' rather than a man with any architectural skill. But the younger one was a competent surveyor and draughtsman who acted as Wren's assistant in connection with the rebuilding of the City Churches and the repair of Westminster Abbey. He was, in the words of the younger Wren, 'a person that has served my father many years with great fidelity, diligence and skill'.[2] His first post, the clerkship of the works at Greenwich, came to an end when that palace became a hospital, but he subsequently served as Comptroller's Clerk at Windsor, and in 1713 returned to the central office as Clerk of the Works at Whitehall.[3] John Scarborough, Dickinson's predecessor at Greenwich and later Clerk of the Works at Winchester, was a measuring clerk rather than an architectural designer in his own right. Henry Winstanley, Clerk of the Works at Newmarket and Audley End from 1679 to 1702, is best known as an engraver and as the ingenious builder of the first Eddystone lighthouse. He had been employed at Audley End by the Earl of Suffolk before its purchase by Charles II, and he therefore had special qualifications for taking charge of the royal palace, of which in 1688 he published a set of engravings dedicated to James II, the Earl of Suffolk and Sir Christopher Wren.[4]

Though most of Wren's clerks were adequately qualified for their duties, there was one who appears to have owed his appointment more to the fact that he was related to Wren than to any special aptitude for his official duties. This was John Ball, whose wife Anne was Wren's cousin.[5] He was Surveyor or Clerk of Works at Windsor from 1671 until his death in 1685, when he was succeeded by his son John Ball, junior. Some years later the younger Ball had to give up his official residence at Windsor, which stood in the way of William III's garden improvements, and was compensated by the additional post of Clerk of Works at Hampton Court, vacant in 1698 by the death of Henry Simmonds. According to Simmonds's widow, Wren had promised to appoint her young son to his father's place, with a suitable deputy to execute the office until he was of a fit age to carry out the duties himself. But, despite the widow's protests, Wren had her evicted in order to make way for his kinsman.[6] Ball's advancement was not yet complete, for 'not thinking [the clerkship of the Works at Hampton Court] sufficient compensation' for the loss of his house, Lord

[1] For Hawksmoor's career and works see Kerry Downes, *Hawksmoor* (1959).
[2] Blenheim Palace archives, F.1.43 (C. Wren to the Duchess of Marlborough, 10 March 1710/11).
[3] For his career, see Colvin, *Biographical Dictionary*, pp. 173–4.
[4] *D.N.B.* It should, however, be noted that the first Clerk of Works at Audley End was John Bennet (perhaps a relative of Lord Arlington), and it was not until 1679 that Winstanley succeeded him, apparently on the nomination, not of Wren, but of Lord Treasurer Danby (*Cal. Treas. Books* v, pp. 1044, 1286).
[5] She was the eldest daughter of Wren's uncle, Matthew, Bishop of Ely. See the pedigree in Monson MS. xxxiv, f. 104.
[6] *Cal. Treas. Books* xv, pp. 57, 62, 272; xvi, pp. 35, 191; *Cal. Treas. Papers 1697–1702*, p. 330.

Treasurer Godolphin was subsequently persuaded to give him the additional post of Auditor to Prince George of Denmark, with a salary of £150 per annum.[1] Although Ball may have been a competent accountant, he was, by his own admission, unskilled in architecture and drawing, a deficiency which at a later date was to prove fatal to his career in the Office of Works.

The two John Balls were not the only members of Wren's family who were indebted to him for office. There appears to have been some relationship between the Surveyor and Thomas Bateman, whom in 1696 he appointed Clerk of the Works at Winchester, and who, on his recommendation, subsequently became Assistant Surveyor and Solicitor to the Commissioners for building St. Paul's Cathedral.[2] And in 1702 it was Wren's own son Christopher who succeeded the elder Dickinson as Clerk Ingrosser. The office was, of course, in the gift of the Lord Treasurer, but in this instance the complaisant Godolphin must have agreed to fall in with Wren's wishes to give his son the senior clerkship of the works. Though Wren evidently hoped that his son would become an established member of the Office, and perhaps even that he would eventually succeed him as Surveyor,[3] the younger Wren never made a reputation for himself either as an architect or as an administrator. In 1716, when Sir Christopher was no longer in effective control of the Office, the son was deprived of his post and retired to the Warwickshire estate which his father had purchased for him.

Over the appointment of his colleagues the Paymaster and the Comptroller Wren had little or no influence. When Philip Packer died in 1686 he was succeeded by Thomas Lloyd, who had obtained a reversionary grant of the office in 1677.[4] He had previously been Solicitor to the Treasury.[5] He did not carry out the duties of either office in person, employing Col. Thomas Taylor as Deputy Paymaster and Philip Burton as Deputy Solicitor.[6] How Lloyd occupied his time, and to whom he was entitled for office, it has not been possible to ascertain. His successor, Charles Dartiquenave (pronounced Dartineuff) was a more interesting character. Reputed to be an illegitimate son of Charles II, he was a well-known figure in London society and a firm supporter of the Whig party. The pleasures of the table were his greatest delight, and his reputation as an epicure was celebrated by Swift and satirised by Pope. In the reign of William III he had been secretary to George, Duke of Northumberland (son of Charles II and Barbara Palmer), and keeper (by purchase) of Bushy Park.[7] His appointment as Paymaster of the Works in 1706 was presumably a reward for political support. Unlike his predecessor, he appears to have performed his duties at the Office of Works in person, and in 1709 the Whig government, 'well satisfied with his faithful and prudent management', increased his salary by £100 per annum.[8]

---

[1] Monson MS. xl, ff. 16, 24.   [2] Jane Lang, *Rebuilding St. Paul's* (1956), p. 198, n. 2.
[3] Below, pp. 36–7.
[4] *Cal. Treas. Books* v, p. 793. In 1685 he claimed that the office was vacant as a result of the king's death, and that his reversion ought to take effect, but he had to wait until Packer died in the following year (*Cal. Treas. Books* viii, pp. 86, 1129).   [5] *Cal. Treas. Books* vi, p. 16, viii, p. 24.
[6] *Cal. Treas. Books* vi, p. 16. For Taylor's military title see *Cal. Treas. Papers 1708–14*, p. 590.
[7] R. R. Tighe and J. E. Davis, *Annals of Windsor* (1858), ii, p. 473; *Cal. Treas. Papers 1557–1698*, pp. 32–3. See also Hist. MSS. Comm. *Portland* iv, pp. 344, 657, 662.
[8] *Cal. Treas. Books* xxiii, pp. 132–3. There is a biography of Dartiquenave in *D.N.B.*, a Kit-Kat portrait in the National Portrait Gallery, and a monumental inscription at Albury, Herts.

During Wren's surveyorship the office of Comptroller was held by three men: by Hugh May until his death in 1684, by William Talman from 1689 to 1702, and by John Vanbrugh from 1702 onwards. From February 1684, when May died at the age of 61, until Talman's appointment in May 1689, the office was left vacant. The omission to make any appointment for five years is difficult to explain, but it suggests that the post was no longer regarded as essential for the functioning of the Office. In 1713 it was, indeed, referred to as having 'commonly been a sinecure',[1] and during his tenure of the office May had certainly been largely occupied in remodelling Windsor Castle. When he died it was Wren who succeeded him as Comptroller of the Works at Windsor, and the need for a new Comptroller at Whitehall may not have seemed very pressing. By the time Talman took office the systematic checking of stores and accounts for which the Comptroller was supposed to be responsible must have been in abeyance for at least five years, and it may be doubted whether he ever resumed the practice, for, like his predecessor, he had special duties elsewhere.

Talman's special responsibility was Hampton Court, and there he enjoyed an independent status as second-in-command to the Earl of Portland, who in June 1689 had been appointed superintendent of all the king's gardens, with powers 'to oversee and direct any plantations and works therein'.[2] This was a new post, but it was the equivalent of the inspectorship of the royal gardens held in the reign of Charles II by Adrian and Hugh May, which had lapsed on the latter's death. The importance of the royal gardens in the reign of William and Mary can be judged from the fact that between 1689 and 1699 expenditure on them amounted to over £88,000, half as much as the total outlay by the Paymaster of the Works on all the royal palaces during the same period.[3] The Hampton Court gardens accounted for well over half the Earl of Portland's expenditure, and must have occupied a large part of his deputy's time.

William Talman was the second son of a gentleman with a small estate at Eastcott, near Devizes. When the father died in 1663, he left the Wiltshire property to his elder son Christopher, but William inherited the lease of three houses in Westminster, and from 1678 onwards he enjoyed the sinecure office of King's Waiter in the Port of London, worth £52 a year. Nothing is known about his education, but by the 1680s he had emerged as one of the leading designers of country houses for the English aristocracy. At Chatsworth he had created a new and grander formula for the facade which was evidently based on Versailles and Marly and was soon to supersede the more insular elevations of Hooke, May, Pratt and Winde, with their hipped roofs and dormer windows.[4] Who was responsible for his recruitment into the Office of Works is not clear: it may have been the Duke (then the Earl) of Devonshire, for whom he was rebuilding Chatsworth, or it may have been Lord Monmouth, who at this time was the principal dispenser of royal patronage.

[1] B.M., Portland Loan, Harley Papers xlvi, ff. 637–42.
[2] *Cal. Treas. Books* ix, p. 102. Strictly speaking, Talman was Comptroller, George London Deputy Superintendent (see below, p. 457).
[3] E 351/3469, 3465, printed in *Wren Soc.* iv, pp. 29–38. During the same period the Paymaster's outlay was £175,500.
[4] On Talman see M. D. Whinney in *Jnl. of the Warburg and Courtauld Institutes* xviii (1955) and John Harris, *ibid.* xxiii (1960).

As an architect of ability who was in touch with developments abroad Talman was a valuable addition to the Office. But as a member of the Board he proved to be difficult and quarrelsome. For Wren he showed no friendship and little respect: indeed his conduct was that of a rival rather than a colleague. His unfriendly attitude soon became apparent when part of the new buildings at Hampton Court collapsed in December 1689, killing two workmen and injuring eleven others. In a written report he did his best to throw the blame on his superior officer, and when both he and Wren were summoned before the Treasury he stuck pugnaciously to his guns. The confrontation was recorded word for word in the Treasury minutes:

> The Surveyor General and Comptroller of the Works called in and their reports were read.
>
> *The Surveyor* objects against Mr. Latham (in the Comptroller's Certificate) for a madman, and sayes the work has stood a new tryal in a hurrycane.
>
> *Mr. Tallman* says My Lord Chamberlaine's lodgings kept the wind absolutely from this building and that Latham is not madd.
>
> *Mr. Banckes* saies there are 24 peers next the Garden and but 4 stones crackt, and the cracks no bigger than a haire's breadth, that the building every day it stands is stronger and grows lighter.
>
> *Mr. Tallman* saies every pier is crackt, that one may putt his finger in.
>
> *Mr. Oliver* says none of the masons Mr. Tallman brought understood so good work as this is.
>
> *Mr. Tallman* sayes that *Pierce, Thompson* and another (in his certificates) are three masons that Sir Christopher imploys,[1] that the piers are all hollow, and crampt with iron to keep them together.
>
> *Sir Ch. Wren* 'What was done for greater Caution ought not to be malitiously interpreted'.
>
> *Tallman.* 'Pray let 6 be chosen by me, and 6 by you to judge in this matter'.
>
> The Lords think they'l never agree, one part will say one thing th'other another.
>
> *Wren.* 'I'le putt it on this, a man cannot put his finger in the cracks'.
>
> *Mr. Tallman* says they are stopt.
>
> The Lords say this is a matter of fact, that they'l appoint indifferent persons to view the same. . . . [2]

In 1699 Talman not only espoused the cause of Henry Simmonds's widow against Wren and his kinsman John Ball, but went so far as to petition the Treasury for the Comptrollership of the Works at Windsor which Wren had held without interruption since 1684.[3] These tactics might in the end have brought Talman some preferment at Wren's expense. But it was not only in the Office of Works that he made enemies. One after another he quarrelled with nearly all his private clients, including the Duke of Devonshire and the Earl of Carlisle. When King William died in 1702 it was Carlisle who became Queen Anne's first Lord Treasurer, and in that capacity

---

[1] At St. Paul's, where Pearce, Thompson and Latham were all mason-contractors. Both Pearce and Latham were, however, at variance with Wren over their contracts at St. Paul's, which explains their readiness to join forces with Talman in giving evidence against him at Hampton Court (cf. Jane Lang, *Rebuilding St. Paul's*, 1956, pp. 114, 129, 138–9).

[2] *Wren Soc.* iv, p. 73.

[3] *Cal. Treas. Papers 1697–1702*, p. 330; *Cal. Treas. Books* xiv, p. 87.

he made it his business to see that Talman's patent was not renewed. On 20 May 1702, at a Treasury meeting attended by the queen, Carlisle and the Chancellor of the Exchequer, Talman was dismissed and Mr John Vanbrugh was appointed to be Comptroller of the Queen's Works in his place.[1]

The death of William III also terminated another appointment which cannot have been altogether agreeable to Wren. The Earl of Portland's responsibility for the royal gardens had lasted until May 1699, when he resigned all his offices at Court.[2] His place as the king's principal minister was taken by his rival the Earl of Albemarle. But Albemarle's interests did not include gardening, and it was the Earl of Ranelagh who took over this part of Portland's functions. Richard Jones, Earl of Ranelagh (d. 1712), was the paymaster of King William's army: but he was considered to have 'a good taste in Architecture, Painting, and Gardening', and fellow-noblemen were in the habit of taking his advice in such matters.[3] The warrant which he received from the king in June 1700 made him 'Sur-intendent generall of oure Buildings & of our Works in our parks, with full & ample power to supervise controul & order all the respective officers in our said Buildings & Works'.[4] The salary was £400 per annum payable by the Paymaster of the Works.[5] Ranelagh's commission was therefore more extensive than Portland's: like Colbert, Louvois and Villacerf in France, he was in effect a minister of works, and both the Officers of the Works at Whitehall and the royal gardeners were subject to his direction. But as Paymaster of the Forces he could not give his undivided attention to the Works, and he does not seem to have concerned himself much with the internal affairs of the Office.[6] What he did was to ascertain the king's wishes and pass them on to the Board. For him, as for Portland before him, Hampton Court was his principal responsibility. It was by his orders that the Water Gallery was demolished to make way for the new river terrace, and he was a party to the contract between the Surveyor-General and Antonio Verrio for painting the king's bedchamber.[7] The relationship between himself as 'sur-intendent', the Lord Chamberlain as the normal channel for communicating the king's wishes, and the Treasury as the authority for all expenditure, appears never to have been thrashed out, and friction might well have arisen had Ranelagh's tenure of office been prolonged.[8] But it came to an end with the king's death in 1702, and the experiment was not continued by Queen Anne.

---

[1] *Cal. Treas. Books* xvii, p. 33.

[2] N. Luttrell, *Brief Historical Relation* iv, pp. 513–14.

[3] J. Macky, *Journey through England* i (1724), p. 46. For his advice to Lord Conway see *Cal. S.P. Dom. 1679–80*, p. 623; *Cal. S.P. Dom. 1683*, i, pp. 105, 128, 166, 172. In 1693 his house at Chelsea was taken as a model for the Earl of Rochester's new house at Petersham, and he was named as arbitrator in the building contract (Surrey County Records S.C. 13/26/102–3). He superintended the enlargement of the Duke of Ormonde's house at Richmond in 1704–5 (below, p. 218).

[4] Works 6/2, f. 125. In *Wren Soc.* iv, p. 66 it is wrongly stated that Ranelagh's commission was limited to Hampton Court. The warrant instructed the Attorney and Solicitor General to prepare a patent, but this does not appear on the Patent Roll. For his position and responsibilities, see also *Cal. S.P. Dom. 1700–2*, p. 90 and *Cal. Treas. Books* xvii, p. 920.

[5] *Cal. Treas. Books* xvii, pp. 7, 61, 125, 298, 477. The first payment was, however, made out of the Secret Service Money (*ibid.*, p. 920).

[6] In June 1701 he did, however, address to the Treasury a memorial 'relating to several particulars in the Office of the Works and Gardens', whose contents are unknown (*Cal. Treas. Books* xvi, p. 82).

[7] *Cal. Treas. Papers 1697–1702*, p. 422; Works 6/14, f. 13; Works 6/2, f. 123. See also Works 6/14, f. 59; *Wren Soc.* iv, p. 60.

[8] *Cal. Treas. Papers 1697–1702*, p. 422 and Works 6/14, ff. 1–2 are cases in point.

For the next decade Wren's closest colleague was to be John Vanbrugh.[1] In 1702 Vanbrugh was in his thirty-ninth year. Already an ex-soldier and a playwright, he was very much a man of the world, consorting freely with the Whig magnates whose architectural patronage he was engaged in diverting from Talman to himself. The Comptrollership was the principal, but not the only, reward of his intimacy with the ruling great. Soon Carlisle, who was acting as Earl Marshal during the incapacity of the Duke of Norfolk, was to make him Clarenceux King of Arms, and as such the bearer of a Garter to the Electoral Prince of Hanover. In 1703 he became a member of the Board of Directors of Greenwich Hospital, and later still the surveyorship of the royal gardens was to be revived for his benefit. As an architect Vanbrugh was still a brilliant novice who needed the technical assistance of Hawksmoor to realise those heroic visions which were his peculiar contribution to English architecture. But his reputation as a designer of country houses was growing rapidly, and during the winter of 1704–5 he was nominated as the architect of the great palace at Woodstock which was intended to be a mark of royal gratitude for the Duke of Marlborough's victories over Louis XIV. This was the greatest architectural commission in England since St. Paul's Cathedral, and made Vanbrugh the leading architect of the age. His influence, if not his hand, was soon to be felt in the buildings erected by the Office of Ordnance, over which the Duke of Marlborough presided, and as the favourite architect of the Whig aristocracy he had by now totally supplanted his rival Talman. The presence on the Board of Works of Benjamin Jackson, the recently appointed Master Mason, who was a protégé of Talman's, was a source of annoyance, but not one that could seriously affect Vanbrugh's equanimity. It looked indeed as if he was destined in due course to succeed Wren as Surveyor of the Works. Many years later the Duchess of Marlborough, anxious to emphasise Vanbrugh's dependence on her husband, asserted not only that it was by the duke's favour that Vanbrugh became Comptroller, but that he 'likewise obtained the promise of giving him Sr. Christopher Wren's employment when he should happen to dye'.[2] Neither claim can be substantiated from the public records, but there may well have been some unofficial understanding that Vanbrugh would be the next Surveyor, and he certainly thought of himself in that light. It was, he told the duke himself, something he thought he 'could not fail of'.[3] But Wren, it seems, had other ideas. This emerges from two coded letters from Arthur Mainwaring to the Duchess of Marlborough, both undated, but evidently written in 1710 or the following year.[4] The duchess was then engaged in building Marlborough House, St. James's, and had snubbed Vanbrugh by employing Wren instead. Vanbrugh's annoyance (so Mainwaring reported) was all the greater because this had, he said, 'been the only encouragement to him (Wren) to think of resigning to his son, by which he (Vanbrugh) should now lose that office'. 'I am not surprised' (Mainwaring wrote in the second letter) 'at his (Vanbrugh's) being round with Shrewsbury, for now he has no more hopes

[1] For Vanbrugh see L. Whistler, *Sir John Vanbrugh* (1938) and *The Imagination of Vanbrugh and his Fellow Artists* (1954). His letters were edited by Geoffrey Webb as vol. 4 of *The Complete Works of Sir John Vanbrugh* (1928).

[2] Chatsworth Archives, Letter 122.3 (to the Duke of Devonshire, 6 May 1721).

[3] Letter of March 1713 printed by Whistler, *Imagination of Sir John Vanbrugh*, p. 241.

[4] The first letter is printed by David Green, *Blenheim Palace* (1951), pp. 248–9. For a transcript of the second (Blenheim Archives E 20(2)) I am also indebted to Mr. Green.

of Godolphin doing anything for him upon several accounts 'tis only by Shrewsbury that he can hope to get the better of the little old man and his son'. Letters at Blenheim show that the younger Wren did in fact assist his father in building Marlborough House, and in *Vitruvius Britannicus* it is 'Christopher Wren, Esquire' who is named as the sole architect.[1] In the light of Mainwaring's letters it looks as if Wren was deliberately giving his son the credit for a major architectural work, in the hope of qualifying him for the succession. In the event, Wren was never voluntarily to lay down his office, and neither Vanbrugh nor the younger Wren was ever to occupy his place.

In the meanwhile Vanbrugh's ambitions were to receive a still ruder shock. For in 1713 a political indiscretion provided a pretext for his dismissal at the hands of the Tory government which had come to power in 1710. At the general election of that year the Marlboroughs' interest in the parliamentary borough of Woodstock had been seriously affected by the huge Blenheim debt, for which many of the electors were, in one way or another, creditors, and only a timely distribution of money had secured the return of their candidate. Before the next election it was essential for some gesture to be made if Woodstock was not to fall to the Tories. So in January 1713 Vanbrugh wrote a letter to the mayor announcing the duke's generous intention of paving the streets—something, he added, which he would long ago have undertaken to do 'but for the continual plague and bitter persecution he has most barbarously been followed with for two years past'.[2] Bad luck and a badly written address delivered this letter into Tory hands, where it was soon represented as an insult both to the government and to the queen. On 31 March orders were accordingly given for Vanbrugh's patent to be revoked, and the Comptrollership was vacant once more.[3] Talman immediately asked to be restored, and Thomas Archer applied for the post with the support of the Duke of Shrewsbury. Hawksmoor and the younger Wren were also regarded by some as possible candidates.[4] But it so happened that a reorganisation of the Office of Works was under consideration at the time, and as one proposal at least involved the abolition of the office of Comptroller Harley evidently decided to make no appointment for the present.[5] Thus it came about that when Queen Anne died, and the Whigs returned to power in the following year, the post was still vacant. Vanbrugh was first knighted (19 September 1714) and then restored to his Comptrollership.[6] By now it was he rather than Wren who was the dominant figure in the Office of Works, and it was his policies that were embodied in the new regulations that became effective from Lady Day 1715.[7] For three more years Wren was nominally to preside over the Board, but 1715 marks the effective end of his Surveyorship. These last years form the subject of a separate chapter. They mark the transition from the Office which Wren had inherited from Denham to the one that was to last until it was swept away by the 'economical reforms' of 1782. These years of crisis and confusion must figure largely in any history of the Office of Works. But in the history of administration it is often

---

[1] Blenheim Archives, F.1.42–3; Campbell, *Vitruvius Britannicus* i (1715), pl. 40.
[2] *The Complete Works of Sir John Vanbrugh*, vol. 4, pp. 53–4.
[3] *Cal. Treas. Books* xxvii, pp. 168, 191; Works 6/5, f. 209.
[4] Hist. MSS Comm. *Portland* x, pp. 96, 145–7; *Bath* i, p. 231.
[5] Below, pp. 49–50.   [6] *Cal. Treas. Books* xxix, p. 325.   [7] Below, p. 51.

inefficiency rather than its opposite that breeds paper, and much more is known about the end of Wren's regime than about its beginnings. It would be rash to claim that under Charles II and James II Wren's management had been faultless, but it would be equally unfair to judge its quality by the 'frauds and abuses' of his declining years.

*Chapter III*

# FINANCIAL STRESS, 1660–1719

FOR THE Office of Works, as for every other government department in post-Restoration England, the fundamental problem was lack of ready money. It was want of money that exposed an immobilised and demoralised Navy to Dutch attack in 1667, and it was the same deficiency that inhibited the Office of Works from completing either of the two new palaces begun by Charles II, and was later to frustrate every scheme for rebuilding Whitehall Palace after the fire of 1698. By 1666 the Office had already spent more than it had received to the extent of £10,988.[1] Between 1675 and 1719 it never owed less than £20,000 or £30,000. In 1692 the debt reached £60,000,[2] and by the end of Queen Anne's reign it had soared to nearly £80,000.[3] The state of the Paymaster's account was therefore of urgent importance to every officer of the King's Works, and provides the clue to many of the troubles that overtook their Office during these years The causes of this perennial shortage of money form part of English political history: it is their consequences for one government department that form the subject of this chapter.

In the finances of the Office of Works there was a basic distinction between regular maintenance on the one hand and new works ordered by the king or his ministers on the other. The former constituted the 'ordinary' expenditure for which a fixed annual allowance was made, while for any 'extraordinary' expenditure appropriate provision was in theory made by the Treasury Lords who authorised it. It was in the nature of things that the 'Extraordinary' of today should become the 'Ordinary' of tomorrow: but accounts do not change their form overnight, and it was twelve years before the maintenance of Audley End, first entrusted to the Office of Works in 1670, was transferred from one category to the other.[4] Much of the 'Extraordinary' in every account was, however, as unpredictable as its name implied, and for this the officers of the Works could have only a limited responsibility: if the king insisted on expensive alterations when his Treasury was empty it was not their fault. But it was their business to keep the 'Ordinary' within the annual total laid down by the Treasury, and any considerable excess was liable to get them into trouble.

---

[1] SP 29/157, ff. 171–2. See also B.M., Add. MS. 22920, f. 186, where the debt is stated to have stood at £26,880 in April 1668.
[2] Works 6/2, f. 35.     [3] Hist. MSS. Comm. *Portland* x, p. 151.
[4] Audley End first appears in the 'ordinary' section of the Paymaster's accounts in 1682–3 (E 351/3296), although it was in 1670 that the Office of Works was instructed to maintain the house.

In April 1663 the 'Ordinary' was fixed at £10,000 a year.[1] It is difficult to say how far the Office succeeded in keeping within this limit, because it was not until 1673 that, by direction of Lord Treasurer Danby, the 'Ordinary' and the 'Extra-ordinary' were formally distinguished in the Paymaster's accounts. But according to the author of the 'Proposalls' submitted to Shaftesbury in 1667 the average 'Ordinary' expenditure was then 'above £12,300' a year, though if his recommendations were put into effect he claimed that, despite rising prices, it could be brought down to £9000.[2] As it happened, 1667 saw a crisis in Charles II's finances which obliged the Treasury to cut the allocation for the 'Ordinary' to £8000.[3] This remained the basic allowance until 1673, when the Board made a case for increasing the 'Ordinary' to £12,000. This rested partly at least on the fact that the list of buildings in their charge had recently received two additions—Audley End, purchased by the king in 1669, and Somerset House, which they had been maintaining at the king's expense since the death of the Queen Mother in the same year. In July 1673 a warrant was issued increasing the 'Ordinary' to £12,000, on the understanding that Audley End and Somerset House would be included under that heading, but in the following year this was superseded by a new 'establishment' under which the Works received £12,500 a year, of which £8000 was for the 'Ordinary', £4000 for the 'Extraordinary', and £500 for Audley End.[4] In January 1676, as part of another scheme of retrenchment necessitated by Charles II's difficulties with parliament, Danby temporarily reduced the total to £10,000,[5] but by August 1677 the full allocation of £12,000 was restored.[6]

In practice the Treasury was rarely in a position to ensure the payment of either the 'Ordinary' or the 'Extraordinary' allowance when it was due. As arrears piled up, the neat distinction between the two categories became less and less related to reality, and both Treasury and Board found themselves preoccupied rather with paying off the accumulated debt and with keeping urgent works going by *ad hoc* issues.[7] As a result Danby's directive to distinguish between the 'Ordinary' and the 'Extraordinary' in the Paymaster's accounts was not invariably obeyed, and ceased to be observed altogether after 1708.[8] But by this time the cost of maintaining the royal palaces and paying the Officers' stipends could no longer be kept below £12,000 a year. Indeed, in 1710 Wren informed the Treasury that the average cost of the ordinary repairs during the previous eight years had been as much as £17,872.[9] Despite Vanbrugh's claims, it was no less under his regime,[10] but when Benson took office a new attempt was made to establish a ceiling of £14,400, which in August 1718 was hopefully promulgated with all the formality of letters patent.[11]

As for the 'Extraordinary', that fluctuated from year to year in accordance with

[1] *Cal. S.P. Dom. 1663–4*, p. 106.      [2] P.R.O. Shaftesbury Papers (P.R.O. 30/24/7).
[3] *Cal. S.P. Dom. 1667–8*, p. 587; *Cal. Treas. Books* ii, p. 131.
[4] *Cal. Treas. Books* iv, pp. 159, 186, 562; T48/32, pp. 224–5, 238; B.M., Add MS. 17019, ff. 11–12.
[5] *Cal. Treas. Books* v, p. 117.
[6] *Cal. Treas. Books* v, pp. 117, 1072. It appears, however, to have been reduced to £6000 at the beginning of William III's reign (T1/5, f. 109).
[7] E.g. *Cal. Treas. Books* xv, pp. 49, 217, 284–5; *Cal. Treas. Papers 1557–1696*, p. 86.
[8] Except in one version of the accounts for 1716 and 1717, where they are distinguished (Works 5/141).
[9] Works 6/5, f. 65.      [10] Below, p. 56.
[11] *Cal. Treas. Books* xxxii, p. 534; Works 6/11, pp. 112–13.

the volume of new works or alterations. Charles II's new buildings at Greenwich and Winchester, James II's additions to Whitehall, and William III's works at Kensington and Hampton Court are each in turn marked by a corresponding rise in the 'Extraordinary' column and in the grand total. In 1702 the Board reckoned that the average cost of the Works since the Restoration had been as follows:

| | |
|---|---|
| Charles II | £20,000 p.a. |
| James II | £30,000 p.a. |
| William III | £45,000 p.a.[1] |

If these figures are taken to include the debt incurred as well as the actual outlay, it is probably a fair approximation. Had a similar calculation been made for Anne's reign the figure could not have been much less than £40,000. In 1718 the Board did in fact produce figures for the last nine years of Anne's reign which gave an average annual expenditure of £43,777.[2] As Anne built comparatively little this continued heavy expenditure requires explanation. Much of it was in fact attributable to the rising cost of maintenance rather than to new construction. In 1703, in a memorandum to the Treasury explaining 'why the charge of repaires of her Majesty's Pallaces and Houses of Access does amount to more at this present, than in the Reign of his late Majestie King Charles the 2nd', the Board had mentioned not only their increased responsibilities (including Kensington and Winchester Palaces, the new gardens at Hampton Court, and the maintenance of the paving in Whitehall, which had recently been put in their charge), but 'the nicety of the age, and the great increase of wages and of materialls, which at this time of warr is exorbitant'. They instanced the cost of 'glazing between quarries as formerly', which had been no more than 1d. a quarry, whereas 'squares now are from 3d. to 17d. a peice', and referred to the increased use of wainscot and marbles.[3] They might have pointed out that both phenomena were ultimately due to the French: for the wars against Louis XIV has undoubtedly brought about a rise in the cost of wages and materials, and it was the example of Versailles that was in large measure responsible for more expensive standards of garden design and of interior decoration.

War and building are two of the most expensive activities in which governments can engage. For neither did the later Stuarts have adequate means, either from their own resources or from the supplies grudgingly granted by parliament. For both they were consequently dependent on credit. By the end of the seventeenth century that system of government credit was beginning to emerge which has since become known as the 'National Debt'. But in the reign of Charles II national finance was in its infancy. The more sophisticated expedients which were available to Georgian governments were barely envisaged, and individual departments were still to a large extent left to fight their own financial battles with the medieval weapons of anticipatory tallies and preferential assignments on specified sources of revenue. Soon after the Restoration, for instance, it was reckoned that £12,000 were needed for repairs to the royal palaces. The way the Treasury proposed to raise this sum was

---

[1] Works 6/2, f. 161ᵛ.

[2] Works 6/7, f. 85. The figures given by the Board are, however, difficult to reconcile with the Paymaster's accounts, which would indicate an average expenditure (excluding debt) of some £37,000 p.a.

[3] Works 6/14, f. 26.

by directing Exchequer tallies to be struck against the proceeds of an assessment on certain Welsh counties. The tax was collected by the sheriffs of the counties in question, and Hugh May, as Paymaster, was expected to get into touch with them (or with their agents at Westminster) and exchange his tallies for equivalent sums in cash. In due course the Exchequer would accept the tallies from the sheriffs in lieu of the cash which had by then been spent on the king's works. What happened in fact was that the sheriffs were dilatory and had to be scolded by the Treasury 'for their remissness in transmitting the moneys upon the 18 months assessment, whereby the service of the Works suffers'.[1] In 1663 the Hearth Tax was selected as the source of revenue upon which to charge the £10,000 for the 'Ordinary', but the yield fell short of expectation, and in the following year May was obliged to borrow £2800 from the London banker Edward Backwell on the security of tallies struck upon the Customs.[2] Backwell had already advanced £5000 to the Works in 1661 on the security of the Excise, and the interest paid to him was an additional burden on the Office's finances.[3] In 1668 the Paymaster was authorised by the Treasury to raise further loans at 6 per cent interest,[4] but in 1673 he found it impossible to obtain funds at this rate, and had to be allowed to borrow at 10 per cent.[5] In 1684–5 the payment of accumulated interest on loans to the Office of Works amounted to £3340.[6]

Another expedient was the sale of tallies at a discount. In 1695 tallies to the value of £30,966 were struck for the benefit of the Works. They bore no interest, but carried with them a guarantee of repayment 'in course', that is in accordance with a known order of priority as the revenue upon which they were charged became available.[7] They did not, however, prove readily negotiable, so Wren, as spokesman for the Board, asked the Treasury to allow 6 per cent interest on the capital, besides 3 per cent discount. This proposal was regarded at the time as totally unacceptable, so much so that the Treasury made a special minute of its 'unreasonableness'.[8] But government credit was at a low ebb, and in the following year the Treasury was obliged to allow the same tallies to be discounted at any rate not exceeding 10 per cent.[9] In the reign of Queen Anne there was similar difficulty over tallies on the revenue from tin to the value of £33,387 which were struck for the benefit of the Works. Their priority was too low to make them generally acceptable, but it was only after much pressure from the Board that the Treasury reluctantly agreed to allow interest on them, on the understanding that they 'shall not be carried to Market, or if the necessity of the Artizans receiving the same be such as to require the selling thereof that they may be put in the hands of some one person to dispose

---

[1] *Cal. Treas. Books* i, pp. 292, 385, 394.    [2] *Cal. Treas. Books* i, p. 654.

[3] E 351/3274. The origin of this loan was a resolution of the House of Commons on 3 September 1660 charging £5000 on the Excise for the repair of the king's houses, with a provision for the payment of interest until the whole sum had been advanced (*Commons' Jnls.* viii, p. 146). This was in addition to a further £2000 already lent by Backwell 'by order of the Committee of Parliament appointed for His Majesty's happy reception' (E 351/3274).

[4] *Cal. Treas. Books* ii, pp. 175, 261, 456.

[5] *Cal. Treas. Books* iii, pp. 481, 632, 941; iv, p. 200. In 1677 a loan at 8 per cent was envisaged (*Cal. Treas. Books* v, p. 460).

[6] E 351/3298.

[7] For the system see P. G. M. Dickson, *The Financial Revolution in England* (1967), chap. 13.

[8] *Cal. Treas. Books* x, p. 1379.    [9] *Cal. Treas. Books* xi, p. 57.

of and in such small sums at a time that the credit of tallys may not suffer by unreasonable discounts'.[1] On another occasion, when entering into a building contract, the Board undertook to pay interest up to 5 per cent on any balance unpaid at the end of 12 months, and agreed that if payment were made in tallies or bills, a discount would be allowed.[2]

By such means the King's Works were carried on, but the complexity of the financial transactions involved was formidable. Even if cash was forthcoming from the Exchequer, it was rarely paid in a lump sum corresponding to the total stated in the warrant, but came in in driblets over a period of months or even years. A warrant of 1677 for £4000 for the 'Extraordinary' took two and a half years to satisfy, and was paid in 15 instalments ranging from £5 to £500.[3] To add to the complications, payments were not infrequently transferred from one source to another, and when money was allocated (as it often was) for particular purposes, the expenditure of each remittance had to be separately recorded. The debt, too, was not just a simple cumulative total, but was to some extent personal to each sovereign, and the Treasury was apt to assign a lower priority to satisfying the creditors of a deceased monarch than to keeping abreast with the current debts of a live one.

All this meant (as Pepys's experience with the Navy accounts shows) hours of wrestling with figures, days of haggling with recalcitrant Exchequer officials, and years of delay in bringing an account to audit. In 1685 Lord Treasurer Rochester said that he allowed the Paymaster three months to prepare his accounts and the Board one month more to examine and sign them.[4] But no Works account between 1660 and 1719 was ever audited within less than two years of its closing date, and delays of up to ten years were not uncommon. May's last account (for 1668) was bedevilled by the loss of a prest certificate for £10,805, Packer's 1677 account by the discovery of a fraud in the Receipt of the Exchequer.[5] When Lloyd died in 1706 none of his accounts for the last six years had passed the auditor, and unaudited they still remain (in various states of incompleteness) among the Exchequer records.[6]

Though the Paymaster or his deputy bore the brunt of this financial stress, he no doubt took care that his own pocket did not suffer. But there were times when everyone connected with the Works was owed money, from the Surveyor downwards: indeed, there were even occasions when senior members of the Works staff were exhorted to lend money to the government and did so.[7] In 1706 Wren's salary was £341 in arrear, and in 1708 he renounced his claim to the debt as an inducement to the Crown to permit him to take a lease of the house at Hampton Court to which he proposed to retire.[8] By 1718 he was again owed an unspecified sum which

[1] *Cal. Treas. Books* xxvi, p. 294; Works 6/5, f. 158.    [2] Works 5/145, f. 223 (1698).
[3] *Cal. Treas. Books* vi, p. 418.    [4] *Cal. Treas. Books* viii, p. 217.
[5] *Cal. Treas. Books* v, pp. 162–3; S. B. Baxter, *The Development of the Treasury* (1957), p. 154. For further complications affecting these and subsequent accounts see *Cal. Treas. Books* iii, pp. 236, 599, 802, 1248; v, pp. 1236–7; vi, p. 228; viii, pp. 643, 650, 654–5, 972, 1149, 1277; xx, pp. 264, 615, 676; xxvii, p. 438; xxx, p. 439.
[6] *Cal. Treas. Books; Introduction to vols. xi–xvii*, pp. dxcviii–dxcix; xviii, pp. cxc–cxci; xix, pp. ccxlvi–ccxlvii: xxiv, p. 54.
[7] *Cal. Treas. Books* ii, pp. 181–2, 194. In 1685 Wren lent £1000 at 7 per cent, in 1694 £1700 at 6 per cent (*Cal. Treas. Books* viii, p. 2178, x, p. 909). These personal loans must not be confused with the fictitious loans by Paymasters discussed by Dickson, op. cit., pp. 351–2. For examples of the latter see *Cal. Treas. Books* ix, pp. 617–18, 669, 697, 794, 821, 824, 1238, 1911, 1913, 1989; x, pp. 1354–5; xi, pp. 184, 194; xii, p. 210; xxiii, p. 389, xxiv, p. 376.    [8] *Cal. Treas. Books* xx, p. 749; xxii, pp. 26, 308, 370.

his successor Benson did his best to withhold from him.[1] But it was the artificers rather than the staff for whom the inability of the Office to make prompt payment constituted a major problem. In the long run the service of the Crown was a profitable business, and even at the worst times there was no lack of competition for the patents which gave the Master Craftsmen a prescriptive right to work for the king. But only craftsmen with extensive capital had the financial stamina to wait for payment from one year to the next. An extreme case was that of Charles Atherton, the Sergeant Plumber, who in 1702 was still owed £1641 for works carried out in the reigns of Charles II and James II.[2] Almost as serious was the case of Richard Stacey, the Master Bricklayer, who in 1705 submitted a memorial claiming that he was owed £13,000, of which only £3550 was for works performed since the accession of Queen Anne, all the rest dating back to the reign of William III.[3] He had, he said, 'exhausted his whole stock and contracted great debts'. At the end of William III's reign the debt to various craftsmen and workmen amounted altogether to £57,910.[4] Charles Hopson, the joiner, was owed nearly £9500, a figure which by 1703 had risen to £10,587.[5] In 1713 it was 'the business of three Months' time' for a clerk to make a 'Generall list of every Person's debt in the Office for two years and a quarter'—a task so arduous that he was paid £10 extra 'for his extraordinary pains and trouble'.[6]

Although debt was a malady from which the Office was never free, it was a condition that was kept under careful control by injections of money that, if never sufficient to satisfy every creditor, were generally enough to sustain the Office's credit. For the Crown, like a modern bankrupt, paid a dividend. 'It hath been my method in the Office of the Workes', Wren told the Treasury in 1691, 'not to permitt any anticipations, but (the Debt upon any work being represented to your Lordshipps) what mony from time to time is Directed is equally divided to every Creditor by a pound rate, and wee pay ourselves noe otherwise: by which means wee keepe up a Credit for his Majestie's Service though wee injure our Selves.'[7] Again, in 1702, Wren and his colleagues insisted that 'payment in course' (that is, in strict rotation) was 'the only way to sustaine the Office in her Majestie's service, which by this meanes hath been done for many yeares, the prices being very reasonable, notwithstanding the many difficulties wee have laboured under'. But for this assurance of equitable if belated payment they considered that it would be 'exceeding hard to make any reasonable bargaines for the future'.[8] There were, however, ways and means whereby a creditor could sometimes succeed in recovering his money 'out of course'. In extremity a petition might be addressed to the Treasury. Such a petition was invariably referred to the Board for comment, and nearly always resulted in some relief, though rarely in the total discharge of the debt. From time to time creditors would be allowed to convert their debt into an interest-bearing loan. In

---

[1] T 27/23, p. 28: a letter from the Treasury to the Paymaster ordering him to disregard an entry made by Benson in the Office books which 'occasioned a stop to be put to some moneys becoming payable to Sir Christopher Wren', 28 October 1719. Some £250 were due to Wren in 1714 (*Wren Soc.* xviii, pp. 169–70).

[2] *Cal. Treas. Books* xvi, p. 262; *Cal. Treas. Papers 1697–1702*, p. 556.

[3] Works 6/14, p. 97; cf. *Cal. Treas. Books* xix, p. 166.

[4] T1/78, no. 66, printed in *Wren Soc.* xviii, pp. 160–3.

[5] *Cal. Treas. Books* xviii, p. 464.     [6] E 351/3318.

[7] *Wren Soc.* iv, p. 56.     [8] Works 6/14, f. 14.

1670, for instance, all the officers of the Works were allowed 6 per cent interest on their arrears of wages, which were treated as a loan.[1] As a rule, however, such concessions were made only in return for a cash advance at least equivalent to the debt. Thus in about 1692 'every artificer or tradesman belonging to His Majesty's Works that would advance double his debts in money by way of loan into the Exchequer, had in lieu thereof tallies struck for the same and his debts included'.[2] Several of the master craftsmen were able to take advantage of this opportunity, but for the small man or the day labourer such transactions were out of the question, and it was they who were undoubtedly the greatest sufferers from the perennial want of money. The 'clamour' of unpaid workmen was a common and embarrassing feature of Works administration.[3] Like the naval ratings, they were frequently paid with promissory notes, or 'tickets', which they were obliged to sell at a discount to anyone who would buy them.[4] From time to time a body of them would get up a petition to the Board of Works, the Treasury, or even the Privy Council.[5] Sometimes the Board took it upon itself to intercede on their behalf, as in 1702, when 'the necessities of the many poor people and families concerned in the Works' were such that they thought it their duty 'to address your Lordship in their behalf for your pitty to them in your honor's directing some money for their releif against Christmas, they having been about 10 months without any'.[6] On this occasion the Treasury responded by directing £4750 to be issued to clear the debt from March to September 1702, but the situation was recurrent, and in 1719, when even the passing of bills was suspended owing to Benson's mismanagement, the Treasury received yet another 'humble petition' pointing out that 'besides the arrear due to them from his Majesty which amounts to about £40,000, there is a debt of £20,294 owing to them from the late Queen, and of £54,910 from the late King William, by which means Your Petitioners' misfortunes are severally heighten'd, insomuch that the greatest part of them and their Familys, are reduc'd to want and misery & some confin'd to the Verge of the Court for shelter [from their creditors]'.[7]

The consequences for the Works of perpetual indebtedness are not difficult to discern. They were bad credit and disadvantageous terms. Hugh May must often have had cause to echo his friend Pepys's complaint: 'no credit, no goods sold us, nobody will trust [us]. All we have to do at the Office is to hear complaints for want of money'.[8] In an appeal to the Treasury in 1710 the Board begged for money 'to help the credit of the Office of Works from being intirely lost'. All the artificers had, they said, exhausted their stocks and they themselves were 'in great difficulty to find materialls or work to answer Her Majesty's commands in her own conveniencys, much more to answer any Lord Chamberlain's warrants'.[9] As the author of the

[1] *Cal. Treas. Books* iii, p. 646.
[2] *Cal. Treas. Papers 1697–1702*, p. 556. For other examples see *Cal. Treas. Books* ix, pp. 619, 1952–4, x p. 11.
[3] *Cal. Treas. Books* iii, p. 927.　　　　[4] Above, p. 14.
[5] PC2/55, ff. 315, 332, 363 (petition to Privy Council from workmen employed at Westminster, 1661); PC 2/61, f. 369 (petition to Privy Council from workmen employed at Windsor, 1669); *Cal. S.P. Dom. 1670*, p. 265 (petition from Greenwich workmen to king, referred to Treasury, 1670); *Cal. Treas. Books* iv, p. 353 (petition to Treasury from day labourers, 1675); *Cal. Treas. Books* v, p. 1371 (petition from widows of four master artisans, c. 1675); *Cal. Treas. Books* viii, pp. 1330, 1988 (petition from workmen, 1687); *Cal. Treas. Papers 1714–19*, p. 443 (petition from workmen, 1719).
[6] Works, 6/14, ff. 14/15.　　　　[7] T1/220, ff. 151/2.
[8] *Diary of Samuel Pepys*, ed. Wheatley, vi, p. 44.　　　　[9] Works 6/5, ff. 78–9.

'Proposalls' submitted to Shaftesbury pointed out in 1667, regular supplies would enable the officers to make favourable contracts and to purchase materials at far easier rates than was actually the case.[1] As it was they were obliged to accept higher rates than were current in the building trades at large. It is not difficult to find complaints that bear out the statements made in the 'Proposalls'. We have the testimony both of Thomas Archer and of Sarah, Duchess of Marlborough, that in the reign of Queen Anne 'crown work' was paid for at the highest rates,[2] and an unknown writer gives an entertaining account of the profiteering that occurred in connection with a royal funeral.[3] It is much less easy to ascertain from the accounts precisely to what extent the Office of Works was obliged to accept unfavourable terms. To be valid, comparisons must be based on the prices of identical materials or identical craftsmanship supplied in identical physical conditions. The available documents rarely permit such exact comparisons, but the evidence, such as it is, supports the conclusion that if the Crown habitually paid more slowly than private employers, it certainly did not pay less for the same product.

It was undoubtedly the Crown's inability to pay ready money that was chiefly responsible for this uneconomical state of affairs. But the very constitution of the Office was inimical to effective bargaining on the part of the Officers. For the Patent Artisans had a prescriptive right to employment by the Crown, and although their monopoly was not complete, it made anything in the nature of competitive tendering difficult if not impossible. The Office was not incapable of driving a hard bargain. In 1711 it cancelled an agreement with one ironmonger in order to make a more favourable bargain with another, and then rejected his terms in favour of a third man who was prepared to undercut both.[4] But it was not until the offices of Master Mason and Master Carpenter had been taken out of the hands of the artisans and given to architects that the Board gave up *ad hoc* contracts in favour of the more business-like practice of contracting with a mason or a carpenter to perform all the Office's work at rates agreed in advance,[5] and it was not until the era of 'economical reform' that the modern system of open and competitive tendering became the normal rule.

[1] P.R.O., Shaftesbury Papers (PRO 30/24/7).
[2] Below, p. 48.
[3] Hist. MSS. Comm. *Downshire* I (i), pp. 456–8. The payments that so scandalised the writer were made by the Wardrobe, not the Office of Works, but the coffin was supplied by Alexander Fort, the Master Joiner.
[4] Works 5/145, ff. 241/5.
[5] Works 5/145, ff. 259, 263.

*Chapter IV*

# THE END OF WREN'S REGIME

IT WAS an auditor's scrutiny which led to the drawing up in 1705 of new Orders governing the conduct of the Works. Edward Harley, the Auditor of the Imprests, pointed out that the instructions of 1663 limited expenditure without warrant to £40 a year at Whitehall, Hampton Court and Greenwich, and £20 elsewhere— figures which had first been fixed in the reign of James I, and were quite unrealistic in that of Queen Anne. Moreover the Orders themselves had ceased to be valid on the death of Charles II.[1] The Treasury had in fact intended to issue new Orders shortly after the accession of James II, and had written to Wren to ask for his views on various points.[2] Wren's reply is not among the Treasury papers, but apart from the abolition of the office of Purveyor, no major change appears to have been contemplated. For some reason these new Orders were never formally drawn up before James's abdication, nor does any further thought appear to have been given to them after the accession of William and Mary.

Though completely rewritten, the new Orders of 1705 were not designed to change the structure or the functions of the Office in any significant way.[3] The restriction on expenditure for routine repairs was removed, but, as before, no expenditure was to be incurred without Treasury warrant, 'except for necessary causes such as mending of Gutters, Cisterns, Pipes, Tiling, Glazing, Plastering, and such like, which will admit of no delay without great damage'. For the rest the new instructions merely confirmed or clarified existing practice in such matters as the receipt of verbal orders from the queen and the routine for paying creditors of the Office a 'proportionable dividend'. Some emphasis was, however, laid on the principle that no Officer might be 'an undertaker of any work himselfe or have any advantage directly or indirectly by it, but shall only be an overseer of such work as shall be agreed at the Board to be left to his perticular care and inspection'. Any officer contravening this order was thereby to 'be rendered incapable of serving us for the future'. This was directed against the Master Mason and the Master Carpenter, who, as members of the Board, were supposed to protect the queen's interests, but who considered that they were entitled, like the other Master Artisans, to act as contractors for their respective trades. The latter was, indeed, precisely what their predecessors had done for centuries, whereas their presence on the Board

---

[1] *Cal. Treas. Books* xx, pp. 136, 271.
[2] *Cal. Treas. Books* viii, p. 112.

[3] The Office copy is Works 6/368/3.

was an innovation dating from 1564. Moreover, their official salaries fell far short of the legitimate profit they made as contracting workmen to the Office, and it was obvious that 'no Artificer of any repute or consideration would quit his Trade and business for the Office-salary and allowance'.[1] It was Vanbrugh who, in a letter to Godolphin, had drawn the Treasury's attention to this conflict between public responsibility and private gain. As Comptroller, he was quite properly anxious to stamp out this abuse, but his zeal was undoubtedly heightened by his personal animus against Benjamin Jackson, the Master Mason, whom he detested as an associate of his rival Talman. Before writing to the Treasurer about this 'shamefull abuse of those very officers doing the work themselves, who rec'd sallarys from the Queen to prevent her being imposed on by others', he had (he reminded Godolphin) 'made severall attempts upon Sr Chr. Wren to perswade him to redress it himself without troubling yr Lordship; putting him in mind; that besides its being utterly against common sense, it was contrary to an Express Direction to the Board upon the Establishment after the Restoration. He always own'd what I urg'd him to was right and often promis'd to join with me in overruling so bad a practice; but when I press'd him to the Execution, he still evaded it, and that so many times, that at last I saw he never intended it, and so I gave your Lordship the trouble of a Complaint'.[2] The result had been an order from the Treasury condemning the employment of any of the Officers as 'very unreasonable and contrary to the ancient usage of your Office'.[3] But, according to Vanbrugh, Jackson had, with Wren's connivance, evaded it by entering his bills in another's name. Summoned before the Treasury, Jackson insisted that 'he had not wrought since the order to the contrary', while Wren protested feebly that the matter ought to have been brought before the Board instead of the Treasury.[4] Despite the formal condemnation of the practice in the Orders of 1705 the name of Benjamin Jackson continues to appear in the Office's books until his death in 1719, and then the problem was solved by appointing as Master Mason and Master Carpenter men who were not tradesmen at all but architects.

Although (as Vanbrugh was at pains to point out) Wren himself had no personal interest in Jackson's evasion of the regulation, his tolerance of such practices lent support to the general belief that at 80 he was no longer capable of running efficiently a department which was spending £30,000–£40,000 a year. 'The frauds and abuses', wrote Thomas Archer, 'are so great that by the price of work set by the Queen's servants the whole nation, but more particularly the city of London, is a great sufferer, and the Queen herself (as I believe your Lordship well knows) is extremely imposed upon.'[5] When Sarah, Duchess of Marlborough, sent for Wren in 1709 and asked him to design her town house at St. James's, she made him promise that he would make the contracts 'reasonable and not as crown work'. 'The poor old man', she continued, 'undertook this business very readily and as everybody says the hous is a very good one and I performed my promise to him as to the money part. . . . Then I began to find that this man from his age was

---

[1] B.M. Portland Deposit, Harley Papers vol. xlvi, ff. 637–42 (observations made in 1713).
[2] *The Complete Works of Sir John Vanbrugh*, vol. 4, p. 11.
[3] *Cal. Treas. Books* xix, pp. 40, 307 (17 July 1704). See also T 1/89, f. 146.
[4] *Cal. Treas. Books* xx, p. 21.        [5] Hist. MSS. Comm. *Portland* x, p. 146.

imposed upon by the workmen and that the prices for all things were much too high for ready money and sure pay, upon which I took the finishing part upon myself. . . .'[1] At St. Paul's there were similar charges of inefficiency and corruption in the management of the works.[2] Worse still, even the 'poor old man's' ability as an architect was now under fire. Far away in Naples the third Earl of Shaftesbury was composing an open *Letter concerning the Art, or Science of Design,* in the course of which he took occasion to deplore the state of architecture in England. ''Tis no wonder', he wrote, 'if so many noble Designs . . . have miscarry'd amongst us; since the Genius of our Nation has hitherto been so little turn'd this way, that thro' several Reigns we have patiently seen the noblest publick Buildings perish (if I may say so) under the Hand of one single Court-architect. . . . But I question whether our Patience is like to hold much longer.'[3] Nearer at hand connoisseurs of architecture were looking with a new appreciation at those drawings by Jones and Webb which before long were to form the basis of the new national style which Shaftesbury demanded but could not define.

But changing taste alone could not bring Wren's regime to an end. It was in the Treasury that the fate of the Office of Works would be decided. Here there was concern as expenditure and debts continued inexorably to mount, annoyance at the perennial discovery of works carried out without prior reference to their Lordships. Time after time the Treasury found it necessary to draw the attention of the Officers of the Works to this much-neglected rule.[4] In October 1700 Wren was summoned to the Treasury and reprimanded for starting to repair the Lord Keeper's house in Lincoln's Inn Fields before he had authority to do so.[5] In December 1709, after an outburst about 'the vast expense' of works 'all done without his participation or knowledge', Godolphin ordered copies of this and the other regulations to be displayed in all the offices of the Works so that no one could plead ignorance of them.[6] But queens and courtiers did not like to be kept waiting, and it was often inconvenient to delay until Treasury sanction came through. 'I shall (as is my method) give my Lord Treasurer an Estimate', Wren told the Lord Chamberlain's office in June 1710, 'and till I have his Fiat, I shall proceed but slowly'.[7] But proceed he would, even if slowly, and in the end it was this persistent evasion of strict Treasury control that in 1715 brought about radical changes in the organisation of the Royal Works.

Although these changes were the work of a Whig government under a Hanoverian king, they were not in any sense a partisan measure. The reform of the Office of Works was, indeed, under active consideration by Queen Anne's government during the last two years of her reign. As early as March 1712/13 Harley had before him 'A Scheme proposed for the Office of her Majesty's Works', whose principal features were the abolition of the Comptrollership on the grounds that it was a useless sinecure, the removal from the Board of the Master Mason and Master Carpenter,

[1] David Green. *Blenheim Palace* (1951), p. 106.
[2] Jane Lang, *Rebuilding St. Paul's* (1956), p. 250 *et seq.*
[3] Shaftesbury, *Characteristics*, 5th ed., vol. 3 (1732), p. 400. The letter is dated 6 March 1712.
[4] E.g. *Cal. Treas. Books* xvi, pp. 8, 13, 42, 71, 149, xviii, pp. 42, 280, xxiii, p. 31.
[5] Hist. MSS. Comm. *Portland* iii, p. 632. cf. *Cal. Treas. Books* xvi, p. 5.
[6] *Cal. Treas. Books* xxiii, p. 33; Works 6/5, f. 22.          [7] Works 6/5, f. 50.

and the appointment in their place of two Assistant Surveyors, who were in theory to be skilled in architecture. This scheme was intended to come into effect on Wren's resignation or death, and in order to encourage Wren to take the former course it was proposed that his son should be one of the two Assistant Surveyors, with a seat on the Board.[1] It was evidently with these proposals in mind that, when Vanbrugh fell from grace in April of the same year, Harley deliberately refrained from appointing anyone in his place. But Wren remained obstinately at the head of a department whose financial liabilities continued to be a reproach both to the government and to the queen. It was, as it happened, in 1713 that the Works debt rose to a peak of £79,469.[2] As no major works were known to be in progress, the Treasury suspected that, as usual, a good deal had been done without their approval, and demanded a statement of all works carried out since December 1709, the date of Godolphin's reprimand.[3] The statement, when it came, was accompanied by a long, lame letter confessing that some orders from the Lord Chamberlain had indeed been put into effect without reference to the Treasury, while a number of 'particulars' would 'appear to your Lordships to be done without warrant' from either Treasury or Lord Chamberlain. In the former cases the Board had thought it 'more becoming us, immediately to give obedience therto, than in any wise to dispute or delay the same'. As for the latter, they were done either by the queen's verbal order, 'which we thought it our duty to comply with', or they were 'indispencably necessary for accommodating the persons concerned', some of whose names were 'such as we hope will need no other justification but the bare mentioning them'.[4] The Treasury's annoyance at this open defiance of its orders was increased by another letter from the Board complaining that because of these irregularities the Auditor would not pass the Paymaster's accounts for the last five years, and cooly requesting that directions should be given 'that there may be no more obstruction in passing the accounts in relation to the Office Orders abovementioned, which we presume your Lordship (according to the 22$^d$ Article of the said Orders) may alter & dispence with at pleasure'.[5] There ensued another confrontation between Treasury and Board as a result of which a privy seal was issued regularising the illegal expenditure 'out of compassion to the Artizans and workmen concerned', but animadverting on the Board's failure to obey its regulations, and formally charging the Auditor to 'take care that the said Paymaster shall not in any future account . . . be allowed any payment for repairs . . . but such only for which an estimate shall first have been presented to the Treasury.'[6] At the same time Wren was directed to 'prepare and present to my Lord such a proposal as he shall think conducive to lessen the exorbitant charges of the Office of the Works'.[7] On 3 March Wren duly submitted to the Treasury a list of 'such Alterations and Additions as occur to me on the present general Model, and that your Lordship may have the easier and clearer view thereof, I lay before you the present Rules in one column,

[1] B.M., Portland Deposit, Harley Papers xlvi, ff. 637–42.
[2] Hist. MSS. Comm. *Portland* x, p. 151.
[3] *Cal. Treas. Books* xxvii, p. 414; Works 6/5, f. 241.
[4] Works 6/5, f. 242 (19 November 1713). The statement itself does not appear to survive.
[5] Works 6/5, f. 257 (February 1713/14).
[6] Works 6/5, ff. 268–70 (29 April 1714); *Cal. Treas. Books* xxviii (2), pp. 159, 224.
[7] *Cal. Treas. Books* xxviii (2), p. 19.

and the Remarks, with the proposed alterations and additions, in another'.[1] On 29 March the Officers of the Works were informed that they would shortly receive new regulations effective from Lady Day.[2] But these new regulations were, it seems, never signed by the queen, whose failing health may well have prevented her from giving them proper consideration. In any case her illness was soon to precipitate a ministerial crisis in which neither Harley nor his rivals had any further time for the affairs of a minor department of state. No copy of the proposed new Orders can be found among the records of either Treasury or Office of Works, nor are they referred to in subsequent edicts, which always cite the Orders of 1705 as the only ones issued in the name of Queen Anne.

One of the first beneficiaries of the new Whig government of George I was Vanbrugh. Not only was he knighted, but soon afterwards he was invited by Halifax, the new First Lord of the Treasury, to submit his suggestions for the reform of the Office of Works. On 29 November 1714 the ex-Comptroller accordingly sent Halifax a list of nine 'Heads for a new Settlement of the Office of Works'.[3] The first (as might be expected) was the abolition of the offices of Master Mason, Master Carpenter, 'and all the other Master Workmen, with the Purveyor and Clerk Ingrosser'. The second recommendation was that 'for a check on the Surveyor, in lieu of the Master Mason and the Master Carpenter, the Paymaster may be join'd with him and the Comptroller, to make Contracts, pass Bills and sign the Books'. The third reduced the number of office clerks to two:

> One to sit at the Board as Secretary, to take minutes, enter Orders, Contracts, Warrants &c. Draw up Reports, Enter the Prises in the Office Book as adjusted by the Board in passing the Bills, and to write out the Books for the Auditor.
> One other Clark to assist the Paymaster.

In all admeasurements, 'two Clarkes of the Works [to] be oblig'd to measure together', and no Clark to be employed 'who is not duely qualifyed for [his] office by his skill in drawing, measurements, workmanship and materials'. The separate establishment at Windsor was to be abolished, and the maintenance of the castle was to be entrusted to a Clerk on the same footing as those in charge of the other royal palaces. No work might be done in any private lodging 'except necessary repairs to keep out the weather, and the building from falling', and stricter control was to be exercised over alterations carried out at their own expense by occupants of lodgings in the royal palaces.

Before the new Orders were signed Vanbrugh was restored to his office. His second patent as Comptroller of the Works was dated 24 January 1715.[4] The delay of four months between knighthood and office may possibly have been due to continuing doubt at the Treasury as to the utility of the Comptroller's post. But

---

[1] T 1/173, f. 100. The list is not among the Treasury Papers.
[2] *Cal. Treas. Books* xxviii (2), pp. 31, 196–7.
[3] T 1/182, ff. 117–19. Vanbrugh (by now once more a member of the Board) was the only signatory of some further comments on the draft orders submitted by the Treasury to the Board for comment in March 1715 (T 1/189, ff. 117, 118).
[4] Patent Roll 1 George I, part 8, no. 12.

with a Whig ministry in office, and a major reform of the Works in hand, it is likely that Wren's future too was under consideration. By all the rules of eighteenth-century patronage the aged Surveyor, for so long the head of an office in whose affairs there was much to find fault with, and a Tory to boot, ought to have been dismissed to make way for the Whig Vanbrugh. Had Vanbrugh pressed his advantage this is almost certainly what would have happened. But although there is no evidence that the two men had ever been intimate, they had been fellow-members of the Board too long for Vanbrugh to feel able to oust his venerable colleague: and so, as he reminded Jacob Tonson four years later, the surveyorship was an office 'which I might have had formerly, but refus'd it, out of Tenderness for Sr Chr: Wren'.[1]

Though Wren was allowed to remain in office, it was clearly out of the question to leave him in sole control. The obvious solution was the appointment of a Deputy. But Vanbrugh, the heir apparent, could hardly be both Comptroller and Deputy Surveyor. The expedient adopted was an enlarged Board, over which Wren presided as Surveyor, but of which he was in practice no more than an honoured member without any special authority in virtue of his office.[2] As he himself put it: 'It was his Majestie's pleasure, on his happy accession to the Throne to continue me in the office of Surveyor of the Works: But soon after, in regard of my great age, He was pleas'd of his Royal Clemency to ease me of the burden of the business of that Office, by appointing other worthy Gentlemen with me in Commission, which was under such regulations and restrictions, as that alltho' I had the honour to be first nam'd with the old title of Surveyor, yet in acting I had no power to over-rule, or give a casting-vote.'[3] The other members of the Board were the Comptroller (Vanbrugh), the Paymaster (Dartiquenave), the Surveyor General of Crown Lands (Hugh Cholmley), the Surveyor General of Woods and Forests (Thomas Hewett), and the two Secretaries to the Treasury. In April 1717 the Surveyor of the King's Private Roads (William Watkins) was added when the roads themselves became one of the Office's responsibilities.[4]

The two outsiders, Cholmley and Hewett, were men whose duties gave them both some knowledge of works and buildings, as well as of government routine. They received no extra remuneration for their attendance at the Board of Works, but were given possession of the official houses in Scotland Yard and Hampton Court previously occupied by the Master Mason and the Master Carpenter.[5] There was to be a quorum of four (later reduced to three),[6] and in the absence of the Surveyor of Works the Comptroller was to preside. Regular minutes were to be kept for the first time in the Office's history, and for this purpose a new post of Secretary to the Board was created, with a salary of £100 a year. This office Vanbrugh secured for Hawksmoor, who was also promoted to the Clerkship of the

[1] *The Complete Works of Sir John Vanbrugh*, vol. 4, p. 123.
[2] *Cal. Treas. Books* xxix, pp. 493–6; Works 6/11, pp. 1–12.
[3] T 1/220, f. 216.
[4] T 1/206, ff. 233–5; *Cal. Treas. Books* xxxi, p. 263. For the Private Roads see below, pp. 459–60.
[5] *Cal. Treas. Books* xxix, p. 551, xxx, p. 105; Works 6/6, ff. 66, 148. When Hewett lost his post in 1716 Dartiquenave took over his house in Scotland Yard (*Cal. Treas. Books* xxx, p. 356). Watkins demanded a house on his appointment in 1717, and was given the old Call House, which was to be repaired for his benefit (*Cal. Treas. Books* xxxi, p. 491).　　　　[6] *Cal. Treas. Books* xxx, p. 76; Works 4/1, p. 50.

Works at Whitehall, Westminster and St. James's in place of William Dickinson. Dickinson's dismissal is difficult to account for, as he appears to have been a competent surveyor and architectural draughtsman.[1] But his deposition was part of a general purge of the existing clerks, some of whom undoubtedly lacked his professional qualifications. To this end, despite Wren's protests, the Treasury reserved to itself the appointment of all Clerks of the Works *pro hac vice*. Except in the case of the Clerk Ingrosser, future vacancies were, however, to be filled by the Surveyor with the approval of his fellow-Commissioners. Guided, no doubt, by Vanbrugh, the Treasury dismissed all the clerks then in office except Hawksmoor, including Wren's son, his cousin John Ball, and his kinsman Thomas Bateman.[2] As a body, the new Clerks were undoubtedly better qualified than their predecessors. Of Leonard Wooddeson, the new Clerk at Winchester, we know only that he had 'faithfully served the [Office] as an Under-Clerk about twelve years'.[3] Thomas Kynaston, who was put in charge of the Tower and Somerset House, had been Vanbrugh's personal clerk since 1708, when he took him over from his cousin William, the Comptroller of the Chamber, and sent him to Blenheim 'to see the manner of measurements in order to qualify himself the better for future business'.[4] Henry Joynes, too, had served his apprenticeship as resident clerk of the works at Blenheim, and was by now thoroughly experienced in building affairs.[5] He took Hawksmoor's place at Kensington. At Hampton Court John Ball made way for Thomas Fort, by trade a master-joiner, but also a competent surveyor who had recently designed a substantial house illustrated in *Vitruvius Britannicus*.[6] At Windsor the new clerk was a man called Rowland who in later life was to publish two useful works on architecture and surveying.[7] Newmarket was entrusted to Andrews Jelfe, an intelligent young master-mason who was also given the post of Clerk Itinerant, with responsibility for making copies of 'such draughts and designs as the Surveyor shall from time to time judge proper for His Majesty's service to the end the same may be kept in the Office to have a recourse to on occasions, together with the plans, elevations and surveys of all the royal palaces and gardens'.[8] It was therefore with justifiable satisfaction that two years later the Board informed the Treasury that 'the Clerks of the Works, whatever they may have been formerly, are now required to be well skilled in all kinds of admeasurements, in drawing, making plans of the palaces, taking elevations, and competently versed in all parts of architecture, which some among them are, to a great degree of excellence'.[9] The Board also put into effect Vanbrugh's recommendation (which became clause 21 of the new Orders) that Clerks were to measure works jointly, specifying that 'Mr. Fort

[1] As Surveyor to the Dean and Chapter of Westminster he was not left without employment. At first it was proposed to transfer him to Winchester, a minor post which he may well have refused, as it was so remote from his principal post.

[2] *Cal. Treas. Books* xxix, pp. 535, 690, xxx, p. 485; T 1/187, f. 22.

[3] T 1/193, f. 82.

[4] *The Complete Works of Sir John Vanbrugh*, vol. 4, p. 223.

[5] For his career see Colvin, *Biographical Dictionary*, pp. 329–30.

[6] *Vitruvius Britannicus* ii, pl. 46, house at Sunbury, Middlesex, 'designed and executed by Mr. Fort, Anno 1712'. A few years later he added the wings to Chevening House, Kent, for the first Lord Stanhope.

[7] Colvin, *Dictionary*, p. 516.

[8] *Cal. Treas. Books* xxix, p. 686. The salary was £50 per annum.

[9] *Cal. Treas. Papers 1714–19*, pp. 309–10; Works 6/7, p. 9.

measure the works done at Windsor with the Clerk there, and Mr. Rowland measure the works at Hampton Court with Mr. Fort', while Kynaston was to be generally available for the same purpose.[1]

Only one of the new appointments proved to be unfortunate, and that was John Mercer, the new Clerk Ingrosser nominated by the Treasury. The duties of his office were now confined to making up the accounts, but by an oversight he received a patent copied verbatim from those of previous Clerks Ingrosser, in which they were styled 'Chief Clerk of the King's Works', and entitled among other things to attend the monthly meetings of the Board. Mercer claimed that this in effect made him a Commissioner, and that 'he could not with any consistency or propriety attend the Board as a Clerk Engrosser (which is in truth but a Copying Clerk, and a substitute of the Chief Clerk)'. The Board assured the Treasury that Mercer's only qualification for office was 'writing a fair hand and keeping books'. 'We do not', they went on, 'doubt of the activity of his genius, [but] he refuses to do the only thing he is fit for, which evidently demonstrates 'twas rather his ambition than his activity he had a desire to gratify.' In July 1717 his patent was accordingly revoked, and his place was given by the Treasury to a more amenable clerk called Edward Wadeson.[2]

As for those other relics of the past, the Purveyor and the Master Workmen, the new Orders were silent. The Purveyorship had for some time been almost a sinecure, because the purchase of materials in advance at favourable prices, which had once been its responsibility, had for many years been impossible because of shortage of ready money, and in practice materials were either supplied by the contracting workmen, or bargained for by the Board itself.[3] As early as 1684 the Treasury had, at the Board's suggestion, agreed to suppress the office, but in the following year a certain Joseph Radcliffe petitioned for it and was, perhaps inadvertently, admitted to office.[4] In 1694 he was succeeded by Charles Hopson, the Master Joiner, for whom the office can have been little more than an additional perquisite, and in 1709 Hopson had handed it over to his son John, who was in possession in 1715.[5] Now Vanbrugh was urging that the Purveyorship was 'absolutely useless', and ought to be abolished together with the places of all the master workmen. Halifax appears to have accepted this reasoning, and to have agreed that whenever any of these offices fell vacant by death or resignation no fresh appointment should be made.[6] The post of Master Carpenter was accordingly 'sunk' when John Churchill died in November 1715, and no one was nominated to take the place of Thomas Robinson, the Chief Smith, when he died in 1716.

The principal changes introduced by the Orders of April 1715 have now been described. The new Board met for the first time on 6 May 1715. All five Commissioners were there, and one of the two Secretaries to the Treasury made a token appearance for the first and last time.[7] At a subsequent meeting the Board asked

[1] Works 4/1, 2 Dec. 1715, 19 November 1716.
[2] *Cal. Treas. Papers 1714–19*, pp. 300, 309–10, 444 (T 1/220, ff. 157–160); *Cal. Treas. Books* xxx, p. 485, xxxi, pp. 466, 499; Works 6/11, ff. 99–102.
[3] T 1/220, f. 144ᵛ.   [4] *Cal. Treas. Books* vii, p. 1039, viii, pp. 112, 502.
[5] *Cal. Treas. Books* x, pp. 265, 694, xxiii, p. 423.   [6] Works 6/7, f. 74; T 1/220, f. 144ᵛ.
[7] Works 4/1, p. 1. The representative of the Treasury was John Taylor. Lowndes attended on two subsequent occasions (31 December 1715 and 7 January 1716).

the Treasury to authorise a change advocated by Vanbrugh in his memorial to Halifax, but not included in the Orders, namely the amalgamation of the separate Office of Works at Windsor with the Whitehall Office. This was approved in August 1715. At the same time formal authority was given for the Royal Mews and the Savoy to be maintained by the Board.[1] The scope of the Board's responsibilities was further extended by the appointment of Vanbrugh as Surveyor of Gardens and Waters in June 1715, and by the addition to its members in April 1717 of William Watkins, the Surveyor of the King's Private Roads. Vanbrugh's appointment was in a sense a revival of the post previously held by Hugh May, but the salary of £400 a year was twice that enjoyed by May, and may have been based on Lord Ranelagh's stipend as Sur-intendant of Buildings and Gardens under William III.[2] This preferment Vanbrugh no doubt owed to his friend the Earl of Carlisle, who in May 1715 had succeeded Halifax as First Lord of the Treasury. As the gardens had since 1702 been in the capable hands of Henry Wise, who continued to maintain them by contract at the rate of £20 an acre, Vanbrugh's new duties cannot have been unduly arduous.[3] Nor was the Board unfamiliar with the management of the gardens, for matters concerning them were almost invariably referred by the Treasury to the officers of the Works, and it was the Paymaster through whom Wise had always received his remittances.

'Lord Halifax's Orders' (as they were unofficially called) remained in force for a little over three years. During that period the Board met on over 200 occasions. Wren missed only 43 meetings, and Vanbrugh and Dartiquenave were also very regular in their attendance. Cholmley and Hewett, with offices of their own to look after, appeared less frequently, and Edward Young, who took Hewett's place as Surveyor of Woods in July 1716, was continuously absent for months on end. Watkins appeared from time to time. Although Wren continued to bear the title of Surveyor, and to preside at the Board, it was undoubtedly Vanbrugh who was now the leading figure in the Office of Works. In a letter to the Duke of Newcastle written in 1719 he referred to this as the period 'whilst I (in effect) presided at the Board of Works', and he thought of himself, with some justification, as the person who both originated the reforms of 1715 and saw them carried into effect.[4]

By article 7 of the new Orders the Board was charged to examine and pass all accounts outstanding since the accession of Queen Anne. As no accounts since those for the year 1708 had been audited, this meant re-examining a great mass of bills, and in May 1715 the Treasury agreed to dispense the Board from examining the bills prior to 1714.[5] Even so, it was many months before the task was finished.[6] As for the Board's own management, it is doubtful whether this was any more economical than had been the case in the past. In 1718, it is true, Vanbrugh, Dartiquenave and Watkins produced some figures designed to demonstrate that the 'Ordinary' expenditure had been 'per Annum les'nd in the last three years about

---

[1] Works 4/1, pp. 14, 47, 50. For the Windsor Office, see below, pp. 117–21.
[2] *Cal. Treas. Books* xxix, pp. 550, 691–2. Above, p. 35.      [3] Below, p. 458.
[4] L. Whistler, *The Imagination of Sir John Vanbrugh* (1954), p. 244.
[5] *Cal. Treas. Papers 1714–19*, p. 109; *Cal. Treas. Books* xxix, p. 265.
[6] In a petition submitted to the Treasury in 1718 Dartiquenave implied that it had taken nearly three years (T 1/213, f. 215).

£17,555'.[1] According to them the 'Ordinary' had been reduced from an average of £41,488 during the reign of Queen Anne to £23,933 during the first three years of George I. The latter figure is consistent with the 'Ordinary' expenditure recorded in Dartiquenave's accounts, which amounted in 1716 to £19,101 and in 1717 to £23,063.[2] But in Anne's reign the 'Ordinary' and the 'Extraordinary' were not distinguished after 1708, and the figure of £41,488 was obtained by an arbitrary deduction from the grand total of only £20,600 for nine years of 'Extraordinary' expenditure, that is a mere £2288 a year. Which items should be treated as 'Ordinary' and which as 'Extraordinary' was to some extent open to question, but as the figures for the 'Extraordinary' expenditure in Dartiquenave's own accounts amounted in 1706 to £14,726, in 1707 to £14,418 and in 1708 to £16,335,[3] the figure put forward in 1718 was ludicrously low, and can be discounted as a piece of not very scrupulous special pleading designed to reinforce Vanbrugh's repeated assertions that the cost of the King's Works had been 'greatly decreas'd' under his management.[4] In fact, if allowance is made for the extra expenditure entailed by the addition to the Board's responsibilities of Windsor Castle, the Mews and the Savoy, amounting to some £3000 a year, the cost of the 'Ordinary' during the three years in question (1715–18) was not very different from what it had been in the days when Wren was in full control of the Office.[5] There had, however, been a genuine reduction in the total expenditure (accounted for by a fall in the 'Extraordinary' to some £5500 a year), and this, enhanced by Vanbrugh's tendentious manipulation of the figures, enabled him to pose as an economical reformer.

Having (as he thought) given this proof of his administrative ability, Vanbrugh must have felt confident that before long he would succeed Wren as Surveyor and preside over the Office of which he was already the effective head. But in April 1718 his expectations were dashed by the announcement that Wren was to be dismissed in order that his place might be given to William Benson.

---

[1] Works 6/7, f. 85; cf. the Board's claim in June 1716 that the expenses of the past year, both Ordinary and Extraordinary, 'does not amount to half what they have done for many years last past, notwithstanding the Extraordinarys have been much greater than formerly' (Works 6/6, p. 252).
[2] Works 5/141. No distinction between 'Ordinary' and 'Extraordinary' was made in the accounts for 1715 or 1718.
[3] Works 5/141.
[4] *The Works of Sir John Vanbrugh*, vol. 4, *The Letters*, ed. G. F. Webb, pp. 96, 104. See also the letters published by L. Whistler, *The Imagination of Sir John Vanbrugh*, pp. 244–5.
[5] By the omission of Windsor, etc., the figures for the 'Ordinary' in 1716 and 1717 are reduced to £16,320 and £19,994 respectively.

*Chapter V*

# WILLIAM BENSON

WILLIAM BENSON was the eldest son of Sir William Benson, a wealthy iron merchant of Swedish descent who had been sheriff of London in the reign of Queen Anne. As a young man he had made a continental tour which included Hanover and Stockholm. When in 1707 he married the daughter of a Bristol merchant, the settlement made by his father included the purchase of lands in Wiltshire to the value of £5000.[1] Among them was the estate at Wilbury upon which he proceeded to build a house. Architecturally, Wilbury House was remarkable in more ways than one: it was a villa (in the Italian sense of the word) rather than a traditional English seat, and its principal elevation derived from Amesbury Abbey, a seventeenth-century house designed by John Webb in the style of Inigo Jones.[2] In the reign of George II the imitation of Palladian villas was to be a common feature of English architecture under the leadership of Lord Burlington, but in the reign of Queen Anne Wilbury was unique. According to *Vitruvius Britannicus* the house was 'invented and built' by Benson himself. Even if this was polite flattery, Benson was clearly an architectural patron whose ideas were ahead of his time. He also appears to have taken some interest in hydraulics. It was the piped water supply (originating on his own property) with which he provided the inhabitants of Shaftesbury that helped to ensure his election as Whig M.P. for that borough in 1715,[3] and in 1716 he is said to have ingratiated himself with George I by 'giving directions' for a 'curious waterwork' in the gardens at Herrenhausen that was reputed to 'excel the famous fountain of St. Cloud in France'.[4] By what other means he may have recommended himself at Court is not clear, but it was 'very well known' (to quote John Ker of Kersland) 'that Mr. Benson was a favourite of the Germans'.[5] As he was also well known as the author of a celebrated pamphlet in which Swedish history was used to denounce a Tory rival, Sir Jacob Bancks, himself a naturalised Swede, for advocating 'the Divine uncontrolled power of Princes', Benson was an obvious candidate for preferment by a Whig government. The office to which he

[1] P.C.C. 147 BARNES (The elder Benson's will).
[2] Wilbury and Amesbury were both illustrated by Colen Campbell in *Vitruvius Britannicus*.
[3] R. C. Hoare, *History of Modern Wiltshire: Dunworth Hundred* (1829), p. 33; Hutchins, *History of Dorset* iii (1868), p. 45. When he was rejected by the electors of Shaftesbury in 1727 he promptly cut off their water supply.
[4] J. Nichols, *Literary Anecdotes of the Eighteenth Century* ii (1812), p. 138. According to U. von Alvensleben & Hans Reuther, *Herrenhausen* (Hanover, 1966), p. 70, the mechanism was constructed in 1718 by an English mechanic called Joseph Andrews, in accordance with Benson's instructions.
[5] *Memoirs of John Ker of Kersland* ii (1726), pp. 110–11.

aspired was one of the lucrative auditorships of the Imprests, held at the time by Edward Harley and Thomas Foley. On 16 November 1717 he duly obtained a reversionary grant of whichever auditorship should first fall vacant.[1] But as neither Harley nor Foley seemed likely to die in the near future, he or his friends looked round for some other office that would serve as a stop-gap. The surveyorship of the Works no doubt commended itself to him, partly because of his architectural interests and partly because the aged Wren could easily be displaced, as (unlike the two auditors) he held his office only 'during the king's pleasure'. On 26 April 1718 Wren's patent was accordingly revoked, and Benson was appointed Surveyor of the King's Works 'until the said William Benson shall be in possession of one of the two offices of Auditor of the Imprests and Forreign Accounts or untill he shall accept of some other office or place from us'.[2]

Although Benson was now in possession of the Surveyor's title and emoluments he was not yet in effective control of the Board, which was still governed by the Orders of 1715. By those regulations the Surveyor's office was virtually placed in commission, a state of affairs that an ambitious man like Benson was not likely to tolerate for long. By August 1718 he had in fact persuaded the Treasury to rescind Lord Halifax's Orders, and return to those of 1705. Since March 1718 the First Lord had been the Earl of Sunderland, and among his papers at Blenheim Palace there is a notebook containing a list of objections to the Orders of 1715 which must have been provided by Benson or by someone acting on his behalf.[3] It begins by denouncing the new Board as 'entirely new and a totall alteration of the Board of Works as it had been constituted for many reigns, that is to say in the Surveyor, Controller, Master Mason and Master Carpenter'. The well-founded objection to the presence on the Board of the two master workmen is dismissed on the ground that all members of the Board are prohibited from being concerned in work for the Crown, and the writer claims that in their absence the Board is 'very much in the dark' in judging prices of materials and labour. 'In the room of these two officers', he goes on, 'the new orders has substituted first the Paymaster of the Works, who never was of the Board before for a very obvious reason, because as he has poundage of all he pays, the more he allows the Workmen the greater is his profitt. Next the Paymaster are the Secretaries of the Treasury who never attend, and the Surveyor Generall of the Lands, who would be a very usefull officer, if it was made worth his while to attend the service of the Board, but at present he has no consideration for it. The Surveyors of the Woods, & of the Private Roads, are likewise of the Board, but as they doe all the business belonging to their respective provinces by their own officers, upon whom the Board has no check, & are afterwards Judges of their Bills & sollicitors for them, in all probability theirs cannot be an Establishment for the service of the Crown.' The document continues in this tendentious manner, incidentally contriving to insinuate that Vanbrugh had not been carrying out his prescribed duties, either as Comptroller or as Surveyor of Gardens and Waters.

---

[1] Patent Roll 4 George I, part 4, no. 23.        [2] Patent Roll 4 George I, Part 5, no. 24.
[3] Blenheim Muniment Room. D.II.7. 'Observations upon the late Queen's and His present Majesty's instructions.'

On 21 August 1718 the new Board was accordingly dissolved, and Benson was invested with all the powers that Wren had enjoyed until 1715.[1] Within a week he had got Hawksmoor dismissed from his posts of Secretary to the Board and Clerk of the Works at Whitehall, both of which he bestowed on his own brother Benjamin, 'lately come from a merchant in Holland'.[2] Vanbrugh's protégé Kynaston was deprived of his Clerkship of the Works at the Tower, which was given to George Sampson. Thomas Fort was allowed to remain at Hampton Court, as was Henry Joynes at Kensington, but at Newmarket Andrews Jelfe was replaced by Leonard Wooddeson, who was moved from Winchester in order that Benson might bestow the clerkship there, with its minimal duties, on David Toomer, the Mayor of Shaftesbury (where Benson was about to seek re-election as M.P. for the borough).[3] Edward Wadeson, whose twelve-year service as an under-clerk had so recently been rewarded by his promotion to the post of Clerk Ingrosser, was removed to make way for another newcomer. This was Colen Campbell, a Scottish gentleman who, having abandoned the law for architecture, had recently begun the publication of *Vitruvius Britannicus*, a manifesto of the new Palladian style of which Benson was an amateur.[4] According to Vanbrugh he was Benson's 'agent', and on 2 September 1718 he was formally appointed the Surveyor's Deputy.[5] On 14 September Vanbrugh replied by announcing that Kynaston was to be *his* deputy.[6] At the same time Benson filled two posts that would have been allowed to lapse if Vanbrugh had still been in control. These were the Purveyorship and the office of Master Carpenter.[7] Of Robert Barker, the new Master Carpenter, little is known beyond the fact that he was soon to show his subservience to Benson: but the appointment of James Moore as Purveyor looks like a calculated insult to Vanbrugh, for Moore was none other than the joiner to whom the Duchess of Marlborough had entrusted the completion of Blenheim after her epic quarrel with her architect.[8]

It was obvious that if Benson had his way Vanbrugh too would soon be dismissed. No efforts were spared to bring about his fall. 'I have reason to believe', he told the Duke of Newcastle, 'the King has had such an unfair Account given him secretly of my Management, both of his Houses and Gardens; As must make me Appear a very bad Officer in the Employments he has been pleas'd to intrust me with. And I am inform'd, This Representation has been follow'd, with an Attempt

[1] *Cal. Treas. Books* xxxii, pp. 97, 535, 564–5.

[2] T 1/216, f. 82; Works 6/11, p. 130, where Vanbrugh and Jackson, as members of the Board, give their formal assent to an appointment of which they must both have heartily disapproved.

[3] Hutchins, *History of Dorset* iii (1868), p. 16. The title-page of Sir Jacob Bancks's *Letter to William Benson* (for which see below, p. 63) promises a further pamphlet about the Shaftesbury election, including an account 'of Mr. Justice Toomer the Tinman's Advancement to be Clerk of the Works at Winchester, for the better Government of the Town of Shaftesbury, of which he is at present Half Mayor at least'. At the inquiry into Benson's election at Shaftesbury it had transpired that Toomer's election as Mayor was disputed, and that he refused to allow anyone to vote in the parliamentary election who did not acknowledge himself as Mayor. As a result 146 voters were disfranchised. The House of Commons found Toomer guilty of 'arbitrary and illegal practices' and ordered him to be arrested by the Serjeant at Arms (*Commons' Journals*, vol. 19, pp. 71–3).

[4] Campbell's Nairnshire origins are discussed by R. Goodfellow in *Architectural Review*, 140 (1966), pp. 195–6. They are confirmed by his will (P.C.C. 243 ABBOTT), and any doubt that the architect was the same as the lawyer is removed by the fact that in the building accounts of the Rolls House in Chancery Lane he is described as 'Colen Campbell, Doctor of Laws' (below, p. 358).

[5] Works 6/11, f. 128.     [6] Works 6/11, f. 140.

[7] *Cal. Treas. Books* xxxii, p. 542.     [8] David Green, *Blenheim Palace* (1951), pp. 148, 265–6.

to have me remov'd from his Service: And that this Attempt, is in a way of Suc-ceeding.'[1] Luckily Sunderland was a good friend to him at the Treasury, and the 'dark Stroaks in the King's Closet' which he so much feared failed to achieve their purpose.[2] But all his reforms were undone, Jackson was back on the Board, and Benson was (as the event will show) already throwing the Office into confusion by his conduct. Benson's next move in his battle with Vanbrugh was formally to lay charges of mismanagement against the former officers, from Wren downwards. In January 1719 Vanbrugh found 'poor Dartiquenave scar'd out of his Witts about a Memoriall given in by Campbell and Benson the Young, to decry the Managements of former Boards, and exalt this precious New One'.[3] This was followed by the Surveyor's own memorial, whose text has not been preserved. The answers to it are, however, still among the Treasury Papers, and from these it appears that there were four charges affecting the Board:

　　1. That the Officers failed to keep a record of measurements of all works.
　　2. That proper Books of Stores were not kept by the Clerks of Works.
　　3. That the Board had ordered private apartments to be fitted up contrary to their Orders.
　　4. That by not employing the Purveyor they had been extravagant in the provision of materials, and in particular that excessive prices had been paid for Portland Stone.

In a joint memorandum Vanbrugh, Dartiquenave, Young and Watkins had no great difficulty in rebutting these charges by a straightforward statement of 'short plain truths, without Art, Evasions or Perplexity'.[4] As for their subordinates, Hawksmoor, Kynaston and Fort were equally effective in their replies,[5] while Wren, from his retirement at Hampton Court,[6] expressed his surprise and concern 'that after haveing served the Crown and the Publick above Fifty years, and at this great Age, I should be under a necessity of taking a Part in answering a Memorial Presented by Mr. Benson to your Lordships, charging some Mismanagements on the late Commissioners of the Board of Works'. Under the Orders of 1715 he had, he said,

> had the honour to be first nam'd with the old title of Surveyor, yet in acting I had no power to over-rule, or give a casting-vote: I did however, as often as my Infirmities would permit, attend the Board, and endeavour'd to doe his Majesty all the service I was able, with the same integrity and zeal which I had ever practis'd.
> 　I doubt not but the Gentlemen concern'd in the late Commission will lay before

---

[1] *The Complete Works of Sir John Vanbrugh*, vol. 4, p. 98.　　　[2] *Op. cit.*, pp. 100, 109.
[3] *Op. cit.*, p. 109. This memorial is also referred to by Thomas Fort in his reply to Benson's charges (T 1/225, f. 229v).
[4] T 1/220, ff. 144–5.　　　　　　　　　[5] T 1/225, ff. 229–38.
[6] In 1706 Wren had asked for a 50-year lease of his official house on Hampton Court Green, which he undertook to rebuild, as it was in a decayed state, at the same time renouncing his right to arrears of salary due to him amounting to £341. This request was granted in 1708, Queen Anne observing that although it would deprive future Surveyors of their lodgings at Hampton Court, she would gratify Wren as 'an old servant to the Crown' (*Cal. Treas. Books* xx, p. 749; xxii, pp. 26, 308, 370). The Old Court House (as it is called) still exists, but has been much altered since Wren's time. A survey drawing of it made for Wren by Dickinson in March 1709/10 is reproduced in *Wren. Soc.* xii, pl. xx.

your Lordships such particular answers to the Memorial of Complaint, as will be satisfactory; I crave leave to Refer thereto, and may presume to say, that notwithstanding the Pretentions of the Present Surveyor's Management to be better then that of the late Commissioners, or Theirs to be better then what preceeded, yet I am perswaded, upon an impartial view of Matters, & fairly distinguishing all particulars, with due consideration had to long protracted payment of artificers, there will be no just grounds for the censuring former Managements; and as I am Dismiss'd, haveing worn out (by God's mercy) a long Life in the Royal service, and haveing made some Figure in the World, I hope it will be allow'd me to Die in Peace.[1]

Wren's dignified appeal was respected, and no further action was taken against him or his former colleagues. By now, indeed, there was little disposition at the Treasury to listen to Benson's accusations. For the Surveyor General had to a large extent been discredited by his own behaviour. His first blunder arose from an ill-judged attempt to assert his supposed rights over the quarries on the Isle of Portland in Dorset, which was Crown land. Ever since the time of Sir John Denham the king's manorial rights had been exercised in such a way as to ensure that his Works were always adequately served with stone. One of the best quarries was actually on the royal demesne, and could not be worked without the permission of the Crown's agents: nor could any stone be exported from the island without the king's warrant, the exercise of which had in 1669 been entrusted to Wren, as it had before been to Denham and Jones. Special privileges, including control of the pier and crane, had moreover, been granted in 1677 to the dean and chapter of St. Paul's, who had delegated their powers to Wren as architect to the cathedral. In this way Wren, in his dual capacity as Surveyor General and architect to St. Paul's, had for nearly forty years been in effective control of the quarries, where he had kept an agent to enforce his authority. This control had not been maintained without occasional friction between the Surveyor and the inhabitants of Portland. What the latter particularly resented was the Crown's exemption from the duty of 12d. a ton charged on stone destined for private purchasers, out of which they were entitled to 9d. as compensation for the damage done to their common land by the quarrying operations. In 1705 Wren had found it necessary to address a very sharp letter on this subject to the Islanders.[2] His special powers were, however, deemed to have been terminated by the Act of 1711 which declared that St. Paul's was legally complete, and in 1714 the Treasury decided to appoint an agent of its own to watch over the Crown's interests in Portland.[3] The Surveyor's rights were now limited to declaring what stone was dug for the royal works and consequently exempt from the 12d. duty.[4] Wren had accepted the new arrangement without demur, but Benson, anxious no doubt to assert himself in a county where he was himself a landowner, proceeded without consulting the Treasury to nominate his own agent, claiming that he had the right to do so by the terms of his appointment as Surveyor General. Outraged at his behaviour, the Treasury peremptorily ordered him immediately 'to recall the authority you have issued with intent to supersede Mr. Tucker [the

[1] T1/220, f. 216.
[2] *Victoria County History of Dorset* ii, pp. 341–2.
[3] *Cal. Treas. Books* xxix, pp. 244–5, 420.
[4] *Cal. Treas. Books* xxix, pp. 699–700.

Crown agent]', and let him know that his behaviour was 'highly resented'.[1] This was in September 1718. In December the Treasury was no less astonished to receive a letter from Benson informing them that it was the king's order that the contract for maintaining the royal gardens should be taken away from Henry Wise and his partner Joseph Carpenter and given to a certain Thomas Ackers. Whatever the king's wishes might be, their transmission to the Lords of the Treasury in a letter from one of their own subordinates was an impropriety that could not for a moment be tolerated. Without hesitation Sunderland summoned Benson to the Treasury, informed him that it was 'an unusual piece of presumption in an inferior officer to write in such a manner to this Board', and ordered his letter to be burnt in his presence.[2]

The attempted dismissal of Wise and his partner was in fact part of a scheme whose essential dishonesty the Treasury had only recently exposed, and Benson's letter must have been a last attempt to achieve his end by invoking the king's personal authority. In the form in which it reached the Treasury the proposal appeared to have much to commend it. It was an offer to maintain the royal palaces by contract for a fixed annual sum. For £12,000 a year, Benjamin Jackson, the Master Mason, Robert Barker, the Master Carpenter, and Thomas Hughes, the Master Bricklayer, would be prepared to carry out the ordinary repairs of the palaces, while Thomas Ackers expressed his readiness to maintain the gardens 'for half what they have hitherto cost'. As the 'Ordinary' had recently been fixed by the Treasury at £14,400, to which Wise's contract for the gardens added another £2960, this represented a saving of several thousand pounds a year to king and Treasury.[3]

But only three of the Patent Artisans were members of the consortium. The Master Joiner, the Master Plasterer, the Master Glazier, the Sergeant Painter and the Sergeant Plumber were left out in the cold, and they stood to lose a large part of their livelihoods if the proposal went through. It was they who exposed the plot. What they told the Treasury was that the whole scheme had been devised by Benson for his own benefit: that the three contractors were bound by indenture to assign the benefit of their contract to Benson's brother and his deputy Campbell, and that these two in turn were to hand over the profits to Benson. In return for the use of their names the three contracting workmen were to be paid £250 (in the case of the bricklayer only £100) each, 'either for Bribes or Hush money'. All this was dubious enough, but what made the fraudulent character of the proposal abundantly clear was a clause whereby all disputes were to be settled by three persons, one to be nominated by the Treasury, one by the Surveyor, and the third by the contractors; so that (to quote Vanbrugh) 'he had 2 Arbitrators against the Treasury's one, and consequently as little money might be expended as he pleas'd, And by the same Contract he is made Judge what Buildings are necessary or fit to be repair'd, or pulld down & rebuilt, whereby to save himself £50, He might put the Crown to £500, And call it Extraordinarys'.[4] This was simply a new and more sophisticated version of Jackson's old game of 'doing the king's work and

[1] T 27/22, p. 351; T 1/220, ff. 25–30; LR 5/9.    [2] *Cal. Treas. Books* xxxii (2), p. 121.
[3] Works 6/11, f. 112.    [4] T 1/216, f. 82v.

judging his own prices'. Benson was to be both Surveyor and contractor, which, as the indignant Artisans pointed out, was 'the most barefaced fraud that ever was attempted on that Board, especially by one who has a sallary to prevent such frauds'.[1] For their knowledge of this elaborate piece of deceit the Artisans were indebted to Jackson. At the last moment he had—not scruples, but doubts: doubts that Benson would take the money and leave him (despite the assignment of the contract) legally liable to the Crown for the performance of the repairs. The elder Benson told him 'that it would be the worse for him if he did not sign', the younger threatened him with the loss of his patent. But Jackson remained obdurate, and in due course his testimony before the Treasury Board helped to demonstrate the truth of the workmen's allegations.[2] Vanbrugh took the opportunity to give the Treasury his own account of Benson's dishonest proposals, as well as of his 'ignorance and obstinacy' in the conduct of the Works,[3] and the Surveyor's discomfiture was completed by his former victim Sir Jacob Bancks, who gleefully made the whole affair public in an entertaining and hard-hitting pamphlet.[4] These disclosures were not without effect. On taking office Benson had been obliged by law to vacate his seat at Shaftesbury. He had just been re-elected, but allegations of bribery had been made by his Tory opponent, Sir Edward Desbouverie, and in January 1719 the case was heard by a parliamentary committee. Benson was unseated, 'though not only all the Germans but the Monarch himself solicited strenuously for him'. It was noted, however, that 'the Prince's party and several of the other Court [i.e. the king's] joined the Tories upon this occasion, which shews that all sides were heartily weary of the sitting member'.[5]

Meanwhile the Office of Works was in confusion. For weeks on end the Board failed to meet, either because Benson preferred to dispense with it, or because its members were too much at odds to transact any business. For six months no bills were examined, ostensibly because Jackson's persistence in performing the mason's work rendered him incapable of assisting in passing them.[6] Early in the New Year (1719) the Treasury received a petition from the workmen complaining that at Christmas 1718 their payments were twelve months in arrear, and that their accounts 'do lye in the said Office unpass'd, to their great and apparent detrement, and contrary to all former usage and custom'.[7] In April Benson had himself to admit that 'the Office of His Majesty's Works is in very great Disorder', that 'some of the best workmen are absented from the King's business, others refuse to goe on with it, and some are unable for want of the money that is due to them from His Majesty

[1] T 1/216, f. 132v.
[2] *Cal. Treas. Books* xxxii (2), pp. 118–19; T 29/24 (1), ff. 129, 130, 137. The extent to which the Crown would have been financially exploited was demonstrated by a rival offer from Thomas Highmore, the Sergeant Painter, Job Bickerton, carpenter, John Woodall, mason, and Henry Cobden, bricklayer, to maintain the same palaces for only £8000 a year (T 1/220, f. 60).
[3] T 1/216, ff. 82/3, unsigned but in Vanbrugh's hand and dated by internal evidence to March 1719.
[4] *A Letter from Sir J. B—ks to W. B—, Esq; S.O. By Birth an Englishman; But Unnaturaliz'd and turn'd Swede, Architect, Hydrographer, and Gardiner; and for a little time M— of the P— P—: concerning a late Contract, that was endeavour'd to be Establish'd by a certain Bold Officer in Sweden, to the utter Undoing of the Board of Works in that Kingdom, Done from the Original Copy at Stockholm, 1718* (London, Printed for A. Moore, near St. Paul's Church, MDCCXIX).
[5] Hist. MSS. Comm., *Portland* v, p. 577 (Edward Harley jr to Abigail Harley).
[6] Works 6/7, pp. 121–3.      [7] T 1/220, ff. 151–2.

by accounts allready past, besides what is due from Accounts not past, and which the Officers cannot proceed upon til they have your Lordships' directions [as to whether Jackson was eligible to sit on the Board or not]'.[1]

The Treasury did not deign to reply, because by now Benson's obstinacy had brought him into conflict with still higher authority. Determined, with the aid of Colen Campbell, to declare the Houses of Parliament unsafe, and thus to have the opportunity of rebuilding them, Benson had thrown the House of Lords into confusion by reporting that their Chamber was in imminent danger of collapse. A ceremonial visit by the king to give the Royal Assent to some Bills had to be cancelled at the last moment, and the peers were obliged hurriedly to move to temporary quarters in Westminster Hall while the roof of their House was shored up under Benson's directions. Benson's warning was supported by his two henchmen, Colen Campbell and his brother Benjamin, and also by Robert Barker, the Master Carpenter. In the circumstances described above, it was not surprising that the Master Mason should not have joined in the report. But someone in the Lords was not satisfied, and orders were given for the Master Mason and the Master Carpenter 'to take such persons as they shall think proper', 'view the walls and timber', and report on oath to the House. Once more Jackson made it his business to expose the folly of his superior officer. His report, supported by some of the best architectural advice in London, was to the effect that the House was basically sound and that Benson's attempt to shore up the roof 'could be of little or no service to that purpose'. The rest of the story is related in detail on another page.[2] Obstinately refusing to admit his error, Benson defied the Lords' express order to remove his shores. By now there could be no doubt that he and his colleagues had misled the House in a manner which it could hardly be expected to overlook, and on 16 March the Lords formally drew the king's attention to Benson's misconduct. On 16 April the Lord Chamberlain reported that His Majesty 'had given Order for suspending the said William Benson from the Execution of his Office; and would give further Order for his effectual Prosecution'.[3]

But Benson, despite private hatred and public disgrace, was not the man to relinquish office without a struggle, and there are indications that his departure from the Office of Works was not accomplished without a certain amount of legal dispute and hard bargaining. In May 'the case of Mr. Benson relating to his patent as Surveyor of the Works' was being considered by the Attorney General, and it was not until 17 July 1719 that he formally surrendered his office to the king.[4] His reversionary grant of the auditorship of the Imprests was of course not affected, and sixteen years later he duly succeeded Edward Harley in that capacity.[5] Meanwhile he had secured for himself the lease of a wharf in Scotland Yard, reputed to be worth £1500 a year,[6] and 'an assignment of a considerable debt due to the Crown in Ireland'.[7] Of prosecution nothing more was heard, so it was not without

---

[1] Works 6/7, f. 123.                                      [2] Below, pp. 395–7.
[3] *Lords' Journals*, xxi, p. 143.                         [4] T 29/24 (1), f. 170; Works 6/11, f. 151.
[5] The grant was confirmed after George II's accession (*Cal. Treasury Books & Papers 1731–4*, p. 688). Benson employed the same deputy, Edward Bangham, as his predecessor (*Gentleman's Magazine* v, 1735, p. 560).
[6] Below, p. 446. Ker of Kersland says it was 'worth yearly above £1500' (*Memoirs* ii, pp. 110–11).
[7] The assignment of the debt rests on the authority of the biographical note in J. Nichols, *Literary Anecdotes of the Eighteenth Century* ii (1812), p. 139.

some substantial salvage from the wreckage of his career that Benson departed from the Office of Works, taking with him a number of 'plans, drawings, elevations and surveys belonging to that Office', which it took several letters and a threat of legal action to recover from his possession.[1]

Benson's surveyorship was beyond question the most disastrous episode in the whole history of the royal works. In the course of fifteen months he had dismissed his ablest subordinates, declared war on his closest colleagues, infuriated the Treasury, and finally brought down upon himself the wrath of the House of Lords. All the benefits of the reforms so recently brought about by Halifax and Vanbrugh had been thrown away, and the Office of Works was once more in a state of confusion and demoralisation far worse than it had experienced under the lax rule of the aged Wren. Conduct so outrageously perverse is hard to explain in rational terms. Vanbrugh, in his memorandum to the Treasury, attributed Benson's behaviour to 'Ignorance and Obstinacy if not worse'.[2] The insinuation of insanity might be dismissed as a characteristic exaggeration but for the fact that in later life Benson was indubitably out of his mind. In 1745 a lawsuit came before the House of Lords to which Benson was a party. In the course of a lengthy submission his own lawyers certified that in September 1741 Benson 'was seized with a violent Disorder of Mind, and deprived of his Understanding and Memory . . . and entirely incapacitated from transacting or doing any business . . . and continued in this Condition until about December 1742'.[3] They were not concerned with their client's past behaviour at the Office of Works. But in the light of this statement it may well be thought that it was a man of unsound mind to whom George I so unwisely entrusted the management of his Works in April 1718.

[1] T 27/23, p. 102. A list of the drawings in question is given in Works 6/7, p. 193. It included 'A Draught of the Island of Portland', 'A new Designe for bringing Kensington Palace into a regular fine Building', and several plans showing the water-supply of various royal palaces.

[2] T 1/216, f. 83.

[3] B.M., Add. MS. 36156, f. 99 (Benson v. Vernon). I owe this reference to Mr. E. L. C. Mullins and the History of Parliament Trust.

*Chapter VI*

# THE OFFICE OF WORKS
## 1719–1782

BENSON'S ADMISSION in his last letter to the Treasury—that the Office of Works was 'in very great disorder'[1]—had been something of an understatement. The disorder was acute, and it was largely disorder of his own creation. With his departure in July 1719, however, the Office of Works returned to normality and settled down to sixty years of comparative somnolence.

During this period the department's framework of regulations underwent no fundamental change. The new constitution of 1715 had been designed primarily to deal with the problem caused by Wren's failing grasp. It had already been set aside at Benson's instance, and no attempt was made to revive it after his fall. The Royal Instructions of 1719 therefore followed almost exactly the system of rules established in the Instructions of 1705.[2] The roster of palaces and buildings remained unaltered, except that Windsor Castle, the Savoy and the Mews at Charing Cross were formally brought under the Board's jurisdiction.[3] Once again the Board was to consist of the Surveyor, the Comptroller, the Master Mason and the Master Carpenter. But this time an extra (and, as it turned out, nominal) member—Tobias Jenkins (1660–1730), Whig M.P. for York in three parliaments[4]—was added to the list; and it was laid down that a quorum should consist of any three, including either the Surveyor or the Comptroller.[5] Once again the Board was to meet regularly each week,[6] with a General Meeting on the second Tuesday of each month, attended by the Paymaster, the Purveyor and all the Clerks of the Works.[7] At these monthly

---

[1] Above, p. 63.

[2] Works 6/368/4, 10 Oct. 1719. The substance of these instructions and those of 1705, 1715 and 1726 is repeated in a memorandum, possibly by Sir Robert Walpole (Walpole/Cholmondeley Papers 91/168/1 and 168/2), deposited in Cambridge University Library).

[3] Clause xxix.

[4] He attended only 94 Board meetings between 1719 and 1729 (Works 4/1–4). His appointment, and his Secret Service pension, seem to have been a reward for his efforts in the election of 1715, on which he claimed to have spent 'near £1500' (R. Sedgwick, *History of Parliament: House of Commons 1715–54* ii, 1970, p. 176). Colen Campbell dedicated a plate of *Vitruvius Britannicus* to him and complimented him on his 'particular Atachment to Architecture' (vol. ii, 1717, pls. 41–2).

[5] Clause i.

[6] Clause ii. Usually on Wednesdays under George I, on Tuesdays or Thursdays under George II and on Wednesdays or Fridays under George III.

[7] Clerks occasionally had to be reminded of this duty, e.g. Isaac Ware's rebuking of William Rice (Works 1/3, f. 90, 13 March 1753).

meetings itemised accounts for the previous month were to be presented, showing 'Days Men . . . Task Work and Materials entered in a Book but with Blanks for the Prices, that the Board may fill up the same according to Contracts or the Current Rates of Things'. These accounts were then to be signed individually by at least three members of the Board and the respective Clerk of Works.[1] Contracts for task work were to be signed by any three members of the Board, including the Surveyor or his Deputy;[2] and orders for work emanating from the sovereign were not to be carried out until estimates had been presented to the Treasury.[3] As before, Clerks of Works were to be appointed by the Surveyor General, with the Board's approval, but were subject to dismissal only by Treasury authority.[4] They retained responsibility for stores and building materials[5] and these were to be supplied as before by the Purveyor under the Surveyor's warrant[6]—except for those supplied by the Master Smith, Painter, Plumber and Glazier 'and other work done by contract'.[7] In other words, the Purveyor's functions continued to be largely nominal.

The Clerks of Works now totalled seven. The Clerk for Whitehall, St. James's and Westminster was to receive an extra allowance, 'he being also as Secretary to attend the Board at every meeting and take the minutes, draw up reports, estimates and memorials, fill up the blanks left for prices in passing the books and cause fair entries to be made by the respective writing clerks of all proceedings of the Board'.[8] These writing clerks were now two in number: 'One to make the paybooks from the bills according to the direction of the officers. One [nominated by the Treasury] to write the Book to be delivered to the auditor and to bind together all the Books of the several houses as vouchers to remain in the office. He shall also keep the Ledger Books and prepare a list (to be put to the end of each book delivered to the Auditor) of the debts remaining due in the office. He is likewise to make monthly and quarterly abstracts of the accounts and deliver the same to the [Treasury].'[9] All Clerks of Works were responsible for measuring workmanship and taking 'weights of lead, iron etc.' used in building. But in special cases the Board might 'appoint another person (pro tempore) to assist . . . in taking measurements and casting up dimensions'.[10]

---

[1] Clauses iii and vi; Works 4/3, 9 Aug. 1726. Tradesmen who failed to submit monthly accounts promptly discovered that their settlement might be considerably delayed, e.g. Works 4/8, 9 June 1741 and Works 4/3, 11 July 1727. Clerk of Works normally signed the accounts prior to their submission to the Board (Works 4/3, 29 Sept. 1726).

[2] Clause iv. Masons' and carpenters' contracts were normally renewed every 1st March (Works 4/3, 8 Dec. 1726). 'Patterns of plumbers' and ironmongers' goods' were deposited in the office (*ibid.*, 13 Dec. 1726).

[3] Clause v.

[4] Clause viii. This clause was immediately 'fairly writ over . . . and pasted on a board and hung up in the office room' (Works 4/1, 9 Nov. 1719).

[5] Clause ix.　　　　[6] Clauses xii and xiii.

[7] Clause x.　　　　[8] Clause xix.

[9] Clause xx. After the books were signed 'no person whatever [was allowed to] make any rasure, interlineation on or alteration whatsoever without laying the same before the Board' (Works 4/2, 8 Aug. 1721).

[10] Clause xxi. In relation to their responsibilities at the new Horse Guards in 1750 the duties of Clerks of Works were defined as follows: 'to make all drawings for the workmen as they are directed, see the works carefully set out, measure all the works, and make up the several accounts, and make fair entries of them in books, to see that all materials and works are sound and good and well performed; and the prices set down in the bills agreeable to the contract; and to certify the same under each tradesman's bill' (Works 6/17, f. 63, 3 April 1750). As regards measuring, the rule was: 'all work that can be measured, must be measured' (Works 4/2, 20 March 1722/3).

The new Instructions re-established that 'each Clerk of the Works may have a Labourer of Trust to his assistance, to hasten work and look after the stores by day and night, which Labourer shall be approved by the Board and shall have his Lodging and a Dogg in the store yard and to have an allowance not exceeding 6d per diem more than other Labourers. But no other person to be permitted to lodge in the store yard and the Clerks to be responsible for their respective Labourers of Trust'.[1]

The Comptroller's duties were clearly specified: to 'keep short entries of the numbers, dates, names and sums of the bills made out and signed by the Board, . . . to compute the interest upon . . . bills'; and to sign, with the Paymaster, all applications for funds addressed to the Treasury.[2]

As for the Paymaster, he was still supposed to pay creditors each month according to strict alphabetical order 'without Preference or Favour'; and to dispatch his accounts to the Auditors within three months of settlement.[3] Moreover, he had 'to notifye in writing to be hung upon the outside of his office door to what number of the bills in course his payments of the money will extend'.[4] Payments from the Exchequer were still to be received, and old bills dealt with according to the 1705 code:[5] riding charges were to be checked collectively by the Board;[6] officers' houses were not to be sub-let without Treasury warrant,[7] nor improved at public expense except by order of the Chamberlain of the Household;[8] and 'grace and favour' lodgings were to be improved only at the incumbent's expense.[9]

As before, the cost of Ordinary works and salaries was limited to £14,400 per annum, excluding gardeners' contracts.[10] Extra works were to be authorised by royal sign manual and countersigned by the Treasury.[11] And the power to alter or add to the code of regulations was vested once more in the Treasury Commissioners.[12] In other words, as regards matters of substance, the Board was to do 'nothing but by the King's and Lords of the Treasury's direction'.[13]

Such were the Instructions issued in the name of George I. Those issued by George II in 1726 were fewer in number and rather more simply phrased.[14] They made no major alteration in the composition or functioning of the department and included only four significant innovations. The Board was now to meet each Thursday.[15] Clerks of Works were required to send in weekly written estimates of necessary works for the Board's written approval.[16] Contracts for specific works were

---

[1] Clause xv. A Labourer in Trust was defined in 1750 as one who is 'well versed in business, can write a good hand and will always attend upon the spot, to keep account of stores and deliver them out as the Clerks on duty shall direct' (Works 6/17, f. 63, 3 April 1750). He had to 'obey the orders and directions of the Clerk of Works so far as relates to H.M.'s service' (Works 4/14, 30 Aug. 1771).

[2] Clause xxii.   [3] Clause xvi.   [4] Clause xvii.

[5] Clauses vii, xxiii and xxxiii.   [6] Clause xviii.   [7] Clause xxiv.

[8] Clause xxvi.

[9] Clause xxviii. This was a recurrent matter of dispute, e.g. T 29/43, f. 35, 22 April 1773; Works 4/1, 11 Aug. 1737. The clause was specifically read out by the new Surveyor General in November 1719, 'for the good government of this office' (Works 4/1, 9 Nov. 1719). For a successful (and highly articulate) claim for repairs at Windsor by Mrs. Henrietta Egerton, see Works 6/19, ff. 20–3, 5 Dec. 1773 and 21 Jan. 1774.

[10] Clause xxx.   [11] *Ibid.*   [12] Clause xxxi.

[13] Works 4/2, 28 Feb. 1722/3.   [14] Works 6/368/5, 20 June 1726.   [15] Clause ii.

[16] Clause iii. Clerks of Works had occasionally to be reminded of this clause, e.g. Works 4/15, 10 Sept. 1774 or, more spectacularly, Ripley and Gill's magisterial rebuke to Thomas Fort (Works 1/2, f. 4, 29 Dec. 1737).

to be renewed every March by both Treasury and Board.[1] And the Surveyor's Deputy was to be paid out of departmental funds and not by the Surveyor himself.[2]

These Instructions were automatically invalidated by the death of the Sovereign in 1760.[3] But new regulations were slow in coming. It was not until 1766, when the Auditors of the Imprests declined to operate under the old Instructions, that any action was taken.[4] In that year the Treasury asked the Board to 'form and digest' a new 'Body of Orders, Rules and Instructions' designed to encourage 'Economy and Regularity'.[5] The resulting memoranda were then passed by the Treasury 'with amendments to make them conformable to those in the year 1726'.[6]

The Instructions of 1767 involved no fundamental reforms.[7] But they did incorporate a number of changes of detail. The Board was now to consist of six members: the Surveyor, Comptroller, Master Mason and Master Carpenter, plus 'Our Two Architects',[8] that is the joint 'Architects to the Crown' appointed in 1761 as a result of George III's personal initiative.[9] There were now eleven Clerks of Works —thanks to new responsibilities in the shape of Buckingham House, the King's Private Roads, Kew and Richmond Palaces and Richmond New Park Lodge, and some additional Labourers in Trust, including one appointed by the Keeper of the King's Private Roads.[10] Clerks might now be temporarily redirected to another location, with a payment of 2s. 3d. per day plus 1s. 9d. per day 'for keeping a horse'.[11] The limit for Ordinary works and salaries was raised to £22,000 per annum, excluding quarterly payments to the royal gardeners.[12] The duties of Secretary and Clerk Ingrosser were clarified. The Secretary to the Board was as before to take minutes, and prepare reports, estimates and memorials.[13] The Clerk Ingrosser was 'to cast up the Books, and to prepare the books to be delivered to the Auditors. And to see that the books of our several houses be bound up, and to take care that the same and the several ledgers of the office be well preserved'.[14] By an oversight, however, the Instructions of 1767 neglected to mention the Tower of London and the Queen's House at Greenwich. Once again it was the Auditors of the Imprests who noticed the omission and the deficiency had to be rectified in 1769.[15] Otherwise these Instructions remained unaltered until the age of Economical Reform—apart from minor emendations, such as the *ad hoc* appointment of a new Clerk of Works for Carlton House in 1775.[16]

Although normality was restored in 1719, Benson's surveyorship had provided a fatal precedent for treating the Surveyor General's office as a sinecure. For the next sixty years it was to be held by a succession of placemen whose choice was determined more by the exigencies of political patronage than by any professional

[1] Clause iii. After 1760 all Clerks of Works kept copies of contracts (Works 4/12, 19 Aug. 1760).
[2] Clause ix. His salary was £100 p.a.
[3] On the death of the sovereign, works in progress temporarily ceased, e.g. Works 4/12, 27 Oct. 1760.
[4] Works 6/18, f. 133, 8 May, 1766.          [5] T 27/29, f. 316, 13 May 1766.
[6] T 29/38, ff. 154–5, 14 Oct. 1766. The Office received a bill for £20 6s. od. from the Treasury clerks (Works 4/14, 15 Jan. 1768).
[7] Works 6/368/6, 17 July 1767; Works 4/14, 24 July 1767.
[8] Clause i.          [9] Below, p. 91.          [10] Clause ii.
[11] Clause v.          [12] Clause xx.          [13] Clause xi.
[14] Clause xv.
[15] Clause xxxiii; Works 6/18, f. 197, 18 April 1769.
[16] Works 4/15, 19 Oct. 1775.

qualifications for the post. The same was true of the Paymastership, the Keepership (or Surveyorship) of the King's Private Roads and the Superintendentship (or Surveyorship) of Gardens and Waters. Henceforth all four offices were to be distributed on an almost exclusively political basis.

In 1719, although the king's wishes could not be ignored, the choice of Benson's successor lay with the Treasury, then presided over by the Earl of Sunderland. Vanbrugh was the obvious candidate: as Comptroller he had been the most responsible member of the Board during Wren's last years. He had already been passed over once in favour of Benson and as a thorough-going Whig he was politically unexceptionable. But although he was backed by his friend the Duke of Newcastle he was not in favour at Court, and once more he saw the coveted post go to another claimant with inferior qualifications: Thomas Hewett (1656–1726) of Shireoaks, Nottinghamshire.

Thomas Hewett had three claims to office. He was a strong Whig. He had previously held the post of Surveyor of Woods North and South of Trent until Sunderland's rival Walpole had dismissed him in July 1716 in favour of Edward Young.[1] And he was an amateur architect. Together with his friend John Molesworth, Hewett had been one of the 'new Junta for Architecture' which paved the way for Burlington and his Palladian revival.[2] The architect whom they patronised was the Florentine Alessandro Galilei (1691–1737), whose design for a royal palace they enthusiastically sponsored.[3]

Hewett's aesthetic interests had been polished by five years' travel during the 1680s in France, Holland, Switzerland, Italy and Germany.[4] Thence he is said to have returned with 'a wife, atheism and many eccentricities'.[5] His wife was a Kentish heiress whom he married in Geneva.[6] His 'atheism' was a part of his Whiggery: he thought, for example, 'there is but one way' to drain the Roman Campagna, 'that is, Restore the Roman Liberty; no great public work can succeed under the worst of tyrannies, I mean Church Tyranny for Life'.[7] His eccentricities eventually caught up with him: he had to disinherit his daughter when she eloped with a local fortune-teller.[8] Still, his interest in architecture was genuine. Before his appointment as Surveyor General, he had made real efforts on Galilei's behalf.[9] After his

[1] *Cal. Treas. Papers 1714–19*, pp. 217–21, 368, 390; *Cal. Treas. Books* xxx, pp. 27, 341. Hewett complained that 'he is turned out of his offices, one of which (very inconsiderable) he has possessed since the Revolution'. He had in fact been Receiver-General of Crown Rents in Lincs., Warwicks., and Leics. (£30 p.a.) since 1695, and Surveyor-General of Woods N. of Trent (£50 p.a.) since 1696 (*Cal. Treas. Books 1693–6*, pp. 1193–4, 1348). In 1715 he was made Surveyor-General of Woods both North and South of Trent by Halifax with a salary of £100 p.a. (*Cal. Treas. Books* xxix, pp. 323–4; Vanbrugh's *Letters*, ed. Webb, p. 115).
[2] See a letter from Molesworth to Stanhope dated 5 Oct. 1717 in which he asks the latter (then First Lord of the Treasury) to allow 'Mr. Hewet, my eldest son, Sign^r Galilei & I, & (if you can engage him) Sir George Markham (who are of the new Junta for Architecture)' to show him Galilei's designs for a royal palace (Chevening House, Stanhope Archives, Cupboard C 34.1).
[3] Ilaria Toesca, 'Alessandro Galilei in Inghilterra', *English Miscellany*, ed. M. Praz, iii (1952), pp. 211–12.
[4] Epitaph in Wales Church, Yorks.
[5] J. Holland, *History . . . of Worksop* (Sheffield, 1826), pp. 176–7.
[6] She was Frances, daughter of Sir Edward Bettinson of Scadbury and Hewett's epitaph records their marriage at Geneva on 7 Sept. 1689.
[7] *Hist. MSS. Comm. Various Collections* viii, p. 368, 12 Dec. 1723 to Molesworth.
[8] Holland, *loc. cit.*
[9] 'I am troubled to part with you, and grieve, I have not estate to give you a good [pension] for life to keep you here . . . I think your fate is worse than anyone . . . I have done all I can to bring you into business and serve you' (*English Miscellany, op. cit.*, pp. 216–17, 13 July 1719).

appointment, he never quite abandoned his dream of sponsoring a splendid royal palace.[1] He may have been the architect of minor works in his own gardens at Shireoaks near Worksop, including the 'greek Tempietto lind with Marbles', noticed by Vertue, with its 'pillasters of 3 greek Orders, the floors marble, ceilings painted by . . . Trench, little Cupids on several Angles prettily design'd [and a] Bust of Sr. Th. in Marble by [Rysbrack]'.[2] But two other works can be more firmly linked with his name: Lord Sunderland's celebrated library in Piccadilly, which was built under Hewett's directions in 1719–20,[3] and the Duke of Kingston's stables at Thoresby House in Nottinghamshire, which Hawksmoor maliciously described as 'the only piece of Building that Sr. Tho. Hewett was Guilty of, dureing his being Architect Royall, . . . [and] the most infamous that ever was made'.[4]

These two works may perhaps provide the clue to Hewett's preferment. For in 1719 the gift of the Surveyor's office was virtually in Sunderland's hands as First Lord of the Treasury, while the Duke of Kingston was Lord President of the Council. With two such powerful patrons behind him Hewett was assured of success. Vanbrugh's claims were set aside; so were those of James Thornhill, the Sergeant Painter, himself an architectural designer of some ability, who put himself forward with (it was rumoured) the backing of Sunderland's mother-in-law, the redoubtable Duchess of Marlborough, and the goodwill (such as it was) of the ex-Surveyor himself.[5] For Vanbrugh it was 'a bitter Pill . . . one of the hardest pieces of Fortune, that ever fell to anybody'.[6] After seventeen impatient years as Comptroller, after actually foregoing the surveyorship once before 'out of Tenderness to Sr. Chr. Wren', he now felt that he had been cheated of the highest office by a mere Court intrigue. To the Duke of Newcastle he talked hopefully of a consolation prize in the form of the reversion of the surveyorship, or the grant of his own office for life.[7] Neither was forthcoming, but in the end Vanbrugh agreed to step aside and acquiesce in Hewett's appointment in the hope that by not pressing his own claim, he might at least induce the new Surveyor to restore Hawksmoor and Kynaston to the clerk-ships of the works from which they had been dismissed by Benson. Kynaston was in fact reinstated at Somerset House and the Tower of London, but for the time being all Vanbrugh's efforts on Hawksmoor's behalf were in vain.[8]

[1] 'I am not willing that you should dispose of the pallace to anyone without my consent' (*ibid.*). 'I have had the Honour to be often with the King who is gracious and the best of men; he has the true taste of Architecture and I hope I shall please him. He hath done me the honour to knight me without my desire. I have not yet had an opportunity to shew him the Pallace. I hope if I live to see you in England again may I flatter myself it will not be very long before I bring that to pass to your ease and content. . .' (*ibid.* pp. 217–18, 21 Feb. 1720).

[2] G. Vertue, *Notebooks* ii, *Walpole Soc.* xx (1932), p. 36. See also *Notebooks* vi, pp. 23, 70. In his will (P.C.C. 99 PLYMOUTH) Hewett directs his executor to complete various garden works at Shireoaks 'according to a draught and designe which I have made and drawn thereof'.

[3] *Survey of London* xxxii, p. 368. 150 feet long, it was described by Macky as 'the finest in Europe, both for the disposition of the Apartments, as of the Books'. In 1724 Lord Chancellor Macclesfield proposed to consult Hewett about fitting up a library at Shirburn Castle, Oxon. (Hist. MSS. Comm. *Various Collections* viii, p. 371).

[4] *Walpole Society* xix (1931), p. 126.

[5] Vanbrugh's *Letters*, ed. Webb, pp. 116–17. See also G. Vertue, *Notebooks* i, pp. 100–1, iii, p. 55. For Thornhill's ability as an architect see Colvin, *Dictionary*, pp. 610–12.

[6] Vanbrugh's *Letters*, ed. Webb, pp. 115, 123.

[7] *Op. cit.*, pp. 114–15.

[8] *Op. cit.*, pp. 117–19, 138, 169. Vanbrugh hoped at one stage to get Hawksmoor onto the Board, presumably as Master Mason in succession to Jackson, who died in May 1719.

As Secretary of the Board and Clerk of the Works at Whitehall, Westminster and St. James's Hewett nominated John Hallam, a protégé of his own from Nottinghamshire, dismissed contemptuously by Vanbrugh as 'a poor mean Country Joyner'.[1] It was not until Hewett's death in April 1726 that Hallam in his turn was sacked and that Vanbrugh's persistent advocacy of Hawksmoor at last resulted in his restoration to the Secretaryship, though not to the clerkship of the works, which went to Flitcroft.

The surveyorship of Sir Thomas Hewett (he was knighted in November 1719) lasted for six and a half years. Architecturally it was marked by nothing of importance except the completion of the new rooms at Kensington, with their 'antique' decoration by Kent. Of these 'three rooms of 36 square feet . . . exactly done according to the Grecian Tast', Hewett was particularly proud.[2] But, like Vanbrugh, he soon found that in the reign of George I architecture was 'not a trade . . . for any body to recommend themselves by at Court'.[3] By 1723 he had lost his earlier zeal for architectural reform, and settled down to a disillusioned old age.

'I am easy as to my office', he wrote to Molesworth from Shireoaks in December 1723, 'for we have nothing but repairs, my deputy [Westby Gill] a worthy careful gentleman, who informs me by letter of everything; I must tell you we have no prospect of fine new buildings and, if there were monys and inclination to build a palace (you know the finest site in the whole world) there are so many weak pretenders, wrong-headed mules that it is impossible to have anything good and of a fine taste . . . I made trial of one room at Kensington, of the fine Grecian taste, which so much fired the quacks, the knaves, the fools, that I was so baited, the work misrepresented to the K[ing], who had seen and approved of the designs and model first, and perfectly well executed, that I am discouraged to a degree sufficient to spoil any man's genius. The worst was my cavillers denied all rules and due proportions. I assure you, Arts, Geometry, Mathematics etc. are out of fashion here . . .'[4]

In other words, Hewett's 'Grecian taste' fell short of the stricter neo-classical standards insisted on by Lord Burlington. What had been a pioneer work in its day was soon outmoded, and when Hewett died in 1726 he was mourned neither by Wren's surviving colleagues nor by the new Palladians. In Nottinghamshire he left the reputation of being 'a litigious and unpleasant neighbour—one who neither feared God, nor regarded man'.[5]

Hewett's death presented Sir Robert Walpole with a convenient vacancy. He

[1] *Op. cit.*, pp. 169–70, evidently written after hearing a premature report of Hewett's death in the autumn of 1725. According to Vanbrugh Hallam never executed his office. 'Sr. Ro : Walpole', he told Lord Carlisle, 'has always reckon'd Sr. Tho: Hewet put him in for form, but gave him only a small allowance out of the Income of the Place, taking the rest to himself'. Hallam did, however, make an estimate for repairs at St. James's Palace in 1722 (Works 4/2, 27 June 1722), and the curious 'Bath Summer-House' which he designed for Sir George Savile at Rufford Abbey, Notts. (Notts. Record Office 202/2, 3, 10, 15, 16, 22 and 211/58/16) is evidence that he was not wholly without ability as an architect.
[2] Ilaria Toesca, *op. cit.*, pp. 217–18. For the works at Kensington see below, p. 198.
[3] Vanbrugh's *Letters*, ed. Webb, p. 149.
[4] Hist. MSS. Comm. *Various Collections*, viii (1913), p. 368, 12 Dec. 1723.
[5] Holland, *loc. cit.* An inventory of his property at Shireoaks Hall survives (Arundel Castle MSS., In. 4). It is dated 15 August 1726 and includes a portrait of Hewett by [Sebastiano] Bombelli and one of Lady Hewett by 'Wisson', presumably Wissing.

HKW—G

chose a young man of thirty with powerful political and architectural connections: the Hon. Richard Arundell (*c*. 1696–1758) of Allerton Mauleverer, Yorkshire. The new incumbent found his Surveyor General's salary increased by £400 a year to a total of nearly £900.[1] A younger son of Lord Arundell of Trerice, son-in-law of the second Duke of Rutland and stepson of the eighth Earl of Pembroke, Arundell was related to the Pelhams by marriage, to the Foxes and Cavendishes by instinct and to the Burlington set by inheritance and interest. Horace Walpole calls him a 'great friend' of his half-brother the ninth Earl of Pembroke, the 'architect Earl'.[2] When Lord Hervey met him at a house-party at Houghton in 1731 he reported that he was regarded as a pundit on matters architectural.[3] He certainly subscribed to books by Leoni, Kent and Ware. And it was Burlington's influence which in his early twenties made him M.P. for Knaresborough, a seat he retained for thirty-eight years.[4] Arundell had great confidence in William Kent, and tried hard to obtain for him the comptrollership at the time of his own appointment as Surveyor General. 'Your Lordship must be sensible', he told Burlington, 'how Necessary Mr. Kent's being at the Board will be to me.'[5] For, unlike Hewett, Arundell was a placeman with architectural connections rather than an architect in his own right. In fact, although he attended Board meetings more regularly than Hewett had done, he seems to have been rather a frivolous aesthete. Horace Walpole even recalls an occasion when the Surveyor General temporarily disfigured the Wilton marbles by marking their torsos with pubic hair.[6]

Arundell's future was political rather than architectural. After leaving the Office of Works in 1737 he moved on to lucrative posts as Master of the Mint, Lord of the Treasury, Treasurer of the Chamber, Clerk of the Pipe and Cofferer of the Household. Though he counted as an 'Old Whig' by the 1750s, he managed to stand well with the next generation of managers. In 1755 Newcastle hesitated to force him out of his treasurership. 'You know how nice Arundell is', he wrote to Hartington, 'I write in fear and trembling lest he should be angry with me.'[7] Still, retire he did, and with an Irish pension.[8]

Arundell's exit from the Office of Works in 1737 left the way open for another member of the Whig establishment, but this time a man of consummate political

---

[1] The Surveyor's total income is difficult to calculate at this date. But Court directories (e.g. *Chamberayne's Present State of Great Britain*, 1731) suggest £900 p.a., and with annual salary, daily wage, extra allowance, Exchequer salary and livery, riding and lodging fees, the total cannot have been far short of this sum. On the other hand the initial cost of the patent was considerable: in 1760 it cost Worsley £82 16s. od. (Worsley Papers at Hovingham, 23 Dec. 1760). But the cost of a knighthood about this time was £81 13s. 4d. (Miège and Bolton, *Present State of Great Britain*, 1748 [p. 27]).

[2] H. Walpole, *Letters*, ed. P. Toynbee iii (1903), p. 420.

[3] Earl of Ilchester (ed.), *Lord Hervey and His Friends 1728–38* (1950), p. 73.

[4] J. B. Owen, *The Rise of the Pelhams* (1957), pp. 51–2, 245, 321.

[5] Althorp MSS., Arundell to Burlington, 14 April 1726.

[6] 'Old Thomas, Earl of Pembroke . . . one day took it into his grave head to give eyeballs with charcoal to all his statues at Wilton, and then called his wife and daughters to see how much livelier the gods, goddesses and emperors were grown'. Lively, indeed! for Mr. Arundel . . . had improved on his Lordship's idea, and with the same charcoal had distributed whole thickets of black hair to the middles of the whole marble assembly' (Walpole, *Letters*, ed. P. Toynbee, xii, 1904, p. 41, 23 Aug. 1781).

[7] L. Namier and J. Brooke, *The House of Commons 1754–90*, ii (1964), p. 28; *Commons Jnls.* xxxii, p. 472.

[8] Walpole, *Letters*, ed. W. S. Lewis, ix (1941), p. 181, Walpole to Montagu, 20 Dec. 1755. See also *Gent's Mag.* xxviii (1758), p. 46 and *Survey of London* xxxii (1963), p. 510. For paintings owned by Arundell cf. G. Vertue, *Notebooks* i, *Walpole Soc.* xviii (1930), pp. 117, 161, and v, *Walpole Soc.* xxvi (1938), p. 78.

talent: Henry Fox (1705–1774), later Lord Holland, the worldly maestro of Holland House. Fox's appointment, like Arundell's, was merely a first step on the ladder. After seven years' intermittent attendance at the Office of Works he became successively Lord of the Treasury, Privy Councillor, Secretary at War, Secretary of State, Clerk of the Pells and Paymaster General, in the mean time sitting in the Commons as M.P. for Hindon, New Windsor and Dunwich. It was Fox's friend Lord Hervey who persuaded Walpole to make the initial appointment to 'an office not only very creditable, but worth above eleven hundred pounds a year'.[1] From that moment Fox's career as a sinecurist never faltered. His profits between 1757 and 1774 alone were reckoned at half a million pounds. George III called him 'a man void of principles'. Horace Walpole thought him 'dark and troubled—yet . . . an agreeable man'. 'Few men', recalled Waldegrave, 'have been more unpopular; yet when I asked his bitterest enemies what crimes they could allege against him, they always confined themselves to general accusation; that he was avaricious, encouraged jobs, had profligate friends and dangerous connexions; but could never produce a particular fact of any weight or consequence.'[2] Macaulay's dictum is perceptive: 'the most unpopular of the statesmen of his time, not because he sinned more than any of them, but because he canted less'.[3] As Surveyor General his sins are at worst 'not proven'. Far from being Hervey's 'Neglector of His Majesty's Works',[4] we know that he lived in Scotland Yard and attended Board meetings in the usual way. And as a patron of architecture this 'public defaulter of unaccounted millions'[5] at least commissioned one major piece of work, his own country seat at Kingsgate, Kent: 'a fantastic habitation, purporting to represent Tully's Formian Villa';[6] 'a fine estate and a magnificent house, with a colonnade such as Ictinus might have raised by order of Pericles'.[7]

Fox's successor as Surveyor General, the Hon. Henry Finch (?1695–1761), had a rather less dramatic career. One of a flight of thirteen Finches produced at Burley-on-the-Hill by the second Earl of Nottingham, he had previously held the post of Receiver General of the revenues of Minorca. A don turned placeman—he began as Fellow of Christ's College, Cambridge[8]—and a silent ministerialist, he sat for thirty-seven years as M.P. for Malton, the pocket-borough of his brother-in-law, Thomas Watson-Wentworth.[9] In 1743 the choice of Surveyor General seems to have lain between two of these 'dark, funereal Finches': Henry and his younger brother Edward. Pelham supported Henry; Carteret backed Edward. Pelham's influence won the day.[10] Seventeen years later, however, George III came to the throne with his own nominee as Surveyor General. Having dutifully fulfilled his obligations as Surveyor General, Finch willingly surrendered his place in return for

[1] R. Sedgwick (ed.), *Lord Hervey's Memoirs* iii (1931), p. 741. The figure of £1100 would seem to be an exaggeration.
[2] L. Namier and J. Brooke, *op. cit.*, ii (1964), pp. 461–6; *Gent's Mag.* xliv (1774), pp. 333–4. For his political career see T. W. Riker, *Henry Fox, First Lord Holland* (1911).
[3] Lord Macaulay, *Essays* (1885), pp. 301–6, 309, 762–4, 767.      [4] Below, p. 242.
[5] *Annual Register* 1769, p. 202 (City petition).      [6] *D.N.B.*
[7] Wraxall, *Memoirs* ii (1884), p. 8; Thomas Gray, 'Stanzas suggested by a View of the Seat and Ruins at Kingsgate, 1776'; *Country Life* cxiv (1953), pp. 1968–9.
[8] Pearl Finch, *History of Burley-on-the-Hill* i (1901), pp. 264–7.
[9] Namier and Brooke, *op. cit.*, ii (1964), p. 425; *Gent's Mag.* xxxi (1761), p. 284.
[10] J. B. Owen, *The Rise of the Pelhams* (1957), p. 203.

a secret service pension of £900 per annum—a generous reward partly dictated by the influence of Finch's nephew and patron, Lord Rockingham.[1]

The new Surveyor General was Thomas Worsley (1710–78) of Hovingham Hall, Yorkshire, a civilised landowner, horse-breeder and amateur architect, 'a creature of Lord Bute, and a kind of riding-master to the King'.[2] On a 'sudden and positive order' from George III,[3] Worsley arrived in Scotland Yard, soon followed by the two new Joint Architects, Robert Adam and William Chambers. All three belonged to the circle patronised by Lord Bute. Although Worsley was nominally M.P. for Orford and Callington, he seems to have been instinctively apolitical. He cursed the time spent as lobby-fodder in the Commons. 'I have well nigh sacrificed my life this last winter to my duty there', he wrote in June 1766, 'having attended four or five days every week sometimes 10 & 12 hours without moving off my seat. The consequence was violent heats and colds going home [which produced] a fever and inflammation on my lungs.'[4] Instead of politics, he lived for architecture and horses. Having travelled—between 1735 and 1737—visiting Vienna, Venice, Naples, Rome, Florence, Leghorn, Dresden and Hanover, he possessed a more than superficial knowledge of the arts. He advised Earl Harcourt, for example, on the rebuilding of Cokethorpe, Oxon.[5] And his own executed designs for the reconstruction of Hovingham exhibit an architectural talent of considerable ingenuity and power.[6] As for horses, after riding with the king one fine May day in 1769, he wrote: 'they are my musick and I thank God I have yet an hand and an ear for them'.[7]

But Worsley's later years at Hovingham, Scotland Yard and Hampton Court were far from happy. Tormented by kidney trouble and saddened by the death of his eldest son, he became increasingly conscious of his inability to perform the duties either of king's servant or of territorial landowner. As early as 1769 he was anxious to resign the surveyorship.[8] From 1770 onward he was tortured by 'frequent and severe attacks of the gravel'.[9] Chambers recommended 'Chadwick's medicine'. But the illness became worse.[10] 'Grief and pain', he told Chambers in 1774, 'have made me quite unfitt for everything. I suffer cruelly and almost constantly, and . . . [Hovingham] now in its highest beauty affords me no consolation, it only soothes my affliction by renewing ideas of my lost happiness! I am in more frequent and higher pain than ever. I have been heard to cry out above 300 yards from the house, in parting with my water . . . my late calamity and shocking disorder together . . . must end my wretched life soon. I have wished it these five years,

[1] L. Namier, *Structure of Politics at the Accession of George III* (1957 ed.), pp. 19–20, 217, 472.

[2] H. Walpole, *Memoirs of the Reign of George III*, ed. D. Le Marchant and G. F. Russell Barker (1894) i, pp. 28–9, 331. 'Worsley is made Surveyor of the Board of Works, he was the King's equerry, and passes for having a taste for architecture of which . . . the King is very fond' (Walpole, *Letters* ed. P. Toynbee, v, p. 9).

[3] 'Register of the Correspondence of the Earl of Bute', B.M. Add. MS. 36796, f. 62.

[4] B.M. Add. MS. 41197, f. 34, 7 June 1766, Worsley to Hamilton in Naples. For his political career see Namier and Brooke, *op. cit.* iii (1964), pp. 659–61.

[5] Harcourt to Worsley, 21 Dec. 1756, Hovingham MSS.

[6] *Country Life* cxxix (1961), pp. 1410–13.

[7] B.M. Add. MS. 41197, f. 101, 26 May 1769. Walpole describes him as 'a rider of the great horse and architect' (*Memoirs of . . . George III, loc. cit.*).

[8] R.I.B.A. MS. 36, 20 Oct. 1769.

[9] Worsley Papers, Hovingham.

[10] R.I.B.A. MS 36, 12 Oct. 1770.

now stronger than ever. The bribe to life is gone. Health and my eldest son, who I saw all virtue and goodness!'[1]

As Chambers put it, the Surveyor General was indeed 'much afflicted . . . both in body and mind'.[2] Still, he paid serious attention to the business of the Office of Works, even at a distance. His correspondence with Chambers, Robinson and Rice displays a close acquaintance with the intricacies of patronage and a deep sense of departmental pride.[3] He was even concerned with the calligraphy of his clerks: 'As you know dear sir', he told Chambers, 'my sole view is the *Service* and credit of the Office . . . It has been observed our memorials from the Office to the Treasury have been ill penned lately, which is rather a disgrace to us, and which I should wish to obviate, as we don't send many'.[4] On another occasion he reminded Chambers: 'The Engine Keeper at Kew should certainly be *resident* there for the sake of the service and the credit of the Board. Another difficulty occurs to me. Mr. Joseph Philipps should not have sole and absolute command at the Tower, he *drinks at times* and is not to be confided in. Pray let this point be duly weighed by the Board. . . .'[5]

One small incident sums up very well the atmosphere of the Office of Works during Worsley's conscientious surveyorship. In the spring of 1764 the Earl of Fife tried hard to persuade the department to stretch their building regulations a little in his favour. But Worsley was not to be persuaded. 'I talked to Mr. Worsley this morning', wrote Jenkinson to Grenville, 'about what Lord Fife desires; [but] I could not get him to say that even the small addition proposed by Lord Fife would not be a nuisance, and incommode the other inhabitants of Whitehall. He said, however, that it would be greatly less so than what had been proposed by Mr. Steele, and that if the King thought it a proper mark of favour to be conferred on Lord Fife, he should have nothing further to say against it. He was, however, very angry with Lord Fife for having written a letter to his clerk, attempting to influence him with a bribe. The clerk had brought the letter to Worsley, and he had shown it to the King, who approved of his rewarding the clerk's honesty by promoting him upon the first vacancy that happened . . .'[6]

It would, therefore, be quite misleading to dismiss the unreformed Office of Works as wholly corrupt. Like other branches of administration, however, it was susceptible to political pressures. In Worsley it was fortunate to have had a Surveyor General who was both conscientious and architecturally minded. But in his successor, Col. James Whitshed Keene (*c.* 1731–1822), the system of politically-based appointments produced its archetypal representative: a negative placeman, ignorant of architecture and uninterested in the welfare of his department.

Colonel Keene, 'an Irish officer of no fortune' who had served with the 5th

[1] R.I.B.A. MS. 36, 3 July 1774. By the autumn of 1777 he was reduced to walking on crutches and told Kenton Couse: 'I am very poorly, suffer most cruelly night and day . . . I bear it because I must. I force myself out to please my family, and indeed I live merely for others. Life has long been a grievous burden to me' (Worsley Papers, Hovingham, 21 Oct. 1777).
[2] R.I.B.A. MS. 37, 24 May 1774.
[3] Worsley Papers, Hovingham, *passim.*
[4] R.I.B.A. MS. 36, 3 July 1774.          [5] *ibid.*, n.d.
[6] W. J. Smith (ed.), *Grenville Papers* ii (1852), pp. 300–1, 21 April 1764. Another request by Fife to extend his river frontage was refused in 1772 (T 29/42, f. 143, 30 June 1772).

Regiment of Foot in Portugal and Germany,[1] owed his appointment to a series of conjugal accidents: he married the first Earl of Dartmouth's granddaughter, Elizabeth Legge, whose mother chose as her second husband Lord North's father, the first Earl of Guilford. Keene's wife was therefore, in Horace Walpole's words, 'a kind of sister to Lord North'.[2] This made Keene himself a kind of brother-in-law to the Prime Minister. His own marriage had been a political gamble. Commenting on this 'droll match', Walpole recorded that 'Miss Legge, smitten with Colonel Keene's black eyes, had consented . . . They must indeed keep a few sheep at setting out but I supposed the shepherd expects that Lord North will enable them to enlarge their flock'.[3] Walpole's prophecy proved correct. Through the combined patronage of the Earl of Hertford (whom he met in Paris), Lady Powis and Lord North, this 'most absurd Irishman' became in turn Secretary to the Lord Chamberlain (1772–82 and 1783), M.P. for Wareham (1768–74), M.P. for Ludgershall (1774), M.P. for Montgomery (1774–1818), a Lord Commissioner of the Board of Trade and Foreign Plantations (1774–7),[4] and finally Surveyor General of the King's Works (1779–82).[5] Keene secured this last plum only after tantalising delay. In June 1777 George III had informed North: 'I have just heard that Mr. Worsley . . . can scarcely outlive the day; I give you this notice, as it will make a very pretty House of Commons employment. I know very well that Adams the Architect formerly applied to you for it, but if his name or any other of the profession comes in question I shall think it hard on Chambers and shall in that case only think he must not be passed by.'[6] The king approved North's nomination of Keene, provided the latter followed Worsley in promising to observe the principle of seniority in departmental promotions.[7] But Thomas Worsley, 'who was dying, and said to be dead . . . was not'.[8] Only on 13 December 1778 was the king able to report: 'early this morning Mr. Worsley died'.[9] Just over a month later, Keene inherited the surveyorship. The best that Walpole could say of him was that although he 'had very little sense, [and] was a great politician; his faults were owing to his head not to his heart'.[10] Not surprisingly, it was during Keene's régime that the Office of Works had to undergo the purging experience of Economical Reform.[11]

So much for the successive heads of the department. What of their fellow sine-curists?

[1] H. Walpole, *Last Journals, during the reign of George III, 1771–83*, ed. A. F. Steuart i (1910), p. 382 n.; *Army List*, 1761–68.

[2] Walpole, *Last Jnls.*, pp. 128, 258n. Guilford's first wife (Lord North's mother) was Lucy Montagu, daughter of the Earl of Halifax.

[3] Walpole, *Letters*, ed. Toynbee viii (1904), p. 50, 23 June 1771. Keene and his friend Sir George (later Lord) Macartney both determined on political marriages: Macartney married Lord Bute's daughter (F. Bickley (ed.), *Diaries of Sylvester Douglas, Lord Glenbervie*, 1928, pp. 6–7).

[4] For the loss of this post and the cost of one election, he received £2000 compensation from the Civil List in 1779 (John Robinson's accounts, B.M. Add. MS. 37836, f. 60).

[5] Namier and Brooke, *op. cit.*, iii (1964), pp. 3–4. For his representation of Montgomery in thirteen Parliaments, and the electoral influence of the Powis family, cf. W. R. Williams, *Parliamentary History of the Principality of Wales* (Brecknock, 1895); *Montgomeryshire Collections* viii (1875), pp. 8–131; *Intimate Society Letters of the 18th Century*, ed. Duke of Argyll, i (1910), p. 175.

[6] Sir J. Fortescue (ed.), *Correspondence of George III*, iii, no. 2013, 5 June 1777.

[7] *Ibid.* no. 2015, 6 June 1777.    [8] Walpole, *Last Jnls.* ii, p. 31, 8 June 1777.

[9] Fortesque, *Correspondence of George III*, iv, nos. 2364, 29 May 1778 and 2471, 13 Dec. 1778.

[10] Walpole, *Last Jnls.*, i, pp. 382, 388–9, 488–9; ii, p. 31, 214, 511–13.

[11] See vol. vi, p. 6 *et seq.*

As the most lucrative appointment in the Office of Works, the position of Paymaster was usually hotly contested and was seldom relinquished without a struggle. Charles Dartiquenave (d. 1737), wit, gourmet and *bon vivant*, would have been the first to admit its considerable benefits. In all, he held office for twenty years, between 1706 and 1726, surviving one political revolution, several departmental crises and innumerable personal intrigues. He seems to have combined engaging manners with administrative competence, and might have stayed in office another decade had it not been for the almost simultaneous deaths of both Hewett and Vanbrugh in the spring of 1726. For this double demise gave Sir Robert Walpole the signal for a general re-shuffle at the top of the department. Dartiquenave felt strong enough to lay down conditions for his retirement. In a letter to Walpole he successfully claimed the 'customary' retrospective perquisites deriving from the outstanding debt to the Works plus ten weeks' stay of execution, as well as life-tenure of an attractive alternative post: the Surveyorship of Gardens and Waters. Such an 'exchange', he told Walpole, 'may effectively secure me from the Casualtys you were pleased to mention yr self . . . [For] by the advantages arising from ye Premises, I shall have wherewithall to defray the heavy charges of passing a new Patent, and it will not I presume be deem'd an unreasonable Indulgence after 20 years Service with the utmost application and Integrity'.[1]

Hugh Howard (1675–1738), Dartiquenave's successor, was a dilettante turned placeman. 'Son to a worthy gentleman . . . a [Dublin] doctor of physic', traveller, connoisseur and bibliophile, he had studied art in Holland, France and Italy, but gave up painting to be Keeper of State Papers, a post worth £200 per annum.[2] Dr. Mead and other *virtuosi* had such faith in his aesthetic judgements that he came to be known as 'their Oracle'.[3] And Matthew Prior came near to immortalising him with an ode beginning: 'Good Howard! emulous of Grecian art.' His chief patrons were the Earl of Pembroke and the Duke of Devonshire: the former arranged for his artistic education abroad; the latter obtained him employment in government service.[4] In the Office of Works he seems to have occupied his time congenially, rummaging through departmental records in search of information about Inigo Jones.[5] 'A very great antiquarian, a great collector of medals, prints, drawings . . . [with] a very fine library', Howard left about £100,000 to his younger brother Robert Howard, Bishop of Elphin in Ireland.[6] And it was with the bishop that the Office of Works had to negotiate when Howard's accounts as Paymaster were posthumously wound up in 1738. 'The Lord Bishop . . . being come to the Pay

---

[1] Cambridge University Library, Walpole (Cholmondeley) Papers, letter 1296, 9 April 1726. Dartiquenave was able to give his daughter a dowry of £2500 (Mrs. Delany, *Autobiography and Correspondence*, ed. Lady Llanover, i, 1861, p. 548).

[2] Hist. MSS. Comm. *Bath MSS* iii (1908), pp. 110–11; *Egmont MSS, Diary* i (1920), pp. 224–5.

[3] G. Vertue, *Notebooks* iii, *Walpole Society* xxii (1934), p. 83.

[4] H. Walpole, *Anecdotes of Painting in England*, ed. R. N. Wornum ii (1849), pp. 630–1 (portrait). It was Devonshire who pressed his claims on Walpole in 1726. From a letter from Arundell to Burlington at Althorp dated 14 April 1726 it appears that Devonshire wanted Howard to be made Comptroller, while others preferred Kent, but Walpole told the writer 'that he was oblig'd to make Ripley Comptroller to obviate the Duke of Devonshire's recommendation, & remove Howard from the Board, who is to have Dartiquenave's place, & Dartiquenave the Gardens, & that he had spoke to the King to put Kent in to Ripley's employment which was agreed to'.

[5] Vertue, *op. cit.*, ii, xx (1932), p. 24.

[6] *Gent's Mag.* viii (1738), p. 165.

Room . . . the gentlemen of the Board . . . ordered their seal to be taken off the iron chest and caused the same to be opened, and found therein . . . some Exchequer tallies . . . [and] several baggs . . . [containing cash relating to the three preceding quarters, and others variously] ticketed Lord Essex . . . Auditor . . . Wardrobe . . . Callmen . . . [and a] note for £500 to pay the Labourers.'[1]

By comparison with Dartiquenave and Howard, the next three Paymasters were no more than birds of passage in the history of the King's Works. All three were Members of Parliament, and their transient presence reflected only minor ripples in the sluggish waters of Augustan politics. John Harris (?1690–1767) of Hayne, Devon, held office from 1738 to 1741—the year he switched his parliamentary seat from Helston to Ashburton and moved up in the court hierarchy to Master of the Household. A silent placeman married to General Conway's sister—his gouty amours much amused Horace Walpole—'Jack' Harris rightly described himself in 1761 as 'an old servant of the Crown'. As late as 1762 Newcastle reported that he still retained the support of 'the Duke of Devonshire's whole family, and all the old friends of Sir Robert Walpole'.[2] In 1741 he was replaced as Paymaster by Sir Robert Brown (d. 1760), a man of rather different stamp.[3] Brown was a successful stockjobber whose miserly instincts were notorious. Arriving penniless in Venice, he sold his wig and stayed on to make a fortune and become British Consul.[4] Returning to England, his financial acumen so impressed Sir Robert Walpole that he was rewarded with a seat for the venal borough of Ilchester. In 1736 Lord Egmont found him 'a devoted man to Sir Robert Walpole, and every day with him (for I'm told he manages money for him in the public fundes)'.[5] Not surprisingly, Brown survived his master only a few months. In July 1742 Horace Walpole noted dispassionately: 'Sir Robert Brown is displaced from being paymaster of something, I forget what, for Sir Charles Gilmour, a friend of Lord Tweeddale.'[6] A 'New Whig', a follower of Carteret, and M.P. for Edinburghshire, Gilmour soon left the Paymastership in 1743 to join the Commissioners for Trade and Plantation.[7]

Gilmour's departure left a choice vacancy. It was quickly filled by Lord Onslow's cousin Denzil Onslow (c. 1698–1765), M.P. for the family borough of Guildford. Onslow was a country gentleman M.P. who stood well with the Pelham–Newcastle regime.[8] Thanks to their long tenure of power he held on to the paymastership for thirteen years, from 1743 to 1756, before moving on to the Salt Office.[9]

[1] Works 4/7, 27 April 1738. Howard's executors eventually handed over a balance of £2017 7s. 6¼d. (*ibid.* 30 Aug. 1738).
[2] Namier and Brooke, *op. cit.*, ii (1964), p. 590; J. B. Owen, *The Rise of The Pelhams* (1957), pp. 50–2; H. Walpole, *Letters*, ed. P. Toynbee, iii, pp. 225, 277, 296; vii, p. 130; ix, p. 115 and xiii, p. 405.
[3] *Cal. Treasury Books and Papers, 1739–41*, p. 623. Harris's accounts show that he held £2161 2s. 6¼d. when he left office (Works 4/8, 12 May 1741).
[4] H. Walpole, *Letters*, ed. P. Toynbee iii (1903), pp. 237, 254, 321; iv (1903), p. 318; xiii (1905), p. 334, *Gent's Mag.* xxx (1760), p. 490.
[5] Hist. MSS. Comm. *Egmont Diary* ii, p. 286, 17 June 1736.
[6] *Letters*, ed. W. S. Lewis, xvii (1954), pp. 384, 493; *Cal. Treasury Books and Papers, 1742–5*, p. 217; *London Gazette* no. 8136, 13–17 July O.S. For Brown's accounts at the time of his removal cf. Works 4/8, 14 and 23 Sept. 1742.
[7] *Gent's Mag.* xx (1750), p. 380; J. B. Owen, *The Rise of the Pelhams* (1957), pp. 77, 113, 115.
[8] Owen, *op. cit.*, p. 55.
[9] *Gent's Mag.* xxxv (1765), p. 539. His accounts showed £1173 13s. 10d. in hand when he left office (Works 4/9, 15 Dec. 1747).

Harris, Brown, Gilmour and Onslow might all be described as minor politicians and middling sinecurists. None of them lent either lustre or notoriety to His Majesty's Office of Works. But in 1756 on Henry Fox's recommendation, the paymastership was secured by one of the most egregious sinecurists of the day, George Augustus Selwyn (1719–91), wit, rake and gambler. From the time of his rustication from Oxford, for misusing a chalice at a wine party, until the day he died 'of a violent urinary complaint',[1] Selwyn waxed fat on the proceeds of half a dozen sinecures. He was Clerk of the Irons and Surveyor of the Meltings at the Mint and absentee Registrar of the Court of Chancery in Barbados.[2] As M.P. for the family boroughs of Ludgershall (1747–54 and 1780–91) and Gloucester (1754–80), Selwyn was not only silent but somnolent, his slumbers punctuated only by the call of the division bell, at the sound of which he would file stoically into the Government lobby. His witticisms—and they bear repetition—were reserved for the bow window of White's.[3] As one of his admirers put it, 'he was delightfully ornamental'.[4] But Selwyn's reputation eventually contributed greatly to the vulnerability of the Office of Works in the era of Economical Reform.[5]

Scarcely less remunerative than the paymastership was the position of Surveyor of the King's Private Roads. In the early eighteenth century it was a post normally held in conjunction with an office of greater distinction. Brigadier William Watkins (d. 1731) held it independently.[6] But between 1731 and 1737 Richard Arundell relied on its annual fees of £200 and its Exchequer salary of £36 10s. od. to supplement his income as Surveyor General.[7] In this he was followed by Thomas Ripley who combined it with the comptrollership between 1737 and 1756.[8] In the following year the keepership assumed a new importance, at least financially: the total salary was increased first to £518 and then to £918 per annum.[9] The beneficiary was John Offley (?1717–84) of Wichnor, Staffordshire, a client of the Duke of Newcastle and M.P. in succession for Bedford, Orford and East Retford over a period of nearly thirty years. Offley certainly had need of the money: a dandy and a gambler, his nocturnal extravagance was notorious.[10] His enjoyment of the increment was brief. But when, in July 1757, he moved on to a position as Groom of the Bedchamber,

[1] *Gent's Mag.* 1791 pt. i, p. 94.

[2] For his life appointments at the Mint cf. *Royal Kalendar* 1782, pp. 114, 134; *Parl. Debates* xiii (1809), Appendix p. cclxxiv. His successor was Spencer Perceval. For sinecures in the West Indies cf. J. H. Parry, 'Patent Offices in the British West Indies', *E.H.R.* lxix (1954), pp. 200–25.

[3] Chesterfield was his only rival. He was popularly considered to hold at least one supernumerary office: the Receiver Generalship of Waif and Stray Jokes (*Gent's Mag.* 1791 pt. i, p. 94). Most of Selwyn's *bons mots* are to be found in J. H. Jesse, *George Selwyn and his Contemporaries*, 4 vols. (1843–4).

[4] *Gent's Mag.* 1791 pt. i, p. 299. He nominated as his fellow M.P. for Ludgershall, Lord Melbourne, another supporter of Lord North. On account of his influence at Ludgershall and Gloucester, Selwyn received a secret service pension of £1500 p.a. (Fortescue, *Correspondence of George III*, v, pp. 469, 480; Christie, *The End of North's Ministry*, p. 93; Namier and Brooke, *op. cit.*, iii, 1964, pp. 420–1).

[5] Vol vi, p. 7.

[6] Works 6/7, f. 335, 11 June 1723. For Watkins's military career see C. Dalton, *English Army Lists and Commission Registers 1661–1714*, iii (1896), p. 189, n.1.

[7] Works 1/1 f. 4, 5 June 1733.

[8] Works 1/2, f. 16; June 1738. As Ripley's son Richard became chief Clerk of the King's Works in the same year it may be suspected that this was the inducement offered to him to relinquish the keepership of the Private Roads.

[9] T. 52/47/546–9; Works 1/3, f. 120a, 8 March 1757, 122a, 18 April 1758.

[10] Hist. MSS. Comm. *Carlisle*, pp. 273, 488, 495, 497, 524. For his career see Namier and Brooke, *op. cit.*, iii (1964), p. 223.

his new salary was supplemented by a secret service pension of £400 'to make up [the value of] his place'.[1]

Offley's successor was a Scottish M.P., Sir Henry Erskine (?1710–65), scion of a family of Clackmannanshire Jacobites who had come to terms with the Whig régime. A proud and courtly soldier, a supporter of Chatham and a confidant of Bute, Harry Erskine had some claims to be considered as a wit and minor poet. To his English enemies, however, he was merely Bute's *sous ministre*. Alexander Carlyle was probably nearer the mark when he described him as 'a truly honest man, but his views were not extensive nor his talents great'.[2] In 1760 he helpfully surrendered his office as part of the departmental re-shuffle which followed George III's accession. Henry Finch made way for Worsley, and Erskine made way for Finch's younger brother Edward. The Hon. Edward Finch, later Finch Hatton (?1697–1771), M.P. for Cambridge University, previously Groom of the Bedchamber and Master of the Robes, held office for eleven years between 1760 and his death in 1771. He seems to have received the post on the recommendation of Lady Yarmouth.[3] In effect, having followed a successful diplomatic career in Holland, Poland, Sweden and Russia, he used the Office of Works as a convenient niche for retirement. Understandably non-resident, Finch contentedly admitted: 'the state of my health . . . my age, way of thinking, and a 25th of October [the date of George II's death] have . . . determined my choice of retirement and quiet'.[4]

Had the surveyorship of the King's Private Roads been anything more than a sinecure, Finch's successor would have been—*mirabile dictu*—actually qualified for the job. For Thomas Whately (*c.* 1728–72) of Nonsuch Park, Surrey, author of *Observations on Modern Gardening* (1770), knew a good deal about the management of estates. Inevitably, however, he received the post as a political gesture. As M.P. for Ludgershall and Castle Rising he had acted the part of George Grenville's *alter ego*. 'The ideal man of business: industrious, efficient and devoted to his chief', Whately was in fact the invisible inventor of the Stamp Act and the visible author of half a dozen pamphlets on trade and finance.[5] But his tenure of the surveyorship was soon cut short by death in 1772. He was succeeded by a man who possessed neither Whately's aesthetic instincts nor his financial acumen nor his political talent: the Hon. Henry Fane (1739–1802), an ex-Treasury Clerk (1757–63), second son of the eighth Earl of Westmorland and M.P. for the family borough of Lyme Regis (1772–1802).[6] It was Fane who eventually, and appropriately, fell victim to Burke's Economical Reform Act.[7]

Last of the department's quartet of major sinecures was the surveyorship of Royal Gardens and Waters, originally worth £400 per annum, but increased in 1726 to £500, and in 1764 to £800.[8] Between 1715 and 1726 it was held by Sir John Vanbrugh as a supplement to his salary as Comptroller. Between 1726 and 1737 it

---

[1] L. Namier, *Structure of Politics at the Accession of George III* (1957 ed.), pp. 217, 448.
[2] Namier and Brooke, *op. cit.*, ii (1964), pp. 402–5.
[3] H. Walpole, *Letters*, ed. P. Toynbee iv (1903), p. 453. See also *ibid.* vi (1904), p. 139.
[4] Namier and Brooke, *op. cit.*, ii (1964), p. 424; Pearl Finch, *History of Burley-on-the-Hill* i (1901), pp. 267–71.    [5] Namier and Brooke, *op. cit.*, iii (1964), pp. 627–8.
[6] I. R. Christie, *The End of North's Ministry* (1958), p. 201; Namier and Brooke, *op. cit.*, ii (1964), p. 413. Fane's deputy was Samuel Warren (Works 4/14, 21 Aug. 1772).
[7] Vol. vi, pp. 16–17.    [8] *Parliamentary Register* xvi (1779–80), p. 325.

was held by Dartiquenave in compensation for the loss of his paymastership. Then in 1738 it was bestowed upon a full-blooded Court sinecurist, the Hon. Thomas Hervey (1699–1775), second son of the first Earl of Bristol, M.P. for Bury St. Edmunds, and previously Equerry to the Queen and Vice-Chamberlain of her Household.[1] A vintage eccentric who eloped with the wife of the Speaker of the House of Commons, Tom Hervey is described by Horace Walpole as 'quite mad', and much given to publishing letters 'full of madness and wit . . . horrid indecency and folly'.[2] Not surprisingly, his political managers found him somewhat unreliable.

His successors were rather more sober, but equally uninterested in the King's Works. For the Hon. George Onslow (1731–1814), who held it from 1761 to 1762, the surveyorship was 'a very genteel office and worth nearly as much as my other' (the Out-Rangership of Windsor Forest). A son of Speaker Onslow, and a nephew by marriage of the Duke of Newcastle, Onslow represented the Treasury borough of Rye for several years before moving over to intermittent and unsuccessful opposition as M.P. for Surrey. Junius called him 'a false, silly fellow', and Horace Walpole thought him 'a noisy indiscreet man'. Indeed he seems to have been better suited to the obscurity of the unreformed Office of Works than to the daily cut-and-thrust of the unreformed House of Commons.[3] Lord Charles Spencer (1740–1820) of Wheatfield, Oxon., second son of the third Duke of Marlborough, was a member of the department for less than five months. A Bedford Whig who supported Bute's ministry, he was rewarded in 1762 with two sinecures together worth £1200 per annum: the surveyorship of Gardens and Waters and the Out-Rangership of Windsor Forest.[4] Over the next forty years, besides sitting continuously as M.P. for Oxfordshire, he moved slowly up the official ladder—Comptroller of the Household, Lord of the Admiralty, Treasurer of the Chamber, Joint Vice-Treasurer, Joint Postmaster General and Master of the Mint—without once falsifying his tutor's verdict: 'the best of hearts but a ductile mind'.[5] His successor's connection with the Office of Works was equally brief. John Marshe Dickinson (d. 1771) inherited from his father—a City lawyer and Lord Mayor—the patronage of the Duke of Bedford. It was Bedford's son, Lord Tavistock, who obtained for him the surveyorship in 1763.[6] Less than a year later he was induced to surrender the post in return for a pension.[7] 'The place', noted Horace Walpole, 'which young Dickinson held . . . is bestowed on Cadogan.'[8] The Hon. Charles Sloane Cadogan (1728–1807), M.P. for Cambridge for a quarter of a century, was responsible for the Royal Gardens and waterworks for five years between 1764 and 1769. An uncommitted Whig whom Rockingham labelled 'Swiss'—a political mercenary prepared to serve any ministry —he moved on to the Clerkship of the Venison Warrant and the Mastership of the Mint before becoming a Pittite peer in 1800.[9] He was succeeded by William Varey,

---

[1] *D.N.B.*

[2] H. Walpole, *Letters*, ed. P. Toynbee i (1903), p. 142; iii (1903), p. 171; v (1904), p. 322.

[3] Namier and Brooke, *op. cit.*, iii (1964), pp. 228–30; *Gent's Mag.* 1814 (i), pp. 703–4.

[4] *Grenville Papers*, ed. W. J. Smith, ii (1852), p. 21, Countess Temple to Earl Temple, 17 Dec. [1762].

[5] Namier and Brooke, *op. cit.*, iii (1964), pp. 458–9; *Gent's Mag.* 1820, pt. i, p. 640; Hist. MSS. Comm. *Fortescue*, ix, p. 125.

[6] T 52/55/18.      [7] Namier and Brooke, *op. cit.*, ii (1964) p. 321; *Gent's Mag.* xli (1771), p. 335.

[8] H. Walpole, *Letters*, ed. P. Toynbee vi (1904), p. 55, 20 April 1764.

[9] Namier and Brooke, *op. cit.*, ii (1964), pp. 169–70; *Gent's Mag.* 1807 pt. i, p. 386.

a man of fashion and an early member of the Society of Dilettanti, but otherwise no more than a shadowy placeman. He emerges into the historical sunlight only at the moment of his own extinction during the avalanche of Economical Reform.

There was one other sinecure of some significance charged to departmental funds during this period: the Rangership and Keepership of St. James's Park, Hyde Park and Green Park. Its salary, as eventually consolidated, was only £80 per annum. But it was always held by a nobleman with suitable political connections. Between 1714 and 1727 it was held by Walter, first Viscount Chetwynd (1678–1736), a Tory M.P. from Staffordshire who temporarily deserted to the Whigs and was rewarded with an Irish peerage. Between 1727 and 1739 it was held by William, third Earl of Essex (1697–1743), who is dismissed by Mrs. Delany as a worthless wretch.[1] Next came Thomas, second Viscount Weymouth (1710–51), who held the post from 1739 until his death.[2] He was followed in 1751 by Thomas, first Earl of Pomfret (1698–1761), 'a sober virtuous, well-bred gentleman [with] a tincture of learning'.[3] Pomfret was succeeded by John, second Earl of Ashburnham (1724–1812), a moderate Whig who later emerged as a Pittite Tory. Walpole describes him as 'a Court cipher . . . close, artful and dangerous', but a man much patronised by the Duke of Newcastle.[4] He held office from 1753 to 1762,[5] and was followed in 1763 by George, third Earl of Orford (1730–91).[6] It was Orford, largely non-resident and intermittently insane, who eventually attracted the attentions of the economical reformers.[7]

These, then, were the major sinecures in the Office of Works and their incumbents between 1719 and 1782. Each of these posts, as George III remarked of the Surveyor Generalship, could be—and usually was—'a very pretty House of Commons employment'.[8] Their duties were light and their profits considerable. When in 1779 the Countess of Kildare was badgering the Earl of Buckinghamshire about an office for one of her relations, she naturally thought of the King's Works: '. . . some small employ . . . I don't mean a place of trust of money; [but the] Board of Works or any not unbecoming a gentleman to execute.'[9] By eighteenth-century standards the department was not noticeably corrupt. But it had become enmeshed in parliamentary politics. And it was these political connections which were eventually to prove its undoing.

Politics are indeed never far from the surface in the records of the eighteenth-century Office of Works. In 1717, after a hotly disputed election, we find John Davis losing his smith's and ironmonger's contract at Windsor 'for his violent temper against the hearty Friends of the Government'.[10] Even the least remunerative posts in the department were subject to political pressure. In July 1725 the Board

---

[1] Works 6/12, f. 117; *Complete Peerage* v (1926), p. 147.
[2] *Cal. of Treas. Bks. and Papers, 1739–41*, pp. 207, 421; Works 6/8, f. 63.
[3] Works 6/8, f. 95; Hist. MSS. Comm. *Egmont Diary* ii (1923), p. 489.
[4] H. Walpole, *Last Jnls.*, ed. A. F. Steuart; (1910) pp. 492, 556. For the circumstances of Ashburnham's appointment cf. Walpole, *Letters*, ed. P. Toynbee, iii p. 171.
[5] Works 6/8, f. 103. Patent renewed 22 April 1761 (Works 6/13, f. 117). For Ashburnham's resignation cf. Walpole, *Memoirs of George III*, ed. G. F. R. Barker, i (1894), pp. 163, 168, 171.
[6] *Cal. Home Office Papers, 1760–5*, nos. 1149, 1579; H. Walpole, *Letters*, ed. P. Toynbee v, p. 277.
[7] See vol. vi, pp. 16, 30.          [8] Fortesque, *Correspondence of George III*, iii, no. 2013.
[9] Hist. MSS. Comm. *Lothian*, pp. 348–9, 25 March 1779.          [10] Below, p. 121.

'received from the Rt. Hon. the Lord Walpole a recommendation of Stephen South junior to succeed Mr. Thomas Sympson in the care of the water that is carried from Longford to supply His Majesty's palace at Hampton Court when the said Mr. Sympson dies or is thought unfit through his great age to act any longer. To which the Board agreed'.[1] But by October the situation had apparently changed: 'Received from the Treasury a letter directing this Board to let their Lordships know under what authority Mr. Sympson was employed to inspect the river that feeds the King's Palace and Gardens with water at Hampton Court, and what allowance; because their Lordships have agreed that Thomas Guilliam, a servant of the Earl of Halifax shall succeed to the said business and allowances in case Mr. Sympson, who is dangerously ill, shall happen to die.'[2] Similarly, Henry Fox secured Thomas Jenners's employment as joiner at Windsor in 1753.[3] And Sir Robert Walpole helped to procure George Devall's plumbing contract at Hampton Court in 1726.[4]

Such arrangements were no doubt the general rule, though—understandably enough—few were explicitly set down in departmental records. Of course politically motivated appointments naturally required reciprocal action on the part of employees. Thus in 1754 the Board 'ordered that Thomas Jew, [a newly appointed] Carpenter on the call, have leave to go to E[ve]sham in Worcestershire to give his vote in the election there'.[5]

One instance of political pressure sums up so well the state of the unreformed Office of Works that it is worth quoting in full. In March 1726 the Board 'received from His Grace the Duke of Newcastle, one of His Majesty's Secretaries of State, a letter setting forth that it is of the utmost importance to His Majesty's service that John Thompson Esq. alderman be chosen Sheriff of London and Middlesex for the remainder of this year, in the room of Sir Jeremiah Murden deceased; and desiring this Board to make use of their credit with the officers and tradesmen employed in this office'. Thereupon the Board obediently 'ordered that the messenger go immediately to the several persons concerned in this office, and not only to insist upon their giving their vote for the said John Thompson Esq. but to use their utmost credit with all others having votes in the election of sheriff, in whom they may have any interest, to engage them to exert themselves in favour of the said Alderman Thompson'.[6] Thirty-five years later, in 1761, it was to 'letters from the Office of Ordnance and the Board of Works' that Beckford's success in the City of London election was attributed by an unsuccessful rival.[7]

As ministerial supporters, the officers of the King's Works might also be expected to demonstrate their loyalty in time of national crisis. In the summer of 1779, as the disastrous American War of Independence drew to its close, a French invasion of Britain was widely feared. Lord North was happy to report to George III: 'Three

---

[1] Works 4/3, 14 July 1725.                     [2] *Ibid.*, 27 Oct. 1725.
[3] Works 4/11, 28 Aug., 6 Sept. 1753.           [4] Works 4/3, 10 Oct. 1726.
[5] Works 4/11, 27 Sept. 1753, 9 April 1754. 'A profusion of trouble and expence has for more than half a century past . . . marked a seat in Parliament for the borough of Evesham' (Mark Beaufoy to Sir John Rushout, 1 Sept. 1767, quoted in Namier and Brooke, *op. cit.*, i, 1964, p. 424).
[6] Works 4/3, 30 March 1726.
[7] Newcastle Papers, ccxxxvi, B.M. Add MS. 32921, f. 190; Namier and Brooke, *History of Parliament: the House of Commons, 1754–90* i (1964), p. 329; ii, p. 76. 'London was probably the most politically conscious constituency in Great Britain.'

hundred of the artificers and workmen employ'd by the Board of Works have offer'd themselves to be associated and trained upon the same footing as the Westminster and Middlesex Corps to be employ'd in keeping the Peace of this City and County; Their Officers to be the Master-Artificers. Although this Corps promises to be full as useful as the twenty four Middlesex Companies, Mr. Keene does not think it proper to take any step towards forming it till he is apprized of your Majesty's pleasure . . . Mr. Sheridan and Mr. Harris have it under their consideration to form a company on the same plan out of the tradesmen and workmen dependant upon the theatres.'[1] Kenton Couse told Mrs. Worsley, 'we are all turning military, the Board of Works have raised a Subscription to the Voluntier Companies in Westminster and [are] learning Military Exercise, but [I] hope providence will take better care of us than we are able to do of ourselves'.[2] Fortunately, perhaps, the valour of the king's workmen was never tested. The French invaders got no farther than the island of Jersey.[3]

* * *

By comparison with the financial and organisational chaos which preceded the changes of 1718–19 and 1814–15, the mid-eighteenth-century Office of Works seems almost a model of orderly administration: an oasis of moderate efficiency flanked by deserts of grosser incompetence. There were several reasons for this relatively calm and ordered state of affairs.

In the first place the Georgian Office of Works suffered far less than its immediate predecessors and successors from governmental improvidence and royal extravagance. The frequent crises of Restoration finance were not repeated under the Hanoverians. And George I, George II and the young George III were in no way addicted to architectural extravagance. All three monarchs were, it is true, responsible for some not inconsiderable expenditure: George I at Kensington, George II at Richmond and Hampton Court, George III at Windsor, Kew and Buckingham House. Then of course there were Kent's Treasury and Horse Guards and Chambers's Somerset House, the greatest public building programme of the eighteenth century. But none of these works dislocated the functioning of the Office of Works in the way that George IV's grandiose projects were to do. In fact the reigns of the first three Georges were less remarkable for palaces which were built than for those which remained an architect's mirage: Vanbrugh's heroic design for Kensington,[4] Pearce's, Kent's and Chambers's successive plans for Richmond,[5] Hewett and Galilei's vision of a royal palace in Hyde Park,[6] the numerous schemes by Burlington and Kent for rebuilding the Houses of Parliament[7]—all these remained no more than drawing-board dreams. They represented the highest aspirations of English architecture in the Georgian era, but added nothing to the responsibilities of the Office of Works.

---

[1] Sir John Fortesque (ed.), *Correspondence of George III*, iv, no. 2768, (?) 8 Sept. 1779.
[2] Worsley Papers, Hovingham, 31 Aug. 1779.    [3] *Annual Register* 1780, pp. 11–15.
[4] See below, pp. 195–6.    [5] See below, pp. 220 *et seq.*
[6] Ilaria Toesca, 'Alessandro Galilei in Inghilterra', *English Miscellany*. ed. M. Praz, iii (1952), pp. 198–200, 210–11.
[7] See below, pp. 416 *et seq.*

In the second place the Office of Works in the middle decades of the eighteenth century was fairly lucky in its personnel. The department might be inefficient. It might even be corrupt. But at least it was spared a William Benson or a James Wyatt. Sinecurists there were, of course, and in plenty. But their role was parasitic rather than predatory. They were passive not disruptive, comatose rather than actively corrupt. And while they slumbered on the back benches of the Commons, the day-to-day burdens of departmental administration settled quietly on the shoulders of men who as architects and administrators were qualified and competent.

Vanbrugh, Hawksmoor and Grinling Gibbons were of course seasoned veterans of the King's Works. So was Brigadier Watkins, the Keeper of the Private Roads. Despite his mercurial temperament—his 'terrible Ruffles . . . Storm and Sunshine'—Vanbrugh regarded him as a person of 'great importance to our Board' whose absence could ill be spared.[1] The experience of these men must have been invaluable in restoring the deparment to normality after Benson's removal. Gibbons survived as Master Carpenter until his death in 1721, missing only half a dozen Board meetings out of a possible eighty.[2] Vanbrugh as Comptroller remained an active member of the Board until his death in 1726, attending well over half the meetings which were held.[3] And Hawksmoor, after three years in the wilderness, lived to enjoy a second period of office, acting first as Deputy Comptroller from 1721 to 1726[4] and then as Secretary between 1726 and his death ten years later.

But the department was also fortunate in most of its new recruits. Nicholas Dubois (*c*. 1665–1735) joined the Board as Master Mason in 1719. This was the first occasion on which the post had been held by one who was not a mason by trade—a triumph for Vanbrugh's long campaign to exclude master artisans from the Board—and perhaps for that reason Dubois appointed James Horne as his deputy in March 1720/21.[5] A French émigré, probably a Huguenot, Dubois had served in the British army in Spain and Flanders before moving to a peacetime post in the Ordnance Office.[6] In his own words, he claimed to be a person 'of a liberal Education, a man of Honour, an old officer to the King and a Gentleman born'.[7] He had in fact once acted as tutor to the Prince of Friesland, father of the Prince of Orange, and later translated Palladio for Leoni's English edition of 1715. Despite his long domicile in Britain, 'Captain Dubois' seems to have remained identifiably foreign: the servants at Stanmer Park, Sussex, which he designed for Henry Pelham, referred to him scornfully as 'the french son of a Bitch'. But his military background must at least have made him a sympathetic colleague for Watkins and Vanbrugh. He attended more than 750 Board meetings during his period in office.[8] Another newcomer to the Board in 1719 was Westby Gill. Of his architectural activities little is known.[9] But he acted as Deputy Surveyor until 1735, when he became Master

---

[1] *The Works of Sir John Vanbrugh*, vol. iv, *The Letters*, ed. G. F. Webb, pp. 100, 112–13, 124.
[2] Works 4/1–2.     [3] Works 4/1–3.     [4] Works 6/12, 5 July 1721.
[5] Works 6/12, 11 and 15 March 1720. For Horne see Colvin, *Dictionary*, pp. 301–2.
[6] He claimed 'he was made Engineer in the year 1709 and served in that station during the last war in Flanders, where he exposed his life in many sieges, etc., and at the Peace of Utrecht was reduced to half pay'. On becoming Master Mason he lost his engineer's pension (Works 6/15, pp. 36–9, 26 Feb. 1723/4). For further details of his career see Colvin, *Dictionary*, pp. 185–6.
[7] Quoted in Colvin, *op. cit.*     [8] Works 4/1–6.
[9] Colvin, *Dictionary*, p. 237.

Carpenter, a position he held until his death in 1746. In both capacities his attendance in Scotland Yard was indefatigable; in all he attended nearly 1000 ordinary
or extraordinary meetings of the Board.[1] He can perhaps be taken as representative
of a new generation of conscientious, administratively-minded members of the Board
of Works.

Thomas Ripley (*c.* 1683–1758), a Yorkshire carpenter who married a servant
of Sir Robert Walpole, moved rapidly up the departmental ladder—Labourer in
Trust at the Savoy (April 1715), Clerk of Works at the Mews (February 1716),
Master Carpenter (September 1721), Comptroller (May 1726), Surveyor of the
King's Private Roads (June 1737)—and ended up by taking as his second wife a
Middlesex heiress worth £40,000.[2] He was an architect of only moderate ability,
and Vanbrugh was contemptuous of his new colleague on the Board. 'When (he
wrote in 1721) 'I met with his Name, (and Esquire to it) in the News paper; such a
Laugh came upon me, I had like to have Beshit my Self.'[3] Pope, too, lost no opportunity of pouring poetic scorn on 'Ripley with a rule'. But, as Horace Walpole
admitted, these censures were the result of 'politics and partiality', for Ripley 'was
employed by the minister [Robert Walpole] and had not the countenance of Lord
Burlington, the patron of Pope'.[4] And even if he did not have the *entrée* to Burlington
House, a methodical and industrious man like Ripley might still be a useful person
to have in the department. In all he attended something like 1800 meetings of the
Board during his long years in office.[5]

His successor, Henry Flitcroft (1697–1769), was an architect of greater distinction. A joiner by trade, he is said to have attracted Lord Burlington's attention by
falling off a ladder while working at Burlington House. 'Noticing his more than
ordinary talent', Burlington took him on as draughtsman and architectural assistant.
This launched 'Burlington Harry' on a career which began with the Clerkship of
Works at St. James's, Whitehall and Westminster (1726) and included the Clerkship
at Kew and Richmond and the posts of Master Carpenter (1746), Master Mason
and Deputy Surveyor (1748) and finally that of Comptroller (1758). His position
was so strong that even a powerful enemy like William Pulteney, Earl of Bath, could
not harm him. 'There is one Flitcroft in the Board of Works', wrote Bath to the Dean
of Winchester in 1742, 'who used me extreamly ill, and whom I intended to get
removed from his Employment if I could. [But] when I came to try my strength, I
found this Flitcroft had many great Supporters, and among others the Duke of
Cumberland, so that I was forced to drop my pursuit against him.'[6] During these
years Flitcroft's tally of architectural works outside government service is impressive,
including for example the church of St. Giles-in-the-Fields, London, and work at
Wentworth Woodhouse, Ditchley, Woburn, Wimpole, Milton, Stourhead and Wind-

---

[1] Works 4/1–9.     [2] Colvin, *Dictionary*, p. 504.
[3] *The Works of Sir John Vanbrugh*, vol. iv, *The Letters*, ed. G. F. Webb, p. 138. Officers and tradesmen
below Board level—apart from gentlemen sinecurists—were always described as 'Mr.'.
[4] Horace Walpole, *Anecdotes of Painting*, ed. Wornum iii (1862), p. 769.
[5] Works 4/2–11.
[6] Bath to Zachary Pierce, n.d., endorsed 'recd. Sept. 1, 1742', Westminster Abbey Muniments, 64662.
Accounts at Althorp show that from 1733 to 1737 Flitcroft acted as the Duke of Cumberland's architectural
tutor at a salary of £50 p.a. In the British Museum there is a volume of architectural drawings by Flitcroft
dedicated to the duke (King's MS. 283).

sor Great Park (where the Duke of Cumberland was Ranger).[1] Inside the Office of Works his greatest contribution was administrative. He attended at least 1100 Board meetings,[2] and was responsible for the training of Kenton Couse (1721–90), not a distinguished architect but for many years a stalwart member of the department, first as Labourer in Trust at St. James's, Whitehall and Westminster (1746–8), then as Clerk of the Works at Newmarket (June 1750) and the Mews (July 1750), then as Comptroller's Clerk (1762), Clerk at St. James's, Whitehall and Westminster (1766), Secretary, Clerk to the Board, Clerk Itinerant and Clerk at Carlton House and Buckingham House (1775), and finally as Examiner (1782).[3]

All three men—Ripley, Flitcroft and Couse—were loyal and active members of the department, 'bred up' in government service. They were also, in different degrees according to their talents, orthodox Palladians. And like most of their architectural contemporaries, they lived under the shadow of Burlington's principal protégé, William Kent (?1685–1748). As Master Carpenter (1726), Master Mason and Deputy Surveyor (1735), 'Signior' Kent dominated governmental design. His Horse Guards, Royal Mews and Treasury Offices imprinted the Palladian image on the metropolis.[4] In fact the Georgian Office of Works was in many ways the centre of Palladianism in England. Though Lord Burlington had no formal control over appointments, his private influence was considerable, first making itself felt in 1722 when he helped to accomplish Thornhill's eclipse as a court painter.[5] Roger Morris (1695–1749), a talented Palladian much patronised by the 'architect Earl' of Pembroke, was made Clerk of the Works at Richmond New Park Lodge in 1727. In the same year Daniel Garrett, afterwards to be Burlington's personal assistant, was appointed Morris's Labourer in Trust, and he later held the same position at Windsor. Another of Burlington's protégés was Isaac Ware (d. 1766), a chimney sweep's boy who lived to translate Palladio, edit Inigo Jones and compose a standard textbook, *The Complete Body of Architecture*, besides designing Chesterfield House and Wrotham Park. He started as Labourer in Trust at the Savoy (1720/1), rose to be Purveyor (1728) and in due course became Clerk of the Works at Windsor (1729) and Greenwich (1732/3), Clerk Itinerant (1728), Clerk to the Board, and Secretary (1736).

Another of the Scotland Yard Burlingtonians was Stephen Wright (d. 1780), an assistant of William Kent, whose Cambridge University Library (1754–8) rivalled his master's highest achievements. Backed by both the Earl of Burlington and the Duke of Newcastle, he naturally rose from Clerk of Works at Hampton Court (1746) and Richmond New Park Lodge (1754) to Master Mason and Deputy Surveyor (1758).[6] 'An honest and worthy man',[7] his career was blessed with every success except one: he never obtained the coveted Comptrollership. Twice, in 1758 and 1766, he came

---

[1] See Colvin, *Dictionary*, pp. 206–9.          [2] Works 4/9–14.
[3] Colvin, *Dictionary*, pp. 155–6 and Appendix D, below.
[4] See below, pp. 213 and 432–7. In 1728 Kent was also appointed Surveyor or Inspector of the King's Pictures at a salary of £100 p.a. (T 29/26, f. 75, 7 Feb., 1727/8; Works 6/11, f. 102, 24 Jan. 1727/8).
[5] Below, p. 198.
[6] Colvin, *Dictionary*, pp. 716–17 and Appendix D, below.
[7] 'It will give you Pain to hear that Mr. Wright of the Board of Works died this morning. A total Breaking up of his Constitution has been coming on for some time, but flattering hopes have supported him through a lingering though not very painful illness. As an honest and worthy man I feel for his loss' (Couse to Mrs. Worsley, 28 Sept. 1780, Hovingham Papers).

HKW—H

tantalisingly near to achieving his ambition. On the first occasion, as Ripley lay dying at Hampton, he sent the Duke of Newcastle this brief note: 'Wednesday morning. S. Wright's duty to his Grace . . . and begs leave to acquaint him of the certainty of Mr. Ripley's being given over; his case being so desperate his Familly expect his last every hour; so the Great Favour his Grace intends seems drawing to a conclusion . . .'[1] But Flitcroft got the job, and Wright had to be content with the title of Master Mason. On the second occasion his plea was rather more fulsome: 'May it please your Grace, The profound duty owing [to] your Grace for the great services already received, make me asham'd [of] giving any further trouble, but from the knowledge of your Grace's general disposition in taking pleasure through the most elevated situation in making numbers in various stations happy. My present seat at the Board of Works as Master Mason I was honoured with by your Grace's immediate appointment, who at the same time was pleas'd to prefer Mr. Flitcroft to the Comptrollership upon Mr. Ripley's disease, such rotation having taken place for several generations, as a usual course in office; and as the present Comptroller's heavy infirmitys seem to declare him near his end, therefore do most humbly pray for your Grace's continued patronage by a timely recommendation to the Marquiss of Rockingham . . .'[2] But Flitcroft survived another three years. And when he eventually died the post went to another candidate, a man whose name is stamped indelibly on the eighteenth-century Office of Works, Sir William Chambers.

It was not merely his responsibility for Somerset House which made Chambers the eighteenth-century government architect *par excellence*. His successors in the position of Joint Architect—Sir Robert Taylor, Thomas Sandby and James Paine—never became involved with the Office of Works to quite the same extent.[3] Sir Robert Taylor (1714–88) and James Paine (1717–89), in Hardwick's classic phrase, 'nearly divided the practice of the profession between them till Mr. Robert Adam entered the lists'.[4] And both had lengthy careers in government service: Taylor later became Master Carpenter (1777) and Master Mason and Deputy Surveyor (1780); Paine had already been Clerk of the Works at Greenwich (January 1744/5), the Royal Mews (1746), Newmarket (1750) and Richmond New Park Lodge (1758). But Taylor was chiefly concerned with his extensive City practice and its villa appendages; Paine—*faute de mieux*—with his proliferating country houses in the North of England.[5] Paine had been one of those aspirants anxiously

---

[1] Newcastle Papers, B.M. Add. MS. 32877, f. 174, 18 Jan. 1758.

[2] *Ibid.*, Add. MS. 32973, f. 336, 1 Feb. 1766.

[3] For their respective careers see Colvin, *Dictionary*, pp. 601–4, 520–3 and 429–34. When Sandby succeeded Taylor as Joint Architect with James Adam it was decided that the latter was 'to take precedence' (Works 6/8, f. 269, 4 April 1777).

[4] Hardwick, *Memoir of the Life of Sir William Chambers* prefixed to J. Gwilt's edition of Chambers's *Decorative Part of Civil Architecture* (1825), p. xlix.

[5] E.g.: 'Ordered that Mr. Paine have leave to go into the country' (Works 4/9, 26 May 1747); 'Mr. Paine desiring the indulgence of the Board for leave to make the Tour of Italy, and proposes to return in about a Twelvemonth, Order'd he have leave, upon his deputing [James Lillyman] a proper person to see the duty of his office done as Clerk . . . at Newmarket' (Works 4/11, 22 July 1755). Occasionally his public and private practice conflicted, e.g.: 'I am in daily expectation of fixing the time for my coming into the North, but waite to know whether a person in our office recovers of a Dropsy that has been tapt three times; should he drop, I have some expectation to succeed him' (Paine to William Wrightson, n.d. [received 7 March 1749], Leeds Public Library, Wrightson Colln. A.22). The invalid in question may have been his namesake Ambrose Paine.

awaiting Ripley's decease.[1] But the death of his patron, Richard Arundell, and the political revolution of 1760, blighted his hopes of promotion.[2] He eventually became Joint Architect only just in time to have his post abolished by Burke's Economical Reform Act.[3] As for Thomas Sandby (1721–98)—an ex-military draughtsman with considerable talents as a topographical artist—he succeeded Taylor as Master Carpenter (1780) but under the Duke of Cumberland's patronage naturally preferred Windsor to Scotland Yard and is therefore best remembered as 'Tommy Sandbank', the creator of Virginia Water. All three gave the Office of Works no more than a sufficient portion of their time in return for a substantial salary. Chambers made the department his principal concern.

Chambers had first entered the department as the result of a political revolution. In 1760 George III's accession was the signal for a government re-shuffle. Under the spell of his tutor, Lord Bute, the young king consciously began replacing the old Whigs whom he had inherited from his grandfather with new men willing to repay royal confidence with loyalty. In this way in 1761 the Board of Works received three valuable recruits: a new and conscientious Surveyor General, plus two young advisory architects, already rivals for the leadership of the profession, Robert Adam (1728–92) and Sir William Chambers (1723–96). Appropriately, the royal patent creating the new office 'called Architect of our Works' referred proudly to the 'ability, skill and prudent circumspection' of its first joint incumbents.[4] Fresh from the Grand Tour, Adam had already begun to publicise the decorative style for which he became famous. His appointment as Joint Architect was an important stage in this programme of self-promotion,[5] but he never seems to have identified himself with the department, and after becoming M.P. for Kinross-shire in 1768, he

<hr />

[1] 'Payne sends me word that Mr. Ripley is extreamly ill . . . and . . . desires me to intercede with your Grace to recommend him among the several alterations (if Ripley miscarries) that may happen' (Arundell to Devonshire, 23 Sept. 1757, Chatsworth Letters, 234/21),

[2] See, however, his attempts to stand well with George III and Worsley in 1761 (letter to Sir Rowland Winn, 19 March 1761, Nostell Priory).

[3] 'His abilities as an architect shone eminently conspicuous in the public and private works raised under his direction, from Alnwick Castle, nearly to the Land's End . . . He designed the human figure, and all the ornaments needful to the decoration of architecture, with taste and judgement . . . His fame furnished him many employments among the great; and the patronage of the Right Hon. Richard Arundell, of Northallerton, procured [him the place of] Clerk of the Works at Greenwich. [On] the first opportunity he was advanced to the Royal [Mews], and again to Richmond New Park, and Newmarket. A very few years after, the unlucky hour arrived that dated the period of his patron's existence, and [his] hope (from promises recorded) of succeeding to the Comptrollership of all the King's Works. A vacancy in that department was likely every day to happen. Such is the uncertain state of man!—a total change of men and measures soon followed. Notwithstanding his acknowledged reputation he was doomed to remain in his then humble situation for a length of years, until the death of Stephen Wright Esq., master-mason, when [he], by his Majesty's most gracious interposition, was advanced to the rank of a board-officer, by the title of Architect to the King. He had scarcely taken his seat at a board . . . ere he found himself displaced by Mr. Burke's Reform Bill. After a service of nearly half a century, in the labour and drudgery of office, his merits were thus unexpectedly overlooked, without gratuity or pension . . . Some months preceeding his decease, finding the infirmities of age steal fast upon him, and a family occurence of a singular nature preying upon his spirits, he retired to the Continent, where he ended his days' (*Gent's Mag.* 1789 pt. ii, p. 1153).

[4] Works 6/8, f. 150, 18 Nov. 1761.

[5] Adam described the circumstances of his appointment as follows: 'During the former reign [of George II] the Duke of Argyle and Earl of Kinnoul had requested the Duke of Newcastle at that time first Lord of the Treasury to appoint Mr. Adam to an office in the Board of Works, upon which Mr. Adam went to the Duke's levee, the Duke then said to him: I have it not in my power at present to appoint you to any office for none of the officers' places are vacant and I cannot offer you a Clerkship—that you would not accept of—which circumstance shews the estimation and respect in which Mr. Adam was held by all ranks, as some of these Clerkships are extremely lucrative. Lord Bute found means to get over the Duke of Newcastle's difficulty of seeing no vacancy in the Board by creating on purpose for him the place of Architect to the King and made

resigned his post in 1769 to his younger brother James Adam (1732–94).[1] That was the year of Chambers's promotion to the Comptrollership. More self-consciously professional than the Adam brothers, uninterested in speculative projects like the Adelphi, and assured of royal favour even after his eclipse by James Wyatt, Chambers remained at the Office of Works and reaped an appropriate reward. Flitcroft died at last in February 1769. 'I blush to . . . find myself . . . overjoyed', wrote Chambers to Lord Charlemont, 'that an old gentleman who has kept me out of a very great place for these eight years past is at length advanced to sing hallelujah's in heaven and has resigned his earthly post . . . to me.'[2]

Chambers's career in the Office of Works may be divided conveniently into two sections.[3] Before 1782 he bore unofficially one of the heaviest burdens in an inefficient organisation, first as Joint Architect (1761–69) and then as Comptroller (1769–82). Between 1782 and 1796, as Surveyor General and Comptroller, he was to be the acknowledged generalissimo of a rejuvenated department. His most valuable administrative services were performed between 1780 and 1785, and are therefore described elsewhere.[4] During the previous twenty years, particularly after he succeeded Flitcroft, Chambers was the linchpin of the system, deputising for an absentee political head: chairing the Friday Board meetings, writing copious reports and official letters, and dealing as effectively with his superiors in the Treasury or Lord Chamberlain's department as he did with contractors, craftsmen and impecunious employees in the Office of Works. Between his arrival as joint Architect in 1761 and the appointment of a new Surveyor General in 1778, there were as many as 830 Board meetings. Chambers missed less than 120.[5] His correspondence reveals him as an urbane and knowledgeable official, witty, worldly and humane. First and foremost he was a professional architect, nervously aware of the new-found dignity of his calling and acutely conscious of his divided responsibility to government, tradesman and labourer. He had in turn to act the part of king's confidant, civil servant and champion of the underdog. And he performed all three tasks most effectively.

The third way in which the mid-eighteenth-century Office of Works turned out to be fortunate was financial rather than personal: by comparison with the beginning and end of the eighteenth century there was less in the way of external economic pressures. Of course the Spanish and Austrian Wars (1739–48), the Seven Years' War (1756–63) and the War of American Independence (1775–83) all had some effect on the department's rudimentary price-fixing mechanism. Carpenters' wages went up from 2s. 6d to 2s. 9d. a day in 1739.[6] In the early 1740s wartime conditions meant that 'freight and insurance of materials' were 'notoriously known to be considerably increased'.[7] Westmorland slating went up from £2 8s. 0d. to £2 15s. 0d.

---

it a joint office to include Sir William Chambers, bestowing on each a sallery of £300' (Register House, Edinburgh, GD. 18/4982).

[1] Works 4/14, 3 Nov. 1769; L. Namier and J. Brooke, *History of Parliament: the House of Commons, 1754–90* i (1964), pp. 7–8.

[2] *MSS. and Corresp. of James 1st Earl of Charlemont*, Hist. MSS. Comm. *12th Repor* (1891), i, p. 292, 22 March 1769; Works 4/14, 17 March 1769.

[3] For a full account, see J. Mordaunt Crook, 'The Office of Works, 1761–96' in J. Harris, *Sir William Chambers* (1970), pp. 108–27.

[4] Vol. vi, pp. 27–48.

[5] Works 4/13–16.

[6] Works, 4/7, 20 Aug. 1739.

[7] Works 6/17, f. 110, 11 April 1754.

per square foot in the spring of 1744 'on account of the extraordinary rise of freight'.[1] Contracting smiths,[2] carpenters,[3] labourers[4] and plasterers[5] all petitioned for higher prices in 1740–2. Turners' and matlayers'[6] and carriers' rates followed suit in 1746.[7] Lead went up by 3s. per cwt in 1754.[8] Wartime freight charges raised the price of stone by 8s. per ton in 1756.[9] Lead went up from 18s. to 19s. 6d. p.q. in 1767.[10] Bricks followed in 1768, hard grey stocks going up to £1 6s. od. per 1000.[11] Tradesmen tried to avoid paying the Paymaster's extra 10% fee in 1769 'on account of the great advance of the price of materials and labour'.[12] The wages of mason's labourers went up to 2s. per day in 1774, Portland stone rising from 2s. 2d. to 2s. 4d. per cubic foot.[13] By 1776 master bricklayers were pressing for higher rates.[14] In 1779 the Office of Works was telling the Board of Ordnance that while war-time conditions lasted 4s. per ton extra freightage would be allowed on Portland and Purbeck stone.[15] But most of these increases were only temporary. The cost of 'painting three times done', for example, was reduced by 1d. per yard in 1740.[16] 'When the war [of Austrian Succession] was at an end, and the reason for a higher price was at an end, the [contractors'] additional allowance[s] ceased at the same time.'[17] And in 1759 we find John Devall and Rober Cutler courteously and volun-tarily reducing their own prices: 'the price of lead being fallen, we have reduced our prices, you was so kind to advance, on the dearness of lead to the contract, and are with due sense of your favours, Your much obliged and most obedient servants . . .'[18]

Clearly government contracting was usually a profitable business, at least for those large contractors with good credit facilities. For every tradesman like Mansell, the Hampton Court carpenter, who was forced by rising prices to withdraw from government service,[19] there must have been many others who found it more than worthwhile to continue. John Mist, 'Pavior to the Royal Palaces, and to the Office of Works, Slater, Cartaker, Thatcher, Scavenger, and Foundation-Digger', died in 1737, at the age of 46, worth £50,000, having been 'a great Undertaker and a slave to Business'.[20] There are few, if any, indications of wartime bankruptcies among

---

[1] Works 4/9, 24 April 1744.

[2] John Davis, Joseph Pattison and Thomas Wagg complained that 'when they were appointed . . . they were obliged to conform to a contract made by the late John Cleave at a time when Iron, Coal and other materials were considerably cheaper than they have ever been known to be since . . . the said contract not comprising one fourth of the articles which occur in their business' (Works 4/8, 23 Jan. 1739/40, 30 Jan. 1739/40, 7 Feb. 1739/40).

[3] Fir timber went up by 2d. per cubic foot, single and double deals by 1d. and 2d. respectively; oak remained unchanged (*ibid.*, 29 Oct. 1740).

[4] The wages of labourers employed by masons and bricklayers went up to 1s. 10d. per day, so did those of general labourers (*ibid.*, 3 Dec. 1741).

[5] George Worrall, Thomas Clark and George Webster petitioned for rates higher than those 'proposed by the late John Minns, which . . . are so low that several are under prime cost' (*ibid.*, 1 July 1742).

[6] Thomas Patterson obtained higher rates 'in consideration of the rise of materials and the long credit he is now obliged to give' (Works 4/9, 18 March 1745/6, 25 March 1746).

[7] Joseph Windsor's carrying rates for the Windsor area were raised from 1s. per load to 1s. 4d., with 2s. per load for materials carried from the waterside. As contractor he in turn had to pay out 1s. and 1s. 6d. per load (*ibid.*, 8 April 1746.)

[8] Works 4/11, 2 April 1754.    [9] *Ibid.*, 6 July 1756.    [10] Works 4/14, 22 May 1767.

[11] *Ibid.*, 12 Feb. 1768.    [12] *Ibid.*, 13 Oct. 1769.

[13] Works 4/15, 28 Jan. 1774, 15 April 1774.    [14] *Ibid.*, 18 Oct. 1776.

[15] Works 1/5, f. 22 verso, 15 Oct. 1779.    [16] Works 4/8, 29 Oct. 1740.

[17] Works 6/17, f. 110, 11 April 1754.    [18] Works 1/3, f. 132, April 1759.    [19] Works 4/15, 5 Aug. 1774.

[20] Abel Boyer, *The Political State of Great Britain* liii (1737), p. 432; *London Mag.* 1737, p. 221; *Gent's Mag.* vii (1737), p. 253. He was succeeded by his sons Charles and Edward (Works 4/7, 19 April 1737 and 4/8, 6 Oct. 1741, 19 August 1743). There is a tablet to his memory in Hillingdon Church, Middlesex.

contracting tradesmen in the mid-eighteenth-century Office of Works.[1] Surviving building accounts are usually unspecific and generalised before 1778. But the evidence available seems to show that the impact of all four wars on the internal economy of the department must be regarded as small in comparison with the acute difficulties caused by the complexities of Restoration finance and the protracted hostilities against Louis XIV and Napoleon.

Still, some contractors occasionally had good cause for complaint. In the first place there were the deductions. Apart from the Paymaster's fee of 3d. in the pound and 10s. in every 100s., each trademan's bill was subject to deductions of 6d. in the pound (Civil List), and 2s. 6d. (Tellers), 2s. (Auditors) and 1s. (Pells) in every £100, plus variable fees for Treasury letters.[2] Then there were the delays. According to 'ancient usage', payment went to the 'Principal Officers, Clerks and Labourers belonging to the . . . office in the first place, and after they are discharged to . . . the several artificers and workmen in due proportion'.[3] This order of preference was not reversed until the reforms of 1782. Meanwhile contractors very often had to wait for their money. In particular, any expenditure above the annual limit required a special Treasury warrant. That for 1765, for example, was not issued until 1771.[4]

In March 1720 two dozen artificers petitioned the Treasury, claiming payment of debts totalling £105,404, some of them dating back to the reign of William III. 'The most part of your petitioners' substance', they claimed, 'being included in the said debts; [they] have extended their abilities and credit to the utmost in performing the said works. [And] insomuch as they are now reduced to very great straits for want of money to support them and their families, . . . without your Lordships' compassion the same will be their utter ruin'. Far from quibbling, the new Board of Works admitted to even larger debts: their records showed a total of £110,983 14s. 10½d. They urged the Treasury to 'lessen the debt by paying such proportions as . . . your Lordships' great wisdom shall think fit, whereby we shall be enabled to make [new] contracts and agreements for the future . . . upon much easier rates and terms than at present'.[5] In other words, now that prices were lower the Board might strike a better bargain with its tradesmen if the Treasury settled at least part of their arrears. That at any rate seems to have been the procedure adopted. But three years later, eleven contractors including Thornhill, Mist and Lance were petitioning for the payment of more bills for Extra works which had accumulated since 1720: they 'might have reasonably expected a moderate gain for their respective works and services . . . but the great sums remaining unpaid makes it become a very great loss . . . and almost a ruin to some of their families'. The Office of Works explained the delay as follows: '1st. for want of warrants from the Treasury, for the Board . . . have no power to pay any bills until they receive warrants . . . 2nd. The warrants from the Treasury do expressly order that the sums

---

[1] Extracts from Thornhill's accounts, showing substantial profits—£2570 for 1720–5—are preserved among Richard Arundell's papers in Nottingham University Library (Galway Collection).
[2] Robinson Papers, B.M. Add MS. 37836, ff. 39 *et seq.* (1775). After some dispute, the Paymaster's fees were eventually commuted to ½% Paymaster's fee plus ¼% Deputy Paymaster's fee (Works 6/8, f. 208, 17 Jan. 1763; Works 1/4, f. 82 (n.d.); Works 1/5, ff. 51–2, 27 March 1783, 4 April 1783; L.C. 1/40, f. 28 July 1783; *Parl. Pap.* 1813, v, p. 363 and 1830, ix, p. 141).
[3] Works 6/7, f. 125, 4 Nov. 1719.                    [4] T 29/41, f. 251, 14 Aug. 1771.
[5] Works 6/7, f. 196–7, 16–19 March 1719/20.

for the said services shall not exceed the estimate; therefore we cannot pass the bills until the works are finished, and know what the sums will amount to.' The remedy suggested by the Board to the Treasury was simple enough: advance payments during the progress of Extra works. But it was never consistently applied.[1]

Twenty years later the same grievances still rankled. Thirty-one contractors, including Worrall and the younger Thornhill, petitioned the Treasury in January 1743. They complained that, following advertisements in the press in 1730, many tradesmen came forward to undertake the king's works, encouraged by the prospect of prompt quarterly payments. Prices had indeed been fixed on that understanding. But now payments were running five quarters in arrear, 'which hath exhausted their substance in such a manner that many of them are obliged to pay exorbitant interest for money to carry on H.M.'s works'. Altogether the bills totalled some £20,000, and some dated back to George I's reign. 'All which', they claimed, 'hath lessened [their] . . . credit, as well as substance . . . so . . . that many of their families are reduced from affluence and plenty to great want and poverty.' The petitioners concluded by reminding the Treasury of 'the great hardship they labour under if an accident should happen to his most sacred Majesty's person (which God forbid) . . .' Quite simply, they feared that the death of the monarch—and this was the year of the battle of Dettingen—might mean the cancellation of his predecessor's debts, if not his own. The Board of Works endorsed the petition—'the allegations . . . are true'—and reminded the Treasury that by the Instructions of 1715, 'when prices allowed in this Office were much higher than they now are, it was ordered that all such bills as were not paid within six months . . . should carry interest after the rate of 5%'.[2]

Here indeed was an incentive for the Treasury. Departmental expenses were running above the agreed limit.[3] But if the old debts could be settled, new contracts might be negotiated at lower prices. Accordingly on three occasions during the 1740s and 1750s—in 1746, 1751 and 1754—investigations were set in train to discover just how much the King's Works had cost during the last few decades and whether any economies might be expected in future. The results were fairly encouraging.

First of all, the Treasury dealt with a minor problem, the payment of call men or registered labourers. Twenty-nine had petitioned in June 1746: 'they have no sort of subsistance but from their daily labour and being now eight months in arrears have exhausted their credit as well as [their] substance, which has reduced them and their families to the lowest circumstances and are become real objects of compassion'. They asked for payment in at least monthly instalments. The Treasury went one better. They impressed £500 to the Paymaster to pay the call men 'their small wages weekly'.[4] And such payments continued regularly into the 1770s.[5]

---

[1] *Ibid.*, ff. 338–9, 3 April 1723. In 1765 Samuel Swain, nephew of a deceased mason, John Woodall, claimed payment of debts due to Woodall totalling £1813 16s. 4d. and outstanding since the reign of George I. Despite Swain's fourteen children and sick wife, the Treasury curtly replied: 'My Lords cannot consider of this demand, as there is no money to answer this debt' (T 29/37, f. 89, 5 Aug. 1765 and f. 1117, 4 Sept. 1765; Works 6/18, f. 107, 6 Aug. 1765).
[2] Works 4/16, ff. 162–3, 31 Jan. 1743. See also Works 4/8, f. 385, 7 Feb. 1743/4; T 29/30, f.26, 22 May, 1744 and Works 4/9, 31 Jan. 1743/4.          [3] T 29/29, f. 47, 18 May 1742.
[4] Works 6/17, f. 18, 27 June 1746.          [5] E.g. Works 6/19, f. 114, 5 June 1776.

Then came the results of their first inquiry. Expenditure by the Office of Works was found to average £31,354 8s. 10d. per annum in Queen Anne's reign, £27,111 13s. 8d. in George I's reign and £26,917 9s. 6¼d. during the first decade of George II's reign—including 'the three great towers at Windsor Castle all new built excepting the outside walls; the great addition of new buildings at Hampton Court; the Mews at Charing Cross; the new Treasury and Secretary of State's office; a great part of the royal apartments at Somerset House rebuilt; great additions of new building at St. James's and the new library'. The additional responsibilities placed upon the department by George II—Richmond, Kew, New Park Lodge, Greenwich House and the King's Private Roads—cost on average another £3308 12s. 10d. per annum.

In other words, far from being unduly high, departmental expenses had actually fallen. This state of affairs, unusual in the history of the King's Works, is further borne out by an undated table of expenditure between 1706 and 1727 probably prepared about this time.

*Queen Anne*

|  | Ordinary | | | Extraordinary | | | Total | | |
|---|---|---|---|---|---|---|---|---|---|
|  | £ | s. | d. | £ | s. | d. | £ | s. | d. |
| 1706 | 11,994 | 19 | 0 | 14,726 | 6 | 9½ | 26,721 | 5 | 9 |
| 1707 | 17,015 | 11 | 0 | 14,418 | 11 | 11 | 31,434 | 2 | 11 |
| 1708 | 15,923 | 17 | 7¾ | 16,335 | 2 | 7¾ | 32,259 | 0 | 3½ |
| 1709 | 35,072 | 2 | 1 | — | | | 35,072 | 2 | 1 |
| 1710 | 21,038 | 12 | 4 | 1,634 | 12 | 1 | 22,673 | 4 | 5 |
| 1711 | 32,912 | 4 | 11¾ | 4,052 | 17 | 8¾ | 36,965 | 2 | 8½ |
| 1712 | 31,879 | 19 | 11½ | 390 | 18 | 5½ | 32,270 | 18 | 5 |
| 1713 | 30,871 | 10 | 11¼ | 2,568 | 3 | 6 | 33,439 | 14 | 5¼ |
|  | £196,708 | 18 | 11¼ | £54,126 | 13 | 1½ | £250,835 | 11 | 0¾ |

yearly average:

£ 24,588 12 4¼    £ 6,765 16 7¾    £ 31,354 9 0

*George I*

|  | Ordinary | | | Extraordinary | | | Total | | |
|---|---|---|---|---|---|---|---|---|---|
|  | £ | s. | d. | £ | s. | d. | £ | s. | d. |
| 1714 (from 1 Aug.) | 8,306 | 7 | 4 | 9,471 | 13 | 8 | 17,778 | 1 | 0 |
| 1715 | 14,115 | 6 | 1¼ | 2,043 | 13 | 0 | 16,158 | 19 | 1¼ |
| 1716 | 15,929 | 1 | 6¾ | 5,511 | 19 | 7½ | 21,441 | 1 | 2¼ |
| 1717 | 19,992 | 11 | 2½ | 3,217 | 2 | 5½ | 23,209 | 13 | 8 |
| 1718 | 27,106 | 12 | 0¼ | — | | | 27,106 | 12 | 0¼ |
| 1719 | 20,872 | 14 | 3¼ | 36 | 7 | 5¼ | 20,909 | 1 | 8½ |
| 1720 | 11,467 | 18 | 7½ | 3,081 | 14 | 6¾ | 15,269 | 13 | 2¼ |
| 1721 | 12,375 | 3 | 1½ | 9,101 | 6 | 2 | 21,476 | 9 | 3½ |
| 1722 | 12,467 | 18 | 8½ | 221 | 9 | 6 | 12,689 | 8 | 2½ |
| 1723 | 14,514 | 5 | 0¼ | 12,373 | 8 | 4¼ | 26,887 | 13 | 4½ |
| 1724 | 18,050 | 0 | 7¼ | 12,537 | 11 | 9 | 30,587 | 12 | 4¼ |

| | | | |
|---|---|---|---|
| 1725 | 21,288 13 11¼ | 3,107 10 4¼ | 24,396 4 3½ |
| 1726 | 20,191 10 7¼ | 6,826 16 0 | 27,018 6 7¼ |
| 1727 (up to July) | 8,244 5 5½ | 3,204 3 0½ | 11,448 8 6 |
| | £224,922 8 7 | £71,454 15 11 | £296,377 4 6 |
| yearly average: | | | |
| | £ 16,065 17 9 | £ 5,103 18 3¼ | £ 21,169 16 0½ |

*Additional palaces*

| | *Ordinary* | *Extraordinary* | *Total* |
|---|---|---|---|
| | £ s. d. | £ s. d. | £ s. d. |
| 1714 | — | — | — |
| 1715 | 1,726 2 2½ | — | 1,726 2 2½ |
| 1716 | 3,173 11 8 | — | 3,173 11 8 |
| 1717 | 3,070 12 5¼ | 2,504 19 6¾ | 5,575 12 0 |
| 1718 | 7,034 5 7¾ | — | 7,034 5 7¾ |
| 1719 | 2,283 17 2 | — | 2,283 17 2 |
| 1720 | 2,674 14 4¾ | — | 2,674 14 4¾ |
| 1721 | 2,755 15 0 | 3,021 5 6¼ | 5,777 0 6¼ |
| 1722 | 2,643 0 11¾ | 458 16 6 | 3,101 17 5¾ |
| 1723 | 2,433 5 4¾ | 2,220 6 10¾ | 4,653 12 3½ |
| 1724 | 4,880 15 7 | 9,955 13 2¼ | 14,836 8 9¼ |
| 1725 | 3,902 18 0¾ | 9,869 2 0¼ | 13,772 0 1 |
| 1726 | 3,170 16 8¼ | 14,042 13 7½ | 17,213 10 3¾ |
| 1727 (up to July) | 690 1 6¼ | 673 13 3½ | 1,363 14 9¾ |
| | £40,439 16 9 | £42,746 10 7¼ | £83,186 7 4¾ |
| | £ 2,888 11 2¼ | £ 3,053 6 5½ | £ 5,941 17 8 |
| Aggregate yearly average: | | | £27,111 13 8½[1] |

In September 1746 the Board of Works therefore felt every justification in demanding that the Chancellor of the Exchequer authorise in full the payment of departmental debts totalling £33,724 16s. 11d.[2] Less than a year later, in March 1747, all payments due to Midsummer 1746 had been met and there was a balance of £1025 12s. 1d. in the Paymaster's hands.[3] During the next few years this favourable situation continued. When in 1751 the Treasury asked to see a table of all accounts since 1705, it was discovered that the cost of the King's Works between 1740 and 1750 averaged only £23,324 12s. 3d. per annum.[4]

In April 1754, therefore, the Treasury thought the time was ripe for some reordering of contracts. The Board of Works was asked what 'abatement of the price of works', that is 'what saving of expense hath arisen or may hereafter be made in consequence of . . . the prompt and regular payment which of late hath been made'.[5]

[1] Works 4/4, f. 1, tipped in.
[2] Works 6/17, f. 25, 5 Sept. 1746.
[3] *Ibid.*, f. 35, 25 March 1747.
[4] Works 4/10, 10 and 15 July 1751.
[5] Works 6/17, f. 110, 3 April 1754; Works 4/11, 9 April 1754.

Back came the following comparative table showing expenditure in the last eight years of Queen Anne's reign, the last eight years of George I's reign and the last eight years of George II's reign:[1]

*Last eight years of Queen Anne's reign:*

| | | | |
|---|---|---|---|
| Total expense | £250,835 11 0¾ | | |
| Ordinary works | | 24,588 12 3 | yearly average |
| Extra works | | 6,765 16 7¾ | ,,     ,, |
| | | £31,354 8 10¾ | ,,     ,, |

*Last eight years of George I's reign:*

A) 'Old Palaces' (*Tower, Whitehall, St. James's, Westminster, Denmark House, Winchester, Newmarket, Hampton Court, Kensington*).

| | | | |
|---|---|---|---|
| Total expense | £169,773 15 9¾ | | |
| Ordinary works | | 14,824 19 6 | yearly average |
| Extra works | | 6,396 14 11¾ | ,,     ,, |
| | | £21,221 14 5¾ | ,,     ,, |

B) 'New Palaces' (*Windsor, Mews, Greenwich, New Park Lodge, Richmond, Kew, King's Private Roads*).

| | | | |
|---|---|---|---|
| Total expense | £ 63,392 3 10½ | | |
| Ordinary works | | 5,030 3 10½ | yearly average |
| Extra works | | 2,893 18 5½ | ,,     ,, |
| | | £ 7,924 2 4 | ,,     ,, |

| | | |
|---|---|---|
| Combined totals: | £233,165 19 8¼ | |
| Combined yearly av. | 29,145 16 9¾ | |

*Last eight years of George II's reign:*

A) 'Old Palaces'

| | | | |
|---|---|---|---|
| Total expense | £140,605 13 8½ | | |
| Ordinary works | | 15,758 17 3 | yearly average |
| Extra works | | 1,816 16 11½ | ,,     ,, |
| | | £17,575 14 2½ | ,,     ,, |

B) 'New Palaces'

| | | | |
|---|---|---|---|
| Total expense | £ 53,266 18 11½ | | |
| Ordinary works | | 6,027 17 4½ | yearly average |
| Extra works | | 630 10 0½ | ,,     ,, |
| | | £ 6,658 7 5 | ,,     ,, |

| | | |
|---|---|---|
| Combined totals: | £193,872 12 8 | |
| Combined yearly av. | £ 24,234 1 7½ | |

Such figures were by no means alarming. But they were regarded by the Treasury as insufficiently precise. The Board of Works was informed 'that their Lordships expect a more full and satisfactory answer, specifying the difference of the Prices of Work etc. at different Periods that their Lordships may see at one view, what particular abatement hath been made in consequence of the prompt method of

[1] Works 6/17, ff. 110 *verso*–111 (adapted).

Payment'.[1] This time the Board of Works did indeed divulge the details. But they prefaced their figures with a reminder that further economies on any significant scale could hardly be expected. For 'when our Contracts were made, with both the Tradesmen and the Workmen it was understood to be with prompt Payment, and when the Payment was postponed, the Tradesmen and Workmen were the only sufferers'. Besides, 'these Contracts were made in the year 1734. And then they were reduced from the Prices then allowed . . . to the Prices they now stand at'.[2] The table of comparative prices ran as follows:[3]

| Carpenter | Queen Anne | George I | George II |
|---|---|---|---|
| | £ s. d. | £ s. d. | £ s. d. |
| Rough oak per ft. cube | 3 6 | 3 0 | 2 8 |
| Framed oak per ft. cube | | 3 6 | 3 0 |
| Plained & framed oak per ft. cube | | 4 0 | 3 2 |
| Rough fir per ft. cube | 2 0 | 2 0 | 1 8 |
| Framed fir per ft. cube | | 2 6 | 2 0 |
| Plained & framed fir per ft. cube | | 3 0 | 2 2 |
| Folding joint floors per sq. | | 1 12 6 | 1 10 0 |
| Clean deal floor dowelled per sq. | 6 0 0 | | 5 0 0 |
| 2nd. best Clean deal floor dowelled per sq. | 3 15 0 | | 3 10 0 |
| Straight joint boarding per sq. | 2 0 0 | | 1 18 6 |
| 3 in. oak plank per ft. | 9 | 9 | 7½ |
| 4 in. oak plank per ft. | 1 0 | 1 0 | 9 |
| 10 ft. whole deals each | 1 6 | 1 4 | 1 4 |
| 10 ft. slit deals each | | 1 9 | 1 7 |
| Whole deal boarding per sq. | 1 6 0 | 1 5 0 | 1 4 0 |
| **Bricklayer** | | | |
| Reduced brickwork per rod | 5 7 6 | 6 4 0 | 5 15 0 |
| Place bricks per 1000 | 17 0 | 18 0 | 15 0 |
| Plain tiling per sq. | 1 10 0 | 1 6 0 | 1 5 0 |
| Pantiling per sq. | 1 4 0 | | 1 0 6 |
| Lime per cwt. | 11 0 | 10 0 | 10 0 |
| Mortar per hod | | 6 | 5 |
| Pantiles per 100 | 10 0 | 8 6 | 10 0 |
| Plain tiles per 100 | 1 10 0 | 1 5 0 | 1 5 0 |
| Laths per bundle | 2 6 | 2 3 | 2 0 |
| **Mason** | | | |
| Portland stone per ft. cube | 3 4 | 2 3 | 1 8 |
| Portland stone plain, per ft. superficial | | 1 2 | 8 |
| Portland stone moulded, per ft. superficial | | 1 5 | 10½ |
| Portland stone slab, 2 in., per ft. superficial | 2 0 | 1 10 | 1 3 |

[1] *Ibid.*, f. 111 *verso* 2 May 1754; Works 4/11, 11 April 1754, 7 May 1754.
[2] Works 6/17, 8 May 1754.      [3] *Ibid.*, ff. 112 and 112 *verso*.

| | Queen Anne | | | George I | | | George II | | |
|---|---|---|---|---|---|---|---|---|---|
| | £ | s. | d. | £ | s. | d. | £ | s. | d. |
| Portland stone slab, 2½ in., per ft. superficial | | | | | 2 | 2 | | 1 | 4 |
| Firestone hearths per ft. | | 1 | 4 | | 1 | 3 | | 1 | 0 |
| Purbeck paving per ft. superficial | | | 9 | | | 8 | | | 7¼ |
| Old Purbeck paving relaid | | | 3 | | | 2 | | | 2 |
| Veined marble slab per ft. superficial | | 6 | 6 | | 7 | 0 | | 5 | 0½ |
| Purbeck step per ft. running | | 3 | 6 | | 2 | 2 | | 1 | 9 |
| Portland astragal step, 17 in. tread | | 4 | 6 | | 4 | 9 | | 2 | 9 |
| Statuary marble per ft. cube | | | | | 1 | 5 | | 1 | 5 |
| Statuary marble plain, per ft. superficial | | | | | 3 | 6 | | 2 | 9 |
| Statuary marble moulded, per ft. superficial | | | | | 6 | 0 | | 5 | 6 |

## Joiner

| | Queen Anne | | | George I | | | George II | | |
|---|---|---|---|---|---|---|---|---|---|
| Deal square work per yd. | | 3 | 6 | | 2 | 9 | | 2 | 7 |
| Deal bead work per yd. | | 4 | 6 | | | | | 3 | 2 |
| Deal and raised panels per yd. | | 5 | 6 | | | | | 3 | 10 |
| Right Wainscot beadwork per yd. | | | | | 9 | 0 | | 7 | 8 |
| Right Wainscot square work per yd. | | 9 | 0 | | 7 | 0 | | 5 | 6 |

## Glazier

| | Queen Anne | | | George I | | | George II | | |
|---|---|---|---|---|---|---|---|---|---|
| Crown glass in sash per ft. superficial | | 1 | 6 | | 1 | 0 | | | 10 |
| English squares per ft. superficial | | | 8 | | | 6 | | | 5 |
| New lead per ft. superficial | | | 3 | | | 3 | | | 3 |
| Lead repaired per ft. superficial | | | 1½ | | | 1½ | | | 1 |

## Plasterer

| | Queen Anne | | | George I | | | George II | | |
|---|---|---|---|---|---|---|---|---|---|
| Stucco on laths per yd. | | | | | 2 | 6 | | 1 | 9 |
| Stucco on brickwork per yd. | | | | | 1 | 9 | | 1 | 4 |
| Common lathing and plastering per yd. | | 1 | 2 | | | 10 | | | 8 |
| Rendering per yd. | | | 4 | | | 4 | | | 3½ |
| Cornices pointed, each | | 2 | 0 | | 2 | 0 | | | 11 |
| Chimneys plastered and blackened, each | | 2 | 0 | | 1 | 0 | | | 9 |
| Whitewashing per yd. | | | 2 | | | 1½ | | | 1½ |
| Window lights pointed, each | | 1 | 0 | | | | | | 5 |

## Painter

| | Queen Anne | | | George I | | | George II | | |
|---|---|---|---|---|---|---|---|---|---|
| Painting three times in oil, per yd. | | | 10 | | | 9 | | | 7 |
| Painting twice in oil, per yd. | | | | | | 6¾ | | | 5 |
| Painting once in oil, per yd. | | | | | | | | | 3½ |
| Sash frames, three times in oil, each | | 1 | 0 | | | | | 1 | 2 |
| Sash frames, twice in oil, each | | | | | 1 | 0 | | | 9 |
| Sash squares, three times in oil, each | | | 1 | | | 1½ | | | 1½ |
| Sash squares, twice in oil, each | | | | | | 1 | | | 1 |
| Casements each | | | 3 | | | 4 | | | 3 |
| Window lights, twice done in oil, each | | | 6 | | | 4 | | | 3 |
| Window lights, three times in oil, each | | | | | | 6 | | | 4 |

| | Queen Anne | | | George I | | | George II | | |
|---|---|---|---|---|---|---|---|---|---|
| | £ | s. | d. | £ | s. | d. | £ | s. | d. |
| **Plumber** | | | | | | | | | |
| Sheet lead and labour per cwt. | | 15 | 0 | | 19 | 0 | | 18 | 0 |
| Lead and solder in pipes and cisterns, per cwt. | | | | | | | 1 | | 3 |
| Solder per lb. | | | 9 | | | 9 | | | 6 |
| Plumbers allowance for old lead, per cwt. | | | | | 14 | 0 | | 15 | 0 |
| Lead for cramping, per cwt. | | 15 | 0 | | | | | 16 | 0 |
| **Smith** | | | | | | | | | |
| Casements per lb. | | | 8½ | | | 7 | | | 6 |
| Cross garnetts per lb. | | | 5 | | | 5 | | | 3¾ |
| Holdfasts & wall hooks per lb. | | | 5 | | | 5 | | | 4¼ |
| Chimney bars per lb. | | | 4½ | | | 4 | | | 3½ |
| Iron grates per lb. | | | | | | 6 | | | 4 |

Unfortunately for the Office of Works—but fortunately for its historians—even such details as these did not satisfy the Treasury.[1] The next requirement was to supply full details of all salaries, allowances and payments to contractors and labourers for the first quarter of 1754. The result was a long and valuable document covering everything from the rate of window tax on the office in Scotland Yard (14s.) to the cost of maintaining all the turret clocks in His Majesty's Palaces (£12 10s. 0d.).[2] This was followed by 'An Abstract of Works in Hand . . . and an Accompt of the Clerks of the Works, Labourers in Trust and other Labourers etc. that are constantly employed . . .'[3] From this equally helpful document it emerged that there were 'no new works in hand at any of His Majesty's Palaces', and that Ordinary Works not yet brought to account totalled only £2806 18s. 2d. The only future economies the Board of Works could bring itself to contemplate were the sale of the materials of Wren's unfinished Winchester Palace and the abolition of two minor posts: those of Clerk of Works and Labourer in Trust for New Park Lodge.[4] And the only economies immediately put into effect by the Treasury were equally trifling: works in St. James's Park, Green Park, and Hyde Park were henceforward to be the responsibility of the Department of Woods and Forests;[5] and one or two prices were reduced.[6] However, the most striking result of the inquiry—though one not commented on officially at the time—was the heavy disproportion of salaries and allowances to building costs. The total expenditure on men and buildings for the first quarter of 1754 was £4564 0s. 10½d. Of this sum, no less than £762 10s. 11d. was spent on 'Allowances to the Board Officers'. Similarly, the cost of works in St. James's Park and Green Park between 1742 and 1753 was found to be £4549 16s. 5½d.,

[1] Works 4/11, 14 May 1754.
[2] Works 6/17, f. 113.
[3] *Ibid.*, f. 115; Works 4/11, 14 May 1754.
[4] Works 6/17, f. 114, 30 May 1754.
[5] Works 4/11, 4 July 1754.
[6] May, the Windsor carpenter, had his price for oak piling reduced from 3s. 6d. to 3s. per cubic foot (Works 4/12, 1 Nov. 1757).

or £379 3s. 0¾d. per annum. Against this, the Ranger's allowance alone came to £80 per annum or £960 over the same period of twelve years.[1] Such anomalies would not escape the vigilant eyes of economical reformers in the 1770s and 1780s.[2]

Yet despite all its delays and all the cost of its sinecures, the Office of Works was neither more cumbersome nor more inefficient than many other government departments. In some respects it was less subject to traditional abuses. It did not, for instance, share in the pernicious system of 'customary fees'. As Isaac Ware explained to the Commissioners of Land Tax in 1760, 'there are no perquisites in this office as arise from fees established by custom or authority, and payable either by the Crown or the Subjects, in consideration of business done, from time to time in the course of executing such offices and employments.'[3] And as a group the king's workmen were by no means always dilatory. The personal relationship between different levels of government did make it possible, on occasion, to accelerate the processes of departmental administration quite remarkably. When an outbreak of plague was feared in 1721, an Order of Council, a Treasury directive, a report on prophylactic measures by Sir Hans Sloane, Dr. Mead and Dr. Arbuthnot, and an Office of Works programme for emergency hospital barracks all followed each other in rapid succession.[4] When Westminster Hall had to be fitted up in 1746 for the trial of the Jacobite peers—Kilmarnock, Cromarty and Balmerino—the hierarchy of command nominally ran from the king, through the Lord Great Chamberlain, through the Lord Chamberlain of the Household, through the Commissioners of the Treasury to the Surveyor General and thence to the Clerk of Works. Yet the works were performed speedily and without a hitch.[5] Small-scale operations were occasionally very swift. When in 1742 the Piccadilly boundary wall of St. James's Park collapsed, the Keeper managed to get a message to the Treasury within an hour, the Treasury instantly informed the Office of Works and temporary fencing was immediately put up 'to keep the deer in and people out'.[6] In 1743 a minor crisis at Charing Cross Mews provoked an urgent exchange of letters followed by speedy action. From George II's military camp at Worms, Edward Sedgwick, secretary to the Duke of Richmond, Master of the Horse, dispatched an urgent note to his subordinate James Adams: 'My Lord Duke commands me to acquaint you that he has told the King of the death of the Turky horse that died of the Glanders, and H. M. commanded His Grace to give positive orders that the stall in the stable in which that horse died may be pulled down and burnt as soon as possible, let it be in whatever stable it will, the rack, manger, sides and pavement must be taken away, and new built, the wall must be very well scraped and new whitewashed . . . take care that they execute every particular of these orders, and that none of the old stuff serve again. As for the copper that covers the manger, the Board of Works may sell that and put new in its room.' Adams asked for instant action—'these orders are so positive'—and at the same time took care to indemnify himself: 'least I should fail in rightly expressing the orders . . . I have sent by the bearer the letter itself, which I must pray you to order to be copied, for your own

---

[1] Works 6/17, f. 115 *verso*.                    [2] See vol. vi pp. 7–8 *et seq.*
[3] Works 1/3, f. 142, 4 June 1760.                [4] Works 4/2, 14 Oct. 1721.
[5] Works 4/9, 8 July 1746, 15 July 1746.          [6] Works 1/2, f. 57, 6 and 12 Oct. 1742.

memorandum and to deliver the original back again to the bearer for my justification.'[1]

It would be wrong to think of the unreformed Office of Works as in any way anarchic. When the Clerks of Works had to produce an inventory of stores in 1721, they were told: 'the Board will admit of no excuse whatever, but expect the same to be punctually complied with'.[2] Discipline could occasionally be severe. In 1720 Charles Williams was 'dismissed . . . for neglect of duty, disobeying Mr. Surveyor's orders, and insolent language'.[3] In 1770 Kirby lost his labourers' contract for Richmond and Kew when he was discovered to be 'behind hand with the payment of labourers' wages'.[4] In 1773 Cobb was deprived of his painting contract for Kew, Kensington and Carlton House because his 'oil and colours . . . were not such as ought to be used in His Majesty's service.[5] Murden forfeited his mason's contract at Windsor in 1775 for 'having neglected to do the business though often pressed to the same by the Board'.[6] John Barnard, contracting carpenter at the Mews, was made to discharge one of his craftsmen, Edward Kelke, after complaints had been sent to the Board—'this not being the first offence he has been guilty of'.[7] Charles Ryder was 'discharged from his labour in trustship at Denmark House [in 1762], he not being capable of doing that duty'.[8] George Blackstone had his similar post at Whitehall 'discontinued [in 1746] for neglecting his duty'.[9] So did Daniel Garrett in 1737 at Windsor and New Park Lodge.[10] And Fuller White, the carpenter at Hampton Court, was temporarily suspended in 1761 when it was revealed that he 'had laid in bad materials . . . and . . . also neglects his duty'.[11]

Sometimes a stern warning was enough. In 1745 'the Board being informed that the Labourers at the Tower do not do their duty [it was] ordered [that] Mr. Kynaston acquaint them that unless they do perform their duty, they will be discharged and others put in their room'.[12] When complaints were received in 1778 about 'the neglect of the carpenter's business' at Windsor, Couse warned Henry Emlyn 'that if immediate care be not taken by better attendance as well as doing the business in a more workmanlike manner, the Board will immediately appoint another person'.[13] In 1765 Isaac Ware sent this stiff rebuke to Engine Maker Ragg: 'I am informed many applications and messages have been sent for you to attend your duty, and perform what repairs are wanting to the engines at Windsor Castle; I am to acquaint you that if you do not immediately go or send to see what is wanting, you will hear from this Board in a manner very little agreeable to you.'[14] That was ten years after Ware had sent an equally powerful admonition to Thomas Jenners, a joiner at the same palace: 'It having been reported . . . that when you receive any direction from Mr. Biggs . . . you frequently do more works than you receive his directions for. And that when the persons for whose conveniences the repairs [ordered] are making, are pressing for more works than is directed, you are always acquainting them that

[1] Works 1/2, f. 75, 11 Sept. 1743.
[2] Works 4/2, 15 Dec. 1721.
[3] Works 4/2, 23 March 1720.
[4] Works 4/14, 3 Aug. 1770.
[5] Works 4/15, 15 Jan. 1773.
[6] Works 4/15, 22 Dec. 1775.
[7] Works 1/3, f. 73, 8 Jan. 1746/7; Works 4/9, 8 Jan. 1746/7.
[8] Works 4/13, 8 Sept. 1762.
[9] Works 4/9, 25 Sept. 1746.
[10] Works 4/7, 11 Aug. 1737.
[11] Works 4/12, 4 Aug. 1761.
[12] Works 4/9, 22 Aug. 1745.
[13] Works 1/5, f. 7, 15 May 1778.
[14] Works 1/4, f. 38, 5 Oct. 1764.

such Extras may be done very conveniently. This manner of behaviour of yours has been considered this day at a full Board; and I am ordered by the Commissioners to acquaint you that you are for the future to follow strictly Mr. Biggs orders, and not to presume anything of yourself or give any advice in these affairs which does not concern you. Otherwise another Joyner will be employed that will pay a due regard to the Board's orders.'[1]

Occasionally offenders were reduced to making public acts of contrition. When in 1726 Arthur Leppington was 'suspended until further order, for not attending this Board as directed', he was only able to regain his position by 'attending the Board and making his humble submission to the Commissioners'.[2] In 1755 John Bender, Labourer in Trust at Windsor, confessed himself similarly penitent: 'upon making his submission and shew of great concern for his misconduct and insolent behaviour to the Clerk of Works, [he] received the Board's indulgence of being continued in his office upon his good behaviour for the future'.[3] And in 1752 a mild reminder from Ware about overdue painting estimates produced a reply from Henry Joynes, Clerk of the Works at Kensington, which indicates clearly enough the great respect minor officers of the department were expected to show for their superiors on the Board: 'I know of no wilful delay, but what occasioned it, I believe, first was the illness of Mrs. Browne [housekeeper], which continued so very bad and so long, and at last with Death; and myself very much out of order in the Discharge of the Gouty Matter, with Extream Pain for sometime, while the affair was doing. Indeed the weather the whole time so very wett, not two dry days together, unfit for outside painting. I'm very sorry its being so long about should give the Board any displeasure, the truth is from the above accidents, and from no disregard to the Orders of the Board. Please to acquaint them, and I hope they will think so. . . .'[4] Two years later Joynes himself was dead, and his son Samuel sent off a humbly cooperative letter to the Surveyor General on the very morning of his father's demise: 'Whatever orders you shall think are necessary for me to obey, I shall receive the same with the utmost attention and regard, and in the mean time I shall lay every paper and matter which belongs to His Majesty's affairs on one side to be disposed of as you shall please to command, and that I may not unknowingly commit any mistake, I most humbly intreat your honour to favour me with your commands in writing.'[5]

The anathemas of the Board were not delivered lightly. When in 1746 complaints were received from the Duke of Richmond against Joseph Phillips, Clerk of Works at the Mews, dismissal was preceded by temporary suspension, pending an investigation by Isaac Ware.[6] The same procedure was adopted when in the same year accusations were levelled against John Vardy, then Clerk of Works at Hampton Court, by Lord Vere Beauclerk. On that occasion, the decision went the other way. Vardy was reinstated and Beauclerk found himself faced with a legal action.[7] Less dramatically, John Wright, a labourer at Kensington, was dismissed for negligence in 1747 and then reinstated.[8] During 1752 the Board spent some time reconsidering

---

[1] Works 1/3, f. 112, 24 April 1755.
[2] Works 4/3, 10 and 15 Oct. 1726.
[3] Works 4/11, 19 Aug. 1755.
[4] Works 1/3, f. 84, 18 Aug. 1752.
[5] *Ibid.*, f. 104, 2 July 1754.
[6] Works 4/9, 27 May 1746.
[7] *Ibid.*, 17 June, 8 July, 20 Nov. 1746.
[8] *Ibid.*, 21 Jan. 1746/7, 17 March 1747.

their decision to prosecute Richard Arding for 'conveying several old building materials from His Majesty's Gardeners' House at Kensington'.[1] And when in the same year Thomas Stone, a carpenter on call at Hampton Court, began to misbehave he was treated with initial leniency. The Board merely 'ordered [that] the Clerk of Works . . . be acquainted . . . that the Board has forgiven Stone . . . for this his first offence of neglect of duty, and that the Clerk care for the future he be kept close to his business and that no time be allowed but what he works'.[2] Seven years later, however, the situation had become rather more serious. 'Mr. Lovibond, one of His Majesty's J.P.s at Hampton Town, having laid before [the] Board an examination taken before him upon oath of Daniel Dyer, laying detestable practices to the charge of Thomas Stone . . . it [was] ordered . . . that . . . Stone be suspended till such time as he can clear up the crime sworn against him . . . which if he does not forthwith do, he will be turned out of the office.'[3] Within a week Stone was 'examined what he had to say for himself'. But 'not having cleared himself to the satisfaction of [the] Board, [it] ordered his suspension to continue'.[4] Not until a fortnight later was Stone dismissed, 'he not being able to clear himself of the crime'.[5] Unfortunately, whatever the crime was, it seems to have been considered far too heinous for inclusion in the records of the King's Works.

Not surprisingly, when it came to administrative wrangling, the Board of Works tended to side with its own employees against the dictates of the Treasury. In 1728, for example, the Board vainly tried to lift from the shoulders of its contractors all responsibility for the payment of Walpole's sixpence in the pound Civil List Tax. A memorial was simply sent to the Treasury Commissioners announcing 'that they have agreed that the Civil List Tax of 6d. per pound shall be made good to their artificers', and therefore desire 'a warrant to the auditors to allow the same on the Paymaster's accounts'. Back came a stern reply: 'My Lords [of the Treasury] do not enter into the consideration of their [Board of Works] agreement, but say it is very extraordinary for them to take upon them to remit or give up a publique tax, the deficiency whereof (if any) . . . will fall on the King's Civil List to make good, without first having their Lordships' consent. . . .'[6]

Particularly in its lower reaches, the Office of Works built up a tenaciously familial structure during the eighteenth century. This network of family relationships lasted long after the reforms of 1782. The Crocker dynasty, for instance, survived through three generations. Edward Crocker I arrived as office messenger in 1751.[7] He moved up to junior writing clerk in 1769,[8] the same year as Elizabeth Crocker received Maundy Money on the Surveyor General's recommendation.[9] Edward Crocker II became 'assistant enterer of estimates with his father' in 1774,[10] Crocker I being made senior writing clerk in the same year.[11] Crocker I died in 1779, leaving room for Crocker II to become the most junior of the three writing

---

[1] His wife Sarah begged 'the Board to extend their clemency to her unhappy husband, which otherwise must end in the utter ruin of both him and her'. Her petition was supported by 'a great number of the principal inhabitants of Kensington' (Works 4/11, 21 Nov. 1752).
[2] *Ibid.*      [3] Works 4/12, 4 Sept. 1759.      [4] *Ibid.*, 11 Sept. 1759.      [5] *Ibid.*, 25 Sept. 1759.
[6] T. 29/26, 17 Dec. 1728; Works 6/15, ff. 199–200, 15 Dec. 1728.
[7] Works 4/10, 19 March 1750/51.      [8] Works 4/14, 21 April 1769.
[9] *Ibid.*, 3 March 1769 (also 11 March 1768, 9 March 1770 and 21 Feb. 1772).
[10] Works 4/15, 13 May 1774.      [11] *Ibid.*, 24 June 1774.

clerks.[1] In 1781 he moved up to second in line,[2] a position confirmed in 1782. In 1794 he temporarily acted as Resident Clerk. And in 1796 he was promoted to Clerk of the Works at the Tower of London, Newmarket, Greenwich and Winchester, an area of responsibility expanded in 1815 to include the Mint, Somerset House, the Rolls House, and the King's Bench, Fleet and Marshalsea Prisons. After a brief responsibility for the Speaker's House and Exchequer Offices in 1811 he became Clerk of the Works at Whitehall, Westminster, St. James's Palace and the King's Mews from 1818 until his retirement in 1829. Edward Crocker III joined as Labourer in Trust in 1815 and stayed on until his resignation in 1827, fifty-six years after his grandfather's arrival.[3] Among contracting tradesmen the names of Hardy, Pratt, Greening, Carne, Holmes, Cobbett, Devall, Eldridge, Barnard, Windsor, Lowe, Phillips, May, reappear again and again. Even if we exclude such contractors—always a group of family concerns—the strength of family ties in the mid-eighteenth-century Office of Works is striking: William and John Robinson, Thomas and Richard Ripley, Joshua and William Kirby,[4] John Collyer snr. and jnr., Robert Brown snr. and jnr. and John and William Allingham—not to mention the Rices, Woolfes and Leaches who carried on the tradition after 1782. Sometimes the network of relationships could be quite elaborate. Charles Bridgeman, for example, Master Gardener, married into the Mist family of contracting paviours who in turn had married into the plumbing family of Devall.[5] The most striking instance of hereditary succession involved successive holders of the office of Sergeant Painter: Sir James Thornhill was certainly the apprentice and probably a kinsman of his predecessor, Thomas Highmore; and he was in turn succeeded first by his son John Thornhill and then by his son-in-law William Hogarth.

Altogether it was a close-knit department, held together by ties of deference, kinship and mutual self-interest. And its documents supply just enough circumstantial detail to personalise its operations: the Board meeting weekly in their refurbished office in Scotland Yard, watched over by a new clock 'that goes a year without winding up';[6] the clerks in a separate room, working away with their black lead pencils supplied by Tycho Wing or Jesse Ramsden,[7] surrounded by 'Closets, Presses etc. for repositing the Books, Drawings and Designs belonging to the several Palaces';[8] Isaac Ware using all his secretarial authority to assert the department's right 'to lay . . . Dust and Soil at the Dunghill in [Scotland] . . . Yard . . . nay even to Noon Day';[9] the office call bell ringing out to summon the labourers to work;[10] Fulling, Ripley, Armourer and Couse earning a five-guinea bonus by staying up 'all night in making out a General Abstract for the year 1763 for the . . . Treasury';[11] all the officers attending the Office Dinner every August 'at the King's Arms in

---

[1] Works 4/16, 30 April 1779.    [2] *Ibid.*, 18 May 1781.    [3] Details in Vol. vi, Appendix D.

[4] Joshua Kirby was something of an authority on perspective and, thanks to Lord Bute's influence, was appointed drawing master to the future George III (Colvin, *Dictionary*, p. 348.)

[5] P. Willis, 'Charles Bridgeman: a Problem in Genealogy', *Blackmansbury* vii (1970), p. 56. John Mist Jnr. worked with Bridgeman at several royal palaces and at Wimpole, Down Hall, Briggens and Carshalton. Together they subscribed to Gibbs's *Book of Architecture* and Kent's *Inigo Jones*.

[6] Below, pp. 449–51.

[7] Works 1/4, 5, 7 April 1762; Works 4/15, 24 June 1774. While the Board was sitting 'no clerk or other person' was allowed to be present, except by invitation (Works 4/3, 5 Jan. 1726/7).

[8] T 56/18, f. 34, 2 July 1717.    [9] Works 1/2, f. 1, 29 Sept. 1737.

[10] Works 4/12, 8 Jan. 1760, 17 Feb. 1761.    [11] Works 4/13, 22 March 1765.

Palace Road, Westminster',[1] or distributing the Christmas Rewards towards the end of December;[2] the Board assembling at 8.00 a.m. one Saturday in order to arrive at Windsor by 10.30, there to examine the 'great engine', but taking care to order in advance their dinner at the White Hart—'where they dined before, part of the dinner to be a good dish of fish, Mr. Surveyor [Henry Finch] named a pike as one thing'.[3] The duties of the department were certainly various, and unlike many government departments they were scarcely alleviated by a summer recess.[4] One day the Board might be giving evidence in the Attorney General's 'action at law in behalf of the Crown' against three members of the Flan family who had 'taken upon themselves to intrude into the [Portland] quarries and to raise stone without . . . licence'.[5] Another day they might be despatching 'H.M.'s arms, carved and painted, to . . . Giberalter, to set up in the Court there',[6] or else considering the location of gunpowder vaults in St. James's Park—evidently a safer spot than a previous depot in the Tilt Yard Guard Room, 'a place not at all safe, being liable to fire, and consequently liable to blow up Whitehall'.[7] Another day they might have to deal with a group of armed men who 'at five in the morning got over the pallisadoes of the King's Palace [at Winchester] and went in and about the buildings with an intent to kill young rooks'.[8] And another day they might be authorising the payment of £1000 to John Rowley, 'Master of Mechanicks to H.M.' for 'an Instrument or Machine . . . for H.M.'s own use representing the Solar System';[9] or else they might be considering a complaint from the Ranger of Bushy Park that local residents—'notwithstanding the severe punishments which may by law be inflicted on offenders'—were cutting into the river bank and diverting water 'from its proper course into their serpentine ditches, canals and ponds'.[10] Such incidents must have supplied a welcome interruption to the humdrum business of departmental routine.

The personal, familial, structure of the unreformed Office of Works even produced an elementary system of social security for its lowest-paid personnel. Departmental charity took three forms. In the first place the Office of Works participated in the allocation of the Royal Maundy. Each Maundy Thursday in the Chapel Royal, Whitehall—Inigo Jones's Banqueting House—the monarch distributed bread and meat, money and clothes to scores of selected paupers. Before 1754 the feet of the poor were also ceremonially washed by the royal almoner. According to 'immemorial custom' the Office of Works nominated two recipients, one at the suggestion of the Surveyor General and one at the suggestion of the Comptroller.[11] Sometimes these were merely neighbouring poor from the parish of St. Martin-in-

[1] Works 4/12, 12 July, 6 Oct. 1757; Works 4/7, 5 Dec. 1738; Works 4/15, 1 Dec. 1775.
[2] By the 1770s these amounted to £15 (e.g. Works 5/66, December Allowances 1778).
[3] Works 1/3, f. 133, 26 June 1759; Works 4/13, 20 July 1770.
[4] Works 1/3, ff. 80, 83, 1 July and 4 Aug. 1782; Works 1/2, f. 58, 3 June 1742.
[5] Works 1/1 ff. 71–2, 21 and 23 Sept. 1737.
[6] Works 4/8, 23 April 1741.
[7] Works 1/2, ff. 66–7, 27 and 31 Jan. 1742/3.
[8] Works 1/4, f. 71, 3 and 6 June 1768; Works 4/14, 10 and 17 June 1768.
[9] Works 6/7, ff. 263–5, 10 May and 7 Nov. 1722. He received another £480 for the addition of 'a new pedestal and sphere' (Works 6/15, ff. 74–5, 25 Feb. 1724/5).
[10] Works 1/3, f. 95, 10 July 1753 and f. 143, 31 July 1760. In particular Dunk Halifax complained of the activities of one 'Mackoon who lives at Langford . . . Who or what this Mackoon is I don't know, but I know he is an invader of the rights of the Crown, and will I conclude suffer accordingly'.
[11] E.g. Works 1/1 f. 1, 14 Feb. 1729/30; 4/14, 6 March 1767; 4/15, 23 Feb. 1776.

the-Fields: Tabitha Pearson, for example, the widow of a distiller turned sailor;[1] or Theodorus Swerdfeger, a half-blind 'distressed artist';[2] or Sarah Gorden, 'a distressed, poor old woman'.[3] Others were employees and dependants of the department itself: Henry Humphreys, for example, whose employment dated back to the reigns of James II and William and Mary;[4] or Hannah Bushnell and Elizabeth Loach, labourers' widows;[5] or the widow of one Seward who served the department 'several years, but being afflicted with long sickness before his death which exhausted his substance', left his wife 'reduced from affluence and plenty to great want and poverty'.[6]

In the second place the Board might authorise specific *ex gratia* payments, usually allocated by the Paymaster from the sale of old building materials.[7] Thus 'Robert Howling a poor labouring man, who broke his leg in assisting at working one of His Majesty's fire engines at the fire which happened near the Old Palace Yard Westminster' in 1754, was allowed £5 'to assist him in his great distress'.[8] Thomas Bragg, a carpenter 'who had the misfortune to fall from a beam at Carlton House' received two guineas.[9] John Bishop, 'a poor carpenter who received a hurt' at the funeral of the Duke of Cumberland, received one guinea.[10] Paul Troy, a bricklayer at the Mews 'who by a fall from the ladder's breaking, broke his arm', was awarded two guineas.[11] So, on two occasions, was Robert Loyd, 'a poor carpenter who had his leg broke by a fall in pulling down the old building at the Record Office, Westminster'.[12] And when his leg 'was obliged to be cut off', he received two further payments.[13] A payment of five guineas and two further payments of two guineas went to Joseph Manning, 'glazier (servant to Carne, carpenter) on account of the unhappy accident he had by a fall of breaking one leg in two places and putting out the ankle bone of the other in so deplorable a manner as to be thought irrecoverable; [and] as he was employed in cleaning of windows at His Majesty's Palace of Kensington . . . it's thought he will be rendered incapable of ever following his trade'.[14] Ann Hutchinson, 'a poor distressed widow, whose husband was a bricklayer's labourer . . . killed at the new building at the Queen's House', received five guineas.[15] So did 'the widow Knott, a poor labourer's widow with five children [who] petitioned the Board . . . in great distress'.[16] So did 'the widow of Davis the slater who was killed by a fall from the roof of Westminster Hall', leaving his wife in a 'mellancholly situation, being very poor and left with two small children'.[17] Margaret Welch, widow of a glazier who fell to his death from a window at the Queen's House,

---

[1] Works 1/4, f. 26, 24 Feb. 1764; 4/4, 3 March 1769.
[2] Works 1/4, f. 42, 1 March 1765. Vertue records that 'Swordfegger' drew a perspective view of St. Paul's Cathedral that was engraved by Fourdrinier (*Wren Soc.* xiv, p. xvii) and a design for a triumphal arch by him is in the Bodleian Library (Gough Maps 44, f, 18).
[3] Works 1/4, f. 53, 1 March 1766.
[4] Works 1/1, f. 1 (original petition stuck in).
[5] Works 1/5, f. 5 *verso*, 28 Nov. 1777 and f. 25, 26 Feb. 1780.
[6] Works 1/1, f. 1; 1/2 f. 38, 12 March 1739/40.
[7] Slate and marble, for example, was sold to the Earl of Burlington (Works 4/3, 11 May 1727; Works 4/5, 22 May 1733).

[8] Works 4/11, 12 Nov. 1754.
[9] Works 4/13, 22 Feb. 1765.
[10] Works 4/13, 15 Nov. 1765.
[11] Works 4/13, 30 May 1766.
[12] Works 4/11, 24 Aug. 1756, 24 Jan. 1758.
[13] Works 4/11, 15 Jan. 1760 and 10 March 1761.
[14] Works 4/11, 8 Aug. 1758.
[15] Works 4/14, 4 Sept. 1767.
[16] Works 4/11, 8 Oct. 1754.
[17] Works 4/10, 4 Oct. 1750.

was awarded fourteen guineas.[1] And Mary Barrett, widow of a carpenter employed at the Queen's Palace for eight years and at St. James's and Kensington for ten years, received twelve guineas, her 'husband [having] died . . . suddenly . . . [leaving] her and three small children in a very distressing condition and she by illness [being] unable to get her living'.[2]

The third method was the award of a regular pension, sometimes disguised as a nominal employment. In November 1744 'John Sullivan, a Labourer at Hampton Court, having lost his sight, applying to be excused from work but to be continued on the call as usual, the Board was pleased in consideration of his having been a faithful and laborious man, to agree to excuse him from labour'.[3] John Sturges an aged labourer at the same palace was 'excused from duty' in 1747.[4] Earlier in the same year John Andrews, Labourer in Trust at Windsor, 'being past his labour and . . . superannuated', had to be replaced. But 'in consideration of his age and infirmities' he was 'continued in the books . . . with an allowance of two shillings per day'.[5] In 1750 John Lewen, porter at Scotland Yard Gate, 'being in a very sick and weak condition and not able to do his duty', was allowed 1s. per night for 'employing a watchman to assist him'.[6] And in the same year, when William Rice succeeded Henry Stallard as Clerk of the Works at Richmond and Kew, he did so on condition that out of his salary he paid '£30 p.a. during her life' to Stallard's widow, she 'being left in very bad circumstances and five children unprovided for'.[7] In December 1761 it was decided that William Morgan, 'a poor carpenter who lost his eye by an accident in His Majesty's service at St. James's, [is to] be employed in His Majesty's Works at Westminster, and to be allowed after the rate of 12s. 6d. per week; and that five guineas be allowed him for the three months past he has not been able to work and under the surgeon's hands'.[8] Five years later this allowance was transferred to the account of John Phillips the contracting carpenter at Westminster.[9] George Wharton, a joiner, received six weeks' sick pay after a fall at Kensington in 1726.[10] Dorothy Lacey, the widow of a labourer at Whitehall, 'left with a helpless child and in a very distressful condition', received five shillings a week from 1773 onwards.[11] In 1759 Brian Dunn's widow, 'being left in very unhappy circumstances, and incapable of getting her bread', had been awarded 'an allowance . . . of £3 per quarter during the pleasure of the Board'.[12] Ralph Clayton, a turncock who lost his job with the demolition of old Somerset House, was given a nominal place worth 1s. 8d. per day in 1776 as office labourer at Whitehall on account of 'his great age and infirmities rendering him incapable of getting a livelihood, [he] having been forty years in His Majesty's Service'.[13] There was no shortage of applicants for such disguised pensions. James King and James Goodchild were both given the status of 'a seven day man on the call books' in 1759.[14] In 1777 it was 'ordered that Henry Goodchild, one of the labourers employed at Hampton Court, be allowed the

[1] Works 4/14, 9 June 1769.
[2] Works 4/14, 6 July 1770.
[3] Works 4/9, 22 Nov. 1744, 11 Dec. 1744.
[4] Works 4/9, 2 June 1747.
[5] Works 4/9, 12 Jan. 1747/8.
[6] Works 4/9, 18 Dec. 1750.
[7] Works 4/9, 29 Jan. 1750.
[8] Works 4/13, 15 Dec. 1761.
[9] Works 4/13, 25 April 1766.
[10] Works 4/3, 23 June 1726.
[11] Works 4/15, 28 May 1773.
[12] Works 4/12, 21 Aug. 1759.
[13] Works 4/15, 15 Nov. 1776.
[14] Works 4/12, 3 July 1759, 4 Sept. 1759.

Sunday in the Room of James King deceased'.[1] Edward Richards was nominally 'entered [as] a Labourer on the Call in the Whitehall books, he having been a labourer many years'.[2] Even troublemakers like John Bender were not excluded: in 1771 he was eventually 'discharged . . . but in considerations of his having been many years in the [department's employ], and now in very poor circumstances, . . . he [was] allowed the pay of a Labourer in Trust (being 2s.2d. per day) till further notice'.[3]

In short, the records of the unreformed Office of Works show all the symptoms of a genuine, if unsystematic, paternalism. Leave of absence was readily granted to officers in need of medical treatment—as when Richard Biggs, Clerk of the Works at Windsor, retired to Bath for a fortnight in 1754.[4] And the widows of labourers dying in the middle of a month always received—via the husband's successor—the residue of that month's wages.[5] When in 1761 Mrs. Love gave 'up to His Majesty the Suttling House bequeathed to her and her son by her late husband', a carpenter at Richmond Lodge, she was awarded 'full recompense' of £10 per annum 'to be paid out of this office during her natural life'.[6] When in 1771 Thomas Beighton, assistant Labourer in Trust at Whitehall, was 'in a very distressed condition, confined in the Fleet Prison for debt [with] a sheriff's officer in possession of the goods in his house', the Board advanced him a loan of £10.[7] Five years later he was dead, and his widow was receiving an allowance of 5s. per week.[8] In times of sickness and disaster the Office of Works looked after its own. And in the end its poorest servants could at least rely on decent burial. Under 29 July 1763 is inscribed this simple entry: £2 'for a coffin for the buryal of Richard Hughes, late a slater to this office, he dying very poor . . .'[9]

Such haphazard charity was a by-product of the fundamentally haphazard system of profits and perquisites. The future was to be more economical. An early straw in the wind appeared in 1747: 'Edward Tuck, labourer on the call, being deceased and application being made by persons to succeed him, the Board took the same into consideration, and finding that several of the call men have been but of little use, it was resolved, and ordered that for the future no labourer should be admitted upon the call books, but such as were able to do their duty.'[10] The office of Master Smith had been abolished in 1716.[11] The Master Bricklayer disappeared in 1768,[12] the Purveyor in 1777[13] and the Sergeant Plumber in 1781.[14] The office of

---

[1] Works 4/15, 7 Feb. 1777.    [2] Works 4/6, 29 Sept. 1737.
[3] Works 4/14, 30 Aug. 1771.    [4] Works 4/11, 10 Sept. 1754.
[5] Works 4/6, 12 Nov. 1734. When Allen Blake succeeded Lincoln as labourer on call at the Tower, Eaton, 'the other labourer', was directed to pay Lincoln's widow 3s. 6d. per week 'instead of paying it to Blake who did the duty for him' (Works 4/10, 23 June 1752).
[6] Works 4/13, 9 Dec. 1761.    [7] Works 4/14, 22 Nov. 1771.    [8] Works 4/15, 25 Oct. 1776.
[9] Works 4/13, 29 July 1763. Robert Lambert, Labourer on Call at Somerset House, received similar burial (Works 4/9, 4 March 1745/6). So did Robert Clark, a labourer at the Tower (Works 4/6, 24 Oct. 1738); Thomson, office carpenter at Denmark House (Works 4/10, 27 Nov. 1750); and James Brown, Labourer in Trust at Kensington, 'he dying in very low circumstances'. Since 'Brown had been at some expense in improving his apartment at Whitehall' and his house at Kensington, the Board agreed to pay over £55 to his executors in consideration of the fittings he had installed (Works 4/11, 2 Jan., 6 Feb. 1753).
[10] Works 4/9, 15 Dec. 1747.    [11] *Parlty. Register* xvi (1779–80), pp. 322–6.    [12] *Parlty. Register*, *loc. cit.*
[13] *Parlty. Register*, *loc. cit.*; Works 6/19, f. 192, 4 July 1778. This saved £102 p.a. Thomas Hardy's widow, Ann, claimed the office was 'originally given as a support to her family' and successfully requested a compensatory pension of £42 p.a.
[14] Works 6/20, f. 19.

Sergeant Painter hovered several times on the brink of abolition before it finally disappeared with the arrival of economical reform. Nominally it carried grand responsibilities; the Sergeant Painter was appointed to 'Our Royal Palaces and Houses as to Our Great Wardrobe, to be Painted and Gilded or Imbellished, and also Appertaining or belonging to Our Office of the Revells and to Our Stables, and to Our Navy's and Ships, Barges and close Barges, Coaches, Chariots, Caroches, Litters, Waggons and close Carrs, Tents and Pavilions, Heralds Coats, Trumpet Banners and also in anything belonging to the solemnization of Burials or Funerals'.[1] Though the office was held by artists as distinguished as Sir James Thornhill, William Hogarth and James Stuart, its profits lay in routine house-painting and gilding rather than in the declining art of decorative painting on canvas or plaster. Thornhill certainly made considerable sums in this unromantic way. When Hogarth died in 1764 he was found to be in receipt of an Exchequer salary worth only £10 per annum and no other regular allowance.[2] It was not for this pittance that he had been so pleased to get the post in 1757, thanks to the influence of 'my friend Mr. Manning and the Duke of Devonshire'.[3] He once stated that the office was worth £200 a year to him, and the records suggest that this was, if anything, an under-estimate.[4] But the indolent Stuart allowed his profits almost to vanish altogether. So there was, and could be, little complaint when in 1782 this ancient office disappeared into limbo.[5] Indeed, George III had already tried to secure its abolition in 1764, but was baulked by Grenville, reluctant to let even an atom of patronage disappear.[6]

During the quiet years of the mid-eighteenth century, therefore, there were several instances of piecemeal reform. Offices disappeared not as a matter of principle, but because their meagre salaries, atrophied since the end of the seventeenth century, made them scarcely worth retaining. But their casual disappearance hardly reduced the departmental salary bill. The details of these salaries altered little between 1719 and 1782 and are best considered in conjunction with Burke's proposals for Economical Reform.[7] Here it is only necessary to note that in the mid-eighteenth century haphazard abolition was more than counterbalanced by haphazard creation. The Surveyor General's extra annual salary of £400 (1726);[8] the Comptroller's annual compensation of £60 (1728) in lieu of a house at Kensington;[9] the Deputy Surveyor's salary of £100 (1718);[10] the Master Carpenter's and Master Mason's salaries of £200 each (1718 and 1719), both in lieu of perquisites;[11] the Joint Archi-

---

[1] Works 6/8, f. 111.                                   [2] Works 4/13, 18 Nov. 1764.

[3] J. Ireland, *Hogarth Illustrated . . . from his own manuscripts* iii (1812), p. 136.

[4] *Op. cit.*, p. 137: cf. RA 16813–5, where Hogarth's receipts from the Office of Works are stated to have amounted in 1763 to £561 and in 1764 to £581.

[5] On Stuart's death in 1788 the artist James Barry belatedly applied for the post (already abolished in 1782), but withdrew when he was told it had been worth only £18 p.a. (*The Works of James Barry* i, 1809, p. 274).

[6] *Correspondence of George III*, ed. Fortesque, i (1927), p. 168.          [7] Vol. vi, pp. 7 *et seq.*

[8] *Parlty. Register* xvi (1779–80), pp. 322–6; full lists of salaries and perquisites.

[9] The Surveyor General's lodgings at Kensington being destroyed by fire, he moved into the Comptroller's, the latter receiving compensation. The Clerk of Works' lodgings were also partly burnt, but were repaired in view of the necessity of his presence (Works 6/15, f. 165, 17 May 1727).

[10] Charged to departmental funds rather than paid out of the Surveyor General's pocket (Works 6/368/5, clause ix).

[11] The Master Mason's salary had previously consisted of an allowance of 5s. 11d. per day, fees of £20 per annum, an Exchequer salary of £18 5s. 0d. per annum, a wardrobe allowance of £5 3s. 4d. p.a., and houses in Scotland Yard and Hampton Court together worth £90 p.a.—making £241 7s. 11d. p.a. in all. Thomas

tects' salaries of £300 each (1761);[1] the Paymaster's expanded salary of £400 (1738);[2] the Chief Clerk's salary of £16 13s. 4d. (1724);[3] the Secretary's salary of £100 (1716);[4] the daily allowance of 7s. 6d. to the Clerk to the Board (1727)[5] and 2s. 6d. to the Comptroller's Clerk (1716);[6] the annual payment of £140 to the Auditors of the Imprests (1716);[7] the annual payment of £80 to the Ranger of the London parks in lieu of profits (1728);[8] the vast consolidated salaries of £918 for the Keeper of the King's Roads (1757)[9] and £800 for the Surveyor of Gardens and Waters (1764);[10] the daily allowances to the Clerks of the Works:[11] 3s. 3d. at Richmond and Kew (1729), 1s. at Hampton Court House Park (1773) and 2s. 3d. at Windsor (1717), Hampton Court and Bushy (1771), the King's Mews (1716), Carlton House (1763) and Buckingham House (1762)—all these are examples of unplanned expansion, substitution or piecemeal reorganisation involving extra charges. Nearly all of these changes were steps in the right direction, in particular the substitution of regular salaries for contractual profits. The unreformed Office of Works had begun to reform itself. But its pace was slow and its direction uncertain, too slow and too uncertain to satisfy its parliamentary critics. The Office of Works may have been run more efficiently under George III than under Queen Anne. But its salary bill appeared to be more expensive.

Admittedly, there had been minor economies as well, apart from the lapsing of certain offices. One of the smaller burdens of the department had been the maintenance of guard houses and barracks at the Tower, St. James's Palace, Kensington, Hampton Court and Windsor. After 1724 they became the responsibility of the Ordnance Office.[12] The office of Keeper of Water Engines at Windsor was discontinued in 1771 and its allowance of 1s. per day transferred to the Clerk of Works.[13] The use of office stationery by Clerks of Works was restricted.[14] As early as 1720 it was 'ordered that the Labourers in Trust be allowed no more nights than they really sit up and watch'.[15] And repeated attempts were made to curtail the cost of improvements to 'grace and favour' apartments.[16] But such peripheral measures consistently evaded the real political and economic issues involved in departmental reform.

---

Ripley therefore successfully claimed riding charges of 5s. 4d. per day since he was 'really upon a worse foot than his predecessors' (Works 6/15, ff. 30–3, 9 Dec. 1723). Nicholas Dubois, as Master Mason, successfully made a similar plea (*ibid.*, ff. 36–9, 26 Feb. 1723/4). But forty years later Ripley's successor, Stephen Wright, found his claim denied by the Treasury (T 29/36, f. 43, 24 July 1764, T 29/37, f. 150, 30 Sept. 1765).

[1] *Parlty. Register, loc. cit.*
[2] The Paymaster's additional allowance of £100 p.a. was discontinued in 1726 and transferred to the Superintendent of Gardens and Waters (Works 4/3, 29 June 1726; T 29/25, f. 168, 14 April 1726). After 1738 his old allowance—excluding Paymaster's percentage—of 6/6d. per day plus £36 10s. od. Exchequer salary was raised to £400 p.a. (Works 6/16, f. 158 *verso*; Works 1/2, f. 32, 15 May 1739).
[3] *Parlty. Register, loc. cit.*
[4] Works 6/368/4, 10 Oct. 1719, clause xix. The joint office of Clerk and Secretary was divided in 1726 when Hawksmoor became Secretary and Flitcroft Clerk (T 29/25, f. 171, 27 April 1726).
[5] *Parlty. Register, loc. cit.*    [6] *Ibid.*    [7] *Ibid.*    [8] E.g. Works 4/11, 18 Sept. 1753.
[9] Works 1/3, f. 123, 18 April 1757. Arundell had received £200 p.a. in the 1730s, excluding perquisites (Works 4/5, 1 June 1731; Works 6/8, f. 29). Offley received £518 p.a. (Works 4/11, 28 Oct. 1756; Works 6/8, f. 108. 7 April 1756 and f. 109, 12 Oct. 1756).
[10] Works 1/4, f. 31, 23 May 1764: £500 salary plus £300 allowance.
[11] *Parlty. Register, loc. cit.*
[12] Works 6/11, f. 28, 14 Oct. 1724; Works 4/3, 20 Jan. 1724/5, 3 Feb. 1724/5.
[13] Works 4/14, 1 Feb. 1771.    [14] Works 4/9, 30 May 1744.    [15] Works 4/2, 10 Jan. 1720.
[16] E.g. Works 1/4, f. 107, 23 April 1773; Works 1/5, f. 14, 6 and 9 March 1779.

Two factors in particular doomed the expenditure of the Georgian Office of Works to repeated scrutiny. Its debts—and by 1777 the department was £53,788 3s. 0¾d. in debt[1]—formed part of the mounting problem of Civil List deficits; and its four major sinecures inexorably drew the whole department into political controversy.

The Civil List had been instituted in 1698 when Parliament assumed responsibility for the national debt and the armed forces, leaving the Crown to cover the cost of civil government and the royal establishments out of a fixed income (mainly from customs and excise) of £700,000 per annum.[2] During Queen Anne's reign, Civil List revenues fell far short of this sum and in 1712 a loan of £500,000 was required to pay the Civil List debts. The Civil List granted by Parliament to George I was £700,000, but various additional sums brought his average Civil List income to £805,000 per annum. George II was granted a minimum of £800,000 per annum. But in fact, as prosperity increased, he received well over this amount: in his last year the figure was £876,988. If George III had received the same dispensation—£800,000 plus any additional surplus revenues—his Civil List income would by 1777 have exceeded £1,000,000 per annum, and by 1798 would have risen to £1,812,308.[3] Unfortunately, in 1760 he was granted £800,000, *tout court*. Inevitably, this sum was soon seen to be quite insufficient to meet the expanding cost of administration. By 1769 Civil List deficits stood at £513,511, a debt Parliament reluctantly agreed to settle.[4] But still the deficits increased. In 1777 the total Civil List was raised to £900,000 per annum and another debt of £618,340 9s. 6¼d. was discharged.[5] This included a debt of £36,788 3s. 0¾d. for H.M.'s Works and Gardens.[6] Throughout the later 1770s the process continued. And as the debts continued to increase—by 1782 they were £300,000—the pressure for Economical Reform grew proportionately.

The Georgian Office of Works was not in fact a conspicuously expensive department. Another inquiry in 1777 confirmed the principal findings of 1754: namely that, apart from a temporary aberration in 1773,[7] expenditure on the King's Works, although frequently exceeding the formal limit, had not been subject to any dramatic overall increase; but that 'salaries and allowances' constituted a sizeable, and perhaps overlarge, proportion of the bill. Expenditure on the Ordinary account for the seven years 1771–7 totalled £228,374 12s. 11¾d. Of this sum, £27,755 13s. 3¾d. went on 'salaries and allowances', a figure far higher than the cost of any individual palace during the same period.[8] A detailed table of expenditure for each year between January 1761 and January 1777 makes this imbalance still clearer.[9]

[1] Works 5/64, 5 Jan. 1777. For debts 1769—72 see Works 6/18, ff. 316—7, 12 Feb. 1773.
[2] For details see E. A. Reiton, 'The Civil List in 18th century politics: Parliamentary Supremacy versus the Independence of the Crown', *Historical Jnl.* ix, 3 (1966), pp. 318–37.
[3] *Commons Jnls.* lvi, pp. 872–3.
[4] *Annual Register* 1769, pp. 62–4*; *Parlty. Hist.* xvi (1765–71), pp. 599, 842–52; *Commons Jnls.* xxxii, pp. 255, 465–603.
[5] 17 G III, *c.* 21; *Parlty. Hist.* xix (1777–8), pp. 103–188, 211–3; 'Debts on the Civil List, 1775–88', B.M. Add. MS. 29470 ff. 34–5.  [6] *Commons Jnls.* xxxvi, p. 334.
[7] T 29/43, f. 35, 22 April 1773. The Treasury suspected that this increase in Ordinary expenditure was due to improvements in 'grace and favour' apartments.
[8] Works 5/64, under Midsummer Quarter, 1778. For a table of Extra account expenditure between Jan. 1769 and Jan. 1777, see *Parl. Pap.* 1812–13, v, p. 388 or Works 5/64, under Ladyday Quarter 1777.
[9] See Appendix B. See also Works 5/106 *passim.* and Works 5/128–9 *passim.*

The expenditure of the Office of Works fluctuated in fact more or less in accordance with other sections of the Civil List. The following table, covering the years 1720 to 1782, suggests that George II was both luckier and more parsimonious than his father and grandson.[1] But the overall level of expenditure is faily consistent:[2]

| | *Works* | | | *Total Civil List* | | |
|---|---|---|---|---|---|---|
| | £ | s. | d. | £ | s. | d. |
| year ending 29 Sept. 1720 | 43,285 | 8 | 0 | 880,485 | 2 | 7 |
| 1721 | 22,924 | 10 | 11 | 890,189 | 9 | 0 |
| 1722 | 36,613 | 2 | 11 | 1,100,842 | 10 | 8 |
| 1723 | 22,041 | 9 | 4 | 847,499 | 2 | 9 |
| 1724 | 36,772 | 15 | 7 | 885,535 | 17 | 9 |
| 1725 | 78,687 | 10 | 4 | 1,157,384 | 16 | 9 |
| 1726 | 32,565 | 11 | 6 | 825,398 | 19 | 2 |
| 1727 | 23,182 | 10 | 2 | 625,160 | 5 | 11 |
| 1728 | 40,598 | 6 | 8 | 1,050,762 | 12 | 0 |
| 1729 | 44,804 | 17 | 11 | 931,912 | 8 | 1 |
| 1730 | 34,712 | 7 | 0 | 853,447 | 3 | 11 |
| 1731 | 37,999 | 5 | 10 | 862,199 | 4 | 6 |
| 1732 | 40,663 | 2 | 0 | 866,672 | 11 | 1 |
| 1733 | 52,405 | 11 | 7 | 892,781 | 7 | 8 |
| 1734 | 48,374 | 19 | 5 | 944,832 | 10 | 1 |
| 1735 | 45,652 | 2 | 0 | 856,485 | 16 | 0 |
| 1736 | 32,182 | 9 | 5 | 852,953 | 0 | 7 |
| 1737 | 37,765 | 19 | 5 | 855,431 | 19 | 0 |
| 1738 | 44,570 | 10 | 7 | 827,567 | 5 | 0 |
| 1739 | 30,672 | 9 | 1 | 876,193 | 2 | 1 |
| 1740 | 34,098 | 7 | 10 | 791,500 | 0 | 4 |
| 1741 | 26,278 | 3 | 1 | 737,780 | 8 | 2 |
| 1742 | 22,662 | 2 | 4 | 782,659 | 12 | 2 |
| 1743 | 22,261 | 10 | 7 | 749,500 | 3 | 8 |
| 1744 | 29,842 | 8 | 0 | 796,749 | 13 | 7 |
| 1745 | 22,783 | 18 | 11 | 762,121 | 11 | 1 |
| 1746 | 23,664 | 8 | 6 | 685,474 | 18 | 11 |
| 1747 | 53,695 | 11 | 11 | 1,213,385 | 11 | 10 |
| 1748 | 31,356 | 15 | 7 | 770,250 | 0 | 8 |
| 1749 | 25,505 | 6 | 1 | 792,599 | 2 | 4 |
| 1750 | 31,293 | 17 | 0 | 812,861 | 0 | 1 |
| 1751 | 36,491 | 1 | 4 | 1,067,558 | 6 | 2 |
| year ending 10 Oct. 1752 | 39,112 | 18 | 10 | 803,404 | 7 | 11 |
| 1753 | 33,984 | 2 | 5 | 853,417 | 11 | 1 |
| 1754 | 28,551 | 4 | 4 | 801,163 | 1 | 2 |
| 1755 | 30,927 | 17 | 10 | 784,929 | 0 | 10 |
| 1756 | 33,761 | 19 | 7 | 849,169 | 12 | 9 |

[1] George II 'lived both within the limits of the Civil List and left a sum of £170,000 at his decease, which was wholly saved from that revenue and which has been received by his present Majesty' (George Grenville, 28 Feb. 1780, *Parlty. Hist.* xvi, p. 844).

[2] Compiled from 'Public Income and Expenditure', *Parl. Pap.* 1868–9, xxxv, pp. 63–187.

|  | Works | | | Total Civil List | | |
|------|--------|-----|-----|------------------|-----|-----|
|  | £ | s. | d. | £ | s. | d. |
| 1757 | 33,619 | 0 | 4 | 840,769 | 11 | 6 |
| 1758 | 29,883 | 15 | 0 | 839,566 | 1 | 11 |
| 1759 | 33,409 | 7 | 8 | 809,111 | 10 | 2 |
| 1760 | 32,989 | 16 | 11 | 852,234 | 7 | 0 |
| 1761 | 35,618 | 17 | 1 | 996,759 | 4 | 2 |
| 1762 | 45,676 | 14 | 9 | 941,661 | 16 | 0 |
| 1763 | 34,478 | 13 | 4 | 867,222 | 7 | 1 |
| 1764 | 38,908 | 0 | 2 | 865,127 | 4 | 4 |
| 1765 | 35,730 | 17 | 4 | 806,058 | 7 | 2 |
| 1766 | 37,799 | 3 | 11 | 815,039 | 3 | 5 |
| 1767 | 50,878 | 1 | 8 | 812,637 | 11 | 9 |
| 1768 | 29,138 | 5 | 8 | 807,019 | 16 | 2 |
| 1769 | 62,535 | 16 | 3 | 1,267,704 | 8 | 1* |
| 1770 | 35,701 | 15 | 2 | 898,187 | 18 | 2† |
| 1771 | 30,523 | 3 | 1 | 795,974 | 17 | 10 |
| 1772 | 40,549 | 8 | 2 | 797,359 | 15 | 11 |
| 1773 | 51,851 | 10 | 6 | 802,646 | 11 | 6 |
| 1774 | 55,329 | 10 | 5 | 809,125 | 8 | 9 |
| 1775 | 55,211 | 5 | 5 | 904,769 | 18 | 0 |
| 1776 | 40,669 | 14 | 6 | 811,237 | 1 | 2 |
| 1777 | 89,055 | 5 | 2 | 1,385,713 | 19 | 3 ⎱‡ |
| 1778 | 49,100 | 6 | 0 | 1,112,215 | 0 | 11 ⎰ |
| 1779 | 55,925 | 16 | 2 | 969,714 | 15 | 1 |
| 1780 | 43,179 | 19 | 7 | 1,039,375 | 7 | 0 |
| 1781 | 53,599 | 7 | 9 | 983,241 | 12 | 0 |
| 1782 | 54,495 | 11 | 1 | 1,004,909 | 15 | 1 |

* including £463,197 16s. 0d. grant for Civil List debts.
† including £50,313 4s. 0d. balance of grant for Civil List debts.
‡ including £618,340 9s. 6¼d. grant for Civil List debts.

The grounds, therefore, for the reform of the Office of Works were as much political as economic. As an integral—and literally visible—part of the Civil List expenditure, the department's expenses would inevitably come under attack. Newcastle once told George II that the spending of his Civil List was entirely his own affair: 'It is Your Majesty's own Money; You may do with it, what you please.'[1] That was precisely what the opponents of George III feared: that the influence of the Crown over Parliament varied according to the largesse distributable from the Civil List. And four senior—if largely nominal—members of the Office of Works regularly sat in the House of Commons, bound in loyalty to the king's ministers by the size and regularity of their salaries.

On the night of 26 May 1780, the House of Commons passed a resolution:

'That for preserving the Independence of Parliament and obviating any Suspicion of its Purity, there be laid before this House, within Seven Days after the First Day

[1] Hardwicke Papers, B.M. Add. MS. 35419, f. 255, 16 Aug. 1760.

of every Session, exact Accounts, authenticated by the Signature of the proper Officers of every Sum and Sums of Money paid in the Course of the preceeding Year, out of the Produce of the Civil List, or any other Branch of Public Revenue to, or to the Use of, or in Trust for any Member of either House of Parliament, by Way of Pension, Salary, or any other Account whatsoever, specifying when and on what Account.'[1]

It was the death knell of the old Office of Works. Five months later the department was asked by the Treasury to supply detailed accounts for the years 1750–80, 'distinguishing under separate heads the establishment salaries, incidental salaries and allowances, repairs at each place, new works, contingencies and other incidental expenses in each year', as well as 'a list of houses held by . . . officers of the Board . . . and if let, at what rents . . . and also what sums of money have been laid out . . . in rebuilding or repair of such houses'.[2] The battle for and against Economical Reform would be waged as fiercely in Scotland Yard as in Westminster. The very existence of the old Office of Works was at stake. Appropriately, John Robinson's peremptory letter was not despatched in the usual way. Instead it was clearly marked 'Private'.

[1] *Commons Jnls.* xxxviii (1780), p. 884; Works 6/19, f. 321.
[2] Works 6/19, f. 319, 17 Oct. 1780.

*Chapter VII*

# THE WINDSOR OFFICE
# 1660–1715

UNTIL 1715 the maintenance of Windsor Castle was in the hands of a local Office of Works distinct from the Office in Whitehall which was responsible for all the other royal palaces. This arrangement was a survival of the past whose perpetuation can be accounted for only by the conservatism of English government under the later Stuarts, for Windsor was far more easily accessible from London than other palaces such as Audley End, Winchester and Newmarket which were the responsibility of the central Office in Scotland Yard. Although the Windsor Office thus maintained its administrative independence of Whitehall, several of its principal officers were at the same time officers of the London Works: in other words Windsor simply provided certain members of the Whitehall staff with a small additional stipend. The Windsor Office was therefore something of an anomaly, and its suppression in 1715 was a piece of rationalisation that had long been overdue.

The establishment at Windsor consisted of a Surveyor, a Comptroller and a Paymaster (each assisted by a Clerk), a Purveyor, a Keeper of the Timber Yard, a Master Mason, a Master Carpenter, and other artisans. The Surveyor and the Comptroller received only 2s. a day, the Purveyor 1s., the Master Mason 1s., the Master Carpenter 6d.[1] These small stipends hardly constituted a livelihood, and most of those who enjoyed them had some other office or employment. William Taylor, appointed Surveyor after the Restoration, was also Steward, Receiver of Rents and Bailiff of the Honor of Windsor,[2] while the Comptrollership was only one of various sources of income granted to Captain Hartgill Baron, adjutant to Prince Rupert, in recognition of his 'hazardous and faithful services' during the Interregnum.[3] In 1668 the offices of Purveyor, Keeper of the Timber Yard and Comptroller's Clerk were all in the hands of the same individual, William Rowlandson, who

---

[1] Works 6/1, f. 11; *Cal. Treas. Books* xxv (1), pp. cdlxii–cdlxiii.
[2] *Cal. S.P. Dom 1660–1*, p. 72. He was the son of William Taylor (d. 1640), who had been deputy Surveyor of the Works at Windsor in Charles I's reign. He was a lawyer by training, and was elected M.P. for Windsor in 1640, but was subsequently expelled on account of his royalist sympathies. He served as colonel with the royalist forces and claimed to have been a 'great sufferer' for the king (M. F. Keeler, *The Long Parliament, A Biographical Study of its Members*, Philadelphia, 1954, pp. 357–8).
[3] *Cal. S.P. Dom. 1660–1*, pp. 288, 522; *1661–2*, pp. 153, 367, 577. He was the eldest son of John Baron of Mere, Wilts. (C. Dalton, *English Army Lists & Commission Registers* i, 1892, p. 126).

managed in this way to achieve a combined income of £48 13s. 4d. a year.[1] The Surveyor and Comptroller held their offices by royal grant, but the Constable claimed the right to appoint the artisans by his own warrant. He also gave orders for repairs to the castle, and thus occupied much the same position *vis-à-vis* the Windsor Works as the Lord Chamberlain did in relation to the Whitehall Office.

Relations between the Constable and the Works officials were not always amicable, and it was a dispute between William Taylor and Lord Mordaunt, who held the former office from 1660 to 1667, that led to the latter's impeachment by the House of Commons. The rights and wrongs of this *cause célèbre* are now impossible to disentangle, but it was Taylor's unsatisfactory conduct as Surveyor of the Works that gave Mordaunt the pretext for the persecution and illegal imprisonment with which he was charged by the Commons in December 1666.[2] Among the offences which Taylor was deemed to have committed were the submission of false accounts, refusing (at a time when the Castle was full of courtiers escaping from the Plague in London) to obey a royal order to give up some rooms in the Timber Yard that were needed for the accommodation of members of the royal household, and urging the inhabitants of Windsor not to cooperate in certain precautions against the Plague set in motion by the Mayor. For these 'contempts and misdemeanours' he was first suspended from his offices (May 1665) and then ordered to be confined to the castle (November 1665).[3] The fact that the Constable gave effect to these orders in a violent and vindictive manner does not necessarily mean that they were not justified, and the king himself was certainly convinced of Taylor's guilt. In October 1666 Denham wrote to Arlington's secretary to say that

> the King hath bidden me speake to his Lordship to gett a warrant for his Majestie to signe to the [acting] receiver of the rents of Windsor who hath money in his hands for the repayres of that Castle and that his Majestie thinks the best way of beginning that worke is to putt out the Surveyor there for having cheated him to such a degree, that it goes beyond all that any accountant ever made.[4]

Steps to this end were taken the following year, and in May the Officers of the Works at Whitehall were ordered to inspect the repairs that Taylor claimed to have carried out and to report what further repairs were needed.[5] Their verdict was unfavourable, and early in 1668 it was decided to place the repair of the castle in their hands. A warrant to this effect was signed in August 1668, and £500 were allocated from the revenues of the castle for the purpose.[6] But Taylor (no doubt encouraged by the parliamentary proceedings against Mordaunt, which had led to the latter's resignation in 1667), still refused to admit defeat, and managed to get his case brought before the Privy Council. Once more the Officers of the Works,

---

[1] Works 6/1, f. 11.

[2] *Commons' Journals*, vol viii, pp. 666–7. For the political background to this affair see D. T. Witcombe, *Charles II and the Cavalier House of Commons* (Manchester 1966), pp. 49–50.

[3] *Cal. S.P. Dom. 1664–5*, p. 362; *1665–6*, p. 79.

[4] SP 29/176, f. 66.

[5] *Cal. S.P. Dom. 1667*, p. 88; *Cal. Treas. Books* ii, pp. 23, 76, 183.

[6] *Cal. Treas. Books* ii, pp. 235, 246, 282, 413–14, 429, 613, 614, 615.

headed now by Wren, were sent to Windsor to inspect the works and to examine Taylor's accounts. On 23 July 1669 they reported as follows:

> Wee the said Officers of Your Majestie's Workes did with all diligence view your Majestie's House of Windsor Castle, but could not finde any considerable parts thereof repayred by Mr. Tayler either in Leadworke, Timber, Stone, Brickworke or flooring, which are the expencefull parts of all Repaires, and must of necessity have appeared, had they been performed. And for Ironworke, Glasse, & Whiting & such other parts as were dubious & not easy to be distinguished, when or by whom they were performed, Wee allowed more then in reason was necessary to the said Mr. Taylor. And for that the Lead Worke seemed easiest to be discovered upon a more particular Examination thereof, Wee did not find at the most with all fair Allowance above twenty squares of Leads new laid by Mr. Taylor amounting to about Ten Tons, And that Mr. Taylor for the same worke had wholly uncovered to the ruine of the Timbers, four of the Towers amounting to about sixteene tons of Lead. And upon the whole matter, it could not be found, that the workes in view could arise in anything in proportion to what were his Receipts, of which he was to clear himself. The said officers likewise having desired Mr. Taylor to produce what Papers, Evidences & Testimonies he could in his owne behalf, for your Majesty's further satisfaction, could not upon the Examination of them finde any tollerable Account, but rather, that the Books were perplext, imperfect & insufficient, and no method or stile used in them, to direct where the particular Expenses were laid out.
>
> And as for Cranburne Lodge, wee could not exactly discover what was laid out upon it by reason it hath been since reedifyed, but by Examination of Workemen, we cannot judge, that One Thousand pounds were expended upon this & the other Lodges.

As a result, the king, 'being very sensible how much he hath been disserved by the said Mr. Tayleur', ordered Prince Rupert (who had taken Mordaunt's place as Constable) 'forthwith [to] oblige the said Mr. Tayleur to leave & resigne . . . all the severall & respective Places he now posseseth belonging either to His majesty's Castle, or Honour of Windsor (except the Office of Steward of the Courts of the said Honour)', and to replace him by 'such diligent & carefull persons . . . as shall be most conducive to His Majesty's services'.[1]

What in fact happened was that Taylor sold his offices to approved persons.[2] The new Surveyor, John Ball, was related to Wren, and no doubt owed his advancement to Wren's good offices.[3] A certain Dudley Rewse had already been acting as Receiver and Paymaster during Taylor's suspension, but the purchaser of the office was Richard Marriott, who from November 1669 accordingly took Rewse's place.[4] Hartgill Baron continued as Comptroller until his death in November 1673, when his office was given to Hugh May.[5] It was May who in 1675 began the great reconstruction of the Upper Ward which continued almost until his death in 1684.[6] He

---

[1] Privy Council Register 61, pp. 300, 302, 368. Taylor claimed that there was a balance due to him on his account of £1881 16s. 9d., but as finally declared in March 1668, it showed a debt due from him to the Exchequer of £3 5s. 0½d. (E 351/3427).

[2] *Cal. S.P. Dom. 1668–9*, p. 531; *1670*, p. 736.    [3] Above, p. 31.

[4] Works 6/1, f. 11.    [5] *Cal. Treas. Books* iv, pp. 212, 237, 485, 504, 647.

[6] Below, pp. 315–28. For his 'Care and pains in the rebuilding and repairing of the castle' he received £500 a year from Sept. 1675 onwards (*Cal. Treas. Books* v, pp. 82, 361, 1036, 1459, vi, pp. 111, 503).

was then succeeded by Wren, who for thirty years thus combined the surveyorship at Whitehall with the comptrollership at Windsor. In this way the Windsor Office became a sort of appanage of Scotland Yard, its nominal 'Surveyor' fulfilling the functions of a mere clerk of works. 'Surveyor or Clerk of the Works' was in fact the title by which the younger John Ball (who succeeded his father in 1688) was sometimes referred to.[1] The relative insignificance of the surveyorship at Windsor was emphasised in 1698, when Wren appointed Ball to the clerkship of the works at Hampton Court.[2] This was intended to compensate him for the loss of his house at Windsor, which was due to be demolished to improve the grounds of the castle, and meant that thenceforth he resided at Hampton Court, and was represented at Windsor by his clerk, Charles Browne.[3] Only the occasional receipt of a warrant from the Constable and the keeping of a distinct account by a local Receiver and Paymaster now served to distinguish the conduct of the king's works at Windsor from those elsewhere.

The formal abolition of the Windsor Office was therefore an obvious economy, and as such it was included in the reforms of 1715, which provided that the Rules and Instructions for the Office of Works in general should in future extend to the Works at Windsor, which were 'to be paid and accompted for from thenceforth from time to time in like manner with the other expences of our Works'. On 2 June 1715 a new Clerk of the Works was appointed by Treasury warrant, and on 3 February 1716 the offices of Comptroller and Surveyor were formally abolished.[4]

The demise of the Windsor Office was accompanied by a good deal of rather unpleasant controversy which seems to have been basically political. The new arrangements were introduced only a few months after the General Election of 1715 in which the younger Wren stood as a candidate for New Windsor, as his father had done before in 1689. He was returned, but was subsequently unseated because of 'illegal practices' and the partiality of the Mayor as returning officer. One of the principal witnesses who testified against him was Thomas Rowland, then foreman to the Master Carpenter (John Churchill). He alleged that James Browne (then the Surveyor's resident Clerk) had provided materials from the king's stores in order to roast an ox for the benefit of Wren's supporters, that he had employed the king's labour to repair the private house of a voter, and had entered on the Call Book

---

[1] *Cal. Treas. Books* xxx, p. 63.                    [2] Above, p. 31.

[3] Browne died in about 1695, whereupon Wren arranged for his office to be held in trust for the benefit of his widow and son, then under age (*Cal. Treas. Papers 1697–1702*, p. 330). The son appears to have been James Browne, who is referred to as 'Clerke of the Works' at Windsor in 1705 (Works 6/1, f. 50ᵛ), and was also Purveyor and Keeper of the Timber Yard (*Cal. Treas. Books* xxv (1), p. cdlxi. On 13 December 1714, his place was taken (with Wren's approval) by another member of the family, Charles Browne (*Cal. Treas. Papers 1714–19*, p. 67), and in September 1715 'the 2 Mr. Browns' were referred to as 'late Clerks' at Windsor (Works 4/1, p. 57). In 1715 they actively supported Christopher Wren junior as Tory Candidate for Windsor Borough (*Commons' Journals*, vol. 18, p. 63), and it was probably because of Charles Browne's political activities that the Treasury directed Wren to dismiss him and appoint in his place first Ralph Bragg, a writing master at Eton who enjoyed the support of the Whig Sir William St. Quintin (T 1/187, ff. 24–5; *Cal. Treas. Books* xxix, pp. 196, 319–20, 355), and then James Brett, a servant of the Duke of Kent (*Cal. Treas. Books* xxix, p. 383). Wren was still strenuously resisting this order when the abolition of the Windsor Office automatically brought Browne's clerkship to an end together with the rest of the Windsor establishment (*Cal. Treas. Papers 1714–19*, pp. 67, 78).

[4] *Cal. Treas. Books* xxix, pp. 535, 690; xxx, p. 63; Works 6/6, p. 65; Works 6/11, ff. 15–16, 76–7. As they had not at that time been audited, the Windsor accounts for 1713–15 were retrospectively included in the Paymaster's Declarations for those years (E 351/3318–3320).

two workmen who were thereby qualified for the franchise although one of them 'did no work there during the said time', while the other was so decrepit as to be incapable. He himself had been dismissed for not voting for Wren and the other Tory candidate, but had since been made Master Carpenter in place of Churchill by warrant from the Duke of Kent, then Constable of Windsor Castle.[1] It was Rowland who on 2 June 1715 was appointed Clerk of the Works at Windsor under the new Regulations.[2] In the light of his allegations it is not difficult to see why, only three weeks after his appointment, Sir Christopher Wren should have accused him of 'many great frauds and abuses' in relation to his office, while he retaliated by complaining that his predecessors, Charles and James Browne (clerks respectively to the Comptroller and Surveyor) had 'insulted him in the execution of his office'.[3] Meanwhile the Duke of Kent, obstinately refusing to surrender his prerogatives, which were nullified by the new arrangements, proceeded to appoint a number of master craftsmen who were not recognised by the Board of Works at Whitehall.[4]

Wren's charges against Rowland were duly reported by the Treasury to the Board of which he was a member, but it was not to be expected that they would be supported by his Whig colleagues, and they appear to have been quietly dropped. They were, as a friend of Rowland's put it, 'trumped up against him during the heats of the last election, but as soon as he gave in his answer, they were entirely slighted by the Board, tho' at [that] time not very favourable to him'.[5] Feeling in Windsor must, however, have continued to run high, for in January 1717 the Board found it necessary to dismiss from the king's service there a blacksmith called John Davis on account of his 'violent temper against the hearty Friends of the Government'.[6]

These animosities had scarcely died down when the reforms of 1715 were set aside at the instigation of William Benson.[7] One consequence of this was the cancellation (30 August 1718) of the order uniting Windsor with the Office of Works.[8] Had Benson remained in office he would no doubt have reclaimed the Comptrollership of the Works at Windsor for himself, but after his dismissal in August 1719 the works at Windsor were placed once more under 'the care and inspection of the Board of Works', and have so remained ever since.

---

[1] *Commons' Journals*, 18, pp. 62–4.
[2] *Cal. Treas. Books* xxix, p. 535.
[3] *Cal. Treas. Books* xxix, pp. 558, 635, 656, 710.
[4] Works 4/1, p. 103; Works 6/6, pp. 164–5; R. Tighe and J. E. Davis, *Annals of Windsor* ii (1858), pp. 498–9, n. 2.
[5] T 1/216, f. 100 (R. Topham to Sunderland, 29 Dec. 1718). They were, however, subsequently revived by William Benson as part of his campaign against the previous Commissioners of Works (*Cal. Treas. Papers 1714–19*, pp. 418, 439). Rowland was eventually dismissed in 1729.
[6] Works 4/1, 8 Jan. 1716/17.
[7] Above, pp. 58–9.
[8] *Cal. Treas. Books* xxxii, p. 565.

# PART II

## The Royal Palaces

# THE ROYAL PALACES
## 1660–1782

THE HISTORY of the English royal palaces in the seventeenth and eighteenth centuries is largely a record of failure: failure to accomplish a single grand design in its entirety, failure to do more than alter and adapt existing buildings which often were palaces only in name. A king whose finances were constrained by parliamentary control could not build palaces like an absolute monarch, and the country which 'Divine Providence' had (as Lord Chatham's monument so proudly proclaims) 'exalted to an height of Prosperity unknown to any former age', failed signally to provide an appropriately magnificent residence for its titular head. What the *Gentleman's Magazine* for 1826 called 'the disgraceful littleness of the metropolitan palaces'[1] was indeed a perpetual source of surprise to foreigners and of embarrassment to Englishmen. 'The palace of St. James's', wrote John Gwynn in 1766, 'is an object of reproach to the kingdom in general, it is universally condemned, and the meanest subject who has seen it, laments that his Prince resides in a house so ill-becoming the state and grandeur of the most powerful and respectable monarch in the universe.'[2]

Exactly one hundred years later, in 1866, in a leader entitled 'Want of Accommodation for Royalty in England', *The Builder* complained that 'the Sovereign of this country has no palace in which fitly to receive either the visits of illustrious foreigners, or the duty paid by those of her own subjects who have the privilege of access to the Royal presence'. The Queen's private houses, wrote the editor, were 'well suited to the stately simplicity that marks the Victorian era, and the old castle, in which so many English crowned heads have kept their Christmas, is a royal abode of which we need not be quite ashamed'. But for state occasions she had no palace worthy of the name. 'For such purposes the rooms at St. James's Palace are simply and notoriously unfit . . . (and) it would be easy to point out many a ducal or princely palace better fitted for the reception of the Sovereign than are the apartments of that old red-brick residence which still gives its name to the Court of Great Britain in diplomatic correspondence.'[3] The contrast between the splendour of the great private houses and the shabby courts of St. James's struck everyone. Queen Victoria herself made a *bon-mot* about 'going from my house to your palace' when she called on the Duke of Sutherland at York (now Lancaster) House, begun by her uncle the Duke of York in the former stable-yard at St. James's and sold to Sutherland in order to pay his creditors. There was, of course, Buckingham Palace, whose

---

[1] *Gent's Mag.* 1826 (2), p. 223.  [2] John Gwynn, *London and Westminster Improved* (1766), pp. 10–11.
[3] *The Builder* xxiv (1866), p. 166.

later aggrandisement is described in volume VI of this *History*. But in the early
nineteenth century no one was prepared to admire or defend that most unpopular
of all George IV's architectural follies. 'Is it possible', wrote an anonymous architect
in 1832, 'that the same nation which has lodged the Marquis of Buckingham in
Stowe House, the Duke of Marlborough at Blenheim, the tax-gatherers in Somerset
House, her madmen in New Bedlam, and her super-annuated seamen at Greenwich,
should provide for the metropolitan residence of his Britannic Majesty, such a gim-
crack as Buckingham House?'[1]

Although nothing effective was done to remedy these architectural shortcomings,
it was not for want of designs. Throughout the seventeenth and eighteenth centuries
the history of English architecture is haunted by unfulfilled projects for palaces. For
years Charles I had cherished the vision of a great classical palace at Whitehall
that might rival the Escorial or the Louvre.[2] Unluckily the old rambling palace
survived Civil War and Interregnum with the minimum of damage. Early in his
reign Charles II contemplated making a clean sweep of its confused buildings and
irregular courtyards. Plans by John Webb and Christopher Wren show a new palace
in which the Banqueting House would be the only surviving legacy of the past.[3]
But action was inhibited by lack of money and also (it may be suspected) by the
difficulty of displacing the many courtiers who enjoyed rooms at Whitehall. Instead,
Charles began a new palace at Greenwich in 1664, only to abandon it in 1672 at a
time of acute financial difficulty.[4] In 1665 he thought of building 'a noble house'
in the royal park at Woodstock,[5] but eventually acquired the great Jacobean house
at Audley End in Essex from the Earl of Suffolk.[6] In his later years the secret subsidies
from Louis XIV helped him to remodel Windsor at a cost of some £130,000, and
to start an entirely new palace at Winchester which was still incomplete at the
time of his death.[7]

For James II, as for his brother, Whitehall remained the centre of government
and the usual home of the court. As Duke of York he had thought of building at
Richmond:[8] as king his only architectural achievement was the erection of a substantial new wing at Whitehall.[9] It was part of the piecemeal rebuilding of the Tudor
palace that went on almost continuously until the fire of 1698 destroyed everything
except the Banqueting House, the Horse Guards, the two Tudor gateways and some
other peripheral buildings. Although grandiose plans for a great new baroque palace
were at once prepared in Wren's office, William III appears to have had no serious
intention of building a new Whitehall. Indeed, he had never favoured the palace,
whose river damps aggravated his asthma. As early as 1689 he had begun to rebuild

---

[1] *Library of the Fine Arts* iv (1832), p. 132.
[2] See vol. iii of this *History*, p. 139.       [3] Below, p. 299.       [4] Below, p. 150.
[5] In December 1665 a correspondent informed Henry Kippax of Slingsby in Yorkshire that 'His Maty &
the D. [of] York is this day gone to Woodstok for ordering ane Noble hows to be build[ed] ther' (archives of
Sir Richard Graham, Bart., at Norton Conyers, Yorks.). The king's intention to build at Woodstock is also
mentioned in a note by John Evelyn in John Aubrey's MS. *Chronologia Architectonica* (Bodleian Library, MS.
Top. Gen. c. 25, f. 165ᵛ).
[6] Below, pp. 131–3. It was never fully paid for, and in 1701 was restored to the earl's heirs in settlement of
the debt.
[7] Below, pp. 304–11.       [8] Below, p. 217.
[9] Below, pp. 286–91. According to Macky, James II 'marked out a seat on the Downs in Sussex' (*Journey
through England* ii, 1724, 22), but no other reference to this project has been found.

Hampton Court and to enlarge a Jacobean mansion which he had acquired at Kensington. Hampton Court was to be the palace of a victorious monarch, Kensington his private retreat. For Hampton Court, therefore, Wren worked out designs of some magnificence which were partially executed before the king lost interest in them after his consort's death in 1694. At the same time the gardens were the scene of lavish expenditure under William Talman. At Kensington, on the other hand, the modest nucleus was progressively enlarged in an *ad hoc* manner with no great regard for architectural effect. A more ambitious scheme for a real Trianon near Hampton Court never got beyond the drawing-board.[1]

By 1702, when Queen Anne succeeded William III, the English court had five houses at its disposal: St. James's, Hampton Court, Kensington, Windsor and Newmarket (where Charles II had built a small house near the race-course). But of these only Windsor and Hampton Court deserved the name of palaces. Whitehall was a ruin, Winchester a shell, and Greenwich was being converted into a naval hospital. Queen Anne showed no disposition to remedy this state of affairs. While her subjects were building Blenheim, Chatsworth and Castle Howard, she was content with minimal alterations to her existing houses. At St. James's (which now perforce took the place of Whitehall as the metropolitan palace) a modest enlargement was carried out to make the house fit for her receptions.[2] At Windsor she turned her back on the decaying splendours of Charles II's state apartments to live comfortably in a 'garden house' outside its walls.[3] George I was equally uninterested in architectural display. Rejecting a series of magnificent designs by Vanbrugh for remodelling Kensington and St. James's, he confined himself to a modest set of new state apartments at Kensington and to a Palladian hunting-lodge at Richmond.[4] George II had somewhat more taste for public life than his father, but the chief memorials of his architectural ambitions are a portfolio of designs for one unexecuted palace by Edward Lovett Pearce and a model for another by William Kent.[5] It was, however, at his expense and with his approval that two important public buildings were erected in Westminster—the Royal Mews and the Horse Guards.[6] Their architect, William Kent, was also patronised by Queen Caroline, who employed him to design an elaborately decorated library for her at St. James's, and by the Prince of Wales, for whom he built a country house at Kew.[7]

The accession of George III gave promise of a régime with greater architectural ambitions. For in George III England had, for the first time for a hundred years, a sovereign with a personal interest in the arts. As a young man he had been taught the grammar of architecture by Sir William Chambers, and he took a close interest in the affairs of the Royal Academy which he founded in 1768. With the aid of Chambers he spent many hours designing a palace for himself at Richmond. The complicated history of this ill-fated venture is described elsewhere.[8] Its failure seems to have been due as much to lack of decision as to want of means. What George III did achieve was the rehabilitation of Windsor and the acquisition of Buckingham House as a private metropolitan residence in convenient proximity to St. James's.

[1] For Hampton Court and Kensington see below, pp. 153–63 and 183–91. For the Trianon scheme see p. 167.

[2] Below, pp. 237–8.    [3] Below, p. 333.    [4] Below, pp. 195–8, 230–2.    [5] Below, pp. 220–1.

[6] Below, pp. 212–13, 436–7.    [7] Below, pp. 227, 242.    [8] Below, pp. 225–7.

Hampton Court he disliked, and it was during his reign that it first became what William IV called 'the quality poor-house'—a collection of 'grace and favour' residences occupied by distinguished but impoverished beneficiaries of royal charity.[1] Kensington was equally out of favour, so George divided his time between Buckingham House, Windsor and Kew (where he had inherited the 'White House' built by his father). It was at Kew that towards the end of his life he began the ugly castellated palace which was still unfinished at the time of his death and was promptly pulled down by his successor.[2]

Although the history of the royal palaces between 1660 and 1782 is so largely a story of abortive projects, this chronicle of architectural casualties should not obscure the fact that the Office of Works was still very much the centre of English architectural atcivity. Wren, like Inigo Jones before him, was for at least thirty years the dominant figure in English architecture, and between 1660 and 1782 almost every architect of eminence sought or obtained a post in the royal works. And even if they were never finished, the palaces that were planned by the officers of the Royal Works were still in the forefront of English architectural design. Webb's Greenwich and May's Windsor have been regarded, in their several ways, as key buildings in the emergence of an English baroque, while Wren at Winchester (and still more in his first design for Greenwich Hospital) demonstrated ideas that were soon to be taken up by Vanbrugh and exploited in his great country houses.[3] Though Hampton Court was architecturally less influential, its interiors were a show-piece of the new Anglo-Dutch taste, while its gardens were among the most elaborate of their age. Even Kensington deserves more attention than it has received from architectural historians, for the Cube or Cupola Room of 1719–22 must be seen as one of the first manifestations of that precociously neo-classical taste that was soon to find expression in the Palladian Revival.[4] In that revival it was a private patron who took the lead. Had it not been for the folly of William Benson, Colen Campbell, the key figure in the Palladian movement, might have worked his revolution from within, rather than from without the Office of Works. As it was, it was under Lord Burlington's leadership that Palladianism prevailed. But Burlington's influence soon extended to Scotland Yard, and by the accession of George II the Office of Works was as much the stronghold of Palladianism as it had formerly been of the native baroque of Wren and Hawksmoor. The Treasury and the Horse Guards remain to prove the point.[5] Had the new Parliament House been built it would have been the supreme achievement of an Office of Works inspired by Burlington's aesthetic principles. With its failure the Office lost the greatest architectural opportunity of the eighteenth century.[6] Somerset House was an unexpected consolation prize.[7] But a block of offices, however handsome, was hardly a substitute (as the Parliament House would have been) for the royal palace which was the unfulfilled dream of every senior Works official from the time of Inigo Jones to that of James Wyatt.

Although the kings of England could boast of no architectural monument to equal Versailles or Caserta, Potsdam or St. Petersburg, the interiors of their palaces

[1] See vol. vi, p. 329.          [2] See vol. vi, pp. 356–9.
[3] John Summerson, *Architecture in Britain 1530 to 1830* (4th ed. 1963), pp. 111–12, 139–40, 163–6.
[4] Above, p. 73, below, p. 198.
[5] Below, pp. 431–9.          [6] Below, pp. 416–25.          [7] Below, pp. 363–8.

contained sequences of state apartments that were handsome and even stately. At Windsor, indeed, Hugh May provided Charles II with the grandest suite of royal apartments that any English monarch enjoyed before the reign of George IV. It was these state apartments that distinguished a royal palace from a private house, and some account of their function is essential to an understanding of the pages that follow. The history of the English court has yet to be written,[1] but its basic function was simple: it was to regulate and formalise contact between the sovereign and his more important subjects. Access to the king or queen was the objective of every courtier, whether to make a present, to ask a favour, to introduce a protégé or to kiss hands on taking up office. In the seventeenth century access to the king was as essential for a member of his government as a seat in parliament is today: in the eighteenth, attendance at court was still obligatory for any politically active peer or Member of Parliament. Occasional absence might be excused, but persistent absence would be indicative of political opposition. Even in the reign of Queen Victoria the *Builder* could refer to those in certain ranks of society for whom access to the sovereign was not 'a matter of choice' and whose position would be injured if they were not presented at court at the proper age.[2]

The essential problem in planning a Stuart or Georgian palace was therefore to arrange a succession of rooms which would ensure an orderly progression for those who had the privilege of access to the king and queen, and at the same time to provide the latter with private rooms into which they could retire from the fatigue of 'drawing rooms' and levees.[3] In continental palaces—especially German ones—the dignity of the prince was enhanced by the grandeur of the staircase up which the courtier had to mount before being received in audience. The vast galleries of Versailles and the Louvre fulfilled the same function. In England the architectural setting was more modest, but the essential purpose was the same.

The precise chronology of the changes which took place in the arrangement of the English state apartments awaits further inquiry.[4] But the principal stages are fairly clear. In the middle ages the only essential rooms were the hall and the chamber. The chamber might be large enough to accommodate councils, even parliaments, but, at any rate in the thirteenth century, it was still the king's bed-chamber. Sometimes, however, as at Clarendon, there would be two king's chambers, side by side, and the queen would also have a chamber and a chapel of her own.[5] By the end of the fifteenth century it seems to have been usual for the king and queen each to have a separate suite of apartments, and this duality was to be basic to every scheme for an English royal palace from the sixteenth century to the end of the eighteenth. In an ideal palace these twin apartments could be ranged symmetrically in matching suites (Fig. 2, Pl. 24B), but in practice they sometimes had to be

---

[1] E. K. Chambers, *The Elizabethan Stage* i (1923), pp. 7–20 and J. M. Beattie, *The English Court in the Reign of George I* (1967) provide valuable introductions to the subject.

[2] *The Builder* xxiv (1866), p. 166.

[3] Levees were for men only. George III held them twice a week, on Wednesdays and Fridays. Drawing Rooms were attended by both king and queen and were open to both sexes. In George III's reign they were held on Thursdays and Sundays (John Brooke, *King George III*, 1972, p. 294).

[4] The only serious treatment of the subject is H. M. Baillie's valuable article on 'Etiquette and the Planning of the State Apartments in Baroque Palaces', *Archaeologia* ci (1967), upon which much of what follows is based.

[5] See vol. i, especially pp. 121–2.

fitted into a much less logical layout (Figs. 5, 10). By now the sequence of rooms was becoming more elaborate. Besides the hall there were in Tudor royal palaces three state rooms with clearly differentiated functions—the Guard Chamber, the Presence Chamber and the Privy Chamber. Tudor rulers gave audience in the Presence Chamber and retired from the Presence to the Privy Chamber, beyond which was the Bedchamber. In the household ordinances promulgated at Eltham in 1526, access to the Presence Chamber was granted to 'lords, knights, gentlemen, officers of the king's house, and other honest personages', that is, in effect, to anyone of birth or anyone holding a position at court. Entry to the Privy Chamber, however, was carefully restricted. It was ordered that 'Noe person, of what estate, degree or condicion soever he be, from henceforth presume, attempt, or be in any wise suffered or admitted to come or repair into the king's privy chamber', except the servants on duty there and anyone invited by the king himself. As for the Bedchamber, no one was allowed into it except the king's personal servants.[1]

Gradually the Privy Chamber became less and less privy. By the reign of Charles I the right of entry to the Queen's Privy Chamber had been granted to the nobility in general, and it is likely that the King's Privy Chamber was likewise accessible to all courtiers. By the time of Charles II all persons who had business with the king, including military officers, were permitted to enter the Privy Chamber. Thus the Privy Chamber had become only slightly less public than the Presence Chamber and in the course of the seventeenth century its place was taken by a smaller 'withdrawing room', between the Privy Chamber and the Bedroom. By the early eighteenth century this Drawing Room had gone through the same process of diminishing privacy, and had become in fact the main room of assembly. In 1669 it was in the King's Drawing Room at Whitehall (here known as the 'Vane Room') that the suite of the Grand Duke of Tuscany was presented to Charles II. The importance that now attached to this room is shown by the size of the new building designed by Wren to accommodate the Queen's Drawing Room at Whitehall (Fig. 23). When Whitehall Palace was burned down and St. James's took its place a new Drawing Room necessarily formed part of the additional wing built for Queen Anne (Fig. 20). Beyond it was a room originally designed as a Council Chamber, but eventually invaded by the court, so that by the reign of George III the throne and canopy of state were in the farthest room (Pl. 4A), and to pay his court a visitor had to traverse first the Guard Chamber, then the Presence Chamber, the Privy Chamber and the former Drawing Room. The innermost sanctum had yielded to public pressure, and the king and queen had retreated to the privacy of a separate building—Buckingham House.

Between the fifteenth and the eighteenth centuries, therefore, the State Apartments went through an evolution not unlike that of the medieval Chancery seals. Just as the Great Seal was soon superseded, as the instrument of the king's private will, by the Privy Seal, so the Privy Chamber took the place of the Great Chamber as the royal sanctum, only to be captured by the courtiers, obliging the king to retreat to what was at first a private withdrawing room and at last a public drawing room in the modern sense. But just as the Privy Seal did not supersede the Great

---

[1] *Ordinances and Regulations of the Royal Household* (1790), pp. 152–6.

Seal, nor the Signet the Privy Seal, but merely added one more stage in the routine of Chancery procedure, so the Drawing Room did not replace the Privy Chamber, nor the Privy Chamber the Presence Chamber, but merely added one more unit to the suite. Each room retained its appropriate attendants—the Yeomen of the Guard in the Guard Chamber (Pl. 4B), the Gentlemen Ushers in the Presence Chamber, the Gentlemen of the Privy Chamber in the Privy Chamber, and the Groom of the Stole in the Drawing Room and the private rooms beyond. Each of the principal reception rooms might still boast its canopy of state, marking the position where the king had once sat, one, two or three hundred years before. The history of the court was therefore encapsuled in the state apartments of the English royal palaces as they existed in the reign of George III. Only when Buckingham Palace became the sovereign's official residence in the reign of Queen Victoria was the ancient sequence broken, and only after the Prince Consort's death in 1861 was the long tradition of Drawing Rooms and levees finally abandoned.

# AUDLEY END, ESSEX

FROM 1669 to 1701 the great house of Audley End near Saffron Walden had the status of a royal palace. Built in the reign of James I by Thomas Howard, Earl of Suffolk and Lord Treasurer of England, Audley End was one of the largest and most ostentatious houses in the kingdom. King James is reputed to have remarked that it was too large for a king, though it might do for a Lord Treasurer.[1] But for Charles II, whose houses had been so sadly depleted by the Civil War, Audley End offered itself as a ready-made replacement. The third Earl of Suffolk was understood to be burdened with debt and anxious to sell. In March 1666 the king and the Duke of York made a tour of inspection,[2] and in 1669, after three years of negotiations, the house passed into royal possession.[3] The price was £50,000, but this sum was never paid in full, and in 1701 the house was reconveyed to the fifth earl in settlement of the balance, amounting to £20,000.[4]

Audley End was therefore a royal palace for little more than thirty years. In October 1670 the Office of Works was authorised to take charge of the king's new house, and John Bennet, the Clerk of Works at Newmarket, was instructed to look after it.[5] When he died in 1678 his place was taken by Henry Winstanley, engraver

---

[1] Lord Braybrooke, *History of Audley End* (1836), p. 82.

[2] *The Diary of Samuel Pepys*, ed. Wheatley, 5, p. 243.

[3] *Cal. S.P. Dom. 1665–6*, p. 392; *1668–9*, pp. 282, 317, 468, 511; *1671–2*, p. 81; *Cal. Treas. Books* ii, p. 640, iii, pp. 171, 228, 341, 542.

[4] *Cal. S.P. Dom. 1689–90*, p. 249; *Cal. Treas. Books* xvi, pp. 70, 82, 333; *Cal. Treas. Papers 1697–1702*, p. 522.

[5] *Cal. Treas. Books* iii, p. 501, iv, pp. 285, 291, 553, 703, 876. In 1670–1 Maurice Emmett, later Master Bricklayer, was sent to Audley End to make a plan of the buildings (E 351/3279).

and lighthouse builder.[1] In 1688 Winstanley published a set of engravings of the house which he dedicated to James II, the Earl of Suffolk and Sir Christopher Wren. It is from Winstanley's engravings that the original layout and appearance of 'the Royall Pallace of Audley End' are known today.

Winstanley's engravings show little evidence of any external alterations that might be attributed to the Office of Works, nor do the Works Accounts suggest that much was done while the house was in its charge except routine maintenance. In 1695 Wren recalled in a letter to the Treasury that

> When this house was purchased by King Charles an Estimate was given of the Charge of Repaires, amounting to abt. £10,000, for little had been done to it from the first foundation: the whole lead of the house was very defective, much of the timber was decay'd, and the Fabric weake, built after an ill manner rather Gay than substantiall; for this an allowance of £500 p. ann. was settled upon the wood farme; while this continued halfe the house was new leaded, and the Roofe substantially repaired, and many Stacks of Chimneys new built, and divers of the necessary defects amended.[2]

Most of the repairs mentioned by Wren can be traced in the accounts. In 1671 Robert Grumbold, a Cambridge master mason, came over to superintend some repairs to the masonry.[3] In 1681 he undertook to rebuild two of the turrets for £15.[4] The roof of the great gallery was repaired under the direction of Richard Ryder, the Master Carpenter, in 1676–7. This was evidently a work of some difficulty, for he was paid 10s. 'for making a modell to direct the strengthening the plattforme over the gallery'.[5] The carpentry was performed by Henry Blowes, who received £204 for his workmanship. In 1686–8 Matthew Banks, then Master Carpenter, repaired the roofs of the Council Chamber and Chapel for £82, and received £64 'for new framing the roofe of the Great Hall and two Porches'.[6] Internally some alterations were required for the accommodation of the royal family, but these were not very extensive. In 1669 part of the Council Chamber was partitioned off to form a Catholic chapel for the queen, while the manorial pew in Walden church was fitted up, presumably for the king's use. Part of 'the great void place intended for the great stairecase' was similarly enclosed to form a room for the queen's waiters to eat in.[7]

After 1688 expenditure on the palace was generally modest, and in 1695 the Earl of Suffolk (who had been appointed keeper of the house) wrote to Wren begging him to draw the king's attention to the increasing dilapidation of this remote palace which William never visited.

[1] According to the *D.N.B.* Winstanley had previously been employed at Audley End by the Earl of Suffolk. This is confirmed by a reference to 'Mr. Henry Winstanley' as Lord Suffolk's porter in 1665 (Saffron Walden accounts quoted by Lord Braybrooke, *History of Audley End*, 1836, p. 266). It may be added that the first year's expenditure on the house by the Office of Works in 1669 contains a payment to Winstanley for timber (Works 5/12).

[2] *Wren Soc.* xviii, p. 122.

[3] Works 5/17: 'to Robert Grumbold Mason for horse and man 6 daies at 5s. per diem'.

[4] Works 5/145, p. 118.                [5] Works 5/27.

[6] Works 5/40 and 41. In 1688–9 a bricklayer was employed to point 'all the cracks in the ceiling of the Great Hall' and to mend 'severall places in the Plastring that was like to fall' (Works 5/42).

[7] Works 5/12. Winstanley's plan shows four staircases in the corners of the inner court, but evidently none of these was a 'great staircase', and it may be noted that in 1667 Pepys thought the staircase 'exceedingly poor' (*Diary*, ed. Wheatley, vii, p. 139).

Those last great windes has soe extreamly shatered the chimneys of this house that it is dangerous to walke either in the Courtyard or in the Garden, great stones falling from them daily, and in that part wee lye in wee are in danger every night. There is one Great pillar in the Cloyster on the Right hand mouldered quite away at the foot of it wch if not speedily repaired the roomes in probability will tumble downe; the Bridge that goes to the Stable is so tottaly decayed that not long since a cart fell into the River, and with great difficulty the Horses wer saved. The Stables and barnes is in a very ill condition, in truth both them and the house itselfe in a very little time will by degrees fall downe. If you please (whose office it is) to represent these things to his Majestie wee have then done our Duty.[1]

Wren did his duty too, but without effect, and it was doubtless with relief that he learned in 1701 that the house was no longer to be his responsibility. A few years later the next Earl of Suffolk solved the problem by cutting the building down to the size of an ordinary (though still considerable) country house. It is this country house, extensively redecorated in the reign of George III, but still externally recognisable as part of the Jacobean palace, that remains today in the custody of the Department of the Environment.[2]

# BUCKINGHAM HOUSE

THOUGH NOW the official residence of the sovereign, Buckingham Palace still bears the name of the peer by whom it was first built in the reign of Queen Anne. Its history is in fact the gradual transformation of a private mansion into a royal palace, and portions of the Duke of Buckingham's original red brickwork still remain embedded beneath the yellow Bath stone of the nineteenth century.[3]

It was in 1702 that John Sheffield, then Earl of Mulgrave, acquired the site from the trustees of the young Duke of Grafton, and by 1705 he was in occupation of his new mansion facing down the Mall. We have Colen Campbell's authority for stating that the building was 'conducted' (and therefore presumably designed) by Captain William Winde, but there is some reason for thinking that Sheffield may first have consulted William Talman, lately Comptroller of the King's Works.[4] The master-bricklayer John Fitch contracted to build the body of the house for £7000,

---

[1] *Wren Soc.* xviii, p. 123.
[2] For the eighteenth-century transformation see J. D. Williams, *Audley End: The Restoration of 1762–1797* (Essex Record Office Publications No. 45, 1966), and the Official Guidebook.
[3] Hist. Mon. Comm., *West London* (1925), pp. 134–5.
[4] For the possibility that Talman was concerned see John Cornforth in *Country Life*, 12 July 1962.

but the great stone staircase, with its ironwork by Tijou and its paintings of the story of Dido and Aeneas by Laguerre, added more than £1000 to the cost.[1] The result was like a great country house on the edge of Westminster, and with 30 acres of garden behind it and the Mall aligned on its forecourt, Buckingham House seemed to have stolen St. James's Park from the old irregular palace half hidden behind its wall on the other side of the Mall. It was, as Edward Hatton declared in his *New View of London* of 1708, 'a seat not to be contemned by the greatest Monarch'.[2] After the duke's death in 1721 his widow was indeed prepared to lease it to the Prince and Princess of Wales. It was, as she wrote to Mrs. Howard, 'too good for any private body to live in', and 'if the Prince is inclin'd to have it he shall, upon my word for a much less price than were I in that station would give for soe pleasant and healthy a place'. At £3000 a year, including the furniture and pictures, her terms were, however, deemed too high even for a prince, and the negotiations fell through.[3] When the redoubtable duchess died in 1742 the house went to her husband's illegitimate son Sir Charles Sheffield. His title was good, but his tenure was prejudiced by the fact that only part of the site was freehold, just over four acres of it being a portion of the old royal Mulberry Garden, held on a 99-year lease granted by the Crown in 1672. A survey showed that more than half the house was built on this leasehold property. In March 1760 Sheffield approached the Treasury with a view to obtaining a renewal of the lease, but after further negotiations he decided to offer the whole property to the Crown, and in 1762 it was acquired by George III for £28,000.[4] Technically it was designed to be a dower house for Queen Charlotte, whom he had married the previous year, but in fact it became the habitual residence of both king and queen, who much preferred its domestic atmosphere to the formality of their court at St. James's.

The task of adapting the house to the needs of the royal family began with a number of 'necessary works and repairs' for which the Board of Works received Treasury sanction in July 1762. These were 'for the immediate reception of their Majestys', and cost less than £800.[5] The existing accommodation was divided horizontally, the king occupying the ground or 'Hall' floor, while the queen took over the whole of the first floor (Fig. 1A). The exact date when the royal family took up residence is not recorded, but in June 1763 the queen gave an elaborate musical entertainment in the garden to celebrate the king's birthday.[6] More considerable alterations followed, partly to accommodate the king's extensive and ever-growing library, and partly to provide for the domestic needs of his increasing family.

The principal structural addition took the form of two balancing blocks which

[1] The Duke recorded 'the Intire Expence about my House' on ff. 9–11 of an account-book now in London University Library (MS. 533).

[2] E. Hatton, *A New View of London* ii (1708), p. 623.

[3] *Letters to and from Henrietta Countess of Suffolk* i (1824), pp. 113–17; B.M. Add. MS. 22627, ff. 49–50.

[4] For the legal history of the site and the negotiations with Sheffield, see a volume of 'Extracts from the Surveys Entrys and Records in the Surveyor General's Office relative to the Estates purchased of Sir Charles Sheffield in 1762', of which there are two copies, one in the Royal Library at Windsor Castle, and one in the P.R.O. (Works 19/2). The notes and transcripts upon which this volume is based are P.R.O. Crest 2/1648.

[5] Works 6/18, pp. 5, 14, 115.

[6] *Gent's. Mag.* xxxiii (1763), p. 300. For the architectural setting, which was designed by Robert Adam, see *The Works in Architecture of R. and J. Adam* vol. i (1773–8), where the date is wrongly given as June 1762, and Oppé, *English Drawings at Windsor Castle* (1950), p. 22 and pl. 25.

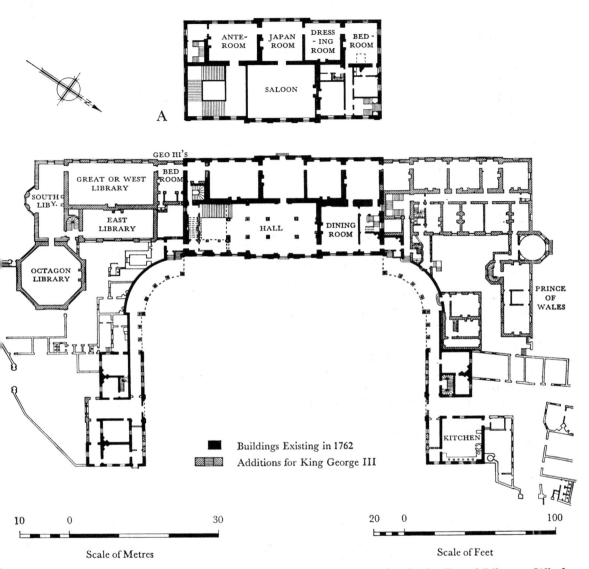

**fig. 1** Buckingham House. A: plan of the first floor in 1762 (from a plan in the Royal Library, Windsor Castle). B: ground floor plan showing the additions made by George III (based on plans in Westminster City Library)

extended the garden front of the house by seven windows at either end (Fig. 1B). The southern block contained the libraries, the northern one provided apartments for various members of the royal household. There were four libraries, approached from the king's bedroom on the ground floor of the house. The Great, or West, Library, 60 feet long and 30 feet wide, was built first, between 1762 and 1764; then came the South Library and the Octagon (1766–7), and finally the East Library in 1772–3. The Great Library and the Octagon extended through two floors, and the latter was provided with galleries at first-floor level (Pl. 5B). The South Library, lit by a bay window, occupied only one floor, and was surmounted by a room of identical dimensions in which the royal collection of drawings and medals was kept. At first the building containing the East Library was only one storey high, but in 1774 its walls were heightened to create a second floor.[1] This was known as the 'Marine Gallery' because it was destined for the display of models of British ships and seaports.[2]

The north wing was built between 1766 and 1768, and was utilitarian in character. A further extension for the Prince of Wales was later added to it, forming a small and nearly insulated block of apartments facing north. The semi-octagonal projection in the centre of this elevation was changed by Blore into a semi-circular porch, and still survives as a feature of the north front of Buckingham Palace.

The internal alterations to the existing buildings are by no means well documented. The king preferred his own apartments to be as simple as possible, and it was only in the queen's suite that there appears to have been any extensive redecoration. All the door-cases and chimneypieces were replaced by new ones in the contemporary taste, and most of the ceilings were altered to match. The chimneypiece in the Saloon was the work of Robert Adam, who also designed the ceiling in the Japanned Room.[3] Several of the ceilings were painted by J. B. Cipriani, whose bill of £180 was among those settled by the Board of Works in 1765.[4] On the stairs, Verrio's baroque paintings had to be extensively restored by William Oram, the Master Carpenter, who had some skill as a painter.[5] It may have been he who painted in *trompe l'oeil* the *exedra* which faced the visitor at the top of the staircase. Though convincingly three-dimensional in Pyne's aquatint (Pl. 7), its illusionist character is demonstrated beyond doubt by a sectional drawing in Sir John Soane's Museum (Pl. 6).[6] It framed a new doorway which gave direct access from the staircase to the Saloon. As a plan made early in the 1760s shows (Fig. 1), the only

[1] For the dates of the libraries and galleries see the tabulated 'Expence of the Queen's House' printed in *Commons' Jnls.*, vol. 35, p. 320. In the Royal Library at Windsor there is a drawing (PA4) which shows all four sides of the Great Library in elevation, complete with bookcases and pictures.

[2] For a description of the gallery see *Sophie in London*, 1786, ed. Clare Williams (1933), pp. 145–6. Two elevations in Westminster Public Library, inscribed 'Marine Gallery' in a modern hand, and filed among the designs for Buckingham House, are in fact designs for the gallery at Gower House by Chambers (Box 39, Nos. 13–14).

[3] *The Works in Architecture of Robert and James Adam* i (1773–8), pls. iv, vii. The original drawing for the chimneypiece is dated 1761 (Sir John Soane's Museum xxii, 56–8).

[4] Works 1/4, p. 48. Horace Walpole, who visited the house in c. 1783, noted that the ceiling of the great room, 'on which were the Poets and Sheffield Duke of Buckingham', 'is effaced, and newly painted in the antique taste by Cipriani, as are two more cielings' ('Journals of Visits to Country Seats', *Walpole Soc.* xvi, 1927–8, p. 78.)

[5] Works 6/18, f. 21.

[6] Drawer 24, Set 5. A variant design for the *exedra* is in Westminster Public Library (Box 39, No. 11A).

entrance to the Saloon had originally been by way of the Ante-Room and the Japanned Room. The new doorway made possible the circulation indispensable in a royal drawing room suite.

Externally the principal alterations were to the east front, which was discreetly remodelled in such a way as to give it a characteristically late-Georgian appearance (Pl. 5A). The old basement was partially hidden by a new raised forecourt, thus reducing the apparent height of the house. Winde's swags and angle-pilasters disappeared, his windows were given architraves and cornices, and the whole facade was tied more firmly together by a continuous string-course and balustrade.[1] The result was to substitute a suave neo-classical villa-front for Winde's grand but old-fashioned elevation. The wings, with their hipped roofs and cupolas, remained, but in 1770 the great gates to the Mall were replaced by a plain iron railing with unobtrusive entrances at either side instead of in the centre (Pl. 5A).[2] Nothing could have demonstrated more clearly that the Queen's House was the private residence of the royal family and not the seat of the court than this deliberate renunciation of a ceremonial approach down the Mall. Of the extended west, or garden, front of the house no drawing or view is known to exist, but the additions were probably plain in character, their brick walls relieved only by stone coins and string-courses.

To the south-west of the house, on the north side of what is now Buckingham Gate, a spacious Riding House was built between 1763 and 1766. This long rectangular building was lighted by lunettes and dignified by a large pediment which in 1860 was to be embellished by William Theed the younger's relief of Hercules taming the horses of Diomedes.

The total cost of the works carried out between 1762 and 1769 was £47,546, of which £16,073 was accounted for by the building of the north wing and the two principal libraries, and £5762 by the Riding House.[3] Throughout they were under the direction of William Chambers, who told Lord Abercorn in September 1762 that he was busy making 'designs for various alterations in the Queen's house'.[4] Some of the drawings made by him or under his direction are preserved in Westminster Public Library.[5] The minutes of the Board of Works do not reveal the mode of communication between the king and the officers of his works, but both Chambers and the Surveyor (Worsley) were on friendly terms with the king, who no doubt discussed the plans with them in person. It may be noted in this connection that an alternative design by Robert Adam for remodelling the main elevation of the house is preserved among Worsley's drawings at Hovingham Hall.

In April 1769 the Treasury gave authority for the Queen's House to be treated as one of the buildings for whose maintenance the Office of Works was regularly responsible, and William Robinson, who had been acting as clerk of works there under Chambers, was formally appointed Clerk of the Works at the Queen's House.[6]

---

[1] A detailed list of the alterations was given by John Carter in *Gent's. Mag.* vol 85 (1), 1815, pp. 36–7. For a description of the interior see *Gent's. Mag.* vol 72 (2), 1802, pp. 1183–5.
[2] Works 6/18, p. 235; Works 4/14, 15 June, 14 & 21 Dec. 1770.
[3] Works 5/142; *Commons' Jnls.* vol. 35, p. 320.
[4] Abercorn Papers, Baronscourt, Ireland. We owe this reference to Mr. John Harris.
[5] Box 39. They were formerly in the Gardner Collection.
[6] Works 6/18, pp. 187, 197, 200.

During the next ten years expenditure on the house averaged £2250 a year, rising to over £4000 in 1771–2 (when the East Library was under construction), and again in 1776–7.[1] One of the surviving plans bears a note to the effect that a copy of it was 'delivered to His Majesty March 23rd, 1776'.[2] As it shows the Prince of Wales's apartments as an addition it may be presumed that it was the building of this new wing that accounted for the heavy expenditure in that year.

# CARLTON HOUSE

THE HISTORY of Carlton House as a royal residence begins in 1732, when it was bought by Frederick, Prince of Wales. It took its name from Henry Boyle, Lord Carleton, a Whig minister who had lived here for many years before his death in 1725. His heir was Lord Burlington, who obtained a new lease of the site in 1730, but soon afterwards handed the property over to his mother. It was the dowager Countess of Burlington who in 1732 sold it to the prince.[3]

Prince Frederick already possessed a town house in Leicester Fields, but the superior situation of Carlton House on the edge of St. James's Park no doubt attracted him. Though in good repair, the greater part of the house was said to be 'very old', and some extensive alterations were called for. They were carried out under the superintendence of William Kent, as surveyor of the prince's works, with Thomas Ripley as comptroller, and Isaac Ware as measurer. Kent also laid out the gardens, where in 1735 he built an octagonal 'saloon', which is said to have been paved with Italian marble brought to England by Lord Bingley and George Bubb Dodington. Among the other embellishments were statues of Alfred the Great and Edward the Black Prince sculptured by Rysbrack.[4] The total cost of the works accounted for by Kent was £5418.

Despite Kent's efforts, Carlton House remained an irregular and not very impressive structure whose only presentable facade was the one (itself of no great distinction) facing the garden. On the other side the entrance from Pall Mall was an architectural muddle which lacked any pretence of formality. A long covered corridor led the visitor into the interior, which may have been comfortable, but was certainly far from dignified. Soon after her son's accession the dowager princess

---

[1] Works 4/142; *Commons' Jnls.* vol. 35, p. 320.     [2] Westminster Public Library, Box 39, No. 16.
[3] *Survey of London*, vol. xx, pp. 71–2.
[4] Duchy of Cornwall Office, Household Accounts of Frederick, Prince of Wales, vol. v, ff. 262–82, vi, ff. 256–73. According to J. P. Malcolm, *Londinium Redivivum* iv (1807), p. 268. 'Flitcroft is said to have drawn a plan for the Prince in 1734, intended as an improvement to Carlton House'. This appears to be the only basis for the statement in Pyne's *Royal Residences* ii (1819), p. 2 and *Survey of London*, vol xx, p. 71, that Flitcroft was in charge of the alterations actually carried out, for which there is no evidence in the accounts. The best view of the garden is an engraving by W. Woollett dated 1774, of which there is a copy in B.M., Dept. of Prints & Drawings, Crace Collection XI, 73.

consulted Chambers about the state of her house. Chambers proposed to impose some regularity on the entrance courtyard by means of a screen wall and two opposed porticos, one of which was to be the main entrance, while the other served merely to relieve the blank wall on the other side.[1] Nothing came of this particular scheme, but in 1762 the death of George Bubb Dodington enabled the princess to acquire his house, which immediately adjoined her own, and in the following year the king ordered the Board of Works to carry out a number of 'necessary works and repairs' for her benefit. These alterations continued for five or six years, in the course of which over £15,000 were spent on the building.[2] No details of the expenditure have been preserved other than the names of the master workmen and the sums paid to them by order of the Board, and it is now impossible to determine precisely what was done. It is, however, clear from views of the house that the entrance gates and porter's lodge was redesigned, that a colonnaded porch was built in front of the main entrance, and that Dodington's house was absorbed into the complex.[3] These works were supervised by William Robinson, the Secretary to the Board, who was also Clerk of the Works at Buckingham House.[4] This led to some bitterness between himself and Chambers, who as surveyor to the princess and one of the two 'Architects of the Works', considered that he had a prescriptive right to be the member of the Office in charge. At the time Chambers accepted the situation as a *fait-accompli*, though later he was to complain of the way in which Robinson had 'seized on Carleton House, my absolute right, as Architect to the Princess and King at the same time, and as an old and favoured servant of both'. In his defence Robinson claimed that he 'never asked or made any interest' for Carlton House, but that 'when I was ordered to that work I thought it my duty to do it'.[5] From whom Robinson received his orders is not recorded, but it may well have been Flitcroft, then Comptroller of the Works, for whom Robinson was a colleague of twenty years' standing, while Chambers was a comparative newcomer.

Robinson continued to act as clerk of works at Carlton House until his death in 1775, when Kenton Couse, the new Clerk of Works at Buckingham House, also took his place at Carlton House. Minor works were accounted for by the Paymaster up to the time of Princess Augusta's death in 1772, and the Office continued to keep the house in repair until 1783, when George III handed it over to the Prince of Wales on his coming of age.[6]

[1] B.M., Dept. of Maps, Crace Plans XII, 8, a plan 'made for the Dowager Princess of Wales 1761. W.C.' (reproduced in *Survey of London*, vol. xx, p. 72).

[2] Works 5/63 (Sept. 1766, March 1767, March 1769); Works 5/142 (1768–9, 'Extraordinarys'); Works 1/4, pp. 37, 39, 49; Works 4/13, 5 Sept 1766, 4/14, 19 June 1767, 26 May, 2 June 1769; Works 6/18, pp. 66, 106, 147.

[3] *Survey of London*, vol. xx, pls. 55–6.

[4] He received 2s. 3d. a day 'for his attendance at Carlton House agreeable to His Majesty's Instructions to this Board' (Works 4/14, 26 May 1769).

[5] B.M., Chambers's letter-book, Add. MS. 41135, ff. 29–30.

[6] The expenditure is tabulated in Works 19/25/1. See also Works 5/64–5, *passim*.

# GREENWICH PALACE

DURING THE first decade of Charles II's reign Greenwich was, outside Whitehall, the scene of the king's most ambitious palace building. Yet when, in 1672, construction came to a halt, although over £44,000[1] had been laid out, not even the first wing of the new palace had been completed. Thereafter Charles turned his attention first to Windsor, and in the last years of his life to Winchester, so that his expenditure at Greenwich proved wholly abortive.

Charles's marriage to Catherine of Braganza took place on 21 May 1661. The first evidence of plans to build at Greenwich can be found in the following month. Arthur Haughton, the Purveyor, received £3 for 'his Extraordinary paines and charges in taking the plott of Greenwich house'. In July a payment of £2 under the Whitehall account was made for 'the draughts with the upwrights for the intended Building at Greenwich'; and on 6 August a warrant was drawn up to pay £1000 to Hugh May, Paymaster of the Works, 'for repairs and additional buildings at the King's house at Greenwich'.[2]

At the outset the king intended no mere adaptation of existing structures, but to build a completely new palace. In October 1661 John Evelyn discussed its siting with the Surveyor of the Works, Sir John Denham. Evelyn had the grandiose but costly idea of building it 'betweene the River & the Queenes house, so as a large Square Cutt, should have let in the Thames like a Baye', and was scornful of Denham's proposal 'for seting it on Piles at the very brink of the water'. On the following 24 January the king himself 'entertaind' Evelyn 'with his intentions of building his Palace of Greenewich & quite demolishing the old'.[3] By that time, it seems, a wooden model existed. The evidence of this comes in a payment in the Works account for Whitehall of December 1661, £3 8s. 'To John Turnor a Turner for 68 dosen of Small Ballisters for a modell of Greenwich &c'.[4]

Who was responsible for this model? John Webb designed the wing which was begun in January 1664; but was he working on the design more than two years before construction started? The evidence is conflicting. We need not suppose that William de Keyser, who in July 1661 received £2 for drawing 'the draughts with the upwrights' (see above), designed what he drew; but it is hard to reconcile Webb's own later statements with what is known of his activities in these first few years after the Restoration. John Webb's official appointment as 'surveyor assistant to

[1] This sum is reached by addition of the totals of expenditure at Greenwich up to May 1665 shown in AO 1/2433/85–2435/89 and the monthly totals in the Extraordinary account from June 1665 to Oct. 1672 in Works 5/7–20.

[2] Works 5/2; *Cal. S.P. Dom. 1661–2*, p. 59. See also Chettle, *The Queen's House, Greenwich* (1937), p. 39.

[3] *The Diary of John Evelyn*, ed. E. S. de Beer, (1955), iii, pp. 300–1, 313.

[4] Works 5/2. A further payment, in Aug. 1661, also under Whitehall, may also be relevant: 'To Hubbard Warfe for his extraordinary paynes in workeing early and late about the makeing of certayne modells at Whitehall by the Surveyor of the Workes appoyntment.'

Sir John Denham, in the erection of the palace at Greenwich', with an annual salary of £200, was made in November 1666, but his salary was back-dated to the month in which work began on the King Charles Block, January 1664.[1] His plans for the building are dated 1663. In 1668 Webb, petitioning for the Surveyorship of the Works, stated that 'After having prepared Whitehall for yr Majesties happy restauration, yor Petitioner withdrew into the country, from whence afterwards in 1663 by yor Royall appointment being sent for, to react for yor Majestie at Greenwich, hee readily obeyed'.[2] Yet Evelyn in October 1661, in recording his disagreement with Denham over the placing of the proposed palace and his conclusion that Denham was 'a better Poet than Architect', added the rider 'though he had Mr. Webb (Inigo Jones's Man) to assist him'. Webb's sketch design for Whitehall Palace dated 17 October 1661 is further evidence that he was putting his mind to the designing of palaces for the king during this period of official unemployment. It is not clear why Webb should have omitted to mention in his petition facts so favourable to his cause, but on the other hand it is almost inconceivable that Charles should have gone forward with major palace-building schemes without using Webb's experience. Webb's designs dated 1663 for the King Charles Block,[3] though closely resembling one wing of his undated designs for a complete palace, yet treat it as virtually a self-sufficient entity. Two further pieces of evidence support the conclusion that by 1663 the proposed palace was not intended to consist of three ranges round a courtyard, in the way Webb's undated plans show, but to be a three-piece palace, two matching blocks facing one another close to the river, and an enlarged Queen's House closing the vista some distance away. M. de Monconys saw the Queen's House in June 1663: 'il ne reste qu'un bastiment à l'Italienne, au bout d'une fort grande basse-cour, qu'on peut plustost nommer un champ'. In place of the demolished Tudor palace, so he was informed, 'l'on fera deux aisles qui accompagneront ce corps de logis'.[4] Three months earlier foundations had been dug of two pavilions to be added to the south-east and south-west corners of the Queen's House. Nothing more was done that year, but in 1667 further foundation-work was put in hand, and this time the scheme was for pavilions at all four corners of the building (see p. 146).

Webb's designs for a unified palace, in three ranges round an open-ended courtyard, superseded by the scheme of 1663, must therefore have been the ones prepared in 1661 and brought to model stage but no further. Two plans survive, one in two variant forms. This latter, for which we also have front and rear elevations, has in the centre a circular hall surmounted by a cupola, which rises behind an attached Corinthian portico, a feature echoed by the end elevations of the side blocks (Fig. 2). The other design, known from a single plan in the Burlington–Devonshire Collection, has a rectangular aisled hall through the depth of the centre block, and extra suites of rooms projecting as wings at the back, perhaps to provide the

[1] *Cal. S.P. Dom. 1666–7*, p. 286.

[2] Webb's petition for the Surveyorship of the Works, S.P. Dom. 29/251, f. 186, quoted in full in *Wren Soc.* xviii, p. 156.

[3] Burlington–Devonshire Collection, R.I.B.A., III/1 (3)–(5).

[4] *Voyages de M. de Monconys*, seconde partie 1666 (Lyon), p. 83. Monconys refers to 'le dessein de Mansal' at this point. Does Monconys here record an otherwise unknown scheme by the Master Mason, Edward Marshall? It seems perhaps more likely that he misunderstood or misheard his informant.

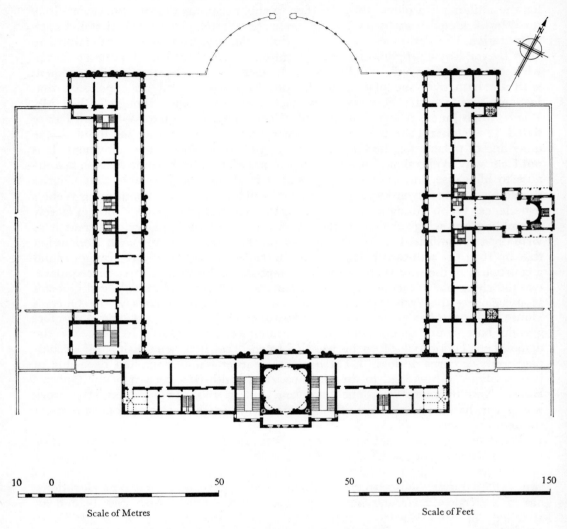

10  0                                    50          50        0              150

Scale of Metres                                    Scale of Feet

Fig. 2. John Webb's design for Greenwich Palace, 1661 (from a plan among the Wren
drawings in the Library of All Souls College, Oxford).

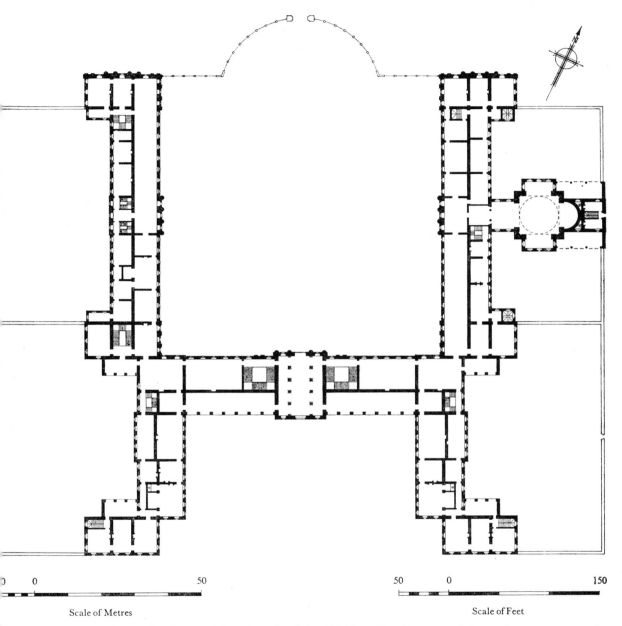

Scale of Metres

Scale of Feet

Fig. 3. Alternative design for Greenwich Palace by John Webb, 1661 (from an eighteenth-century copy in R.I.B.A. Drawings Collection, Burlington–Devonshire III/1(1) )

Duke and Duchess of York with state suites in addition to those for the king and queen in the main wings (Fig. 3).[1]

So much for intentions. In the event the Office of Works carried out three things for Charles II at Greenwich. The Tudor palace was demolished, the Queen's House enlarged by the addition of the two bridge rooms, and the shell built of one range of the proposed new palace, the range today known as the King Charles Block. For the layout of the park, undertaken in 1661–2 and again in 1664–5, the Office of Works was not responsible.

During 1662 the greater part of the Tudor buildings came down. At the palace proper demolition began with the Conduit Court, the guard chambers and long gallery, and, in December 1661, the 'Presence chamber in the old Buildings next the waterside'. In the new year carpenters began to dismantle 'the brick Building turned with an Arch over the way next the Thames', and a Thames-side range 106 feet long is mentioned in February in combination with a range (presumably the main west range) extending 230 feet from the Thames to the garden. In May demolition of the 'Privy Gallery next the Garden' and its staircase is accounted for. Finally, in October 1662, the carpenters were paid for 'takeing downe the high roofe and fflowers by the waters side'. Meanwhile in the Tiltyard one of the towers, the Green Gallery and the Bear Stake Gallery were all pulled down. Wherever possible old materials were saved for re-use. A stone chimneypiece, for instance, was set up in a ground-floor room in the Queen's House, and the roof of the Guard Chamber was shipped to Whitehall. In the nine months February to October 1662 nearly 450,000 whole bricks were cleaned and stacked and a further 750,000 brick-bats heaped up, all no doubt later used in the king's new buildings.[2]

The Tudor hall and chapel however were allowed to remain standing, together with lodgings in the south-west corner of the palace. Of these the most important belonged to the Earl of St. Albans, who in October 1662 was granted the custody of Greenwich House and Park.[3] Glazing here, in the lodgings of the Countess of Denbigh and Sir Henry Wood, in the queen's kitchen, the office of works and the wardrobe was paid for in August 1662. But in June of the following year these lodgings too had to be partly demolished, to make way for the New Road, running north to south across the site of the friary gardens west of the Tudor palace. The rest of the lodgings, together with the friary and wardrobe, came down in the early summer of 1664, and later that year the Prince's Lodging in the Tiltyard followed suit.[4] The Tudor hall survived until April 1666, but the chapel, pressed into service as a storehouse, was still standing in 1694, when the palace site finally passed out of royal hands.[5]

The enlargement of the Queen's House which went on as the Tudor palace was being demolished was intended to make Henrietta Maria's hunting villa suitable for her son by creating in it a King's Side and a Queen's Side. Work began in August

---

[1] Cupola design: plan, with flap showing double-pile centre block, in Worcester College, Oxford (reproduced in *Wren Soc.* vi, pl. xviii); copy of this plan, following variant on flap, All Souls College, Oxford, V, 21; front and rear elevations, All Souls, V, 25, 26 (reproduced in *Wren Soc.* viii, pl. xvii and xx). Columned hall design: *R.I.B.A. Drawings Catalogue: Jones & Webb*, fig. 119.

[2] Works 5/2 and 5/3.                    [3] *Cal. S.P. Dom. 1661–2*, p. 535.

[4] Works 5/4 and 5/5.

[5] Works 5/9; survey plan of *c.* 1695, E 5/1 in R.I.B.A. Drawings Collection.

1661 on the construction of a new east and a new west room, each carried across the road on a bridge. The significance of this beginning was emphasised by the transfer of Greenwich palace in this month to the Extraordinary account. The Ordinary account was not reopened until August 1665. Building and decoration of these additions were complete and paid for by September 1662. The total expenditure during these fourteen months recorded in the Greenwich works accounts was £5067 15s. 1d., the majority spent at the Queen's House. Taskwork and special items cost £730 9s. 6d., i.e. bricklayers' taskwork £509 10s. 4d. (Isaac Corner, Master Bricklayer, £251 8s. 11d., Thomas Pattison, £258 1s. 5d.), Joshua Marshall £78 for three marble chimneypieces, George Drew, smith, £30 12s. 6d. for two balconies, and John Grove, Master Plasterer, £112 6s. 8d. for the enriched plasterwork of four ceilings.[1]

The Queen's House survives today essentially as Charles II left it, the east and west additions indistinguishable in structure and style from Inigo Jones's building. The rusticated walling below and smooth walling of the principal floor are both of brickwork rendered. Payment was made in July 1662 for 'whiteing and putting all the old and new finishing of the outside the buildings into a collour'. But whereas Jones's central bridge spans the road in a single arc, the new bridges form a segment-headed central arch 11 feet 6 inches wide, flanked by two small square-headed openings for pedestrians, with 'little chambers' in the mezzanines above. The iron balconies to the centre windows of the two bridge rooms, clearly visible in, for instance, Vorsterman's painting of the palace in *c.* 1680, now in the National Maritime Museum, were removed in 1807–10 at the time when the colonnades were constructed.[2]

Internally, the rearrangement of the building for its new use was at the expense of the ground storey, where from 'the paved roome one the east side the Hall' masons removed 'the marble neech and tearmes with the marble head'. They also took down 'a marble Chimny peice with the white marble pillars in another lower roome' in order to set it up 'in the new roomes above staires', and replaced it with a freestone chimneypiece taken from the demolished part of the Tudor palace. A second freestone chimneypiece went into 'the roome where the marble head stood'.[3]

From the evidence in the Works accounts it is clear that the east side of the upper storey was the King's Side, and the west the Queen's. The suites on both sides seem to have been arranged so that the north-east and north-west rooms, retaining their Jonesian decoration, became respectively the King's and the Queen's Presence Chambers, the new bridge rooms became the Privy Chambers, and the south-east and south-west rooms were both partitioned to form state bedrooms measuring 20 feet by 17 feet, with closets beyond only 12 feet wide and reduced in height by the insertion of a mezzanine floor. Decoration in the new suites was confined to the major rooms. For the Presence Chambers nothing further was needed. Presumably they had enriched marble chimneypieces of the 1630s which have since disappeared. The new-built Privy Chambers, on the other hand, were each embellished by an 'Egipt marble' chimneypiece worth £26, and the still

[1] Works 5/2 and 5/3.     [2] Chettle, pl. 11. The balconies were remade in 1694, *ibid.* p. 112.
[3] Works 5/2, Feb. and March 1662; Works 5/3, April 1662.

surviving enriched plaster ceilings. John Grove, the Master Plasterer, received, in March 1662, £41 10s., for 'one new frett Ceiling in the new roome on the Kings side' (Pl. 9A). The ceiling in the new room on the Queen's Side cost only £33 10s., but it may be that its central oval was intended for the 'ovall picture' for which carpenters were making a 'strayning frame' in the following June. In May Robert Streater, the Sergeant Painter, had received £3 10s. 'ffor mending the ceeling peice which came from St Jameses house XI foote Diameter'. The King's and Queen's Bedchambers also had their fret ceilings, made by Grove for £37 6s. 8d. the pair. Both were coved; and the present ceiling in the south-east room may be an adaptation of part of the former.[1] White marble chimneypieces were set up in both bedchambers, an 'enriched' one supplied by Joshua Marshall in the King's, but in the Queen's, it seems, a re-used chimneypiece from the demolished palace.[2]

In July 1662 Thomas Bagley, the Master Glazier, received £52 9s. for glazing all the windows, carpenters were paid for putting up 'ledges for hangings' in fourteen rooms and labourers for sweeping and cleaning the rooms. So, although two chimneypieces and a circular ceiling painting had still to be set up and the wainscot needed mending in the 'Guilded roome by the hall', as the king's Presence Chamber was called in August, the house was fit for occupation.[3] Thus somewhat precipitately completed it was ready: to receive not Charles II and his consort, but the house's former owner, Queen Henrietta Maria. The Queen Mother landed in England at the end of July and is known to have stayed at Greenwich until Somerset House should be ready for her occupation.[4] From this date onwards the Works accounts refer to the building no longer as the 'King's new building' but as the 'Queen's building'.

A room in the house was adapted as a chapel; but the accounts make it clear that the kitchen and other service rooms were free-standing, formed from some of the structures still remaining at the south end of the Tiltyard. It was probably to remedy this inconvenient arrangement that a start was made in May 1663 on further enlarging the Queen's House. Pavilions, or towers as the accounts call them, 44 feet by 48 in plan, were to be added to the south-east and south-west corners. Foundations were dug, and in July the two south quoins of the building were underpinned; but with that work stopped.[5]

Four years later, when the first block of the king's new palace had risen practically to its full height, the scheme was revived, but in a larger form. Now pavilions were to be added to all four corners. In May 1667 carpenters were paid for staking out the ground, and bricklayers for underpinning the quoins of the Queen's House. A joiner, William Cleere, sent in his bill in October for sixty-one days' work in making 'a large moddell for the addition to the Queens buildings'.[6] Three variant plans by John Webb presumably date from this year. The added pavilions would not house the kitchen but give on each storey four self-contained lodgings. One of the plans indicates a refacing of the north and south fronts with a continuous

---

[1] Nothing in the accounts can be connected with the enriched plaster ceilings which exist in the north-east cabinet and over the south-west staircase.
[2] Works 5/2 and 5/3.     [3] Works 5/3.     [4] Chettle, p. 41.
[5] Works 5/4.
[6] Works 5/10, ordinary account of May, extraordinary of Oct.

pilaster order.[1] Webb's only elevation, a quick sketch, records a different idea, a pedimented loggia of four columns in the centre, similar frontispieces to the flanking pavilions, and a central cupola.[2] But this scheme too proved unattainable. No further payments for constructing the pavilions are entered in the Works accounts, and as early as April 1670 there occurs the entry: 'Labourers imployed in wheeling and filling in the earth that lay about the Cellar and foundation that was digged at the east quoine of the Queenes buildings in the parke cont. LII foote square and five foote ½ deepe'.[3]

By this time also construction of the new block of the king's palace was slowing down. More than six years' work had brought the shell of the King Charles Block almost to completion. The design was finalised during 1663, and a model made. The earliest certain reference to the model however is the 'Moddell of the house' in the list of items stored in the King Charles Block in 1696 and handed over in that year by the Clerk of the Works at Greenwich to the Commissioners for the Hospital.[4] Webb's surviving plans, dated 1663, differ in several significant ways from the executed building. A one-storeyed link is shown at the south-east corner, but the block is already conceived as essentially free-standing and self-sufficient, not as a mere wing of a larger building.[5] In execution the link was omitted altogether. The plan and the executed building provided for a King's Side only. The queen's state rooms were to be in the answering block to the east. The main two-storeyed part was designed with rooms two deep, the three-storeyed pavilions, with the belvedere rooms at the top, being extended by a third room on the west side. The king was allotted two suites, a state suite on the first floor extending through all the rooms on the east side of the building, and a private suite on the ground floor running north from the centre of the east front and occupying the width of the north pavilion. There were therefore two entrances. The apse-ended vestibule, entered through a trio of arches in the centre of the east front (Pl. 9B), led into the private suite, a sequence of rooms labelled by Webb 'wayting roome', 'Anti roome', 'Dining roome', 'withdrawing roome' and finally a groin-vaulted 'Cabinett' in the centre of the north front. At the south end the single-storey arcaded loggia led, according to a modification of the 1663 plan close to the executed arrangement, to the grand staircase. From there the state suite on the principal floor began with presence chamber and privy chamber, bedchamber, cabinet, and finally a gallery longer than half the length of the facade.

Webb's elevational treatment for the long, rather low range, two-storeyed except for the end pavilions, was developed from a plate in Vincenzo Scamozzi's treatise *L'Idea dell'Architettura Universale* (1615).[6] The two important facades, the long east front and the north end facing the river, are given a giant Corinthian order, supporting a central pediment (Pl. 8B). This bold use of a giant order, making it weld each facade into a visual whole, was something new to English classical architecture. The rusticated wall surface is a reminiscence of the treatment accorded by Webb's master, Inigo Jones, to the Whitehall Banqueting House; but the window openings,

[1] *R.I.B.A. Drawings Catalogue: Jones & Webb*, figs. 166–8.
[2] *Ibid.*, fig. 165.
[3] Works 5/15, Ordinary account.
[5] R.I.B.A. Burlington–Devonshire Collection, III/1 (3–5).
[4] Works 5/48 under Jan. 1696.
[6] I, Lib. iii, Cap. xv, p. 284.

crowned by powerfully projecting voussoir blocks are, although Palladian in origin, stronger and more dramatic in their effect than Jones ever allowed himself to be. The south end and the west front are treated more simply, although the former contained the entrance to the state rooms. Webb's surviving elevation drawings are almost precisely followed in the executed building.[1] Since its erection only two alterations have been made, the demolition of the one-storey entrance loggia at the south end, and the refacing in stone of the brick walling of the west or back-side.[2]

Construction of the shell of the building went forward steadily from February 1664, when labourers were employed in 'begining to digg the three foundations for the new building 250 foot in length and 6 foot wide and 6 foot deepe' and in 'filling up the damm with marsh earth 80 foot in length and 7 foot deep and 4 foot wide'—for the foundations extended into the bed of the river itself.[3] In August 1664 the foundations, the Kentish stone and 'Scottish' stone footings and the brick vaults were complete.[4] Above that level brick walls and Portland stone facings were exclusively used. Over one million nine hundred thousand bricks were bought, from Sir Nicholas Crisp of Hammersmith and his executors, and almost exactly two thousand four hundred tons of Portland stone, supplied by a partnership of masons on the Isle of Portland, Christopher Gibbs and Robert Attwooll, and after April 1665 by Attwooll and his new partner, Robert Benfeild.

The master bricklayers throughout were Maurice Emmett and Thomas Pattison; but the masonry was divided between three teams. The south pavilion was built by Stephen Switzer and Thomas Wise; the master masons for the long central portion of the building were Joshua Marshall and John Young; and Marshall was solely responsible for the erection of the north pavilion. Marshall also carved the figures of Fortitude and Dominion of the Sea in the east pediment, and Mars and Fame in the north pediment.

The ground storey walls had risen up to the 'upper side of the fascia against the first ffloore' by July 1665, when the first instalment of masons' and bricklayers' taskwork was entered in the accounts.[5] The second task 'up to the under parte of the architrave' was complete by April 1666, and the entablature and pediments by November of that year.[6] After that, the progress of the work was somewhat slower. The masons' bills for constructing the upper pavilions were not presented until May 1668, and work dragged on at the north pavilion until March 1669, the month in which the taskwork carpenters completed roofing the whole building.[7]

The decoration of the exterior was executed as work progressed, and entered item by item in the accounts. For example John Young and Joshua Marshall were paid for the enrichment of the entrance arches of the east vestibule, for 'the Golosse with flowers in the sofito of the arches . . . the molding cut with egs & anchors in the sofito . . . XII Roses in the squares . . . laurell leaves & small Roses in the bottome of the middle keystones' and so on.[8] Payment for scaffolding for the carvers signifies that some of the carving was done *in situ*; but much was carved on the

---

[1] *R.I.B.A. Drawings Catalogue: Jones & Webb*, figs. 124–7.
[2] The loggia is visible in early views of the palace, e.g. Vorsterman's and Danckerts's, both reproduced by Chettle, pls. 11–12.
[3] Works 5/4.    [4] Works 5/5.    [5] Works 5/7.
[6] Works 5/9.    [7] Works 5/12.    [8] Works 5/9, April 1666.

ground, in one end of the great work shed, in particular the four pediment figures, which required the removal of the shed side when they were ready to be set in position.[1]

Internally a number of stone doorways survive, in particular on the north staircase at all three levels, simple classical surrounds bearing open pediments on brackets. The south staircase, on the other hand, has at ground level two round-headed doorways with console-keystones formed as pedestals for busts, clearly in imitation of those in the hall of the Queen's House. The lower girder here, carved with laurel leaves, is the item for which Henry Phillips and Richard Cleere were paid £1 18s. 8d. in October 1666. Webb turned his attention to designing the interior decoration during 1665 and 1666. Both dates occur on the surviving drawings, and the payment in January 1665 to Richard Gammon 'for bringing two Boxes out of Sommersetshire with books prints and drawings of Mr Webbs for his Majesties use' probably marks the preparation for this new design campaign.[2] Among the surviving drawings there are as many as thirteen for the King's Bedchamber, which was to have been a sumptuous room, the main area under a coved ceiling enriched with foliage, the opening to the bed alcove arched over by the fronds of a pair of palm trees. Of the ceiling designs the most interesting (although marked 'not taken') is for the king's state cabinet. The spandrels formed by a circle inscribed in the square area are filled by cartouches of the four Continents, over which pairs of eagles spread their wings, an allegorical conceit explained by Webb in the margin: 'The Allusion, that his Majestys Eagles—vizt. his shipping, spread their wings (their sailes) over the whole world.'[3]

Of Webb's designs for internal fittings one set was put into execution, that for marble chimneypieces, which his 'Particular of the Chimneys sent for to Lygorne' shows to have been for rooms of lesser importance.[4] This was a special order, negotiated by Joseph Kent, the consul at Leghorn, and his deputy, Charles Chillingworth, for the benefit of a company of British merchants at Leghorn headed by Thomas Dethick. Hugh May, the Paymaster, remitted to Chillingworth £1000 in advance, an arrangement which alarmed the Secretary of State, Lord Arlington: 'His Majesty is likely to be much wronged by the latter (Chillingworth) keeping the money, sending an extravagant account, demanding unreasonable allowances, and not sending the marbles, for want of disbursing the sums remitted.'[5] In the event the marbles reached Greenwich, but the bill fell far short of £1000. Designs were dispatched to Leghorn in 1667, postage being paid in March on a 'packet of molds for Chimny peices', and in July carriage on 'a box with molds for Chimny peices'.[6] Two years later, in March 1669, the marbles arrived at Greenwich 'in his Majesty's Frigate called the Victorie' and were unloaded into the cellar of the Queen's House, not only the twelve marble chimneypieces to Webb's specifications, but over four thousand hexagonal marble paving stones and seven blocks of marble as well. The bill came to £390 4s. ½d., and an additional £119 7s. 9¾d. for carriage. What Chillingworth did with the £490 surplus is not recorded.[7] The marbles re-

[1] Works 5/9, Feb. 1667.　　　　　　　　　　　[2] Works 5/5.
[3] R.I.B.A. Drawings Catalogue: Jones & Webb, fig. 141.　　[4] Ibid., III/1 (44).
[5] Cal. S.P. Dom. 1665–6, p. 171. Arlington's letter is undated.　　[6] Works 5/9, 5/10.
[7] Works 5/12, 5/14, 5/17 extraordinary book 'Marbles from Leghorne to Greenwich April 1671'.

mained in store in the Queen's House until May 1693, when they were removed 'ffor the Use of their Majesties new Building att Hampton Court'.[1]

Greenwich Palace was the victim of the king's perilous financial position in the late 1660s and early 1670s. Money for the earliest operations came from the normal Treasury grants to the Office of Works for the upkeep of the royal palaces, supplemented by the special grant of £1000 in August 1661 for the additions to the Queen's House and a further £1000 the following February for the demolition of the old palace.[2] Since the Paymaster of the Works was able to balance his books until 1663–4, the King Charles Block was begun without any special grant until letters of privy seal for a further £5000 were issued in May 1664. Of this however only £3000 was paid, for the next financial year was a bad one, leaving arrears of over £12,000, including a debt to a long list of purveyors and workmen at Greenwich totalling £1485 17s. 4¼d., a debt which was not cleared until 1675.[3] Thereupon a new account, confined to the Extraordinary work at Greenwich, was opened on 1 June 1665, and fed primarily from the sale of prizes, which between January 1664 and November 1667 realised in all £14,781 7s. 11¾d. for the works at Greenwich.[4] But with the end of the second Anglo–Dutch War in July 1667 that source of revenue dried up.

After the dispatch of the order to Leghorn preparation for decorating the interior of the King Charles Block stopped, and as the king's finances progressively deteriorated during the ensuing few years, construction work at Greenwich became slower and slower; for the Works accounts bear out Pepys's observation in March 1669, that the king's house 'goes on slow'.[5] In July of that year all the lower windows of the King Charles Block were boarded up.[6] A year later Webb received his last month's salary as surveyor, and the Extraordinary account for Greenwich closed. This marked the virtual cessation of work, although the completion of the north pavilion dragged on for a considerable time and the final payment to Joshua Marshall for completing the balustrade was made only in October 1672. With that the Paymaster concluded his account, recording a total expenditure since June 1665 of £27,755 12s. 2¾d.[7]

Certain preparations for building a second block to match the King Charles Block were made. A sketch plan by Webb for the chapel proposed to project eastwards from the centre of the block is dated 10 March 1670.[8] The warrant dated 9 June 1673 to pay £10,000 towards the works at Greenwich specified that it was not only for 'finishing part of the palace' but also for 'laying the foundations of another part'; but no money was ever paid out on this warrant.[9] One final fruitless effort seems to have been made in 1682 to fit up the interior of the King Charles Block. In February a little glazing was done, and two marble chimneypieces set up; in May preparations were made for joiners and carvers to begin work.[10]

In official documents there is no evidence that any of the Stuart monarchs showed

---

[1] Works 5/46, June 1693.
[2] *Cal. S.P. Dom. 1661–2*, pp. 59, 273. E 351/3247 ff. and AO 1/2433/85 ff.
[3] E 351/3278 and AO 1/2435/89.     [4] E 351/3438.
[5] Pepys, *Diary* ed. Wheatley, viii, p. 262.  [6] Works 5/13.
[7] E 351/3438.
[8] *R.I.B.A. Drawings Catalogue: Jones & Webb*, fig. 120.
[9] *Cal. S.P. Dom. 1673*, p. 358.    [10] Works 5/33 and 5/35.

further interest in Greenwich Palace until it passed out of royal hands. The King Charles Block remained boarded up and fenced around, used increasingly as a storehouse, as the Tudor chapel and ante-chapel fell into decay.[1]

James II was the first to suggest that the shell of his brother's palace should be put to some other use. It was reported in a newsletter of 10 December 1687 that the king had 'given his house at Greenwich to that of the Trinity to be fitted for the service of impotent sea Commanders and others'.[2] During the next reign this idea bore fruit. First, after the Battle of La Hogue in 1692, the King Charles Block was fitted up as a temporary hospital for the sick and wounded.[3] On 25 October 1694 letters patent vested the King Charles Block and adjoining lands in trustees to convert them for use as a hospital,[4] thereby ending both the royal ownership and the responsibility of the Office of Works for the uncompleted palace.

The Queen's House on the other hand continued to be maintained by the Office of Works. Until 1690, when it became the official residence of the newly-appointed Ranger of Greenwich Park, Charles, Earl of Dorset and Middlesex,[5] it was unoccupied for long periods, and some if not all the windows were boarded up. In the Works accounts the only certain evidence of occupation is in entries under March 1675 and 1678 for 'boarding parte of the floore in a lower roome next the park where the dutch painters work',[6] and references in 1687 to the lodgings of the Marquis de Ruvigny, the French Ambassador. Between April and August of that year an unusual amount of work was done in the house, culminating in the laying of '1105 ffoot of Artifisciall glassie paveing one the flower of the Gallery over the South porche', for which Kenrick Edgbury received £27 12s. 6d.[7] On two occasions late in 1687 John Evelyn met Ruvigny in the Queen's House, the first time at the christening of a son of Sir John Chardin, who was apparently also occupying rooms in the house at the time.[8]

Work on the new Hospital began in 1696, and as its buildings began to rise between the Queen's House and the river, it was natural that the Commissioners responsible for its management should hope eventually to appropriate this last relic of the former royal palace. With this end in view, Prince George of Denmark, the chief Commissioner of the Hospital, purchased the lease of the house from the Ranger, Lord Romney. His intention was eventually to settle the house on the hospital, but he died in 1708 with the lease still in his possession. The Commissioners had, however, already laid out a considerable sum of money on the house 'to fit the same up for the reception of a Governor . . . nominated by his Highness'. One of the alterations carried out by the Commissioners consisted in cutting down the sills of the ground-floor windows and substituting sashes for the casement windows, a change which considerably altered the proportions of the original design.[9] In 1710 Sir William Gifford, the first Governor of Greenwich Hospital, took office. At the same time he was appointed Ranger of the Park, and granted the use of the Queen's House. Responsibility for the maintenance of the building was now assumed

[1] First in Sept. 1684 (Works 5/38).          [2] Hist. MSS. Comm. *Downshire* I(i), p. 280.
[3] N. Luttrell, *Brief Historical Relation*, iii, p. 21 under 26 Jan. 1692/3.
[4] J. Cooke and J. Maule, *Royal Hospital at Greenwich* (1789), pp. 1–7.
[5] Chettle, p. 47.                                    [6] Works 5/25 and 5/29.
[7] Works 5/41.          [8] Evelyn, *Diary*, iv, pp. 561, 565.          [9] Chettle, p. 49.

by the Commissioners, and William Dickinson's post as Clerk of the Works at Greenwich Palace was allowed to lapse.[1]

The ownership of the Queen's House had, however, never been formally renounced by the Crown, and its status as a royal palace was reasserted in 1714, when George I was accommodated there on his first night on English soil, before his state entry into London on 20 September. The cost of fitting up the interior of the house for the occasion was borne by the Hospital, but the Office of Works made itself responsible for erecting additional temporary buildings, including 'kitchens, larders, scalding office, pastry, confectionary, Groom Porter's Office and other necessary offices'.[2] Repairs continued to be carried out by the Hospital throughout the reign of George I, but soon after his death the governing body of the Hospital decided to spend no further funds on the repair of a building which they now saw no prospect of acquiring, and in November 1729 they asked the Crown to relieve them of the responsibility for maintaining it.[3] Their request was granted, and in 1730 Queen Caroline obtained from George II a grant of the house which had been so closely associated with former queens consort.[4] It continued, however, to be occupied for the time being by the Governor of the Hospital, Sir John Jennings, in his capacity as Ranger of the Park. Responsibility for its upkeep now reverted to the Office of Works, whose Board obtained authority from the Treasury to revive the post of Clerk of Works at Greenwich.[5] On 24 February 1730 Leonard Wooddeson was appointed to the office at £100 per annum.[6] Some extensive repairs to the roof were found to be necessary, and were carried out in 1730 at a cost of £440.[7] In 1736 it was at the Queen's House that Princess Augusta stayed before her marriage to Frederick, Prince of Wales.[8] Further repairs costing over £4500 were carried out in 1745–6 after the death of Sir John Jennings and the appointment of Lady Catherine Pelham as his successor in the Ranger's office.[9] After her death in 1780 the road which separated the grounds of the Queen's House from the Hospital was widened by agreement between the Office of Works and the Hospital authorities. The boundary was set back 19 feet and a new wall was built at the expense of the Hospital. The Board at first required this wall to be 12 feet high, but eventually agreed to lower it (in the middle) in order to preserve the vista from the Queen's House through the Hospital.[10]

[1] On 30 Sept. 1715 the Board of Works 'Order'd that the King's Timber Yard belonging to the Palace at Greenwich, and the House and Buildings belonging to the late Clerk of the Works be put into the Custody of Mr. Nicholas Hawkesmoor [Clerk of Works to the Commissioners of the Hospital], and that he take care that no damage or waste be committed in the said yard, and that noe persons be permitted to lodge in the said Timber Yard, or House (late the Clerk of Works) without the Consent of Mr. Nicholas Hawkesmoor' (Works 4/1, 30 Sept. 1715).
[2] AO 1/2448/148; Works 6/5, p. 4.
[3] *Cal. Treas. Books & Papers 1729–30*, pp. 163, 167, 319, 329, 393, 397; T 98/2, ff. 123–6.
[4] *Cal Treasury Books & Papers 1729–30*, pp. 412, 442.
[5] *Cal. Treasury Books & Papers 1729–30*, pp. 319, 329; Works 4/4, 23 Dec. 1729.
[6] *Cal. Treasury Books & Papers 1729–30*, p. 609; Works 4/4, 5 March 1729/30.
[7] Works 4/4, 21 May, 7 July 1730; T 56/18, p. 329; Works 5/58, Sept. 1730.
[8] *Gent's. Mag.* vi (1736), p. 230.
[9] Works 5/141, years 1745 and 1746.
[10] Works 4/16, 20, 25 July 1781, 26 April, 31 May, 7 June 1782; Works 6/19, pp. 370–1. The plan reproduced by Chettle, *op. cit.*, pl. 25 was evidently made in connection with this improvement.

# HAMPTON COURT

## 1. THE PALACE, 1660–1702

AT THE Restoration the fabric of Hampton Court was in poor condition. The monthly accounts of the Office of Works, which begin in October 1660, record during the ensuing decade constant payments to the plumbers for relaying lead and soldering drips by the dozen. Neither Charles II nor James II favoured the palace as a regular place of residence, although between 1670 and 1674 over £6000 was spent on new-built lodgings for the former and newly-converted lodgings for the latter, then Duke of York. Monthly totals of expenditure on the Ordinary account rarely exceeded £200, and the noteworthy works under this heading can be briefly catalogued. In 1660–1 the present tennis court was extensively refitted; in September 1663 the hall lantern was removed; during the early summer of 1667 a tower over the outer gateway was reconstructed and the following season saw a wholesale renewal of pinnacles and battlements.[1]

Only in 1661 were special grants authorised towards expenditure on the buildings at Hampton Court. In July a warrant for £628 was issued for the repair of the stables, in accordance with an estimate drawn up by Simon Basill, the Clerk of the Works at Hampton Court, and in September £500 was issued to Hugh May, Paymaster of the Works, for repairs to the house 'for His Majesty's speedy remove', and towards building a new foot-guard house in the tilt yard.[2] In May the following year Hampton Court was the setting for the honeymoon of the newly-married Charles and Catherine of Braganza. The sharp increase in the monthly totals of expenditure, which average over £500 between March and June 1662 and then fall back to their former level, reflects the preparations made for their visit. Now, for the first time since the Restoration, the palace was made habitable for royalty, by a great deal of whitewashing and matting, by putting up ledges for hangings, by painting and even gilding a balcony, but without any significant structural alterations.[3] The king's mistress, Lady Castlemaine, had lodgings at Hampton Court by mid-1665.

The first major work authorised by the king at Hampton Court was not at the house but in the park, the long canal aligned on the centre of the east front. The contract with Joshua Marshall, for 'the severall parts of Masons Worke about the two ends of the Canale' was drawn up on 9 October 1668, and exactly six years later he received his last payment for tidying the job up.[4]

[1] Works 5/1; 5/4; 5/10; 5/12.    [2] *Cal. Treas. Books* i, pp. 259, 296.
[3] E. Law, *The History of Hampton Court Palace* (1888), ii, p. 209; Works 5/2; 5/3.
[4] Works 5/145, p. 9; Works 5/23, Oct. 1674.
H K W—M

The Duke and Duchess of York were at first allotted the three-storeyed range between the inner courtyard, then still known as Cloister Court, and the middle or Fountain Court.[1] Late in 1669, however, plans were drawn up for creating new lodgings for them in the disused tennis court on the east side of Chapel Court, at an estimated cost of £3000. Treasury warrants were passed in November–December 1669 and July 1670 for two-thirds of this sum, but the third part was delayed by the financial stringencies of the period until 1674, the final £400 being issued in December 1674 to Sir Allen Apsley, the treasurer of the duke's household, for hangings.[2] Of the two Extraordinary accounts for this building the first, for £2281 12s. 5¼d., is dated February 1669/70–6 June 1673, the second amounts to £584 2s. 6¾d. and is closed at September 1674.[3] Contracts with the carpenter, John Wratten, and John Grove, the Master Plasterer, were drawn up on 31 May 1670. Thomas Kinward, the Master Joiner, contracted on the following 12 September to fit deal wainscot in the duke's bedchamber, presence and privy chamber, and the duchess's presence chamber, chapel, bedchamber and closet.[4] From the accounts it is clear that only the duchess was to be accommodated in the old tennis court, the duke's lodgings presumably occupying the north range of Chapel Court. The ranges were completely refenestrated, the tennis court heightened to three storeys (five on the east side, where there were 'little back rooms' on each floor[5]), but not deprived of its buttresses. The most telling parts of the fabric surviving today however are the simple rusticated doorways, with scroll-flanked windows above, which stand at the east and west ends of the passage beneath the duchess's lodgings. For this pair of 'dores with lights over them' Joshua Marshall received £20.[6]

The new block for the king himself, which went up at the same time, had a life of less than twenty years.[7] In the accounts it is referred to as 'His Majesty's New Building next Paradise', and Wren's outline plans of the palace as he found it in 1689 make clear that it formed a rectangular projection at the south-east corner of the palace, where the privy-garden and park fronts met.[8] As for the facing materials, the contract (27 May 1670) of Isaac Corner, the Master Bricklayer, specified 'the outsides of the House to be of rubbed Bricks with clean white small Joyntes', and the mason, Joshua Marshall, contracted (on 12 July 1670) for water-table and quoins of old stone, and for working and setting architraves for the windows, the 'Bastard Cornish' ten inches thick, cornices over the windows eleven inches thick and for the upper architrave and cornice with 'Denticles'.[9] The main block seems to have been of four by four bays; but slightly recessed to the north on the privy-garden front was an open loggia, with a balcony. Joshua Marshall

---

[1] Streater's bill for painting in September 1664 (Works 5/6) makes this clear. These contemporary names of the courtyards will be used here. The Cloister Court became known after its rebuilding as Quadrangle Court, until the erection of the fountain there in 1702 (see p. 170).

[2] *Cal. Treas. Books* iii, pp. 164, 166, 625; iv, pp. 244, 623.

[3] Works 5/14 and 5/24.  [4] Works 5/145, ff. 42, 44, 54.

[5] Works 5/24, 'Second booke for his Royall highness', Kinward's bill.

[6] Works 5/14, 'Booke ffor his Royall Highnis the Duke of Yorkes lodgings: and the Old Tennis Court'.

[7] The Extraordinary accounts for this building are in Works 5/17 (1670–1, total £4811 0s. 10d.), Works 5/21 (September 1671–November 1673, total £800 6s. 6¼d.) and Works 5/27 (July 1676, total £147 0s. 1d.).

[8] All Souls iv, 4 and 5 (*Wren Soc.* iv, pl. 5).

[9] Works 5/145, pp. 41, 47.

received £62 5s. for '4 peers with pilasters capitalls and bases', £27 12s. for a stone balcony 21 feet 6 inches long and 5 feet wide with a return at one end, £13 for four 'Cartooses of portland stone carved' and £5 for working four Ionic capitals.[1]

Internally, as the accounts show, the new building adjoined the queen's eating room and a long gallery, and was linked to Paradise by a passage. The main rooms which it contained were a great staircase, a withdrawing room, bedchamber and closet for the king. On the ground floor was the 'Marble Room'. The staircase was toplit from a twelve-sided lantern. The windows throughout both the main storeys and the garrets were casements. Mention is also made of 'the halfe-round roofe and the windows at the ends, . . . the windows being 16 lights long; and two halfe-round lights under them'.[2]

The standard required in the internal decoration is suggested by the clause in the contract with the Master Joiner, Thomas Kinward, 'That all the wainescott Doores, and shutters be of extraordinary good clapp bourd of equall Coulour and workemanlike doone, in goodnesse, stuffe and workemanshipp at least equall to the lower Apartement of the Lord Berckeleys house', that is of Hugh May's Berkeley House, Piccadilly.[3] In 1670–1 Marshall provided marble chimneypieces, some white, some veined; John Grove, the Master Plasterer, charged £28 17s. 9d. for 'fret ceilings' in the withdrawing room and great staircase. In 1673 the joiner's bill amounted to £293, and Henry Phillips, the Master Carver, received £106 1s. 7d. for carving on the great stairs, in the room next the backstairs, the king's closet, bedchamber and room adjoining, and for 'iiii large Cantalavers done after the Corinthian order each iii foot long' to carry the balcony on the front of Paradise. The final account, of July 1676, records the decoration of Paradise itself, with four fluted pilasters with 'Compositive Capitalls', and 'a very Larg imbosement of drapery fruit and flowers about the chimney peece', for which Phillips charged £10, the wainscot and carving being painted by Robert Streater, the Sergeant Painter, 'white veined in nut oyle'. The total sum spent on the building was £5758 7s. 5¼d.

During the rest of Charles's reign and that of his brother nothing beyond maintenance was carried out by the Office of Works. With the accession of William and Mary, however, there began the third great building campaign at Hampton Court, the complete reconstruction of the royal apartments. Their majesties' decision is reported in a newsletter dated 2 March 1688/9: 'The bed of state is removed from Windsor to Hampton Court, and Sir Christopher Wren hath received orders to beautify and add some new building to that fabric.' Wren sketched out his vision of a palace completely new-built except for the Tudor great hall, which was to be the central feature of a grand approach from the north (Fig. 6).[4] The royal apartments were to be rebuilt on their old site in four ranges round a large rectangular

[1] Marshall's task in Works 5/17, Extraordinary book. For the position of this structure see All Souls iv, 4.

[2] Works 5/17, Extraordinary book, Wratten's second measurement.

[3] Works 5/145, p. 57. The use of Berkeley House as a standard of excellence for the joinery should probably not be taken as evidence that Hugh May designed the Paradise building. Wren, as Surveyor-General, will have been expected to provide designs, although there is nothing among the surviving Wren drawings which can be connected with it. No doubt May's position as Paymaster of the Works will have enabled him to get royal craftsmen to work for Lord Berkeley.

[4] Hist. MSS. Comm. *Portland* iii, p. 431; *Wren Soc.* iv, pl. 4.

grand or privy court aligned on the long canal, and this part Wren worked out in more detail, and eventually executed in a modified and truncated form.

The surviving drawings belong to at least four separate schemes.[1] Wren's design suffered from two major constraints, financial retrenchment which withered the north and west ranges of the grand court so much that it was impossible to provide the required accommodation in three storeys, and the king's asthma, which made him demand that his state apartment should be set as low as possible, above a ground storey only 12 feet 6 inches high instead of the normal 16 feet.[2] Hence the excessively narrow spacing of the bays in the Quadrangle Court, hence the round-windowed mezzanine, which Wren introduced at a late stage in the design, hence the unduly low ground storey, hence the awkward scooping back of the cloister arches (Pl. 13). Nothing suggests however that the unbroken horizontal skyline of the palace, another feature which came in for contemporary criticism, was not deliberately chosen by Wren, in imitation of Louis XIV's Versailles.[3]

In planning the principal floor of the new quadrangle Wren repeated the essential features of the Tudor royal suites, placing the king's state apartment in the south range overlooking the privy garden and the queen's facing east across the park, so that they met at their inmost closets in the south-east corner of the palace. The north range provided the outer rooms of the queen's apartment and the west range became a mere linking gallery between the two suites. The arcaded ground-floor walk round the courtyard repeated the Tudor arrangement with cloisters. The north-east pavilion, projecting beyond the north range of the court, housed a subsidiary state apartment, intended for Princess Anne. The private apartment of the queen occupied the courtyard side of the east range, but on the king's side a gallery occupied the corresponding space. Here the Raphael cartoons were to be hung, but it is not clear whether William intended to use this room as a council chamber. His private apartment was placed on the ground floor, with an orangery in the centre open to the privy garden, and behind that a grotto. The top two floors of all three full-height ranges were to provide lodgings for some of the principal courtiers.

The Extraordinary monthly account was opened in April 1689. In that month a temporary apartment for the queen was fitted up in the east range of the Tudor Fountain Court.[4] In May foundations were dug for the range of brick guardhouses which still survive along the north side of the outer court, from the palace to the road.[5] In July Maurice Emmett, the Master Bricklayer, and James Groves, the carpenter, were paid for erecting the Horse Guard, Foot Guard, and hay barn there.

---

[1] *Wren Soc.* iv, pls. 11–18 and vii, pl. 23. These drawings are analysed by E. Sekler, *Wren and his Place in European Architecture* (London 1956), pp. 159–63.

[2] The elevation drawings can be grouped according to the greater or less height of the ground storey. The king admitted that his requirement had spoilt Wren's design (see the passage in *Parentalia*, quoted in *Wren Soc.* iv, p. 19). A. T. Bolton's suggestion, *ibid.* p. 20, that the principal floor-level was raised from the level of the imposts of the court arcade to the existing intermediate height during the course of building, ignores the fact that the principal floor level of 12 ft. 6 ins. above ground, entailing a ground floor aperture height of 11 ft. 4 ins., was established before the final design was arrived at and hence before building began.

[3] Wren's preferred elevation may be that in *Wren Soc.* iv, pl. 15 upper.

[4] Works 5/55. The position of the new apartment is fixed by the payment to Thomas Hill for a marble chimneypiece in the 'Clossett next Fountaine Court'.

[5] A plan showing the original internal layout of the guardhouses is All Souls iv, 2.

By this time demolitions had already started to make way for the new royal apartments in the palace. Contemporaneously the so-called Thames Gallery, or Water Gallery, was converted into a *maison de plaisir* for the queen. This elaborate Tudor brick water-gate at the south end of the privy garden is very clearly represented in Anthony van den Wyngaerde's mid-sixteenth-century drawing of the palace as seen from the river. Unfortunately no late seventeenth-century drawing is extant to show the effect of the remodelling, and the building itself survived no later than 1700, when William III ordered its demolition. It survives then most vividly in the descriptions of Defoe and Celia Fiennes.[1] Although Defoe says that the building was quickly fitted up 'that here their majesties might repose while they saw the main building go forward', he makes it clear that it belonged to the queen and expressed her taste and interests. Both writers mention the 'gallery of beauties' filled with full-length portraits by Kneller of the queen's ladies in waiting, and the ubiquitous Chinese porcelain and Delft-ware.[2] Defoe speaks of her majesty's 'fine apartment, with a sett of lodgings, for her private retreat only', but from Celia Fiennes we learn the layout of rooms on the principal floor. The gallery with the portraits was at the river end of the building and 'opened into a ballcony to the water', and beyond were a large room and four closets in the corners, 'one pannell'd all with Jappan another with Looking Glass and two with fine work under pannells of Glass'.

The payments for work at the Thames Gallery recorded in the monthly accounts make a more concrete visualisation of the building possible. The Tudor skyline of battlements was retained, although mention is made of 'cutting downe the Battlements in the inside next the Flatt and raiseing upp Brickworke for the new floore round the whole Building'.[3] The four projecting polygonal turrets also survived, new-capped with cupolas; and two larger cupolas, octagonal and domed, were erected over the main body of the building, one above each end of the long gallery on the upper floor. Charles II's balcony and pilasters next to Paradise were brought across and re-erected at the Thames Gallery, and the existing iron balcony at the river end was taken down and remodelled. But the most effective modification to bring the exterior up to date must have been the remodelling of the windows to take sashes, at least twenty-one of which were inserted in the upper storey. The two large cupolas were crowned with wrought-iron weather vanes for which Tijou received £80 in March 1691. Internally, the queen's bathing room and dairy (with accommodation for the dairy woman) were in the lower storey, and a grotto was formed apparently in a Tudor staircase turret. On the principal floor there were the two major rooms, the gallery and a 'great room next the Thames'. Closets are also mentioned, in particular the 'queen's closet', which Maurice Emmett in December 1691 was 'altering . . . to a sextigon and rounding the angles'. At first the splendour of the interior derived more from the contents than from any integral

[1] D. Defoe, *A Tour through England and Wales* (1725), Everyman edition, i, p. 175; *The Journeys of Celia Fiennes*, ed. Morris, pp. 59–60.

[2] For Queen Mary's china collection see A. Lane in *Transactions of the Oriental Ceramic Society*, vol. 25 (1949–50), pp. 21–31.

[3] Works 5/55, Oct. 1689, taskwork of Maurice Emmett. The plan of the Thames Gallery is known only from a tiny outline plan in William Talman's set of drawings for a proposed 'Trianon' at Hampton Court (R.I.B.A. B4/1).

decoration. The carving by William Emmett consisted merely of enriched cornices, and in the great room 'Italian Picture frame Mouldings with 3 Inrichments' over the two chimneypieces. Reference is made to looking-glass put in some of the rooms and closets, but only the queen's closet was enriched with plasterwork, for which 'Mr. Nedoe' was paid £50.[1]

The building was ready for use by the end of 1690; but in the last year of the queen's life it was further beautified. In the queen's bedchamber, Glass Closet and Delft Ware Closet Gerrard Johnson installed mirrors, Thomas Davis supplied seven marble chimneypieces, and made a marble basin with a 'Back Neech and Cornish', and expensive painting was done by John Cooke in the 'Marble Closett' (£50) and by James Bogedain, the flower painter, in the 'Queens Looking Glasse Closett' (£60).[2]

To return to the palace itself, in June 1689 joiners began to remove wainscot from the royal apartments, and in the same month foundations were dug.

The south range, facing the Privy Garden, was the first to be tackled. By October 1689 the western two-thirds of the range as far as Paradise were up and the timbers of the roof in place. The work was in the hands of Thomas Hill and John Clarke, masons, Maurice Emmett, the Master Bricklayer, and James Groves, carpenter, who received respectively £1117, £856, £2878 and £917 for workmanship alone.[3] Most of the facing stone came from Headington, supplied by John Townesend, Richard Piddington and Bartholomew Peisley.[4] In all the later parts of the palace, by contrast, Portland stone (from the quarries of Thomas Gilbert and Thomas Wise) predominated. All decorative carving was done on the ground, and the carved blocks inserted as work proceeded, with the exception of the circular lion-skin windows towards the Quadrangle Court.

This was fast work: too fast, for in early December the roof over the centrepiece collapsed, killing two carpenters and injuring eleven others.[5] On 12 December Robert Hooke noted in his diary that Wren was 'troubld about fall at Hampton Court',[6] and during the next month his professional competence was called into question, his second-in-command, the Comptroller William Talman, displaying characteristic disloyalty to him. At the end of the month the king, believing the building to be in a bad condition, ordered Wren and the other Officers of the Works to submit a report. Wren, seeing trouble ahead but believing the new range to be structurally sound, suggested an impartial report by 'able men not interested . . . that have left off their aprons', but in the end submitted. Thus when the matter was next considered by the Treasury Lords in January, Wren and Talman sent in conflicting reports. The other chief Officers of the Works, Bankes the Master Car-

---

[1] Works 5/55, July 1689–March 1691/2, passim. The payment to Mr. Nedoe is in AO 1/2482/296 (the name wrongly transcribed in *Wren Soc.*). He is presumably the 'Frenchman' mentioned as beating plaster, etc., in the Thames Gallery in Aug. and Sept. 1691. He should probably be identified with 'Nadauld', the Huguenot plasterer and stone-carver employed at Chatsworth and Castle Howard *c.* 1699–1705.

[2] AO 1/2482/297, printed in *Wren Soc.* iv, pp. 26–9.

[3] Works 5/55, Oct. 1689.

[4] Reigate and Beer stone were also used, the latter for the shafts of the columns, Portland stone mainly for plinths and cornices. The stonework of this part of the palace has worn badly, and in spite of restoration in 1882 was in 1970 almost completely renewed.

[5] Works 5/55, payment to James Groves in Feb. 1689/90 for the cost of burial and for doctor's fee.

[6] Diary of Robert Hooke 1688–93, in *Early Science in Oxford*, ed. R. T. Gunther (Oxford, 1935), x, p. 171.

penter, and Oliver, the Master Mason, stood by Wren; but Talman insisted that certain cracks in the piers of the privy garden front were both more numerous and wider than the others made out and eventually the argument became so acrimonious that the Treasury Secretary in his minutes transcribed the exchanges as dramatic dialogue.[1] Finally an independent committee of three was set up, consisting of Philip Ryley, Surveyor General of Woods and Forests South of the Trent, Sir Samuel Morland, the noted hydraulic engineer, and Mr. Fitch, no doubt John Fitch, the eminent master-bricklayer. These three paid several visits to inspect the new buildings, but their report does not survive.[2] The monthly accounts however seem to support Wren against Talman, for no payment for reconstructing this range was made, beyond repairs to the carved pilaster capitals of the centrepiece, damaged when the roof collapsed, and the reconstruction (for £9 17s. 4d.) of the Portland stone facing to two piers on the garden front.[3]

It is however noticeable that the remainder of the shell of the new buildings was erected at a considerably slower pace, and the masons' and bricklayers' work paid for, and thereby measured and checked, at more frequent intervals. Lack of money also began to delay progress. The first grant of £40,000, authorised on 22 May 1689, was at first issued at a rate of £500 per week, until the following December. Thereafter the flow was much more sluggish so that the full sum was not issued until Easter Term 1694. In 1691 the Officers of the Works estimated that the debt was already £24,000, and, unrealistically, that only £23,500 was needed to complete the work. They requested a regular £450 per week in order to carry on the new building and clear the debt.[4] During the five years up to 31 March 1694 covered by the first two declared accounts, £52,108 was issued for building at Hampton Court Palace, but the total expenditure amounted to £114,660. Queen Mary's death late in 1694 halted work, so that the third account, closed on 31 March 1696, showed an expenditure of only £17,015 and a slight reduction of the arrears to £54,093 (a sum which included over £4000 spent at Hounslow and Richmond Old Lodge).[5]

The detailed monthly accounts survive up to March 1692, so that the progress of building can be closely followed only as far as that. Foundations for the south-east pavilion and the centre of the park front were completed in April 1690, and by August, Emmett, Clarke and Hill had worked up the ground storey. The park front did not reach its full height before October 1691, and in November 1691 Hill was paid for setting the cornice and balustrade on the south-east pavilion and the centre of the park front. In August 1691 demolitions were started to make way for the north range of the new Quadrangle Court and in September foundations were laid there.

The first of the circular windows, prepared for carving, were set in the Quadrangle Court between February and April 1691, and the first of several payments

[1] See p. 34.
[2] *Cal. Treas. Books* ix, p. 1226.
[3] Works 5/55, payments to Clarke in May and to Hill in June 1690. Attention should however be drawn to a payment in Oct. 1690 of £100 for taking down and rebuilding 88 rods of brickwork in some unspecified part of the building.
[4] Works 6/2, f. 20ᵛ. Undated entry, placed in the volume under the year 1691.
[5] AO 1/2482/294, 296, 297.

to William Emmett for carving the lion skins on them, at the rate of £20 per window, was made the following July. The same month Hill was paid for setting and preparing the 'blank round windows' in the south wall of the Quadrangle Court. In the second declared account, for 1691–4, payment to Laguerre is recorded for painting these to represent the twelve Labours of Hercules, paintings which can still in their present faded condition just be descried. Laguerre's bill amounted to £86, for these and eight other windows, four representing the Seasons and four painted in imitation of glass, presumably the eight dummy bullseyes in the centre of the privy-garden front.[1]

The major route of access to the new state apartments had to lead to the foot of the king's great stairs. The staircase pavilion was formed out of pre-existing Tudor structures. Work began here in October 1690, when an old buttress of brickwork was removed from the great staircase and the timber truss for the halfpace was inserted. At the same time rubbish from the new buildings was used to fill up the moat on the west side where the colonnade was to be sited. Payment was made to Maurice Emmett, the Master Bricklayer, in November 1690 for 'cutting way through severall Walls in the old Building into Fountaine Court for the new Cloyster'. A delay now ensued, for in December James Groves, the carpenter, was paid for taking down the roof, half-pace and steps of the great stairs, and in February 1690/1 for shoring the west wall and roof there. In March the old west wall was taken down, and in April Emmett was paid for 'cutting downe the old Walls att the great Stair-case that the new wall may have Roome to splay and not to hang on the old wall'. Thereafter work went quickly ahead: in July William Emmett received £4 10s. for carving the keystones of the three round-headed windows of the staircase, and in October the Master Bricklayer's bill includes the item: 'the back-wall of the Cloyster in the Fountaine [i.e. Clock] Court'.[2]

By this time however attention had been diverted to the other major entrance into the state apartments, by the south-east corner of the great hall, where in April 1691 a new passage was cut through the Tudor east range of the middle court into the new court. The great entrance doorway of Portland stone in axis with the two outer gateways was erected by John Clarke later in the year.[3] This doorway was swept away by Kent's remodelling in the 1730s, but its position is known from Kip's bird's-eye view of the palace (Pl. 10), and from a set of drawings by Hawksmoor of this range. The surviving design for the doorway is also drawn by Hawksmoor, who, besides being Clerk of the Works at Kensington throughout this period, received a daily wage as Mr. Surveyor's Clerk at Hampton Court.[4]

The queen's great stair, to which this entrance way directly led, began to be remodelled early in 1692. In January Emmett was paid for 'makeing a Scaffold in Feasant Court in order to reforme two Windows to the great Staires to goe up to the Queens Guard Chamber'.[5]

At this point the monthly accounts break off without recording the construction of the Ionic colonnade across the south end of what is now Clock Court, Wren's

[1] Works 5/55; AO 1/2482/296; Law, *op. cit.*, iii, p. 49.      [2] Works 5/55.
[3] Works 5/55, Clarke's bill, daywork item, and Emmett's bill April 1691; Clarke's bill Nov. 1691.
[4] *Wren Soc.* vii, pl. 25 and iv, pl. 22.
[5] Works 5/55.

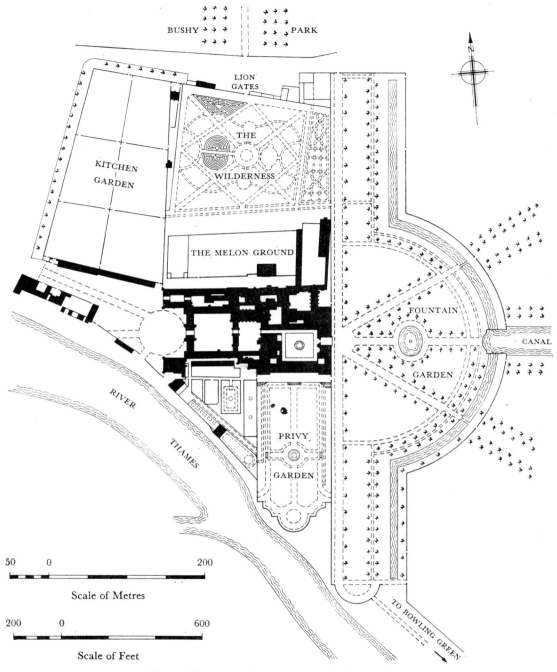

Fig. 4. Hampton Court: general plan of the palace

BUSHY PARK

LION GATES

THE WILDERNESS

KITCHEN GARDEN

THE MELON GROUND

RIVER THAMES

FOUNTAIN GARDEN

CANAL

PRIVY GARDEN

N

TO BOWLING GREEN

50 0 200
Scale of Metres

200 0 600
Scale of Feet

ingenious way of giving a grand frontispiece to an entrance in a corner. The declared account for 1691–4 however records payment to Caius Gabriel Cibber for the pair of carved stone crests over the centre of the colonnade.[1]

The internal fitting out of the state apartments had just begun by March 1692, when the monthly accounts terminate. The single payment to Alexander Fort, the Master Joiner, for work in the new building, was made in May 1691: for 'Shasses in 12 Windowes . . . in the kings Gallery' he received £85 8s., and for the wainscot shutters there £72; otherwise his work was confined to the wainscot and windows of the attic storey.[2]

A year later, in March 1693, the Office of Works submitted an estimate for 'the remainder of the Buildings to complete the new Quadrangle at Hampton Court'. It amounted to £35,315.[3] It is possible to deduce, particularly from the small bricklayers' estimate (£920), that work was by that time already well advanced on the north and west ranges of the court, although masons' work on the former was estimated at £2400 and on the latter at £1200. The estimate for the interior, which included the entire glazing, came to £20,100, with additional sums of £3225 for paving the quadrangle, passages and cloisters with marble, £460 for carving the great pediment and £300 for the iron gates in the vestibule.

By the end of 1694 the finishing touches had been put to the exterior of the south and east ranges. Cibber for instance had by March not only set up the coats of arms on the colonnade, as mentioned above, but had supplied metal figures, probably the four statues to crown the centre of the privy garden front.[4] Then he moved to the park front, and executed the pediment sculpture of the triumph of Hercules over Envy, receiving a round £400 for 'insculpting the Relieve on the Timpan of the great ffrontispeece, with Iconologicall ffigures, and for severall Journies of himself and men to look after the performance'. During the same period Jean Tijou supplied the three iron gates for the vestibule of the park front.[5]

Tijou's bill, which came to £1153 12s. 6d., also included 'Iron Rail to the King and Queens Back-Stairs, the Kings Privy Stairs, the Princess's, Lord Portland's and severall other Stairs in the said Buildings'. How much of the internal fitting of the new ranges had been completed by the time of the queen's death? In May 1693 the marble chimneypieces designed by John Webb for Greenwich in 1669, but never set up there, were removed for use at Hampton Court.[6] Whether they were set up this time is not clear; but the marble altarpiece from James II's chapel at Whitehall, dismantled and transported by Gibbons to Hampton Court in 1695, languished in the stores until 1706, when it found a new home in Westminster Abbey.[7] The main effort of the period however must have been to complete the queen's apartment, both the state rooms and the privy suite. This can be deduced

[1] AO 1/2482/296; Works 5/145.  [2] Works 5/55.
[3] Works 6/2, f. 34. The estimate can be dated only by its position in the volume.
[4] For the coats of arms and for 'severall Statues and ffigures in Mettall . . .' Cibber received £530 (AO 1/2482/296). The statues were removed in 1829. It is probable that one was a figure of Victory and another of Fame (see E 351/3315, payment to Richard Osgood in the house account for 1710 for repairs). Celia Fiennes (*op. cit.*, p. 356), however, identifies the figures as Hercules, Jupiter, Mars and Neptune. She also thought that they were of stone. They may have been painted stone colour.
[5] AO 1/2482/297, declared account for April 1694–March 1696, printed in *Wren Soc.* iv, p. 28.
[6] Works 5/45, Greenwich account for June 1693.
[7] AO 1/2482/297 and *Cal. Treas. Books* xx, p. 583.

from the enormous sum received for wainscoting by Alexander Fort, the Master Joiner, £9406 10s. 3¼d. in all. For carving William Emmett received £918 3s. 5d. and Grinling Gibbons £1265 3s. 4d.[1]

After Mary's death the king decided to shut the palace up and divert his limited funds to improving Kensington. Thus a number of designs remained on paper. There survives in the Soane Museum a series of drawings, probably in Grinling Gibbons's hand, for bravura wood-carving on doorcases, friezes and in particular chimneypieces in both the royal suites. In the same collection are two alternative designs for decorating the queen's closet in the south-east corner of the *piano nobile* with carving and flower-paintings and landscapes in brilliant hues on the wainscot.[2] In September 1694 a design was made for a bridge and steps leading out of this room down to the Privy Garden.[3]

For over four years after the queen's death nothing but maintenance work was done at Hampton Court. Money was regularly ordered however to pay off the debt, which had by Christmas 1697 been reduced to a little over £7000.[4]

In 1697 the Treasury thought of moving to Hampton Court for the summer. Charles Montagu, created First Lord of the Treasury on 1 May, was allotted the lodgings previously occupied by the Earl of Portland, and John Smith, another of the treasury lords, was given Marriott's, the housekeeper's.[5] Small payments for items in these lodgings, e.g. for wainscot, occur in the monthly accounts, but as Luttrell reported in late May, the scheme was soon abandoned.[6]

During the same year 1697–8 (the only one in this interim period for which the detailed accounts survive), a modest beginning was made towards taking the royal apartments in hand again. In July scaffolding was erected for the plasterers and painters in the king's great staircase, and in December the queen's great staircase was similarly prepared so that the carpenters could begin their work there. The Raphael cartoons were even set in place in the king's gallery: they are first mentioned under May, and in November carpenters and labourers were paid for 'helping Mr. Norris to hang up the 7 Cartoons in the Kings Gallery'.[7] Marble chimneypieces were installed at this time in the king's guard chamber and privy chamber, and the floor boards for the state rooms were prepared but not laid.[8]

In April 1699 the king decided to push on once more with the completion of the palace, and first of all to have his own state apartment fitted up. So William Talman, the Comptroller, gained his greatest opportunity. Wren, as Surveyor, presented the first estimate, dated 28 April, for 'fitting the Inside of the Roomes of State at Hampton Court, from the entrance out of the Portico to the roomes already finished above stairs, Containing the Great staires, the Guard-Chamber, the Presence-Chamber, Privy-Chamber, Drawing roome, Anteroome, Great Bedchamber

---

[1] AO 1/2482/296 and 297. Fort's total includes £268 9s. 8½d. for work executed in the Thames Gallery in May 1691 (Works 5/55).
[2] All these drawings (except one overmantel design) are reproduced in *Wren Soc.* iv, pls. 27–46.
[3] Soane Museum. Reproduced in *Wren Soc.* iv, pls. 21 and 22.
[4] Works 6/2, f. 100r.     [5] Luttrell, *Brief Histor. Relat.* iv, p. 220.
[6] Works 5/49; Luttrell *op. cit.* iv, p. 228.
[7] Works 5/49. John Norris held the post of Joiner to the Privy Chamber (P.R.O.L.C. 5/165, p. 15).
[8] Works 5/50, see under 'A Booke of the Estimate of the Workes in the Kings new Apartment att Hampton Court. December 15th, 1699', which is the complete account for the work done under Talman's first estimate.

Lobby & Gallery for the pictures'. Wren reported that the cost of this based on designs prepared in 1694 (for 'the Insides of these Roomes have been long since designed') would be £6800. Wren also pointed out that lodgings for members of the court and installation of services would be needed before the king could use his palace.[1] When however on 12 May the Treasury Board discussed the matter, it was not Wren's, but Talman's estimate of £5500 for completing all these rooms except the bedchamber and lobby, which was laid before them; and the Chancellor of the Exchequer announced that the king had 'appointed Mr. Talman to have the care and overseeing of this work'. Talman's request for issues of £200 per week was granted.[2]

By June four hundred men were reported to be at work, attempting to complete the royal suite before the king returned from Holland at the end of August. That proved impossible, but on 12 September Talman wrote to William Blathwayt: 'The 5 Roomes are almost finished, the great stone staires is done and the ironwork put up, the Gallery for the Cartoones of Raphell is so forward that I shall fix up the pictures in a week; the Kings Great Bed chamber and two Clossetts are in hand that his Majestie will find I have made use of my time, for it proves a greater work than I expected, and I hope it will be to his Majestie's satisfaction.'[3] Before the year was out Talman had successfully concluded his assignment. His account for the gallery and first five state rooms amounted to £5240 11s. 11d.[4]

The pre-existing designs for the state apartments seem not to have been followed in detail. The carving as executed does not correspond with any of the surviving Gibbons drawings for overmantels, doorcases and friezes, and is in general less ornate than those designs. Gibbons executed all the wainscot enrichments and attached carving over doors and windows, in the guard-chamber (£39), privy chamber (£102), ante room (£100), drawing room (£99) and cartoon gallery (£572, including £150 for the twenty-five Corinthian capitals); in the presence chamber however he executed only the festoons over the two doors (£28), and John Le-Sage received £70 for the rest of the carving in that room.

Wren's estimate had envisaged the wrought-iron balustrade for the king's great staircase, executed by Tijou for £265; and the decoration of the guard-chamber with 'Armes as at Windsor and other Houses'. But Talman omitted the especially elaborate decoration of the drawing-room ('as having the best Furniture') and the marble overmantel for the presence chamber. For the gallery Wren had intended a similar 'Marble Chimney', and here John Nost carved and set up a polychrome piece, of purple, black and white marble, with gilt-brass attachments, the 'Triumph of Love' carved in relief on the lintel, costing £235.

Talman succeeded in removing from the Household Locksmith, Richard Greenway, the contract to supply the door furniture in the king's apartment, and gave it to Josiah Key, the Master Smith, who was paid for the locks throughout the king's apartment.[5] Presumably Talman was also responsible for effecting a change in joiners. Alexander Fort, the Master Joiner, who had been so heavily employed

[1] T 1/60/78, printed in *Wren Soc.* iv, pp. 58–9.
[2] *Cal. Treas. Books* xiv, p. 80.
[3] B.M., Add. MS. 20101, f. 69, printed in *Wren Soc.* iv, pp. 59–60.     [4] Works 5/50.
[5] See Talman's letter to Blathwayt, *Wren Soc.* iv, p. 60.

in earlier years, received from this time onwards only minor contracts. Charles Hopson, who combined his craft as joiner with purveying on a large scale, now gained all the big jobs, beginning with work worth £2695 in this first instalment of the state rooms.

By autumn, as Talman's letter to Blathwayt shows, the inner rooms of the king's state apartment were being fitted up. The bills for these, the king's great and little bedchambers, first and second closet and lobby, were made up and entered under the date 24 January 1699/1700, and amounted to £1846 in all.[1]

These rooms must have been already partly fitted, for Hopson's bill for joinery amounted to only £457, and includes payment for altering the wainscot in the great and little bedchambers, while Gibbons received only £214, a sum which did not include payment for the rich limewood frieze, the most remarkable feature of the great bedchamber, which must therefore have been supplied by 1694. A major loss to the great bedchamber as now completed is Nost's chimneypiece, costing £275, moved (except for the purple marble chimney surround) to the queen's gallery in 1701.[2] The 'Pannell of Glass 13 ft long with a Glass in it of 52 inches with a Crown and Cypher in Glass and other ornaments', for which Gerrard Johnson charged £200, remains, occupying the wall-space between the two windows. Johnson supplied glasses for the little bedchamber, at £50 for the panel, and £10 for the glass over the chimneypiece, and the tripartite glasses in the closets at £12 each.

No time was lost in making rooms habitable for the chief members of the court. During the second half of 1699 the Earl of Albemarle's lodgings were fitted up at a total cost of £765. They were situated in the southern part of the park front, above the queen's apartment, and linked to the king's bedroom and closets by a staircase.[3]

On 14 November 1699 Talman was ordered by the Treasury to prepare an estimate for the remaining works needed to make the palace usable by the king. A fortnight later the estimate was ready. It came to £5514 3s. 1d. The king was by now in such a hurry that the other Chief Officers of the Works, Wren, Oliver and Bankes, had less than twenty-four hours in which to scrutinise it. Nevertheless they suggested economies which would reduce the total by £606 18s.[4] Economies in his own apartments the king would not accept, but he agreed to all the reductions suggested elsewhere.[5] Yet it seems that Talman had the last word, for although it

[1] Works 5/50.
[2] Described in the account as follows: 'a purple marble Chimney peice, foot pace and slipps of the same, a border of Dove Colour marble and pillaster on each side with a freeze and two scrowles and a pannell between and over them, and a pedastall all of the same marble with a Venus head upon the said pedastall cutt in white marble, two doves underneath the said head cutt in the same marble, a looking Glass frame over the said Chimney of Black marble, two laurell Branches under the same guilded in water Colour being cast in brass, a Cupid sitting on each side of the said scrowle with festoons cutt in white marble over the said boys'. The king seems to have rejected this chimneypiece for his bedchamber at once, for in Jan. 1699/1700 carpenters were paid for 'makeing 5 ruff boxes to put up the Chimney Peice and Ornaments taken down in the King's great bed Chamber'.
[3] Works 5/50, Dec. 1699. The position of the lodging is fixed by a reference under April 1700 (Works 5/51, carpenters' day bill) to 'my Lord Albemarle' lodgings over the Queens gallery'.
[4] T 1/65/1; *Cal. Treas. Books* xv, p. 227.
[5] The king at first accepted that the cornice of the Communication Gallery should be plain, not carved; but Hopson's bill for Jan. 1699/1700 (Works 5/50) shows that he changed his mind. The sum involved was only £37.

was agreed that the old mullioned windows in Lord Overkirk's lodgings should be left, sashes in accordance with the original estimate had been inserted there by March 1700[1]. By midsummer all the items on the estimate had been dealt with. Most important, the king's routes of access were completed. The Communication Gallery, the 'Eating Room at the End of it' and the king's backstairs were finished off, as were lobbies by the old council chamber and the chapel closet. The way through from the gallery of the queen's great staircase was also completed 'that the King may goe to Chappell', and in March 1700 Joseph Jolly received £436 for paving, mostly in the outer Green Court, 'part of which must be done that the King's Coach may come well into the ffountaine Court', i.e. into the middle court to land him at the colonnaded portico.[2] Finishing touches were also put to the new Quadrangle Court at this time. Wise made gravel paths and borders, laid turf and planted it up with evergreen shrubs trimmed into spheres and pyramids. A brass figure of Diana repaired by Osgood was erected in the court, on a Portland stone pedestal 4 feet high and 3 feet square.[3]

Fitting up several important lodgings for members of the court made up the bulk of the rest of the estimate. They were the Lord Chancellor's and the Secretary of State, the Earl of Jersey's, in the new buildings, and in the Tudor part of the palace lodgings for the Lord President, for the Archbishop of Canterbury, for the Master of the Horse, Lord Overkirk, and for Mr. Van Hull, the last two identifiable as being in the south range of the Green Court. A further series of lodgings was also fitted up in the rooms above the as yet unfinished queen's guard chamber, presence chamber, etc., one of which had by July 1700 been assigned to Lord Overkirk's son, the Earl of Grantham.

After January 1699/1700 the work done under Talman's November estimate was not kept separate in the accounts; but a summary of 16 February makes the financial position clear: £6500 had by then been paid towards the works carried out the previous year, leaving £1352 outstanding, plus the £4800 of Talman's reduced estimate.[4]

On 7 May 1700 a new estimate was submitted, on a warrant of the Duke of Shrewsbury, the Lord Chamberlain, for £3550.[5] The major item (£976) was 'To finish the Court before the Guardhouse', i.e. the outer court, and £240 was estimated to build the three-bay sutlery which links the two guardhouses. For the repair of the Tennis Court, ordered by the king in January, and estimated by Horatio Moore, Master of His Majesty's Tennis Courts, at £365, £300 was set aside.[6] For the king himself cellars, sideboard and confectionery were to be fitted up, and £224 was

---

[1] Works 5/50, James Groves's daybill, March 1700.

[2] The quotations in this paragraph are from Talman's estimate, T 1/65, ff. 3–6.

[3] The pedestal is mentioned in the garden estimate of 19 December 1699 (T 1/67/12). For payments see Works 5/51, garden account. Nost received £5 more than the £20 estimated for the pedestal 'for the Diana to stand on being made larger half a foot every way than was Estimated'. See C. Fiennes, *op. cit.*, p. 354 for the topiary.

[4] T 1/67/38, copied in Works 6/2, ff. 104/5, and printed in *Wren Soc.* iv, p. 61.

[5] T 1/68/47, copied in Works 6/2, ff. 112v.–16.

[6] See Works 6/2, f. 103 for Moore's report of 19 January 1699/1700. He advocated a stone floor 'without which no Ball can give a true bound', and that the tennis court lodgings should also be repaired, for an extra £160. The officers of the Works reported to the Treasury the king's verbal direction, that only £200 should be spent, and that the floor should be of brick. In May 1700 however Thomas Hill was paid £62 for laying 1070 feet of Ketton stone in the Tennis Court (Works 5/51).

earmarked to fit up his winter closet with a room over it for the clerk of the closet. Expenditure on lodgings was also included, in particular for the Lord Steward and Secretary Vernon.

The execution of some of this work can be traced in the works accounts for 1700; but it was during May of that year that for the first time the king, with the white staff officers, was in residence in the new apartments at Hampton Court.[1] The visit engendered further work, to embellish and enlarge the king's apartment and improve the view from it. Improving the view entailed razing the Thames Gallery. To replace it, a new, much smaller, waterside banqueting house was created out of a Tudor garden-tower, and a new pavilion begun beside the new bowling green at the far east end of the newly formed Thames-side terrace. This latter building perhaps represents a drastic reduction of a much more ambitious proposal which never got beyond the paper stage. This was for a Trianon, a substantial house of retirement in the French manner, a mile and a half away across the Thames at Ditton. Numerous drawings for the Trianon survive, by both William Talman and his son John, culminating in a set of presentation designs now in the R.I.B.A. collection.[2]

On 16 July Ranelagh, newly appointed by the king 'Sur-intendent generall of our Buildings and of our Works in our parks', sent to Wren and the officers of the works a 'Draught of a building to be Erected at the End of the new Terras Walk', which, he said, had received the king's approval before he left Hampton Court. He requested an estimate for its construction, allowing for the re-use of materials from the Thames Gallery.[3] This 'draught' is presumably represented by a set of drawings in the Soane Museum for a one-storey pavilion with a transparent Tuscan portico in the centre, between a great room and an apartment, all surmounted by a martial relief on a panel between the ends of a big open pediment.[4] By late September the foundations for the pavilion were laid, using old bricks, although 'not intended to be carryed higher then the Levell of the Terras this yeare'.[5] The laying of the foundations of the pavilion, and their protection with straw for the winter, can be followed in the works accounts until December 1700.[6] But by spring 1701 the plan had been changed, for in April Richard Stacey, the Master Bricklayer,

[1] Luttrell (*Brief Histor. Relat.* iv, p. 636) reports that the king intended to leave London on 19 April and remain at Hampton Court for a month or six weeks.

[2] R.I.B.A. Drawings Collection B 4/1. The drawings have been analysed by J. Harris in *Journal of the Warburg and Courtauld Institutes*, 23 (1960), pp. 139–49. It has been suggested that the Trianon scheme should be dated to the early months of 1699 (by M. Whinney, *ibid.* 18 (1955), p. 128); but this is not supported by the evidence cited, correspondence between the Earl of Portland and Matthew Prior, the secretary to the British embassy in Paris, in which mention is made of 'the design which His Majesty is now forming'. Prior had been in negotiation with J. H. Mansart on Portland's behalf for plans of Louis XIV's palaces at Versailles, the Trianon and Marly. In excusing the delay in their delivery Prior writes (1 April 1699): 'As to the plans, he [Villeroy] told me that Mansard is working at them, that the King intended you should have them perfect, and according to the design which His Majesty is now forming.' That the design was Louis' and not William's is made clear by the context and by Portland's reply (9 April 1699): 'Je suis bien aise que les nouveaus desseyns de Marly soyent adjoutés au plans' (Hist. MSS. Comm. *Bath*, iii, pp. 329, 332). A letter from Mansart to Portland apologising for the delay is among the Portland papers in Nottingham University Library (Pw A.843). It is dated at Versailles, 5 April 1699.

[3] Works 6/2, f. 123.

[4] Reproduced in *Wren Soc.* iv, pls. 25 and 26. The hand is not Talman's, but he may nevertheless have been responsible for the design.

[5] Works 6/2, f. 125v.

[6] Works 5/51.

received £250 for the foundation and first storey of 'the 4 pavilions . . . by the Bowling green'.[1]

The four pavilions, each a tiny three-by-two-bay house crowned by a prominent pyramid roof, a chimney stack and six urns, stood two at the near end, two at the far end of the bowling green, linked by the curving walls which enclosed the green (Pl. 15A).[2] Payments in September 1701 were made for fitting the pavilions up, to Thomas Hill for marble chimneypieces, to Josiah Key for locks in two of the houses 'with fine borders chased and water gilded' and to Charles Hopson for joiner's work in 'the great Roome next the Bowling Green'. In October Nost, Richard Osgood and Thomas Highmore were paid for respectively designing and casting the urns and painting them stone colour.[3] Gibbons was paid for work in the 'King's Pavilion', £30 for 100 foot of carved hollow cornice in September and in November and January 1701/2 for glass frames. Final payments, for setting old wainscot and erecting iron railings, were made after the king's death, in March 1702.[4]

Meanwhile, nearer the house, the new pavilion in the Glass Case Garden also reached completion about the time of the king's death. This little building, a slightly irregular rectangle into which are squeezed a great room overlooking the river, a vestibule and two closets, survives unaltered, memorable for Verrio's paintings, allegorical figures of the arts in the ceiling, the loves of Jupiter on the walls of the great room (Pl. 16).

The king's order to demolish the Thames Gallery was transmitted to the Officers of the Works on 30 July 1700. Payments for the demolition were made in August and September. Glass, china, chimneypieces, joinery and carving were all boxed up and stored for re-use.[5] For bricks and stones new uses were at once available, both by the bowling green (as we have seen) and in the new garden pavilion. The Officers of the Works reported on 25 September that 'the little Tower in the glass Case Garden', ordered to be 'augmented, by adding a Room and Clossett' was 'now covering in, and is made for the most part out of materialls taken from the Water Gallery'.[6] In October Richard Stacey, the Master Bricklayer, was paid for the 'Cornish and base in the chimneys', and in November one of the old iron vanes was reset there. In December Charles Hopson installed the window sashes and shutters, Thomas Hill set up three marble chimneypieces 'new polished and cleaned', that is old ones from the Thames Gallery, and the interior was made ready for the painters to begin work.[7] Verrio's bill does not survive, but he was at work in the Glass Case Building during the early months of 1701—payment was made for carrying the elderly artist to and from his work. In May the bill of Peter Cousin

[1] Works 5/52.

[2] A design in Hawksmoor's hand for the bowling green flanked by four domed pavilions, their channelled walls reminiscent of the contemporary service ranges of Castle Howard, is in the collection of Mr. Paul Mellon. It was reproduced in *Illustrated London News* 29 Sept. 1962, p. 489.

[3] Payments relating to the urns only are in the garden account in Works 5/52.

[4] Works 5/52.

[5] Works 6/2, f. 123; payments in Works 5/51, in Aug. to Stephen South and Thomas Hill, and in Oct. to Charles Hopson.                                                                                    [6] Works 6/2, f. 125ᵛ.

[7] Works 5/51. In March 1700/1 the accounts mention the construction of tables and steps for Kneller and Laguerre as well as for Verrio. Laguerre was employed restoring the Mantegna Triumphs of Caesar, and sent in his bill for £360 in March 1701/2 (Works 5/52).

was entered for the copious gilding of the great room, amounting to £79 9s. 2d. Gibbons was paid for the carved cornices and mouldings in the painted room, outward room and closet in September.[1]

At the other end of the Glass Case Garden, the long plain greenhouse was constructed at this time, backing onto the south range of the Green Court. In June 1701 payment was made for '3 windows stopt up in the wall by the new Green-house', and the bill of Richard Stacey, the Master Bricklayer, for brickwork in the 'new Orangery', submitted in August, amounted to £376. In September Charles Hopson's bill for wainscot, sashes and window frames came in.

Within the palace itself a warrant of the Duke of Shrewsbury, the Lord Chamberlain, shortly before his resignation late in June 1700, authorised the completion of twenty more rooms for lodgings, sash windows for Dr. Radcliffe, the king's physician, six rooms for the Board of Greencloth, and for the king himself the East Gallery. By this last item, estimated to cost £629, the king would gain from the queen's apartment a new long gallery, perhaps because his own, the Cartoon Gallery, was now in use as the council chamber.[2] In August 1700 the gallery floor was being boarded, and in October the bills for wainscot there came in, £276 for Hopson, and £122 for Gibbons.[3] At this time Nost's sculptured overmantel made for the king's great bedchamber was removed to the newly finished gallery: in July 1701 the sculptor was paid £30 for a 'Dove Colour marble Chimney Peice in the Queens Gallery' and for 'takeing down a purple marble Chimney Peice in the long Gallery . . . and puting up the Venus'.[4]

In the king's great and little bedchambers Verrio was painting the ceilings in September 1701, the subjects being Diana and Endymion in the former, Mars and Venus in the latter; and by February 1701/2 he had moved on to the king's great staircase. Here the ceiling and walls are devoted to a single theme, that of Julian the Apostate and his satire, *The Caesars*, in which Alexander the Great is preferred to Romulus and all the Caesars. Alexander represents the Protestant William, introduced to the banqueting gods by his patron, Hercules, and the Roman emperors are equated with Roman Catholics. It has also been shown that, according to Whig thinkers such as Locke, Somers and the third Earl of Shaftesbury, Julian was a 'symbol of toleration and freedom', which helps to explain this choice of subject at this particular time.[5]

In the portico leading to the foot of the king's great stairs a doorcase from the demolished Thames Gallery was re-erected in September 1700 (but has since been removed), and in October Gibbons carved the brackets for the three doorways in the back wall of the portico at £1 apiece. At the same time wainscot was put up in the orangery which occupies the centre thirteen bays of the ground floor on the king's side: in October Hopson put in his bill for £407.[6] The three-bay grotto behind the central bays of the orangery remained a design on paper; the rough brick-work of the arched recesses remains exposed to this day.[7] In front of the

[1] Works 5/52.      [2] Works 6/2, f. 121.      [3] Works 5/51.      [4] Works 5/52.
[5] E. Wind in *Journal of the Warburg and Courtauld Institutes*, iii (1939), pp. 127–37.
[6] Works 5/51.
[7] Elevations of the entrance and back wall, with a statue of Neptune striding over the central fountain and basin, are in the Soane Museum (reproduced in *Wren. Soc.* iv, pl. 24). They may well date from *c.* 1694.

orangery Josiah Key erected the iron rail 'with scrowles, pillers, spikes, bottom darts and 2 large scrowles att the ends of the rayle', charging £258, and an extra £2 8s. for 32 spikes to go on a panel by Tijou there.[1]

In the last months of William's reign considerable progress was made on the queen's great stair. The vaulting under the half-paces, the paving and the stone steps, Tijou's iron balustrade, Hopson's wainscot and doorcases, with Gibbons's heraldic carving in the pediments (now lost), were all in place by January 1701/2.[2]

Finally, the Quadrangle Court became the Fountain Court; for among the works under way at the time of the king's death was the 'fountain in the Quadrangle Court', paved with Kentish ashlar and coped with white marble.[3]

The total cost of the works described above, executed between mid-1699 and March 1702, was £43,155 14s. 4¾d. Although monthly issues of £1000 were made from the beginning of 1700, the paper debt on 28 February 1701/2 amounted to £15,702 16s. 4¾d.[4]

## 2. THE GARDENS AND PARK UNDER WILLIAM III

In the gardens and parks over the same period £40,714 13s. 6¼d. was spent, in addition to the £44,000 odd which had been expended on them during the period 1689–94.[5] Great formal gardens, as Le Nôtre had demonstrated at Versailles, were as potent as palaces in creating a splendid ambience for a monarch. William was himself an enthusiastic gardener, and had formed magnificent gardens at both Loo and the Huis ten Bosch. In England he indulged his horticultural ambitions at Hampton Court as nowhere else.[6]

For the earlier period of garden work no detailed accounts survive, merely a single declared account.[7] The major works in these years seem to have been the mighty semi-circular parterre called the Fountain Garden stretching from the terrace in front of the east facade of the palace to the long canal, and the Wilderness on the north side of the palace beyond the melon ground (formerly tilt yard) (Fig. 4). All the works came under the supervision of the Earl of Portland, Surveyor General of His Majesty's Parks and Gardens, whose executants were the two deputy superintendents, William Talman and George London, who were paid annual salaries of

[1] Works 5/52, May 1701.

[2] Works 5/52, bills of Richard Stacey, bricklayer, Aug. and Sept. 1701; Thomas Hill, mason, Sept. 1701; Tijou, for £200, in Oct. 1701; Gibbons, £59 for mouldings in Nov. 1701 and £23 for the 'embossments' in seven pediments, five on the staircase, two in the passage, in Jan. 1701/2; Charles Hopson, joiner, Dec. 1701.

[3] Works 5/52, March 1702, bills of Stacey for £25 17s. 9d. and Jackson for £156 3s. 9d.

[4] Works 5/50–52 for monthly bills; Works 6/2, ff. 119–61 *passim* for monthly statements.

[5] For the earlier period AO 1/2482/298; for the later, monthly totals in Works 5/51 and 5/52 garden accounts.

[6] No complete plan of the gardens created by William III survives, although in March 1702 Thomas Cleer received £50 'for making a large Mapp of the Parke, Canalls ffountaines at Hampton Court by his late Majesty's directions' (Works 5/52 garden account). Two plans of c. 1701 showing the Privy Garden and the small gardens west of it are in the Soane Museum (*Wren Soc.* iv, pls. 2 and 3).

[7] AO 1/2482/298, printed in *Wren Soc.* iv, pp. 29–36. It covers the period 1 May 1689 to 25 March 1696.

£140 and £200 respectively. Evelyn recorded in July 1689 that a beginning had already been made on a 'spacious Garden with fountaines . . . in the Parke, at the head of the Canale'.[1]

The design of the parterre however was provided by Daniel Marot, the French Huguenot decorative designer already employed by the king in Holland both as architect and garden designer.[2] His design survives in two variants, an engraving, and a drawing of the parterre seen in perspective as if from an upper room of the palace, signed and dated August 1689. How much of Marot's design was executed is not clear. None of the fountains was yet constructed, but ironwork, railings, two great ornamental gates and other decorative panels, separating the eastern curve of the garden from the park, were supplied by Jean Tijou for £2160.[3] At the entry to the parterre was set a pair of marble vases on Portland stone pedestals, the work of Edward Pearce and Caius Gabriel Cibber.[4]

For the Privy Garden also important sculptured ornaments were provided at this time. The centrepiece was Pearce's new base, with scrolls, festoons and shells, for Fanelli's fountain figure of Diana. This cost £1262 3s., and a further £121 19s went on Josias Iback's recasting and repair of the original brass shells on the fountain. Pearce also carved a white marble urn decorated with a relief of the Judgement of Paris, and Cibber a matching urn with a relief of Meleager hunting the Calydonian Boar, a spectacular pair, now on the East Terrace at Windsor Castle.[5] The other conspicuous object in the Privy Garden must have been the round domed arbour, erected by the carpenter Edward Wilcox. Built of oak posts and fir 'rails', the arbour cost £449, and was decorated in 1701 by Thomas Highmore, who painted it green and gold, and Louis Laguerre, who for £25 painted inside it '4 Figures and 3 Neeches and 3 heads' and '2 great Figures of Each side of the Arbour with 2 Consoles etc.'[6] This perishable structure was taken down c. 1870, but its appearance survives in a drawing attributed to Thomas Fort, Clerk of the Works at Hampton Court during George I's reign.[7]

In the summer of 1699 the unfinished garden works were resumed. A great new enterprise was also undertaken, the creation of the Bushy Park avenue and the circular basin there four hundred feet across. The avenue, aligned on the great hall, implied a major approach to the palace from the north, as Wren had envisaged in his earliest schemes. Talman's design was ready by September, and before the year was out Henry Wise, who was responsible for all the earth-moving and planting

---

[1] Evelyn, *Diary*, ed. de Beer, iv, p. 645.

[2] Kip's view largely corresponds with Marot's published design for the parterre, as has been pointed out by A. Lane in *The Connoisseur*, vol. 123 (1949), pp. 23–4. For Marot's drawing, in the Boymans Museum, Rotterdam, see *Burlington Magazine*, vol. 92 (1950), p. 234 and fig. 19.

[3] Tijou received this sum for 'ii pair of great Iron Gates, with ii other little Gates on each side thereof, for viii square Pillars of Ornaments, xii pannells for the Circle of the ffountaine Garden at Hampton Court with Ornaments . . . and for x Pilasters between xii Pannells'. These are the panels now facing the Thames at the lower end of the Privy Garden (see below p. 173).

[4] The pedestals are still in situ, the vases were in 1829 removed to the east terrace at Windsor Castle.

[5] In 1701 John Nost transferred the urns from the Privy Garden, setting them up 'att the head of the Canal', whence they were taken in 1829 to the east terrace at Windsor (Works 5/52, garden account, July 1701).

[6] Works 5/52, garden account, Sept. and Oct. 1701.

[7] In a volume of drawings in the Library of the Department of the Environment.

in the gardens and parks, had dug the avenue and basin and planted the lime and horse-chestnut trees, at a cost of £4102.[1]

For the further development of the gardens Talman submitted an estimate in December 1699, for just under £9000.[2] Under it the walls flanking the park front of the palace were completed and the great gravel terrace constructed from the Kingston Road to the Thames. New rectangular borders beside the terrace to north and south of the parterre were dug and planted up with 30,000 odd bulbs, snow-drops, crocuses, narcissi and tulips, as well as polyanthus, irises and ornithogalums.

At this time Benjamin Jackson constructed (for £719 12s. 10½d.) the basin in the centre of the Fountain Garden parterre, coping it with grey marble. Matthew Roberts, the master-plumber, connected up the fountains so that in May 1700 the king could watch 'Experiments of severall jed'eaeu's and jerts of Water'; but nothing was done yet to execute the fountain for Jackson's basin for which John Nost had made a model 'with 4 shells, 4 Dolphins, one Sea-horse and 11 other ffigures', and indeed the basin itself was not finally sealed nor the brasswork fitted until November 1700.[3]

The enclosure of the great terrace and the Fountain Garden was completed during 1700. Tijou supplied iron railings, piers and pedestals for the return walls flanking the circle of the parterre and for the semi-circular wall which terminated the terrace at the Thames. That cost £1315, while the Portland stone gatepiers at the other end of the terrace, beside the road, cost £336 8s. 1d., Jackson working the piers, and Nost the carved panels and the bronze basket-bearing putti on top.[4]

The following year it was the turn of the Privy Garden. With the demolition of the Thames Gallery it became possible to redesign the garden completely. The main problem was to relate the far end of the garden, where the Gallery had stood, to the southern end of the terrace, which had been raised behind a retaining wall to a considerably higher level. Talman first considered forming a wedge-shaped termination and an enclosed triangular garden beyond, backing against the terrace wall, from which a wall-fountain might issue into a basin 70 foot broad.[5] This idea was eventually set aside in favour of the excuted scheme, which partly survives.[6]

In March 1700/1 Charles Hopson, the joiner, was paid for making 'a moddle for the new Glass Case and moddles for the Privy Garden'.[7] Already in February the Diana Fountain and Pearce's base for it were being dismantled.[8] By the end of

---

[1] Talman to Blathwayt, 12 Sept. 1699 (*Wren Soc.* iv, p. 60); sketch design, All Souls iv, 1 (*Wren Soc.* iv, pl. 6). Wise's estimate is in T 1/67/14, f, 107, and his bill in Works 5/51, garden account.

[2] T 1/67/12.

[3] Works 5/51, garden account, bills of craftsmen named and of Robert Aldersey.          [4] *Ibid.*

[5] Plans are All Souls iv, 15 and 16, the former reproduced in *Wren Soc.* iv, pl. 8. The fountain and basin appear only in All Souls iv, 13 and 16, both unpublished.

[6] The final design for the privy garden is shown on *Wren Soc.* iv, pl. 2.

[7] Works 5/51, house account.

[8] Works 5/51, garden account. In February Josiah Key was paid for 'fileing and cutting the Revetts for the takeing down the brass figures from the fountain in the Privy Garden'; in March Stephen South's bill included the cartage of '35 load of marble, nymphs, dolphins and shells from the fountain in the Privy Garden to the Carpenters yard by the ship'. It is possible that the Diana from the Privy Garden now took the place of the Diana already set up in the Quadrangle Court, for in this latter account labourers are paid for 'helping the mason and Carver to put up the Golden figure in the Quadrangle Court', and carpenters for 'setting up a paire of sheres to raise the figure of Diana and helping to raise the same'. In July 1701 however John Nost was paid for 'taking down the Diana in the Green Court and setting up the great Diana in the same place'. It seems therefore that there may have been three statues of Diana at Hampton Court during this period.

April Wise had excavated the garden, 'begining by the fountaine there and Sunk to 8 foot perpendicular from the last Levell Sunk'. The basin of the fountain survived until September, when it was filled in. In the summer of 1701 Wise continued his work, levelling the ground at the palace end of the garden, gravelling, turfing, laying down 'a Coat of good Earth upon the Naturall gravell', and planting the beds up with bulbs and with round-headed and pyramid hollies and yews.[1] At the water's edge Stacey completed the 'foundation of the circular walls att the end of the Privy Garden for the great iron to stand on', and the following month the twelve sumptuous panels made by Tijou *c.* 1693 for the circle of the parterre were transported from his shop and unloaded for erection at this new site.[2] At the beginning of 1702 a statue of Apollo was set up, on a pedestal by Nost, in the circular grassplot in front of the ironwork.[3] This was among the seven Italian marble statues supplied for the Privy Garden by Robert Ball, merchant of Turnham Green, shortly before the king's death and never paid for. In June 1703 Ball petitioned for the £600 due to him. The Treasury proposed to return the statues, but the matter had still not been cleared up by July 1711.[4]

During 1701 Nost and Richard Osgood, the figure caster, were busy mending statues, some of them collected from Windsor, Whitehall and St. James's Park, and in setting them up in various places about the gardens. Nost supplied pedestals for sundials, a pair in black marble, and two metal sundials, one in the form of a blackamoor, the other an Indian slave. The Fountain Garden received the two marble vases from the Privy Garden, and at least four statues; and Benjamin Jackson constructed four more fountains there.[5] For the central fountain new ideas were mooted. Nost cast two metal models for fountains, one to re-use the base of the Diana Fountain, the other having 'four figures of young men, each sitting on a Dolphin, and 4 Swans between them, a Pedastall of four Scrowles in the middle, and a Mercury on the top of it'. He also received £20 for 'severall drawings of the kings statue for the marble fountain'.[6]

In 1701, when William's great schemes were nearing completion, appropriate gateways were set in hand. The north terrace gate, already erected, was not intended for everyday use, and the main entrance continued to be from the west, up to the Tudor west front of the palace. On the gatepiers here the lion and unicorn were erected in July and the trophies of armour on either side in November. John Oliver, the Master Mason, received £115 for 'imbossing and casting the imperiall

---

[1] Works 5/52, garden account, Wise's garden accounts and South's bill, Sept. 1701.

[2] Works 5/52, garden account, Stacey's bill in April 1701 and South's in May for transporting '6 large Pannells of wrought iron from Tijou's shop on the Green to the Privy Garden' and '6 lesser Pannells from the same place'. Tijou's *Nouveau Libre de Desseins*, 1693, pl. 20, illustrates two of the panels in question. Attention should also be drawn to the payment made in 1700 to Thomas Highmore for 'painting all the rich Iron Work that was made for the Circle of the Fountaine garden before the front of the house, it containing 12 large pannells and pilasters' (Works 5/51, garden account).

[3] Works 5/52, Nost's bill in Feb. 1701/2; see also *Cal. Treas. Books* xvii, p. 130.

[4] T 1/86/76; Works 6/3, f. 7.

[5] Works 5/52, garden account *passim.* Jackson's bill for £622, is under Jan. 1701/2. Nost's marble sundials cost £45 apiece, his metal ones £30 and £35. The layout of the Fountain Garden during the period 1702–7 is recorded in Wise's plan, reproduced in D. Green, *Gardener to Queen Anne* (1956), pl. 21.

[6] See J. Physick, *Designs for English Sculpture 1680–1860* (1969), figs. 30 and 31, for drawings by Nost representing these ideas and variations on them. Nost's bill is in Works 5/52, garden account, Aug. 1701.

supporters the Lyon and Unicorn in Hard Metall . . . and two imperiall sheilds', and, after his death in November, his widow was paid a further £130 for the trophies.[1]

## 3. WORKS FOR QUEEN ANNE

Queen Anne regularly held councils at Hampton Court in the early years of her reign, and towards the end of it carried out a thorough modernisation of the chapel; nevertheless her reign marks a drastic drop in the level of expenditure there. At her accession Verrio was in full swing painting the king's great staircase. The queen allowed him to complete this, and then commissioned him to paint the walls and ceiling of the central room of the east front, which she was having fitted up as her Drawing Room. By December 1703 he was at work there, and for this garish and ungainly production, allegorising Britain's naval power while Anne occupied the throne and Prince George held the baton of Lord High Admiral, he was paid the huge sum of £1660.[2] But when Verrio, on completing the Drawing Room early in 1705, made so bold as to ask the queen for further tasks she turned him aside by saying that 'there was no haste of any more painting', and he had to be content with a pension of £200 per annum.[3]

In the gardens there was retrenchment. During the year following William's death a mere £380 was spent on them.[4] In 1703 the statues supplied for the late king were ordered to be returned to their vendor, as has been mentioned above. A proposal for sinking, new making and altering the Fountain Garden was rejected in August 1703 as too expensive.[5] In 1707 all the plumbing for the fountains, except in the Privy Garden, was removed and re-used in Bushy Park and four of the fountains themselves were dismantled.[6]

Towards the end of Anne's reign this trend was reversed. In 1710 an estimate for £873 10s. was passed for improving the head of water to the gardens, so that the *jets d'eau* would rise 8 feet higher.[7] The following winter Henry Wise dug the unfinished canals which enclose the east end of the Fountain Garden and put in order twenty miles of chaise rides through the parks, at a cost of £1004.[8] In March 1711 the Lord Chamberlain, the Duke of Shrewsbury, ordered Wren to reset Tijou's ironwork on the near side of the newly dug canals.[9]

Inside the palace the queen commissioned one major undertaking, the redecoration of the chapel. On 31 January 1710/11 the Lord Chamberlain authorised Wren and the other Officers of the Works 'to Give Orders for fitting up Her Majesty's

[1] Works 5/52, house account Aug. and Nov. 1701, also mason's bill in July and James Groves's daybill in November.
[2] *Cal. Treas. Books* xix, pp. 369, 495.
[3] *Cal. Treas. Books* xx, p. 18. It is doubtful whether Queen Anne ever used this Withdrawing Room, for Celia Fiennes, who visited the palace *c.* 1711, found the state rooms in use in the south range only (*op. cit.* pp. 354–6).
[4] Works 5/53.          [5] *Cal. Treas. Books* xviii, pp. 76, 357.
[6] *Cal. Treas. Books* xxi, pp. 449–50, xxii, pp. 340; Works 6/14, f. 150.
[7] Works 6/5, pp. 52–4.
[8] Works 6/5, pp. 82–6; T 1/126/21 and 21A, which includes a plan of the canals.
[9] Works 6/5, p. 94.

Chappel at Hamton Court with all convenient Speed according to the Design you prepared, and which Her Majesty has been pleased to approve of'. The ensuing estimate was for £2735 9s. 4d. (£1116 being for joiners' and carvers' work), which the Treasury Lords on 7 February sent back to the Lord Chamberlain with a request to lay it before the queen, to ask whether she still wanted these works performed 'notwithstanding the great expense they will amount to'.[1] This warning did not prevent work commencing at once, continuing at speed, and costing £4052 17s. 8¾d., as the declared account for 1711 reveals.[2] The joinery was Hopson's, the carving by Gibbons, and the painting by Thornhill. Thornhill's sketch for the east wall of the chapel survives,[3] but no payment to him is recorded in the Works accounts.

In the same year Gibbons was paid for carving in the queen's dressing room and in 1712 Hopson received over £1200 for wainscot there, in the state room, Lord Chamberlain's and Groom of the Stole's. Thornhill also painted the ceiling of the queen's closet, for £140.[4] The final major work of the reign was the erection of the Diana Fountain in the centre of the great basin in Bushy Park. The account for this, dated March 1713/14, totalled £1300.[5] The Lion Gates, so much more grandiloquent than the west gates, and reinforcing the implication of the Bushy Park avenue that the main approach ought to be from the north, were not completed until George I's reign. Queen Anne's monogram is on the monumental stone piers, and that of her successor appears on the gates themselves, a copy of those at the end of the Fountain Garden and clearly too small for the piers. Among the ironwork finished by Tijou at William III's death but not erected was a pair of gates 18 feet high with a 'finishing Topp' about 6 feet high, valued at £400, gates of a size commensurate with the piers.[6] By March 1713/14, according to the accounts, the gates had not been delivered, so that the present unsatisfactory substitute had to go up in their place.

## 4. THE GEORGES, 1714–1782

George I's known preference for a retired life held out little hope that his reign would see a resumption of major building activity at Hampton Court. The fact that he took up residence there did, however, ensure the maintenance of the palace, and suitable accommodation had also to be provided for the Prince and Princess of Wales and their children. In the absence of a queen, they took over the unfinished apartments in the east wing that had been intended for Queen Mary.[7] The disposition of the rooms is indicated on a contemporary plan preserved at Windsor

[1] Works 6/5, pp. 96–7; *Cal. Treas. Books* xxv, p. 161.
[2] AO 1/2447/145 (E 351/3316).
[3] In the Courtauld Collection. See E. Croft-Murray, *Decorative Painting in England 1537–1837*, i (1962), p. 269.
[4] AO 1/2447/146 (E 351/3317).
[5] Works 6/6, p. 28. For the composition of the fountain see J. Harris, *Burlington Magazine* cxi (1969), pp. 444–7.
[6] Works 5/52, garden account, Tijou's bill under March 1701/2.
[7] See plans of them in *Wren Soc.* iv, pl. x.

(Fig. 5). The princess's Bedroom, Drawing Room and Privy Chamber were the first to be tackled. The ceiling of the Drawing Room had already been decorated by Verrio in the previous reign, but that of the Bedroom was as yet unadorned by painting, and a good deal of joinery remained to be done in all three. During the first nine months of 1715 the three rooms were accordingly made ready for occupation at a cost of £1536, while Thornhill painted the ceiling of the Bedchamber.[1] The Duke of Shrewsbury, as Lord Chamberlain, had intended to employ Sebastiano Ricci, but Halifax, who was then First Lord of the Treasury, urged the claims of Thornhill as a fellow-countryman, and told the duke that 'if Ricci painted it, he would not pay him'.[2] Thornhill accordingly had the commission. The Board of Works, to whom his account was referred, reported in October that the work was 'skilfully and laboriously performed', and advised that '£457 10s. might be allowed him, including all guildings, decorations and history painting, being at the rate of £3 15s. per yard, which price is inferiour to what was always allowed Seignior Vario for works in our opinion not so well executed'.[3] The ceiling is indeed a very competent performance. The subject is Leucothoë restraining Apollo from entering his chariot.[4] In the cove are portraits of George I, the Prince and Princess of Wales, and of their eldest son Frederick, then a boy in his ninth year. Work on the remaining rooms began in the summer of 1716. On 13 July Vanbrugh told the Duchess of Marlborough that on the following day he was 'to attend the Prince to Hampton Court, where he goes to view the House, distribute the lodgings and direct (I believe) all the unfinish'd rooms to be compleated'.[5] On 19 July Hopson the Master Joiner was directed to 'measure and make draughts of the 6 unfinished roomes at Hampton Court, that are intended to be finished on the Prince and Princess's side', and on 15 December the Board received authority from the Treasury 'for finishing six rooms and a little oratory at Hampton Court estimated at £6600'.[6] The six rooms in question appear to have been the Prince's Guard Room and Presence Chamber, the Music Room, and the three smaller rooms in the angle at the northern end of the east wing. The 'little oratory' is a windowless room in the north-east corner of Fountain Court lighted from above by a glazed lantern.[7] Further directions were given to erect a partition across the western end of the Music Room, and to make a doorway in the northern wall of the small room thus formed.[8] This was to provide a means of communication between the princess's apartment and those on the east side of Chapel Court allotted to the young princesses Anne, Emily and Caroline.[9]

[1] T 54/22, p. 369; Works 5/141, 1715; AO 1/2448/149. Drawings for the panelling of the Bedchamber, Privy Chamber and Drawing Room survive among Wren's drawings at All Souls (*Wren Soc.* vii, pl. 26).

[2] H. Walpole, *Anecdotes of Painting*, ed. Dallaway ii (1862), p. 664, n. 2; *Vertue Note Books* (Walpole Soc.) p. 45.

[3] T 1/192, no. 68.

[4] E. Croft-Murray, *Decorative Painting in England* i (1962), p. 269, where the common description of the subject as 'The triumph of Aurora' is corrected. Thornhill's *modello* for the ceiling hangs in Sir John Soane's Museum.

[5] Complete Works of Sir John Vanbrugh, *The Letters*, ed. G. Webb (1928), p. 73.

[6] Works 4/1, 19 July, 15 Dec. 1716.

[7] Though the plasterwork in this room dates from 1716–18, the wooden entablature beneath it appears not to have been added until 1728 (Works 4/3, 28 March, 3 April, 1728).

[8] Works 4/1, 7 Feb., 12 Feb., 6 March, 14 April, 15 May, 16 May, 10 Dec. 1717.

[9] At Windsor there is a contemporary plan showing how these rooms were allotted to the young princesses and their governess, etc. (Portfolio 58). It is reproduced in *Wren Soc.* xix, pl. lxvi.

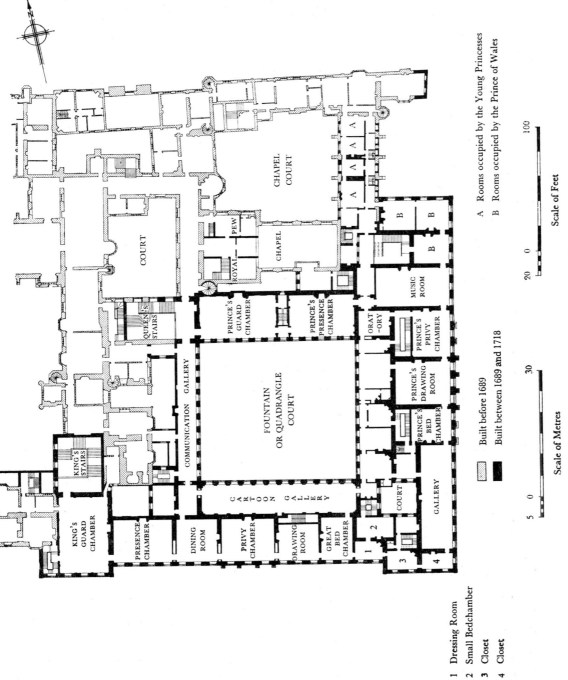

Fig. 5. Hampton Court: the royal apartments in the reign of George I.

These works were completed by 1718, when the Paymaster accounted for an expenditure of £4354 on the Prince of Wales's apartment. The principal craftsmen employed were Benjamin Jackson (mason), Matthew Churchill (bricklayer), John Hopson (joiner) and Grinling Gibbons (carver). The plasterer's work was divided between David Lance, the Master Plasterer, and Robert Wetherilt. The Guard Chamber and Presence Chamber were entrusted to the latter, the Music Room and the three smaller rooms to the former. Gibbons's workmanship may or may not have included the singular chimneypiece in the Guard Chamber in which life-size figures of yeomen of the guard do duty as caryatids, but the chimneypiece in the Music Room is embellished with an achievement of the royal arms for which he was no doubt responsible.[1]

With their boldly modelled ceilings and their massive marble chimneypieces the prince's rooms have a distinctive character that marks them off from the works of the two previous reigns, and indicates the hand of an architect other than Wren. The coved ceiling of the Guard Chamber may be compared with that of the contemporary kitchen at St. James's, but it is the chimneypieces which point most clearly to Vanbrugh as the designer of these early Georgian interiors at Hampton Court. No exact parallel in Vanbrugh's work can, it is true, be cited for the yeomen caryatids of the Guard Chamber, but the chimneypieces in the Prince of Wales's rooms beyond closely resemble chimneypieces at Blenheim, Grimsthorpe and other houses of which Vanbrugh was the architect.[2]

To Vanbrugh must also be ascribed a final attempt to gain acceptance for the project for a grand northern entrance to the palace, which had been in abeyance since William III's death. Instead of the stepped recession of Wren's projected forecourt, he proposed two long arcaded wings stretching out to terminal pavilions in a manner that he was soon to demonstrate in stone at Eastbury, Grimsthorpe and Seaton Delaval (Fig. 6). This plan cannot have been drawn before July 1716, for it shows the alterations to the Prince of Wales's apartments that were not settled until that date, and in all probability it was a by-product of the renewed building activity at the palace in 1717–18. The only other record of it is a poorly-drawn perspective in a volume of drawings thought to have been made by Thomas Fort, Clerk of the Works at the palace from 1714 to 1745.[3] This omits the arcaded cloisters shown on the plan, but appears in other respects to be a tolerably accurate representation of what Vanbrugh must have intended (Pl. 14B).

Though their apartments were not all complete until 1718, the Prince and Princess of Wales had already taken up residence at Hampton Court in the summer of 1716.[4] Both here and at St. James's, their readiness to hold public court emphasised the retirement of George I's daily life, and was a potential source of embarrass-

---

[1] AO 1/2449/152; Works 5/56, Sept. 1718. Gibbons received £533 'for carved work in the Bed Chamber, Angle Room, Presence, Great Presence, Musick Room and Guard Chamber', while Benjamin Jackson was paid £617 'for white and veined marble, Egyptian marble, fire hearths, coving stones and workmanship in the Musick Room &c.'.

[2] Cf. K. Downes, *English Baroque Architecture* (1966), pls. 279–82 and *Architectural Drawings at Elton Hall*, ed. Colvin & Craig (Roxburghe Club, 1964), pl. xliii.

[3] Department of the Environment Library. The plan (Works 34/32) was reproduced by E. Law, *History of Hampton Court* iii (1891), p. 80, but with a misleading inscription attributing it to Wren.

[4] *Diary of Lady Cowper* (1864), p. 121.

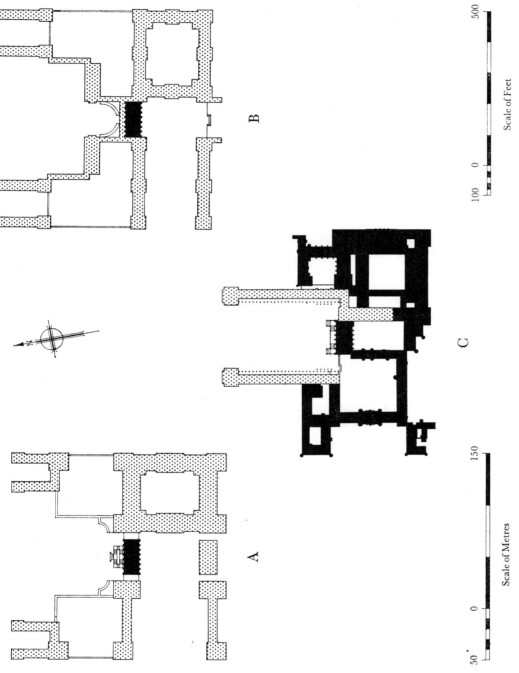

Scale of Feet

Scale of Metres

Fig. 6. Hampton Court. A and B, projects for a new palace by Sir Christopher Wren (based on drawings at All Souls College, Oxford); C, a project attributed to Sir John Vanbrugh *c.* 1718 (P.R.O., Works 34/32). The Great Hall and other existing buildings are shown in solid black.

ment to the government, which saw in the prince's court a rival centre of political influence. When, in 1717, the ministry was threatened by a split within the Whig party, the danger of a new opposition, loyal, not to the king, but to the prince, forced George I to behave in a manner more calculated to make his court the centre of social and political life. In December 1717 a family quarrel resulted in the banishment of the prince and princess from the royal palaces, and during that winter the king maintained a public table at St. James's and held an evening assembly three times a week. When, in August, he moved to Hampton Court, he went so far as to dine in public and to appear every evening at assemblies held either in the Tennis Court or in the Cartoon Gallery. Extra musicians were engaged, and at least twice a week there was a ball in the Music Room so lately fitted up for the benefit of the banished prince. When it was rumoured that the latter was constucting a theatre at Richmond, the king, not to be outdone, ordered a stage to be erected immediately in the Great Hall at Hampton Court. The order was received on 11 September, and the work was carried out in time for seven plays to be performed between 23 September and 25 October.[1] Though never again used except once in 1731, the theatre continued to block up the hall until 1798, when James Wyatt obtained George III's permission to remove it.[2] A plan of it is preserved in the book of drawings attributed to Thomas Fort, the Clerk of Works at the palace.[3] Orders had already been given in April for the Tennis Court to be 'fitted up for a Drawing Room', for an additional 'side kitchen' to be constructed, and for many other minor works such as the provision of a 'Necessary House for Persons of Quality'.[4] These extra works, together with the completion of the Prince of Wales's apartments, brought the total expenditure on building at Hampton Court in 1718 up to £8272.[5] As George I spent the next two summers in Hanover, the expenditure in 1719 and 1720 fell back to normal, and in the latter year a reconciliation between king and prince brought to an end the competition between their respective courts that had led to such unwonted activity in 1718.[6]

After his accession George II regularly resided at Hampton Court during the summer, and considerable sums were spent on the maintenance and improvement of the palace. For some time the range on the east side of Clock Court had been in a more or less ruinous state, and in June 1731 the Treasury authorised the Board to take it down and rebuild it at an estimated cost of £3454.[7] The front to Clock Court was rebuilt in a Tudor Gothic style matching the adjoining parts of the

---

[1] Works 4/1, 11 Sept. 1718, 10 Nov. 1719. The installation of the theatre cost £526 (Works 5/141, 1719). The canvas scenery was painted by Thornhill (AO 1/2449/153) Designs for stage scenery by Thornhill that may have been connected with the Hampton Court Theatre are reproduced by R. Southern, *Changeable Scenery* (1952), pl. 29 and E. de N. Mayhew, *Sketches by Thornhill* (Victoria and Albert Museum, 1967), pl. 1.

[2] D. Lysons, *Account of those parishes in Middlesex which are not described in the Environs of London* (1800), p. 67.

[3] This volume also contains a plan of the Tennis Court (f. 24), and a plan and elevation of an octagonal timber structure of unknown size and purpose, which appears to be the same as 'the Octagon roome, made by His Majesty's directions to the late Surveyor of the Works (Benson), intended to be put up at Hampton Court', which the Board ordered to be sent down there from London on 4 Nov. 1719 (Works 4/1, 4 and 10 Nov. 1719).

[4] Works 6/7, pp. 52–3.                                          [5] Works 5/141, 1718.

[6] For the whole episode, see J. M. Beattie, 'The Court of George I and English Politics 1717–20', *E.H.R.* lxxxi (1966).

[7] Works 4/3, 7 March 1728; Works 4/5, 6 June 1731; T 56/18, p. 396. This part of the palace is coloured brown on a plan (Works 34/43) datable to 1718 in which that colour was intended to denote those portions of the building that were 'ruinous' (Works 4/1, 14 Oct. 1718).

palace, and the former entry leading through to Fountain Court was replaced by a tower gateway complete with semi-octagonal turrets and a Gothic archway. This bears the initials G II R and the date 1732. As usual the minutes of the Board of Works do not throw any light on the authorship of the design, but there can be no doubt that Horace Walpole was correct in ascribing it to William Kent. According to him, Kent at first proposed a classical design, but was 'overruled' by Sir Robert Walpole, then First Lord of the Treasury, who insisted that the new work should be in harmony with the old.[1] This was the first time the Georgian Office of Works was called upon to build in the Gothic style, and the Board was soon confronted with a demand from Andrews Jelfe, the mason, for an extra 5½d. a foot 'for Portland molded work in the Gothic way.'[2] Kent did not venture to vault the entry in stone, but designed a flat plaster ceiling with Gothic mouldings and a quadrant of fan tracery in each corner.[3] The interior of the range, consisting originally of several large rooms, was divided up into smaller rooms 'for the more commodious reception of His Majesty's family'.[4] Three of the first-floor rooms form a suite, and were dignified by elaborately moulded plaster ceilings, one of which was embellished with Gothic pendentives. This suite is traditionally—and no doubt correctly—believed to have been occupied by the Duke of Cumberland.

Beyond the new entry was the Queen's Staircase, leading to the State Apartments on the north side of Fountain Court. This still remained in an unfinished state, and in May 1734 the Board pointed out to the Treasury that it

> was never yet compleatly finished, and the wainscot thereof much out of repair, for which reason we humbly are of opinion that it would be adviseable to take away the wainscot, and embellish the walls and ceiling of the said staircase, which are at present only whitewashed, with ornaments painted on canvas, in chiaro oscuro, the charge whereof, if it be your Lordships' pleasure to have it performed, will amount to the sum of £450.[5]

Their Lordships' approval was received on 14 May, and the accounts show that payment of the £450 was made in 1735.[6] The artist was William Kent, for Vertue noted in that year that 'Mr. Kent finisht a small staircase with ornaments, bass relievos at Hampton Court'.[7] The large framed painting on the west wall of the Arts and Sciences presented to Apollo and Diana is of earlier date, but the decoration of the remaining three walls and that of the ceiling, painted to represent a dome, are Kent's work. George II's initials appear in the angles of the cove.

After the death of Queen Caroline in 1737, Hampton Court ceased to be regularly visited by the king, and no further alterations or embellishments were called for. A project for some new offices, for which designs had been made in March 1737, was evidently abandoned, and on 29 November the Clerk of the Works reported that there were 'no works standing out at Hampton, nor any jobs doing but what

[1] *Anecdotes of Painting*, ed. Dallaway ii (1862), p. 564.
[2] Works 4/5, 9 Jan. 1732/3.
[3] For a detailed description of the gateway see C. L. Eastlake, *A History of the Gothic Revival* (1872), pp. 55–7.
[4] T 56/18, p. 396.          [5] Works 6/16, p. 19.
[6] Works 5/141, 1735.          [7] *Vertue Note Books* (Walpole Soc.) iii, p. 76.

is done by the men on the call'.[1] According to Vertue one of Kent's last projects was 'some alterations at Hampton Court Gallery',[2] but these too came to nothing, and the only work of any importance carried out during the remainder of George II's reign was the restoration of Verrio's paintings on the King's Staircase, undertaken by William Oram and Stephen Wright in 1750–1 at a cost of £590.[3]

George II was the last king to live at Hampton Court. The palace had distasteful associations for George III, and he never took up residence there.[4] In 1770, when a fire in the outbuildings was successfully prevented from spreading to the palace itself, the king told Lord Hertford, who brought the news, 'that he shou'd not have been sorry if it had been burnt down'.[5] The State Apartments were accordingly disused, and most of their furniture was taken elsewhere, while the remainder of the palace was divided up into grace-and-favour residences.[6] The absence of the court did not, however, mean that the buildings were neglected, and throughout the reign between £1000 and £2000 a year were regularly spent on their maintenance by the Office of Works. The gardens were also kept in good order, and in 1769–70 a dining-room was added to the Master-Gardener's house for the benefit of Launcelot Brown.[7] The only major work of the reign was the rebuilding of the main gatehouse at the entrance to the palace. In 1769 the old gatehouse was inspected by the Board and found to be 'in so dangerous a condition . . . that we ordered it to be immediately taken down and the walls to be shored up to prevent any accidents that might happen from their falling'.[8] An estimate for rebuilding the gateway and the adjoining walls was submitted to the Treasury, but in 1770 the Board reported that they had 'found it necessary to alter their design for rebuilding the Tower and walls to the entrance of the Palace (& which will lessen the expense), which design has been shewn to the King by the Comptroller, and his Majesty has been pleased to approve of the same'.[9] The work was carried out in 1770–2 at a cost of £2268, £282 more than the original estimate of £1986.[10] The new gateway, though similar in plan and corresponding in style to the old one, was considerably lower in height, and differed in silhouette. In 1882 the flat ceiling over the entry was replaced by a stone vault, and the squat proportions were improved by carrying octagonal buttresses up on either side of the archway on the outer face.[11]

[1] Works 4/7, 17 March, 29 Nov. 1737.

[2] *Vertue Note Books* (Walpole Soc.) iii, p. 140.

[3] Works 4/10, 5 July, 10 July, 3 Aug. 1750, 11 June 1751. The paintings were again repaired in 1781 at a cost of £400 (Works 4/16, 29 June, 6 July, 10 Aug. 1781; Works 6/20, p. 2).

[4] J. H. Jesse, *Memoirs of the Life & Reign of George III*, i (1867), p. 11.

[5] *Letters & Journals of Lady Mary Coke*, ed. Hume, iii (1892), p. 242.

[6] For a list of their occupants for 1760 onwards, see E. Law, *History of Hampton Court Palace* iii (1891), Appendix G.

[7] Works 6/18, pp. 205–6, 221; Works 4/14, 2 June, 16 June, 1 Sept. 1769. The house is now known as Wilderness House, and the dining-room is the projection on the east side, built of yellow stock brick.

[8] Works 6/18, p. 219.

[9] Works 4/14, 27 July 1770. Works 34/95 is a contemporary plan of the new gateway.

[10] Works 5/142, 1771–2.

[11] E. Law, *History of Hampton Court Palace* iii (1891), pp. 390–1. Lysons (*Middlesex Parishes*) shows the W. side of the gatehouse before alteration.

# KENSINGTON PALACE

THE BUILDING histories of Kensington House and Hampton Court complement one another during the reign of William III. Hampton Court was to be a country palace, Kensington a suburban retreat; Hampton Court was to be expensive and lavish, Kensington utilitarian and cheap. Circumstances which made the one desirable inhibited enjoyment of the other. But at the outset the overriding consideration at both was speed.

William III and his consort both wished to spend as little time as possible at Whitehall, where the king's health and the queen's spirits were affected. As early as February 1689 they were at Hampton Court. But the day-to-day conduct of state and court affairs forced their Majesties to spend considerable periods at Whitehall, so they decided to find a new residence closer to London. In early June therefore the Lords of the Treasury negotiated with the Earl of Nottingham to purchase his house and estate at Kensington, on the western edge of Hyde Park, one of a number of moderate-sized houses standing in small estates which had sprung up close to London in the earlier part of the seventeenth century. For this 'villa', as Evelyn called it, with its beautiful gardens, the king paid £14,000.[1] Narcissus Luttrell, reporting the purchase, asserted that the king 'designs it for his seat in winter, being near Whitehall'.[2]

Nottingham House had been built soon after 1605 as a two-storyed building with attics and a semi-basement. In plan a simple rectangle, it provided about six rooms on each floor. Its most prominent architectural features were shaped gables and a bow window in the centre of each facade.[3]

For royal use such a house needed enlargement. This was immediately put in hand. The main contracts, with Thomas Hughes, the bricklayer, and John Hayward, the carpenter, were agreed on 3 July 1689. In the course of the next seven months £14,000 was issued in instalments by the Treasury to Thomas Lloyd, Paymaster of the Works.[4] As early as 24 December the king and queen moved in, notwithstanding the collapse of part of the new work early in November.[5] To provide extra rooms without sacrificing any in the existing house only one type of addition would preserve a symmetrical appearance, a pavilion at each corner, such as John Webb had suggested in the 1660s for the enlargement of the Queen's House, Greenwich. A new entrance-court and extensive new kitchens were also planned. From the very

[1] Evelyn, *Diary* v, p. 8; Pepys, *Diary*, ed. Wheatley, iv, p. 160; *Cal. Treas. Books* ix, pp. 42, 73. N. Luttrell, *Brief Histor. Relat.* i, p. 549, however states that the purchase price was 18,000 guineas.
[2] Luttrell, *loc. cit.*
[3] The appearance of the house can be reconstructed from John Thorpe's plan (*Walpole Society* xl, p. 43), the late 17th-century engraving by Sutton Nicholls (Pl. 19B) and a plan of the mid-1690s among the Wren drawings (*Wren Soc.* vii, pl. xvii).
[4] Works 5/146; *Cal. Treas. Books* ix, pp. 170 *et seq.*
[5] Luttrell, *Brief Histor. Relat.* i, pp. 602, 618.

detailed Extraordinary account which survives, covering the period from the commencement of work in the last week of June 1689 to March 1694/5 it is possible to trace with a fair degree of accuracy both the original scheme and the successive modifications made to it during the lifetime of Queen Mary.[1]

The new additions were built of stock brick, with the window heads and the stringcourse between the main storeys of rubbed brick. The cornices were executed in deal with simple 'cantilavers'. Sashes were used in the windows of both main floors in the pavilions, and casements elsewhere. Plainness, utility and speed of construction were the primary objects (Pl. 19B).

In plan however the new building was in some ways highly idiosyncratic. Lord Nottingham's house had been entered from the north and south, and its outbuildings extended to the north-west.[2] But now a new approach was made from the west, consisting of a timber *porte cochère* of elongated Doric columns, which survives to the present day, and a covered, stone-flagged passage about 180 feet long, the 'Stone Gallery' running the length of the 'long gallery range' to the south-west pavilion of the house. Between the old service buildings and this new range the Great Court was formed, entered through an archway upon which stood a low brick tower bearing a concave-sided pyramidal roof and a timber, lead-covered cupola with a clock and weathervane. This complete gatehouse structure also survives, a surprisingly unambitious and indeed almost provincial affair (Pl. 20A).

By this arrangement no close view of the house could be had by anyone approaching the state apartments, for the Stone Gallery was entirely enclosed and led directly to the foot of the great staircase in the south-west pavilion. From this point the state apartments commenced. Up three steps from the stair-foot lay the ground-floor chapel. At the head of the staircase, above the chapel, was the guard-chamber, still within the south-west pavilion. The arrangement of rooms within the old house cannot be determined; but the accounts refer to the king's pavilion (south-east) and queen's pavilion (north-west), both containing a bedchamber and two closets on the state floor. In the north-east pavilion the council chamber was situated. There was a single audience chamber, 'theire Majesties presence Chamber', which had 'compasse windowes' and so must have been the great chamber of the Jacobean house. The king had a dining room, the queen a drawing room and an ante-room, the latter certainly in the old house. The Earl of Portland, the king's closest adviser, and the Countess of Derby, the queen's Groom of the Stole, had spacious apartments close to the monarchs whom they served.

As for decorative features, Thomas Hill, the mason, erected two Portland stone entrance doorways on the west side of the house (presumably in the Stone Gallery), with rusticated pilasters and arches with keystones carved with 'huskes and scrowles'. He also put up numerous marble chimneypieces, white, veined or coloured, but none of them particularly expensive, the costliest being for the council chamber, at

---

[1] Works 19/48/1. For a preliminary analysis of this period of the building history, using the Extraordinary account, see G. H. Chettle and P. A. Faulkner in *Jnl. of the British Archaeological Association* 3rd ser. xiv (1951), pp. 1–10.

[2] These were in part at any rate retained. The accounts refer to the 'old long Wing on the North side of the great Cort' and to the 'old chapell building', converted into lodgings for Lord Overkirk (Works 19/48/1, Feb. 1689/90 and Oct. 1689).

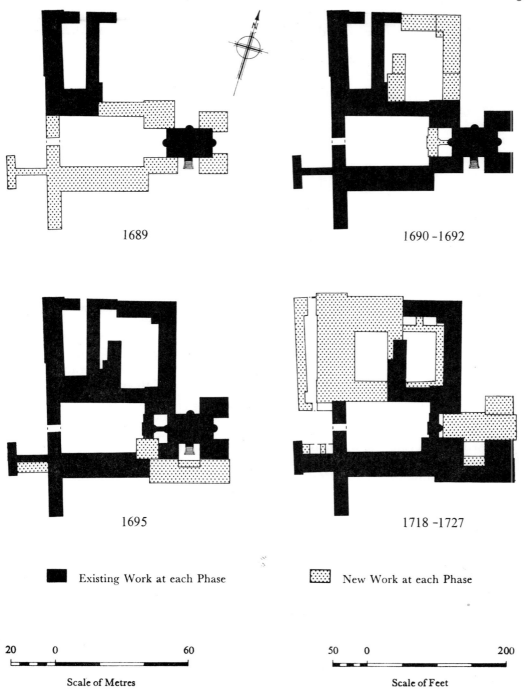

1689

1690 –1692

1695

1718 –1727

■ Existing Work at each Phase

▨ New Work at each Phase

20　0　　　　　　　60
Scale of Metres

50　0　　　　　　　200
Scale of Feet

Fig. 7. Kensington Palace: plans showing the development of the palace.

£14 10s. Jacobean chimneypieces in the old house were cleaned and reset. For the royal apartments cornices, overdoors and chimney-frames were carved by Nicholas Alcock and William Emmett, to a total cost of £206 11s. 2½d. Emmett's work included '6 bracketts with halfe boyes and foliage' in the queen's closet 'for shelves to sett China on'.[1]

The new kitchens were on the north side of the Great Court. They consisted of the 'King's new kitchen', with 'hammer-beame roofing', a window 11 feet 6 inches high and eleven dormers, a hammer-beamed side kitchen, and 'Mr. Lamb's kitchen', fitted with racks for sweetmeats.[2]

On 7 November 1689 Richard Stacey, bricklayer, and Edward Wilcox, carpenter, contracted to erect 'their Majesties guard houses and stables'.[3] These stood apart, comprising a range opposite the main entrance to the Great Court, which was probably for the foot-guards, and stables and quarters for the horse-guards. The latter probably included the thirteen-bay range which still survives at the south end of Palace Green. Garden works, mainly the gravelling of walks, were carried out concurrently, by George London 'by the appointment of the Right Honourable the Earle of Portland Superintendent of their Majesties gardens and plantations'.

When the accounts were closed in April 1690, London's 'outworks' had cost £1540 3s. 1d., the stables and guardhouses £5002 11s. 2d. and the main building account amounted to £26,049 11s. 4d.[4] The house was now complete and ready for its new function as a royal palace.[5] The road through Hyde Park to Kensington had also been constructed under the supervision of Captain Michael Studholme, Surveyor of their Majesties' Roads. It was the first continuously lit road in the kingdom.

The queen however at once decided that her apartment was too cramped, and during the king's absence in Ireland during the summer of 1690 work began again, to enlarge her pavilion and construct a gallery range linking it with a pre-existing block.[6] In June William Edge, labourer, was paid for 'taking downe the wall next the Buttery Office and . . . taking downe the walls in the Queen's Lodgings', and in August for 'carrying the old floors downe to the Yard that were taken up in the Queen's Bedchamber and Closetts and Backstairs'. The main bills for construction work were submitted in October 1690, John Hayward the carpenter's for £1889 3s. 1d. and Thomas Hughes the bricklayer's for £1126 1s. 1d., the latter specified as for 'worke done in the Queen's new Gallery and Lodgings adjoineing Containing the Range from the Queen's Dressing roome unto the Garden gate and soe returning unto the Chandlery'.[7]

This new suite of rooms provided the queen with a spacious private apartment, approached at the north end by a wainscoted staircase with heavy turned balusters. The present Portland stone doorcase at the north end of the east wall was executed

---

[1] Works 19/48/1, mason's bill March 1690/1, carvers' bills April 1690.
[2] Works 19/48/1, capenter's bill Feb. 1689/90.   [3] Works 5/146.
[4] Works 19/48/1: monthly totals up to April 1690, with the addition of the joiner's and plasterer's bills submitted in the following Sept. and Oct. respectively. The joiner's bill however includes some work done after April. Stables and outworks are entered at the end of the volume, ff. 104–7.
[5] During the Stuart ownership the building was known as Kensington House. But there are several early official references to it as 'palace', e.g. *Cal. Treas. Books* ix, pp. 776, 808 (Aug. and Sept. 1690); *Cal. Treas. Books* x, p. 514 (1694); also Luttrell, *op. cit.*, vol. ii, p. 305 (1691).
[6] This may possibly have been the fifth pavilion mentioned in the accounts (Chettle and Faulkner, *op. cit.*, p. 3).   [7] Works 19/48/1.

by the mason Thomas Hill and cost £46 2s. 11½d., of which sum Hill charged £15 for carving the 'Sheild and festoones' and £1 10s. for 'carving 2 little Scrowles' and 'fluting the 2 Cartoozes there and cutting the Dropps'. The staircase and the rooms on the principal floor have been preserved with little alteration, complete with the carved wood cornices for which William Emmett and Nicholas Alcock received £185 3s. 5d. in March 1691.[1] The staircase leads immediately into the Queen's Gallery, for which Hill provided the two purple marble chimneypieces, at £40 the pair, and Grinling Gibbons the overmantels 'in Wood on Glasse' for £50. Nicholas Alcock carved for the gallery 'the King's Armes with the Garter and Imperiall Crowne 2 boyes holding Trumpetts at Topp and a Lyon and Unicorne couching at bottome, £10', Emmett executing a similar piece for the queen's bedchamber. The most expensive chimneypiece, a 'redd and purple marble' one, costing £23, was in the bedchamber. Gibbons was also paid £70 for '2 Carved Chimney pieces in [the queen's] Closett [one] on a Glasse ground and the other on a Gold ground in her Dressing roome'.[2] The precise disposition of the rooms in the queen's apartment cannot be determined: her withdrawing room was not affected by the new building; other rooms given new marble chimneypieces were her supping room, chocolate room and 'passage roome next the Garden', in her privy apartment on the ground floor. The queen's 'little garden' itself apparently extended along the east side of the new gallery range, and was reached from the garden room by a 'marble bridge'.[3]

The opportunity was taken during the king's absence in the summer of 1690 to paint the house. As early as 22 July/3 August Queen Mary was writing to her husband to report: 'Your own apartment, lord Portland's, Mr. Overkirk's, and Lady Derby's are done, but mine is impossible to be used, . . . your closet as yet smells of paint, for which I will ask pardon when I see you.' A fortnight later she was able to announce 'Kensington is ready'. Her own new apartment however was not furnished for occupation until the following November.[4] With that work stopped for a year, the cost for the first two years' work being £55,575 3s. 2¼d., according to the declared account for the period up to 30 September 1691.[5]

On 11 November 1691 a serious fire broke out in the Stone Gallery range. The cost of repairing the damage was estimated at £6502 6s., and during the next six months the range was reconstructed and the gallery and the various apartments there were repaired.[6] In the same month however there arrived the first of a series of large consignments of place bricks, not the cheaper stock bricks used previously. This must mark the beginning of preparations for yet another phase of building. In April 1692 a new account was opened, 'Expences in the Alterations of the Queen's Apartment and great Staircase'. Now for the first time the main house was given a suitable entrance, at the inner end of the Great Court. This, the Stone Portico, as it was called, was a two-storeyed structure, linking the queen's pavilion

[1] Works 19/48/1, mason's and carver's bills, March 1690/1.
[2] Works 19/48/1, mason's and carver's bills, March 1690/1, Gibbons's bills, March and July 1691.
[3] Several references in Works 19/48/1, Dec. 1690–March 1690/1, suggest this.
[4] Sir J. Dalrymple, *Memoirs of Great Britain and Ireland*, 2nd ed. (1773), ii, pp. 150, 155; Works 19/48/1. Nov. 1690, smith's bill.   [5] AO 1/2493/402.
[6] T/1/16 no. 31. Fire account bills specified Dec. 1691–June 1692 total £5261.

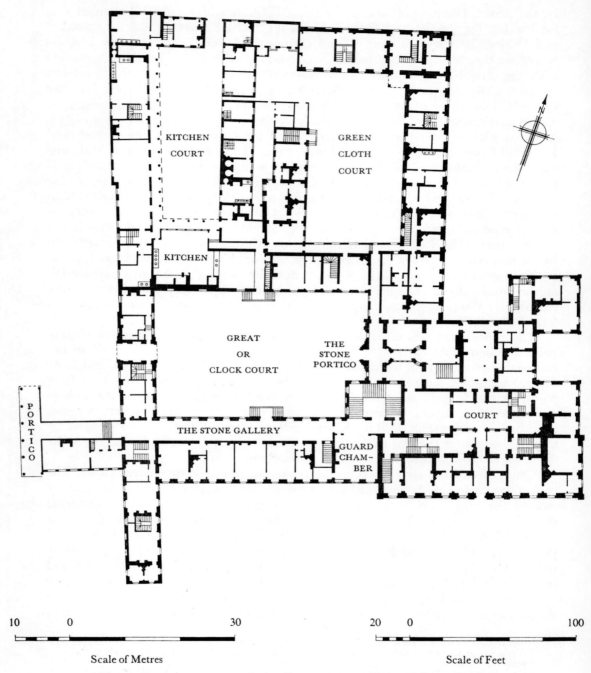

KITCHEN
COURT

GREEN
CLOTH
COURT

KITCHEN

GREAT
OR
CLOCK COURT

THE
STONE
PORTICO

COURT

P O R T I C O

THE STONE GALLERY

GUARD
CHAM-
BER

10      0                                    30

Scale of Metres

20      0                                    100

Scale of Feet

Fig. 8. Kensington Palace in 1717 (based on P.R.O., Works 34/115).

to the staircase pavilion, with rubbed and gauged brickwork, Portland ashlar pilasters and carved scrolls, two on the door, two reused from the dismantled doorway in the Stone Gallery and two 'upper Cartoozes'. Decorative carving was paid for, three large and six small roses and 'small Lace' in the 'Pannells under the Pediment' there. Behind this rich facade lay at each level a broad, shallow room, with a big bow in the centre of the inner wall. Payment was made for three brick niches 2 feet wide within the bow, and to Alexander Fort, the Master Joiner, for '2 double Arches in the 2 Galleryes, 11 foot by 8 foot each twice with Pillasters and Ornaments'.[1]

By this portico easy access was given both from the Great Court and from the principal staircase to the queen's apartment, which must hitherto have been inconveniently approached through the body of the old house or at the far north of the palace up the queen's privy stairs from her garden. The apartment was also rearranged for a second time, giving the queen once more a 'new bedchamber', in which Thomas Hill installed a purple marble chimneypiece costing £20. No new carved cornice however was required for it; so the room must already have been part of the queen's apartment. Yet on the other hand, the apartment was enlarged at this time, as a payment for bars for 'Chimneys in the new Building by the Queen's Bedchamber' makes clear. So it must have been at this time that the two eastern bays of the north range to the Great Court were raised to the height of the Queen's Pavilion.[2]

To the south of the new portico too remodelling took place, thereby creating a new ground-floor guard chamber.[3] The Guard Chamber had a wainscotted gallery 'hanging over' it, and Richard Osgood was paid £6 for 'a large Caesar's Head & Busto broonsed sett up in the Guardroome'. Other rooms which required completely new wainscotting were 'their Majesties Eating roome' and the chapel, ante-chapel, vestry and 'Women's Seates'.[4] But it seems clear from the accounts that the main staircase was not enlarged at this period.

With that it seems their Majesties were satisfied. The riding charges of the Surveyer and Comptroller and their clerks, which had been at the rate of twelve days per month, were reduced in March 1694 to six and in April to two. But at the end of that year the queen died. With her death William's enthusiasm for Hampton Court temporarily waned and he decided to increase his own accommodation at Kensington and thereby improve its external appearance. As early as February 1695 an estimate of £9363 'for the severall alterations and additionall buildings at his Majesty's house at Kensington' was drawn up. The contract of Richard Stacey, his Majesty's bricklayer, is dated 29 April, Stacey agreeing 'to fitt the Walls for the Roofe according to the designes at or before the end of June next ensueing, . . . in case of failure . . . it shall be lawfull for Mr Surveyor to putt on such number of Workmen as hee shall judge may performe the same by the tyme appointed'.[5] Work went ahead at speed: in mid-August, Lord Godolphin reported to Portland 'the

---

[1] Works 19/48/1, bill of Thomas Hughes, bricklayer, Oct. 1692; bills of Thomas Hill, mason, June 1692 and March 1692/3; joiner's bill, Dec. 1692.
[2] Works 19/48/1. See mason's bill, March 1692/3, and carver's bill, May 1693, where only is 'theire Majesties Bedchamber' referred to, and a cornice for it 98 ft. long; smith's bill, April 1692.
[3] Works 19/48/1, Nov. 1692, smith's bill refers to the 'doors at the Stair foot by the Guardchamber'.
[4] Works 19/48/1, Sept. 1692 and joiner's bill, Dec. 1692.
[5] *Cal. S.P. Dom. 1695*, p. 307; Works 6/2, ff. 65–6; works 5/146.

joyners are now in every roome of the house, and Sir Chr. Wren who lies there, told mee last night, they should be out of it in one months time'.[1] The king's apartment was due to be 'fully compleat in 30 working dayes' after 3 September, and before the year was out the king, assisted by Constantijn Huygens, was arranging the paintings in his new gallery.[2]

The 'new gallery building' greatly improved the king's apartment. Besides the picture gallery which occupies almost the entire state floor level of the new building, he gained two closets for his state bedroom and enlarged privy lodgings on the floor below. Evelyn, who visited the palace in April 1696, found the galleries 'furnished with all the best Pictures of all the Houses', and also 'a pretty private Library'. It is not known to what uses the other rooms in the range were put. Several rooms were elaborately decorated with wood carving: Grinling Gibbons received £839 4½d. 'for Worke done in the New Gallery Building in the Kings Great and little Closset in three Rooms under the King's Apartment in the Kings Gallery, etc.' None of this survives except the enriched cornice in the gallery, where too, over the fireplace, is the map of William III's kingdoms, drawn by Robert Norden for £5, and the wind dial. The vane to which the dial was linked was set up by Isaac Thompson for £54 8s. 4d., and this also survives.[3]

Externally the King's Gallery was of even greater value in establishing the new status of Kensington House, as it gave it, for the first time, a facade, restrained but of adequate dignity, facing not only the gardens but also the public highway beyond. There are a few sparing stone enrichments, a stringcourse with three carved key-stones, and the 'iiii great fflowerpots of Portland Stone richly carved' on the attic for which Caius Gabriel Cibber received £187 10s., but the classical orders are reduced to mere pilaster strips and a deep wooden bracket cornice with 'metopes' originally 'finished' and 'enricht' in paint.[4] There is some evidence that a more ornate exterior was at first designed, if one can trust an early nineteenth-century description of two large drawings for Kensington owned by John Carter, the antiquary, but now lost. The first is described as being for a new east front, with a centre and wings divided by giant pilasters, the windows given architraves, and in the basement treble key-stones. To the second drawing 'the present South front owes its origin', being 'similar in arrangement' to the first, 'but simplified in all the parts'.[5] The design of the King's Gallery has been attributed to Nicholas Hawksmoor, the Clerk of the Works at Kensington, but the declared account records no special payment to him above his clerk's salary beyond £5 for 'making up an account of the Kinges new Gallery' and £5 2s. for 'pastboard and other Materialls for making a Modell of the said Gallery for the King'.[6] It was part of Wren's normal duties as Surveyor of the Works to design the king's new palaces, and as has already been noted, Wren undertook personal responsibility for the work and was present on site.

---

[1] B.M. Add. MS. 28103, f. 74, printed with slight errors in *Correspondentie van Willem III en van Hans Willem Bentinck* ed. N. Japikse, iii, part 3, 's–Gravenhage (1937), p. 363.

[2] Luttrell, *op. cit.*, iii, p. 520; *Journaal van Constantijn Huygens, den zoon.*, Utrecht (1876), pp. 551–7.

[3] Evelyn, *Diary* v, p. 237; AO 1/2493/403 (E 351/3467).

[4] AO 1/2493/403 (E 351/3467); Works 4/1, 5 March 1716/17, a minute ordering the cornice, etc., to be painted plain in future, as it remains today.

[5] *Gentleman's Magazine*, 1814 (2), pp. 133–4.     [6] AO 1/2493/403 (E 351/3467).

It is however true that the one surviving plan of Kensington House which bears freehand alterations is altered in Hawksmoor's hand.[1] The proposal is to reconstruct the great staircase in an enlarged south-west pavilion, and the drawing makes it clear that this improvement of access to the king's apartments, which so upsets the building's balance as seen from the Great Court, was worked out after the plan of the new gallery building was settled. The estimate of February 1694/5 does, admittedly, include a new great staircase, but only a carpentry one. The present staircase, with its marble steps and wrought iron balustrade, must have been constructed in the first half of 1696. The first order for payment to Jean Tijou, the smith, for work at Kensington is dated September 1695; and during 1696 his bills amounted to £160. On 4 August 1696 the Earl of Portland informed the king: 'I have also been to Kensington, where I was assured that everything would be finished in three weeks, or a month at latest . . . the stair case is well enough; the little bedroom is practically finished, and I think you will be satisfied with it all.'[2]

It was in this year that the marriage with the Princess of Brandenburgh was being negotiated. In August £4000 was issued to the Wardrobe for the purchase of furniture for Kensington, by which people concluded that the king was going on with the marriage. A plan for adding a range of state apartments running out at right angles from the west end of the King's Gallery may also have been made in anticipation of this match. Nothing was done, as the marriage never materialised, but this plan certainly antedates the last significant improvement to the king's apartment, the resiting of the backstairs in 1699 to create a second bedchamber on the principal floor in the south-east pavilion. This is probably related to the painting of spacious lodgings for the Earl of Albemarle, Portland's successor as the king's closest adviser. These were at the east end of the house and included a 'passing Roome next the King's Closett'.[3] However the sum of £900 which was set aside in the budget for the year 1698–9 for 'Lord Albemarle's buildings' was for a free-standing service block. This 'Kitchen building' which Thomas Hill, the mason, John Churchill, the carpenter, and John Grove, the Master Plasterer, agreed on 30 July 1698 to erect for £877 17s. 7d. 'according to the Designe given them signed by Mr. Surveyor', was to measure 60 feet by 40 feet externally and to have a cellar storey 9 feet high, a ground storey of 11 feet and an upper storey measuring 10 feet 'to the topp of the Garrett floore'. A pastry, a confectionery and a laundry figure in the terms of the estimate. This must be the building shown on early eighteenth-century plans lying north of the palace, between the service courts and the surviving stables.[4] These stables, so much closer to the palace than those erected in 1689–90, must be the New Horse Guard house erected in 1696 at a cost of £1551.[5]

In the last months of King William's reign the gardens received renewed

[1] *Wren Soc.* vii, pl. xvii, left. The plan is misdated by Chettle and Faulkner. The amendments shown in this drawing are incorporated in another in the Wren collection (*Wren Soc.* vii, pl. xxi, lower).

[2] Works 6/2, ff. $67^v$, $68^v$, $77^r$; *Cal. S.P. Dom. 1696*, p. 319.

[3] *Cal. Treas. Books* xi, p. 47; Luttrell, *op. cit.* iv, p. 106; *Wren Soc.* vii, pl. xix; Works 5/50, Sept.–Oct. 1699 *passim*; AO 1/2446/137 (E 351/3310), Streater's taskwork. A plan at All Souls (*Wren Soc.* vii, pl. xx), entitled in Hawksmoor's hand 'Plan of the Kings ffloor as at present' shows the south-east corner of the house in its final form.

[4] Works 6/2, f. $87^v$; Works 5/145, pp. 223–6; All Souls I, 9 and Works 34/114 (reproduced in *Wren Soc.* vii, pl. xviii and p. 240).

[5] AO 1/2445/135 (E 351/3308).

attention. Henry Wise's work 'in trenching, new making and planting that part of Kensington Garden that formerly was an old Orchard' began on 12 September 1701, and by the following March he had planted over 3500 shrubs there in 'a Plantation of Ever-greene hedges and flowering Shrubbs in the Quarters', at a cost of £371 14s. 7d.[1]

With the accession of Queen Anne the garden works redoubled. In April 1702 a wilderness was begun beyond the gardens to the north, and for planting up this and the other parts of the gardens Wise was owed £682 16s. 8½d. in January 1703. By December of that year he had carried out further tasks, 'planting the Coach Court at Kensington [on the west side of the house] into a garden, cleansing the mud out of the canal there and raising with earth and new laying with turf several grass walks etc.', for which he sent in a bill for £358 14s. 6d.[2] In June 1706 Wise negotiated a contract for maintaining the enlarged gardens: 'the old Gardens . . . from the New Greenhouse downe to the Road', 17 acres, the 'New Plantation, Kitchen Garden, Coach-Court and peice before the Stoves', 38 acres, and 30 acres in the new wilderness.[3]

Far more expensive than Wise's planting however were the new building works in the gardens during 1703 and 1704. The first became something of a test case in Vanbrugh's campaign against the patent artisans, for it was at Kensington that Benjamin Jackson, the Master Mason, took a contract contrary to the principle that members of the Board were not supposed to work for the Crown.[4] But in the absence of all but an incomplete series of terse declared accounts for this period it is not clear what this job was, unless it included the black and white squared paving in front of the King's Gallery visible in early eighteenth-century engravings of the palace but unmentioned in the surviving accounts. Jackson's estimate for £1402 7s., 2d., presented in late May 1703, was considered by the Officers of the Works to be somewhat too high. Nevertheless, by this time, early in June, work was already 'farr advanced, and much materialls delivered upon the place'. At the completion of work the following December the bill which Jackson presented was for no less than £2003 10s. 7½d.; but this in its turn was cut down on the advice of the Officers of the Works to £1651 5s. 7½d., the sum he eventually received—not too far above his original estimate![5]

The most expensive, and the most spectacular, of the garden works was the New Greenhouse or orangery, built north-east of the house, at the north end of the gardens, and happily still surviving practically unaltered (Pl. 18). The first estimate, of £2599 5s. 1d., for a greenhouse 170 feet long and 30 feet wide 'from out to out', was passed by the Treasury on 17 June 1704. On 10 July, however, William Lowndes, the Secretary to the Treasury, wrote to the Officers of the Works: 'I am commanded by the Lord Treasurer to acquaint you it is her Majesty's pleasure that the Green

[1] Works 5/52, Wise's extraordinary account.
[2] Works 5/53; *Cal. Treas. Books* xviii, pp. 374, 485.
[3] Works 6/14, ff. 130–1.
[4] T 1/87, no. 48. Above, pp. 47–8.
[5] *Cal. Treas. Books* xviii, p. 282; T 1/86, no. 24; *Cal. Treas. Books* xviii, p. 483; T 1/87 no. 48. Relevant here perhaps is the payment under 1704–5 of £2786 6s. 4d. to Jackson 'for copeing the walls, at the end of the Baytree walk, before the South ffront of the House, makeing xv flights of Stepps in the Gardens, with Pedestalls on each side' (AO 1/2446/140).

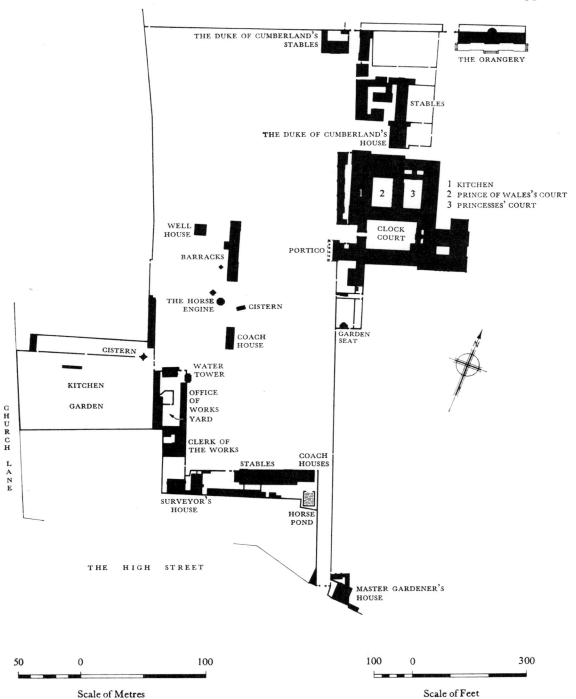

THE DUKE OF CUMBERLAND'S
STABLES

THE ORANGERY

STABLES

THE DUKE OF CUMBERLAND'S
HOUSE

1 KITCHEN
2 PRINCE OF WALES'S COURT
3 PRINCESSES' COURT

1  2  3

CLOCK
COURT

PORTICO

WELL
HOUSE

BARRACKS

THE HORSE
ENGINE

CISTERN

COACH
HOUSE

GARDEN
SEAT

N

CISTERN

WATER
TOWER

KITCHEN
GARDEN

OFFICE
OF
WORKS
YARD

CLERK OF
THE WORKS

COACH
HOUSES

STABLES

C
H
U
R
C
H

L
A
N
E

SURVEYOR'S
HOUSE

HORSE
POND

THE   HIGH   STREET

MASTER GARDENER'S
HOUSE

50        0                    100

Scale of Metres

100      0           300

Scale of Feet

Fig. 9. Kensington Palace and its outbuildings in 1754 (based on P.R.O., Works 34/118).

House at Kensington be made according to the alteration of the Draft proposed by Mr. Vanburgh.'[1]

How radical was this alteration is suggested by the steeply increased estimate for the bricklayer's work, from £697 12s. to £1560.[2] It seems reasonable to suppose that the very elaborate rubbed brickwork of the south facade, the banded columns in the centre, the concave channelled window surrounds at the ends and the sculptural attic features, constitute Vanbrugh's afterthought. Internally the twenty-four giant Corinthian half-columns also seem too expensive to have figured in the totals of the first estimate. So one should probably conclude that it was Vanbrugh who persuaded the queen to contemplate a structure that would give the gardens a grandeur lacking in the palace itself. At the completion of work at the end of 1705 the total cost had risen to £6126.[3]

During 1705 walls round the garden were under construction. The north wall partly survives, with two pairs of lofty brick gatepiers bearing stone vases. At the same time an elaborate Portland stone seat or 'summer-house' was placed at the south end of the middle walk of the garden facing the King's Gallery. This seat, now resited at the north end of the Serpentine, consists of a lofty niche breaking up into a broad pediment borne on pairs of composite half-columns. The cost of this also seems to have risen far above the estimate of £160, for 'the Seat at the lower end of the middle Walk of the Garden'. This is dated 26 April 1705, but bills for the last quarter of that year include £409 9s. 5½d. for the 'New Sommerhouse [at Kensington], and taking downe an old one'. Furthermore, John Smoute, mason, was paid £555 7s. 9d. in 1706 for work done and stone used at the 'New Summer House at the lower end of the Garden'.[4]

John Bowack, writing in 1705 while the garden works were still in progress, stressed the constant use made of Kensington by the late king and queen, and continued: 'Her Present Majesty with her Royal Consort, are pleas'd often to spend two or three Days here in good Weather, and in all probability, design to reside here oftner, when 'tis Finish'd.'[5]

In 1704 a staircase was built at the east end of King William's gallery, and in June 1706 Wren submitted an estimate for £650 for 'severall new Roomes' then being added to the queen's apartment 'in the little Court behind the Gallery', i.e. across the south end of the White Court. The declared account refers to a new library under construction for Prince George in the year of his death. The sole recorded luxury item in which the queen indulged was a 'Marble inlayd Table upon a Carved guilded fframe', supplied by John Nost in 1704 and valued at £80.[6]

Kensington continued to be used by George I, chiefly as a summer residence,[7] and it was during his reign that the last traces of Nottingham House were removed to

[1] Works 6/14, f. 65 and T 1/91 no. 9; T 27/17, p. 407.
[2] Works 6/14, ff. 65 and 70. The engraving in *Britannia Illustrata* (1707), which differs from the executed building, can hardly represent the first design, as the two-storeyed centre bays which it shows look very improbable in a greenhouse.
[3] Works 6/14, f. 109. The charge for Oct.–Dec 1705 includes the item 'Remainder of the new Greenhouse at Kensington, being now finished, 3600 li. paid before, £2526 10s. 0½d.'
[4] Works 6/14, ff. 88, 109; E 351/3311.
[5] John Bowack, *The Antiquities of Middlesex*, London (1705), p. 20.
[6] Works 6/14, ff. 63, 76; T 1/98, no. 85; see survey plan of 1717, Works 34/115; E 351/3312.
[7] C. de Saussure, *A Foreign View of England in the Reigns of George I and II* (1902), p. 136.

make way for buildings of a more palatial character. By now the surviving portions of the original fabric were beginning to show their age. On 13 June 1716 the Board of Works ordered repairs to 'the Old front . . . being much Crakt and out of Repair, espetially the Bow Window'. In July the Treasury authorised the Board to 'take down the front wall, roof and floors of the Privy Chamber, where necessary, and to rebuild the same in a plain and substantiall manner'; and in August an estimate for £1050, which included altering the king's backstairs and rebuilding the Water Tower, was approved.[1] Work began, but when Henry Lowman, the house-keeper at Kensington, reported that all the Jacobean walls were ruinous, a halt was called by order of the Board of Works 'until His Majesty's Pleasure be further known therein'. The king now asked the Lord Chamberlain (the Duke of Newcastle) to conduct an inspection of the building, meanwhile instructing the Treasury to direct 'such Repairs as He shall find absolutely necessary (and no other).[2] Nothing was done to implement this order for more than a year until, in December 1717, the Board of Works was requested by the Lord Chamberlain to make 'an exact and particular survey' of the palace, which he described as 'very much out of repair'. The survey confirmed the Lord Chamberlain's opinion, and some repairs were immediately put in hand. But the letter which the Board addressed to Newcastle in April of the following year shows that more ambitious proposals were now under consideration by the king. 'We have', they wrote, 'surveyed the Palace at Kensington, the ill state of which your Grace is allready fully apprized off upon your own view. Wee have directed several common & necessary repairs to be done out of hand: but as to those roomes in the Body of the House, which are at present in a ruinous condition, 'til His Majesty shall please to determine which of the designes now lying before him shall be pursued, wee can neither proceed thereupon nor make estimates of the charge the new building may amount to'.[3]

By whom these alternative designs had been made is not recorded in the Board's minutes. Wren, as Surveyor-General, may well have submitted one.[4] His colleague Vanbrugh was certainly the author of an ambitious plan for rebuilding the palace in a style reminiscent of Blenheim, and on a comparable scale. One copy of it, labelled in French for the king's benefit, is preserved in the royal archives at Windsor; another is among Wren's drawings at All Souls.[5] If it had been carried out only Wren's gallery would have survived as the central feature of a south front flanked by boldly projecting pavilions. Two opposed hemicycles, linked by a towered gate-way, formed the outer entrance, leading the visitor through a series of courtyards in which Vanbrugh had exercised all his genius for architectural pomp and circum-stance. Unfortunately George I had little taste for ceremonial, and what he wanted

[1] Works 4/1, 13 June 1716; Works 6/6, pp. 131–2; *Cal. Treasury Books* xxx, pp. 386, 391. The Water Tower was designed by Vanbrugh and built in 1722–4. It was demolished in the 19th century, but there is a drawing of it by Stukeley in a sketchbook formerly among the Craggs MSS. in the Record Office at Lincoln (inscribed 'Vanbrug invt. 1722') and it is also illustrated in *Gent's Mag.* xci (1), 1821, p. 497 (see Pl. 19A).

[2] Works 4/1, 3 Oct. 1716; Works 6/6, p. 196, letter of Hugh Boscawen, Comptroller of the Household, to Robert Walpole.

[3] Works 6/7, pp. 34–5. The 'old Body of the House' is also described as 'very Ruinous and out of Repair' in a minute of 14 Feb. 1717/18 (Works 4/1, 14 Feb. 1717/18).

[4] Among his portfolios there were several older projects that could have served as the basis of a new design for George I: cf. *Wren Soc.* vii, pls xviii, xix.

[5] *Wren Soc.* xii, pl. xvii; xix, pl. lxvi.

at Kensington was a suburban residence, not a national monument. Vanbrugh's scheme therefore remained on paper: no elevations corresponding to it are known to exist, and very likely none were ever drawn. As for Wren, his dismissal in April 1718 no doubt carried with it the rejection of any proposals for Kensington that he may have submitted. A plan is recorded which would have provided two large state apartments while respecting Wren's pavilions.[1] It may well have had his blessing, but the two large tripartite (presumably 'Venetian') windows are features which he is unlikely to have introduced himself, and the dimensions are in a hand that is not his, and may be Hawksmoor's.[2] It too was rejected when in June 1718 the king at last made up his mind. The plan which he approved was transmitted by the Lord Chamberlain to the Treasury, and by the Treasury to the Board of Works, who took the precaution of having a copy of it inserted in their minutes.[3] Internally it provided a handsome new suite of three rooms, but externally it thrust out a pedimented projection between Wren's pavilions in a manner which aggravated the awkward asymmetry of the eastern elevation (Pl. 20B). No clue as to the authorship of this design is provided by the Works records, but its architectural character points to someone who shared the tastes of William Benson, the new Surveyor of Works, who had assumed office in April. Benson's sympathies lay in the direction of Palladianism and away from the native baroque of Wren and Vanbrugh, and Colen Campbell was the architect whom he patronised. As the central window of the new east front is treated in a manner particularly favoured by Campbell,[4] he may perhaps have made the design at Benson's behest. This supposition receives some support from the presence among Colen Campbell's drawings of a duplicate copy of the plan approved by the king in 1718.[5] When Benson was dismissed in his turn in August 1719 he took with him a number of drawings belonging to the Office of Works, for the return of which the Board had to invoke the aid of the Treasury. Among them was 'a new design for bringing Kensington Palace into a regular fine building'.[6] This has not survived, but it is permissible to guess that it included the addition of an extra wing or pavilion to the north of the east face, balancing the end of Wren's gallery.[7]

Meanwhile the new work had been put in hand at once. On 25 June 1718 the Master Bricklayer, Thomas Hughes, was ordered to 'attend the Board tomorrow morning and be ready to inform the Commissioners of the price of materials and workmen for the New Brickworke His Majesty has been pleased to order to be done at Kensington, in order to come to a contract', and on 23 July, in obedience to a request from the Treasury, Hawksmoor was directed to 'make an estimate of the shell of the New Building erecting at Kensington against Tuesday next'.[8] On

[1] Reproduced by G. H. Chettle and P. A. Faulkner, *op. cit.*, pl. iv. The original is now missing.

[2] 'Twenty-seven designs of Kensington Palace,' none of which are now known to be in existence, were in the sale catalogue of Hawksmoor's drawings in 1740 (*Burlington Mag.* Oct. 1953, p. 333).

[3] Works 6/7, p. 68. A wooden 'moddal for the New Building' was made by the joiner John Hopson (AO 1/2449/153).

[4] Cf. *Vitruvius Britannicus* iii (1725), pls. 33, 50, 55.

[5] R.I.B.A. Drawings Collection.          [6] Works 6/7, p. 193.

[7] The idea of a balancing wing was revived in 1832 by Sir Jeffry Wyatville in a set of plans now in the Royal Library at Windsor, but was not carried into effect. It is also indicated in pencil in another early 19th-century plan in the Public Record Office (Works 34/117).

[8] Works 4/1, 25 June, 23 July 1718.

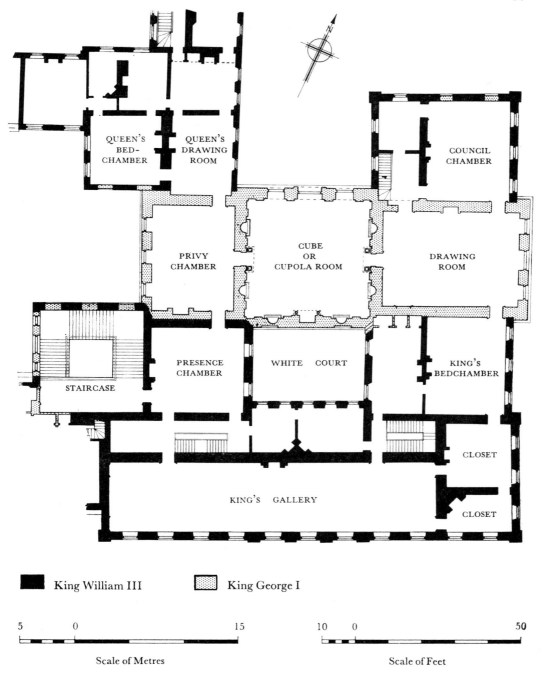

King William III    King George I

5    0    15
Scale of Metres

10    0    50
Scale of Feet

Fig. 10. Kensington Palace: the State Apartments

20 August the Board was able to inform the Treasury that they were 'of opinion that the charge of erecting the shell, being 3 story high & containing severall roomes of state exclusive of the wainscott and finishing the inside will amount to £5827'.[1] By September the provision of pantiles for the roof was already being considered, and by the following summer the building must have been structurally complete, for on 1 September 1719 Smallwell the joiner was to 'be writt to forthwith to measure his worke in the New Building'.[2] In January 1720 the king gave verbal orders to Hewett (Benson's successor as Surveyor-General) to finish the two lower floors 'in the cheapest and plainest manner', and in February he 'signified His pleasure to Mr. Surveyor General that the upper & best story of the New Building at Kensington be fitted up by March 1721 according the designes approved off by His Majesty'. The estimated cost of these works was £330 for the ground floor, £789 for the 'middle story', and £2230 for the main floor.[3] This presumably included the architectural decoration of the Cube or Cupola Room with its tabernacle doorcases and pilastered walls (Pl. 17)—a 'Grecian' design for which Hewett claimed some degree of personal credit.[4] It did not, however, include Rysbrack's relief of a Roman Marriage, which was not commissioned by the Board until January 1723/4,[5] nor the decorative painting of the walls and ceilings, which was under consideration early in 1722. Thornhill, as Sergeant Painter, had a prescriptive right to be the artist employed, and submitted sketches which were at first accepted, but later rejected in favour of rival designs by William Kent, the protégé of Lord Burlington. How this 'mighty mortification' befell the Sergeant Painter is told by George Vertue:

> 'The affair', he says, 'happen'd thus. Sir James haveing made designs of several forms, one having been pitch'd on, they ask'd him what he must have for one Room in that Manner. He said £800 (for only ornaments on the ceiling and about the pictures), which being by the Vice-Chamberlain Coke thought too extravagant and so represented to the King—he without more adoe takes Mr. Kent to Kensington and ask'd him what he would have for the same painting to be done. After having considered he answered £300 which was agreed to & he sett to work. [Too late Thornhill] sent a letter to the Vice-Chamberlain that he would do it for what any other would do it, but was rejected'.[6]

It was on the last day of February 1722 that 'la proposition de Mons. Kent pour peindre la voute de la grande Chambre a Kensington' was submitted to the king, and the estimate was £300 if Prussian Blue was used, £350 if ultramarine was substituted. The more expensive alternative was at once accepted by the king, and by the middle of May the work was well on the way to completion.[7]

[1] Works 6/7, p. 70.    [2] Works 4/1, 15 Sept. 1718, 1 Oct. 1719.
[3] Works 6/7, pp. 150/1. See also pp. 198–9.
[4] Above, p. 73 and cf. Vanbrugh's *Letters*, ed. Webb, p. 149. In Kensington Public Library there are two early 18th-century elevations of the interior of the Cube Room as built (2019, 2228). These are endorsed 'Drafts of ye 2 sides of the Cube room at Kensington' in a hand that appears to be William Kent's. If so, they were perhaps procured by him for use in connection with his decorative schemes.
[5] Works 4/2, 22 Jan. 1723/4.
[6] Walpole Society, *Vertue Notebooks* i, pp. 100–1. A design by Thornhill 'For the Cieling of the Great Room at Kensington' is in the Print Room of the Victoria & Albert Museum (E. de N. Mayhew, *Sketches by Thornhill*, H.M.S.O. 1967, pl. 38).
[7] Works 6/7, p. 272. The dimensions given in the estimate (37 ft. × 37 ft.) make it clear that the 'grande chambre' was the Cube Room.

Vertue attributed Thornhill's discomfiture partly to the influence exerted by Lord Burlington in favour of his protégé, partly to Thornhill's recent candidature for the Surveyorship of the Works, which had aroused the hostility of his colleagues in Scotland Yard. This is not perhaps the whole story, for Kent's handsome if not very accomplished ornamentation was far more sympathetic to the neo-classical aspirations of the room than anything in Thornhill's baroque repertoire, and the taste that preferred the style of Campbell to that of Wren or Vanbrugh would naturally prefer the work of Kent to that of the Sergeant Painter. Whether that taste was the king's own it is difficult to say, but Vice-Chamberlain Coke evidently played an important part in the affair, and seems to have been the person responsible for bringing Kent on the scene. As for the alleged hostility of the Officers of the Works, there is little evidence to suggest that it was a significant factor. Hewett, the Surveyor-General, was so far from nourishing any grudge against Thornhill that a year later he was induced by the latter to send the Treasury a memorial which supported his, rather than Kent's pretensions.[1] The Board certainly showed no great confidence in Kent's workmanship, for in May 1722 they invited 'several of the best artists' to inspect it, and promptly forwarded their report to the Treasury. Messrs. Van der Vaart, Nisbett and Rambour were artists of the old school, and they were unanimous in their disapproval. They declared that

> having examined the particulars thereof, we have observed and 'tis our opinion, that the perspective is not just, that the principall of the worke, which consists in ornaments and architecture, is not done as such a place requires. Mr. Nesbot adds that the boys, masks, mouldings, etc., farr from being well, he has seen very few worse for such a place, and Mr. Rambour affirms that the said worke, farr from being done in the best manner . . . is not so much as tollerably well performed, as for the quality of the blew used in the worke Mr. Vandervaart & Mr. Rambour declare that they cant judge whether it is true Ultramarine because it does not look fine enough, but Mr. Nesbot's opinion is that it is nothing but Prussian Blew, in which perhaps there may be some Ultramarine mixt.[2]

Undeterred by these signs of disapproval, Kent continued to paint, and by August he was in a position to ask for payment. The Board now resolved to take the opinions of Messrs. Dahl and Jervas, but 'Mr. Dahl sending a letter to the Board desiring to be excused, and Mr. Gervice not being in town', they proposed 'to make choice of some other proper persons to survey the same'. Kent, understandably 'uneasy for want of his money', complained to the Treasury, who wrote on 22 August 'directing Mr. Kent to be paid his money immediately without any further exceptions or delays whatsoever', whereupon the Surveyor capitulated and signed the necessary warrant forthwith.[3]

Whatever the Office of Works thought of Kent's abilities, his workmanship evidently met with the approval of the king, for in the course of the next five years he was commissioned to decorate or redecorate nearly all the royal apartments,

[1] *Cal. Treasury Papers 1720–8*, p. 201.
[2] Works 6/7, pp. 273-4. The original letter signed by the artists is T 1/241, part 2, ff. 282–3.
[3] Works 4/2, 8, 15, 17 & 22 Aug. 1722.

including the King's Gallery and the main staircase. The order in which the work was carried out was as follows:

1722        the vaulted ceiling of the Cube or Cupola Room (£350)
1722–3      the Great Drawing Room (£500)
1723        the Privy Chamber (£300) and the King's Bedchamber (£150)
1724        the Presence and Council Chambers (£300)
1725        the walls of the Cube or Cupola Room (£324 2s. 7d.)
1725–7      the King's Gallery (£700), the Great and Little Closets (£150) and the Staircase (£500).[1]

The staircase was treated by Kent in elaborate *trompe-l'oeil*, painted on canvas. On the north and east walls he represented an arcaded loggia crowded with members of the Court. According to eighteenth-century guide-books the figures include George I's two Turkish grooms of the chamber, Mehemet and Mustapha, a dwarf named Ulrich, Peter 'the wild boy', and a Quaker. The ceiling is designed to give the idea of a dome pierced by balustraded openings, from which further spectators look down on the stairs, among them Kent himself and an actress with whom he is said to have lived. In the oval ceilings of the Great Drawing Room and the Privy Chamber Kent attempted mythological subjects (Jupiter and Semele and Minerva and the Arts) of a kind for which he scarcely possessed adequate technical ability. The same may be said of the scenes from the Odyssey with which he decorated the ceiling of the King's Gallery.[2] The ceilings of the King's Bedchamber, the Presence Chamber and the Council Chamber, on the other hand, are specifically stated in the Board's records to have been done 'in grotesque painting', that is in the elegant neo-antique style which Kent had no doubt seen in Raphael's Vatican loggie. How well he learned to reproduce it can be judged from the surviving ceiling of the Presence Chamber. The ceiling of the King's Gallery also survives, but those of the two closets (the two small rooms at its eastern end, communicating with the king's bedroom) do not. All three were seen and approved of by the king a few months before his death, which took place at Kensington in June 1727.[3]

Kent's responsibility for the redecoration of the royal apartments did not stop at painting, for he also designed new doorcases in the King's Gallery, and it was he who in August 1726 'represented to the Board His Majesty's special directions for making two pedistalls & 4 tables of marble at Kensington'.[4] No doubt it was Kent too who supplied the drawings for the chimneypiece in the Great Drawing Room which was carved by James Richards in 1724 'according to a Designe ordered by His Majesty and approved by the Board',[5] for it was in his

---

[1] Works 4/2, 29 May, 16 Oct., 1723, 3 June, 11 Nov., 1724; Works 6/15, pp. 15, 103, 108, 168–9.
[2] When these paintings were restored in 1955 one of the canvases was found to be signed on the back: 'Gulielmus Kent Pinxit April ye 2, 1726. Franciscus de Valentia Ornamenta Pingebat.'
[3] 'His Majesty has seen the paintings, and has been pleased to approve thereof' (memorial of W. Kent to the Treasury, Works 6/15, pp. 168–9).
[4] T 1/257, f. 38; Works 4/3, 23 March 1725, 25 Aug. 1726.
[5] Works 4/2, 6 May 1724: Richards agrees to carve 'all the Ornaments of the chimney of the Great Drawing Room at Kensington according to a Designe ordered by His Majesty and approved by the Board' for £45. This chimney-piece was removed to 'Queen Anne's Room' at St. James's Palace in 1822 but restored to Kensington in 1974. It is illustrated in Kent's *Designs of Inigo Jones* i (1727), pl. 65.

characteristic style, and a bill submitted by him in 1727 shows that he was responsible for the entire *décor* of this room:

> For drawing the sides of the Drawing Roome with all the Pictures sketcht in proper Colours designing & drawing the mouldings & ornaments for all the picture frames, glasses, etc.[1]

In the Gallery (for which Kent made similar drawings) the new scheme of decoration included the painting and gilding of the wainscot, which originally had probably been only varnished and grained. This task was given by the Lord Chamberlain to an outsider named Howard, who may be identified as Hugh Howard, the gentleman artist who a year later was to achieve a greater coup by getting himself made Paymaster of the Works. Thornhill at once protested at this fresh infringement of his patent. 'I can not help thinking', he wrote to the Board of Works, 'it [is] a great incroachment on your Office, as well as my patent'. The Treasury agreed, and Thornhill, though ousted by Kent as the king's decorative painter, had the consolation of vindicating his right to the profitable, if more mundane, business of gilding.[2]

Meanwhile, some signs of structural unsoundness had been observed in the new buildings, for on 15 May 1723, 'the 3 Roomes at Kensington built by Mr. Benson, being in great dainger', it was 'ordered that Mr. Joynes view and give the Board an account of the condition, & [by] what method he thinks the same may be secured, with an estimate of the charge of performing the same'.[3] But no report or estimate follows, and it looks as if the minute may have been due to a false alarm.

One other alteration to the main buildings of the palace remains to be mentioned. In 1725, before Kent began his operations on the staircase, it was enlarged at the south-west corner so as to prolong the landing. The fenestration was also altered, the three northern windows being blocked up to provide wall-space for the paintings, while a larger 'arch window' with two 'side windows' took the place of the two original windows in the west wall. This 'arch window' is the one still to be seen to the right of the main entrance in Clock Court.[4]

While the new state rooms were being decorated, major changes were being carried out to the subsidiary courts to the north. These, as the plan (Fig. 8) shows, were of an irregular character, and incorporated portions of the out-buildings of the old Nottingham House. Between 1724 and 1726 the whole of the western, or Kitchen Court, was demolished and replaced by a new arcaded court built of purplish-grey brick, while the eastern, or Green Cloth Court, was altered and provided with an arcade at ground level round three sides (Fig. 7). The new arcade in the eastern court was built under a Treasury warrant dated 17 March 1723/4, which authorised the construction of 'a colonnade of communication between the Dutchess of Kendal's and the young Princesses' lodgings'. Soon afterwards the Board was instructed 'to build two Roomes over the new Arcade in the Green Cloth Court, for the Dutchess of Kendall, two closetts for the young princesses, and one roome over

---

[1] Works 6/15, pp. 168–9.
[2] *Cal. Treasury Papers 1720–8*, p. 367; Works 6/15, pp. 108–9. Thornhill's original letter is T 1/253, f. 232.
[3] Works 4/2, 15 May 1723.     [4] Works 6/15, pp. 94, 95.

them for the Countess of Portland'.[1] The 'young princesses' were the daughters of the Prince of Wales, and the dowager Countess of Portland was their governess. They had taken up residence at Kensington in May 1719,[2] and it was evidently due to them that Green Cloth Court became known as Princesses' Court.

The rebuilding of the Kitchen Court was carried out in 1725–6, after the Board had found that the existing kitchen and offices were 'in so mean and decaied' a condition and in so much danger of fire 'that it would not be advisable to lay out any money on their repair'. The estimate for rebuilding them 'in a plain and substantial manner' amounted to £7850 and was accepted by the Treasury on 16 June. The work was supervised by Henry Joynes, the resident Clerk of Works, who prepared the estimates and may well have made the designs. The new kitchen was situated on the west side of the new court. Over it was a 'garret floor' divided into rooms for members of the royal household.[3] The removal of the old kitchen also entailed rebuilding part of the north-west side of Clock Court, where the new Georgian frontage can readily be recognised by its grey brickwork. The north side of the new court was occupied by a self-contained house whose interior was very handsomely fitted up in the style of William Kent. It has been suggested that this was the residence of the Duchess of Kendal, George I's mistress, whose previous apartment in Princesses' Court would have been close by.[4] If so, she cannot have occupied her new house for more than a year or two before she was deprived of it by the king's death in 1727. Its subsequent history is uncertain, but the person most likely to have taken it over is Frederick, Prince of Wales, who came of age soon after his father's accession, and is known to have had an apartment at Kensington.[5] Indeed, it was presumably as a result of his residence in this part of the palace that the former Kitchen Court came to be known by its present name of Prince of Wales's Court. As Prince Frederick was an enthusiastic patron of William Kent, the interior decoration could have been ordered by him rather than by the Duchess of Kendal. In either case the work may have been a private commission, for there is nothing in the records of the Office of Works to suggest that it was carried out at the king's expense.

The total expenditure on works at Kensington during George I's reign (including routine maintenance) amounted to upwards of £49,000, of which at least £17,000 may be specifically attributed to the new buildings.[6]

Though George II and Queen Caroline were frequently at Kensington, no further alterations of importance were carried out during their reign. In 1728 the roof of the Queen's Gallery was reported to be 'very much out of repair', and the defects were remedied at a cost of £309. This was over £200 less than the estimate, as the roof 'did not prove so bad as was expected'.[7] Three years later the ground floor

[1] Works 6/15, pp. 16, 94–5: T 56/18, p. 189; see also Works 5/141, where the 'Extra Works' accounted for in 1724 include 'several new works at Kensington Palace per warrant 17 March 1723/4 & 16 June 1725', amounting altogether to £4302 10s. 7½d.

[2] *Historical Register* iv (1719), 'Chronological Diary', p. 28.

[3] Works 6/15, pp. 99–100, 126, 142–3; Works 4/3, 16 Feb. 1725/6.

[4] Christopher Hussey in *Country Life*, 1 Sept. 1928, where the house is fully illustrated. The house was damaged by bombs during the Second World War, and still awaits restoration.

[5] H. Walpole, *Memoirs of the Reign of George II*, ii (1822), p. 207; *Egmont Diary* (Hist. MSS. Comm.), ii, pp. 265, 272, 310.

[6] Works 5/141.                                                      [7] Works 6/15, p. 182; Works 5/104.

of the palace was found to be so badly affected by damp that it was necessary 'to take away the floors, turn brick arches and lay new wainscot floors on top'.[1] In 1740 the Board reported that the tower at the entrance to the palace was 'in a very bad condition, and that the clock is so very old and decay'd that we are informed it cannot be repair'd'. They therefore proposed to rebuild the tower and instal a new clock at a cost of £750.[2] The Treasury did not, however, accept the recommendation, apparently with good reason, since the original tower still remains, and it was not until the early nineteenth century that the clock was replaced by one from Carlton House.

While the palace itself underwent little change after 1727, the grounds continued for some years to be the scene of extensive alterations. These had been initiated by George I, and were continued with enthusiasm by Queen Caroline. The plan was to extend the gardens eastwards into Hyde Park, forming an ornamental lake—the 'Serpentine'—out of an existing series of ponds. The boundary between the extended garden and the curtailed park was to be defined by a ha-ha or 'fosse', whose excavation provided the material for a mount from which the whole layout could be surveyed. Nearer the palace a large basin of water—the existing 'Round Pond'—formed the focus of a series of intersecting avenues radiating (as at Hampton Court) from a double semi-circle of trees.[3]

The water-works were the responsibility of Charles Withers, the Surveyor of Woods and Forests, assisted by James Horne as clerk of works,[4] but most of the tree-planting and landscaping was carried out by Charles Bridgeman (until 1728 in partnership with Henry Wise) under a contract for £3800 dating from April 1727. Works valued at £1668 had been performed by the time of George I's death, and the final payment was made in August 1729. Meanwhile in August 1728 Bridgeman entered into a further contract with the Office of Works amounting to £5000.[5] The landscaping was complete by 1731, when two yachts were placed on the Serpentine 'for the diversion of the Royal Family'.[6] The total cost of the whole operation was over £39,000.

The amenities of the gardens included a revolving summer-house placed on top of the mount. Defoe describes a similar seat at Windsor, which was evidently the first of its kind, for another at Dyrham Park in Gloucestershire is referred to by Switzer in 1718 as a 'Windsor Seat'.[7] A drawing by Bernard Lens shows that the one at Kensington was embellished with a pediment supported by caryatids,[8] and enables it to be identified with a 'garden seat at Kensington Palace' designed by William Kent and illustrated in Vardy's *Designs of Mr. Inigo Jones and Mr. William*

---

[1] Works 6/15, p. 246.   [2] Works 6/16, p. 104.

[3] For the gardens see Daniel Defoe, *A Tour thro' the Whole Island of Great Britain* (1724), P. A. Faulkner, 'A Note on the Gardens of Kensington Palace', *Jnl. of the British Archl. Assn.* 3rd ser. xiv (1951), and David Green, *Gardener to Queen Anne* (1956), pp. 73–8.

[4] AO 1/2480/282–3. The second of these two accounts is printed by W. L. Rutton, 'The Making of the Serpentine', *Home Counties' Magazine* 5 (1903), pp. 81–91, 183–95.

[5] Works 4/3, 14 March, 1727; Works 4/4, 13 August, 1728, 17 March, 17 April, 26 June, 5 August, 1729; Works 5/141; Works 16/39/1 (an office letter-book concerning the royal gardens from 1726 to 1731, duplicating Works 6/114).

[6] *London Journal*, 1 May, 1731. The whole layout is shown in two engraved plates published by John Rocque in 1736 and 1754.

[7] Green, *op. cit.*, p. 78.   [8] Reproduced by Faulkner, *op. cit.*, pl. ix.

*Kent* of 1744. A note accompanying Lens's drawing states that it was erected in 1733, and 'Kensington's fair Mount' was the subject of some laudatory verses in the *Gentleman's Magazine* for April of that year. There can be little doubt that it was also Kent (by now a member of the Board of Works) who designed the ornamental building known as the Queen's Temple which still survives as a park-keeper's lodge. This was probably built in 1734–5, for it was in October 1734 that their Majesties having 'ordered Designs to be laid before them for making a piece of ground in Kensington Gardens & erecting a seat of stone therein', drawings were 'made and laid before them which they were pleased to approve of & directed the works to be forthwith put in execution'. The estimate amounted to £500, and the accounts for building the 'new Stone Building in Kensington Gardens' were passed by the Board in September 1735.[1] According to John Buckler, who drew it in 1828, it was 'a favourite retreat of George II'.[2]

Another, and more utilitarian, addition to the grounds was the stable-block built in 1740 for the Duke of Cumberland, who occupied the detached house (now demolished) on the north side of the palace that had been built for the Earl of Albemarle in 1698–9.[3] These stables still stand immediately to the north-west of the palace, but were altered in 1799 for the benefit of Edward, Duke of Kent, and have since been converted into a residence. They were built by the Office of Works at a cost of £956 18s. 1¼d.[4]

George II was the last king to reside at Kensington. In 1756 he offered to have the apartment formerly occupied by Frederick, Prince of Wales, fitted up for his grandson, who had just come of age, but the prince declined to be parted from his mother,[5] and after his accession he preferred to live at Buckingham House, which was conveniently near to St. James's, and did not suffer (like Kensington) from damp walls and bad roads. During his reign Kensington Palace was regularly surveyed by the Board, and essential repairs were carried out from time to time, but it was not until George III's sons began to need an establishment of their own that it became once more a royal residence.

---

[1] Works 4/6, 24 Sept., 2 Oct., 3 Dec. 1734, 4 Sept. 1735; Works 6/16, f. 25ᵛ.
[2] B.M., Add. MS. 36370, f. 128: B.M., Dept. of Prints & Drawings, Crace Collection, ix, 24.
[3] It is identified as the Duke of Cumberland's house on a survey of 1754 (Works 34/118).
[4] Works 5/141, 1740 'Extraordinary Works'; Works 5/60, June 1740; AO 1/2457/175. Thomas Kynaston (Clerk of the Works at the Tower of London) measured the workmanship and made up the bills. The stables were intended originally for 13 horses, but in 1799 were adapted to hold 10, and were thereafter known as the 'ten stall stables' (see vol. vi of this *History*, p. 340).
[5] H. Walpole, *Memoirs of the Reign of George II*, ii (1822), p. 50.

# LYNDHURST, HAMPSHIRE: THE KING'S HOUSE

THE KING'S House at Lyndhurst was 'a house of the king's when he comes to hunt in the New Forest'.[1] At the beginning of Charles II's reign it consisted of a modest brick house built by his father in 1635.[2] Immediately to the east stood the Verderers' Hall, a brick structure of the late sixteenth century.[3] Between 1669 and 1671 Charles spent over £4000 on enlarging the house and building new stables for his horses. The two operations were separately accounted for, the work on the house by Charles Pawlett, Lord St. John (afterwards Duke of Bolton), who held a grant of the manor, and the building of the stables by Sir John Norton, Chief Woodward of the New Forest.[4] By the king's order the Officers of the Works were called in to superintend the building of the stables, and there is evidence that Richard Ryder, the King's Master Carpenter, was concerned in the repairing of the house.[5] William Cousins, 'a Master Builder at Lyndhurst', contracted to build the stables, for which he received in all nearly £3000.[6]

The new stables were demolished early in the nineteenth century, but a survey plan exists which shows that they formed a quadrangle about 120 feet square with an entrance in the middle of each side (Fig. 11). For the site on which they were built (now occupied by the local school) £55 were paid.

The enlargement of the house cost £1057. One Ferdinand Knapton of Southampton appears to have acted as surveyor or clerk of works, and the principal building craftsmen employed were John Ockeford, carpenter, and Thomas Swyer and Daniel Grantham, who are described as 'masons', but were probably in fact bricklayers.[7] The work carried out appears to have included the building of the present south and west fronts of the house, whose windows have moulded brick architraves of a type characteristic of the period. The additional accommodation comprised two large and two smaller rooms on each floor, and gave the house the character of a 'double pile', with a central corridor from one end to the other.

The enlarged house served as a residence for the Warden of the Forest or his deputy, and in 1711 a survey of it was made by the Surveyor of Woods and Forests, Edward Wilcox. He estimated that an expenditure of £630 would be needed to make

---

[1] *The Journeys of Celia Fiennes*, ed. C. Morris (1949), p. 50.
[2] See vol. iv of this *History*.
[3] This building is clearly shown in a panoramic view of Lyndhurst as seen from the church tower dated 1843 and hanging in the offices of Messrs. Pasmore, surveyors and estate agents in Lyndhurst.
[4] E 351/3406 (St. John); E 351/3444 (Norton); *Cal. Treas. Books* iii, pp. 553, 695, 1010, 1015.
[5] *Cal. Treas. Books* iii, pp. 50, 452; *Cal. S.P. Dom. 1670*, p. 407; *1671*, p. 217.
[6] *Cal. Treas. Books* iii, p. 539; E 351/3444.      [7] E 351/3406.

206

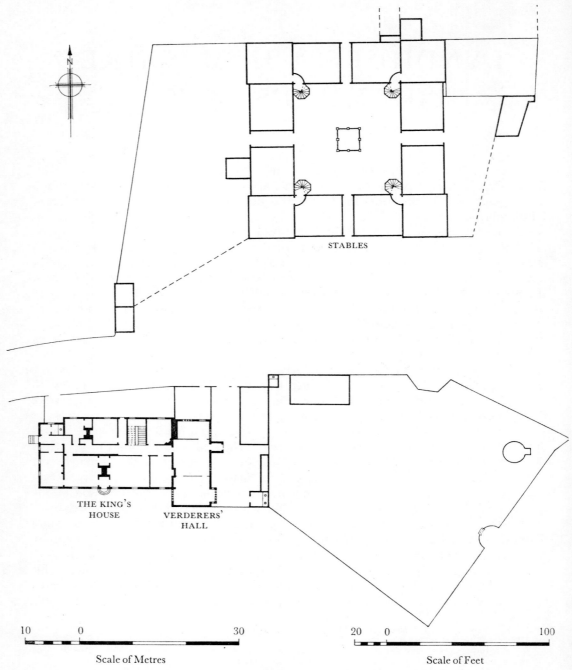

STABLES

THE KING'S
HOUSE

VERDERERS'
HALL

10        0                    30

Scale of Metres

20    0                    100

Scale of Feet

Fig. 11. Lyndhurst, Hants.: the King's House in 1851 (based on P.R.O., F 17/201).

the house fit for the reception of the Warden, then the second Duke of Bolton.[1] The repairs that followed are commemorated by rainwater heads dated 1712. Two other rainwater heads record a further repair in 1748. It may have been at this date that the narrow space that had hitherto separated the King's House from the Verderers' Court was filled in to form an additional bay uniform with the brickwork of the house. The pedimented doorway in the middle of the south front was probably inserted at the same time.

By 1818 the house was said to be in need of repairs costing £2422,[2] but nothing was done until 1849, when on the death of the last Warden, the Duke of Cambridge, control of the Forest passed to the Commissioners of Woods and Works. In 1851–2 the upper floors of the building containing the Verderers' Hall were demolished under the direction of John Phipps, the Assistant Surveyor of Works and Buildings, and the Hall itself was repaired and extended towards the north.[3] In 1904 a new upper floor was built over the Hall to provide offices for the Deputy Surveyor of the New Forest, thus approximately restoring the arrangements that had existed before 1851.[4] Finally in 1965 the house was converted into offices for the Forestry Commission.

# THE ROYAL MEWS, CHARING CROSS

THE LAYOUT of the Royal Mews during the period covered by this volume is shown by several survey plans.[5] The area now occupied by Trafalgar Square was divided up into three principal yards, each surrounded by ranges of heterogeneous buildings which no topographical artist of the day thought it worth while to record (Fig. 12). The 'Great Mews' was more or less rectangular in shape, with a long range of stables on the west and a large hay barn on the east. In the middle was the Horse Pond, and near the pond stood a detached equerry's house which, being in bad repair, was pulled down in 1725.[6] Entries on the north and west sides led to the Green or Upper Mews and to the Back or Dunghill Mews, respectively. The latter

[1] T 1/131, No. 24; *Cal. Treas. Books* xxv, pp. 173, 405; xxvi, p. 268.
[2] Works 19/17/4, ff. 1–4.
[3] Works 19/17/4, ff. 6, 15–15, 22; plan by Phipps dated Sept. 1851 in F 17/201.
[4] G. Lascelles, *Thirty-five years in the New Forest* (1915), pp. 112–13.
[5] See especially P.R.O., MPE 560 of *c.* 1695, Works 30/455 and 456, a plan among the Worsley drawings in the R.I.B.A. Library, and B.M. King's Maps XXIV, 15 i.a. The last is reproduced by A. Stratton, 'The King's Mews at Charing Cross', *Architectural Review* xxxix (1916), p. 120, where it is dated 'about 1730'. It cannot in fact be later than 1725, the year in which the detached house in the middle of the Great Mews was pulled down.
[6] Works 4/3, 3 and 31 March 1725.

was very irregular in shape as its western boundary was defined by the curve of Hedge Lane (now Whitcomb Street). Part of the frontage to the street was occupied by the Master of the Horse's Lodging, a large house with a symmetrical facade built (it would seem) by the Earl of Newburgh soon after the Restoration and purchased from him by the Crown in 1662.[1] To the east another and even more irregular area contained an extensive granary and a small Riding House. In 1686 Wren reckoned that there was accommodation for 300 horses and 30 coaches.[2] Another list drawn up about the same time given a total of 279 stalls and 33 coach houses.[3] But some of these were appropriated by individual officers, so the total available for the royal horses was somewhat smaller. By the reign of George I the total was reduced still further by the collapse of several stables, and there was now room for only 177 horses, of which 76 belonged to the king, 85 to the Prince of Wales, and 16 to the latter's daughters ('the Young Princesses'). In addition there were 27 coach houses, a porter's lodge, and various dwelling for equerries and others connected with the Mews.[4]

For the maintenance of these buildings the Office of Works had in 1660 no direct responsibility. Their fabric was in the charge of a Surveyor of the Mews who received money by warrant and accounted independently at the Exchequer.[5] Some building was also done by equerries and others at their own expense,[6] and some by special grants to favoured individuals. In 1673 the Duke of Buckingham, then Master of the Horse, obtained a warrant for £1134 for a new building to house the royal coaches, and £575 for repairs to the stables. This 'new building', for which the duke employed William Samwell as architect, was completed by his successor the Duke of Monmouth in 1674.[7] But expenditure incurred in this somewhat irregular fashion had ultimately to be audited, and it was Wren who was called upon to sort out the accounts of the works done by the two dukes.[8]

Soon afterwards the Treasury decided to put the works at the Mews on a more regular footing. The Office of Works was instructed to submit estimates both for the repairs immediately needed and for the annual charge of maintaining the buildings, and in 1676 a Privy Seal laid down that 'the repairs and buildings of our Mews and Stables shall from henceforth be put into the charge of the officers of our Works, and the former way and course for performing the said repairs by the surveyors of our Mews and Stables do from henceforth cease and be superseded'.[9] The expenditure was now entered annually in the Office books and accounted for by the Paymaster

[1] *Cal. S.P. Dom. 1661–2*, pp. 417, 542; *Cal. Treas. Books* i, p. 590. The earl's house was stated to contain 11 rooms, which corresponds with the plan of the house in Hedge Lane as shown in Works 30/456. The Earl of Newburgh was Captain of the Guards.

[2] Report of Oct. 1686, printed in *Wren Soc.* xviii, p. 56.

[3] B.M., Add. MS. 16370, f. 117. In 1681 Nicholas Barbon claimed that the Mews could accommodate fewer than 200 horses and 20 coaches, but he was doing his best to minimise their utility (T 4/1, pp. 212–13).

[4] B.M., King's Maps XXIV, 15 i.a.

[5] The Surveyors in question were John Bayspoole (1660–4), Col. Ambrose Norton (1664–88), and Col. Francis Negus (1688–1716). Numerous references to their expenditure on the Mews will be found in the Calendars of *State Papers Domestic* and *Treasury Books*. Bayspoole's enrolled account for 1660–2 is E 351/3361.

[6] E.g. *Cal. S.P. Dom 1661–2*, p. 64; *Cal. Treas. Books* xxx, pp. 252, 586; *Cal. Treas. Books & Papers 1731–4*, p. 398.

[7] *Cal. Treas. Books* iv, p. 151, v, pp. 28–9, 51, 56, 699, viii (1) pp. 119–20. For an equerry's house designed by Samwell see SP 30, Case C, No. 18 (*Cal. S.P. Dom. 1670*, p. 635).

[8] *Wren Soc.* xviii, p. 38.     [9] *Cal. Treas. Books* v, pp. 255–6.

MASTER OF THE
HORSE'S HOUSE

HEDGE          LANE

(WHITCOMB          STREET)

THE
BACK
OR
DUNGHILL
MEWS

THE          GREAT          STABLE

THE
GREEN
OR
UPPER MEWS

THE          GREAT          MEWS

HORSE
POND

CASTLE          STREET

HAY
BARN

GRANARY

RIDING
HOUSE

DUKES          COURT

STRAND

ST. MARTIN'S          LANE

Fig. 12. The Royal Mews, Charing Cross, in the eighteenth century (based on P.R.O., Works 30/456).

Scale of Metres

50          0          100

CHARING          CROSS

STATUE OF
KING CHARLES I

100          0          100          300

Scale of Feet

under the heading of 'Extraordinary Works'.[1] The Surveyor of the Mews continued, however, to occupy what must by now have become largely a sinecure, and in 1688, when Col. Francis Negus succeeded Col. Ambrose Norton in the post, a new routine was established whereby the Surveyor of the Mews once more carried out the repairs, but submitted his accounts to the Surveyor of Works for auditing and was in due course authorised by Treasury warrant to claim the money due to him from the Paymaster of the Works.[2] This arrangement continued until the general reorganisation of the Office of Works in 1715–16, when the office of Surveyor of the Mews was abolished. A Clerk of the Works was appointed in his place, and thereafter the Mews were on exactly the same footing as any other building in the Office's care.[3]

Whether supervised by a Surveyor or by a Clerk of the Works, the recorded repairs were mostly of an *ad hoc* character, and the whole complex of buildings, irregularly laid out, with many alterations and additions of various dates, looked, in the words of a Georgian topographer, 'like a common inn-yard'.[4] Unimpressive to look at and uneconomic to maintain, the Royal Mews clearly invited some bold scheme of replacement that would provide the royal household with better and more dignified quarters for its coaches and horses. Among Wren's drawings there is indeed just such a scheme, in which accommodation for 388 horses and 42 coaches is arranged in an orderly fashion round a courtyard dignified by a curved end culminating in a domed gateway.[5] But no date can be assigned to this drawing, and the first scheme for rebuilding the Mews that is known to have been seriously considered emanated not from the Surveyor of His Majesty's Works but from the speculator Dr. Nicholas Barbon. In the winter of 1680–1 he approached the Treasury with an offer to build new stables and coach houses for the king if he were allowed to pull down the old Mews and develop the site for building. The 'draught' which accompanied his paper is lost, but the new stables were evidently to be sited further south, for they were to be 'nearer his Majesty's Palace [of Whitehall] & nearer the Thames & feilds for the breathing & good watering of Horses', while 'the appartments for the Master of the Horse to the King & Queen for the Equerries & other Persons who have right to lodge in the Mews wilbe larger & pleasanter scituated then now they are, being designed in the range of building next the Park'. As 'the front' was 'to conforme to his Majesty's Walkes' the site envisaged by Barbon must have been somewhere on the edge of St. James's Park, perhaps in the neighbourhood of Spring Gardens. The remainder of Barbon's paper is characteristically devoted to plausible financial calculations designed to show how advantageous the scheme would be to the Crown.[6] Although it was alleged in February 1681 that the king had 'sold the Mews for £30,000' (roughly the figure at which Barbon valued their site and materials),[7] nothing came of this project, and the Mews remained as they were.

The idea of selling the Mews for building was, however, revived by James II, who in December 1687 was reported to have 'lately surveyed with Sir Christopher

[1] Works 5/23–42.
[2] E.g. *Wren Soc.* xviii, p. 65, *Cal. Treas. Books* x, pp. 616, 1053, 1071, xi, p. 169, xiv, p. 208, xv, p. 251, xvii, pp. 1066–8, xix, p. 284.
[3] *Cal. Treas. Books* xxix, p. 318; Works 6/6, f. 148. Works 6/11, pp. 78, 107. For a list of the Clerks see below, p. 474.
[4] J. Noorthouck, *History of London* (1773), p. 724.
[6] T 4/1, pp. 212–13.
[5] *Wren Soc.* xii, pl. xxvi.
[7] *Cal. S.P. Dom. 1680–1*, p. 186.

Wren the ground of the Mews at Charing Cross, considering it to be an ancient and incommodious building, and intends to erect a noble structure for his coach houses and stables, and an apartment for a Court of Horse and Foot Guards'.[1] Now the idea was to site the new stables on the west side of St. James's Palace, and to build a new street on the edge of the Green Park linking them with Piccadilly (Fig. 13). It was reckoned that 'the ground in the Mews which his Majesty intends to let . . . to be built upon' would bring in £9640, to which the new street would add £11,622, whereas the cost of building 'the new intended Mews' exclusive of fittings, etc., would be only £884.[2] The new street was to be built by Richard Frith, a leading master-builder who had been concerned in the very successful development of the adjoining estate of the Earl of St. Albans, and in January 1688 Lord Dartmouth, as Master of the Horse, was ordered by the Treasury to send Frith to see Wren in order to discuss his proposals. In March Wren was directed to attend the king at the Treasury with his 'draughts' for the new stables, 'and all your papers concerning that whole business'.[3] This is the last reference to the scheme in official records: no doubt it was a casualty of the political revolution then imminent. But two plans in Hawksmoor's hand remain to show what was envisaged (Fig. 13), and among some papers of Dartmouth's now in the British Museum there is a plan of the housing-plots in the new street drawn up by Frith together with a detailed specification and estimate for the Mews themselves.[4] They were to be uniformly built of brick, with a stone plinth and a stone fascia marking the division between the first and second stories. Beneath the eaves there was to be a 'large modillion cornish', and in the roof there were to be 'convenient Luterne lights'. All the windows were 'to be wrought with Architrives to resemble stone, to stand out before the Range of Brickwork for ornament all of oak', and alternate windows were to be pedimented. The cost was estimated on a basis of £41 per 'square' (of 10 feet) for the stables and £40 per square for the houses for equerries and others, and came to £33,425. The value of the ground in the new street was estimated at £865 11s. a year, or £17,311 at 20 years' purchase. To this £15,380 was added as the value (at 20 years' purchase) of the ground in the old Mews, making a total of £32,691. The cost to the Crown of the whole street was therefore to be £734. For this modest outlay (if the calculations were correct) the king could have had a handsome new stable accommodating 400 horses, 28 coaches and 32 equerries and stable staff.

Soon after Anne's accession an Act of Parliament allowing the Crown to grant building leases for up to 50 years encouraged the Treasury to think once more of a profitable building development on the site of the Mews. Wren and Travers, the Surveyor of Crown Lands, drew up two successive plans for new streets, 'and reckoning the fronts of the said streets containing 2400 foot to be worth one with another a ground rent of 10s. per foot, the same amounted to £1200 per annum, and wee judged the old materials standing on the premises (to be sold to such

[1] Hist. MSS. Comm. *Downshire* i (1), p. 282.
[2] T 27/11, f. 290; *Cal. Treas. Books* viii, p. 1704.
[3] *Cal. Treas. Books* viii, pp. 1716, 1801.
[4] Add. MS. 16370, ff. 115–24. Hawksmoor's plans are All Souls IV, 92 (*Wren Soc.* vii, pl. xxx) and B.M., King's Maps XXVI, 2 i. Mention should also be made of an elevation of a design for a new mews, and of a plan of 'An Adittion to the King's stable-yard at St. James' ', both in the volume of drawings from the Dartmouth Collection now in the library of the Department of the Environment (vol. iv, no. 12).

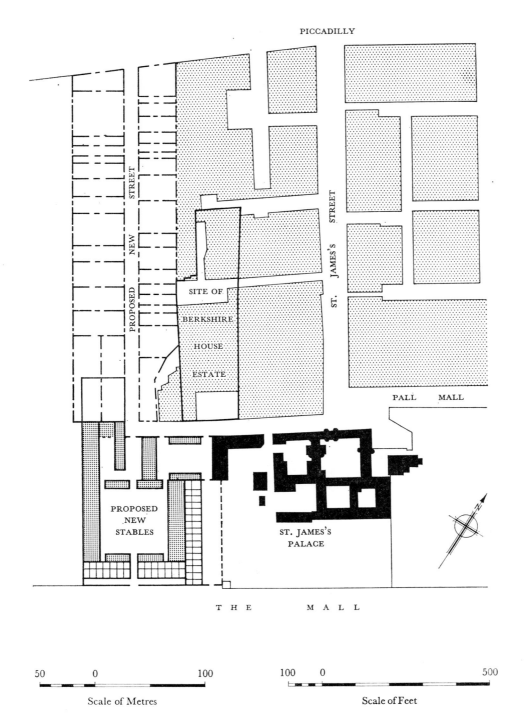

PICCADILLY

NEW STREET

PROPOSED

ST. JAMES'S STREET

SITE OF

BERKSHIRE

HOUSE

ESTATE

PALL MALL

PROPOSED
NEW
STABLES

ST. JAMES'S
PALACE

N

THE        MALL

50        0                    100          100      0                        500

Scale of Metres                              Scale of Feet

Fig. 13. An unfulfilled project of 1688 for resiting the Royal Mews at St. James's Palace
(based on *Wren Society* vii, pl. xxx, B.M., Add. MS. 16370 and King's Maps xxvi, 2–1).

persons as should undertake the new building the ground) well worth £2000'. 'Wee have,' they went on, 'seen some other designes of men skil'd in building, for making handsome streets and good houses on the greatest part of the premises, and smaller where the ground grows narrow. And by their computation the whole is thought likewise to be worth about £1200 a year ground rent.' If the site was sold at fee farm they estimated that the return would be £30,000, more if the prospect of rebuilding Whitehall became a reality.[1] Once more, however, nothing resulted, and it was not until the reign of George II that king and Treasury were at last induced to authorise something more than piecemeal repairs. In February 1731 the Master of the Horse (the Earl of Scarborough) wrote to the Treasury complaining of the ruinous state both of the stables at Charing Cross and in the Mews at St. James's Palace. The Treasury asked the Board of Works to prepare estimates for putting the buildings into good repair, but the Board replied that they found them 'in so ruinous a condition that we think it not adviseable for his Majesty to lay out money to repair' them. Instead they offered 'a General Plan which may be pursued as occasion shall require'. Of this general plan they proposed for immediate execution only 'that part that devides the Great Mews from what is called the Green Mews, with lodgings & accommodations for grooms, coachmen etc.'. This could be built for £5700, but if the new stables were to house the horses from St. James's as well, the total cost would be £6500.[2] On 15 June the Board 'received from the Treasury their Lordships' order, signifying His Majesty's pleasure for rebuilding part of the Great Mewse at Charing Cross, estimated at £6500'.[3] Work began the same summer, but while it was in progress the plan was further enlarged, apparently as a result of the king's personal intervention. The circumstances were set out in a letter from the Board to the Treasury dated 3 August 1732:

> We humbly beg leave to acquaint Your Lordships that after we had laid an estimate amounting to £6500 for building the new stables at the Mews before you and for which we had a warrant from your Lordships, His Majesty was pleased to order the Front and plan to be enlarged, and a large walk to be made in the middle between the horses, which obliged us to put two rows of piers and pilasters, and to raise the whole building much higher in order to get grainaries & arch the same over the heads of the horses; which alterations will greatly add to the building (there being now 140 square of building upon the ground plan) and will increase the expence to about the sum of £13500 for which excess we humbly pray your Lordships' warrant.[4]

Reference to the plan (Fig. 12) will show the central walk mentioned in the letter, together with the two rows of pilastered piers on either side. Authority to proceed on this basis was given a week later, and the building was eventually completed in 1733 at a cost of £14,118.[5] The principal workmen employed were Andrews Jelfe, mason, Thomas Churchill, bricklayer, and John Norris, carpenter. Isaac Ware

---

[1] *Cal. Treas. Books* xviii, p. 292, xix, pp. 54, 386; Crest 6/22, pp. 198/9, 6/23, pp. 42–5.
[2] *Cal. Treasury Books & Papers 1731–4*, p. 19; Works 6/15, p. 231–2.
[3] Works 4/5, 15 June 1731; *Cal. Treasury Books & Papers 1731–4*, p. 63.
[4] T 56/18, p. 399; T 29/27, p. 144.
[5] Works 5/141, Extraordinary Works 1733.

acted as clerk of works.[1] There is no reference in the Board's minutes to the author-ship of the plans and elevations, but 'Guilielmus Kent, Archit: et Pict: Invenit et Delin[t]' is the signature on a contemporary engraving of the elevation by Four-drinier,[2] and in a manuscript once owned by Kent there is a note recording the fact that on 12 January 1733/4 he accompanied the king and queen to the Mews 'to look upon that Building of my Designe'.[3] There are, moreover, two preliminary drawings for the building in Kent's hand in Sir John Soane's Museum.[4] One is for a grand entrance to the Great Mews from the south (Pl. 21B). This of course was never built, but it incorporates as flanking features duplicates of the two cupola'd towers that marked the centres of each wing of the building actually erected. The second drawing is for the stables itself, but shows a different treatment of the facade, with a simple pedimented centrepiece. A third drawing, probably in Ware's hand (Pl. 21C), is of interest because it shows a building of similar dimensions to the one erected, but without the central aisle, in place of which there are cross-walls con-taining staircase-wells. This may well represent the plan approved in 1731, but modified in the following year. The elevation also differs from the one finally adopted, but introduces a central feature resembling the one actually built, which was based on Colen Campbell's gateway to Burlington House. The introduction of this feature from Lord Burlington's town house recalls the fact that in his *Picturesque Tour through London and Westminster* of 1792 James Malton states that the Mews were erected 'from the designs of the Earl of Burlington', while Joseph Gwilt, in his edition of Chambers's *Treatise* (1825), says that 'the architect is generally understood to have been Lord Burlington, though Kent has the credit of it'. This claim is not borne out by the evidence cited above, but the association between Burlington and Kent was so close that it may be taken for granted that the designs were seen by Burlington and dis-cussed with him before being submitted to the king.[5]

Of the 'General Plan' referred to by the Board in 1731 no copy has survived in official custody, but among the drawings left by Thomas Worsley, Surveyor of the Works from 1760 to 1779, there is a plan for rebuilding the remainder of the Great Mews which may have been based upon it (Pl. 69). This plan provides for two wings, decorated with columns and pilasters, one of which was to contain a large riding-house, the other additional stables and coach houses. In the event Kent's 'Great Stable' was the only portion of the 'General Plan' that was ever carried out, and the subsequent history of the Mews is a story of piecemeal repairs and replace-ments that it would be tedious to recount in detail.

---

[1] Works 4/5, 9 and 14 Sept. 1731, 22 June, 19 Dec. 1732. In June 1732 Norris was dismissed for neglecting his work, and the carpentry was given to Leonard Phillips.

[2] There is a copy of it in the Soane Museum (Fauntleroy Pennant, vol. ii, f. 245).

[3] Bodleian Library, MS. Rawlinson D 540, at the end.

[4] Fauntleroy Pennant, vol. ii, pp. 241–4. There is another drawing (a section) by Kent in the Collection of Mr. Paul Mellon.

[5] In this connection it may be noted that in May 1733 the Board ordered that 'five tonns of the slates at the Mewse Charing Cross be deliver'd for the Earl of Burlington at Cheswick' (Works 4/5).

# NEWMARKET, SUFFOLK

WHEN CHARLES II's courtiers took stock of the royal hunting seat at Newmarket they found that the old palace with its additions by Inigo Jones had been almost completely demolished by the regicide Colonel Okey.[1] The stables were rebuilt by John Bayspoole, Surveyor of the Mews,[2] but no attempt was made to reconstruct the house itself. Instead, in 1668 the king bought a house further east on the same side of the High Street which belonged to the seventh Earl of Thomond (Fig. 14), and proceeded to enlarge it.[3] The Officers of the Works were not employed to supervise the works, which were entrusted to the gentleman-architect William Samwell. In 1669 Samwell was stated to 'have the ordering of the workmen at Newmarket', and he is known to have charged £40 'for his first Journy and Designes'.[4] To whose recommendation he owed this commission is not clear, but he may have been sponsored by Lord Arlington, then Secretary of State.[5] His accounts do not survive among the public records, but it appears from a subsequent report on them by Wren that between December 1668 and Midsummer 1671 he received and spent over £8000 on 'the king's buildings at Newmarket'.[6]

No view of these buildings appears to be extant, but two survey plans of them exist, one made in the first half of the eighteenth century, probably by Thomas Fort, Clerk of the Works at Newmarket from 1719 to 1745, the other by Thomas Chawner of the Office of Woods and Forests in 1816.[7] These both show the street frontage occupied by an old timber-framed house of Jacobean character which was doubtless the one bought by the king in 1668. Behind it was a courtyard, one side of which consisted of a long brick range stretching south. The ground floor of this range was occupied entirely by vaulted offices and by an elaborately compartmented corridor which led in one direction to a staircase and in the other to a projecting wing containing four rooms, two on each floor. In the reign of Charles II the king and queen, the Duchess of York and the Duke of Monmouth each had their own lodgings,[8] but it is impossible to reconstruct the original allocation of all the rooms. It is evident, however, that the main suite of royal apartments was on the first floor,

[1] *Cal. S.P. Dom. 1660–1*, pp. 239–40. In 1676 Wren described the site of the old palace as a 'vacant yard' (*Wren Soc.* xviii, p. 46).
[2] *Cal. Treas. Books* i, p. 590.
[3] *Cal. S.P. Dom. 1667–8*, pp. 326, 597; *Cal. Treas. Books* iii, p. 591.
[4] *Cal. S.P. Dom. 1668–9*, p. 393; SP 29/303, f. 245.
[5] An undated statement of moneys paid to Arlington begins with £4266 to 'Lord Arlington & Mr. Samwell' (P.R.O., Shaftesbury Papers 24/VI B, No. 394), and it has been claimed that Samwell designed Arlington's house at Euston in Suffolk (*Wren Soc.* xix, p. xiii).
[6] SP 29/303, f. 245. For the duration of the work, see SP 29/302, f. 116.
[7] The former plan forms part of a volume preserved in the Library of the Department of the Environment. Chawner's plan is P.R.O., MPE 630.
[8] Works 5/25, 29, 35 &c. Lists of those occupying rooms in the palace in 1672 and 1674 will be found in one of the Lord Chamberlain's Warrant Books (LC 5/139, ff. 5 and 7 at the end).

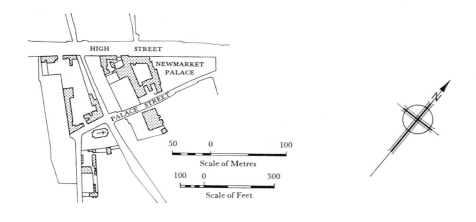

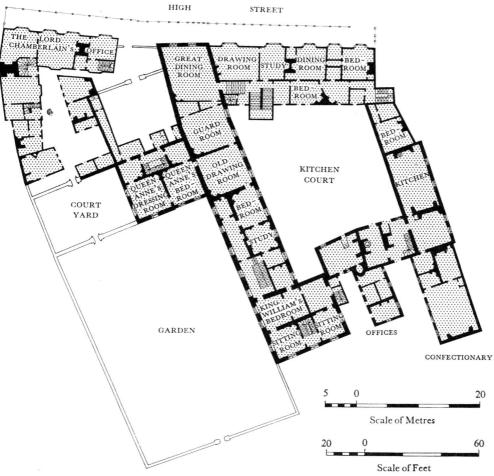

Fig. 14. Newmarket Palace, from an eighteenth-century plan in the Library of the Department of the Environment and a survey of 1816 (P.R.O., MPE 630).

where in 1816 Chawner marked the 'Guard Room', 'Old Drawing Room', 'Bed Room' and the octagonal 'Study'. Seventeenth- and eighteenth-century documents also mention the Presence Chamber, the king's closet and the king's back-stairs.[1] Chawner's plan indicates that William III occupied the rooms at the south end of the building, while Queen Anne preferred the projecting wing. Evelyn, who saw the building in the summer of 1670 when it was still unfinished, admired 'the arches of the Cellers beneath', which 'are exceedingly well turned, by the Architect Mr. Samuel', but considered 'the rest meane enough, & hardly capable for a hunting house'. He also disapproved of 'the Chimnies plac'd in the angles & Corners, a Mode now introduc'd by his Majestie which I do at no hand approve of', and criticised the situation 'in a dirty Streete; without any Court or avenue, like a common Burgers: whereas it might & ought to have ben built at either end of the Towne, upon the very Carpet, where the Sports are celebrated'.[2] Newmarket was certainly an unpretentious house, but its modest accommodation seems to have been found adequate for its informal purpose, for Charles was often there for hawking, cock-fighting and racing, and William III was reported to have expressed satisfaction with it when he went there—not for the first time—in 1698.[3]

Early in 1675 Samwell's account was finally settled after some difficulty,[4] and in March the building was handed over to the Office of Works for maintenance.[5] A Clerk of the Works was appointed, and a modest sum was spent annually on repairs and such minor tasks as 'making a seat at the playhouse for the King, Duke of York & Prince of Orange to sitt in' (1676–7) or 'making a large box for a Bitch to lye in the King's Bedchamber' (1682–3).[6] The King's House was not affected by the fire which burned down half the town in March 1683,[7] and no major addition or altera-tion was called for by any succeeding sovereign. In 1705, when Queen Anne spent a fortnight at Newmarket in April, it was reported in a newsletter that she has 'ordered her house to be rebuilt',[8] but what in fact she asked for was much less radical. It comprised the general redecoration of her apartment, new sash windows, an alteration to the staircase, the renewal of the floor in her bedroom, and the removal of a forge and coach house 'that hid the prospect of the country' from the windows of her privy lodgings.[9] Comparison of the early eighteenth-century plan with that of 1816 shows no significant change other than the demolition in 1814 of the former Lord Chamberlain's office, a timber-framed building which occupied the street frontage immediately to the west of Charles II's building, and

[1] Works 4/2, 5 Feb. 1724; Works 5/35, 37 and 51.
[2] *Diary of John Evelyn*, ed. E. S. de Beer (1959), p. 542.
[3] N. Luttrell, *Brief Historical Relation* i, p. 125; *Cal. S.P. Dom. 1698*, p. 200.
[4] Two of the principal workmen, Edward Roman, bricklayer, and John Scudamore, carpenter, complained in 1672 that Samwell refused to pay 'their moneys due remaining upon just accompts', and accused him of trying to defraud them. Samwell's integrity was sustained by Wren, to whom the complaint was referred by the Treasury, but his own claim for £928 16s. 'for his service in surveying and attending the king's buildings at Newmarket for 6 years past' was eventually cut down to £730 (SP 29/302, f. 116, SP 29/303, ff.245–6; *Cal. Treas. Books* iv, p. 726).
[5] *Cal. Treas. Books* iv, pp. 291, 698. For the Works Yard see *Cal. S.P. Dom. 1676–7*, p. 427.
[6] Works 5/29 and 35.
[7] Luttrell specifically states that 'his Majestie's house received no damage' (*Brief Historical Relation* i, p. 253). See also John Cole, *A Particular Account of the Late Fire with the several losses at Newmarket* (1683).
[8] Luttrell, *op. cit.*, v, pp. 539, 544.
[9] *Cal. Treasury Books* xx, pp. 67, 620; Works 6/14, ff. 89, 110; Works 5/145, p. 236.

which must have been part of the property acquired in 1668. Today the northern part of the site of the palace is occupied by the International Stores, but the south-eastern block of Charles II's building can still be seen from Palace Street, where it forms the two lower storeys of the nineteenth-century house known as 'Palace House Mansion'.

# RICHMOND LODGE AND KEW HOUSE

IN 1664 Charles II granted the manor, park and 'capital messuage' of Richmond to his brother James, Duke of York.[1] The duke thus became possessed of what survived of the Tudor palace. Precisely how much of the fabric remained standing is uncertain, but it is clear that much had been destroyed.[2] In these circumstances the duke contemplated building himself a completely new house, for which he obtained a design from France. In 1707 the architect François Bruand communicated to the Académie Royale d'Architecture the plan and elevation of 'le château de Riche-mont, qui a esté basti en Angleterre, suivant les mêmes desseins que feu M. Bruand fit en 1662 pour le duc d'York'. The date given is two years before the duke's grant, and the house was certainly not built, either at that or at any subsequent date, but two versions of the design survive to substantiate the partial truth of Bruand's statement. One, evidently dating from the 1660s, may probably be attributed to Libéral Bruand, the architect of the Invalides, the other being a revision of it made by his son François in 1705. Both represent a large symmetrical building of the villa type, surmounted by a central dome.[3]

After his accession to the throne in 1685 James II settled Richmond on his queen, and after the birth of his son in June 1688 he had some parts of the old palace fitted up by the Office of Works as a nursery for the infant prince. The accounts refer to the king's and queen's apartments, to the Guard Chamber, the chapel, the banqueting house, and to the prince's Presence Chamber, bedchamber and kitchen. Apartments were provided for the prince's governess, the Marchioness of Powis, and for the under-governess, Lady Strickland. The work involved was chiefly joinery, plastering, painting and glazing, but a decayed tower 16 feet high near the gover-ness's kitchen had to be taken down and rebuilt, a brick wall 33 feet long and 15 feet high was erected 'betwixt the lodgings and the garden, dividing the two Courts',

[1] *V.C.H. Surrey*, iii, p. 543.
[2] *Cal. S.P. Dom. 1660–1*, pp. 71, 140–1, 394.
[3] Patrick Reuterswärd, 'A French Project for a Castle at Richmond', *Burlington Mag.* civ, Dec. 1962, pp. 533–5. The original drawings are in the Nationalmuseum at Stockholm.

and masons were employed 'in cutting two chimneys, and two door cases, in the Trumpeting House, and setting the battlements over the great gate'. The total cost was approximately £1800.[1]

William III appears to have taken no interest in the remains of the palace, but enlarged the lodge in the Old Park for his personal use. Work began in the summer of 1693 and continued in 1694 and 1695. According to a newsletter, the king was 'so well pleased with the situation of the house in the park where he lay', that on returning to Kensington after a short stay at Richmond in January 1695, he immediately 'gave orders for some additional apartments and enlarging of the gardens'.[2] The expenditure, amounting in all to about £3500, was charged to the Hampton Court account. The detailed books have not been preserved, but the enrolments show that the usual Office of Works craftsmen were employed, the largest payments being to James Groves, carpenter, Richard Stacey, bricklayer, and Alexander Fort, joiner. Henry Simmonds, the Clerk of Works at Hampton Court, was in charge, and Nicholas Hawksmoor claimed riding charges for at least one visit to the lodge.[3] The gardening works, accounted for by the Earl of Portland as Superintendent of the King's Gardens, cost £572, of which £120 was paid to George London for 'makeing and levelling the great Walke leading from the House to the Thames, planting it with trees, and other services'.

Soon after William III's death a lease of the lodge was acquired by the Duke of Ormonde, who was ranger of the park.[4] He rebuilt the south-west, or garden, front of the house (Pl. 22) employing the Earl of Ranelagh to superintend the works.[5] Ormonde's tenancy was abruptly terminated by his flight in 1715, and in 1719 the house was offered for sale before the Commissioners for Forfeited Estates. It was bought by the Prince of Wales as a summer residence, a function it continued to serve throughout his reign as George II.[6] If we are to believe John Macky, the prince's new house was 'a perfect Trianon'.[7] In actual fact its pedimented facade concealed an irregular plan (Fig. 15) that hardly justified so exalted an epithet. The walls, moreover, were damp, and so thin that, according to Lord Hervey, who was often there, 'what was said in one room might be often overheard in the next'.[8] But in summer-time the gardens and riverside walks made it a delightful retreat, and the lack of accommodation enforced a degree of privacy which a genuine Trianon might have prejudiced.

---

[1] Works 5/42 contains the detailed account: cf. *Cal. Treasury Papers 1708–14,* p. 590 and Narcissus Luttrell, *Brief Historical Relation* i, pp. 443, 453, 455. Rainwater heads with the date 1688 were still visible in the early nineteenth century (J. Evans, *Richmond and its Vicinity,* 1825, p. 23).

[2] *Cal. S.P. Dom. 1695,* p. 307; Luttrell, *op. cit.,* iii, p. 430.

[3] AO 1/2482/296–7; Works 6/2. For the furnishings of the house see T 1/34, ff. 279, 281.

[4] *Cal. Treasury Papers 1702–7,* pp. 115, 212. The duke acquired the unexpired term of a lease granted in 1694 to John Latten, and a report made in that year by the Surveyor-General of Crown Lands refers to the lodge as having been 'lately repaired and additions made thereto for his Majestie's reception when he shall be pleased to hunt thereabouts' (Crest 40/28, pp. 301–2). There can therefore be no doubt that the Lodge enlarged by William III was the one afterwards known as Ormonde Lodge.

[5] See Ranelagh's letters to Ormonde (1704–5), printed in Hist. MSS. Comm. *Seventh Report,* Appendix, pp. 774–6. For this reference we are indebted to Mr. Alan Bean.

[6] J. Thorne, *Handbook to the Environs of London* ii (1876), p. 493. The prince subsequently obtained a 99-year renewal of the Crown lease (*V.C.H. Surrey* iii, p. 536).

[7] J. Macky, *Journey through England* i (1724), p. 66.

[8] *Memoirs of the Reign of George II by John, Lord Hervey,* ed. Croker, ii, (1884) pp. 88, 107, 249. For its reputation for dampness, see J. Gwynn, *London and Westminster Improved* (1766), p. 116, note †.

219

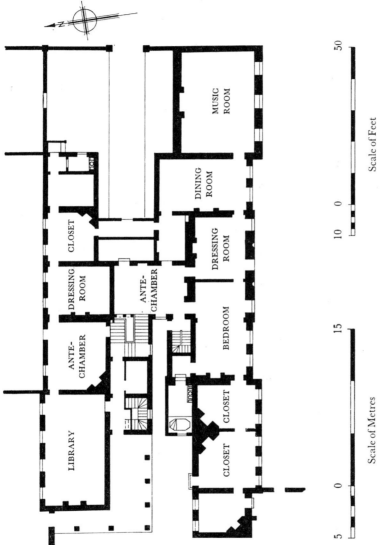

Fig. 15. Richmond Lodge (from a plan in the Royal Library, Windsor).

Proposals for a building more consistent with royal dignity were not, however, wanting. A set of plans and elevations for a royal 'lodge' at Richmond is preserved among the drawings of Sir Edward Lovett Pearce, the Surveyor-General of Ireland.[1] This is an essay in the Palladian manner of which Pearce was an early advocate, and might, but for its provenance, be mistaken for a project by Colen Campbell, who had held the post of architect to the prince before the latter's accession.[2] The exact date of the scheme is not known, but Pearce died in 1733, and it may be conjectured that it was drawn up soon after George II's accession, when the question of a building more suited to the royal dignity would naturally have arisen. No request to Pearce to prepare plans has been found in the royal archives, but the accompanying text implies that it was not merely an unsolicited essay, for the lodge is stated to be 'by command confined to conveniency and proper use without magnificence, ornament or great expense'. It was, nevertheless, a building of some size and consequence that Pearce envisaged, for it was to have four facades, each 173 feet in length and terminating in corner pavilions emphasised by Venetian windows. Within, the layout was admirably logical: a grand staircase, itself divided on either side of the main entrance, led to duplicate sequences of state apartments, each consisting of Guard Chamber, Ante-Chamber, Presence Chamber and Bedchamber, one for the king, the other for the queen. The two suites united in a grand 'gallery for public assemblies' which occupied the whole of the front on the side opposite the entrance. The normal circulation from one room to another was supplemented by a circular gallery which ran round the courtyard at first floor level. This gallery also served a visual purpose, by 'breaking that disagreeable elevation usual in small courts and hiding the want of other ornaments'. Ample accommodation for the household officers was provided on the ground floor and in the attics, but the offices were to be banished somewhat inconveniently to a detached building 150 yards distant from the main block. As Pearce was 'unacquainted with particular rates now in England', he did not submit an estimate, but hazarded a guess that 'in all probability it can not exceed £18 or £20,000 at the highest computation'.

Pearce was followed by William Kent, whose design for a full-scale palace is represented by a pearwood model now exhibited in the Dutch House at Kew, but formerly kept at Hampton Court. In the past this model has been connected with the project for a palace in Hyde Park, but its real destination is indicated by the following entry in the minutes of the Board or Works for 1 October 1773:

> Order'd that the Model of a Palace (design'd by the late Mr. Kent) proposed to be built at Richmond which has been deposited in this office several years be sent to Hampton Court Palace.[3]

It is a characteristic composition in which the mass is broken up into a number of architecturally independent elements, and has features in common with Chiswick

[1] *Architectural Drawings in the Library of Elton Hall*, ed. H. Colvin & M. Craig (Roxburghe Club 1964), pls. 74–6.
[2] B.M., Add. MS. 24387, f. 76 (Register of Warrants of George, Prince of Wales).
[3] Works 4/15. It was doubtless this model that Count Kielmansegge saw in one of the summer-houses at Richmond in 1761 (*Diary of a Journey to England*, 1902, p. 74).

House, Holkham Hall and the Horse Guards. The abruptness of the flat top of the central pavilion suggests a missing dome, like the one which surmounted Kent's project for the Houses of Parliament (Pl. 59). This is presumably the model referred to in the *London Daily Post and General Advertiser* for 15 September 1735, where it is reported that 'last Saturday' Richard Arundell went to Kew to show the queen a model 'made by Mr. Marsden of Vine Street, Westminster, joiner to H.M. at Hampton Court, designed for a Hunting Seat for His Majesty to be built either at Richmond or Bushy Park'.[1] In the Paymaster's accounts for 1736 there duly appears a payment to John Marsden 'for making a wainscot moddel finneered with pear tree for Richmond, with a frame, case, and repairing several times . . . £120'.[2]

Neither project was, of course, adopted, but considerable sums were spent on the lodge, and still larger ones on the grounds. According to Rocque the house was 'not quite finished' at the time of Ormonde's forfeiture, and it underwent several alterations during its period of royal occupation. The library wing at the rear (Pl. 23B) was clearly an addition, and one probably to be attributed to the reign of George II. The Music Room seen in Sandby's water-colour (Pl. 22B) replaced an earlier wing with five windows matching the one opposite, but dated probably from the early years of George III.[3] From the accession of George II onwards works here were supervised and accounted for by the Office of Works, but only summarised statements of expenditure are recorded, amounting during the whole reign to a total of £36,171, an average of £1130 a year.[4] The heaviest expenditure was, however, incurred during the lifetime of Queen Caroline, for the property had in 1727 been settled on her as a potential dower house should she survive her husband, and it was she who created the extensive gardens. They covered some hundreds of acres, and were a notable example of English landscape-gardening. The entire layout is shown in a series of engravings by John Rocque, and in an original plan, probably by the hand of Charles Bridgeman, now in the Public Record Office.[5] It consisted of three principal landscaped areas, charmingly interspersed with fields and parkland so as to create a great variety of scenery (Fig. 16). The whole was linked together by a 'Forest Walk' stretching from Richmond to Kew, and by a parallel terraced walk along the banks of the Thames. Formal vistas framed the two facades of the lodge itself, but otherwise the aim was (to quote the queen herself) 'to help nature' rather than to regiment it.[6] Informality did not, however, mean the exclusion of architectural embellishment, and a variety of buildings beckoned the visitor on or

---

[1] For this reference we are indebted to Mr. Geoffrey Beard.

[2] AO 1/2455/170 (Paymaster's enrolled account).

[3] The original wing, with its five windows, is shown in a survey plan in the P.R.O. (Works 32/94), and in a similar plan in the Royal Library at Windsor (Portfolio 58). An engraved elevation decorates the title-page of Badeslade and Rocque's *Vitruvius Brittanicus* (1739). Fig. 15, based on a later plan in the same portfolio at Windsor, shows the Music Room as in Sandby's water-colour.

[4] Works 5/57–62, 141. Throughout George II's reign the expenses of the royal household at Richmond formed a separate account in the Civil List (*Commons' Journals* vol. 32, pp. 470, 478, 485 etc.; B.M., Add. MS. 30205, ff. 10, 11, 12, 13). One surviving account (P.R.O. T 1/319, no. 19) includes payments only for minor maintenance works, but if the whole series could be found it might well throw further light on the history of the lodge and its grounds.

[5] Works 32/96. For a variant layout for the 'Wilderness' at the Richmond end see B.M., King's Maps xli, 16-e. Rocque's engraved plans are (i) *Vitruvius Brittanicus* iv (1739), pls. 9–10; (ii) a large sheet dated 1748; (iii) a small sheet dated 1754.

[6] *Egmont Diary* (Hist. MSS. Comm.) ii, p .138.

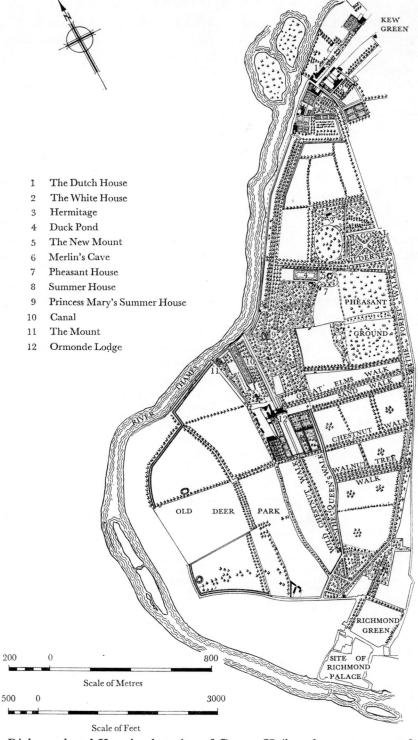

1     The Dutch House
2     The White House
3     Hermitage
4     Duck Pond
5     The New Mount
6     Merlin's Cave
7     Pheasant House
8     Summer House
9     Princess Mary's Summer House
10    Canal
11    The Mount
12    Ormonde Lodge

Scale of Metres

Scale of Feet

Fig. 16. Richmond and Kew in the reign of George II (based on an engraved map by
J. Rocque dated 1754).

1   The Dutch House
2   The White House
3   Orangery
4   Menagerie
5   Hermitage
6   Temple of Victory
7   Gothic Cathedral
8   Pagoda
9   New Menagerie
10  Site for Royal House
11  Obelisk
12  Observatory

Scale of Metres

Scale of Feet

Fig. 17. Richmond and Kew in the reign of George III (based on Works 32/99 and other sources).

offered him a point of vantage from which to survey the landscape. They included a Hermitage (Pl. 31 B), a Dairy, a small domed Temple, complete with altar, a summer-house at the end of the river-walk, another in one of the woods, and a bizarre building with a thatched roof, known as Merlin's Cave. This last contained wax-work figures sitting round a table. The significance of this group is not altogether clear, but one figure apparently represented Elizabeth of York, the wife of Henry VII, and another the magician Merlin, who was supposed to have prophesied the accession of the Hanoverian dynasty to the English throne. Both the 'Cave' and the Hermitage were designed by William Kent, who was no doubt responsible for most of the other garden buildings.[1] Some of them may have been commissioned by Caroline before her husband's accession to the throne, but others were of subsequent erection, and these were built under the direction of the Board of Works. Thus in October 1729 the Board passed the accounts 'for building a new pavilion [i.e. a summer-house] in the wood at Richmond', and in November 1730 'took into consideration the Hermitage to be built for His Majesty at Richmond and gave the necessary directions to Mr. Flitcroft and Mr. Jelfe for proceeding thereon'.[2] Henry Flitcroft held the office of Clerk of Works at Richmond, and Andrews Jelfe was the mason employed. The cost of the Hermitage was £1114.[3] Merlin's Cave was built in 1735: the *Gentleman's Magazine* refers to it as 'carrying on' in that year,[4] and it may have been the 'new building in the wood at Richmond' for which the accounts were passed in August. The river terrace was an extension of one already existing in Ormonde's time. Work on it appears to have been begun in October 1729, when the Board 'ordered the New Terrass Wall at Richmond to be proceded upon', and it was finished by April 1734, when they passed the books for the 'Tarras wall from Kew to Richmond'. The original estimate was £614.[5]

Any further embellishments were prevented by Queen Caroline's death in 1737, and for the next twenty years nothing more than maintenance is indicated by the Works records. George III's accession gave promise of new works at Richmond to match those of his mother the dowager Princess of Wales at Kew. As early as October 1761 a foreign visitor to Richmond was told that the king 'has decided to begin the building of an entirely new palace in February', but that the site had not been settled.[6] As at Kew, so at Richmond the architect was to be William Chambers, whose drawing of 'the North front of a villa for a particular situation near London', exhibited at the Society of Artists in 1762, was identified by Horace Walpole as a

---

[1] Merlin's Cave and the Hermitage are the subject of plates in Vardy's *Designs of Inigo Jones and William Kent* (1744). For the Hermitage see Judith Colton in *Architectura*, 1974, pp. 181–191.
[2] Works 4/4, 9 Oct. 1729, 5 Nov. 1730.
[3] Works 5/58, March 1731.
[4] *Gent's. Mag.* vol. v (1735), p. 331, where it is also stated that 'Her Majesty has ordered Mr. Risbrack to make the Bustos in Marble of all the Kings of England from William the Conqueror, in order to be placed in her New Building in the Gardens at Richmond'. Owing to the queen's death this commission was never completed, but terracotta models of 10 of them survived at Windsor until 1906. For these and the busts for the Hermitage by the sculptors Guelfi and Rysbrack see M. I. Webb, *Michael Rysbrack, Sculptor* (1954), pp. 145–54. They are not referred to in the Works Minutes, nor do the four busts originally commissioned for the Hermitage (Newton, Locke, Clarke and Wollaston) seem to have been paid for by the Paymaster. But in 1732 he paid Guelfi £68 'for a Busto of the Honble. Robert Boyle in Statuary Marble with a neck of veined marble & for carriage & repairing the antique statue of Venus' (AO 1/2454/166).
[5] Works 4/4, 9 Oct. 1729; Works 4/6, 9 April 1734.
[6] Count Frederick Kielmansegge, *Diary of a Journey to England in the Years 1761–2* (1902), p. 73.

design for George III at Richmond.[1] In the Royal Library at Windsor there are numerous alternative plans and elevations for houses and palaces made by Chambers for George III. None of them is dated, and it is impossible to identify with certainty the 'villa' projected in 1762. There is, however, a more ambitious design, for which a number of drawings exist, whose markedly Palladian character suggests that it should be placed early in the reign, before architectural taste had moved far in the direction of neo-classicism.[2] Its principal features were pavilion towers at the corners, a Corinthian portico flanked by ranges of conventionally pedimented windows, and a great apsidal hall dividing the internal space into two equal courtyards (Pl. 24B). This design evidently owed a good deal to Holkham, though the monotonous simplicity of the fenestration is in marked contrast to the studied variegation so characteristic of Kent's architecture. In terms of size, the royal palace would have been considerably larger, some 328 × 225 feet as against Holkham's 160 × 110 feet. An undated estimate for a palace 'to be erected in the Royal Gardens at Richmond' enumerates features which appear to correspond to this design, and gives the cost as £89,320.[3] This design was also represented by a wooden model, formerly preserved at Hampton Court, but unfortunately destroyed in 1922 (Pl. 24A). It is likely that this was the model of a royal palace, 'designed by William Chambers Esq., and executed by Benoni Thacker Esq.', which was presented to the king in 1765.[4] Neither in 1762 nor in 1765, however, was the king in a position to embark on so ambitious a project, for he had just spend £28,000 on the purchase of Buckingham House, and still larger sums were needed to adapt it to the purposes of a royal residence.

The idea of building at Richmond was, however, postponed rather than abandoned, and in the meanwhile 'Capability' Brown was given a free hand with the grounds, which he completely remodelled, doing away not only with Bridgeman's walks and wildernesses, but also with the river terrace and most of Queen Caroline's garden buildings. In October 1765 Kirby, the Clerk of Works, reported to the Board 'that great alterations and improvements were making in Richmond Gardens by Mr. Launcelot Browne', and a year later a quantity of old lead from Merlin's Cave was sold to Devall the plumber for £31 14s. 9¼d.[5] Thus the delightfully varied layout which Bridgeman and Kent had created for Queen Caroline was swept away, presumably with the full approval of the king, though not with that of the Reverend William Mason, whose *Heroic Epistle to Sir William Chambers* sadly records its demise:

> To Richmond come, for see, untutor'd Brown
> Destroys those wonders which were once thy own.
> Lo, from his melon-ground the peasant slave
> Has rudely rush'd, and levell'd Merlin's Cave;

---

[1] *Walpole Society* xxvii (1939), p. 63.

[2] Windsor Castle, Royal Library, PA 2/1–2. See also B.M., King's Maps cxxiv, 59, 60 and Sir John Soane's Museum, Dance Cabinet, Slider 3, Set 7, No. 7.

[3] This estimate is loosely inserted within the cover of a survey (1771) of Richmond in the Royal Library at Windsor.

[4] *Court Magazine* 1765, p. 801, when it is stated to have 'four fronts which will, if executed, be one of the grandest palaces in Europe'. Benoni Thacker was a London carpenter and joiner.

[5] Works 4/13, 11 Oct. 1765, 10 Oct. 1766.

> Knock'd down the waxen Wizzard, seiz'd his wand,
> Transform'd to lawn what late was Fairy land;
> And marr'd, with impious hand, each sweet design
> Of Stephen Duck, and good Queen Caroline.[1]

Presently the place of Queen Caroline's follies was taken by a building destined for more serious purposes. In order to enable the king to observe the transit of Venus in 1769, a Royal Observatory was erected in 1768–9 to Chambers's designs. It was conceived in terms of a small villa with octagon rooms expressed externally by canted bays. The original silhouette was altered in the nineteenth century by raising the one-story wings to the same height as the central block, but the interior has been little changed to serve the meteorological purposes to which the Observatory is now devoted. The Office of Works appears to have had no responsibility for the construction of this elegant but strictly functional building, and the only known account connected with its erection was one submitted direct to the king by William Kirby on behalf of James Arrow, joiner, Solomon Brown, bricklayer, and two other craftsmen. This was presumably settled out of the Privy Purse.[2]

At the same time the project for a new palace or 'villa' was revived. A site for a house is indicated on one of Brown's plans for the new landscape of grassland interspersed with clumps of trees,[3] and Mrs. Papendiek (whose husband was a member of the household staff at Richmond) recalls that 'in this year, 1769, we remained late in the season at Richmond, as his Majesty was greatly occupied in digesting plans with Sir William Chambers for a new palace at Richmond, the lodge now occupied being too small for the increasing family'.[4] An 'elevation of one of the flanks of a royal palace' was exhibited by Chambers at the Royal Academy that summer, and in 1770, in an autobiographical note, he stated that he was 'at present engaged on the plans for a Royal Palace in Richmond'.[5] The foundations were laid in the summer of 1770, 'very near' the site of the old lodge (Fig. 17).[6] According to Lady Mary Coke the building was to have a frontage of 140 feet, and was to be 'built on arches in order, as I suppose, to command a greater prospect'. It was, she understood, to cost 'no more than five and twenty thousand pounds'.[7] The 'arches' are also mentioned by Lysons:[8] a vaulted basement is presumably what is meant. Mrs. Papendiek says that 'the model of the elegant design fixed upon' was to be seen at Hampton Court. This would seem to identify it with a second model, also

[1] *Satirical Poems of William Mason*, ed. P. Toynbee (1926), p. 49. Stephen Duck, the 'Thresher-Poet', was a protégé of the queen's who looked after Merlin's Cave.

[2] Windsor Castle, RA 55656–7. It was, however, the Office of Works which in 1778 set up three Portland stone obelisks in the Old Deer Park in order to mark the points of the compass in relation to the Observatory (Works 5/66, June 1778). For the history of the observatory see R. H. Scott in *Proceedings of the Royal Society*, 1885.

[3] Works 32/96. The outline appears to envisage a house about 200 ft. × 100 ft. Another plan by Brown in the library of the Royal Botanic Garden at Kew shows an outline about 400 ft × 200 ft. This plan is dated December 10, 1764, and thus relates to the earlier schemes of 1762–5.

[4] *The Journals of Mrs. Papendiek*, ed. Mrs. V. Delves Broughton, i (1887), pp. 42–3.

[5] Uppsala University Library.

[6] The 'foundation of the intended house' is marked in this position on a 'Plan of Richmond and Kew Gardens' made in 1771 (B.M., King's Maps xli, 16 i), and on a plan of this part of the garden in the Royal Library at Windsor (Portfolio 58). The area is now a golf-course and the exact site cannot be discerned.

[7] *Letters and Journals of Lady Mary Coke*, ed. J. A. Home iii (1892), pp. 268–9.

[8] S. & D. Lysons, *The Environs of London* i (1810), p. 329.

unhappily destroyed in 1922, of a house raised on a high rusticated basement, with quadrant colonnades stretching out to detached wings in the manner of Palladio's Villa Mocenigo, already imitated in England in the designs for Nostell Priory and Kedleston Hall. A plan at Windsor shows that the front of this house measured about 130 feet, which is within 10 feet of Lady Mary Coke's figure of 140 feet. The model destroyed in 1922 is, however, almost certainly to be identified with one known to have been made in 1775,[1] and it is possible that Mrs. Papendiek was wrong to associate it with the design adopted in 1770. On the other hand there are among the drawings at Windsor several variant versions of the house with the quadrant colonnades,[2] and it may well be that the designs of 1770 and 1775 were essentially similar. As the foundations had actually been laid it would, indeed, be understandable if Chambers's later proposals were variations on the same basic plan. However this may be, no royal residence, whether villa or palace, was destined to be built at Richmond. Already in August 1770, Lady Mary Coke commented on the slow progress of the works, and in 1773 Thomas Worsley lamented that the king 'cannot go on with so small a design'. 'If', he observed, 'it was a grand *Caserta*, I should not be surprised, but [for] so modest an undertaking to stop, or go on so very slow is hard'.[3] As the house, like the Observatory, was apparently paid for out of the Privy Purse, the records of the Office of Works throw no light on the operations at Richmond. According to Mrs. Papendiek the difficulty was that in order to complete the amenities of the house, the king desired to purchase a small piece of adjoining ground that did not form part of the royal manor, but belonged to the inhabitants of Richmond. This they refused to part with. 'The building nevertheless went on as far as the ground floor, but was then stopped, and their Majesties determined to remove to Kew.'[4] Here they took over both the 'White House', for many years the residence of the Dowager Princess of Wales, and the adjoining 'Dutch House', the lease of which had been acquired by the Crown in the previous reign. The latter served as an annexe for some of the royal children, others of whom occupied houses on Kew Green.[5]

Kew House, which thus succeeded Richmond Lodge as the royal residence, had been built by Frederick, Prince of Wales, between 1731 and 1735. William Kent had been his architect, with Thomas Ripley as Comptroller of his Works, and over £8000 had been spent on the building under their direction.[6] The result was the mansion, commonly known as the White House in order to distinguish it from the

---

[1] J. Gough, *British Topography* i (1780), p. 357, note f, mentions all three models, and says that the third was 'made in 1775 by Mr. Goldsmith, of Rose Street, Covent Garden, from a model of Sir William Chambers'. Chambers refers to his 'model for Richmond' as 'finished' in a letter to Thomas Worsley dated 4 August 1775 (B.M., Add. MS. 41135, f. 72ᵛ).

[2] For these see J. Harris, *Sir William Chambers* (1970), pp. 77–8 and pl. 112. One possibility is that the central block was originally to stand alone, and that the wings and colonnades were envisaged only in 1775. This would explain the awkwardness of the junction between the colonnades and the main block.

[3] B.M., Add. MS. 41134, f. 30.

[4] *The Journals of Mrs. Papendiek* i (1887) pp. 42–3.

[5] According to Mrs. Papendiek the princess gave up the White House to the royal family in 1770 or 1771, and lived at the Dutch House until her death in 1772. But other evidence indicates that it was not until after her death that the king and queen moved from Richmond to Kew, taking over both houses at the same time. On this and other points concerning the royal residences at Kew see R. L. Rutton's articles in *Home Counties Magazine* vol. 7 (1905).

[6] Duchy of Cornwall Records, Accounts of Frederick Prince of Wales, vol. ii, f. 206, vol. iv, f. 222, vol. v, ff. 262–282; Analysis of his expenditure (Cupboard Y1).

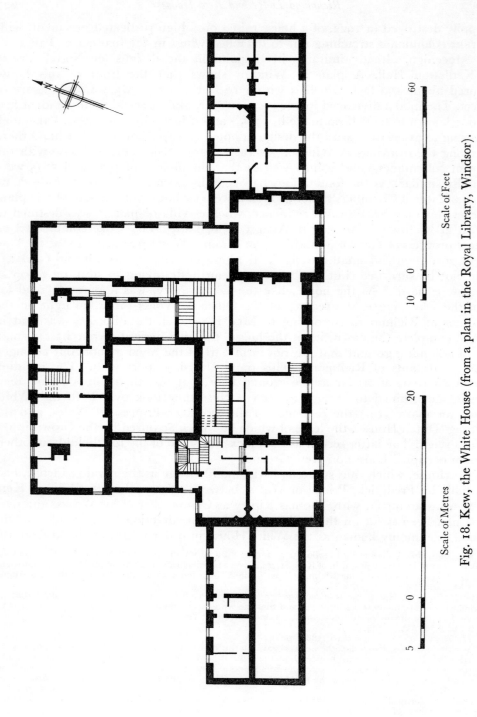

Scale of Metres

Scale of Feet

Fig. 18. Kew, the White House (from a plan in the Royal Library, Windsor).

0

5

0

20

10

0

60

red-brick Dutch House opposite, shown in Plate 23C and Figure 18. More recently Sir William Chambers and the botanist Aiton had created for the Dowager Princess the celebrated gardens of which Chambers had published a volume of engravings in 1763.[1] Now, as Comptroller of the King's Works, he was commissioned to adapt the house for occupation by the royal family. No details of the works carried out in 1772–3 are afforded by the accounts, but the expenditure exceeded £9000, and a good deal more was spent during the next few years.[2] Plans in the Royal Library at Windsor show that what was envisaged was the conversion of the left-hand wing into a library and of the right-hand wing into what was almost certainly a music-room. The north side of the house, facing towards the Dutch House and the river, was to be entirely rebuilt, with a new facade 18 feet wider than the old one, and corresponding exactly in plan (and therefore presumably in elevation) to the garden facade seen in Plate 23C. How far these alterations were carried out it is difficult to say, as topographical artists invariably chose to draw the garden, rather than the entrance, front.[3] Some later views of the house from the south do, however, show a building which evidently formed part of the works carried out in 1772–3. This was a small clock-tower, terminating in a cupola, which stood a short distance to the north-east of the house. In January 1773 the accounts passed by the Board of Works included 'an Extra for Richmond and Kew Tower'.[4]

As soon as the White House was ready, Ormonde Lodge was demolished,[5] and Richmond and Kew Gardens were united by doing away with the road known as Kew Lane, which hitherto had separated them.[6] The 'beautifying and enriching' of the combined gardens became one of the queen's favourite pastimes, and it was for her pleasure that the half-timbered *cottage orné* which still survives was erected near the southern end of the gardens. Neither the exact date of its construction nor the identity of its designer is known, but it already existed in 1774, for it was mentioned in the *London Magazine* of that year.[7]

[1] *Plans, Elevations Sections and Perspective Views of the Gardens and Buildings at Kew in Surrey.*
[2] Works 5/142; Works 5/64, June 1772, under 'Extra Works'; Works 4/15, 19 Feb. 1773.
[3] For a description of the White House during its occupation by George III, see *A New Display of the Beauties of England*, 3rd. ed. 1776, vol. i, pp. 5–6.
[4] Works 4/15, 29 Jan. 1773. A view of this tower forms part of a rare set of coloured aquatints of Kew Gardens by C. E. Pependiek of which there is a copy in the Abbey Collection now owned by Mr. Paul Mellon.
[5] Windsor Castle, RA 15981 is an estimate for its demolition, dated 3 July 1772.
[6] J. Watkins, *Memoirs of Queen Charlotte* i (1819), p. 235.
[7] *London Magazine* vol. 43 (1774), p. 361.

# RICHMOND NEW PARK LODGE

ALTHOUGH THERE were deer in the Little Park adjoining Ormonde Lodge, it was only in the New Park created by Charles I that there was adequate space for kings to hunt. Here, however, satisfactory accommodation was altogether lacking. The old Carlile Lodge had indeed been handsomely rebuilt by the Earl of Rochester, but as a private residence.[1] Meanwhile the Ranger's Lodge on the edge of Spanker's Hill was falling into decay.[2] When William III hunted in Richmond Park he used the lodge in the Little Park, but by George I's reign this was in the hands of the Prince of Wales,[3] and the king himself had no base for hunting or shooting expeditions in either park.

It was in these circumstances that towards the end of his reign George I gave orders for the building of a new lodge in the New Park. The design which he approved in the winter of 1726–7 was made by Roger Morris, the architectural protégé of Lord Herbert, afterwards ninth Earl of Pembroke. Herbert was on good terms with the king, and it was presumably due to his influence that Morris was employed. Horace Walpole, indeed, implies that he designed the building himself, but it is probable that the plans, though sponsored by Herbert, were worked out on paper by Morris, and that the editors of *Vitruvius Britannicus* were right to refer to the latter as the 'architect'.[4] In February 1727 the 'draughts' were sent by the Treasury to the Board of Works, with a request for an estimate. In their reply the Board stated that, 'not being appriz'd of the manner of finishing' the lodge, they could furnish an estimate only 'for building the carcase faced with stone, digging, and making the terrass round the house, which may amount to about the sum of £5780 2s. 3½d.' £953 could, however, be saved by using bricks and timber available in the Park, and a further saving of £375 could be effected by not using stone above the level of the basement, except for ornaments. By these means the total cost might be reduced to £4450. In addition, it would be necessary to appoint a Clerk of Works at £100 a year, and a Labourer in Trust at 2s. 2d. a day, as none of the Board's existing staff could be spared to supervise the work. On 5 March

[1] Rochester's contract with Matthew Banckes, the King's Master Carpenter, is in the Surrey County Record Office, S.C. 13/26/102–3. The house was destroyed by fire in 1721. There is a plate of it in Kip's *Britannia Illustrata* (1714).

[2] *Cal. Treasury Papers 1714–19*, p. 231. In the reign of George II it was largely rebuilt at the expense of Sir Robert Walpole, who used it as a country retreat throughout his ministerial career. Nominally it belonged to his eldest son Robert, as Ranger of the Park. Walpole added the wings with canted bow-windows seen in the engraving published in Watts's *Views of Seats* (1780). It was subsequently occupied by Princess Amelia (1751–61) and Philip Meadows (d. 1781). By 1807 it was reported to be in poor repair, and it was eventually pulled down in 1839–41 (C. L. Collenette, *History of Richmond Park*, 1937, 46–7). Block plans of it exist in the P.R.O. (MR 296) and the R.I.B.A. Collection (E 6/3³), and there is a drawing by Buckler in B.M., Add. MS. 36388, f. 274.

[3] Above, p. 218.

[4] Walpole, *Anecdotes of Painting*, ed. Wornum iii (1862), p. 772; Woolfe & Gandon, *Vitruvius Britannicus* iv (1767), pls. 1–4.

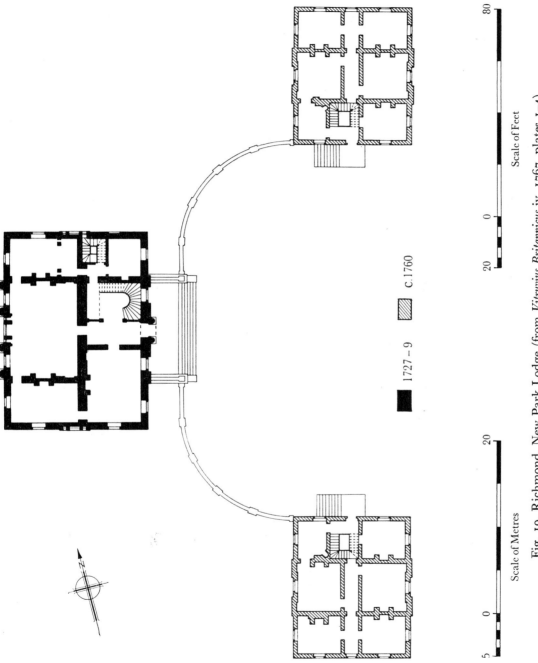

Scale of Metres

Scale of Feet

Fig. 19. Richmond, New Park Lodge (from *Vitruvius Britannicus* iv, 1767, plates 1–4).

1727 the Treasury authorised an expenditure of £4450, and the appointment of the Clerk of Works and his assistant. On 30 March Roger Morris was accordingly nominated as Clerk of Works, with Daniel Garrett as Labourer in Trust. John Mist contracted to dig the foundations at the rate of 10d. per cubic yard, while Thomas Rogers, brickmaker, undertook to deliver 30,000 picked grey stock bricks at 22s. a thousand. The bricks were laid by Thomas Churchill; Christopher Cass was employed as master-mason.[1] The site was on rising ground about a quarter of a mile to the north of the Old Lodge.

The operations in Richmond Park were not interrupted by George I's death in June 1727, but continued until the 'carcase' was finished early in 1728. The expenditure then reported to the Treasury totalled £6483, of which £1959 was attributed to the reign of George I, and £4524 to that of his successor.[2] In 1729 the Treasury authorised a further expenditure of £500 on making an approach to the lodge, fitting up the kitchen and providing the Great Room with a floor and a Portland Stone chimneypiece.[3] In fact the sums spent in 1729 amounted to £1176, raising the total cost of the building to £7659.[4]

The result was an elegant Palladian villa, faced (despite the Treasury's initial directive to save money by using brick) with the Portland Stone to whose colour the building owes its present name of White Lodge. The accommodation was clearly intended only for brief, informal visits, consisting of no more than four rooms on the principal floor, with offices below and a few bedrooms above (Fig. 19). Horace Walpole, indeed, says that it was designed 'merely as a banquetting-house, with a large eating room, kitchen and necessary offices, where the king might dine after his sport'.[5]

In 1751 the rangership was given to Princess Amelia, who lived at the Old Lodge, but also made use of the new one. In 1751–2 the house was repaired and redecorated at her expense under the direction of Stephen Wright,[6] and she subsequently employed Wright (formally appointed Clerk of Works in 1754) to add the existing wings. These are of brick and were connected to the main block by curving tunnels whose vaulted roofs did not rise above basement-level. These additions cannot yet have been complete in 1761, when Princess Amelia gave up the rangership, for they were stated still to be unfinished when in 1767 they were illustrated in volume IV of *Vitruvius Britannicus*.

Soon after the accession of George III some extensive repairs had, however, been carried out by the Office of Works for the benefit of Lord Bute, the new Ranger. The expenditure amounted in 1761–2 to £2128, in 1762–3 to £1688, and in 1763–4 to £2130.[7] Bute was not, however, permanently resident, and during the earlier part of their reign King George III and Queen Charlotte were in the habit of

---

[1] Works 4/3, 26 Jan., 2, 14, 16 Feb., 23, 30 March, 1727; T 56/18, p. 245; Works 5/57, Jan. 1727/8.
[2] Works 4/3, 11 July 1728; Works 5/141, 1728; Works 6/15, p. 187.
[3] Works 4/4, 15 May, 12 June 1729; T 56/18, p. 300. The existing chimneypiece, though Georgian, is of wood.
[4] Works 5/141, 1729.
[5] *Reminiscences of Horace Walpole*, ed. P. Toynbee (1924), pp. 16–17.
[6] The accounts for the work done in 1751–2 are among the papers of Richard Arundell now in Nottingham University Library (Galway Collection, 12873).
[7] Works 5/142; Works 1/3, p. 156.

withdrawing to the White Lodge on Sundays, when the royal gardens at Richmond were open to the public.[1] This practice was, however, discontinued later in the reign, and in 1801 the king offered the lodge to his Prime Minister, Henry Addington, afterwards Lord Sidmouth.

# ST. JAMES'S PALACE

## 1. THE PALACE

DURING THE last years of the Interregnum St. James's Palace had served as a barracks and military headquarters. On the eve of the Restoration it was occupied by troops under the command of General Monck, and two clerks of the works, Richard and Leonard Gammon, subsequently accounted for 'worke done at St. James's from the xij^th March 1659 [i.e. 1659/60] unto the last of Aprill 1660 for [Moncke] himselfe, his officers and souldiers'.[2] There is evidence that steps to make the palace fit for royal occupation were taken as soon as the Restoration was certain,[3] but the surviving accounts cover works carried out from June 1660 only.[4] These indicate that a general repair was in progress. While bricklayers were 'worcking upp with brick the walles of the out side of the house which were verey much brocken; and hueing of all the morter which was layed on the said walles by reason of courts of Guard and shedds built up against itt when itt was a Garrison', carpenters were engaged on various tasks, including 'repaireinge the roofe and sceelinge of the Long Gallery; the principall timbers beinge rotten in severall places' and 'takeinge down a large bourded partition in the Anti-Chapell'. Plasterers were finishing off work already begun at the Great Stairs and making good in the Long Gallery after the carpenters. In the chapel Henry Phillips repaired the 'modern [i.e. Gothic] church worke in the canopy over the staules'.

It was the Duke and Duchess of York for whose residence the palace was designated, and during the next few years a good deal of money was spent on their apartments. These occupied the garden front, and were considered to have been 'very nobly trimed up' for their occupation.[5] Indeed, a French visitor considered that the duke and duchess were 'better lodged than the king or the queen'.[6] The

---

[1] *Letters & Journals of Lady Mary Coke*, ed. Home (1889–96), ii, p. 319.
[2] Works 5/1: duplicate in B.M., Harleian MS. 1656, ff. 255–8.
[3] *Commons' Jnls.* vol. 8, p. 29: a payment of £200 to John Embree, Cromwell's Surveyor of Works, for the repair of St. James's.
[4] Works 5/1, under 'St. James's'.
[5] Rugge's Diurnall (B.M., Add. MS. 10116), f. 237.
[6] *Les Voyages de M. de Monconys en Angleterre* iii (Paris 1695), p. 38.

most elaborately decorated room was the duchess's bedchamber. Her bed stood in an alcove ornamented with festoons and trophies carved by Henry Phillips, and was surrounded on three sides by a balustered rail. Four wreathed columns each 7 feet 6 inches high were an important feature of the room, but it is not clear where they stood in relation to the bed: they do not appear to have been bed-posts. The walls were painted to look like 'white marble', and the mouldings were lavishly gilded by the Sergeant Painter.[1] The alcove had a 'frett ceiling' made by John Grove, the Master Plasterer, who subsequently made a similar ceiling in the bed-room itself.[2] The old stone mullioned window was taken out and replaced by a new window divided by two wooden transomes so as to have four square lights in the upper part and two casements below.[3] In 1663 a similar window was set up in the adjoining 'Withdrawing' or 'Balcony' Room, but with doors to give access to the balcony.[4] These doors and the window were painted stone colour, as also was the rail of the balcony.[5] The encroachment of a new chimney-stack on one end of the balcony seems to explain a further payment to Robert Streater, the Sergeant Painter, for 'imitating the rayle and bannister on the wall and shadowing it'.[6] When the duchess died in 1671 her bedchamber was hung with black, and the doors and doorcase were coloured black to match. The new duchess, Mary of Modena, had the room redecorated by Streater. The wreathed columns were removed, and the floor was made good 'whither they were taken away'.[7] In 1677 the old balcony outside her Withdrawing Room was replaced by a new one 'with a timber rayle and ballaster'.[8] In 1680 a little oratory or 'chapel closet' was made beside her bedroom. William Emmett carved a 'ritch picktur frame wrought with flowers' to go over the altar, and 'a cherubin's head with a compartment about for two festoones of leaves' to decorate the window, while Robert Streater painted 'all the wainscott worke carveing & window shutters' to resemble 'lapis lazuli & raince marbell & white & black marbell'. In the bedroom itself a new 'frett ceiling' was made by John Grove and William Emmett supplied carved architraves for the five doors with picture frames over them, 'a foliage pannell with a Cipher of the Dutchess of York's name in it' and 'one ornayment about the chimney peece rought with drapery freued [fruit] and flowers and a Dukeall Coronett'. The cost of £219 was defrayed by the king.[9]

The position of the duke's apartment is not clear. He may have occupied the king's lodgings immediately to the east of the duchess's apartment, but this would leave the symmetrical brick building which stood immediately to the west of her apartment unaccounted for, and it is possible that this was occupied by the duke. The date of its erection is not known, but it must have been built before the death of Charles II, for it is visible in Ogilby and Morgan's map of 1682, as well as in a late seventeenth-century painting in the Royal Collection (Pl. 26). A survey of *circa* 1700 shows that it was 68 feet long, and that it contained three interconnecting rooms on the principal floor.[10] The external distribution of the windows into three

[1] Works 5/2–3.          [2] Works 5/3 and 11.          [3] Works 5/2.
[4] Works 5/3 (March 1663).       [5] Works 5/4.          [6] Works 5/4 (Feb. 1664).
[7] Works 5/29.          [8] Works 5/29.
[9] Works 5/32 (at the end); E 351/3293.
[10] Bodleian, MS. Gough Misc. Ant. 17, f. 92ᵛ, a note-book of the clerk of works, William Dickinson.

pairs of two may be compared with Wren's design of 1688 for the Queen's Drawing Room at Whitehall (Pl. 37). No expenditure commensurate with the erection of such a building has been found in the Works accounts, but if the duke built it at his own expense the accounts would not necessarily appear in the Works series.

Wherever the duke's apartment was, the accounts do not suggest that it was so lavishly fitted up as the duchess's, but his rooms were wainscotted, and in 1663 Joshua Marshall supplied 'a large chimney piece of Portland stone . . . with an architrave and swelling frize and a black marble table and a cornice six inches thick & nine foote long' for his Presence Chamber.[1] In the spring of 1667 his apartment was further embellished and was enlarged by adding three new rooms over the passage to his back-stairs. His withdrawing room was provided with a 'frett ceiling' made by Edward Martin, plasterer, for £23 16s. 3d., and the space over the chimney-piece was decorated by a picture frame carved with 'french leaves', 'folding leaves', 'a knot of ribbon' and 'a foliage pannel' 4 feet 8 inches long and 1 foot 2 inches broad carved by Henry Phillips. The expenditure was shared between the king and the duke, the latter contributing £300 to the total of £622 9s.[2] When Pepys saw the room in May 1667 he admired the 'fretted' ceiling and the chimneypiece, and thought it 'one of the noblest and best-proportioned rooms that ever, I think, I saw in my life'.[3] New stables for the duke's horses had already been built in 1661 at a cost of over £500,[4] and in 1664–6 two old houses 'belonging to the Tennis Court at St. James's' were altered for the duke at a cost of some £300. The work included linking the two houses by a brick gallery built across the space which separated them.[5] In 1666–7 a 'snow well' was built for the duke 'in the field by Berksheire garden nere St. James's' at a cost of £84. It was 24 feet deep and 20 feet wide, and was sited in such a way that the melted snow drained into the horse-pond in the stable-yard of the palace.[6]

References to the 'nursery' and to the 'Rockers' lodgings'[7] recall the births of the ladies Mary (April 1662) and Anne (Feb. 1665), for whom separate apartments were in due course provided. Mary's Presence and Closet were both referred to in 1673–4, when a new closet 11 feet square was made for Anne.[8] Both suites underwent extensive alterations in 1677, when the old mullioned windows were replaced by large sash windows, and Anne's closet was given a parquet floor made by Thomas Kinward, the Master Joiner. The 'fine brass locks and keys' were supplied by John Wilkinson, the Master Smith.[9] In 1666 the old Council Chamber was converted into a nursery for another of the duke's children, the short-lived Duke of Kendal,

[1] Works 5/4.
[2] Works 5/9 (extraordinary); *Cal. Treas. Books* ii, p. 517.
[3] *Diary of Samuel Pepys*, ed. H. B. Wheatley, vi, pp. 300–1.
[4] Works 5/2; *Cal. S.P. Dom. 1661–2*, p. 203; *Cal. Treas. Books* i, pp. 233, 296. The roof was repaired in 1674 (*Cal. Treas. Books* iv, pp. 249, 265, 556, 620; Works 5/23 and 24; Works 5/145, p. 92).
[5] Works 5/9 (extraordinary). The account also refers to an 'old gallery crosse the highway'.
[6] Works 5/9 contains two duplicate accounts for building this 'snow well'. One is headed 'a snow well for his Majestie', the other 'a snow well for his Highness the Duke of York'. In view of its proximity to the latter's lodgings at St. James's it was presumably built for his benefit. In 1668–9 a new well 19 feet deep and 19½ feet in diameter at the top was built, and the old one was reconstructed after its thatched roof had been burnt (Works 6/11, pp. 188–90; Works 5/145, p. 3). The remains of a seventeenth-century ice-house were discovered in this vicinity in 1956 (*The Times*, 19 Sept. 1956).
[7] Works 5/3 and 5.                                    [8] Works 5/21.
[9] Works 5/29; cf. *Cal. Treas. Books* v, p. 1152.

and some lodgings were adapted for occupation by the Countess of Rochester, sister-in-law to the duchess and afterwards governess to the Lady Anne.[1]

When James succeeded to the throne in 1685 he moved to Whitehall, but gave St. James's to his queen as her official residence.[2] Mary of Modena proceeded to have a room fitted up for meetings of her Council. Wren submitted 'an estimate for the alteration of some rooms att St. James's to make a roome fitt for a Counsill Chamber to bee 22 fo$^t$ long and 17 fo$^t$ 10 in. broad'. The floor, ceiling and windows were to be renewed and the room was to be wainscotted and furnished with a new chimneypiece. A new staircase was to be built to give access to it, and there was also to be an office close by for a clerk. The estimate, amounting to £238 13s. 0d., was accepted by the queen's Council on 6 March 1685/6, and the work was carried out soon afterwards at the queen's expense.[3] Some associated repairs to the roof were, however, charged to the 'ordinary' account of the Office of Works, which continued to be responsible for the routine maintenance of the palace.[4] King James himself appears to have retained his own apartment at St. James's, for in 1687–7 he had a new 'stool-room' fitted up there. The stool, set in a surround of white Dutch tiles, was flushed by means of a cistern and a force-pump. The brass-work, ironwork, and ivory handles of this early water-closet were supplied by Peter Thompson, engine-maker.[5] James's abortive scheme for removing the Royal Mews from Charing Cross to St. James's is discussed elsewhere.[6]

During the reign of William III the palace served chiefly to provide lodgings for various courtiers, including the Earl of Danby (Lord President of the Council), the Earl of Bath (a Privy Councillor), Lord Selkirk (a Gentleman of the Bed-chamber), the Countess of Plymouth (Danby's daughter), Lady Wentworth, and the Dutch Secretary.[7] In 1695 the king invited Princess Anne, the heir presumptive, and her husband Prince George of Denmark, to remove from Berkeley House to St. James's. Danby (now Duke of Leeds) moved out to make way for them, and in 1696–7 over £2200 were spent on fitting the palace up for their reception.[8] The detailed accounts for this year are missing, but the works are known to have included the building of 'a large room to dance in'.[9] This is the existing Ball Room on the south side of Green Cloth (now Ambassadors') Court. Then, as now, it stood on an arcaded basement, and was lighted by four large sash windows in its north wall.[10] Access to it was by means of a rectangular staircase which projected from the centre of its facade, but has since been removed. Its place is now occupied by a fifth window. Two rainwater heads still bear the date 1697. In November 1698

---

[1] Works 5/9 (extraordinary).

[2] *Cal. Treas. Books* viii, p. 498. Somerset House was the house usually reserved for the queen, but at this time it was still in the occupation of the dowager Queen Catherine.

[3] The estimate is printed in *Wren Soc.* vii, pp. 208–9 from a volume of Queen Mary of Modena's papers in the Bodleian Library (MS. Rawlinson C 987, ff. 12–14).

[4] Works 5/40: 'an account of workes taken out of the severall workemens' Bills for the building of her Maties Councell Chamber at St. James's and placed on the Ordinary'.

[5] Works 5/40.                                          [6] Above, pp. 209–10.

[7] Works 5/46 records alterations to their respective lodgings in 1693–4.

[8] N. Luttrell, *Brief Historical Relation* iii, pp. 475, 531–2, 551; E 351/3308.

[9] *Cal. S.P. Dom. 1697*, p. 293.

[10] 'The Princess's sashes . . . in the ball-room at St. James Palace' are referred to as a model in the contract for the Duke of Leeds's country house at Kiveton, Yorks., dated 3 March 1697/8 (*Jnl. of the Warburg & Courtauld Institutes* xviii, 1955, p. 131, n.).

the king's birthday was celebrated by a great court and a ball 'in the new Great Room.'[1] It is likely that the works carried out for the Prince and Princess of Denmark also included the elaborate external staircase which gave direct access from the royal apartments to the garden (Pl. 27), taking the place of an old winding staircase in one of the projecting turrets.[2]

In 1698 it was announced that Princess Anne's eldest son, William, Duke of Gloucester, was to have an apartment of his own.[3] Sketch plans of the palace by Wren's assistant William Dickinson[4] show that the duke was given the symmetrical building with six windows at the south-west corner of the palace which may previously have been occupied by his grandfather the Duke of York (p. 234). But the building was soon vacant again, for the young duke died in 1700. In January 1698 the destruction by fire of Whitehall Palace constrained the king to make use of the Chapel and Drawing Room at St. James's,[5] and this presumably explains the expenditure of £1553 on 'enlarging and repairing' the Chapel Royal in 1698–9.[6]

When Anne came to the throne in March 1702 she continued to reside at St. James's, and it became necessary to provide a full suite of State Apartments for her use. In June the Office of Works accordingly submitted an estimate for enlarging the Council Chamber (£459), the Drawing Room (£1034) and the Chapel (£1317), fitting a room below for a Guard Chamber (£199), fitting a room for the Queen's lesser bedchamber (£103), and 'erecting a porticoe leading from the Great Gate' (£662).[7] The portico, comprising 24 Portland stone columns (probably in couples, as in the Clock Court at Hampton Court), was designed to provide a covered walk from the Great Gate to the royal apartments. The estimate, amounting in all to £3775, appears to have been accepted, but in July the Officers of the Works were informed that the queen had 'put a stop to the works she intended'.[8] Evidently their first proposal for the adaptation of the existing apartments was not considered adequate, for in March 1703 a more ambitious scheme was submitted and approved. This consisted of a new wing projecting westwards from the south range of the palace, across the site of the Duke of Gloucester's lodging, which must have been demolished to make way for it.[9] The estimate now came to over £5000.[10] On 17 March the queen agreed to an expenditure of £1000 a month, and demanded

[1] *Cal. S.P. Dom. 1698*, p. 413.

[2] Owing to the loss of the detailed accounts for 1696–7 this cannot be substantiated by documentary evidence, but in Charles II's reign the site of the staircase was occupied by the Duchess of York's balcony, (Pl. 26.). The new staircase is seen in Kip's view (Pl. 27), which appears to date from *c*. 1705, and on a plan by W. Dickinson made soon after the accession of Queen Anne, and before her major alterations of 1703 (Bodleian, MS. Gough Misc. Ant. 17, f. 92).

[3] Luttrell, *Brief Historical Relation* iv, p. 328.

[4] Bodleian, MS. Gough Misc. Ant. 17, ff. 91, 92ᵛ, inscribed 'D. of Gloster'.

[5] *Cal. S.P. Dom. 1698*, pp. 36, 69.

[6] E 351/3310.

[7] Works 6/2, ff. 72–3, printed in *Wren Soc.* vii, pp. 210–12.

[8] *Cal. Treas. Books* xvii, pp. 60–1, 479.

[9] Its demolition may be referred to in a payment to the Master Bricklayer 'for making a scaffold and pulling and carrying downe the brick of the front of the Council Chamber that was to be' (Works 5/53). If so, the original intention must have been to adapt one of the Duke of Gloucester's rooms for use as a Council Chamber.

[10] Works 6/14, f. 21. The estimate for the building itself was £4967, but various 'contingencies' brought it up to £5468. Several alternative plans for the new building are reproduced in *Wren Soc.* vii, pls. xxx, xxxi, xxxiii. It was evidently designed either by Wren or under his immediate supervision. Pl. xxix is a scheme for the colonnade by Hawksmoor.

completion by the beginning of September.[1] This the Office appears to have accomplished, though at a cost which substantially exceeded the estimate.[2] The principal contractor was Richard Stacey, the Master Bricklayer, who on 12 March 1702/3 undertook to build 'a large Brick building at St. James's . . . according to the Designe given him . . . observing the manner of building which may suit with the old Buildings contiguous, that is to say, with rubbd Coines, streight arches and window jambs with staff mouldings, and battlements & rubb'd Chimney shafts'.[3] The estimated cost of the brickwork was £1186. John Churchill was responsible for the carpentry (estimated cost £968), Benjamin Jackson for the masonry (£443) and Charles Hopson for the joinery (£733). £89 was allowed for carving by Grinling Gibbons and £54 for plasterwork by John Grove.[4] Jackson was responsible for building the colonnade across the west side of the Great (now Colour) Court. Dickinson's plans show that there was already an open porch in the south-west corner of this Court, at the foot of the Great Staircase.[5] This was supported by five columns, and the accounts show that five columns were taken down and reset as part of the new colonnade. Jackson supplied ten new columns at £8 10s. each, making 15 in all.[6] Eighteenth-century plans, however, show that the colonnade consisted of 14, not 15, Doric columns equally spaced.[7] These were reduced to nine in 1865, when the south side of the court was rebuilt 18 feet further north.

The new wing contained, on the first floor, a large Drawing Room, a Council Chamber, and a room for the Clerk of the Council. Beyond these, on the west side of Paradise (now Friary) Court, were the Guard Chamber, Presence Chamber and Privy Chamber (Fig. 20). These arrangements can still be traced today, but only the Drawing Room retains its original function under the name of the Entrée Room, the former Council Chamber now serving as the Throne Room, and the room now known as the Council Chamber having been created by remodelling the south-west end of the building.[8] The apartment now known as 'Queen Anne's Room' was not built until 1822, and occupies the site of her Privy Chamber.

The estimate of June 1702 included an item of £1317 for enlarging the Chapel. This recalls Narcissus Luttrell's statement in April 1702 that the queen proposed to restore the Banqueting House at Whitehall (then serving as a royal chapel) to secular uses, and 'to enlarge her chappel at St. James's, turning it into the form of a cathedrall'.[9] The Chapel Royal at St. James's does not in fact appear to have undergone any structural alterations at this date, but in October 1703 Luttrell records that 'the Bishop of Rochester has by Her Majestie's order declar'd St.

[1] *Cal. Treas. Books* xviii, pp. 20, 26, 167.

[2] *Cal. Treas. Books* xix, p. 339, which shows that the total cost was £6961.

[3] Works 5/145, p. 231 (possibly only a draft).

[4] Works 6/14, f. 21.

[5] Bodleian, MS. Gough Misc. Ant. 17, f. 91. See also f. 92, where one column is evidently omitted.

[6] Works 5/53. The account is for work done during the winter of 1702–3.

[7] Works 34/121, reproduced in *Wren Soc.* vii, p. 244, and a plan in the Soane Museum reproduced *ibid.*, p. 246.

[8] Comparison of the eighteenth-century plans of the palace shows that these alterations (which involved extending the range by 2 bays) were effected between 1712 (plan at Windsor) and 1729 (*Wren Soc.* vii, pp. 244–5). Owing to the loss of the detailed Works accounts for these years it is not possible to point to any relevant payments. In 1729 the old Council Chamber still bore that name, but George III used it as a Drawing or Throne Room and George II may have done the same.

[9] *Brief Historical Relation* v, p. 159.

James's Chappel to be the Chappel Royal and all the singing men & boys belonging to that of Whitehal are to remove to St. James's'.[1]

Expenditure on the palace continued to be quite heavy throughout Anne's reign, amounting between 1704 and 1714 to an average of some £3700 a year. After 1703 no detailed accounts survive, but much of the expenditure appears to have been accounted for by alterations to the apartments of the Duchess of Marlborough and other members of the Court.[2] In February 1714 Wren was directed to enlarge the gallery between the Guard Chamber and the royal pew in the Chapel Royal.[3] Hitherto this had been little more than 4 feet wide,[4] and Wren had already envisaged enlarging it soon after Anne's accession.[5] Later plans show that in 1714 he increased its width to approximately 10 feet.[6]

The palace continued to be the king's principal residence throughout the reigns of George I and George II. Despite its lack of magnificence—unfailingly noticed by every foreign visitor[7]—its irregular brick ranges apparently satisfied the needs of the Georgian court, and its architectural history during the eighteenth century is one of piecemeal alteration and adaptation rather than of any major scheme of rebuilding. Early in the reign of George I an architect who can without difficulty be identified as Vanbrugh did, it is true, draw up two grand schemes, one for a complete rebuilding, the other for a new south front, which, inscribed in French for the king's benefit, still repose among the royal archives at Windsor.[8] But there is no evidence that either was ever seriously considered by the king, and throughout the eighteenth century it continued to be a source of surprise and regret to many that royalty should 'reside in a house so ill-becoming the state and grandeur of the most powerful and respectable monarch in the universe'.[9]

The story of the king's works at St. James's in the Georgian period is therefore for the most part one of orders for new backstairs, laundries, wardrobes and dressing-rooms for members of the Court; alterations of to guard-rooms, kitchens, stables and wine-cellars; of the gradual encroachment on the Tudor courtyards which is so apparent in the eighteenth-century surveys of the palace (Fig. 20). In the minutes of the Board of Works the accession of George I is marked by nothing more notable than 'a parquetted floor' for his mistress the Countess of Schulenberg (afterwards Duchess of Kendal), upon whose apartment in the garden front over £4000 were to be spent in the course of the reign.[10] A good deal was also done for the comfort of the lady known to the officers of the Works as 'Madame Kilmansack', and many minor repairs and alterations were ordered for the benefit of Baron Hattorf, the Hanoverian resident, for the staff of the German Chancery which dealt

[1] *Op. cit.*, p. 350.
[2] Cf., e.g., *Cal. Treas. Books* xxiv, p. 296; *Wren Soc.* vii, pp. 213–14.
[3] *Wren Soc.* vii, p. 215, xviii, p. 164.      [4] *Wren Soc.* vii, pl. 33.
[5] *Wren Soc.* vii, pl. 31.      [6] *Wren Soc.* vii, p. 245.
[7] E.g. *Letters of Baron Bielfeld*, trans. Hooper iv (1770), p. 98; C. de Saussure, *A Foreign View of England in the Reigns of George I and II* (1902), p. 41.
[8] Portfolio 58. The complete scheme has been reproduced by K. Downes, *English Baroque Architecture* (1966), fig. 19a. A companion plan showing the palace 'as it is, 1712' might suggest that the grand project was made in the same year, but one of the drawings is inscribed 'Appartement pour le Roy', showing that it must have been made—or at least presented—after the accession of George I.
[9] J. Gwynn, *London & Westminster Improved* (1766), pp. 10–11.
[10] See the Paymaster's Accounts for 1717, 1718, 1721 and 1723.

with Hanoverian affairs, for the king's German tailor, for his two Turkish servants, and for 'Mr. Ulrick', his dwarf. The Prince and Princess of Wales and the young princesses their daughters also had apartments at St. James's, and these too were decorated, altered and enlarged under the direction of Dickinson and Hawksmoor, successively Clerks of Works at the palace.[1]

It was in the stables that the first alteration of any architectural importance took place. On 14 February 1716 the Board resolved that 'the king's two eighteen-horse stables at St. James's be repaired immediately for grooms, coachmen, etc., and a scheme and estimate be prepared to lay before the Board of such new works as are required'. On 29 February it ordered 'that an arcade of brick be drawn by Mr. Hawksmoor, to the stables at St. James's in a double story for the service of the said stables'. The Treasury fiat 'for several extraordinary works to be performed in His Majesty's Stable Yard at St. James's, estimated at £1800', was received on 2 August, and the work was immediately put in hand. It was completed in 1717 at a cost of £1771, and the result was the existing arcade on the north side of Stable Yard. Originally intended for 23 horses, it has long since been converted into offices. There was some further work in the Stable Yard in 1725, when the lodgings of Colonel Negus, the commissioner for executing the office of Master of the Horse, were rebuilt, but by 1731 the remaining stables were found to be so ruinous that the Board thought it 'not adviseable for His Majesty to lay out money to repair them', and it was decided to rebuild the Charing Cross Mews on a scale large enough to accommodate the horses from St. James's as well.[2]

While the arcade was building in Stable Yard, a request was received from the Lord Chamberlain for a new kitchen for the Prince of Wales's household, 'great inconveniences' having been experienced 'in dressing dayly great quantities of provisions for His Majesty and the Prince's family in the same kitchen'. The Royal Household at first proposed that the new kitchen should be built adjoining the existing one in the south-east corner of the palace. But the Board of Works rightly thought this site very inconvenient, and found a better one in the Back Court on the west side of the palace. Before the work had been put in hand relations between the king and the prince deteriorated to such an extent that the latter was banished from the court, and what had been intended for the prince's household was in fact built for his father's. Besides the kitchen proper, the building was designed to contain also 'a Livery Cellar, Silver Scullery, Common Scullery, the Master-Cook's roome, Children of the Kitchin's roome, Clerk of the Kitchin's Office and other necessary conveniencys'. Beneath it was to be 'a large vault for Rhenish wine'. It was erected in 1717–19 at a cost of £2076, and is an insulated building whose massive brickwork is boldly handled in the manner of Vanbrugh, by whom it was in all probability designed. The main room, containing the cooking ranges, rises to the

---

[1] The Prince's apartment was in the eastern part of the palace, adjoining Marlborough House. This is shown by the fact that in 1727 the Paymaster accounted for the building of a wall 'between the Prince of Wales's Lodgings and the Dutchess of Marlborough's Buildings' (AO 1/2452/161). The young princesses' apartments were close by in Pheasant Court (AO 1/2448/150).

[2] Works 4/1, 1 Feb., 14 Feb., 29 Feb., 2 Aug., 1716, 18 Dec. 1717; Works 4/3, 6 Feb., 23 June 1725; Works 6/15, pp. 231–3. It is doubtful whether the sketch reproduced in *Wren Soc.* xii, pl. v has anything to do with this arcade.

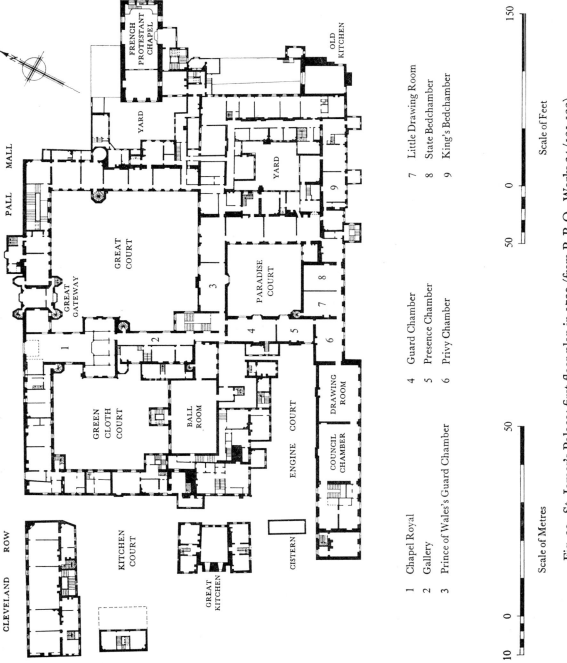

CLEVELAND ROW

PALL MALL

FRENCH PROTESTANT CHAPEL

YARD

GREAT COURT

GREAT GATEWAY

GREEN CLOTH COURT

BALL ROOM

KITCHEN COURT

GREAT KITCHEN

CISTERN

ENGINE COURT

PARADISE COURT

YARD

OLD KITCHEN

COUNCIL CHAMBER

DRAWING ROOM

1   Chapel Royal
2   Gallery
3   Prince of Wales's Guard Chamber

4   Guard Chamber
5   Presence Chamber
6   Privy Chamber

7   Little Drawing Room
8   State Bedchamber
9   King's Bedchamber

Scale of Feet

0          50          150

Scale of Metres

0    10          50

Fig. 20. St. James's Palace: first-floor plan in 1729 (from P. R. O., Works 34/121,122).

full height of the building, and has a coved ceiling straddling a clerestorey of *oeil-de-boeuf* windows.[1]

In 1723 a large new laundry with vaults beneath and rooms above was built for the Duchess of Kendal at a cost estimated at £2182, and two rooms on the ground floor on the south side of the palace facing the garden were thrown into one and fitted up as a library for the king at a cost of £451.[2] The old library had been in a room over the kitchen in the south-east corner of the palace.[3] The new library was one of the rooms destroyed by the fire of 1809, but it is indicated on Soane's survey of 1793, and from Flitcroft's survey of 1729 it can be seen that it was on the ground floor immediately to the east of the king's bedroom on the floor above (cf. Vol. VI, Fig. 8). Nearby the king also had a smoking room, which in 1724 was lined with 'slitt deal'.[4]

The principal work of the next reign was the building of a library for Queen Caroline, who had a taste for books and intellectual company. A site was found for it on the west side of the palace, overlooking the park, where the Office of Works had had its store-yard.[5] It was designed by Kent, whose original drawings are preserved in Sir John Soane's Museum.[6] They are for a single-storey building 60 feet long, 30 feet wide and 30 feet high, in other words a double cube. No drawings of the exterior survive, but the interior was highly ornamented in the Palladian manner (Pl. 30A). At first Kent envisaged projecting bookcases whose ends were to contain niches for busts of poets and philosophers, but in the end these were dispensed with, and the books were accommodated in arched recesses set in the walls. Between each pair of arches a wall-bracket supported a bust of a former queen of England sculpted by Rysbrack. Overhead was a coved ceiling with a richly moulded cornice and at either end was a marble chimneypiece in the style of Inigo Jones. This exquisite room—at once library and garden pavilion—was begun in 1736 and completed in October 1737. A premature announcement that all was ready for the queen's books provided the Vice-Chamberlain, Lord Hervey, with an excuse for a facetious letter to his friend Henry Fox, who had just succeeded Richard Arundell as Surveyor of the King's Works:

> Henry Fox Esq. Neglecter of His Majesty's Works
>
> St. James's, Thursday night, 1737
>
> Which of all the Devils in Hell prompted you to tell the Queen that every thing in her library was ready for the putting up of her Books? Thou abominable new broom that so far from sweeping clean, hast not removed one grain of Dirt and Rhubbish come to me to-morrow morning to take the rest of your scolding, and go with me to scold all your odious dilatory subalterns.
>
> Bad night.[7]

The work was, indeed, completed only just in time, for it was 'at her new library in St. James's Park' that on 9 November 1737 the queen was taken ill.[8] After her

---

[1] Works 6/6, pp. 196–8; Works 6/7, pp. 12ᵛ–13, 54ᵛ–55; Works 5/141, 1719.
[2] Works 6/7, pp. 282–3, 298. The 'Old Library' is marked in this position on Soane's plan of 1793 (Vol. V Fig. 8).           [3] See a plan of it made by Wren in 1706 (T 1/100, f. 184).
[4] Works 4/3, 4 Nov. 1724.           [5] Works 1/1, p. 44.
[6] Fauntleroy Pennant vol. ii, pp. 296–302.           [7] B.M., Add. MS. 51396, f. 185.
[8] Hervey, *Memoirs of the Reign of George II*, ed. Croker, iii (1884), p. 294.

death it was little used, and in 1825 it was pulled down to make way for the Duke of York's new house. The two chimneypieces were then transferred to the State Apartments, where they can still be seen, minus their overmantels, in the Throne Room and the adjoining Entrée Room. Queen Caroline's heraldic badges are carved on the leaves of the swags with which they are decorated. Busts of the king and queen which once surmounted these two chimneypieces are now preserved at Windsor Castle.[1]

Kent's only other work at St. James's was of an even more ephemeral character. This was the fitting up of Inigo Jones's chapel for the marriage of Princess Anne to the Prince of Orange on 14 March 1734. Lord Hervey thought the decorations showed 'an extreme good taste', and Kent, having successfully prevented his rival Hogarth from recording the ceremony, himself published a print which shows the velvet-covered galleries and gilt lustres and sconces so much admired by the vice-chamberlain. For the procession from the Drawing Room to the Chapel the Office of Works erected a boarded gallery which went south to the bottom of the garden, then east along the garden wall, and finally north to the chapel. Hervey says that the king spared no expense on this occasion, and the Paymaster's accounts show that the gallery alone cost £3980.[2]

In the following year the impending marriage of the Prince of Wales resulted in the creation of a new 'apartment' or suite of rooms for him and his bride. This is stated in the *London Daily Post* of 24 September 1735 to have faced Cleveland Row, and to have been on the site of the former Guards' suttling-house. This would identify the prince's apartment with the range on the north side of Kitchen Court (now part of Ambassadors' Court), and an examination of the various surveys of the palace indicates that this was extended westwards by three bays, while a return elevation was built facing onto the former Stable Yard, the northern range of which (the one rebuilt by Hawksmoor in 1716–17) was converted into offices for the prince's household.[3] Owing to his breach with the king the prince's occupation of these rooms must have terminated in 1737. In George III's reign they were used in 1764 to accommodate the newly-married Prince and Princess of Brunswick, and in 1768 they were prepared for the reception of the King of Denmark and his suite.[4] They have since been occupied successively by the Duke of Cumberland (d. 1851), the Duchess of Cambridge (d. 1889), the Duke of York, afterwards King George V (1893–1910), Lord Kitchener (1914–19), the Prince of Wales, afterwards King Edward VIII (1921–36), and the Duke of Gloucester (d. 1974), and are now known as York House.[5]

---

[1] M. I. Webb, *Michael Rysbrack, Sculptor* (1954), pp. 154–5, Figs. 73–6. Rysbrack's authorship of the 'bustos' in the Queen's Library is confirmed by entries in Works 4/7, 11 Jan. 1738 and Works 1/2, p. 7ᵛ. The Paymaster's account for 1737 includes payments for workmanship connected with the library to Andrews Jelfe (mason), James Richards and Richard Lawrence (carvers).
[2] Hervey, *Memoirs of the Reign of George II*, ed. Croker, i (1884), pp. 312–16; Works 5/58, March 1734. Isaac Ware received £2646 for 'deals, uphirs, baulks, standards &c. by him provided' (AO 1/2454/1680). For Hogarth's discomfiture see *Vertue's Notebooks* (Walpole Soc.) iii, p. 68.
[3] Hervey, *Memoirs* ii, p. 228; Works 4/6, 16 March, 21 June 1736; Works 6/16, p. 43. See the contemporary elevation in Works 34/135.
[4] Works 1/4, p. 73; Walpole, *Memoirs of the Reign of George III* (1894), iii, p. 159.
[5] E. Sheppard, *Memorials of St. James's Palace* i (1894), pp. 105, 418–20. The house was extensively altered in 1892, when a third storey was added to accommodate servants.

In 1736 the first move was made to disengage the north and east sides of the palace from the heterogeneous buildings which in the course of time had been allowed to encroach on its walls. To the west of the main gateway there was a guard-room, while to the east there were a barber's shop, an alehouse, and (just round the corner) a coach house belonging to the Duke of Marlborough.[1] The alehouse stood close to the apartments occupied by the young princesses Anne, Emily and Caroline, and during the winter of 1735–6 'the stench of a necessary house belonging to it' became so offensive that the princesses were obliged to move their rooms. At a cost of £846, and an abusive letter from the dowager Duchess of Marlborough, who feared some encroachment on her property by the 'insolence and folly of the workmen', the Office of Works was able to remove this nuisance in 1736, and in 1748 the expiration of the leases made further demolitions possible in this area. But the scars remained on the external walls, and the question arose 'how to hide the bad appearance the Palace now makes to the street'.[2] Before his death in 1747 Kent had given some thought to this problem, and in 1748 John Vardy, the Clerk of the Works at St. James's, made a design for tidying up the facade which he exhibited subsequently at the Society of Artists.[3] All that in fact was done was to substitute for the demolished houses a two-storied building whose very plain elevation can be seen in a view by Sandby dated 1766.[4] After George III's accession this was assigned to Lady Charlotte Finch, the governess of the royal children, who in 1768 asked for the addition of a third story and a bow window. This was approved by the king, and resulted in the existing elevation to the street at the north-east corner of the palace (Pl. 31A).[5]

## 2. THE QUEENS' CHAPEL

Though physically attached to St. James's Palace, the Catholic Chapel built by Inigo Jones for Queen Henrietta Maria formed, with its satellite Friary, a separate establishment, and as such requires separate treatment. It appears to have escaped serious damage during the Interregnum, but was no doubt stripped of all its fittings. A good deal of work was therefore required in 1662 in order to enable Catholic worship to be resumed for the benefit of Queen Catherine of Braganza. The organ loft had to be taken down and was completely rebuilt, including its outside wall, its floor and its 'plattforme' or flat roof. Internally the loft was supported by two wooden columns with stone bases. This organ loft was presumably in the same position as the existing one on the south side of the Chapel. The dimensions tally,

---

[1] A plan and elevation showing these buildings are reproduced by E. Sheppard, *Memorials of St. James's Palace* i (1894), p. 10. See also London Survey, *St. James's, Westminster* i (1960), p. 384.
[2] Works 6/16, p. 45, Works 6/17, pp. 40ᵛ, 45ᵛ, 48ᵛ, 49ᵛ, 50ᵛ; Works 1/1, p. 56.
[3] Vertue says that one of Kent's last projects was some alterations to the front of St. James's Palace (*Notebooks*, Walpole Society, iii, p. 40); A. Graves, *The Society of Artists of Great Britain &c.* (1907), p. 266.
[4] Reproduced by E. Sheppard, *Memorials of St. James's Palace* i (1894), p. 8.
[5] Works 6/18, pp. 175, 179. See also a contemporary plan and elevation among the Works records (Works 34/133 and 135).

and the organ can be seen in this situation in a seventeenth-century engraving (Pl. 28). It was approached by means of the 'Great Staircase' which also gave access (via an intermediate room) to the gallery at the west end of the chapel (Fig. 21). This staircase (which still exists, though rearranged to occupy a smaller space) does not appear to have been altered in 1662, but 'a new paire of staires with raile and ballaster containing xvij stepps' was made 'to go up to the musicke roome there'. This Music Room was lighted by a new 'compasse window of iiij lights', but its exact position is not clear.[1]

Iron bars were inserted in the 'great windowes' of the Chapel in order to fix painted glass made by Thomas Bagley, the Master Glazier. This included 'a Crucifix of paynted glasse iij foote broade and 4 foote deepe' and '2 coates of Armes each 3 foote 5 inches deepe and 2 foote 7 inches broad'.[2]

Further fittings paid for by the Office of Works in 1663–4 included 'a portall of deal wainscot' set up in the ante-chapel, a simple deal pulpit 'with a foote pace for it to stand on and a broad stepp ladder to it with 7 stepps', a 'confessing howse . . . devided into three parts with arches 7 foote wide 7 foote 8 inches high two foote 3 inches deepe with an Architrave freeze and cornish', and a new 'closct' for the queen. This last was made by Thomas Kinward, the Master Joiner, at a cost of £64 18s. 9d. It was a framed structure faced with wainscot both inside and out. There were three doorways 'going into the closett', one with double and two with single doors. These doorways were ornamented with 'waved leaves and berries' carved by Henry Phillips. There was a cornice at the top both outside and inside, and 'at the end of the Closett looking into the Chappell'. The ceiling was provided with a 'strayneing frame' for a painting.[3] The spacious gallery still existing at the west end of the chapel is marked as 'the closet' on a seventeenth-century sketch-plan (Pl. 25). The exact relationship between the closet made by Kinward and the gallery is not clear, but it would appear that what he was asked to provide was a large enclosed pew standing in the gallery. This pew would seem to be the 'tribune' referred to in other sources, notably a description of the chapel written by M. de Monconys, a French visitor who attended a service in the chapel in May 1663:

Le 20 nous fûmes a S. James oüir la Messe de la Reine, dans une Chapelle faite lors du marriage de la Reine mere. Elle est fort bien entendue, la voûte fort haussée a compartimens dorez jusqu'au tiers qui couvre l'Autel, lequel est placé tout simple-ment dans le milieu de la Chapelle, sans autre ornement que six Chandeliers, & un Tabernacle d'argent. Il y a au milieu un parfaitement beau Dais de velours rouge cramoisi en broderie d'or, de la plus belle que j'aye jamais vûë, que la Reine à ap-portée de Portugal. La Reine étoit dans une Tribune à main droite, tapissée de damas rouge avec de grands rideaux de même, qui la ferment. . . . Nous étions dans une petite Tribune vis-à-vis de celle de la Reine, qui est dans une Chapelle haute, où souvent elle fait ses devotions, & dans laquelle sont 24 grands coffres de velours, garnis de trois grandes plaques d'argent cizelé, avec des ferrures, anses, & clous

[1] Works 5/3, May and June 1662. The round window in the Music Room overlooked 'Mr. Walker's garden'.

[2] Works 5/3, Aug. 1662.　　　　　　　　　　[3] Works 5/4, Dec. 1662.

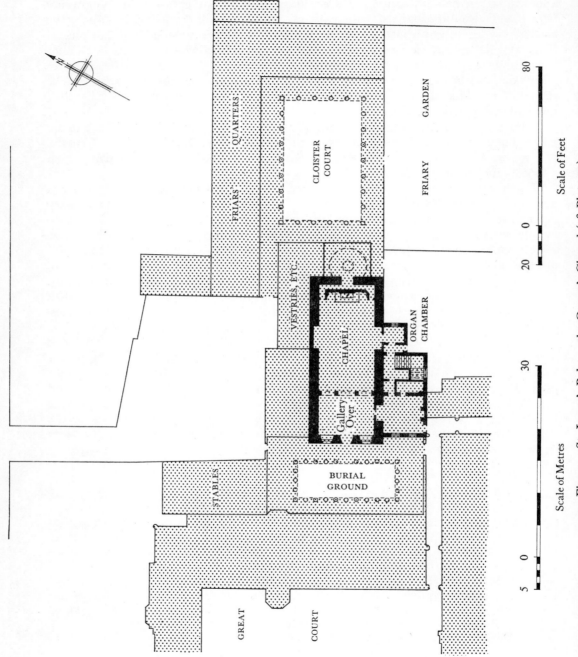

FRIARS'
QUARTERS

CLOISTER
COURT

FRIARY
GARDEN

VESTRIES, ETC.

CHAPEL

Gallery Over

ORGAN
CHAMBER

STABLES

BURIAL
GROUND

GREAT

COURT

Scale of Metres

Scale of Feet

80

0

20

30

5

0

Fig. 21. St. James's Palace: the Queen's Chapel (cf. Plate 25).

d'argent, que la Reine a apportés, & qu'elle a donnés à la Chapelle, avec 24 couvertures de Mulets de velours rouge, brodés d'or alentour, & les armes d'Angleterre, &
de Portugal au milieu; lesquelles couvertures tapissent la Chappelle.[1]

The 24 coffers presumably contained relics. Whatever their purpose they must
have taken up a good deal of space, and as M. de Monconys states that they were
kept in 'an upper chapel' (une Chapelle haute), they can hardly have stood any-
where but in the capacious west gallery. It follows therefore that the 'great tribune'
occupied by the queen projected from the right-hand end of this gallery, while
the little one 'opposite' (vis-à-vis) must have projected from the left-hand end.

From another foreign visitor, Cosmo, Duke of Tuscany, we learn that 'at the
entrance of the church are two lateral chapels, of which that on the right is dedicated
to the most blessed Virgin, and in it her majesty recites the rosary on holy days,
when she is present at divine service'.[2] These two lateral chapels may possibly have
been outside the existing west door, but were more probably on either side beneath
the gallery. This space beneath the gallery is apparently what is referred to elsewhere as the 'ante-chapel'.

Pepys, who visited the chapel in September 1662, admired 'the fine altar,
ornaments, and the fryers in their habits'.[3] The Portuguese Capuchin friars occupied
a cloistered quadrangle immediately to the east of the chapel (Fig. 21). This appears
to have been rebuilt by Queen Catherine, for in January 1667 Pepys was shown
'the new monastery', with its 'dortoire', 'refectoire', kitchen, library and cells for
the individual friars, all of which he thought 'mighty pretty'.[4] It is likewise stated
in the journal of the Duke of Tuscany, who inspected the chapel in 1669, that the
Friary had been 'built at her Majesty's expense'.[5] The work must have been paid for
by the queen's Treasurer, for it was not accounted for by the Paymaster of the
Works.

The works carried out for the queen at this time probably also included the
addition to the chapel of an eastern projection, externally rectangular, but surmounted by a circular dome covered with lead (Pl. 29B). This addition contained
two principal rooms, one at ground level, and another above for the choir where
the Capuchins said their offices. It is marked as 'built by the Queen Dowager' on
a plan made soon after her death,[6] and its outline can be recognised on the sketch-
plan of 1689 (Pl. 25). When the Duke of Tuscany visited the chapel in 1669 he
noted that masses and vespers were sung by the Capuchins 'in the upper choir'.
Unless the choir was then in a different part of the building altogether, this implies
that the eastern extension had been built in the 1660s together with the Friary
with which it interlocked.

In 1679–80 some extensive repairs and alterations were carried out for the
queen by the Office of Works. Although detailed accounts exist for these works,
it is difficult to relate all the entries to the fabric of the chapel as it exists today.

---

[1] *Les Voyages de M. de Monconys* iii (Paris 1695), pp. 36–7.
[2] *Travels of Cosmo, Duke of Tuscany, through England*, ed. Magalotti (1821) p. 169.
[3] *Diary of Samuel Pepys*, ed. H. B. Wheatley, ii (1893), p. 342.
[4] *Op. cit.*, vi (1895), pp. 142–4.
[5] *Travels of Cosmo, Duke of Tuscany, through England*, ed. Magalotti (1821), p. 170.
[6] P.R.O. MPE 485.

This is especially so in the case of the ante-chapel, where a good deal of work was done whose purpose is not readily apparent. Its roof was repaired after 'mazer-scourers' had been employed to 'throw downe all the garden tubbs off earth from of the leads'. Bricklayers were paid for

> workeinge up a sollid wall 2 Bricks thick tenn foot long, 11 foote high in the lower roome of the Anty Chappell & bringing up of two brick peeres to fasten the cheekes of the Stone Dore case in the said roome there, makeing up with brickworke a Dore-way leading out of the Lady Isabella's Lodgings into the said Anty Chappell 7 foote high 4 foote 9 inches wide, workeing up with brick work a great hole which was broken in the Chappell to sett the Shores to take up the Lead for the plombers & lesstening two Dore wayes with brick on each side the Ante-rome belonging to the Chappell & makeing up with brick worke 4 substantiall peeres 11 ffote high 5 ffotte deepe two bricks thick & splaying the inside of the two said Dore wayes.

The stone doorcases themselves were taken down 'out of the partition wall in the Anty-Chappell' by the masons, and one of them was then 'set up into the said walle againe'. Two new chimneys and chimney-stacks were constructed in the ante-chapel, and 'the great stone chimney-piece in the Queen's Great Clossett' was repaired. The 'stone dore case at the head of the great staires leading into the Queen's Trybunall' was mended, and a raised floor with two circular steps was constructed 'to sett the railes & ballisters round the Queen's seat'. The 'compas raile & ballisters in the Queen's Clossett' were duly reset on this platform. Two panels in the screen between the columns under the queen's closet window were repaired. Finally the altar in the ante-chapel was taken away and a new altar from Somerset House was set up in its place.

The principal altar was also temporarily removed in order that its steps might be lengthened and its rails brought forward five feet in order to provide more space in front of it. Upon it stood a 'tabernakle' made by the joiner Kinward, 'being wrought with an Arch & Arketrave round & Cornish with a foot for it to stand on being 5 fot. 4 in. high one fot. 8 in. wide & 10 inches deepe'. The outside of this tabernacle was gilded and the inside was painted blue with gilded stars. Kinward also supplied 'a wainscott pullpitt . . . with a ladder of broad stepps of wainscott, the pullpitt being 6 cants with Archetrive frees and cornish'. Its angles were embellished with cherubims' heads and festoons carved by William Emmett, and underneath it terminated in a 'great ogee' with a rose at the apex (cf. Pl. 28). The coffered ceiling was cleaned and repainted by Robert Streater, the Sergeant Painter, who charged 6d. for painting each of 49 panels white with nut oil, and 4s. each for washing and cleaning the gilding of the 28 panels at the east end and 'picking in' the white ground.

The Sacristy was provided with presses for altar-cloths, and on top of 'the great chest of drawers' a 'degree' or step seven inches high was made 'to sett candle sticks on'. In the 'Privy Sacristy' Kinward made 'a napkin rowle with a pedement over it'. In the friars' choir 16 old stalls were repaired and 4 new ones were made. Two door cases were set up there and two more in 'two little rooms in the dark passage leading out of the Chappell into the Friery'.

Within the Friary itself alterations were carried out to many parts of the building, including the Kitchen, the Refectory, the Friars' Gallery (which contained two chimneypieces and a clock) and the two great staircases. The Library was furnished with 48 bookcases each 3 feet 10 inches long, 14 inches broad and 16 inches deep and a folding ladder 9 feet 4 inches long. In 'the Friars' Great Cloister' 27 columns, capitals and bases were made good with plaster of paris. This was probably the cloister round the 'Burying Place' at the west end of the Chapel, for the sketch-plan of 1689 shows that its roof was supported by precisely 27 columns (Pl. 25). In the walls of the Great Cloister there were four niches, and these were 'washed, stopped and whitened' by a plasterer. The chambers of several of the friars were each provided with an inner 'cell' framed in timber and measuring 6 or 7 feet by 4 feet. These 'cells' appear to have been for the friars' personal servants, since one of them is said to have been made 'for Father John's man', and another 'for Father Hudleston's man'. Several of the friars had a number of small picture frames 8 inches square made for them by Thomas Kinward: Father John had as many as 20, the 'Father President' twelve.

The total cost of these repairs and alterations was £1569.[1] Although entered in the Office Books, they were not accounted for by the Paymaster, and were evidently paid for by the queen herself.

In March 1682 a fire broke out in the Friary which 'consumed severall lodgings, and had it not been timely stopt by the blowing up of houses, it would have endangered the whole palace'.[2] The chapel itself does not appear to have been seriously damaged, but in restoring the Friary the opportunity was taken further to embellish the former building. The work was paid for by the queen's Treasurer, and there is no record of it in the books of the Office of Works. Wren was, however, in charge, and the accounts were kept by Leonard Gammon, the Clerk of Works at Whitehall and St. James's Palaces. Both the detailed account of the 'Charges in repaireing & adorning her Majesty's Chappell & Rooms adjoining &c at St. James's from the first of May 1682 to the last of July 1683', signed by Wren, and many of the original bills certified by him survive among Catherine of Braganza's papers in the Public Record Office.[3] A supplementary account for works done in the chapel in January 1683/4 bears a note by Wren to the effect that it was examined by him 'at the request of Mr. Deias', that is Father Emanuel Diaz, the Treasurer of the Queen's Chapel.[4] The total expenditure amounted to over £1800. The principal craftsmen named were all men regularly employed by the Office of Works, and included Thomas Wise (the Master Mason), Matthew Bankes (the Master Carpenter from May 1683), Maurice Emmett (the Master Bricklayer), Robert Streater (the Sergeant Painter), John Grove (the Master Plasterer) and William Bache (the Master Smith).

Although the works in the chapel were chiefly decorative, they included 'taking

---

[1] Works 5/32 (5 books bound up at the end).
[2] N. Luttrell, *Brief Historical Relation* i, p. 172.
[3] They are scattered among unsorted papers in LR 6/204, 205, 206, 209, 210 and 213. The 16-page account (and a supplementary one for work in January 1683/4) is in LR 6/213. Two stray documents from the series have found their way into the class of Exchequer, Accounts Various (E 101/674/31 and E 101/675/17). The joiner's contract for refitting the choir is entered in Works 5/145, p. 145.
[4] E. Sheppard, *Memorials of St. James's Palace* ii, p. 233.

downe the 2 Architrave stone windows on the north side the Chappell', taking down and resetting one of the inside jambs of a window 'that was blowne out' (presumably by the gunpowder used to stop the advance of the fire), and cutting away the external 'cornish and frontispiece' of that window to make it 'even with the wall'. The master mason also made 'a great new architrave window on the north side the Chappell'. This was carved with festoons and scrolls inside and out, and had a cherubim's head on its keystone. It is not easy to relate these entries to the three existing windows on the north side of the chapel. All three are decorated externally with architraves and pediments. These have been restored, but the authenticity of their design is vouched for by the corresponding window on the south side, which appears to be the original workmanship of the time of Inigo Jones. There is now no trace on any window of festoons or scrolls or of a keystone ornamented with a cherubim's head, but all these features formerly decorated the window, now no longer in existence, in the recess on the north side of the chapel, opposite the organ chamber (Pl. 28). This window, therefore, with its segmental head, now blocked, but externally restored, may have been the one whose cornice and pediment were shorn away, perhaps because it was wholly or partly covered up by the row of sacristies and other buildings erected close to this side of the chapel (cf. Pl. 25).[1] If it were effectively deprived of light in this way, the need for a new window further east would be understandable. The Master Mason also charged for 81 feet of Portland stone 'in the 2 round Architrave windows of the Choire'. One of these can be seen in Gasselin's view of *circa* 1700 (Pl. 29B).

Inside the domed extension the choir was now arranged in a circle or quadrant. The '14 stalls of right wainscot' made by John Turner, joiner, were 'wrought circular with a cornish'. In addition, there were '2 stalls made to open in the choir', and 'one large stall against the door with the wainscott & cornish over it answerable to the door'. The occupants of the stalls were provided with 'compasse [i.e. segmental] kneeling boards & restingboards'. In the centre there was a 'large reading deske of wainscot turning upon a pillar', and at one side (presumably the eastern) there was an altar standing on deal steps. Communication between the domed choir and the body of the chapel was by means of a door which appears to have been centrally placed beneath the Venetian window in the east wall. This gave access on the west to a narrow passage behind the principal altar, from which doors opened at each end into the main body of the chapel (Pl. 28). The superstructure of this passage formed (and still forms) the architectural background to the altar itself.

The altar was the work of Grinling Gibbons, who received in all £307 for his workmanship in the chapel:

> To Grinling Gibbons Carver for carving the Altar in her Majestie's Chappell according to a designe approved of by her Majestie, Vizt. one large picture frame with ornaments on the topp, festoones on the sides relating thereto: 2 figures over the

---

[1] These appear to be the rooms enumerated in one of Streater's accounts for paintings in 1682–3 (LR 6/ 213). Evidently reading from E. to W., he charged for work in the choir, the 'passage behind the Altar, in the next roome, the cistern roome, the Sacrary, the roome next it, the farthest roome, the passages, the porch, the Chappell, the Queen's Closett, the passage by it, the great staires. . . .'.

doorway next the wall: 2 ornaments over the doores: 2 suitable ornaments over the neeches. The parapett with the moldings inricht. The pannells partly carved partly pierced through with a lattice of foliage, the cornish & all other moldings inricht relating to the Architecture of the screene, a compartment & 2 figures supporting it over the arch with festoons, two little figures holding festoons in the suffetas betweene the pillasters. In all as by Contract signed June 10th 1682, the summe of CClxv li.

Whether the design was made by Wren or by Gibbons himself does not appear, but Gibbons also made a 'modell for the altar piece' for which he charged £1 17s. Gibbons's workmanship was painted and gilded by Robert Streater:

> To Robert Streeter
> For guilding the Architrave of 2 doors & pedaments & the raffleafe cornish on both sides the Altar, the molding there & 12 great pannells that are carved, the great frame & glory & 2 small festoones that the boyes hold & 2 great festoones over the Arch & 4 festoons that the 2 flying boyes holds & 4 great ones that hang on the sides of the great pillars.
>
> £106 0s. 0d.

> For guilding the Queen's armes & the festoons over the great frames & the 2 Angells & pedestalls and crowne & branches in their hands & 8 Capitalls & the carved pannell over the door: & 2 boys guilded by the great frame & the guilding in the great Cornish over the Pillers & the moldings in the degrees & the Virgin Mary in the private Chappell & 3 small frames & one great one, writing 2 little tables with gold & other small things done there         £40 0s. 0d.

One feature was apparently altered in plaster, for John Grove was paid £3 'for making a carved peice over the picture frame of the Altar instead of the Glory'.

Some of these baroque incrustations have disappeared, including the two angels kneeling on either side of the altar (presumably the '2 figures over the door[s] next the wall' made by Grinling Gibbons), but the arms of Portugal impaling Stuart still appear on the 'compartment' over the arch of the Venetian window, complete with the '2 figures' (of flying angels) supporting it and the 'two great festoons' which depend from it (Pl. 29A).

The altarpiece itself (a Holy Family) is not mentioned in the building account. It was, however, by Jacob Huysmans, a painter much patronaged by Queen Catherine. Vertue says it was 'the most famous piece of his performance'.[1] Huysmans was also responsible for painting the tabernacle on the altar, and the surface of the dome over the choir. On 7 July 1683 Wren certified that the work was 'painfully don and like an able Artist', and the accounts duly record the payment:

> To Jacob Huysman for Painteing the Coupelo ceiling of the Choire and the Tabernacle within the Alter according to designe the summe of         £230 0s. 0d.

An obscure painter called Parry Walton received £15 15s. 'for 5 Altar peices and 3 peices putt in each picture'. There is no payment in the account for the large

[1] *Vertue's Notebooks* (Walpole Soc.) ii, p. 124.

religious paintings which occupied the spaces originally intended for the glazing of the great east window (Pl. 28). Their frames are, however, evidently the ones referred to in Streater's account. The presence of this pictorial barrier makes it clear that the choir was intended primarily for the private offices of the friars. But choral music was a feature of the chapel and the arrangements for its performance remain somewhat obscure.

At the west end, the queen's closet or 'tribune' (as it is invariably called in the account) underwent some further alterations. Its floor was shored up in order to enable the eight posts which supoorted it to be taken down and reset.[1] The tribune itself was altered by William Cleare, joiner:

> For 14 dayes worke allowed in taking downe the old wainscott in the Queen's Tribune next the Chapell, cutting away to inlarge for shasse frames, making good the old wainscott & laying on an Astrigall at ij s. viij d. per diem.        £1  17s.  4d.

> For the screene in the Chappell before the Queen's Tribune by Agreement
> £23  0s.  0d.

The front of the screen was carved by Grinling Gibbons 'by verball agreement' for £60.[2] New rails and balusters for the tribune were supplied by William Emmett, carver. The old rail and balusters were taken down and put away in the stable. John Grove, the plasterer, carved 'the Armes over the Chimney in the Queen's Tribune' (probably in plaster added to the old cartouche), while Streater painted what was presumably the same 'carved sheild in the Tribune'. Gibbons supplied 'a carved panell under the organ', evidently the one still existing in that position.[3]

The two niches seen in the engraving (Pl. 28) also formed part of the alterations of 1682–4. They were 'hewed out' by Maurice Emmett, the Master Bricklayer, and formed in brick 'with a staff moulding on the edge of the brick'. The festoons and frame of leaves with ribbons and berries were added in plaster by John Grove. No reference is made in the account to the two figures of St. Benedict and St. Augustine which are seen occupying the niches in Plate 28, but they may have taken the place of figures of Saints Peter and Paul for which Grinling Gibbons provided pedestals. These figures may well have been those of Saints Peter and Paul made for Queen Catherine by the sculptor John Bushnell, who in 1687 claimed that £100 was still due to him for his workmanship.[4] It should be noted that certain unspecified 'figures' were in 1682–3 removed from the chapel at Somerset House to the one at St. James's.[5] and that the painting of '6 great glaz'd white figures' is

---

[1] Only four posts or piers are, however, shown supporting the gallery in Flitcroft's survey plan of 1729 (Works 34/121).

[2] This does not survive. The three existing openings in the front of the gallery appear to have been given their present form in the eighteenth century.

[3] It is appropriately decorated with two trumpets, etc. The initials MR for Mary of Modena which appear on it in the engraving (Pl. 28) were no doubt added in 1685 and have since been obliterated.

[4] *Cal. Treas. Books* viii, pp. 1299–1300. In this petition he refers to them as being then at Somerset House. This is not inconsistent with their having been made originally for St. James's, for many of its fittings were removed to Somerset House Chapel in 1685 (see below, p. 253).

[5] 'For taking downe the figures at Denmark House Chappell & bringing them to St. James's and carrying them up into a roome, 5 men one day at 2s. 8d. each man'.

one of the items in Streater's account. The front of the altar and the front of the queen's seat were also painted a glossy white.

Though some details remain unaccounted for, it is thus possible to relate many of the surviving features of the chapel's decoration, and most of those seen in Plate 28, to the building account of 1682–4. The result was an interior almost unique in the history of English ecclesiastical architecture, and one that is of especial interest as an example of English seventeenth-century craftsmanship in the service of the Catholic Church.

Queen Catherine did not long enjoy the use of this sumptuously-furnished chapel. After the death of her royal husband in February 1685 both palace and chapel passed into the possession of the new queen, and the queen dowager had to withdraw to Somerset House. Wren's estimate for fitting up Somerset House as her permanent residence includes a provision for redecorating the Catholic chapel there, 'restoring the necessary things which were taken from thence to the Chappel at St. James's', and 'removeing the necessarys of the Fryery at St. James's' to Somerset House.[1] However, Queen Mary of Modena evidently bought some of the fittings, for in 1686, when they were transferred to the new Catholic chapel which James II had built at Whitehall, her Treasurer received £1263 from the king's Treasury 'to reimburse her for several provisions bought by her Majesty for her Chappell at St. James's which provisions are and are to be removed . . . to the King's Chappell at Whitehall.'[2]

No record of these 'provisions' appears to survive, but alterations to the chapel at St. James's carried out by the Office of Works in 1685–7 included making a curved altar-rail, two tabernacles for the side altar, two pedestals for the great altar, two confessing seats ('mitred with an O:G: the panells raised, the forsides wrought compas with architrave, freese and cornice'), and a new pair of stairs up to the queen's tribune.[3] In 1686 a 'great niche' was 'cutt out of the maine wall' of the chapel 'to set the front [*sic*] in'.[4] It was no doubt in this font that Prince Charles Edward was baptised on 15 October 1688.

In 1689 the use of the chapel as a place of Catholic worship was finally brought to an end. For some years no use appears to have been found for it, and in 1699 the organ was presented to the parishioners of St. Anne's, Soho.[5] In 1700 use of the chapel was granted to French and Dutch Protestants, and in 1702–3 a new altar-table, altar-rail and reading-desk were provided at Queen Anne's expense. They were made by Charles Hopson, joiner.[6] Queen Catherine, who had obtained a lease of the site of the Friary in 1671,[7] retained her property in it until her death in 1707, but soon afterwards a new lease was granted to the Duke and Duchess of Marlborough, who proceeded to demolish the monastic buildings to make room

[1] *Wren Soc.* xviii, pp. 146–7.

[2] Bodleian Library, MS. Rawlinson C 987. f. 31 (printed, with some textual errors, in *Wren Soc.* vii, p. 132).

[3] Works 5/39 and 5/40 (Extraordinary Works).

[4] Works 5/40 (Extraordinary Works). In 1938 a plastered niche was discovered behind the panelling on the north side of the ante-chapel immediately to the west of the pier supporting the north end of the gallery (photograph at Dept. of Environment). This does not, however, appear to have been as large as the niche made in 1686, which was 8 ft. high and 6 ft. wide.

[5] *Cal. Treas. Books* xiv, p. 365.      [6] Works 5/53.

[7] *Cal. Treas. Books* iii, pp. 897, 916.

for Marlborough House. It was presumably at this time that the domed choir was removed and the east end restored to its original appearance. The chapel itself continued to be used by the French Protestant congregation until 1781, when they exchanged with the German Lutheran congregation, who had the use of a room in Great Court which they used as a chapel. The German Chapel (as it was henceforth called) was then repaired and redecorated by the Office of Works at an estimated cost of over £600.[1]

# SOMERSET HOUSE

AFTER THE Restoration, Denmark House—the name by which Somerset House was still generally referred to in the Works accounts—became once more the queen's dower-house. As such it was in turn the residence of the queen-mother from her return to England in 1660 until her departure for France in 1665, and of Catherine of Braganza from her widowhood in 1685 until her return to Portugal in 1692. Although Catherine's actual residence was limited to seven years, the house belonged to her from 1669 onwards, and was used by her partly to accommodate various members of her household (including her Capuchin friars), and partly for ceremonies such as the annual distribution of Maundy money.

From the point of view of the Office of Works, a house belonging to a queen consort might form part of its regular responsibilities, but one occupied by a queen dowager did not. In practice it carried out works for both queens more or less continuously from 1660 to 1685, but whereas the expenditure for Queen Catherine was accounted for and enrolled in the same way as works on other royal palaces, the expenditure for the queen-mother was financed from her Privy Purse, and did not appear on the Paymaster's enrolled accounts. Often one copy of the detailed accounts would be bound up in the Office's annual book, but this was not always the case, and the second copy was no doubt retained by the queen's treasurer.[2] After 1685 no further works were performed by the Office of Works on the queen's behalf, and it was not until after her death in 1705 that its officers resumed possession.[3] Continuity was, however, maintained by Thomas Rotherham, the Clerk of the Works at the Tower of London, who held the same office at Somerset House without a break from 1678 until 1714.[4]

[1] Works 4/16, 23 May and 25 Aug. 1780; Works 6/19, pp. 310–11, 317, 354. In their petition the ministers stated that the chapel had not been redecorated since the marriage of the Prince of Orange, for which see above, p. 243. Works 34/137 is a plan showing the chapel in use by the German congregation.

[2] Thus detailed accounts survive in Works 5 for the years 1660–1 and for nearly every year from 1664–5 until 1684–5. One duplicate book of expenditure on alterations to the greenhouse in the garden at Somerset House in 1678 remains among Queen Catherine's accounts in LR 6/204, the Office copy being in Works 5/31.

[3] *Cal. S.P. Dom. 1668–9*, p. 511; *1671*, p. 290; *Cal. Treas. Books 1669–72* (i), p. 501; Works 6/5, f. 193.

[4] He received a salary of £45 a year as Clerk of the Works to Queen Catherine, and also supervised the works at her house at Hammersmith (see accounts &c. scattered throughout the queen dowager's papers in LR 6/196–217. His name as 'Clerke of the Works to Her Majesty' occurs in a list of persons having lodgings in Somerset House in 1705 (B.M., Add. MS. 20726, f. 41).

When Henrietta Maria arrived in London in November 1660, her palace was already undergoing a general repair and redecoration costing some £1300.[1] In January 1661 she went to France, and when she returned in July 1662 she was obliged to stay at Greenwich because Somerset House was undergoing extensive alterations.[2] No detailed books of expenditure are extant for works at Somerset House in the years 1661–2, 1662–3 or 1663–4, but the total outlay on building during these three years can be ascertained from the annual accounts of the queen-mother's treasurer, drafts or summaries of which survive among her papers.[3] It amounted to £23,501, of which £14,381 was represented by

> Payments made upon the workmens monethly books for wages signed by Sir John Denham Kn[t]. and others the Officers of the works and for comodities bought and used about Denmarke House and allowed by her Mats. warrant,

while the remaining £9119 was paid

> to severall persons as Masons Bricklayers Carpenters &c. according to severall Contracts made with them by the right hono[ble] the Earle of St. Albans [the queen's treasurer] and S[r] Robert Long [her receiver-general] and others and allowed by her Mats. warrant.

For 1661–2 the treasurer's account is supplemented by a list of the workmen to whom payments were made under the heading of 'contracts'. The names include Maurice Emmett, bricklayer (£1000), John Angier, carpenter (£1000), William Allenby, bricklayer (£200), Nathaniel Brackenbury, carpenter (£200), Thomas Shadbolt and Abraham Story, masons (£87 8s. 0d.), John Young et al. masons (£500), William de Keyser, sculptor (£140), Henry Phillips, carver (£10), 'Mounsieur Ambrey' (£109 1s. 6d.), and 'the French Joyners' (£15).[4] Under a separate heading of payments 'made for her Majesty's service upon the signification of her Majesty's pleasure', is found the name of Hugh May, while Peter Besnier, sculptor, and Leonard Gammon, the clerk of works, occur in a third category of 'payments made by order of Her Majesty's Council'.

No details of any kind throw light on the expenditure of 1662–3, but in 1663–4 the summary refers to 'work and materialls had and used about her Mats. new stone building in the Garden at Somerset house and also the Stables Coachhouses and Mr. Gamon's house in Somersett Yard And the new brick building at the end of the Crosse Gallery in the Back Court of Somersett house'. The identification of the 'new brick building at the end of the Crosse Gallery' presents some difficulty, but there can be no doubt that the 'new stone building' was the suite of state rooms facing the Thames whose facade is familiar from *Vitruvius Britannicus*, from a

[1] E 351/3274: details in Works 5/1.     [2] *D.N.B.*     [3] LR 6/190.
[4] 'M. Ambrey' has not been identified. The reference to 'French joiners' recalls a statement in Rugge's 'Diurnall' under April 1662 that the chapel of Somerset House was being 'paved by French men against the Queen mother comes' and that 'the stones that paved this place came out of France' (B.M., Add. MS. 10117, f. 325); also a plate in Godfrey Richards' translation of Le Muet's French edition of Palladio's *First Book of Architecture*, 3rd ed. 1676, showing the 'floors of small squares of carpentry work' at Somerset House, described as 'a novelty in England'. A French joiner named Charles Godelier had been employed by the queen in 1628 (LR 6/191).

water-colour by Sandby (Pl. 32), and from many views of London from the river.[1] From the plan (Fig. 22) it can be seen that the new suite comprised a staircase leading to a Presence Chamber and a Privy Chamber, beyond which were the private apartments built for Anne of Denmark. Colen Campbell explicitly states that the arcaded facade was 'built Anno 1662', while in 1663 a French visitor noted that Somerset House was the queen-mother's residence, 'qu'elle fait rebatir a present pour la rendre un peu plus agreable'.[2] In October 1664 Samuel Pepys 'saw the Queene's new rooms, which are most stately and nobly furnished',[3] and about the same time Edmund Waller addressed to the queen-mother some flattering verses 'Upon Her Majesty's new buildings at Somerset House'. According to Waller the new buildings were 'by the Queen herself designed', but Campbell says that the front 'was taken from a Design of Inigo Jones, but conducted by another Hand', and Macky tells us that it was 'built upon a Plan of Inigo Jones by his Son-in-Law Mr. Webb'.[4] The payment to Hugh May in the account for 1661–2 might suggest that he was the architect, but it is equally likely that this was a recognition of the services he had rendered as Paymaster of the Works.[5] The elevation—based apparently on an engraving of Tibaldi's Palazzo Magnani in Bologna[6] —is certainly of a kind more characteristic of Webb than of May, and the probability is that it was the former whom the queen-mother employed to design her new suite.

The final addition to the palace was the building in 1664–5 of 'a new Bricke building three stories high for her Majesty the Queene-Mother adjoyning to the Stone gallery next the Garden containing about 97 foote long 17 foot ½ wide & 31 foote high up to the plate with a Roofe upon it, & making the said Gallery into lodgings with cellars under them, working up a new brickwall before the building 80 foote long, & paving the passage there with Purbacke stone'. This appears to have been the long range at the back of the Cross Gallery described in the plan of 1706 as 'French Buildings', and was presumably the same as the 'new brick building' referred to in the previous year. It consisted of sets of apartments separated by staircases, and probably resembled one of the contemporary ranges in the Inns of Court. It faced north towards the backs of the houses in the Strand, from which it was separated by the new brick wall, and must have had the least attractive outlook of any part of the palace. The cost amounted to £1431.[7]

The palace was again overhauled in 1671–2 for the benefit of Queen Catherine.

[1] The most accurate view would, however, appear to be that of James Basire, made for the Society of Antiquaries in *c.* 1776 (Pl. 32A). The engraving in *Vitruvius Britannicus* is quite untrustworthy, and Sandby, although reliable in most details, seems to have followed Campbell's rendering of the masonry of the arcade.

[2] C. Campbell, *Vitruvius Britannicus* i (1715), p. 4; *Les Voyages de M. de Monconys* iii (1695), p. 15. He criticised the old lodgings, 'tant pour la petitesse des chambres, que pour le laideur des planchers' (p. 35).

[3] *Diary*, ed. H. B. Wheatley, 4 (1894), p. 270.

[4] J. Macky, *Journey through England* i (1724), p. 172.

[5] At the time of the queen mother's death in 1669 May was receiving a salary of £30 a year as Comptroller of her works (*Cal. S.P. Dom. 1671*, pp. 561–2.)

[6] We are indebted to Mr. John Harris for pointing out the resemblance between the facade of the English palace and its Bolognese prototype. The ultimate source for the arcade on the ground floor was presumably the one illustrated by Serlio, Book IV, p. 131 (edition of 1619).

[7] Works 5/8. Maurice Emmett was the bricklayer, Joshua Marshall the mason, Nathaniel Brackenbury the carpenter.

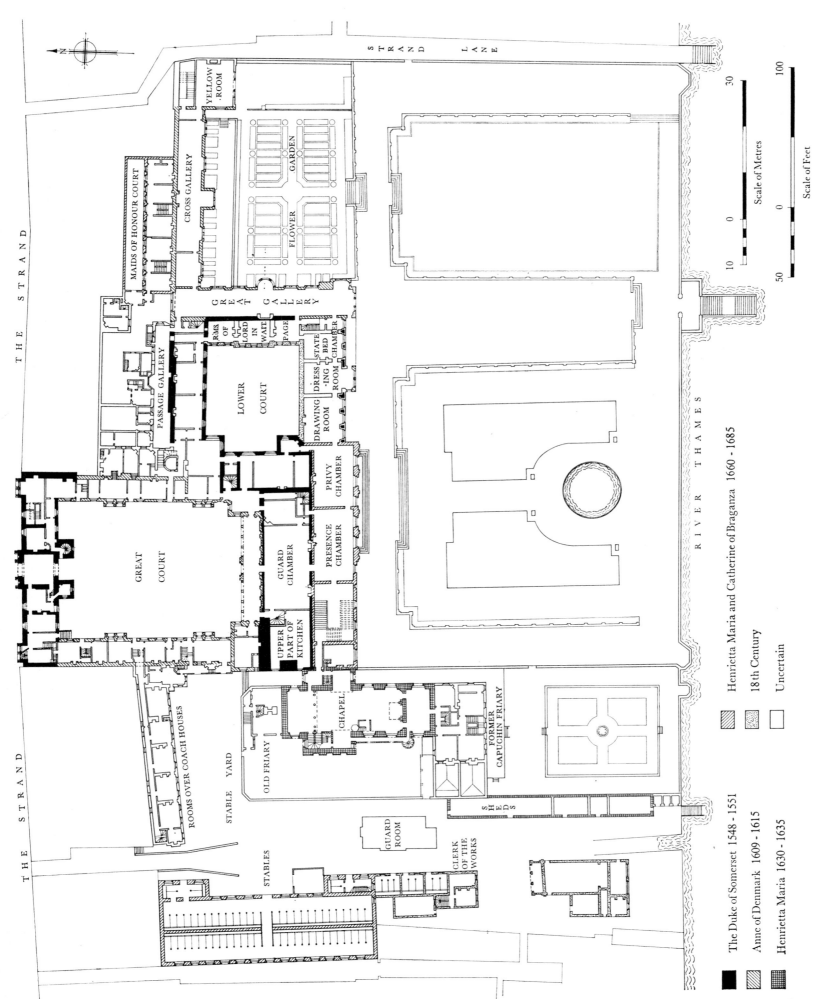

THE STRAND

THE STRAND

STRAND LANE

N

YELLOW ROOM

MAIDS OF HONOUR COURT

CROSS GALLERY

FLOWER GARDEN

PASSAGE GALLERY

GREAT GALLERY

RMS OF G LORD IN WAIT PAGE

LOWER COURT

DRAWING ROOM

DRESS-ING ROOM

STATE BED CHAMBER

ROOMS OVER COACH HOUSES

GREAT COURT

PRIVY CHAMBER

STABLE YARD

GUARD CHAMBER

PRESENCE CHAMBER

UPPER PART OF KITCHEN

OLD FRIARY

CHAPEL

FORMER CAPUCHIN FRIARY

SHEDS

STABLES

GUARD ROOM

CLERK OF THE WORKS

RIVER THAMES

Scale of Metres

Scale of Feet

30

10

0

100

50

0

Fig. 22. Old Somerset House, based on an eighteenth-century survey by Kenton Couse (Works 30/261)

The Duke of Somerset 1548 - 1551

Anne of Denmark 1609 - 1615

Henrietta Maria 1630 - 1635

Henrietta Maria and Catherine of Braganza 1660 - 1685

18th Century

Uncertain

In the queen's great bedchamber Henry Phillips, the Master Carver, took down the arms of France from the alcove and put up those of Portugal. The chapel was redecorated by the Sergeant Painter with white paint and gilding and Joshua Marshall supplied a new white marble chimneypiece for the queen's tribune or closet. The old and new friaries, one at the north, the other at the south, end of the chapel were repaired, as was the friars' 'banqueting' or summer-house at the bottom of their walled garden running down to the Thames.[1]

More work was done in the chapel in 1674–5. The '21 paintings of the sceeling' were let down by ropes, so that Robert Streater could 'new paint the Clouds on all the Clothes in the Chappell seeling'. The 'great carved ceeling' itself was washed and cleaned and two plaster statues were 'coloured white in distemper'.[2] At the same time two external lean-to galleries or corridors were built, one on each side of the chapel, each leading to a new circular staircase which projected from the wall on either side of the altar.[3] The purpose of these galleries is not entirely clear, but there was evidently an upper room over the space behind the altar, and the staircases and galleries would have enabled the officiating friars to pass to and fro between this upper room and the two side chapels without going through the sanctuary.

The palace underwent another general repair and redecoration in 1685, when the death of Charles II meant that Catherine of Braganza would leave Whitehall and take up permanent residence at Somerset House. Wren drew up an estimate amounting to £1813,[4] and between February and May £1933 were spent on painting, carving, wainscotting, lathing, plastering, whiting and glazing.[5] The detailed book for these works has not survived, but the enrolment shows that Charles Hopson received £203 for joiner's work in the chapel, and that William Emmett was responsible for 'carveing about the Alter and Pulpitt'. Between June 1685 and May 1688 Robert Streater, the Sergeant Painter, was employed by the queen to carry out further work in the chapel, including 'painting the clouds & cherubims' heads betweene the Altar & great Quire & mending the Clouds in the Ceiling', and 'painting 3 peices to be under the 3 Altarpieces at 30s. each'.[6] Bills also survive for the repair and embellishment (at the queen's own expense) of the grotto and the greenhouse. In connection with the former, John Settle, mason, submitted an account for various items, including £10 'for the Pilasters and Great Arch', £4 'for the little Arch that bears up the Marble Bason', £5 'for the Compasse Bason', £7 'for the Dolphin of White Marble', and £7 16s. od. 'for 26 Pedestalls at 6s. per pedestall', while John Palmer charged £21 5s. o. 'for severall Parcells of Curious Shells, and Varietie of Corall & other things for the use and Ornament of Her Majestie's Grotto'.[7] After 1685 no further work was accounted for by the Office of Works until 1707, when the palace reverted to the Crown after the queen dowager's death. As there was evidently no plan of the palace in the Office, one

---

[1] Works 5/17.
[2] Were these the figures of Sts. Peter and Paul for which the sculptor John Bushnell was claiming payment in 1687? (*Cal. Treas. Books* viii, pp. 1299–1300).    [3] Works 5/24.
[4] Works 3/1, f. 6, printed in *Wren Soc.* xviii, pp. 146–7.    [5] E 351/3298.
[6] LR 6/204. Details of some earlier alterations to the greenhouse in Feb. 1678/9 will be found in Works 5/30, ff. 188–9, and Works 5/31 (at end).    [7] LR 6/214.

was commissioned from a certain Francis Bickerton, who was paid £20 'for plotting down in a mapp the whole Pallace of Denmark House by agreement'. William Dickinson was then paid a further £5 'for contracting the said plott into less scale and fixing it neatly into a frame with copying the Book of the Inhabitants for her Majesty's use'.[1] This must evidently have been the original of the plan printed by Samuel Pegge in his *Curialia*, which is accompanied by a list of rooms and their occupants, drawn up in 1706.[2]

One important building that appears on this plan has not so far been mentioned. This is the great stable, with stalls for 56 horses, that stood on the west side of the palace. Knyff's view (Pl. 33A) shows its pedimented facade in perspective, and it can be recognised also in Ogilby and Morgan's map of 1682. No reference to its erection has been found in the Works accounts, but the original plan and elevation are preserved in a volume of drawings associated with Robert Hooke.[3] Both architectural style and draughtsmanship are characteristic of Hooke, who must therefore be regarded as its architect. Hooke was not active as an architect before 1666, but there is no reference to the stable in his diary, which begins in 1672. It therefore seems likely that it was built in 1669 or 1670, soon after the palace came into the hands of Queen Catherine of Braganza. It may be noted that several entries in Hooke's diary show that in the 1670s he was friendly with John Hervey, then the queen's treasurer, and with Richard Gammon, the clerk of her works.[4]

Catherine of Braganza was the last queen to inhabit the palace, and in the course of the eighteenth century it came to be used for a variety of purposes. Many of the rooms were occupied by court officials, or by favoured individuals.[5] Some were for a time assigned to the Duchy of Cornwall,[6] others were used for the storage of surplus pictures from other royal palaces.[7] The stables were under the jurisdiction of the Master of the Horse, at whose request arrangements were made in 1722 for the accommodation of horses belonging to the Horse Guards, in 1729 for the horses and coaches of the Prince of Wales.[8] From 1756 onwards the amenities of the palace were not improved by the quartering there of a battalion of Foot Guards.[9]

But from time to time the State Apartments were still made use of. In 1706 the palace was designated by Queen Anne for the reception of foreign embassies,[10] and in 1714 it was at Somerset House that the Dutch ambassadors were entertained after their public entry into London. The Prince of Orange was lodged in the

[1] E 351/3311 (under 'Whitehall').      [2] S. Pegge, *Curialia* iv (1806), p. 93–100.

[3] B.M., Add. MS. 5238, no. 89, reproduced in *Wren Soc.* v, pl. xxxii.

[4] *The Diary of Robert Hooke*, ed. H. W. Robinson and W. Adams (1935), pp. 7, 156 for Gammon and for Hervey *anno* 1677 *passim*. On 18 Oct. 1673 Hooke went to Somerset House with Wren (pp. 65–6).

[5] For lists of the occupants of Somerset House in the reign of Anne see B.M., Add. MS. 20726, f. 41 and S. Pegge, *Curialia* iv (1806), pp. 93–100. In 1710 Narcissus Luttrell noted that the queen had given the Bishop of Bristol lodgings in the palace, 'with leave to convert the popish chappel there for the use of the Church of England' (*Brief Historical Relation* vi, p. 668).

[6] The 'Prince's Council Chamber' was fitted up by the Office of Works in 1716–17 at a cost of £75 (Works 5/141), and the Duchy Council met in it for the first time in February 1717 (Duchy of Cornwall Records V.4.SR). The Duchy gave up these quarters in 1751.

[7] See a list of 328 pictures 'in the Store Rooms at Somerset House', dated 28 Oct. 1714, in B.M., Add. MS. 19933.

[8] Works 4/2, 15, 20, 23, 24 Oct., 14 Dec. 1722; Works 5/141; Works 6/7, pp. 280–1; Works 4/4, 9 Jan. 1729/30; Works 5/141; T 56/18, pp. 289, 291.

[9] Works 6/17, p. 148ᵛ; Works 4/11, 30 Nov. 1756.

[10] Works 6/14, f. 144; N. Luttrell, *Brief Historical Relation* vi, pp. 11, 172–3.

palace when he came to marry the Princess Royal in 1733, and in 1764 the same apartments were got ready for the Prince of Brunswick, who was to become the husband of Princess Augusta.[1] Elaborate entertainments were also given at Somerset House. One celebrated masquerade, mentioned by Addison, was given in 1712 by the French ambassador; another, in honour of the royal birthday, is referred to by the same writer in 1716; and yet another, in which Miss Chudleigh made herself notorious, was held in 1749.[2] In 1755 the Russian ambassador had permission to give an entertainment and ball in the palace, and in 1763 there was an official reception in honour of the Venetian ambassador.[3]

These brilliant occasions could not, however, conceal the fact that the palace was falling gradually into ruin. On the Strand front the ornamental features had by now become 'much defaced by time and the smoke of the city': within, the passage to the garden had become 'extremely disagreeable, the broken staircase, the appearance of the walls, the darkness, and the filth, rendering it like the descent into a prison'.[4] Already in 1718 Somerset House was regarded by Vanbrugh as the 'most out of repair' of all the royal palaces, and in a report to the Lord Chamberlain he and the other members of the Board of Works expressed their apprehension at its condition.[5] 'We find it,' they wrote, 'generally very much out of repair; but the most danger wee apprehend is from the decay and bulging out of some of the front and back walls, which unless speedily taken down and rebuilt, may expose great part of the fabrick to ruin.' Other parts of the building which they specified as urgently in need of replacement were the sash windows in the royal apartments, which 'are no longer able to resist the gusts of wind or keep out the weather', the floor of the 'gallery of communication', which was 'rotten throughout', and the 'ceilings, roofs, windows and window jaumbs of stone' which, 'being much decayed, stand in great need of repeiring'. They concluded by drawing the Lord Chamberlain's attention to the 'great and considerable damage' which the building was receiving 'from several irregular wooden buildings which have from time to time been erected upon the roofs and leads, the said leads being often cut, and carryed off, the stone copings defaced, the building in dainger of being crusht by the pressure of such additional weights, or of being set on fire, by carelessness of servants & mean officers, together with many other injuries ensuing therefrom'.[6]

The estimate for making good these specific defects amounted to £1500, but in Colen Campbell's opinion £8000 would not be enough to put the building as a whole into good repair.[7] In fact the expenditure during the next five years amounted only to £2262, and it was not until 1723 that the Treasury agreed to the repair of the sashes in the royal apartments, which by then were 'so very bad that the furniture in some of the roomes are exposed to the weather and have very much suffered by the late storms'.[8] In 1725–6 the lead roofs of the Picture Gallery and the Long Gallery were taken up and relaid and the painting and gilding in the ceiling of

[1] Lord Hervey's *Memoirs*, ed. Croker, i, p. 277; Walpole, *Memoirs of the Reign of George III* i, p. 276; Works 4/13, 25 May 1764; Works 6/18, pp. 46, 61, 62.
[2] E. B. Chancellor, *Annals of the Strand* (1912), pp. 195–6.
[3] Works 4/11, 28 Jan. 1755; Works 4/13, 25 March 1763.
[4] *London & its Environs Described* (R. & J. Dodsley, 1761), vi, pp. 42–3.
[5] T 1/216, f. 82v.          [6] Works 6/7, pp. 34v–5.
[7] T 1/216, f. 70v.          [8] Works 4/2, 7 Dec. 1720; Works 6/7, p. 309.

the 'Royal Gallery' (presumably the Great Gallery) was repaired.[1] In 1730 steps were taken to rebuild one of the walls in the Lower Court, which was reported to be 'in a very dangerous condition'. When the wall was taken down an adjoining wall and stack of chimneys were found to be in danger of falling, while the roof of the royal suite was 'in a very dangerous condition occasioned by the weight of an apartment very injudiciously placed upon it, now in the possession of the Black Rod'. The cost of making good both walls and of rebuilding Black Rod's apartment in a more substantial manner was estimated at £2155. This expenditure was authorised by the Treasury in August 1730, but the state of the roof over the royal apartments on the south side of the court was found to be worse than had been expected, and in April 1731 the Treasury received another communication from the Board of Works informing them that

> we have pursuant to your Lordships' order dated 31 August 1730 rebuilt the walls o two sides of a court at Denmark House and new leaded and repaired so much of the roof as in that memorial we apprehended in danger, and think it our duty to acquaint your Lordships that upon opening the roof of the great apartment, we find it necessary to repair that whole roof, and that it will be proper to take down an old rotten wooden staircase at the end of the Royal Apartment very dangerous in case of fire, and build one of stone in the room thereof with proper walls to carry it. And if it be your Lordships' pleasure to have the whole royal apartment [i.e. the whole royal suite] reaching as farr as the Gallery put in thorough repair and the rooms under it & over it wainscoted, which we think our duty to represent to your Lordships as necessary, the expence may amount to the sum of £2300.

The expenditure was approved on 15 April, and was carried out forthwith.[2] The walls in question were those on the south and east sides of the court (Fig. 22). The eastern wall lost its two prominently projecting bays, and was replaced by what appears to have been an elevation of straightforward Georgian character. The new southern wall was, like its predecessor, windowless and utilitarian in character. The northern and western walls remained as they were until forty years later when they, too, were reported to be in danger of collapse.[3]

In 1733 the Board turned its attention to the Chapel, which since 1711 had been used for the worship of the Established Church and was now served by a minister appointed by the Bishop of London as Dean of the Chapels Royal.[4] The roof was new boarded and leaded, the cornice was painted, and 'the whole put in thorough repair' at a cost of £642—£10 less than the estimate approved by the Treasury on 3 May 1733.[5]

In 1743 the royal apartments in the Lower Court once more demanded attention. The south-east angle, forming the end of the Great Gallery, was found

---

[1] Works 4/3, 24 Feb., 23 March 1725/6.

[2] Works 4/2, 7 July, 20 Aug., 24 Aug. 1720; Works 4/4, 2 Feb., 16 March 1731; Works 4/5, 20 April, 1731; T 56/18, pp. 330, 332, 347; Works 5/141.

[3] Below, p. 261.

[4] R. Needham & A. Webster, *Somerset House Past and Present* (1905), pp. 176–7. The Board's minutes refer in 1724 to a room at Somerset House' 'built by the late Bishop of London [John Robinson] for his servants to dine in' (Works 4/2, 29 Jan. 1723/4).

[5] Works 4/5, 6, 30 March, 3, 15 May, 1733; Works 6/16, p. 1; Works 5/141.

to be in so bad a state that it was thought to be 'in great danger of falling', and it was accordingly rebuilt at an estimated cost of £1365.[1] Comparison between Knyff's engraving of *c.* 1705 (Pl. 33A) and later views such as that of Sandby (Pl. 32B), show that the plain southern elevation of the gallery was replaced by a new Palladian design incorporating a Venetian window, and crowned by a pediment. There can be little doubt that William Kent was the member of the Board responsible for this characteristic architectural emendation.

The repairs of 1725–43 represented the last major attempt to keep pace with the decay of the fabric. Minor repairs continued to be carried out yearly, and there was some extra expenditure in connection with events such as the reception of the Venetian ambassador in 1763 and the Prince of Brunswick's visit in 1764.[2] But the prince was the last royal personage to be lodged in the palace, and in 1771 George III handed the royal apartments over to the newly founded Royal Academy for the accommodation of their schools of design. By now the gardens had been spoiled by use as a parade ground for the troops quartered in the palace, and much of the original architectural detail had perished or been removed for the sake of safety. In the Great Court the parapet and the upper order of columns had long ago been taken down because of their dangerous condition, and in 1764 the front of the Great Gallery had to be shored up to prevent its collapse.[3] Sooner or later some decision would have to be taken, either to spend a very large sum on restoring the building or else to pull much or all of it down.

It was on 6 May 1774 that the Board submitted to the Treasury the report which brought the problem of Somerset House to a head:

> We humbly beg leave to represent to your Lordships that we have caused a survey to be made of His Majesty's Palace of Denmark House and find it to be in the following condition, vizt.
> The East Building of the Great Court is in a very ruinous condition, the West front of which we have shored up to prevent its falling. The North building of the said Court (which is next the Strand) is greatly out of repair and much decayed.
> The walls of the buildings on the North and West sides of Well Court are greatly crackt, bulg'd and out of an upright.
> The Buildings on the North and West side of the Flower Garden are in a very ruinous condition, part being fallen down and the other parts are shored up to prevent their falling.
> The greatest part of the covering of the roofs and flats are out of repair, and many of the chimney shafts, window frames, sashes, casments, window lights &c., are in a ruinous condition.[4]

By 17 May the king had agreed that the palace should be pulled down to make way for public offices, and that Buckingham House should take its place as the queen's official dower house.[5] Demolition began in 1776, and was carried out in

---

[1] Works 4/8, 29 March, 8, 14 June, 1743; Works 6/16, p. 150; Works 5/141.
[2] Works 4/13, 25 March, 18 Nov. 1763; Works 1/4, p. 21.
[3] Works 4/1, p. 77 (removal of columns, 1718); Works 4/8, 7 Sept. 1742 (removal of parapet); Works 4/13, 29 June 1764 (gallery shored up).
[4] Works 6/19, p. 27.                                    [5] Below, p. 365.

stages as the building of the new Somerset House progressed. Some valuable measured drawings of the main elevations of the Tudor quadrangle were made by James Hunter in 1775,[1] but the most evocative picture of the old palace is to be found in the *European Magazine* for 1802, where Joseph Moser, son of the first keeper of the Royal Academy's rooms, describes how he and others accompanied Sir William Chambers on a last tour of the building before demolition began.

> At the extremity of the royal apartments . . . two large folding-doors connected the architecture of Jones with the ancient structure; these opened into a long gallery, on the first floor of a building which occupied one side of the water-garden. . . . This old part of the mansion had long been shut up (it was haunted of course), when Sir William Chambers wishing . . . to survey it, the folding-doors of the royal bedchamber (the Keeper's drawing-room) were opened; a number of persons entered with the Surveyor. The first of the apartments, the long gallery, was observed to be lined with oak, in small pannels; the heights of their mouldings had been touched with gold; it had an oaken floor and stuccoed ceiling, from which still depended part of the chains, &c., to which had hung chandeliers. Some of the sconces remained against the sides, and the marks of the glasses were still to be distinguished upon the wainscot.
>
> From several circumstances it was evident that this gallery had been used as a ball-room. The furniture which had decorated the royal apartments had, for the convenience of the Academy, and perhaps prior to that establishment, . . . been removed to this and the adjoining suite of apartments. It was extremely curious to observe thrown together, in the utmost confusion, various articles, the fashion and forms of which showed that they were the production of different periods. In one part there was the vestiges of a throne and canopy of state; in another, curtains for the audience-chamber, which had once been crimson velvet fringed with gold. What remained of the fabric had, except in the deepest folds, faded to an olive colour; all the fringe and lace but a few threads and spangles had been ripped off; the ornaments of the chairs of state demolished; stools, couches, screens, and fire-dogs, broken and scattered about in a state of derangement which might have tempted a philosopher to moralise upon the transitory nature of sublunary splendour and human enjoyments.
>
> With respect to the gold and silver which were worked in the borders and other parts of the tapestries with which the royal apartments were, even within my remembrance, hung, it had been carefully picked out while those rooms were used as barracks. Some very elegant landscapes, beautifully wove in tapestry, adorned the library of the Royal Academy until the dissolution of the building.
>
> To return from this short digression to the gallery; I must observe, that treading in dust that had been for ages accumulating, we passed through the collection of ruined furniture to the suite of apartments which I have already stated formed the other side of the angle, and fronted the Thames.
>
> In these rooms, which had been adorned in a style of splendour and magnificence which was creditable to the taste of the age of Edward the Sixth, part of the ancient furniture remained, and, indeed, from the stability of its materials and construction, might have remained for centuries, had proper attention been paid to its preservation.

[1] Works 30/263–4.

The audience chamber had been hung with silk, which was in tatters, as were the curtains, gilt leather covers, and painted screens. There was in this and a much longer room a number of articles which had been removed from other apartments, and the same confusion and appearance of neglect was evident. Some of the sconces, though reversed, were still against the hangings; and one of the brass gilt chandeliers still depended from the ceiling. . . . The general state of this building, its mouldering walls and decaying furniture, broken casements, falling roof, and the long range of its uninhabited and uninhabitable apartments, presented to the mind in strong, though gloomy, colours a correct picture of those dilapidated castles, the haunts of spectres and residence of magicians and murderers, that have, since the period to which I allude, made such a figure of romance.

# WHITEHALL PALACE

## 1. 1660–1685

FROM THE Restoration onwards Whitehall, essentially one and a half centuries old, underwent a constant process of alteration and piecemeal rebuilding without approaching to any significant degree the clarity and order of planning which a late seventeenth-century metropolitan palace might be expected to embody. Thus the destruction by fire on 4 January 1698 of the greater part of the buildings rendered an architectural palimpsest indecipherable, and the surviving documentary material, though more copious than for any previous period in its history, is still not sufficient for a reconstruction of the appearance of the palace after the additions of Charles II and James II.

James II was the last king to live at Whitehall, and while it retained many official and court lodgers at the time of the 1698 fire it was a palace in little more than title: the Thames-side atmosphere was too damp for William III's chesty constitution and he could see no cogent reason for rebuilding it. A number of outlying offices were retained; portions of the ruins and undamaged peripheral buildings were leased, and Whitehall became synonymous with administration. If the minor fires of 1661 and 1662 had caught hold, the history not only of Whitehall but of English architecture would have been different.[1]

Charles II's intentions for Whitehall in the early years of the Restoration greatly exceeded what was achieved. The revival of projects made for his father by Inigo Jones and John Webb was in Charles's mind by the autumn of 1661, and ideas of

---

[1] *Cal. Treas. Books 1660–7*, p. 296; *London Survey*, xiii, p. 37. On the windy night of 17 February 1662 the palace caught fire four times.

rebuilding recurred through the 1660s. The detailed survey of the old palace made in 1669–70 was perhaps related in the king's mind to the abandonment of such ideas in favour of making do with what was already there. By 1670 he was in serious financial difficulty and the nation was suffering from the destruction of three quarters of the City of London in the Great Fire of 1666.[1] The king may have felt it wise that economies should be seen to be made; at the same time the piecemeal alterations and costly maintenance at Whitehall continued.

Accommodation was needed not only for the Royal Household (including the king's brother James, Duke of York and his duchess and the king's cousin Prince Rupert) but also for some of the mistresses who added piquancy to Charles's life, public as well as private. On certain days when the king dined at Whitehall the public were admitted to watch him.[2] He continued the customs of the Royal Maundy and of touching for the King's Evil in the Banqueting House, and he was often to be seen, and spoken to, as he walked in St. James's Park. In 1682 Charles began a new palace at Winchester, far from London and the eye of Parliament. But throughout the 1670s Whitehall was the principal seat of king and court, and the gaiety and splendour of life there were as real, if not as irresponsible, as popular imagination has held them to be.

The two prime documents for the appearance of Whitehall in the last period of its history are the plan of 1669–70 (Pl. 36) and the bird's-eye view of c. 1695–7 (Pl. 37).[3] It is therefore both convenient and illuminating to consider the history of the buildings in relation to these two documents, the one dating from the period soon after the Restoration, the other from the last decade of the seventeenth century, after the substantial works undertaken for James II and William and Mary.

The ground floor plan of the palace is recorded in an engraving titled 'A Survey & Ground plot of the Royal Palace of Whitehall with the Lodgings & Apartments belonging to their Majesties Ao D. 1680. Surveyed by Ino Fisher'. The plate was drawn and published by George Vertue in 1747. Two manuscript plans survive which can be shown to depend with the engraving on a lost common source which may be the original drawing used by Vertue.[4] It can also be shown that the original plan must have been made in 1669–70.[5] It is extremely detailed and, as far as can be checked, very accurate—far more so than the bird's-eye view in which the wedge-shaped site is reduced to a parallelogram. It is unlikely that so comprehensive a plan was undertaken twice in a short period, and it seems reasonable to connect it with the substantial payment of £60 entered in October 1670 to Ralph Greatorex for three quarters of a year in 'surveighing & describing in vellom a Exact Ground plott of

---

[1] During the fire the danger to Whitehall was sufficient for a great quantity of large timber to be jettisoned from Scotland Yard into the Thames; subsequently workmen were employed to recover it (Works 5/9, Sept., Dec. 1666, March 1667).

[2] *Diary of John Evelyn*, ed. E. S. de Beer (1955), iii, pp. 490–1.

[3] The versions, date and authorship of these documents are discussed in *London Survey*, xiii, pp. 41–4, 111–13; for the bird's-eye view see also below, p. 285). Vertue's engraving of the plan is reproduced *ibid.*, pl. 1, and in *Wren Soc.* vii, pl. vi. It is not suitable for reproduction in half-tone, and the version reproduced here (Pl. 36) is the one in the Library of the Society of Antiquaries. A large-scale plan based on Vertue's engraving, but incorporating the evidence of archaeological investigations in 1939, 1950 and 1960–2, will be issued with vol. iv of the *History*, whose text will describe the building of the Tudor palace.

[4] *London Survey* xiii, p. 42. The drawings are B.M. Crace Plans xi, 65, and Society of Antiquaries, 196 G. A later version of the key to the plan, in B.M. MS. Lansdowne 736, is a copy dated 1739 of a list made in 1689.

[5] *London Survey, loc. cit.*

the whole house of Whitehall, Cockpit, & parts adjacent'.[1] No indication is given of the nature or the height of the upper storeys, whose disposition remains to a large extent in doubt.[2] Whether or not the plan reflects a decision on the king's part not to rebuild, the force behind the survey is likely to have been Wren, whose responsibility the palace officially became on his appointment as Surveyor on 29 March 1669.

The palace in 1670 may be divided into three areas:

(1) The nucleus, consisting of two main courts, the Great Court and the Pebble Court, divided by an east-west terrace over which a gallery was built in 1668–9. On the west they were bounded respectively by the Palace Gate leading to the street called Whitehall and the Banqueting House; on the east they were bounded jointly by the Great Hall and a complex of apartments fronting the river. The Great Court was bounded on the north by a range of kitchens and offices, backing on to Scotland Yard. The Pebble Court was bounded on the south by the range of the Privy Gallery.

(2) The Privy Garden, to the south of the nucleus (1), bounded on the west by The Street between the Holbein Gate and the King Street Gate and on the east by superimposed galleries and further riverside apartments. The orchard south of the Privy Garden was made into a bowling green and separated from it by a terrace walk and a row of trees; in 1673 these were removed and the green, which was bordered by several houses connected with the palace, was added to the Privy Garden.[3]

(3) West of the Privy Garden and The Street between the two gates, and extending into St. James's Park, were the Tennis Courts and the Cockpit, both of which gradually became converted to lodgings and offices.

North of the nucleus (1) lay Scotland Yard, an irregular complex of courts and yards. To the west, in what had been the Tilt Yard, Charles II built quarters for Horse and Foot Guards.[4]

After Cromwell's death at Whitehall on 3 September 1658 an abortive attempt was made to put the palace up for sale.[5] It then stood empty until the Restoration, when John Webb, while holding no confirmed office, made the most immediate preparations for the reception of the monarch.[6] To judge from the number of items accounted for during the rest of 1660, the old door furniture of Whitehall must either have been past use or have been stripped in the period before the Restoration.[7]

---

[1] Works 5/15 (*London Survey*, xiii, p. 43). Greatorex was a mathematical instrument maker known to Wren's circle. In December 1660 Richard Daynes received £5 12s. 6d. for drawing fair three drafts and scales of the ground plot of Whitehall (Works 5/1). A plan of Whitehall was made 'as ordered by the King' in 1668 or early 1669 by Daniel Fabureau de la Fabvolière, chief engineer to the Ordnance. It is mentioned in his letter of 5 March 1669, written from prison where he seems to have been placed for debt, but is not otherwise recorded (*Cal. S.P. Dom. 1668–9*, pp. 128, 224, 460, 463, 567). In March 1671/2 the Gentlemen Ushers were ordered by the Lord Chamberlain 'to take an exact survey of all the lodgings within the palace of Whitehall and the names of the occupants entered in a book' (LC 5/140, p. 67).

[2] The account in *London Survey* is arranged topographically and not chronologically.

[3] *London Survey*, xiii, p. 230.

[4] For Scotland Yard and the Horse Guards, see below, pp. 433–40, 443–51.

[5] *London Survey*, xiii, p. 34.

[6] Webb's petition for the Surveyorship (*Cal. S.P. Dom. 1660–1*, p. 76); *Commons' Journals*, viii, p. 27 (Estimate of 15 May 1660 'for Repair of the King's Majesty's Houses' not to exceed £30,000) and p. 29.

[7] Works 5/1.

HKW—T

The sum of £1251 17s. 2d. spent in June 1660[1] was not to be exceptional: the Works books give the impression of ceaseless work all over the palace. Most of the first month's work comprised general repairs, including cleaning and repairing the Chapel, making a wooden screen for the king's closet there and providing a wooden pulpit 7 ft. by 2 ft. 7 in. The Cabinet rooms were also attended to, and Emanuel de Critz's bill included mending letters and making new badges in gold picked in with 'fair bice'. Repairs were also begun on the sun dial in the Privy Garden, a practical object which was also one of its principal ornaments.[2] In October the carver Henry Phillips made three gnomons for the great dial, so that they could be cast in brass, for 28s. In October and November joiners were at work on another useful ornament in the Privy Garden, 'the King's Tube' or astronomical telescope. It was 36 ft. by 10 in., had two wainscot boxes 'to put the glasses in' and was supported by two trestles and an easel to raise or lower it. The interior, which was blackened, had 24 baffles with round holes.

Decorating work had also started in the king's private apartments in the eastern half of the Privy Gallery range. This work included in November a marble chimney-piece and wood-carving in the king's bathing room; the carving, by Phillips, included an elaborate architrave and cornice and the decoration of the alcove with a 'frutidge' hanging across and down the sides, a large drapery and eagle and two whole pilasters and capitals and four corner capitals. There was also 86 ft. of lace moulding carved in the fret ceiling, which may have been a wooden roof to the alcove. The bathing room was painted and gilt in June 1662, paved in black and white marble in April 1663, given a waste pipe and curtains in June and July and further embellished with carving in September.[3]

Similar refitting was given early in 1661 to the king's bedchamber, with a black and white marble chimneypiece made by Thomas Burman, 'sculptor'.[4] This designation and the price of £21 10s. suggest a certain amount of figurative work. William Dekeser (de Keyser)[5] was paid £40 in the same month (February 1661) for carving two great 'Draperyes' with two flying boys in them holding the curtains before the bedchamber alcove, and for two great eagles and a shield with a head on it. In May several bills, including that of the joiners for a floor 26 ft. by 15 ft. in the bedchamber, mentioned night work, an indication of work under pressure of time often found at Whitehall. In 1661 the ceiling was provided with an oval allegorical canvas of the Restoration, painted by John Michael Wright. This was saved from the 1698 fire and now belongs to the Nottingham Castle Museum.[6]

[1] Works 5/1. The Extraordinary accounts in this volume include one titled 'Lord General Monke and his Officers and Souldiers Jan 1659 March and April 1660' comprising work at Whitehall in January 1660 and St. James's in March–April, with 678 man-days for carpentry, 295 for bricklayers, 56 for plasterers, 93 for masons, 325 for plumbers, 34 paviours, 35 sawyers, 610 labourers.

[2] *London Survey*, xiii, pp. 91–4. In July 1660 Emanuel de Critz was paid for whitening in oil the dial. See also below p. 271.

[3] Works 5/3, 5/4.

[4] Thomas Burman (1618–74), pupil of Edward Marshall. His epitaph in St Paul's Covent Garden bore the title of 'sculptor' (R. Gunnis, *Dictionary of British Sculptors*, 1953).

[5] William de Keyser, b. 1603, brother-in-law of Nicholas Stone the sculptor; in England c. 1621–40 and 1658–74; Amsterdam City stonemason 1647–53 (M. Whinney, *Sculpture in Britain 1530–1830*, 1964, p. 240 n. 30; E. Neurdenberg, *De Zeventiende Eeuwsche Beeldhouwkunst in de Noordelijke Nederlanden*, 1948, pp. 143–5).

[6] It measures 90 × 56 in. E. Croft-Murray, *Decorative Painting in England 1537–1837*, i (1962), p. 229. Evelyn mentions Wright's work at Whitehall on 3 Oct. 1662, and it is reasonable to suppose that the bed-

The bedchamber was probably not the old one in the Privy Gallery facing the garden, but a room referred to in January 1664 as 'the king's new bedchamber in the turk's gallery'.[1] The exact position of the Turk's Gallery is uncertain but as references place it at the east end of the Privy Gallery and next to the Countess of Suffolk's rooms it must have approximated to an eastward extension of the Privy Gallery range. It included among other rooms a small bedchamber for the queen. Most of the Turk's Gallery was demolished in 1667 and the rest, including the king's bedroom, in 1682 to make way for new buildings (p. 276).[2] None of it appears in the 1670 plan because it was above stairs, presumably over the queen's wardrobe.

In April 1662, in anticipation of the arrival of Catherine of Braganza, work was extended to the queen's side, the series of upper rooms between the Privy Gallery range and the river and south-east of the Great Hall and Presence Chamber and the king's other state rooms. The accounts for that month mention carpenters framing a roof for the queen's new Privy Chamber, 36 ft. by 25 ft.[3] In the following months Phillips and the joiner Thomas Kinward completed the woodwork of her bedchamber, including festoons of tulips and other flowers, 'a rich laurell in the middle of the Acove' and two oval frames containing pedestals for heads to stand on. The queen's sleeping arrangements are not clear from the accounts. In September 1664, while mats were taken up in the queen's alcove and new ones laid in 'her bedchamber in the Turks Gallery', the chimneypiece in the queen's chamber was taken down; in October John Grove made a new fret ceiling in the bedchamber and alcove, and Phillips was altering the carving of flowers, laurels and festoons in the alcove and work continued in the bedchamber and alcove until December.[4] It seems therefore that she occupied the little room in the Turk's Gallery during alterations to the proper room with its alcove in the queen's side further north.

In July 1662 Thomas Rotherham the Clerk of Works earned an 'extraordinary pains' payment for extra attendance on the workmen who 'wrought over hours in making ready the Queen's privy lodgings'. Charles's match with a Catholic princess necessitated the provision of a separate chapel, which was probably a room on the queen's side.[5] A wooden altar was provided in August 1662, and from the fact that existing silvered rails were altered in October[6] it may be that the same room was used as had served Charles I's Catholic queen. In November the king's new closet was painted red, white, blue and yellow and his supping room white marble veined.

December 1662 also saw carcase work in progress in the Countess of Castlemaine's lodgings.[7] Work was to continue there until 1667; in an account for painting and gilding in April and May 1663 the rooms are named as closet, bedchamber

---

chamber ceiling was part of the account of Sir Robert Howard, the Sergeant Painter, for £500 imprest for 'severall paynting workes' in the bedchamber and bathing room, May–June 1661 (AO 1/2492/394).

[1] Works 5/4.

[2] See *London Survey*, xiii, pp. 75, 78, 97, and references there, differently interpreted.

[3] Works 5/3.    [4] Works 5/5.

[5] This is more likely than the 'intended chapel in the cockpit' mentioned in Aug. 1661 which was connected with Albemarle's lodgings (below, p. 273 and n. 2).

[6] A silvered rail 2 ft. 7 in. high by 30 ft. round the Duchess of York's bed is mentioned in July 1662 (Works 5/3). On 22 March 1668 Pepys went to the queen's chapel and 'did hear the Italians sing'.

[7] Barbara Palmer, née Villiers, became the king's mistress soon after the Restoration. In 1661 her husband was unwillingly created Earl of Castlemaine on his wife's account; in 1670 she became Duchess of Cleveland *suo jure*.

and ante-chamber, dining room, passage and nursery. Although the king's involvement with Lady Castlemaine was well known at court the affair was at first observed with enough reticence to leave some uncertainty as to the location of her lodgings. Her grandmother lived in a house known as Hance's House on the east side of King Street, backing on to the Bowling Green, and Pepys's entries of 1 January and 1 February 1663 imply that the king's visits to his mistress were outside the palace.[1] However, on 25 April Pepys noted from hearsay that her bed had been moved 'to a chamber in White Hall, next to the King's own' and on 11 May a Mr. Pierce told him that her lodgings were now 'near the king's chamber at court'. It has been suggested, largely on the common mention of a dining room balcony, that the rooms painted in April–May 1663 were in the King Street house, and that the move mentioned by Pepys was to a temporary lodging in Whitehall.[2] But from accounts for repairs to the countess's rooms after a fire on 25 January 1664, in which the same rooms are enumerated but with variations of detail, there can be no doubt of the identity of the 1662–3 rooms with those repaired in 1664, which were over the west end of the Privy Gallery and the Holbein Gate and extended to the upper floor on the park side.[3] It is not however certain when the countess moved into the apartment prepared for her.

In March and May 1666 two new doorcases and three new marble chimney-pieces were provided.[4] Carving is mentioned in subsequent months, extending in November to the countess's oratory (Pepys records in 1663, with scepticism, a conversion to Catholicism). In February 1667 some of this work was painted and gilded by Robert Streater; the account bears a note explaining a price increase by a rise in the cost of materials.[5] In July 1667 joiners worked in the room 'that was the Countess of Castlemaine's bedchamber', which may relate to a gradual decline in favour although she went on living at Whitehall, and the following month there is mention of new stairs to her lodgings and carver's work in her library.[6] However, in April 1668 the king gave her Berkshire House, St. James's, to which she moved.[7] The Whitehall lodgings still bore her name in 1683, though in 1676 they seem to have been occupied by her daughter Anne, Countess of Sussex.[8]

In 1662–3 two new rooms were built for Prince Rupert at the south-east corner of the Privy Garden, backing on to the Stone Gallery.[9] This lodging was enlarged after 1670 (p. 279). During 1664–5 the group between the Stone and Matted Galleries and the Thames, known as the Prince's Lodging, was prepared for the Duke and Duchess of York.[10] These adaptations included 'charges in building part of the Lodgings one story higher'.[11] There is some evidence that the lodgings were more extensive on the upper floor than at the level of the 1670 plan,[12] but the 1664–5 accounts

---

[1] *London Survey*, xiii, pp. 233–4. The Duke of Cleveland was born (June 1662) at the King Street house (*D.N.B.*).  [2] *London Survey*, xiv, p. 16.

[3] Feb.–March 1664, Works 5/4. *London Survey*, xiv, p. 17, quotes an account of April 1683 (Works 5/37) referring to lodgings over the Privy Gallery, *i.e.* on the east side, but the kitchen, on the west side ground floor, is shown on the 1670 plan.

[4] Works 5/8, 5/9.  [5] Works 5/9.  [6] Works 5/10.

[7] The king had bought Berkshire House in 1661–2 (*Cal. S.P. Dom. 1661–2*, p. 606). An account for fitting up the house for the reception of the French Ambassador in March–May 1665 (Works 5/7) includes payment for boring holes through the presence chamber ceiling 'to hang a statue there'.

[8] *London Survey*, xiv, p. 17.  [9] *London Survey*, xiii, p. 87.  [10] Works 5/5.

[11] Duplicate account, B.M. Harl. MS. 1618.  [12] *London Survey*, xiii, p. 81.

also mention work in rooms next to the Tennis Court. In 1665–6 a new three-storey brick building was added for the duke 'in the Privy Garden'.[1] This building, which is not identifiable on the plan, was probably near the south-east corner of the garden but across the Stone Gallery from it, and related to a new staircase from the Matted Gallery down to the Bowling Green mentioned in April–May 1666.[2] Later work in the York apartments included carving in 1668[3] and the relining of the duchess's rooms and the removal of her bedroom alcove (1670). For the latter work the duchess paid £97 10s. out of a total of £186 11s. 5½d.[4]

From 1664 extensions were made to the queen's lodgings in the neighbourhood of the Shield Gallery, which seems to have been a short gallery running east and west over the passage to the Privy Stairs.[5] The new closet built in 1664 was 'over the Sheild Gallery' and there was a small room under it, so it was presumably on the second floor. It had a fret ceiling, a chimneypiece of 'Egiptian marble' and the customary carving.[6] The carver's bill implies a balcony window, probably opening on to the roof of the Shield Gallery, for which a wooden rail was made with pedestals and 23 dozen turned balusters.[7] The 'Queen's room at the end of the Shield Gallery' for which Phillips did carving in 1666–7 was perhaps below this roof.[8] A further extension in 1668 comprised 'severall new Roomes for the Queenes majestie by the Privie Staires', which were certainly on the waterfront between the apartments marked on the 1670 plan as Sir William Killigrew's and Mr. Chiffinch's.[9] The last account mentions two upper rooms, one next the bedchamber and the other the closet next the Thames, and a bathing room; from details in the account of white marble chimneypieces and fret ceilings, and from the extant contracts, these rooms must be entirely additional to those of 1664,[10] and answerable to the Volary building further south (p. 270). In 1666–7 Phillips also executed carving in the queen's older apartments, in the little oratory, bedchamber and alcove, including a large chimneypiece ornamented with festoons, letters (royal cyphers?) and a crown.[11]

The most important new buildings of the 1660s architecturally were the palace gate and gallery and the Volary building. The Volary Garden, in which the king's aviary was kept, was situated between the river and the Stone Gallery, and extended about 140 ft. south of the Privy Stairs.[12] Some new rooms in this area were joisted and boarded in 1663 and 300 ft. of purbeck paving was laid in the garden in front of them.[13] In 1667 an altogether larger scheme was undertaken.[14] The aviary was moved to St. James's Park and part of the Turk's Gallery was demolished, and new lodgings for the king were built across the garden, leaving a small garden on the

---

[1] Works 5/9 (Extraord.).     [2] *Ibid.* (Ord.).
[3] Works 5/11, Sept.–Oct. Carpenter's work in Mr. Wren's office in Nov. 1668 and July 1669 (Works 5/11, 5/13) was for the duke's secretary, Matthew Wren.
[4] Works 5/15, July–Sept. (Extraord.).     [5] *London Survey*, xiii, p. 73.
[6] *Ibid.*, p. 70; Works 5/5 (Extraord.).
[7] Works 5/7 (May–Nov. 1665), 5/9 (May 1666), Ord.
[8] Works 5/9 (Dec. 1666), 5/10 (Oct. 1667), Ord.
[9] References to these apartments as adjacent: Works 5/11 (Extraord.), Sept. 1668–Jan. 1669.
[10] Works 5/13 (Extraord.), March–Aug. 1669. Contracts for bricklayer, mason and joiner, Works 5/145, pp. 6–8, 14, 21.
[11] July 1666, March–April 1667, Works 5/9, 5/10 (Ord.).
[12] *London Survey*, xiii, p. 74.
[13] Works 5/4, Sept.–Oct. 1663 (Ord.).
[14] Works 5/9, 5/10, 5/11, March 1667–March 1668 (Extraord.).

south and making the new Volary Court or Square Court on the north between the new range and the queen's buildings of 1668–9. An engraving of Whitehall from the river in 1682 by Ogilby and Morgan (Pl. 34B) shows both these ranges to be similar, of two main storeys with a dormered attic,[1] and uniform with the third range on the west of the Volary Court which was not built until 1682 (p. 276). Nevertheless the extent, rather than the exact site, of the new buildings is 'difficult to define';[2] the rooms known as the Volary Lodgings seem to have ranged further west. They included a bedchamber by the waterside, a withdrawing room nearer the Privy Gallery, a library, the king's new laboratory and a new great staircase.[3] The accounts for September 1667 mention lodgings for the Maids of Honour, which may be part of their main lodging shown on the 1670 plan on the south and west sides of the Volary Garden. The north range was built over the ground floor passage to the Privy Stairs to the river.

The accounts of the main contractors for the Volary building comprise Maurice Emmett, bricklayer; John Angier, carpenter; Thomas Joyner and Thomas Turner, joiners; Henry Phillips, carver; Robert Streater, painter; Joshua Marshall, chimney-pieces and paving; Edward Martin and John Grove, plasterers, and Thomas Heath, brick paving.[4] In the accounts of joiners, carver and painter the rooms are numbered first to ninth, with the addition of an upper and lower stool room each with an adjacent room and approach passage, a 'closet below' and the staircase. The interiors were lined with wainscot, painted either white or 'timber colour' and finished with leaf or modillion cornices and other mouldings and vegetable panels. Some of the ceilings were fretted.[5] The joiners also altered the wainscot of the seventh room for the setting of a statue; there are several other references to sculptures in the Volary area. In October 1670 carpenters made ten panels of chequer work $4\frac{1}{2}$ ft. square at the king's 'stattue room by the vollery new lodgings'.[6] In 1668 five statues had been set on Portland bases near the corners and in the middle of the court, which is subsequently referred to as the Statue Court.[7] The bases are shown on the 1670 plan.

A larger, though no more identifiable, collection of sculpture stood in the Privy Garden. The 1670 plan shows the garden divided into sixteen plots each with a pedestal and all but one supporting a statue. Twelve figures of bronze or marble were brought from St. James's Palace in 1651, and in 1659, when they were in the Privy Garden, were seriously damaged by a fanatic with a hammer.[8] It seems likely that most of them were replicas of antique figures, and that some were bronze

[1] There is a reference to the *middle* storey in Works 5/11, April 1668.

[2] *London Survey*, xiii, pp. 75–6, where the new buildings are assumed to include 'those on the north and south sides of the Square Court'. But the May 1667 book (Works 5/10) includes, as if extraneous, alterations to the queen's little bedchamber and rooms adjacent 'lately made in the Turk's Gallery'. The present identification is based on a comparison of the accounts with the 1670 plan and Ogilby and Morgan's view (B.M. Crace ii, 58) (Pl. 34B).

[3] *London Survey*, xiii, pp. 76, 100. Another new laboratory was set up in the Cockpit (below, p. 273). A laboratory under the Privy Gallery was built or rebuilt in 1672–3 (p. 275). For the king's scientific interests see above, p. 266, *London Survey*, xiii, p. 101, and T. Sprat, *History of the Royal Society* (1667).

[4] Works 5/12 (Extraord.): a single account for each completed contract. Their work came to £4697. The total cost of the new buildings was £6034 (E 351/3438). Emmett was allowed £12 for 'extraordinary price of lime by reason of the dearness of Coles in the time of the dutch warrs'.

[5] Pepys admired the ceilings and houses of office (*Diary*, 29 June 1668).

[6] Works 5/15 (Ord.).

[7] Works 5/11 (Extraord.), June, Aug. 1668) 5/13 (Ord.), March 1669; *London Survey*, xiii, p. 75.

[8] *London Survey*, xiii, p. 90; *The Diurnal of Thomas Rugg* (Camden Society, ser. 3, xci, 1961), pp. 10–11.

casts made for Charles I by Hubert Le Sueur including those now in the East Garden at Windsor.[1] It is assumed that the damaged figures were mended or replaced soon after the Restoration, for statues were being carried into the Privy Garden in August 1660.[2] In April 1662 masons made a new pedestal, and in March 1668 four figures were set up on new bases then made for them; if eleven of the original twelve were reinstated in 1660 this would make up the number shown on the 1670 plan.[3] However, further work probably of a conservative nature was undertaken in November 1672 (two stone pedestals and a plinth for a third) and June–July 1673 (pedestal and three brick foundations, and removal of two statues and pedestals).[4]

In 1661–2 the fountain which previously stood in the Privy Garden was dismantled.[5] In 1663 repairs were made by masons to the great sundial, which is presumably the one shown on the 1670 plan. Three gnomons had been cast in 1660.[6] In 1664 a new dial was designed, drawn and made for the apparatus by William Marre.[7] In 1669 an additional dial (not shown on the plan) was installed, to the design of the Jesuit Dr. Hall; this elaborate object was largely made of glass, and was damaged by frost and in 1675 irreparably by 'My Lord Rochester in a frolick'. The pedestal of Caen stone in the 1669 accounts must be for this short-lived contrivance.[8]

In 1662 a new double organ costing £900 was ordered from John Hingston for the chapel; the following year the erection of a large organ loft was ordered, and this entailed the demolition of a stone window in 1664. In March 1665 Phillips carved 22 ft. of 'arcutts' under the organ.[9]

The hall, which had been used for entertainments on occasion before the Civil War, was again in use by August 1660, when the king watched 'dancing on the ropes'.[10] In 1665 major steps were taken at a cost of £737 6s. 2¼d. to make the hall more suitable for a permanent theatre 'for Masking Playes and Dancing'.[11] Four 'tiring rooms' were made at the north end, and several rooms under the stage. Degrees and boxes were built, with a gallery at the south end. The windows were boarded up. There was 'provision to draw the Ovall shutters before the musicke and to tacke up and let

[1] Whinney, *Sculpture in Britain*, p. 28; M. Whinney and O. Millar, *English Art 1625–1714* (1957), p. 120 n. 4. For the statues in the Privy and Volary Gardens among others, see A. H. Scott-Elliot, 'The Statues from Mantua in the Collection of King Charles I', *Burlington Magazine*, ci (1959), pp. 218–27.

[2] *London Survey*, xiii, p. 90. The 'Dutch Gift' to Charles II included 'a greate number of statuers of white marble of excellent sculpters' (*Diurnal*, p. 126, Nov. 1660).

[3] Works 5/3, 5/11. Other references are to carpenters shoring up figures in the garden (Oct. 1665, Works 5/7) and the removal of figures from the Matted Gallery in Feb. 1665 and Aug. 1668 (Works 5/5, 5/11). The Matted Gallery may have been used for temporary storage, for in March 1667 a brass figure was taken there on the demolition of the Volary (Works 5/9, Volary Building account).

[4] Works 5/19, 5/22 (Ord.). Pedestals were still being re-set in March 1687 (Works 5/54). See also below, p. 297.

[5] *London Survey*, xiii, p. 90; masons taking down the fountain and carrying out the 'great bason', Dec. 1661 and March 1662 (Works 5/2).

[6] Works 5/4, April 1663, and above, p. 266. The dial had been constructed in 1622–3.

[7] *Cal. S.P. Dom. 1663–4*, pp. 537, 580; *Cal. S.P. Dom. 1665–6*, p. 156; *Cal. Treas. Books 1660–7*, p. 721. Marre was 'new delineating' it again in 1688 (below, p. 294).

[8] *London Survey*, xiii, p. 94; Works 5/13, July 1669.

[9] References in *London Survey*, xiii, p. 56, where the Surveyor is prematurely identified as Wren and where the new organ is presumed to have been given 'a different position' from the old; also Works 5/5 and 5/6, June 1664 and March 1665.

[10] *London Survey*, xiii, p. 51.

[11] Works 5/7 (Extraord.). The antern was repaired in March (Works 5/6, Ord.) and again in Dec. 1670 (Works 5/15).

down the curtain'. The carpenters also built 'a Stage for the Screens' 39 ft. long, 33 ft. wide and 5 ft. high, a 'frontispiece' and 'several frames, shutting upon the said stage'. This was in essence the deep Baroque stage with a proscenium arch, wings and borders and sliding shutters. The work was completed in February–April, and the foreman carpenter received a gratuity of £5 for his pains 'early and late in hastening the carpenters work'. Temporary additions were later made, such as a stage for a 'Drollery' (the clerk first wrote 'puppet play') in October 1666[1] and a dance floor of five squares in February 1667.[2] In November 1668 and on later occasions the carpenters were paid for attendance for several nights 'when the Players were there'.[3]

On 30 July 1668 Pepys 'met with Mr. May, who was giving directions about making a close way for people to go dry from the gate up into the House, to prevent their going through the galleries'.[4] This new brick gallery ran from the junction of the Great Gate and the Banqueting House to the complex containing the Great Hall and the entrance to the state rooms, following the line of the old terrace that marked the drop in level from the Great Court to the Pebble Court.[5] Halfway along it were doors into the courts on either side. The accounts show that the work was finished in July 1669 and included the provision of staircases at each end, to the Banqueting House and the King's Guard Chamber, and the recasing of the lower part of the Great Gatehouse.[6] The gallery appears, from the bird's-eye view of the 1690s (Pl. 37), to have been a plain one-storey building, but the additions to the gatehouse were, although restrained, something of a showpiece. A shed was built in the Pebble Court for the working of the cut, rubbed and gauged brick.[7] The central carriage gateway was fronted and backed by triangular pediments resting on piers; the street side was flanked by quadrant pedestrian passages 15 ft. high projecting into Whitehall and surmounted by smaller pediments. The mouldings were 'hewn' in brick, and the concave faces of each quadrant had two 'circular' (round-headed) and two square niches. Phillips was paid 12s. for carving four 'cartookes' for the frontispiece.[8] The upper part of the gate was rebuilt in 1676 (p. 273).

Pepys's remark raises the question of the authorship of these works, and it is perhaps worth noting May's fondness for simple relief devices such as niches and blind panels, and the combination of restraint and a strong sense of plasticity in the projecting quadrants which would accord with his certain works and in particular with the quadrant colonnades he introduced at Berkeley House, Piccadilly (1663–5).[9]

The area on the west side between The Street and St. James's Park is loosely referred to by its two chief features, the Cockpit and the Tennis Court. The old Cockpit Theatre was refurbished in November 1660 with a new stage floor and pavilions in the gallery for musicians and players; night work was necessary to finish the theatre for the first performance on 19 November.[10] After the conversion of the Great Hall to a permanent theatre in 1665 the Cockpit was abandoned, and

[1] Works 5/9.                                    [2] *Ibid.*
[3] Works 5/11.                                   [4] *The Diary of Samuel Pepys, sub die.*
[5] *London Survey*, xiii, pp. 62–3.              [6] Works 5/11, 5/13 (Extraord.).
[7] Carpenter's account, Works 5/11.             [8] No views show this detail.
[9] Niches and blind panels appear in the garden front of Eltham Lodge (1662–4), at Cornbury (1663–8) and Cassiobury (c. 1677–80, destroyed).
[10] *London Survey*, xiv, pp. 26–7.

was demolished probably in 1675.[1] The building seems to have been under the jurisdiction of the Duke of Albemarle who, as General Monck, had moved at the Restoration into the Cockpit lodgings south and east of the theatre. Accounts during 1660–1 mention a 'new hall' and 'intended chapel' among these lodgings but it is clear that the work done was conversion and not new building.[2] An Extraordinary account (December 1662–January 1664) covers the building of several animal houses in the park (of which Albemarle was the keeper) and stork-nests on Adrian May's house, as well as general repairs.[3] The extent of Albemarle's lodgings is shown on the 1670 plan. He died there on 3 January 1670, and in October the lodgings were cleaned, painted and fitted for the reception of the Prince of Orange (afterwards William III) on his first visit to England.[4]

Of the various tennis courts at Whitehall two are of importance in the 1660s. A new covered court was built in 1662 near The Street and south of the passage to the Cockpit Theatre. This appears to have been modelled on the one at Hampton Court; it is shown on the 1670 plan and survived until 1809. Thomas Cooke, Master of the Tennis Courts, was allowed £1500 in advance for its construction, for which the Works were not responsible.[5] On the other (north) side of the Cockpit passage, adjoining The Street, was a building which then became known as the Old Tennis Court, and which in 1663 was altered to provide lodgings for the Duke of Monmouth. It appears to have been partly used already for lodgings,[6] but the work undertaken between October 1663 and July 1664 included an additional floor, two pair of stairs, chimneys, new lanterns, and the replacement of the old stone windows by rectangular wooden ones; Portland chimneypieces were provided for the dining and withdrawing rooms.[7] In or before about 1670 Monmouth's lodgings were extended as other tenancies were vacated. By 1670 there was also a laboratory in the Cockpit.[8]

By 1670 the state of the palace was certainly much improved, although there was constant need for maintenance of many old buildings, some of them timbered and plastered. There were also constant alterations for convenience or for changes in the palace population. But whereas the Ordinary expenditure for June 1660 alone had been over twelve hundred pounds, the total for the year March 1675–February 1676 was £3782 1s. 7½d.

The new gate to Whitehall is shown still incomplete in the view drawn in connection with Cosimo de Medici's visit to England in 1669.[9] The upper part probably formed a recasing of existing masonry, but the only extant accounts are some among the Ordinary. In July 1672 four Portland cills were provided for the 'neices' (niches) at the gate.[10] The upper part appears to have been 'taken in hand' in 1676; the accounts from July onward record only the finishing stages.[11] In July Streater painted

[1] *Ibid.*, p. 29; Works 5/1 (Ord.). The same month's accounts mention posts and stands in the tilt yard for bear and bull baiting.

[2] *London Survey*, xiv, p. 50; Works 5/1, 5/2 (Ord.).

[3] Works 5/4 (Extraord.). Storks are naturally restricted to the Continental land-mass and the birds in question belonged to the colony of 'outlandish fowl' in St James's Park. For Adrian May, see p. 457 below.

[4] *London Survey*, xiv, pp. 50–1. Works 5/15 and 16 contain an account for Albemarle's funeral.

[5] *London Survey*, xiv, p. 42. Warrant for payment, March 1663 (*Cal. S.P. Dom. 1663–4*, p. 95).

[6] *London Survey*, xiv, p. 68 n.

[7] Works 5/4, 5/5 (Extraord.); *London Survey*, xiv, pp. 68–9.

[8] Works 5/15, Dec. 1670; *London Survey*, xiv, pp. 69–70.

[9] *London Survey*, xiii, Pl. 4 (b).

[10] Works 5/19.

[11] *London Survey*, xiii, p. 14; Works 5/27.

a device of four crossed C's and a crown, gilded them and painted blue the figures of '2' which accompanied them; he also painted the carved stone pedestal of leaves and the lead around it. They were set up on the pyramidal roof in August, and something like them appears in Terasson's print of 1713 (Pl. 38). In September the lodgings over the gatehouse were painted, and the bills included carpenter's work there; works in October included the hipped roof over the 'portugue'.

The accounts of the 1670s imply continued activity in the area between the Volary Court and the Stone and Matted Galleries, generically known as Volary and extending as far as the king's backstairs, which were near the junction of those galleries with the Privy Gallery at the north-east corner of the Privy Garden. A door was made in July 1672 from the backstairs into the Vane Room, which was upstairs at the intersection of the lines of the two galleries; the following month saw carpentry and brickwork in a new room at the back-stairs with eighteen window lights.[1] In 1671 new rooms were built adjacent to the Volary on the south-west (94 and 97 on the 1670 plan) for the Countess of Suffolk and Lord Gerard, Gentleman of the Bedchamber.[2] Some of Lady Suffolk's rooms were in use by the queen by 1681[3] and the accounts probably give an incomplete picture.

In October 1671 Diocinto Cowey (the clerk made two attempts at this presumably Italian name) produced two chimneypieces with 'counterfitt marble' in the king's little bedchamber and the withdrawing room in the new Volary building.[4] The 1672 accounts contain several references to the king's new great bedchamber in the Volary, including a framed panel with an oval glass (July), carpentry, joinery and carving in a partition 14 ft. by 22 ft. long (November–December); it is difficult to tell whether this is the same room as that described in January 1664 as in the Turk's Gallery.[5] During the construction in 1682 of the west range of the Volary building, including a new bedroom, the king slept in the Duke of York's; his previous bedroom was, if not demolished, at least incommoded by the work.[6]

The 1670s saw considerable enrichment of the Tudor chapel. It was painted in July–September 1674; in August Thomas Kinward the joiner and Henry Phillips provided an altar rail with carved balusters and foliage panels.[7] In December 1675 Streater decorated the king's canopy with a gilt crown, and with 32 yards in fine lake representing crimson velvet with gilding 'flickered' to represent embroidery and the pile of the material.[8] The canopy was altered or replaced in March 1678 when Kinward, Phillips and Streater were paid for work on a canopy and throne. The throne incorporated a circular pedestal with three gilt boys three feet high on a round carved base. The canopy had a cupola, with gilded brackets at cornice level and a shield with festoons below it. There were panels and pilasters with gilding on either side, and Streater was also paid for 'Shadoeing the Crotesco in the Cupelo' and 'paynting the Tortoyce shell'. It is as difficult to visualise this object as it is the grander throne finished later the same year for St. George's Hall at Windsor.[9] The ostentation of the latter may be the key to the provision of that at Whitehall.

[1] Works 5/19 (Ord.).                    [2] Works 5/18 (Extraord.); E 351/3285.
[3] *London Survey*, xiii, p. 77 n.        [4] Works 5/18 (Ord.).        [5] Works 5/19 (Ord.); above, p. 267.
[6] *London Survey*, xiii, pp. 75, 78, 80; N. Luttrell, *Brief Historical Relation*, i, p. 177.
[7] Works 5/23 (Ord.). Contract 25 June, Works 5/145, p. 90.
[8] Works 5/25 (Ord.).                    [9] Below, p. 327.

The same three craftsmen were responsible for the new altar-piece, for which a preliminary drawing exists in the Wren Collection at All Souls (Pl. 39A).[1] Their account for this work, dated December 1676, is bound into the Ordinary accounts for Hampton Court.[2] Kinward's contract of 28 July 1676 includes wainscot on the east wall the same as work already done, four pilasters with pedestals, the cornice and mouldings and carving above the oval.[3] The altar-work was similar to that now at Hampton Court but it can be shown that drawing and accounts agree in major dimensions and that neither agrees with the chapel at Hampton Court. The drawing can be placed in Charles II's reign as the books on the altar display crossed C's. The scale on the drawing gives a width of slightly over 28 ft. which accords with the width in the 1670 plan and in Stukeley's 1718 survey of the hall and chapel;[4] the Hampton Court chapel is about 4 ft. wider. The drawing also shows a considerably taller building in proportion than Hampton Court, and the 1676 account describes a wall considerably more elaborate. The drawing does not agree in all details with the account, but this is not unusual. However, there is agreement on the dimensions of the oval, the 'compass cornice' and other parts of the segmental pediment, the provision among 'Imbostments' of 'a cherubims head', two palms, 26 ft. of 'Frutidg' and the oval and four festoons in the spandrels around it. Streater finished the wainscot in cedar colour, with gilding and shading or colouring in the relief work, and the columns and friezes were painted tortoiseshell. The drawing is of further interest as the nearest we have to a visual record of any of Phillips's work; the upper festoons around the oval show that he was considered capable of considerable skill in under-cutting.

Some confusion surrounds the king's bathroom and laboratory on the ground floor on the north side of the Privy Garden, under the Privy Gallery. 'The King's Laboratory & Bath' are marked on this site on the 1670 plan. At that date there were two other laboratories at Whitehall and it has been inferred that the Privy Garden one was vacant.[5] The king subsequently installed Dr. Edmund Dickinson, alchemist and his own physician, in the Privy Garden premises.[6] The wall between Lord Arlington's office and 'the new Elabouratory' is mentioned in October 1672, and in 1678 there are references to the 'Kings old Bathing Roome where the New Elaboratory is Made for Doctor Dickinsons use' with various alterations for its new occupant.[7] These included work on furnaces and the taking down of ceiling boards and provision of a new cupboard.[8] In August–September 1683 a chimney was reduced and a screen, shelves and pigeon-holes for papers were provided in the 'old bathing room by the Treasury' for the use of Treasury clerks.[9] On the 1670 plan the bath-laboratory complex was bounded on the east by Arlington's office and on the west by Treasury chambers but it is not clear whether references to these rooms in accounts indicate the whole or individual parts of the complex, which evidently

[1] All Souls ii. 66; *Wren Soc.*, v, Pl. xliv, as 'Hampton Court'.
[2] Works 5/27, between Jan. and Feb.
[3] Works 5/145, p. 104. *East* must be interpreted ritually as the chapel ran north-south.
[4] *London Survey*, xiii, repr. p. 48.
[5] *Ibid.*, p. 100; there were laboratories in the Volary and the Cockpit (above, pp. 270, 273).
[6] *London Survey*, xiii, p. 101.                [7] Works 5/19, Oct. 1692; 5/31, April 1678.
[8] Works 5/29, Feb.–March 1678; 5/32, April 1679.
[9] Works 5/37; *Cal. Treas. Books 1681–5*, pp. 850, 898.

contained a number of rooms; moreover, as often happens in the Works books, the currency of the terms *old* and *new* is hard to determine. The fullest, if incomplete, evidence is to be drawn from an Extraordinary account of May 1673 for several months' work 'in altering the Kings bathing roome & fitting the walls & Ceiling to be sett with looking Glasses & altering the rooms within it according to Sir Samuell Morelands directions'.[1] In 1679 Morland and others petitioned for payment which for undisclosed reasons had been delayed; a note on the duplicate account shows that the work was not allowed for payment until 1682.[2] From Matthew Banks's contract for carpentry in February 1672 it is evident that the 'Elaboratory by the Privy Garden' consisted of at least three rooms as well as what are described as 'pavilions'.[3]

On 26 June 1671 Evelyn records a proposal by the king for a council room to be built in the Privy Garden for the Council for Foreign Plantations; the building was ingeniously to be financed by a loan from the members. On 24 July Wren showed a plan for the room to the Council but no more was heard of the scheme.[4]

Charles II's last campaign of work at Whitehall was the king's new building of 1682; it was contemporary with the beginning of Winchester Palace and included an attempt to modernise some existing apartments. The Extraordinary accounts show considerable alterations to joinery and doors in the Presence Chamber, closet chapel or private oratory, Privy Chamber and the east end of the Privy Gallery next to the Vane Room, thus bringing the area between the king's and queen's apartments and the hall and chapel into a semblance of conformity with the newer buildings.[5] The accounts are in fact more precise about the additional works than about the new building itself, which formed (a) the west range of the Volary, joining and conforming with the north and south sides of 1667–9,[6] and (b) a building at the king's backstairs which must have been behind (a) to the west and adjacent to the end of the Privy Gallery. Parts of the buildings were on new foundations, but contracts with John Gibson, joiner and Maurice Emmett, bricklayer, on 10 March 1682 include the dismantling of parts of the Volary lodgings, rooms formerly belonging to the Countess of Suffolk and then to Lady Sayers, and the king's backstairs and 'low rooms' adjoining them.[7] The bricklayer's contract specifies new work with a ground storey and 17 ft. storey according to a design and draught drawn, agreed and signed by Wren.

In March 1682 the five figures set up in Volary Court in 1668 were moved to a safe corner of the court.[8] In April masons were sorting out good stone from the demolitions.[9] Gibson's contract engaged him to re-use old joinery where possible. Those contracts which survive include three others for joinery on the principal floor of the new Volary building, with Roger Davis, Alexander Fort and John Turner; division of labour to this extent implies that speed was important.[10] Fort's contract specified sash frames 11 ft. by 5 ft. 11 in. for the new bedchamber. On

---

[1] Works 5/22.                                                     [2] Works 5/21; petition at end of Works 5/22.
[3] Works 5/145, p. 80; bricklayer's contract of same date, p. 82.
[4] *Diary of John Evelyn*, iii, pp. 582–4.                         [5] Works 5/36, especially May, June, Aug.
[6] See above, p. 270. The account runs from May 1682 to Jan. 1683.
[7] Works 5/145, pp. 126, 127. Rooms had been built for Lady Suffolk in 1671 (above, p. 274).
[8] Works 5/33 (Extraord.).
[9] Works 5/35 (Ord.).                                              [10] Works 5/145, pp. 134–9.

25 July William Emmett contracted for carving, according to patterns to be approved, in the four principal rooms: the September account specified these as the great and little ante-rooms, king's bedchamber and king's eating room.[1]

The main construction was the taskwork of Matthew Banks and Maurice Emmett.[2] The bricklayer's account included the foundation of the backstairs building; the carpenter's refers to the king's new high building (the 17 ft. first floor was surmounted by the usual dormered roof but the straight lines and regular bays of the Volary elevations still contrasted with surrounding Tudor work) and includes 64 window lights, 63 lintels over doors and windows, and the rough boarding of a pediment roof. Both versions of the 1695–7 bird's-eye view (Pl. 37) show a small pediment on the west Volary range and this is compatible with the supposition that Ogilby and Morgan's view of 1682 (Pl. 34B) shows an approximation of what was about to be built during that year. The uniformity of the west range with the north and south ones, which had been built not only earlier but separately, was to the credit of Denham or May. Excavation has revealed some of the foundations of the three ranges, showing that the south side of the court was about 5 ft. deeper than the north, and while those two ranges were parallel, the west building thus ran at an angle of about seven degrees to the river side (Fig. 25).

Some significant work was carried out in the 1670s for members of the royal circle. The Duke of York's lodgings suffered a small fire in November 1673, but this seems to have had no connection with the building of a new riverside room and approach passage in January–April 1674.[3] The accounts mention brick walls, 40 ft. of outside cornice, and a floor 22 ft. by 18 ft. In March Streater painted the windows stone colour inside and out. In September 1676 the duchess's dressing room was embellished with the usual carving by Phillips and a plaster ceiling including two spandrels of foliage.[4] In June 1677 Streater charged £20 for 'paynting the Ceiling in the Duchess of Yorks dressing roome being in an 8 square frame 12 ft long by 9 ft wide by agreement'.

Henry Fitzroy, Duke of Grafton, came of age in 1684 and in December the Lord Chamberlain's lodgings in the west end of the Privy Gallery range (facing the south end of the Banqueting House) were repaired and fitted for his use.[5] His father-in-law, the Earl of Arlington, had been Lord Chamberlain since 1674; he had other lodgings at Whitehall by the river, which on his death in December 1685 were transferred to Grafton.[6]

There appears to be no official record of the allocation of lodgings to the Duchess of Portsmouth, and little of the subsequent work on them figures in the accounts, presumably because it was not financed and perhaps not carried out through the Works. Louise de Kéroualle (1649–1734), anglicised at Whitehall as Madam Carwell, was at court by November 1670; by the next October she was the king's *maîtresse en titre* and known to be lodged in the palace.[7] Her apartment, which was at the south end of the river front adjoining the Bowling Green, was destroyed on 10

---

[1] *Ibid.*, p. 143; Works 5/36 (Extraord.).
[3] Some of the work is accounted for in Works 5/22 and 23.
[4] Works 5/27.
[6] *London Survey*, xiii, p. 72.
[7] *Ibid.*, p. 85; *Diary of John Evelyn*, iii, pp. 589–90.

[2] Works 5/36, July.

[5] Works 5/38. (Extraord.)

April 1691 in a fire which began in it and spread to adjacent rooms to the north; after the Revolution of 1688 it had been taken over by Princess Anne for her children and at the time of the fire it was in course of preparation for her son the Duke of Gloucester.[1] The Duchess of Portsmouth had effected several enlargements and transformations of her apartments, which were remarkable for the extravagance of their furnishings. At the time of the fire they comprised 24 rooms and 16 garrets.[2] The duchess could certainly afford to employ her own workmen: she had a pension of £12,000 a year from the Secret Services account, amounting by 1681 to over £136,000.[3]

It can be deduced from evidence of the position of the duchess's lodgings that their nucleus was an apartment constructed for Henry Jermyn, Earl of St. Albans.[4] This had been built in October 1670–April 1671, and could have become super-fluous soon after completion since the earl's appointment as Lord Chamberlain on 13 May 1671 afforded him other accommodation. One result of this was a contract with William Cleare for wainscot and chimneypieces in the Lord Chamberlain's lodgings, dated 24 June 1671.[5] The 1670–1 apartment is described by the account as 'at the end of the Matted Gallery'; this identifies the rooms as on the upper floor, and there is reference to the already existing staircase down to the Bowling Green at the south end, part of which was removed and replaced. Carpenter's work included four lucerne (dormer) windows, 50 ft. of outside cornice and 44 ft. of eaves, but five lucernes were also inserted into an existing roof which is twice described as over Prince Rupert's lodgings.[6] The latter are shown on the 1670 plan on the west side of the Stone Gallery (i.e. on the ground floor) next but one to the south end. The joiner's account for St. Albans included work in the great bedchamber, alcove and closet and a dining room next to the Matted (or upstairs) Gallery, and four garrets; the third of these was next to the Bowling Green and the fourth adjoined the house-keeper's lodgings and stairhead. The housekeeper's lodgings must have been identi-cal with, or over, rooms between the gallery, the Bowling Green and the river, marked on the 1670 plan as 'Mrs Kirks'; she was the wife or widow of George Kirke, appointed Housekeeper in 1663 and succeeded in that office in due course by two sons and probably a grandson.[7]

Some alterations were made to 'Mrs Carwell's lodgings at the end of the Matted Gallery' in April–August 1672, and the mention of the alcove and closet is consistent with the composition of the St. Albans apartment.[8] At the same time (April–June) a separate account was made for several new rooms and a cellar 'for Mrs Carwell for an apartment added to her other lodgings at the end of the Matted Gallery'.[9] No foundations are mentioned but the walls were of brick and the joiner's work in-cluded two lower (i.e. ground floor) and two middle rooms and garrets. These last

[1] *London Survey*, xiii, p. 86. The extent of the fire damage can be seen in the bird's-eye view (Pl. 37).
[2] *Ibid.*, quoting LC 5/196, ff. 1–9ᵛ, a list compiled in May 1691 of rooms at Whitehall other than the king's and queen's sides.
[3] *Diary of John Evelyn*, iv, p. 410, and J. Y. Akerman, *Moneys Received and Paid for Secret Services of Charles II and James II*, (Camden Society, 1851).
[4] *London Survey*, xiii, p. 85. Accounts in Works 5/17 and duplicate 5/18 (Extraord.).
[5] Works 5/145, p. 61.
[6] As noted in *London Survey*, xiii, p. 84. Prince Rupert's lodgings were built in 1662–3; above, p. 268.
[7] *London Survey*, xiii, pp. 81, 214, 238.
[8] Works 5/20 (Extraord.).
[9] Works 5/19 (Extraord.).

were at third floor level, and Kinward subsequently contracted on 26 September 1672 for the wainscot of the two 'upper' rooms beneath them on the second floor.[1] The two first floor rooms (one the bedchamber) had the customary enriched mouldings and mantel panels carved by Phillips, with fret ceilings and marble fireplaces. Further work took place between August 1673 and March 1674 in the form of carpenters' and joiners' alterations to the ante-room, next and inner rooms 'at the further end of the Privy Garden'.[2]

A reference in the account for April–June 1672 to the closet over the Stone Gallery may be literally accurate.[3] It seems probable on the evidence of proximity that the Portsmouth apartments included, or came to include, the southernmost 60 or 70 ft. of what had been the Matted Gallery,[4] and rooms on the upper floor on both sides of this extent, that is abutting or overlying the lodgings of Prince Rupert and those adjacent at the south end on the garden side, and those of Mrs. Kirk and Sir Edward Walker on the river side. The staircase, which is not shown on the plan but was called new in 1666,[5] gave access to the Bowling Green area. In this context may be mentioned the northward extension of Prince Rupert's lodgings on the garden side of the galleries into the walled court shown on the 1670 plan: three ground floor rooms were under construction in 1671–2 and upper rooms and a staircase in 1672–3.[6]

The Duchess of Portsmouth also had a kitchen south of the Bowling Green on the river side.[7] Characteristically the site was changed after work had begun and payment was made for filling in the foundations and digging new ones.[8] The kitchen was of one storey with an attic and dormers; it was finished in February 1673 and was joined to the lodgings by a gravel walk which was cleared away in 1674–5.[9]

On 10 September 1675 Evelyn saw the apartment 'luxuriously furnished, & with ten times the richness & glory beyond the Queenes, such massy pieces of Plate, whole Tables, Stands &c: of incredible value &c'. His later notices describe the lodgings as 'twice or thrice puld downe, & rebuilt' (4 October 1683) and 'rebuilt to please her no lesse than 3 times' (10 April 1691). These statements must be factual notwithstanding his dislike of the duchess, and a news letter probably of June 1678 refers to her as having begun to pull down her Whitehall lodgings.[10] Evelyn's longest notice is largely concerned with the furniture and includes references to Gobelins tapestries which it is known were sent by Louis XIV, and a profusion of cabinets, screens, clocks, vases and silver furniture of all sorts which would have left little room for architectural embellishment.[11]

Some, but by no means all work in connection with events in the Hall Theatre

---

[1] Works 5/145, p. 72.    [2] Works 5/22 and 23 (Ord.).
[3] Works 5/19 (Extraord.).
[4] In March 1675 Streater was painting in rooms in what had been the Matted Gallery (Works 5/24).
[5] Works 5/9, May.    [6] *London Survey*, xiii, p. 87; Works 5/21.
[7] *London Survey*, xiii, p. 246.
[8] Works 5/20 (Extraord.).
[9] Below, p. 283. Account in Works 5/25 (Extraord.).
[10] *Cal. S.P. Dom.* 1678, p. 262.
[11] *Diary of John Evelyn*, iv, p. 343. Some of Charles II's silver furniture is still at Windsor (C. C. Oman, 'An XVIIIth Century Record of Silver Furniture at Windsor Castle', *Connoisseur*, xciv, 1934, pp. 300–3). Louis XIV's silver furniture from Versailles was melted down in financial straits in 1689 (A. F. Blunt, *Art and Architecture in France 1500–1700*, 1953, p. 236).

appears in the Works books.[1] In March 1673 Streater painted a rustic background, arch and crosspiece; scenery was kept and altered for new uses, but these pieces were probably initially for an amateur performance of Elkanah Settle's *Empress of Morocco*.[2] In May 1673 he painted rock work, sky and sea and carpenters provided shutters, a trap door, a wooden horse and a platform in the clouds; between May and September a foreign company played under Tiberio Fiorelli.[3] In May 1674 ten porters returned scenery to Whitehall from the Theatre Royal in Drury Lane which had been borrowed by Louis Grabu on a warrant from the Lord Chamberlain on 27 March. The account refers to the theatre by the name of its predecessor, the King's Theatre in Bridge[s] Street, which had burned down on 2 January 1672.[4] In July 1675 scenery was sent to Windsor by water.[5]

Substantial works were undertaken in the theatre in November 1674–February 1675.[6] The stage was extended one yard forward into the pit. A new door and frame were inserted in the stage floor 'for the sincking underneath the same'; in February 1679 carpenters made a new trap door in the middle of the stage.[7] Alterations were made in 1674–5 to the musicians' seating and to the scenes and moving shutters; a new pair of shutters with grooves was made to represent clouds. Other additions of a celestial nature were steps behind the back clouds to take lights, and seats in the clouds for goddesses to sit. Several scenes are mentioned in the alterations: Denmark House, 'the arbour' and 'Florybanke'. Lights were also put behind 'the glory' and in order to conceal light sources a number of canvas scenes were backed with boards. A frame or floor was made for kettledrums, and the order of the account suggests that this was also in the upper regions for the creation of storms and supernatural effects.

The new gallery for which masons cut fixing holes was probably also connected with the stage, but alterations were made to the king's seat and the Lord Chamberlain's and Lord Newport's boxes. Steps for seats were provided in the audience galleries. The box made for the Surveyor of Works was temporary as it was taken down in June.[8] In November–December 1675 a new ceiling of boards, lath and plaster was installed, primarily for acoustical reasons—Pepys in 1666 had found 'the House, though very fine, yet bad for the voice, for hearing'.[9] The reference in the carpenter's account to 'quarters about the hammer beams' confirms the supposition that part at least of the Tudor roof construction was tidily hidden above the new ceiling, a treatment not uncommon for visual reasons in the later seventeenth century.

The diversification of the Cockpit area west of The Street continued after 1670. The area is shown on the plan of that year as largely occupied by Albemarle, who died on 3 January 1670; the major exception is the Duke of Ormonde's rooms at the

[1] The accounts and Lord Chamberlain's papers have been used by theatre scholars for a fuller record of performances than is here appropriate. See E. Boswell, *The Restoration Court Stage (1660–1702)* (1932); J. L. Hotson, *The Commonwealth and Restoration Stage* (1928); A. Nicoll, *History of English Drama 1660–1900*, i (1961); W. B. van Lennep, *The London Stage 1660–1800*, i (1960).

[2] Works 5/19 (Ord.); Boswell, *op. cit.*, pp. 182–3, 285.

[3] van Lennep, *op. cit.*, pp. 205–7.

[4] Account in Works 5/23 (Ord.); Drury Lane opened on 26 March 1674 and the scenery was used for Pierre Perrin's opera *Ariane* (Nicoll, *op. cit.*, pp. 354–5; van Lennep, pp. 214–15).

[5] Works 5/25 (Ord.).      [6] Works 5/24 (Extraord.).

[7] Works 5/30 (Ord.).      [8] Works 5/25 (Ord.).

[9] *London Survey*, xiii, pp. 52–3. Pepys, *Diary*, 29 Oct. 1666. The account is in Works 5/25 (Extraord.).

north end next to the Holbein Gate. While rooms were prepared in October for the Prince of Orange the Albemarle premises were subsequently divided into three sections. The western section facing the park and the disused Cockpit Theatre were allocated to the Duke of Buckingham, the eastern part towards The Street and the Privy Garden to the Duke of Monmouth, and the central part was probably assigned subsequently with the theatre to the Earl of Danby.[1]

In March 1671 work began on demolitions and alteration of rooms at the Cockpit for Buckingham; in this month the total was £35 13s. 8d. but in addition stores to the value of £41 15s. 10½d. were used, and the work included both the re-roofing of the gallery between the western range and the theatre and the dismantling of parts of the auditorium.[2] In April there are references to foundations, and by May the account is headed 'New Rooms'; work continued to the end of 1671 when the carcase of the new building had been roofed and provided with eight dormers.[3] The position and appearance of the building can be established with certainty by reference to a view of Whitehall from St. James's Park attributed to Danckerts (Pl. 35) which is datable on other evidence *c.* 1674.[4] It replaced the Albemarle rooms projecting into the park at the south-west corner of the palace site and was six bays long to the park, of two brick storeys with garrets, of what may be called the standard domestic style of the Works as exemplified in the Volary buildings. It must have extended further east than the two bays' thickness shown in the painting, for in the interior flooring and fitting, undertaken in August 1672–August 1673, the joiner's account comprises twelve rooms and closets.[5] A pale fence on a brick base was erected by May 1674 enclosing a rectangular garden from the park.[6] This appears in the Danckerts view.

The subsequent history of the Buckingham lodgings and the theatre building is brief but mysterious. The theatre received a new vane painted with *CR* and a crown, and the lantern was leaded, in 1672.[7] An order was made in 1674 for £200 for repairs to the Cockpit, and flooring and roofing repairs took place later that year.[8] However, the theatre was probably pulled down towards the end of 1675.[9] By 1677 the main part at least of Buckingham's lodgings had not only been demolished but replaced by another building, extending further into the park and with its major dimension running from west to east, that is at right angles to the block it replaced. A plan of the new block, dated 10 April 1677, is attached to the grant (31 May 1677) of ground and buildings to the Earl and Countess of Lichfield.[10] There is no record

---

[1] *London Survey*, xiv, pp. 27–8, 51. Work done in 1666–7 to the value of £500 in Clifford's lodgings was allowed in 1671 (Works 5/9 and 18, Extraord.). These lodgings were north-east of Whitehall Gate and designated *The Comptroller* on the 1670 plan.

[2] Works 5/15 (Extraord.); *London Survey*, xiv, pp. 27–8, 113.

[3] Works 5/17 (Extraord.).

[4] *London Survey*, xiv, pp. 101–2 and Pl. 2.

[5] Works 5/22 (Extraord.).

[6] Works 5/23 (Ord.).

[7] Works 5/19 (Ord.). The payments (*ibid.*) of £10 in July to Robert Streater for painting 'a peece for his Majesties bedchamber over which the new vaine is put' and 22s. for gilding the carved frame more probably refer to the old bedchamber next to the Vane Room in the palace. *Cf. London Survey*, xiii, p. 97.

[8] *London Survey*, xiv, p. 28; *Cal. Treas. Books 1672–5*, p. 239; Works 5/23 (Ord.), Sept., Dec.

[9] *London Survey*, xiv, pp. 28–9.

[10] Edward Henry Lee, cr. Earl of Lichfield, married in 1677 Charlotte Fitzroy, Charles II's daughter by the Duchess of Cleveland. *London Survey*, xiv, pp. 114–15.

either of the destruction of the old building or of the construction of the new, but the countess's old and new buildings are mentioned in the Ordinary account for March 1677.[1] It is conceivable that the new building was outside the Works' authority, but this does not explain the destruction of the Buckingham building and some calamity such as fire or even collapse has been suggested.[2]

A documented example of a grant of property subsequent to the erection of new buildings is offered by the case of the Earl of Danby, Lord High Treasurer. The area granted to Danby on 28 March 1676 included the theatre site, his lodgings recently erected adjacent to it on the south and to the Buckingham–Lichfield area on the west, the remains of the old Cockpit garden (shown as a courtyard with columns down the east and west sides on the grant plan) and the offices at the southern extremity of the Cockpit site.[3] The new building consisted of a block 73 ft. by 32 ft., recessed in the centre of the principal front which faced south to the courtyard; it was probably of one main storey and an attic with ten dormers.[4] The principal floor contained a lobby leading to the old round staircase shown on the 1670 plan, the dining room and withdrawing room which had the usual carved foliage over the chimneypieces. The lobby walls were finished 'sceeder colour' and the dining room in 'walnut tree colour pencill grained'. The accounts also refer to work on the old buildings at the south end of the court or garden, along the east and west sides of which the carpenter built the 'culumnes' shown on the grant plan, eight on the east and five more widely spaced on the shorter west side.

Danby's grant included the site of the Cockpit proper, and he seems almost at once to have set about rebuilding there. The evidence for this is pictorial: two views of Whitehall from the park datable 1675–6 and 1677 show a nearly square four-storey building in place of the theatre.[5] The views differ in details, and as other evidence separates them by at least a year it is possible that the earlier of the two paintings was made very soon after the commencement of the new block.[6] Its construction was evidently at Danby's expense; after his dismissal from the Treasury in 1679 he seems to have let part of his Cockpit premises, and subsequently to have disposed of the lease to the second Duke of Albemarle, from whom the whole was repurchased by Charles II in 1684 for Princess Anne's use. The building on the theatre site was used for the Treasury after the Whitehall fire of 1698 and until 1732 when it was declared dangerous—perhaps as a result of hasty, ill-founded and sub-standard workmanship—and it was replaced by Kent's Treasury building.[7] While Danby's building may have been carried out independently of the Works, it is disturbing to find implications of bad work within the general jurisdiction of Wren as Surveyor; it would be the more so if the Buckingham building, which was put up by the Works, were to prove deficient in the same respect.

One further alteration should be mentioned. On 1 February 1674 an order was

[1] Works 5/27; *London Survey*, xiv, pp. 115–16.
[2] *London Survey*, xiv, pp. 116 n., 28 n.
[3] P.R.O. C 66/3185; *London Survey*, xiv, p. 51 and Pl. 37.
[4] Accounts April–Sept., Oct.–Dec. 1674; Works 5/23 (Extraord.).
[5] *London Survey*, xiv, pp. 28–9, 102–3, and Pls. 3–4.
[6] There is a reference in November 1677 (Works 5/28, Ord.) to the Monmouth nursery as 'next the Lord Treasurers new building'.
[7] *London Survey*, xiv, pp. 28–9, 51–2.

given for a new brick building to be erected for the Earl of Ossory, son of the Duke of Ormonde, whose lodgings formed the north-east corner of the Cockpit site. The building, which was to be paid for by Ossory, was about 70 ft. long from west to east and about 21 ft. (three bays) on the side elevation facing the park. It lay immediately south of Ormonde's range running between the Holbein Gate and the stairs to the park.[1]

The remainder of the Cockpit area continued in the occupancy of the Duke of Monmouth. There are accounts for alterations to make additional rooms in July–November 1673 'over against the Privy Garden', that is in the Old Tennis Court across The Street from the Privy Garden.[2] Further alterations were made to the Cockpit lodgings in January 1674–December 1675.[3] The work consisted mainly of offices and accommodation for members of Monmouth's household (for example 'escriptories' for Mrs. Davis and Major Watson) and improvements to the duchess's bedchamber. At an unknown date the Monmouth lodgings included an elaborate bedchamber and probably other rooms on the upper floor on the south side of the passage from The Street to the Cockpit (given on the 1670 plan to Captain Cooke).[4] The bedroom is described and illustrated in Ackermann's *Microcosm of London* (1809); it was then used as an office by the Board of Trade. Drawings by Soane (1823) show that it had a rich fret ceiling with an oval blind dome in the centre, and plaster relief monograms in the corners with a ducal coronet and the letters (of which there is a replica in the Soane Museum) JAMB (for James and Anne of Monmouth and Buccleuch). These rooms were pulled down to make way for Soane's Board of Trade building of 1824–7. Minor works were carried out for the duchess in 1682, and in the following year the Cockpit laboratory was converted into a kitchen for her.[5] In October 1683 the lath-and-plaster wall to the park of Lord Doncaster's lodgings (formerly the nursery) was renewed.[6]

The principal outdoor work in the 1670s was the extension of the Privy Garden south into the Bowling Green area. Work began in August 1673 and was resumed the following spring, on demolishing the terrace walk dividing the south end of the garden from the green, on digging up the green to make a fountain basin, and on constructing a new raised terrace on the river side of the basin.[7] The new terrace was some way in from the river bank; the north end of it can be seen in the Westminster version of the bird's-eye view (Pl. 37), together with the fountain and part of its basin, which were on the axis of the centre walk of the Privy Garden. In the following account (November 1674–April 1675) the existing gravel walk nearer the river was taken down and levelled, and the basin was dug and lined.[8] In the second half of 1675 New River water was piped from Charing Cross for the fountain; the fall of about 75 ft. from Islington made possible the high jet shown in the view and mentioned by Delaune in 1690.[9] The 1674–5 account refers also to a grotto at

[1] *Ibid.*, pp. 56–7.
[2] Works 5/21 (Extraord.). For the various tennis courts see above, p. 273.
[3] Works 5/21 and 23 (Extraord.).     [4] *London Survey*, xiv, pp. 80–1 and Pls. 62–5.
[5] Works 5/35 (Extraord.); *London Survey*, xiv, p. 70.
[6] Works 5/37 (Ord.).     [7] Works 5/23 (Extraord.).
[8] Works 5/25 (Extraord.); 5/22 (Ord.), Jan. 1675.
[9] Works 5/25 (misdated) and 26 (Extraord.). T. Delaune, *Angliae Metropolis* (1690), p. 94. The fountain basin is shown in Ogilby and Morgan's London map of 1682 (B.M. Crace ii, 58).

the south end, although those details given imply a remarkably urban structure. The masonry included two Ionic columns *in antis* supporting a full entablature 18 ft. wide, without a pediment. Two scrolls and plinths were also made. Within this structure were a seat and three 'seated niches'. An oval pavement of 60 square feet was provided and the grotto had an oval ceiling 11 ft. by 8 ft. 6 in., also described in the plasterer's account as a 'compass ceiling' which suggests that it was domical. The basin was filled in in 1714,[1] but its approximate size and shape can be reconstructed. From the amounts of earth excavated and materials used it was probably about 4 ft. deep, lined and paved with brick, oval in shape and about 110 ft. by 85 ft. including a Ketton stone coping; the mason's account also provided for a stone pyramid encasing the fountain jet.[2]

In 1672 negotiations began between the fourth Earl of Portland and the king for the purchase of the bronze equestrian statute of Charles I cast by Hubert Le Sueur in 1633 for the first earl's garden at Roehampton but never set up, preserved during the Civil War and Protectorate and claimed by Portland after the Restoration. The sale to Charles II was completed in April 1675.[3] The following month Robert Streater was paid £2 10s. for making '2 designes on paper . . . in order to the setting up of the Statue of King Charles the first upon a stone pedestall by Master Surveyors Direction'.[4] A wooden model was also made of the pedestal, for which William Cleare, joiner, sent an account in April 1678.[5] This was two years after the erection of the statue at Charing Cross, and it might be asked whether the model was preparatory or a replica; however, since the previous month's accounts include the carriage of stones and rubbish away from the figure, the Office seems to have been finally clearing up a matter which had begun to drag. The foundation for the figure was prepared in July–October 1675 and the pedestal was built by Joshua Marshall, who received in addition £100 for 'carveing the Relieves of the pedistall'.[6] The pedestal was closely surrounded by an iron fence with ten twisted and 167 plain bars.[7] The figure was set up and given a new bridle and sword, and several loose parts were secured. Two designs for the pedestal in the Wren Collection at All Souls, neither corresponding to the executed work, are usually attributed to Wren although for no adequate reason.[8] The ultimate responsibility was his as Surveyor, but Marshall's contract merely contains the common unhelpful formula 'according to a design'.[9] William Cleare, who made the model, is unlikely to have designed it and the most likely candidate is Streater.

[1] *London Survey*, xiii, p. 231.
[2] Bricklayer's contract, Works 5/145, p. 92 (26 Oct. 1674); mason's contract, *ibid.*, p. 95 (4 Jan. 1675). The oval shape is mentioned in the first contract and confirmed by Delaune and other sources. The overall dimensions are taken from the survey plan on the drawing at All Souls (Vol. v, 2; *Wren Soc.*, viii, Pl. ii.), which is reasonably in agreement with the circumference of 290 ft. given in the accounts.
[3] *London Survey*, xvi, p. 264. For the statue see M. Whinney, *Sculpture in Britain 1530–1830* (1964), p. 36.
[4] Works 5/25 (Ord.).
[5] Works 5/30 (Ord.).
[6] Works 5/25 (Extraord.).
[7] *London Survey*, xvi, Pl. 85, shows the statue *c.* 1720.
[8] Vol. iv, 55, 54 (*Wren Soc.*, v, Pls. xxxviii, xxxix).
[9] Works 5/145, p. 99.

## 2. 1685–1698

The chief visual document for Whitehall under James II and William and Mary is the bird's-eye view datable *c.* 1695–7 and now attributed to Leonard Knyff (Pl. 37). One version is in the extra-illustrated Pennant's *London* in the British Museum, another is in Westminster Public Library.[1] Comparison with other evidence shows that the drawings give an accurate record of many individual buildings, in particular those elevations shown parallel to the picture plane. On the other hand, in some places the draughtsman has sacrificed literal exactness to the desire to show as much as possible. In foreshortened parts he has tended to suggest the essential features, such as windows of a particular kind, rather than their correct number. Where buildings are partly obscured by others he may have made adjustments so as to show what could not have been seen from the imagined viewpoint. The crucial example of these deficiencies is in the details of James II's Privy Garden range and the buildings between it and the Banqueting House, where some of the lines in the British Museum version appear to show more than the other drawing but cannot be deciphered. In general the British Museum version is more complex, better drawn and apparently more detailed, but it is also unfinished both in the delineation of buildings and in the incidentals such as traffic which, together with the somewhat arbitrary rendering of glazing bars, have been filled in in the Westminster version. The two drawings seem to be largely independent, being of different construction, scale, extent and viewpoint.

In the absence of any real aerial station such perspectives were of necessity artificial views made from plans and elevation sketches; this has two consequences. First, in the case of new buildings the draughtsman could show unfinished or projected work as it would be when completed, or equally he might use drawings that had been superseded. Both versions show north of the Horse Guards the new Admiralty building erected in 1694–5 on the site of Wallingford House (demolished in 1724 for the present building) and this, as the latest construction shown, may be taken with the 1698 fire as termini for the date of the drawing.[2] On the other hand, discrepancies between the two versions in the extent and details of James II's chapel are probably due to errors in setting out rather than connected with the alterations to the chapel of 1687. As a second consequence, the draughtsman has regularised the whole site to a rectangle, whereas it was wedge-shaped and narrower at the south end; the garden, Stone Gallery, Banqueting House, The Street and Whitehall were all oblique to the river front. Concealed adjustments thus introduce incalculable errors into the interpretation of all foreshortened distances, and here also the confusion is worst in James II's buildings, whose foundations for the most part lie inaccessibly under more recent structures or thoroughfares.

The bird's-eye views show the considerable modernisation effected in the last

[1] B.M. Print Room, Crowle Pennant, iv, 8 (*Wren Soc.* vii, Pl. vii); Westminster Public Library, E 134.1 (24).

[2] *London Survey*, xiii, pp. 112–13; xvi, pp. 51–3. The scale ratio between the two drawings is about 5 : 8.

thirteen years of the palace's history: besides the new Privy Garden range, which took account of the axis though not the orientation of the sundial and the fountain of 1674–5, James II's building included the famous Roman Catholic chapel at the end next to the Street, a new Council Chamber facing Pebble Court and roughly on the site of the old one, and some buildings between it, the Holbein Gate and the Banqueting House. The Privy Garden range included new rooms for the queen, and this made it possible to rebuild the river front of the old queen's lodgings north of the Volary; this new building, begun early in 1688 and not finished until after the Revolution, is shown in the views, together with the garden terrace built out into the river in front of it for Queen Mary in 1691–3. The southern half of the Stone and Matted Galleries, the old lodgings of the Duke of York and Prince Rupert and those of the Duchess of Portsmouth, were burned down on 10 April 1691, and their site is shown cleared and levelled.

James II acceded to the throne on 6 February 1685 and was crowned on 23 April. As Duke of York he had occupied rooms south of the Volary buildings and between the Stone Gallery and the river, and the character of the palace was familiar to him. Good reasons may be inferred for a new campaign of improvement at Whitehall: besides the prestige of the sovereign by Divine Right, the personal prestige of the new monarch stood to benefit from new buildings, regular and modern in style and in contrast to the old. The range on the north of the Privy Garden was now, as can be seen from its outlines in the 1670 plan, the most irregular in the palace and an obvious place for improvements. Even prestige building needs another *raison d'être*, and two in particular were appropriate. James came to the throne committed to the restoration of Catholicism in England: on 15 February, the second Sunday of his reign, he heard mass in his oratory at Whitehall with the doors wide open.[1] A new chapel next to The Street expressly designed for Catholic worship in a Baroque setting would be more prestigious and more convenient, and probably no more expensive in the long run, than altering the old Chapel Royal. Further, rebuilding the Council Chamber with the Privy Gallery range would accord with the primacy of Whitehall as the seat of government of a king who intended, however ineffectively, to be seen to govern.

Some of the ambiguities and omissions of the bird's-eye view can be repaired by the accounts, which refer to individual blocks and buildings adjacent to them.[2] Two preparatory drawings are extant, one a plan of the chapel (Pl. 39B) and the other an east elevation of the Council Chamber with a section of the Privy Gallery block (Pl. 40A).[3] The latter is designed on a bay width of 8 ft. and a cornice level with that of the lower order of the Banqueting House, and it is very probable, both from notions of architectural regularity and from an interpretation of documents, that both these dimensions were constant norms for the other elevations. The largest single block was a range of apartments, facing the Privy Garden and running for 200 ft. (or 25 bays) westwards from the north end of the Stone Gallery. It was continued to the west by the chapel, extending as far as The Street, something over 80 ft. A door

[1] *Diary of John Evelyn*, iv, p. 416.
[2] Works 5/54 contains Extraordinary accounts for these buildings. Extracts, with unspecified omissions, are printed in *Wren Soc.*, vii, pp. 93–130.
[3] Chapel, All Souls, ii, 115*; Council Chamber, All Souls, iv, 142.

opened from the apartment range to the garden on the axis of the sundial and fountain, in the sixteenth bay from the east, that is in the centre neither of this range nor
of the whole complex. This axis, however, coincided approximately with the east
wall of the Banqueting House and also with the west end of the new Privy Gallery
which lay on the upper floor behind (north of) the apartments. The eastern 80 ft. of
the Privy Gallery overlooked the Pebble Court on the north and was lit by ten windows.[1] The western end adjoined the Council Chamber block and was lit by a large
window in the west end. On the east both the gallery and the apartment range led
to the old Vane Room, which was reconstructed and enlarged. The Council Chamber
also had access, as did the Banqueting House, to a new stone staircase in the angle
formed by these two structures.[2] From the staircase a second gallery appears to have
run along the end of the Banqueting House and continued westwards as far as the
Holbein Gate; for the westernmost 80 ft. or so it was doubled to the south, leaving a
long narrow court between it and the chapel, referred to as the Chapel Court.
Either the second gallery or the doubling block was known as the Lesser Building,
but the structure so described had two storeys, a half storey and garrets like the
Privy Gallery range.[3]

The bird's-eye view shows the garden and the new buildings as rectangular,
but it is clear from excavations of the east end of the latter that they followed the
axes of the Banqueting House and were thus oblique to the garden and the Stone
Gallery (Fig. 23).[4] In fact Wren was presented with an insoluble conflict of align-
ment, and while taking account of the Privy Garden axis in placing the doorway he
chose to align the new work with the most regular existing building, the largest in
scale and the most important aesthetically and ideologically. It was also the one
most likely to survive in any further rebuilding programme, and it would be logical
to relate it as closely as possible with the new Council Chamber and Chapel.

The progress of the work is well documented. James's intentions were serious by
15 May 1685, when Wren estimated for 'the whole South side of the privy Garden
double, the ground story 11 foot high, the Second Story 19, containing the Gallery
& the Queens apartment, & the Chapell the highth of both stories. The ground
story to be fitted with deale wanscote into lodgings & offices for the Treasury,
Secretaries, Ld Chamberlain & others. The 2d story & galleries to be finished as the
Kings new Lodgings, and the Chapell decently adorned.'[5] The offices were to replace those on the ground floor of the old building, which is wrongly described in
the estimate as south, not north of the garden. The estimate mentions lodgings
for the queen, and a number of rooms were fitted for her on the first floor; early
accounts refer to the 'queen's' chapel either because that was the original purpose or
because for some time James discreetly concealed his real intentions.[6] The estimate
is costed on area but also includes alterations to the Vane Room and those consequent on 'peecing the old Works to the new'; the total, after a deduction of £1020

---

[1] Works 5/54, Nov. 1685.    [2] *Ibid.*, Feb., July 1686.    [3] *Wren Soc.*, vii, pp. 109, 112.
[4] Drawings made in 1939–40 by H.M. Office of Works.
[5] Bodleian MS. Clarendon 6, f. 301; first printed in *Clarendon State Papers*, i, p. 271, and subsequently in
*London Survey*, xiii, pp. 102–3, where the estimate for two storeys is interpreted as a lower building than the
final design. But the latter has two main storeys and in some parts a mezzanine.
[6] Evelyn's notice of the building works, 18 Oct. 1685, also refers to 'a new Chapel for the Queene, whose
Lodgings this new building was' (*Diary of John Evelyn*, iv, p. 480).

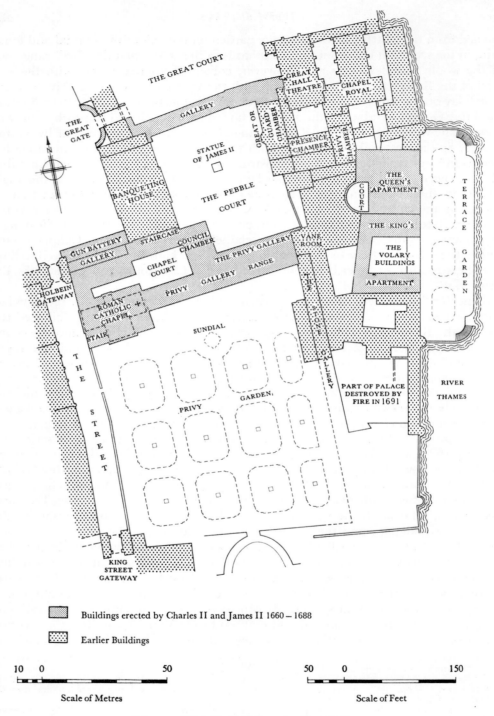

THE GREAT COURT

THE GREAT GATE

GALLERY

GREAT HALL THEATRE

CHAPEL ROYAL

GREAT OR GUARD CHAMBER

PRESENCE CHAMBER

PRIVY CHAMBER

STATUE OF JAMES II

THE QUEEN'S APARTMENT

COURT

TERRACE GARDEN

BANQUETING HOUSE

THE PEBBLE COURT

THE KING'S

GUN BATTERY GALLERY

STAIRCASE

COUNCIL CHAMBER

THE PRIVY GALLERY

VANE ROOM

THE VOLARY BUILDINGS

APARTMENT

CHAPEL COURT

GALLERY RANGE

HOLBEIN GATEWAY

PRIVY GALLERY

ROMAN CATHOLIC CHAPEL

THE STONE GALLERY

STAIR

SUNDIAL

THE STREET

PRIVY GARDEN

PART OF PALACE DESTROYED BY FIRE IN 1691

RIVER

THAMES

KING STREET GATEWAY

Buildings erected by Charles II and James II 1660 – 1688

Earlier Buildings

10    0                                50

Scale of Metres

50    0                              150

Scale of Feet

Fig. 23. Whitehall Palace in about 1695.

for old materials, comes to £13,305. This sum was far exceeded, the accounts total-ling £35,343 12s. 3½d.; an appreciable part of the increase was spent on a chapel more than 'decently adorned'. The mention of rooms 'to be finished as the Kings new Lodgings' must, in the context of the estimate, be read as concerned with likeness and not with function: it indicates a degree of intentional conformity, not with the Banqueting House but with the domestic style of the Volary.

Demolition of the old buildings began on 18 May 1685 and by the end of June involved the whole site; fittings were stored in the Banqueting House.[1] In July and August the gun platform facing Whitehall was taken down, and in August work began on altering the Vane Room.[2] In July an average of over a hundred men per day were working on the new foundations. Progress was so good that in January 1686 carpentry was under way in the Council Chamber and the queen's rooms, and in February the chapel was roofed with blue slates. In that month work began on the 'great stone stairs' next to the Banqueting House.

In July 1686 six firms of joiners were at work. John Smallwell worked in the Lesser Building and the rooms allotted to the Duchess of Mazarin next to the Privy Garden.[3] John Heysenbuttel and Edward Cannell were also working in the Lesser Building. Charles Hopson was in the queen's rooms, Roger Davis in the chapel, John Gibson in the Treasury and other offices, William Cleare in the Council Chamber.

Some of the rooms were elaborate. The ceilings of the queen's great bedchamber, closet and private chapel were painted by Verrio and gilded by René Cousin.[4] The great bedchamber had a chimneypiece whose decoration included two large and two smaller pieces of drapery, a crown and a coat of arms, carved by Grinling Gibbons and gilded. Evelyn saw this in January 1687 and also admired the expensive em-broidery of the crimson velvet bed.[5] Routine carving was executed by William Emmett in the rest of the queen's apartment, the Privy Gallery, the Council Chamber and the reconstructed Vane Room.[6]

The great stone staircase provided, for the only time in its history, an adequate access to the Banqueting House, leading to the south end and also to the new build-ings. It was lit by a glazed wooden lantern 7 ft. 4 in. high and 8 ft. 8 in. wide; the ceiling was executed by John Grove and Henry Doogood. The lantern ceiling was 'enricht with a goloss [guilloche] on the Ribs with a large foliage flower' and the main ceiling included '4 large pannells with mouldings enricht with Sheilds and Trophies in the Pannels' and '4 large Wreaths of flowers'. The total area of the ceiling with the lantern was 812 sq. ft.[7] While not emulating the richness or the illusionism of Hugh May's staircases at Windsor the device of the lantern had its

---

[1] *Diary of John Evelyn*, iv, p. 492.

[2] In August 1686 a marble chimneypiece was brought from store at Greenwich for the Vane Room (Works 5/54).

[3] Works 5/145, p. 178. His contract mentions 'Designes of each roome drawn & approved off by Sir Christopher Wren knight'.

[4] Oct. 1687, Oct. 1686.

[5] Accounts Dec. 1686, Feb. 1687; *Diary of John Evelyn*, iv, p. 537; *Wren Soc.*, vii, p. 133.

[6] Oct. 1686. The most elaborate carved work for Mary of Modena was in the waterside building; see below, p. 295.

[7] Carpenter's account July 1686; plasterer (£49 17s. 4d.) Dec. 1686. A lantern, apparently rather too small, can be seen behind the Council Chamber roof in the bird's-eye view.

nearest prototype there. In January 1687 a rail was made for the staircase and keys were issued for the queen's apartment.[1]

In July 1686 John Heysenbuttel was paid £4 for a model of the altarpiece of the Popish Chapel, for the making of which Grinling Gibbons and Arnold Quellin had contracted in March. The contract stipulated that the work was to be finished by 25 September subject to a penalty of £100, and the contractors were to employ fifty men or as many as were necessary to finish the work in time. More men could be required by the Surveyor, who was responsible for the draft, design and direction of the whole. The materials are specified as white marble with veined pilasters and purple rance columns.[2] The chapel was first used for midnight mass at Christmas 1686, and the fullest eye-witness account of the interior and its ceremonies was given four days later by Evelyn.[3]

By April 1687 considerable alterations to the chapel were desired.[4] These involved an addition towards the garden with roof, side walls and south end, and the need for extra space for musicians and for the side altar must have been serious to offset the disruption of the recently completed interior. At the same time a new staircase and vestry were built flanking the extension and replacing the original south vestry. Moreover, while the centre was screened off from the new work on the south,[5] alterations were also made to the altar steps and chancel floor in the summer of 1687 and later (October) to the throne and altarpiece. The accounts end in November 1687. A year later James II left England for ever and the chapel, in which the last mass was celebrated on 17 December 1688, was no longer needed.[6] Some of the fittings were soon removed and thus escaped the 1698 fire which destroyed James's buildings.

The surviving plan of the chapel appears to show its final state after the additions. The marble altarpiece stood at the true east end on the ground floor, with a door from the space behind it into a room in the Privy Gallery range. The altar bay was balanced by the ante-chapel on the west, facing The Street at an oblique angle. Above this, at first floor level, was the royal pew (according to Evelyn, 'The Thrones where the K: & Q: sits is very glorious in a Closset above just [i.e. exactly] opposite to the altar'). A model for the throne was charged for in October 1686, when the work was already partly installed. Gibbons's and Cousin's bills included gilt carved work: nine boys over the canopy, a crown, sceptre, tassels, eight festoons on the pilasters, and '4 Antiquos'.[7] On the second floor above the ante-chapel was the priest's lodging.[8] The original side altar, mentioned in the joiner's account in December 1686, was probably against the middle of the south wall. It was probably replaced by one at the east end of the new southern arm, for which carving was included in Gibbons's bill of October 1687. In the same month Cousin charged for

---

[1] *London Survey*, xiii, p. 105 n.    [2] Works 5/145, p. 184.

[3] *The autobiography of Sir John Bramston* (Camden Society, 1845), p. 253; A. Wood, *Life and Times*, iii (Oxford Historical Society, xxvi, 1894), p. 201, misquoted in *Wren Soc.*, vii, p. 75 as 1685; *Diary of John Evelyn*, iv, pp. 534–5. A view of the chapel was in Sir James Thornhill's sale (*Burlington Magazine*, lxxxii (1943), p. 136).

[4] Order to Wren to enlarge, 10 April; *Wren Soc.*, vii, p. 134. A newsletter gives the purpose of enlargement as 'to make several alcoves therein' but no other details (Hist. MSS. Comm. *Downshire* i (1), p. 238).

[5] Account, June, 1687.

[6] Evelyn's letter to his son, 18 Dec. 1688 (*Diary and Correspondence of John Evelyn*, ed. W. Bray (1894), iii, pp. 288–9).

[7] Nov.–Dec. 1686.    [8] *Wren Soc.*, vii, p. 130.

gilding on the carving round the three tribunes in the chapel; later in the same account these are described as the tribune and the two organ lofts. The small organ
would have stood in the small gallery in the middle of the north side.[1] The larger
instrument must have been made for the first floor gallery in the new southern arm;
René (Renatus) Harris received £1100 between December 1686 and July 1688 for
an organ for the chapel, with part of an added sum for 'fitting and preparing' it,
and Gibbons was again paid (October 1687) for carving 'before the great Organ on
the side of the Chappel'.[2] In 1691 Queen Mary gave the great organ to the church
of St. James, Piccadilly, where the case remains.[3]

The chapel plan is ambiguous and probably does not show a consistent single
level; it is however reasonable to suppose that the staircase in the south-west corner
gave access to the southern tribune rather than to the royal gallery which would be
accessible only from the first floor—in this case from the passage on the north side.
The paired columns at the front of both these galleries were supported in the lower
storey by piers; according to the plan they reached the chapel ceiling at four angles
of an elongated octagonal ceiling fret or moulding.[4] The appearance of this fret and
a certain spatial similarity with Wren's oval-octagonal church of St. Antholin have
led to the suggestion that the centre of the ceiling opened into an oval lath-and-plaster
dome.[5] On the other hand the two outline elevations of the altarpiece at All Souls[6]
show a section of a half-oval barrel vault which must, if carried out, have covered
the central and chancel parts of the chapel in a continuous surface (Fig. 24). Evelyn's
reference to 'the Volto, in *fresca*, the Asumption of the blessed Virgin . . . painted
by Verrio' is not sufficiently precise evidence. However, while the roof space could
have accommodated either construction, the absence of exceptional items in the
accounts suggests the barrel vault rather than the fret and dome. In October 1687
Verrio's bill included £1250 for painting by contract the ceiling and walls (excluding the organ lofts).[7] The ceiling at least must have been finished a year earlier, when
Cousin used 8132 leaves of gold in gilding it.[8]

The central portion of the massive altarpiece, about 18 ft. wide, was concave and
of two storeys; the extant drawings show a picture frame about 8 by 7 ft. and its
terminal ornaments reached almost to the full height (39 ft. 6 in.) of the chapel.
The painting in the frame according to Evelyn's description was an *Annunciation*; he
does not identify the artist though in the context it might be Verrio. However,
Benedetto Gennari was to be paid £420 in January 1687 for 'several pictures by him
drawn and delivered for the chappel at Whitehall'. The side altar had a carved
picture frame and the *Annunciation* may have been moved there after the alterations

---

[1] William Emmett's account of Oct. 1686 included work on the outside of the organ loft to the court.
Gibbons was paid for the organ front in Dec. 1686.
[2] Payments to Harris, Akerman, *Secret Services of Charles II and James II*, pp. 144, 169, 180, 196.
[3] C. Clutton and A. Niland, *The British Organ* (1963), p. 214. The chaire organ case was added in 1852.
[4] Two more columns are pencilled in on the chancel side, which cannot have been incorporated in the
chapel as it is known from the documents.
[5] M. Whinney and O. Millar, *English Art 1625–1714* (1957), p. 217 n; K. Downes, *English Baroque Architecture* (1966), p. 22. St. Antholin, built 1678–82, was recorded at the time of its demolition in 1875 in a water-
colour frequently reproduced in the Wren literature (*e.g.* Downes, *op. cit.*, Pl. 22).
[6] Vol. ii, 69; vol. iv, 97; *Wren Soc.*, vii, Pls. xiii, xiv.
[7] 'Fresco' was normally oil on set plaster in England at this time. Wren's report on Verrio's bill is printed
in two versions in *Wren Soc.*, xviii: pp. 147–8 (Works 3/1, f. 7) and pp. 63–4 (MS. in Soane Museum.)
[8] Nov. 1686.

ELEVATION

LOWER PLAN  UPPER PLAN

| 1 | 0 | 2 |
Scale of Metres

| 5 | 0 | 5 |
Scale of Feet

Fig. 24. Whitehall Palace: Wren's design for the altarpiece of James II's Catholic Chapel
(based on *Wren Society* xiv, plate xiii).

and been replaced by 'a picture representing the Nativity of Our Lord, for the great altar in the chappel at Whitehall' for which Gennari was paid £150 in October 1688.[1] The sculptural work included, besides cherubs in the round and in relief, four life-size statues and two adoring angels; most of this work survives in varying states of preservation. Cousin was paid for 'the silver figures in the great Barlief over the Altar'; this was presumably the panel shown in the top of the lower storey, under the picture frame.

The altarpiece was dismantled about 1695 by Gibbons and taken to Hampton court.[2] In 1706 Queen Anne gave it to Westminster Abbey where it was set up, again by Gibbons, without the four statues; these were, however, sent to Westminster and now stand, very weathered, in the College Garden of Westminster School.[3] Evelyn's identification as St. Peter, St. Paul, St. John and the Church is certainly mistaken since two figures are female and probably represented Faith and Hope, flanking SS. Peter and Paul on the outside.[4] The statues must have stood on the cornice of the outer one-storey sections of the altarpiece; the two angels were placed (at least in the Abbey reconstruction) on the corners of the upper storey. Soon after 1820 the altarpiece was given to Walter King, Vicar of Burnham, Somerset, who installed as much of the work as would fit in Burnham church; the angels and some relief panels are still there. Two reliefs with medallions of Christ and the Virgin Mary are in Dean's Yard, Westminster.[5]

The pulpit for which Gibbons received £90, and which had relief figures of the Evangelists as well as cherubs and vegetation, was given to the Danish Church in Wellclose Square in 1696; it appears in Kip's engraving of the interior (1697) but has not been identified since the demolition sale of that church in 1869.[6]

On 1 January 1687 Sir John Bramston recorded the setting up in the Pebble Court of the bronze statue of James II which is shown in position in the bird's-eye view and is now, on a modern base, outside the National Gallery in Trafalgar Square. The statue was made by Gibbons and assistants, by agreement with Tobias Rustat, Yeoman of the Robes.[7] Rustat is known to have commissioned Gibbons's equestrian *Charles II* at Windsor (dated 1679) and is reputed also to have paid for the standing *Charles II* at Chelsea Hospital, a work traditionally (but without evidence) dated 1676 and believed (again without evidence) to have been made for Whitehall and removed to make way for the *James*.[8]

Ordinary expenditure in James II's reign was about £250 per month, a sign of

[1] Akerman, *op. cit.*, pp. 175, 209; the latter payment was accompanied by £20 for two pictures of 'Our Saviour and the blessed Virgin, for the new vestry'. No religious pictures by Gennari can now be found in the Royal Collection but there are a number of secular ones (M. Levey, *The Later Italian Pictures in the Collection of Her Majesty the Queen*, 1964, pp. 21–3, 81).

[2] E 351/3464.

[3] *Wren Soc.*, xi, Pl. xxix.

[4] Identification proposed by Rudolf Wittkower, *Wren Soc.*, xi, p. 119.

[5] See D. Green, *Grinling Gibbons* (1964), pp. 59–62; Whinney, *Sculpture in Britain*, pp. 55–6; *Wren Soc.*, vii, pp. 236–9.

[6] *Cal. Treas. Books 1696–7*, p. 214; *London Survey*, xiii, pp. 109–10.

[7] *Autobiography of Sir John Bramston*, p. 253. Vertue (*Walpole Society*, xxvi, 1938, p. 59) quotes the contract. See also Green, *Gibbons*, pp. 56–7; Whinney, *Sculpture*, p. 55. According to F. Colsoni, *Le Guide de Londres* (1691, reprinted ed. W. H. Godfrey, 1951), p. 11, the base was inscribed *Jacobus . . . rex d. fid. anno 1684*; since James acceded on 6 February 1684/5 the date would appear to refer to his reign and not to his statue.

[8] If it was made before the foundation of Chelsea in 1682 it must have had another destination. See C. G. T. Dean, *The Royal Hospital, Chelsea* (1950), pp. 51–2; Whinney and Millar, *op. cit.*, p. 247.

the continued improvement in the state of the palace. The unusual number of sash-cords renewed in the winter of 1686–7 probably relates to the life-span of those installed in the 1660s. In the autumn of 1687 the sutlery on the north side of the court towards Scotland Yard was rebuilt; in 1688 the lodgings over the buttery were enlarged by the addition of an extra storey.[1]

In 1687 the King's Guard Chamber was fitted with wainscot and with wooden frames and iron hooks and holdfasts to make a display of armour on the pattern of that at Windsor. William Emmett carved a pedestal for a cap-à-pie armour over the door into the Presence Chamber and Charles Hopson and Robert Streater II repaired the drops and 'pendelums' of the Tudor ceiling.[2] The ceiling was silvered and lacquered, the wainscot was colour grained and the chimneypiece marbled. In September-December the old chapel was cleaned and made good, the joiner renewing 25 ceiling pendants of various sizes; in September Arnold Wallwin was repaid 31s. 6d. expended on gratuities to painters, carpenters and glaziers for overtime and night work there.[3]

The gun platform to Whitehall which had been demolished in the preparations for the Privy Gallery building was rebuilt in 1688, in brick with a stone base, fascia and coping. The carpenter provided centres for seven large arches on the inside of the structure and for nine gun portholes.[4] The following year the board roof over the guns, 90 ft. by 18 ft., was rebuilt more commodiously and 6 ft. higher. Thomas Woffington received £42 for taskwork in covering the roof 'with plaster of Puzzola'.[5] The new platform is seen in Terasson's view of 1713 (Pl. 38).

On the completion of the Privy Garden buildings the great sundial in the garden was repaired in May 1688 and William Marre, who had made the apparatus in 1664, was paid for 'new delineating' the dials, Streater for painting and Emmett for a new carved gnomon.[6]

As a result of the provision of new lodgings for the queen in the new building, a warrant was issued on 16 February 1688 for the rebuilding of her older privy lodgings on the riverside.[7] Work began almost immediately, and the bricklayer's contract of 10 March refers to work already in hand near the Old Volary.[8] Contracts were made with joiners in March, with the carver Emmett on 25 April and the plasterer on 28 May.[9] The joinery was divided among six firms. One drawing survives with two elevations of the new building; the right-hand one agrees fairly well with the river front in the bird's-eye view.[10] Nevertheless the 'new building' from which Evelyn watched King James's final departure on 18 December[11] was barely completed at the time—the main account runs from February to December—and was to be of use to Mary Stuart rather than to Mary of Modena. In the absence of William III the machinery of government obliged Queen Mary to spend a considerable amount of time there during the early 1690s.

[1] Works 5/42 (Extraord.). Contracts for Sutlery, Works 5/145, pp. 188–90.
[2] Works 5/41 (Extraord.); joiner's contract, Works 5/145, p. 186.
[3] Works 5/42 (Ord.).          [4] *Ibid.*, (Extraord.).                    [5] Works 5/43 (Ord.).
[6] Works 5/42 (Extraord., and May, Ord.).
[7] LC 5/148, p. 112, quoted in *Wren Soc.*, vii, p. 134. First Treasury payment Feb. 1688 (*Cal. Treas. Books 1688–9*, p. 1758).          [8] Works 5/145, pp. 195–6.          [9] *Ibid.*, pp. 200–9.
[10] All Souls, i, 85 (*Wren Soc.*, vii, Pl. xv). The warrant of 16 Feb. 1688 approves the draughts and designs.
[11] See the letter to his son cited above, p. 290, n. 6.

Parts of the foundations of the queen's building have been excavated.[1] The river front had an elevation of six bays in a basement, first floor and blind attic, with a low pitched roof concealed by a balustrade. The bird's-eye view shows six panels in the attic, whereas the preparatory drawing shows four, presumably those 'in the Outside of the Brickwall over the windows in fresco fronting the Thames' painted by Verrio.[2] A further payment was made in August 1691 to Henry Cooke for '2 Pannells in fresco upon the front of the Queen's new lodgings next the Thames'.[3] That these panels concealed the upper part of the first floor is confirmed by Roger North's criticism that 'in exceeding high rooms it is best for them and us to have high windoes square above the others to light the Roof' and Wren's explanation to him that at Whitehall the light reflected from the river would perform this function.[4]

The bird's-eye view appears to show two ridge roofs corresponding to the front and back of the building, with dormers in the west roof facing east towards a central gutter (Pl. 37). The carpenter made a total of 19 pedimented lucerne windows; this figure seems enough for inner dormers on both halves of the roof and a further row at the back on the west side. The main cornice of the river elevation was massive, 2 ft. 4½ in. thick and enriched with flowers between the modillions, and mouldings of lacework and of eggs and anchors. Its length of about 105 ft. allowed a return along the sides of about 5 ft.[5] The mason was also paid for carving the shield with festoons, crown and scrolls in the broken pediment over the centre windows, for six faces in keystones and for four cantilevers under the balcony. The dressings and the basement were of stone while the surface wall was of rubbed and gauged brick.

The elevation drawing is inscribed in pencil 'Front of the Drawing Room'; this was the largest room on the first floor, occupying the northern two-thirds of the river front, lit by four windows and measuring, according to the drawing and to excavations of the basement, about 52 ft. by 29 ft. For this room Edward Strong provided an Egyptian marble chimneypiece; the walls were wainscotted by Charles Hopson with pilasters framing the door and windows. The other principal rooms were the presence chamber, privy chamber and great bedchamber; Emmett carved enrichments for these, for the drawing room and also for the eating room, little bedchamber, dressing room, closet and lobby. Grinling Gibbons carved wooden chimneypieces for the last four costing together £100; he also provided picture frames in most of the rooms and three doorcases in the great bedchamber. His showpieces were in the drawing room, two marble figures 'as big as the life a Crowne and Cushion and a pedistall over the chimney' (£180) and in the great bedchamber 'a Baserleave of Galleth [Goliath] in marble cornice and base' (£110) and '2 marble Boyes and cornucopes and ——' [blank in account] over the chimney.[6] These overmantels might seem not to have pleased William and Mary, for the account for the first quarter of 1689 includes wooden chimneypieces for both rooms. That in the drawing room, however, is likely to have been for a second fireplace since the marble

[1] Drawings made by H.M. Office of Works.

[2] Works 5/42.

[3] Works 5/45 (Ord.). For Cooke see E. Croft-Murray, *Decorative Painting in England 1537–1837*, i (1962), pp. 245–6.

[4] H. M. Colvin, 'Roger North and Sir Christopher Wren', *Architectural Review*, cx (1951), p. 259.

[5] Account of Thomas Hill, mason.

[6] Wrongly connected by Green, *Gibbons*, p. 62, with the Privy Gallery rooms.

piece was cleaned *in situ* in March 1692.[1] Gibbons carved a wooden 'ffreass' around the bedchamber early in 1689 for £70. Some rooms were given coved ceilings; the plasterer's account included alterations to 'characters' and crowns in the ceiling of the little bedchamber, which may have resulted from the change of queen.

One curious feature of the building was a D-shaped court of 54 ft. diameter described in the accounts as the 'compass [i.e. round] court' and confirmed by excavation to have stood at the south-west corner of the building joining it to older buildings on the west (Fig. 23). The enclosing wall was of brick with a stone coping and enriched cornice, and the court was paved in January–March 1689. Alterations were also made to adjacent older buildings, such as joinery (John Heysenbuttel) in lodgings 'on the other side of the circular court' and outside lath and plaster work at an unspecified location.

In 1691 a new terrace garden was begun, projecting into the river about 70 ft. from the walls of the queen's and Volary buildings and about 285 ft. long. It can be seen in the foreground of the bird's-eye view and is shown on a plan of Whitehall of 1804.[2] A plan of a preliminary design shows[3] a different layout and confirms that the terrace was centred on the old passage under the north wing of the Volary building that gave access to the privy water stairs. The site of these stairs was covered by the terrace, and new stairs were built at the outer corners.[4] The mason's contract was signed on 2 November 1691 after several months of preparatory work: a newsletter of 17 July refers to work in hand and gives the information that the débris from the fire of 1691 was used for the foundations.[5]

Work on the terrace was completed by 1693, when further alterations were made to the queen's riverside building.[6] Modifications were made to the joinery, and picture frames were carved by William Emmett, in the great withdrawing room and in what is called the queen's new bedchamber, 'which was the eating room'. The account also includes the rebuilding of the queen's vice-chamberlain's lodgings and the private oratory, and a new staircase to give access to the water stairs. Some or all of these rooms were in the building of three bays abutting on the north end of the queen's building and visible in the view; the latter also shows the 'portico' or covered way running out to the stairs at the corner of the terrace and built simultaneously with it. The pillars for which a number of capitals were made cannot be made to match numerically those visible in the drawing, but a good deal of the passage work is invisible there. The alternative supposition, that the 'New portico to the Waterstairs' of the account was not that shown in the view, is difficult to reconcile with the date of the drawing; their identity is supported by the payment in the final account for the terrace (April 1694) to William Bache for an iron railing over the portico,[7] since one is shown in the drawing.

There are further references to the statuary population of Whitehall. In May

---

[1] Works 5/42 (Ord.). Further alterations were made in 1693 (see below).
[2] *London Survey*, xiii, Pl. 2.      [3] All Souls iv, 59 (*Wren Soc.*, vii, Pl. xvi).
[4] The north-east stair is shown in the bird's-eye view and the 1804 plan; the south-east stair was evidently destroyed before 1804. The preliminary drawing also shows alternatives in pencil for a more elaborate stair in the centre of the terrace.
[5] Contract, Works 5/145, p. 215; Luttrell, *Brief Historical Relation*, ii, 287, iii, 174; Hist. MSS. Comm. *8th Report*, Appendix I, p. 563, quoted *Wren Soc.*, vii, p. 79.
[6] Works 5/46 (Extraord.).      [7] Works 5/47 (Extraord.).

1693 carpenters mended fences in the garden 'where the figures lie'.[1] An account for the queen's building of June–September 1693 includes £4 to Gabriel Cibber for mending four statues in the queen's garden and £3 for mending one in brass, and in August figures were set up in the Volary garden.[2] The accounts of 1701 and 1702 contain a number of references to the movement of statuary and other marble work, some of it new, to Hampton Court, including 'the figure' in St. James's Park which was almost certainly Le Sueur's bronze copy of the Borghese Gladiator now at Windsor.[3]

Between them the fires of 1691 and 1698 virtually destroyed Whitehall Palace. That of 10 April 1691 began 'at the end of the Stone Gallery next the Privy Garden' according to the Works account, and specifically in the lodgings there formerly belonging to the Duchess of Portsmouth. These were burnt out and with them the southern half of the gallery and the lodgings on either side of them.[4] The account begins in April with the extinguishing of the fire over a period of 48 hours, and the repair of windows broken when buildings were blown up in an attempt to contain the fire. The remainder of the Stone Gallery was boarded off and a dry brick wall was built next to the river. The account continues with a more permanent framed partition at the end of the gallery (May 1691) and in later months with a shore against Lord Portland's lodgings 'next the ruins' and repairs to the roof and interior of these and the Earl of Monmouth's rooms. None of the destroyed buildings was replaced.

The fire of 4 January 1698 was yet more serious. The Works books for 1698–9 are lost, but the Ordinary account to the end of March 1698 includes work at the time of the disaster and the initial stages of salvage.[5] Besides a large deployment from Whitehall, help came from seven outside forces. A special payment of £5 was made to a bricklayer named John Evans for working 'in the high window of the Banqueting House against the flame'; this was the window still existing at gallery level in the south end. In 1714 Evans petitioned for some additional reward, claiming that his part in saving the Banqueting House was worth more than beer money; his persistence finally gained him Wren's recommendation for a reward.[6] The fire began 'over the Kings Lodgings' and spread to consume the whole of the palace proper: the riverside buildings, the theatre, the old chapel and all of James II's buildings with the great staircase to the Banqueting House. The front of the queen's building remained as a shell until 1701 when it was taken down.[7] However, the south side of the Volary building and the south end of what remained of the Stone Gallery and adjacent rooms were not damaged beyond repair. These buildings, which were occupied by the Earls of Albemarle and Essex, were reported still standing on 7 January, and on 19 January a project was entertained for fitting up the remains of

---

[1] Works 5/46 (Ord.).

[2] *Ibid.* (Extraord. and Ord.). There was also in the Queen's Building a 'room for the statues' for which joiners made a door in 1688 and carpenters shelves for heads to stand on in 1689 (Works 5/42, Extraord.).

[3] April, Nov., Dec. 1701, Jan. 1702. *London Survey*, xiv, p. 102 and Pl. 2.

[4] Works 5/45 (Extraord.); *Diary of John Evelyn*, v, p. 47; Luttrell, *Brief Historical Relation*, ii, p. 206.

[5] Works 5/49. For descriptions of the fire and damage see *Cal. S.P. Dom. 1698*, pp. 8–15; Luttrell, *Relation*, iv, p. 328.

[6] T 1/175, No. 46; T 1/176, No. 17; printed in *Wren Soc.*, xviii, pp. 165–7 (*Cal. Treas. Papers 1708–14*, pp. 584, 590). Evans had already petitioned for the place of Master Bricklayer (*Cal. Treas. Books 1714*, p. 256).

[7] Works 5/51 (Ord.).

the Volary (Albemarle) building for the king and buildings in the Cockpit area for offices.[1] It is clear from the accounts of January–March that immediate accommodation was adapted in the Cockpit for the Treasury and Council Chamber.[2] On 3 March Narcissus Luttrell reported that Wren was to construct a Council room and five lodgings at the south end of the Banqueting House; this one-storey building, which can be seen in Terasson's print (Pl. 38) and other eighteenth-century views, was included in an Extraordinary account of which there is only a brief Declared version.[3] Luttrell's note that other rebuilding 'will be omitted till the parliament provide for the same' marks the end of serious thoughts of reconstruction.[4] Between July 1698 and March 1702 the Albemarle rooms were augmented by a new kitchen, laundry and other rooms.[5]

With the abandonment of Whitehall as a palace there was an increase in the mingling of official and private quarters in the remaining buildings and in the leasing of buildings beyond the purview of the Works.[6] Early in 1703, after the death of the Duchess of Richmond, old Richmond House on the river side of the Bowling Green was taken over for the Earl of Nottingham as Secretary of State; in 1708 it was refitted for the controllers of army accounts.[7] In 1705–6 the area around the fountain in the garden was enclosed and added to the house in the Bowling Green occupied by the Secretaries for Scotland, the Earls of Loudoun and Mar, who continued to live there after the abolition of their office in 1707.[8] A different procedure occurred on the Cockpit side, where the upper rooms of the Danby Treasury building, fitted up in 1709 for the Duke of Queensberry as Secretary of State, were absorbed into the Treasury after his death in 1711.[9]

Subsequently much of the palace site was leased for building. One of the earliest lessees was Vanbrugh, recently turned architect and not yet in the Works, who obtained permission in July 1700 to build a house, at his own expense but making use of demolition materials, on the site of the lodgings of the vice-chamberlain of the Household.[10]

---

[1] *Cal. S.P. Dom. 1698*, pp. 18–19; *Cal. Treas. Books 1697–8*, p. 228; *London Survey*, xiii, pp. 180, 189; Works 6/2, f. 86.

[2] Works 5/49 (Ord.); *London Survey*, xiv, p. 29.

[3] Luttrell, *Relation*, iv, p. 351. E 351/3310. An abridged account of expenditure on repairs to Whitehall between 1697 and 1700 is among Sir Stephen Fox's papers: B.M. Add. MS. 51321, ff. 25–6.

[4] On 20 January 1698 Luttrell had reported that Wren had surveyed the site in accordance with the king's desire for a 'noble palace' (*Relation* iv, p. 334). An outline survey of the site appears on the rebuilding plan at All Souls (Vol. V, 2, *Wren Soc.* viii, Pl. ii).

[5] Works 5/52 (Extraord.); contract for kitchen 40 × 60 ft., July 1698, Works 5/145, pp. 223–6. Albemarle returned to Holland on the death of William III but the house was still in his possession in 1708 (*London Survey*, xiii, p. 181).

[6] The changes in occupancy and consequent building works are dealt with in *London Survey*, xiii, xiv and xvi.

[7] Richmond House was new in 1662, occupied and enlarged by the Duke about 1667–8 (*London Survey*, xiii, pp. 243–6; Luttrell, *Relation*, vi, pp. 406–7).

[8] This house was built *c.* 1688–93 on the site of two houses of the 1670s (*London Survey*, xiii, pp. 240–1; Luttrell, *Relation*, vi, p. 3).

[9] *London Survey*, xiv, p. 29. These rooms had previously, in 1706, been arranged for the Commissioners of Union, and in that same year Wren suggested that they should be used for the State Paper Office which was inadequately housed over the Holbein Gate (*Cal. Treas. Papers 1702–7*, pp. 455–6; *Cal. Treas. Books 1705–6*, pp. 699, 750). On 9 January 1707 Wren further reported the feasibility of a plan to house the papers on the ground floor of the Old Tennis Court building fronting The Street, and moving the Secretary of State's rooms upstairs (T 1/101, art. 4, ff. 13 and (plan) 15; *Cal. Treas. Papers 1702–7*, p. 483) but this was not carried out.

[10] *Cal. Treas. Books 1700–1*, p. 48; T 27/16/324, 13 March 1700/1. These documents are quoted in *Wren Soc.*, iv, pp. 74–5 as a year earlier; see also *London Survey*, xvi, pp. 168–9.

The idea of a regular, modern and uniform Whitehall was conceived by Inigo Jones and Charles I in the late 1630s and lasted longer than the old buildings. John Webb, who had started with Jones's designs, produced new drawings in the 1660s.[1] One of these is dated 17 October 1661: it records a scheme related to and reduced from one made in Charles I's last years. It was made at a time when Webb (although as yet without any official standing in the Works) was already assisting Denham with designs for the new palace at Greenwich.[2] Webb also produced several undated drawings for a smaller palace with the Banqueting House doubled on either side of a central portico to form the middle side of a court facing the river.[3] This arrangement is similar to that projected by Webb for Greenwich, and both schemes may have been conceived about the same time. The Whitehall scheme can be related to a number of drawings in the Wren Collection at All Souls, which can be presumed to have come from Wren's office but only one of which is datable.[4] This shows half a portico and the end of the Banqueting House; it implies a similar doubling of the latter and the details of the drawing can be related to an account for a model façade made in January–June 1665 but charged for in November 1667.[5] It must therefore have been drawn late in 1664 and recalls Evelyn's note of 28 October 1664 describing how the king himself drew for him 'the plot for the future building of White-hall'. If the customary ascription of the drawing to Wren is correct, it would imply that Wren, like Webb three years earlier, was working on Whitehall without any post in the Works.[6]

The fire of 1698 cleared the site for wholesale rebuilding, and a number of schemes were produced. The best known and probably the earliest are the two sets of drawings at All Souls College now generally attributed to Wren.[7] The first and larger scheme is for a number of courts centred on the Banqueting House on the lines of the projects for Charles I; the second derives from the schemes of the 1660s. The larger scheme also includes a new parliament building north of Westminster Hall, linked to the palace by a long ceremonial corridor.[8] These drawings were probably made very soon after the fire, before ideas of rebuilding faded and certainly before William III's death early in 1702, since the relief decoration contains references to him. Luttrell reported in October 1702 that Queen Anne intended to rebuild Whitehall,[9] and intermittent public interest in the idea can be found for some years. A number of other schemes for palaces are recorded, all from outside the Works, some by foreigners, and indeed not all of them certainly for Whitehall.[10]

[1] M. Whinney, 'John Webb's Drawings for Whitehall Palace', *Walpole Society*, xxxi (1946), esp. pp. 88–95.  [2] Whinney, *op. cit.*, Pl. xx(a); see above, p. 140.
[3] Whinney, *op. cit.*, Pls. xxi, xxii(a), xxiv, xxvi(b) and pp. 87, 89, 93–4.
[4] Vol. ii, 73 (*Wren Soc.*, vii, Pl. x. The scheme and its implications are discussed by K. Downes, 'Wren and Whitehall in 1664', *Burlington Magazine*, cxiii (1971), pp. 89–92.
[5] Works 5/10 (Ord.), Nov.
[6] *Diary of John Evelyn*, iii, pp. 386–7. Another drawing at All Souls with the Banqueting House doubled (ii, 106, *Wren Soc.*, vii, Pl. xi) is more likely to date from the same period than from the reign of James II as suggested in *Wren Soc.*, vii, p. 250.
[7] All Souls v, 1–9 and 10–14 (*Wren Soc.*, viii, Pls. i–x). Further drawings are All Souls ii, suppl. nos. 1–3 (from the Bute sale, Sotheby's 23 May 1951, lot 16); Soane Museum, Hampton Court volume, no. 13x (*Wren Soc.*, vi, Pl. li (left)). Recent discussions of the schemes include J. Summerson, *Architecture in Britain 1530–1830* (1963), pp. 161–2; K. Downes, *Christopher Wren* (1971), pp. 102–10. See also E. F. Sekler, *Wren* (1956), pp. 175–8; J. H. V. Davies, 'Nicholas Hawksmoor', *R.I.B.A. Journal*, lxix (1962), pp. 368ff.
[8] The elevation of this is All Souls ii, suppl. no. 1.
[9] Luttrell, *Relation*, v, p. 222.    [10] K. Downes, *English Baroque Architecture*, pp. 46–9.

## 3. THE BANQUETING HOUSE

While the Banqueting House was no longer used for masques, it continued to be a ceremonial hall. The accounts record annually the preparations for the Royal Maundy. In November 1662 ledges were put up for hangings round the room and in December a large number of curtain rods were provided.[1] On the queen's birthday (16 November) in 1664 a chariot was driven several times round the interior.[2] In April 1667 carpenters were paid for tables and a music stage for the St. George's Day feast of the Order of the Garter which was that year held at Whitehall.[3] In 1668–9 the construction of the new gallery (p. 272) included an improved staircase to the north end of the building.[4] In September 1674 and again in May 1677 rope dancing was staged there.[5]

In 1678 the gallery, described as 'much decayed', was repaired and strengthened; in May Richard Ryder, Master Carpenter, worked a sample portion and Phillips carved one cantilever, evidently as a replacement, and in June the repair was completed as contract work by John Syrat.[6] In 1686–8 the nine Rubens panels were taken down, cleaned and restored by the painter Parry Walton, and replaced.[7] In September 1688 Streater charged for cleaning and gilding the ceiling, cornice and frieze, and in the same years the gutters outside were repaired and renewed.[8]

The room served a variety of occasional purposes; material from the old Privy Gallery had been stored there in 1685 and there was a payment in June 1693 to masons for removing chimneypieces stored there.[9] In January 1695 the room was fitted for Queen Mary's lying in state.[10]

In March 1695 carpenters were paid for boarding up ten windows next to the street.[11] Since each floor has seven windows the blocking must have been on more than one level and it was presumably symmetrical from the ends. After the 1698 fire all the windows, upper and lower, on both sides were boarded up.[12] This was an emergency measure, but that of 1695 may not have been intended as permanent. Terasson in 1713 shows all the basement windows apparently bricked up from the outside and the lower halves of the main lower end windows also blocked (Pl. 38). These changes and the replacement of the original four-light windows by sashes presumably formed part of the conversion of the Banqueting House into the Chapel Royal, an operation which was reported by Luttrell four days after the fire, and

[1] Works 5/3.                                    [2] *Cal. S.P. Dom. 1664–5*, p. 74.
[3] Works 5/10 (Ord.). The occasion is described by both Pepys and Evelyn; the former thought its purpose was to impress the Swedish Ambassadors.
[4] Works 5/13; *London Survey*, xiii, p. 126.
[5] Works 5/23, 5/29 (Ord.).
[6] Works 5/30; the contract is not extant.
[7] Warrant for scaffolding, LC 5/147, pp. 151, 306. Accounts for scaffolding only. Walton received £212 in Oct. 1688 (Akerman, *Secret Services*, p. 206). See also *Wren Soc.*, xviii, pp. 54, 67.
[8] Works 5/42 (Ord.), 5/41 (Ord.), Aug.–Sept. 1687, March 1688.
[9] Works 5/46 (Ord.).
[10] Luttrell, *Relation*, iii, p. 420.
[11] Works 5/47 (Ord.). The fenestration of the Banqueting House is discussed by P. Palme, *Triumph of Peace* (1956), pp. 201–19; J. Charlton, *The Banqueting House, Whitehall* (1964), p. 45.
[12] Works 5/49.

completed during the year.[1] Queen Anne's intention of restoring it to state use, reported by Luttrell early in 1702, came to nothing.[2]

In the course of the eighteenth century some extensive repairs were found to be necessary both to the fabric and to the painted ceiling. As one of the principal works of Inigo Jones the Banqueting House was a building of special interest to the Georgian Board of Works, and as such it received more attention than its function as a Chapel Royal might otherwise have ensured. In October 1726 the Board obtained leave to put up a scaffold in order to examine the state of the ceiling, and in July 1728 wrote to the Treasury about the 'decayed state' of the roof, 'which upon examination we find to be so very bad that it is dangerous for people to congregate there'. They asked for authority to spend £185 on setting up a scaffold which would support the roof for the present and also enable them 'to see better what repairs will be wanting'.[3] Four years later they reported that 'on taking down the pictures . . . we found the ends of the beams . . so very much decayed, by the badness of the covering that we are of opinion they should be thoroughly repaired and the lead new cast'. The pictures themselves were 'in so bad a way that unless they are soon new lined, cleaned &c. we fear they will be in danger of totally perishing. . . . We also humbly acquaint your Lordships that the Masks, Festoons, and other ornaments painted all round the room in yellow and heightened with Gold are almost quite defaced.'[4] The estimate of £1100 was accepted by the Treasury, and the work of restoration was carried out by William Kent, who in 1728 had been appointed inspector of paintings in the royal palaces. In January 1734 the king and queen paid a visit to the building in order to inspect the paintings from the scaffold, and complimented Kent on his handiwork.[5]

In 1748 one of the side panels was cleaned and mended by Stephen Wright,[6] and in 1776–7 the paintings were again restored by J. B. Cipriani. The circumstances of this last repair are not clear, for the Board's minutes record only that on 26 April 1776 'Mr. Cipriani acquainted the Board that he was now at leisure to proceed with the painting of the ceiling at Whitehall Chapel', and that on 28 November 1777 the Board 'went to Whitehall Chapel to view the painting which Mr. Cipriani had compleated'.[7]

Meanwhile nothing had been done to the exterior of the building since its erection, and by 1761 the frieze of masks and swags was stated to be 'soe corroded as to be scarce intelligible'.[8] It was, however, the basement which first received attention. In 1773 the Board pointed out to the Treasury that its stone facing was 'greatly decayed owing to its having been originally built with soft stone', and received

---

[1] Luttrell, *Relation*, iv, p. 329. See *London Survey*, xiii, pp. 122, 129; Works 5/50 (Ord.). The main account is only found in short Declared form in E 351/3310.    [2] Luttrell, *Relation*, v. p. 159.
[3] Works 4/3, 25 Oct. 1726; Works 6/15, p. 172.    [4] T 56/18, pp. 394, 402.
[5] The occasion was recorded by Kent himself at the end of a MS. of Ovid's *Metamorphoses* now in the Bodleian Library (MS. Rawlinson D. 540):' The 12th day of January 1733/4 the King & Queen came to the Banquiting House at Whitehall, and came upon the scaffold forty foot high to see the paintings of Ruben's, that I had restor'd—his Majesty was pleas'd to tell me I had done them exceeding well the Queen told me I not only deserv'd thanks from the King but to all lovers of Painting'.
[6] AO 1/2458/179, a payment of £48 10s. to Stephen Wright for 'cleaning and mending one of the side panels to the ceiling of Rubens in the Banquitting House and strowing pounded glass on thick colour on the back'.
[7] Works 4/15, 26 April 1776, 28 Nov. 1777.
[8] *London & its Environs* (R. & J. Dodsley, 1761), vi, p. 315.

authority to reface it with Portland stone at an estimated cost of £510. The work was carried out in 1774 at a cost of £524.[1]


## 4. THE PALACE GATEWAYS


The inconvenience to wheeled traffic caused by the two gateways across Whitehall is obvious, and both were demolished in the course of the eighteenth century. At Westminister the Great Gate between King Street and New Palace Yard was taken down in 1707, and the growing use of coaches by Members of Parliament and others meant that sooner or later there would be a demand for the removal of the two gateways which obstructed the road between King Street and Charing Cross. In 1718 the House of Commons appointed a Committee 'to consider of proper methods for preventing the inconveniences to the Members of Parliament in their coming to and going from this House'.[2] Among those consulted by the Committee were the Officers of the Works, who gave it as their opinion that 'the Gate next to the Banquetting House cannot be made wide enough for Coaches to pass, but must be taken down to give sufficient roome, the expence of which as to what relates to the building only, will not be considerable, the materialls being worth rather more than [what] the charge of taking down the Gateway will amount to'. As for the King Street gateway, they thought that it could be 'inlarged to a proper wideness for Coaches to pass' at a cost of £150.[3] The outcome was a humble address asking His Majesty 'to give such directions, that the gates in the passage between Whitehall and King Street, Westminster, may either be taken down, or made wider', and in July 1719 the Lord Chamberlain was instructed to get the Office of Works to pull down the northern gateway if it could be done without undue expense and before the next session of Parliament.[4] There was, however, one member of the Board who was determined to preserve the gateway as an ancient and picturesque relic of Whitehall. This was Vanbrugh, who had the ear of the Lord Chamberlain, and was, after Benson's disgrace, in a strong position to press his point. On 6 August he wrote to Newcastle to express the surprise felt by himself and others that 'there shou'd be no other Expedient found to make way for Coaches &c, than destroying one of the Greatest Curiostys there is in London. . . . The Chancellr. of the Excheqr. said much of this to me last night being entirely of opinion it ought not to be destroy'd, if an other Expedient can be found'. The expedient he proposed was to take down the buildings which extended eastwards from the gate to the Banqueting House, and to make a new and wider road by taking in part of the Privy Garden.[5] Vanbrugh's point of view prevailed, for on 31 August the Board informed the Treasury that by taking away the flat inner arch the passage could be widened sufficiently to allow two coaches to pass one another 'without weakening, disfiguring, or pulling down' the

[1] Works 6/18, pp. 329–30; Works 4/15, 16 July 1773, 27 Jan. 1775; Works 5/142, year 1774–5.
[2] *Commons' Journals*, vol. 19, pp. 22–3, 37.
[3] Works 6/7, p. 117.                                    [4] Works 6/7, p. 126.
[5] *Complete Works of Sir John Vanbrugh*, vol. iv *The Letters*, ed. G. F. Webb, pp. 114–16.

gateway itself. In the case of the southern gateway similar results could be obtained by cutting away the jambs and inserting corbels to carry the arches.[1] Although these proposals were accepted by the Treasury, nothing appears to have been done until 1723, when fresh instructions were received. These were to pull down the southern gateway, and to set back the wall of the Privy Garden in the way suggested by Vanbrugh.[2] The southern gateway formed part of a house occupied by the Earl of Clarendon, and this was resumed by the Crown as a preliminary to its demolition.[3] The Office of Works was also authorised to demolish the gun platform which faced north immediately to the east of the northern gate. As for the latter, its arch was to be 'cleared off the floor or segment that now cutts the same so as the passage through that arch may be open and clear as at first when it was built'.[4] It was found, however, that the outer arches 'did not go thro' the thickness of the wall', so it was necessary to turn 'two sufficient brick arches' in order to support the gateway.[5] The destruction of the southern gateway divided the Earl of Clarendon's house into two, one part of which now stood in isolation on the east side of the widened street facing onto the curtailed Privy Garden, while the other remained on the west side of the street facing east. The eastern portion was fitted up for the Commissioners of Trade and Plantations (who since 1698 had been located on the Cockpit side of Whitehall in rooms that were now granted to the Bishop of London), while the western one was allocated to Horatio Walpole, the Auditor and Surveyor-General of H.M. Revenues in America, who said that he was 'in very great want of roome to keep the books and other accounts relating to the revenues of His Majesty's dominions in America, which are grown very voluminous, as allso for transacting the business of his said office'.[6] The cost of the whole operation amounted to £3945.[7] It is of some importance in the history of Whitehall, for it was the beginning of the process which in the course of the next hundred years was to transform the constricted way through the old palace into a single broad thoroughfare all the way from Charing Cross to the Houses of Parliament.

Meanwhile the 'Holbein Gateway' remained as a partial obstruction to the flow of traffic. Once the improvements effected farther south by the Westminster Bridge Commissioners were completed it was inevitable that this relic of the past should disappear. In 1755 the Treasury asked the Board to consider whether it could be taken down and rebuilt somewhere in the vicinity. The Board's reply was that the 'ornaments, battlements and several other parts of it' were 'so decayed, that if it be taken down, rebuilt, and restored to its ancient form, and placed at the end of the new street leading from Westminster Bridge, which is the properest place we can think of, the expence will amount to about the sum of £1374'.[8] This was evidently more than the Treasury was prepared to spend, and the case for demolition

---

[1] Works 6/7, pp. 126–8.

[2] The new wall can be seen in Canaletto's well-known view of Whitehall from Richmond House, painted in 1746. It was built of brick, with stone pilasters to the street and brick ones to the gardens, and was to be 11 ft. high.

[3] For the history of this house, and the topography of Whitehall in general, see *London Survey*, vol. xiii. Lord Clarendon received £6000 from the Privy Purse in compensation (B.M., Add. MS. 34327, p. 19).

[4] Works 6/15, p. 3.  [5] Works 4/2, 10 Sept. 1723.

[6] Works 6/15, p. 10.  [7] Works 6/15, p. 73.

[8] Works 6/17, p. 135ᵛ.

was strengthened by a complaint from Sir Matthew Featherstonehaugh, who was then building what is now Dover House, that the proximity of this 'ruinous gateway' made it impossible for him to clear away an old building on his own site 'for fear of endangering part of that side of the gateway to which it is joined'. The State Papers which were preserved in the upper storey were accordingly removed elsewhere, the lessee of the lower room was given notice to quit, and on 21 June 1759 the Board of Works was authorised to demolish 'that obstruction in the way to both Houses of Parliment'.[1] In 1760 some at least of the old materials were sold for £58.[2] According to J. T. Smith, however, the stones and ornamental features of the gateway were begged by the Duke of Cumberland, who intended to re-erect it as a feature at the end of the Long Walk in Windsor Great Park, of which he was Ranger.[3] Although there is no reference to the duke in the Board's minutes, there can be little doubt that Smith's information was correct, for he reproduces a design made by the duke's architect, Thomas Sandby, for the reconstruction of the gateway with the addition of supporting wings. The duke's intentions were never carried out, but some of the ornamental features were incorporated in lodges and other park buildings at Windsor.[4]

# WINCHESTER PALACE

LATE IN 1682 Charles II ordered preparations to begin for what was to prove the last in the series of palace-constructions which he entrusted to the Office of Works. His first recorded visit to Winchester was in early September of that year, and it must have been on that occasion that he decided to demolish the medieval castle on the high ground to the west, just outside the city wall, and erect a new palace on its site. In the following month expenses were incurred 'for surveying and measuring the Ground att Winchester Castle', when Sir Christopher Wren, Surveyor General of the Works, and John Scarborough, later appointed Clerk of the Works at Winchester, paid two visits to the city with a brickmaker.[5]

It is not entirely clear why the king felt in need of a new palace outside London, at a time when Windsor was newly complete and Newmarket was his favourite resort for country sports. Although the serious fire which damaged the town of Newmarket in March 1683 did not destroy the royal house there, Evelyn considered

[1] Works 6/17, pp. 150, 154, 188.                    [2] Works 4/12, 8 May 1760.
[3] J. T. Smith, *Antiquities of Westminster* (1837), p. 21.
[4] Two of the terra-cotta medallions now at Hampton Court were among the portions of the gateway formerly incorporated in buildings at Windsor by Sandby. See Hist. Mon. Comm., *Middlesex*, p. xxxiii. Another version of Sandby's design for reconstructing the gateway at Windsor is in the Royal Library (Oppé no. 167).
[5] Works 5/36, f. 101.

that the fire 'made the King more earnest to render Winchester the seat of his Autumnal field diversions for the future, . . . infinitely indeed preferable to New-Market, for Prospect, aire, pleasure, & provisions'.[1] Other early commentators agree that Winchester was intended as a 'hunting-seat'.[2] Defoe, however, while allowing that the king's design 'would certainly have made that Part of the Country, the New-market of the ages to come', added with justice that it included 'a noble Palace, sufficient like Windsor, for a summer residence of the whole Court'.[3] It was with the whole Court that Charles, during the last two years of his life, visited Winchester, even though the building of his palace was far from finished. In 1683 the Court spent almost the whole month of September there, the king lodging with Dr. Beeson, the queen with the Dean of Winchester, Dr. Megot.[4] On 21 September the Earl of Sunderland reported to Sir Leoline Jenkins in London: 'We are like to be here twice a year, the King growing fonder of his building and the country every day', and in 1684 the king not only spent three or four days in June at Winchester, but returned with the Court for a month, from 26 August to 25 September.[5] Charles was certainly anxious to have his palace built with the utmost speed. Roger North's story of the king's impatience[6] is amply supported by the records of construction, which was, so far as it went, exceptionally expeditious.

Wren, given his first opportunity to design a complete new palace, conceived a building round three sides of a courtyard open on the east side where the land dropped and the view opened over the city and the cathedral. At the junctions of the three ranges a thickening allowed for two small internal courtyards. This stepped arrangement made the plan strongly reminiscent of Versailles as first enlarged, by Louis Le Vau, for Louis XIV. Wren's first elevation design has a convex pavilion roof in the centre, after the French fashion, and in its handling of the high ground storey and the diminutive portico attached to the centre of the principal storey, has a surface prettiness which is also typical of Versailles.[7] The executed design was simpler and stronger, and must have been inspired by the king's earlier abortive palace, for John Webb's design for Greenwich had the central feature, a large cupola over an attached giant portico, with a grand staircase inside, which was adopted by Wren.[8] For the centre of each of the three outer facades Wren designed a giant three-bay portico, giving scale to the three-storeyed ranges, which were otherwise simply handled, the brick walling enlivened by Portland stone for the window surrounds, the rusticated angle quoins and the balustraded parapet which made a continuous crown to the building. Three-quarter columns also marked the entrances

---

[1] Evelyn, *Diary*, iv, p. 341.
[2] *Parentalia* (1750), p. 325. Cf. *The Journeys of Celia Fiennes*, ed. C. Morris (1949), p. 47; J. Macky, *Journey through England*, ii, p. 19.
[3] D. Defoe, *A Tour through England and Wales*, Everyman edition 1928, i, p. 185.
[4] *Cal. S.P. Dom. 1683* (2), p. 352.
[5] *Cal. S.P. Dom. 1683* (2), pp. 410-11; N. Luttrell, *Brief Historical Relation*, i, pp. 315–16.
[6] Above, p. 23.
[7] East elevation drawing in the Winchester Museum (reproduced in J. Summerson, *Architecture in Britain 1530-1830* 4th ed. 1963, pl. 98A). The only complete surviving plan, *Wren Soc.* vii, pl. 1, corresponds with this early design.
[8] The cupola is mentioned in *Parentalia* (1750) p. 325. Its exact form is not known, since the 18th-century engravings (reproduced in *Wren Soc.* vii, pl. iv and p. 231) are inconsistent with one another and with the building as otherwise recorded, although Milner's (Pl. 41B) is said to have been 'copied from a coloured drawing, made by the architect himself'.

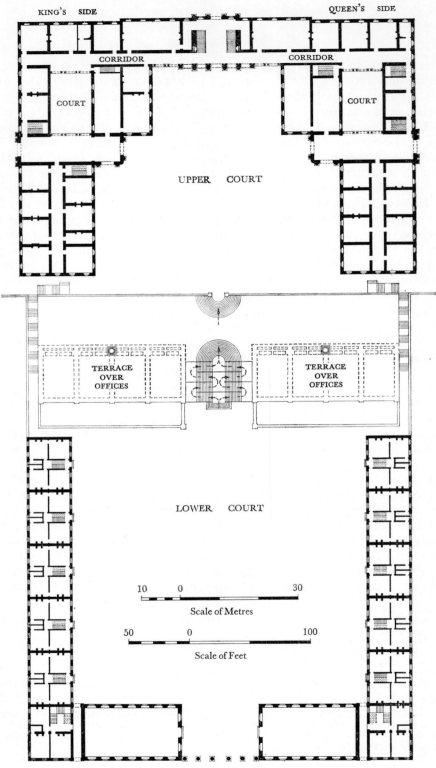

KING'S SIDE            QUEEN'S SIDE

CORRIDOR        CORRIDOR

COURT                COURT

UPPER COURT

TERRACE OVER OFFICES          TERRACE OVER OFFICES

LOWER COURT

10    0           30

Scale of Metres

50    0           100

Scale of Feet

Fig. 25 (see opposite).

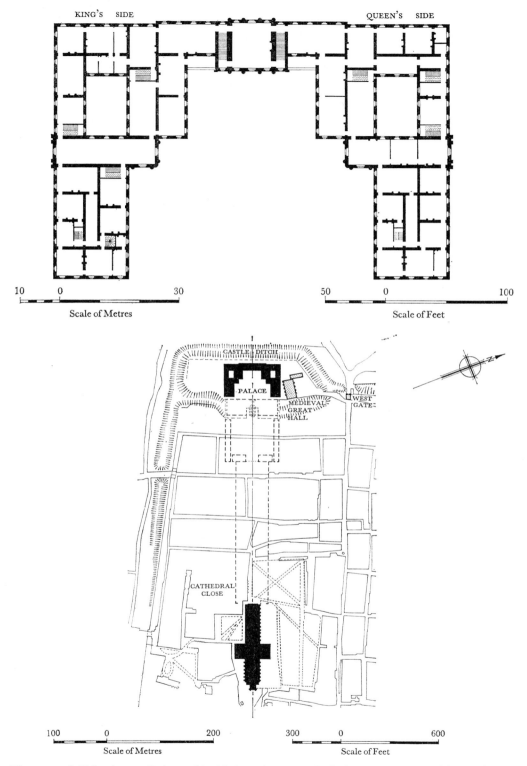

KING'S SIDE

QUEEN'S SIDE

10    0            30

Scale of Metres

50    0          100

Scale of Feet

CASTLE DITCH

PALACE

WEST GATE

MEDIEVAL GREAT HALL

CATHEDRAL CLOSE

100    0      200

Scale of Metres

300    0      600

Scale of Feet

Figs. 25–26. Winchester Palace: Sir Christopher Wren's design reconstructed from plans at All Souls College (*Wren Society*, vii, plate i), the Bodleian Library (MS Top. Gen. a. 7, No. 8) and the R.I.B.A. Drawings Collection. Ground floor on left, upper floor above.

from the courtyard to the system of internal loggia-corridors, which were a remarkable feature of Wren's planning of the ground floor (Fig. 25).

The plan, unlike the elevation, seems not to have been significantly changed after the preliminary design stage. The piano nobile was to be devoted to five sets of state apartments. The king's side was to include, besides the state suite of presence chamber, privy chamber, drawing room, bedchamber and cabinet, and a chapel, also a council-chamber with ante-room, closet and privy gallery. There was to be a somewhat curtailed queen's side with a second chapel, suites for the Duke and Duchess of York and a further full state suite presumably intended for the king's mistress, the Duchess of Portsmouth. How the suites were to be distributed about the principal storey it has not been possible to determine precisely. Below the council rooms were to be the secretaries' rooms, and the queen's ladies and the servants of the duke and duchess under their respective suites. 'Under the Side next the Privy Garden', however, 'as his Majesty shall direct'. On the top storey Wren envisaged sixty rooms 'for accommodation of the Family'.[1]

The main block was placed within the confines of the medieval castle site, to the east of which the ground dropped sharply, and here, at a lower level, long ranges of lodgings were planned to enclose an outer courtyard. They were to be linked to the main block by an elaborate flight of thirty steps, flanked by eight kitchens on either side.

The main outline of the palace's building history can be made out from the contract book and the single declared account. The latter is brief and even incomplete, for the death of Philip Packer, the Paymaster, in December 1686, when many bills were still unpaid, greatly inconvenienced the auditors, and the account was not finally declared until 21 July 1709.[2]

Negotiations to obtain vacant possession of the site of Winchester Castle were initiated on 8 February 1682/3, and the following day a royal warrant was issued for letters of privy seal authorising the Treasury to issue £36,000 for the purchase of land and the building of the palace.[3] On 28 February the Grand Jury of the county of Southampton granted the king 'all their right, title and interest in their county hall and the ground thereto belonging, they being assured of his intention to build a palace where formerly the castle stood, in which he cannot proceed without the entire use and possession of the said hall and ground, and he having promised to rebuild another place for the accommodation of the county'.[4] To clear the site the entire castle, already ruinous, seems to have been demolished with the exception of the great hall itself. Labourers were paid for 'pulling downe the East Wall of the Castle, for digging, and Wheeling away the ffoundation of the Castle, throwing downe the wall of the West End of the Countie Hall, . . . pulling down the North Wall of the Castle, and the black Tower, the East wall joyning to the Chapple, digging downe the south east Bulwarke, the Crowne of the Arch, at the North East

---

[1] For the preliminary plan see p. 305 note 7. A half-plan of the *piano nobile*, probably as executed, is in the R.I.B.A. AF 2/17; a plan of the foundations of the main block, is in *Wren Soc.* vii, pl. ii. The disposition of the ground floor is known from a late 18th-century plan, Bodleian MS. Top. Gen. a.7, no. 8 (reproduced in *The Country Seat*, ed. H. Colvin and J. Harris, 1970, fig. 35). The schedule of rooms drawn up by Wren is printed in *Wren Soc.* vii, pp. 17–19.

[2] The contract book is in the library of the R.I.B.A., MS. 725:71), published in part in *Wren Soc.* vii, pp. 22–67. The declared account is P.R.O. AO 1/2493/401 and E 351/3460. See also Works 6/1,

[3] *Cal. Treas. Books* vii, pp. 705, 707.                    [4] *Cal. S.P. Dom. 1683* (1), p. 84.

Tower, digging and Wheeling away the Call House wall, and a wall at the southeast Angle of the Keepe to make way for the midle line'.[1]

For supervising the construction of the new palace Sir Christopher Wren received, by a warrant of 13 December 1683, £500 per annum, a salary in line with Hugh May's at Windsor. Wren was also paid travelling expenses for 78 days during the period of construction. Since the salary was backdated only to the preceding 29 September, it did not represent payment for Wren's labours in designing the palace, or indeed during the laying of foundations.[2] Wren's design was embodied in a model, executed by the joiners Bongrace Jack and Roger Davies. Celia Fiennes saw the model at Winchester in 1696 and thought it 'very fine'; but shortly afterwards it must have been removed to Kensington, since the Kensington accounts for November 1697 include an entry for 'makeing a bottom for the Modell of the Kings house at Winton and a Case to Enclose it'.[3] This is the last that is heard of it.

In January 1682/3 arrangements were made with the farmer, Robert Forder, to dig brick earth in Painter's Field, on the south side of the city, from which Nicholas Goodwin of Hammersmith and Nicholas Rufford of Islington were to make two million bricks. The same brickmakers contracted, as work progressed, to make a further 700,000 stock bricks and 1,200,000 place bricks in the following November, and in November 1684 one million stock bricks and two million place bricks, on land in Painter's Field, or in Oxford Close belonging to Dulcibella Ford.[4]

These three contracts correspond with the phases of construction. The foundations of the main block of the palace were laid during 1683. By their contract dated 13 March, Christopher Kempster and Edward Strong, 'Citizens and Masons of London', undertook to complete this task by the following Michaelmas, raising the walls as high as the water-table, using 'the old Ashler of the Castle, being Isle of Wight Stone', and new Isle of Wight stone as necessary, and Portland stone for the cellar windows. The contract for Portland stone was not signed until 9 July, but the contractors, Thomas Wise Jnr. and Thomas Gilbert, undertook to deliver stone by the end of the following month, and it was to include 300 quoin-stones and stones ready prepared 'to a mould for Cornices, Columns, Capitolls, or the like'. Everything was certainly ready for the next phase of construction by the end of 1683, for the five teams of masons and the single bricklayers' team contracted to begin on 2 January 1683/4 the raising of the walls. The finishing date specified in these contracts was the end of the following July. Maurice Emmett, the Master Bricklayer, who had the bricklayer's contract, was due to begin only on 1 March, yet he too contracted to complete his work by the end of July. He undertook to keep at least thirty-two bricklayers and sixteen labourers on the job, and estimated the cost at £996.

The masons divided the work between them as follows: Christopher Kempster contracted to execute the masonry of the west front, for £608 13s. 2d., William Wise and Samuel Fulkes the north front, and the end and inner side of the north wing for

---

[1] AO 1/2493/401 (E 351/3460) (labourers' taskwork).
[2] *Cal. Treas. Books* vii, p. 985; AO 1/4293/401 (E 351/3460).
[3] AO 1/2493/401 (E 351/3460) (joiners' taskwork, payments of £12 1s. to Jack and £17 6s. 4d. to Davies, and a reward of £66 12s. 7d. to Jack 'for makeing severall Modells of his Majesties house'; Celia Fiennes, *loc. cit.*; Works 5/49 (payment to Alexander Fort). See also p. 312, n. 2 below.
[4] *Wren Soc.* vii, pp. 22–67, *passim*, for this and the two following paragraphs.

£451 3s. 9d., John Thompson the south front and wing for the same price, William Bird the front and inner side of the south wing, west of and including the intermediate columnar porch, for £444 7s. ½d., and Edward Strong the central section of the east front continuing along the inner side of the north wing as far as and including the columnar porch there, but omitting the central portico itself, which was not at this stage contracted for. Strong's estimate was for £828 1s. 8½d. and included parts of the cross corridors and small courtyards, which he shared with the other contractors, whose estimates thus included this extra work. The contracts stated that the giant order was to be Composite, with an enriched entablature having modillions and panels of roses, and that the small order of coupled columns was to be Doric. Parts of the Composite capitals, in the Winchester City Museum, are the only identifiable remains of the palace to survive today.

The wording of the declared account is precise enough to allow one to say that the contract prices proved to have been underestimated. Thus Thompson received £722 15s. 2d. for executing the masonry of the south front, Bird £607 11s. 10½d. for his task on the south wing in spite of its being left incomplete, and Wise and Fulkes no less than £1207 2s. 6½d. On the other hand the payment of £2726 11s. 11¼d. to Kempster for 'the ffoundations . . . at severall Angles and Walls' and the £1378 5s. 9d. paid to Strong for 'makeing Pillasters and Collumnes makeing Windowes and ornaments on severall Pillasters &c. Carving the top of the Capitalls &c.' do not allow any comparison to be made. The payment to Strong may include the six columns of the central portico, which eighteenth-century views show to have been erected, although the relevant contract is not preserved. But the three-quarter columns of the intermediate porches appear not to have been fully erected.[1] At any rate the porches and the portico, with the grand staircase behind it, in spite of being the major architectural accents, destined to be crowned by cupolas, were clearly omitted for the time being in the drive to make the palace habitable as fast as possible. The six white marble columns presented to Charles by the Duke of Tuscany for the staircase were laid up in the stores.[2]

Contract dates must have been fairly successfully adhered to, for by the death of Charles II on 6 February 1684/5 the masons and bricklayers had long completed their tasks so that the carpenters and plumbers had all but roofed in the building. James Groves, the principal carpenter, received £2451 14s. 4¼d. for '. . . raising ffloors, Roofs, and door-cases, Windows, fflooring . . about the said building', and the plumbers too received substantial sums, Matthew Roberts and John Haley £1809 15s. 2d. and Charles Atherton, the Sergeant Plumber, £1755 14s. ¾d.[3] Indeed on the Sunday before his death the king could use the 'fatal expression': 'I shall be most happy this week, for my building will be covered with lead'.[4] Instructions issued on 11 March 1685 show that little remained to be done to the roof: some of the flashes had not been laid down and some lead required to be seamed, but that was all.[5]

---

[1] See the views by Buck and Peak reproduced in *Wren Soc.* vii, pl. iii. An 18th-century sketch recently acquired by the Winchester Museum shows a closer view of the central portico.
[2] J. Macky, *Journey through England* (1722), ii, p. 21; R.I.B.A. MS. 725:171, quoted in *Wren Soc.* vii, p. 58.
[3] AO 1/2493/401 (E 351/3460).
[4] *Memoires of Thomas, Earl of Ailesbury* (1890) i, p. 23.                     [5] *Wren Soc.* vii, p. 59.

The plasterers, John Grove and Henry Doogood, made their contract for plastering the interior of the main block a week before the king died. Meanwhile the third contract for brick-making suggests that, had the king lived longer, the terraces and the ranges round the outer court would have been undertaken during 1685.[1]

On 28 January 1685 letters of privy seal authorised the issue of a second £36,000 towards building the palace, and the day before the king's death the Treasury ordered the first £10,000 of this to be paid to Packer, the Paymaster. However, before the month was out the new king, James II, had summoned Wren to appear at the Treasury Chambers 'with an account of the expence requisite to make tight and preserve from damage the buildings at Winchester and to work up all the materials that lie ready there, as his Majesty was pleased to order you the last time you attended him'.[2]

So James's decision to call a halt to the Winchester works seems to have been immediate, although it is probable that at first the halt was meant to be only a temporary one. In April James authorised the allocation of £10,000 for the buildings at Winchester, more than enough to cover Wren's estimate of 2 March, 'to conclude the whole outside Shell of the Fabrick'.[3] A design which must date from this period envisages completing the exterior of the palace as cheaply as possible, crowning the central portico with a mere pavilion roof and omitting the subordinate cupolas and the pediments on the north and south fronts altogether.[4] Nothing further however was done, and although the king spent five days in September staying in the house of the dean at Winchester, Evelyn entered in his diary under that month that 'his now Majestie did not seeme to encourage the finishing of [the palace]; at least for a while; & it is like to stand'.[5]

In 1687 James finally decided to abandon the palace. The accounts had been closed on 31 May 1686, up to which date £44,623 9s. 10¼d. was declared to have been spent. Orders were given in November 1687 to sell the unused, and by then rotten, timber to help pay off the debt to the workmen.[6] The ordinary account opens with the striking of the scaffolding.[7] In April 1688 carpenters were paid for boarding up the windows and from then onwards the shell of the palace was deserted except for two labourers and a dog—5s. for dogsmeat was a regular monthly expense.[8] In August of that year the saleable stores were removed. In August 1689 Wren was ordered to deliver to the inhabitants of Alresford the small scaffolding which 'may be spared', to assist them after a fire in the town, and in May 1691 William and Mary gave away for the same purpose the 'great Ladders, and poles' stored in the palace.[9]

It remained to restore to their former owners the lands purchased to create a park for the palace. Negotiations to purchase over 352 acres in the parishes of St. Cross and St. Thomas had been initiated at the end of 1683. This land, held in twenty-five lots, was then valued, overvalued in the opinion of the Deputy Surveyor

---

[1] *Wren Soc.* vii, pp. 59, 42–3, 41.
[2] *Cal. Treas. Books* vii, p. 1527; viii, p. 17.
[3] *Cal. Treas. Books* viii, p. 133; *Wren Soc.* vii, p. 58.
[4] Alan Cook in *The Country Seat*, ed. H. Colvin and J. Harris, p. 62, n. 5 and fig. 37.
[5] Evelyn, *Diary*, iv, pp. 468, 472.
[6] *Cal. Treas. Books* vii, pp. 1504, 1606.
[7] Works 5/41 (Jan.–March 1687/8).
[8] Works 5/42.
[9] *Cal. Treas. Books* ix, p. 217; Works 5/45.

of Crown Lands, at £7180. Wren's plans for the park are said to have included a cascade 'of 30 Feet fall', but there was no time to execute anything, and the land was leased back to its former owners in 1691–2, with the proviso that 'the Crown may have occasion of it again for the use it was at first purchased for'.[1]

William III and Anne both considered the possibility of completing the palace, but neither did more. William visited Winchester in March 1694, taking Wren with him, but no decision was taken.[2] When Anne succeeded, Winchester was included in the settlement made on her husband, Prince George of Denmark, and in July 1704 Wren was reported to have 'computed the charge of furnishing the prince's pallace at Winchester, which amounts to £18,000'.[3] In August of the following year the queen and Prince George visited Winchester in person. A staircase was erected to enable them to mount to the first floor of the palace, and Wren was sent for 'to view the buildings there which the Queen has a mind to finish'.[4] But nothing more was done, nor did anything come of a later proposal to fit the palace up for the Electoral Prince, afterwards King George I. According to Thomas Worsley, Surveyor of the King's Works in the reign of George III, the queen 'did not chuse to have her successor so near her'.[5] George I himself had no intention of completing the palace, for in 1723 he made a present of all the unused marble and freestone to the third Duke of Bolton, who had just succeeded his father as the owner of Hackwood, and was intending to build there. It proved to be a handsome gift, for when the materials were valued by the Office of Works they were found to be worth £1389.[6]

Although it was now most unlikely that the palace would ever be completed, the Office of Works continued to appoint a Clerk of Works and a Labourer in Trust, and to carry out such minor repairs as were needed to keep the structure wind and water tight.[7] From time to time it was suggested that the cost of maintaining the empty shell might well be spared,[8] and in 1766 there was a proposal from a Southampton builder to pull the building down and develop the site.[9] But the builder was evidently not prepared to pay the sum of £5245 which the Office of Works declared to be the value of the materials 'to any builder who proposes to use them on or near the premises', and after 1760 all such proposals were in any case vetoed by George III, who appears to have cherished the idea of completing the unfinished palace. In 1767, when the High Sheriff of Hampshire asked for permission to remove some prisoners to the palace in order to escape a contagious fever then ravaging the county goal, he was told by the Lord Chamberlain's Office that healthy prisoners

---

[1] *Cal. Treas. Books* vii, pp. 972–4; *Parentalia*, p. 325; *Cal. Treas. Books* ix, pp. 1399, 1693.

[2] N. Luttrell, *Brief Historical Relation* iii, p. 280. It may be significant that in April 1693 Hooke had seen 'module of Winchester house at Sr Christoph Wrens' (R. T. Gunther, Hooke's Diary from 1688 to 1693, in *Early Science in Oxford* x, Oxford 1935, p. 233).

[3] Luttrell, *op. cit.* v, pp. 242, 450.

[4] Hist. MSS. Comm., *Portland* vi, p. 174; *Wren Society*, xix, p. 114; Boyer, *History of the Reign of Queen Anne* iv, pp. 178–80.

[5] B.M., Add. MS. 41135, f. 66ᵛ (letter to Chambers dated 1775).

[6] Works 6/7, pp. 328–9, 361; Works 4/2, 24 April, 22 May, 15 June 1723. For an inventory of the materials presented to the duke, which included six marble columns, see Works 6/7, p. 329. In 1738 they were reported to be still lying at Hackwood, unused (Hist. MSS. Comm., *Portland* vi, p. 174).

[7] The expenditure recorded in the Paymaster's accounts (Works 5/141–2) rarely exceeded £150 in any year, and most of it was accounted for by the salaries of the two officials. In 1778–9 the repair of a defective beam accounts for an abnormal expenditure of £314 (cf. Works 1/5, p. 18.)

[8] E.g. in 1754 (Works 6/17, p. 114) and in 1775 (B.M., Add., MS. 41135, f. 66ᵛ).

[9] Works 6/18, pp. 143–5; Works 1/4, p. 58; P.R.O., Crest 2/1676.

might be lodged there, but that 'as it is the King's intention to make use of the palace some time hence His Majesty would not have any infected person admitted therein under any pretence'.[1] On another occasion the king countered a scheme to turn the palace into a permanent prison of war by declaring firmly that he did not 'approve of the House being made over to anybody'.[2] So nothing came of these economical proposals, and it was not until 1796 that the palace finally passed out of the control of the Office of Works into that of the military.[3]

Meanwhile, during both the Seven Years War and the American War of Independence, the palace had, with royal permission, been occupied by French prisoners of war. During the Seven Years War there were up to 5000 prisoners, guarded by a troop of Hessian soldiers, and during the American War more than 6500 French and Spanish prisoners were confined, many of whom died in an epidemic of fever.[4] On both occasions the Office of Works handed the building over to the Commissioners for Sick and Wounded Seamen who were responsible for the custody of the prisoners. During the first period, which lasted from December 1757 to May 1764, the Commissioners adapted the interior for their purposes by inserting floors and ceilings, doors, windows and partitions to the value of £1015.[5] In 1769 the War Office considered plans for converting the palace into barracks,[6] and on the outbreak of war with the French in 1778 it was actually occupied for some time by a large body of Militia, much to the disgust of the Labourer in Trust, who wrote to the Board of Works that the men were 'daily committing mischief', and that he had complained in vain to their officers.[7] Later in the year the palace was again taken over by the Sick and Wounded department of the Admiralty for occupation by French prisoners, and continued to be used for that purpose until it was handed back to the Office of Works in January 1785.[8]

# WINDSOR CASTLE

WINDSOR WAS of all Charles II's non-metropolitan palaces the one where he spent most time and most money and the only one where his building projects were brought to completion. Windsor Castle was of particular significance to the restored monarch in three different ways. First, alone among his palaces it was also a fortress which could be effectively garrisoned. Secondly the castle housed St. George's Chapel and St. George's Hall and was the headquarters of the Order of the Garter,

---

[1] Works 1/4, pp. 64–6.      [2] Works 6/20, f. 268 (1784).
[3] See Vol. vi, p. 372.      [4] Milner, *op. cit.*, pp. 177–8.
[5] Works 1/3, p. 121; Works 6/18, pp. 44–5; Works 4/13, 18 May, 13 July 1764. A plan in the Bodleian Library (MS. Top. Gen. a. 7, no. 8) shows the building at this period. See also P.R.O., Crest 2/1676.
[6] P.R.O., W.O. 30/56, pp. 89–92.      [7] Works 1/5, pp. 8–9.
[8] Works 6/19, p. 189; Works 4/16, 10 July, 6 Aug. 1784, 28 Jan. 1785.

England's prime order of chivalry, which the Stuart monarchs fostered with especial enthusiasm.[1] Finally, it had the personal significance of being the burial place of his martyred father, Charles I.

Unfortunately Charles II's work at Windsor Castle is not as well documented as it might be. The monthly accounts of the Windsor Office are lost, so the building history of the castle in this period must be reconstructed from the declared accounts, an unbroken run from 1660 to 1713. Little that is eloquent is left now of the great works executed for Charles II. Three rooms survive relatively intact, but almost everything else, except the fabric of the walls, was swept away by the remodelling of the state apartments for George III and George IV.

During the 1660s the Windsor Office had little to do. Garter installations were held in 1661 and 1662 but not thereafter until 1671. The first grant of the reign, of £5000 in October 1660, for 'the necessary Repairations and amendments of our said Castle and Lodges there', was made to the constable of the castle, Viscount Mordaunt. A warrant was issued to the Lord Chamberlain, the Earl of Manchester, on 25 March 1662, to fit up the constable's lodgings, 'his attendance being absolutely necessary, as often as the King repairs there'.[2]

Mordaunt himself declared the first account, based on a book signed by Hartgill Baron, Comptroller of the Windsor Office. This covered work done up to 4 November 1662 costing £3743 15s. 5d., almost entirely, the account suggests, repairs to the walls and roofs of the castle.[3]

In April 1662 the Surveyor of the Honor and Castle of Windsor, William Taylor, opened his first account, £2000 having been granted for 'the repaires, fitting and making ready the Lodgings which belong to our Selfe, and dearest Consort, and other Offices in that our Castle for our better Reception there'. This account closed in September 1664, by which time only £1663 18s. 3½d. had been spent. Little can have been done to embellish the royal apartments, for the painter's taskwork, for painting staircases and balconies and 'the Pulpit in the private Chappell' came to a mere £22 1s. 4d. One of the few other luxury items was £1 7s., expended on 'Pennyroyall, Camomile and turfes for the Tarras Walke'.[4]

During this period, on the other hand, according to an estimate of 1661, the cost of maintaining the garrison in the castle was nearly £5000 per annum.[5] Normally three companies seem to have been stationed at Windsor. The Constable, Mordaunt, and from 1668 his successor Prince Rupert, commanded one of them.[6] From 1663 there are a number of references in the State Papers to political prisoners being detained in the castle; but during 1668 and 1669 they were being transferred to other castles.

Prince Rupert's appointment as constable was soon followed by improvements in the fortifications of the castle. In May 1670 a warrant was issued to the Com-

---

[1] Elias Ashmole, *The Institution, Laws & Ceremonies Of the most Noble Order of the Garter*, London (1672), pp. 475, 477, 483.
[2] AO 1/2477/262 (duplicated by E 351/3426); *Cal. Treas. Books* i, p. 89; *Cal. S.P. Dom. 1661–2*, p. 320.
[3] AO 1/2477/262 (E 351/3426).
[4] AO 1/2477/264 (E 351/3427). Painter's taskwork entry printed in Hope, p. 307. Throughout Hope quotes from the Pipe Office series of declared accounts (E 351), whereas all quotations here are from the duplicate Audit Office series (AO 1).
[5] *Cal. S.P. Dom. 1661–2*, p. 21.                           [6] *Cal. S.P. Dom. 1667–8*, p. 608.

missioners of the Ordnance for the strengthening of the walls round the Middle Ward and Keep. This work was to be carried out under the supervision of Prince Rupert and the Surveyor-General of the Ordnance, Sir Jonas Moore.[1]

Further repairs were carried out during this period. In July 1668 an estimate was presented for £510 for renewing roofs over the queen's lodging, the king's wardrobe and part of the king's lodgings, and in August and September warrants for £1000 were issued.[2] In the following March Wren reported that £1000 would be needed to put the castle into a fit condition to hold the St. George's feast, and a Treasury order to provide £500 for that purpose was issued.[3] It is not certain however that these works were carried out, since the next declared account covers a fifteen-month period beginning only on 1 September 1669. It shows during that period an expenditure of £2349 19s. 8½d.[4] Once more this was basically maintenance work; among the necessary tasks performed was slating the roofs of the Chancellor's (now Salisbury) Tower and Garter's Tower.[5] Nevertheless Evelyn, on his visit in August, thought the Castle 'exceedingly ragged and ruinous'.[6]

In spite of the Garter installations and feasts in the early 1670s, expenditure at Windsor continued at a relatively low level, less than £4500 during the period January 1670/1 to March 1674. In small ways however the amenities of the castle were improved, in painting and wainscotting, in the digging of an ice well, and in particular by the installation in 1673 of an organ in the King's Chapel, for which Bernard Smith received £310, and William Dickinson £5 10s. for carved work about the organ loft.[7]

From 1669 onwards Richard Ryder, the Master Carpenter, received a fee of 6d. a day for 'directing the works', a fee which he drew until his death in 1683, when it was continued to Matthew Bankes, his successor as Master Carpenter.

In November 1673, however, Hugh May was appointed Comptroller of the Windsor office. May was a practising architect and no mere placeman, as his immediate predecessors seem to have been. In the great remodelling which was shortly to be initiated May was the true and effective director, whereas up to the month of his appointment the Surveyor-General, Wren, was giving estimates and adjusting prices at Windsor, in accordance with the Treasury instruction of 1668.[8]

The year 1674 marks a new interest shown by the king in Windsor Castle. New furniture was ordered from the Officers of the Works at Windsor for St. George's feast that year, to be stored for future use: a table 12 ft. by 3 ft. 6 ins. for the king, tables 10 ft. by 3 ft. for the Knights of the Garter 'to be placed two att a Messe', with a cupboard per mess and serving tables, the king's table and the knights' tables to be made 'very stedfast', with 'a very strong Rayle before [them] to keepe of the Crowde'.[9] From May to August the Court, for the first time in Charles's reign, was in residence at Windsor.[10] In July a stage was erected in St. George's Hall 'for the

[1] *Cal. S.P. Dom. 1670*, pp. 195, 222.
[2] Works 6/1, f. 4ᵛ, printed in Hope, pp. 307–8; S.P. 44/30, f. 85ᵛ.
[3] *Cal. Treas. Books* iii, p. 45.   [4] AO 1/2477/265.
[5] *Cal. Treas. Books* iii, p. 447, 10 June 1670.   [6] Evelyn, *Diary* iii, p. 560.
[7] AO 1/2478/266, E 351/3447 and AO 1/2478/267 (E 351/3446 and 3448); *Cal. Treas. Books* iv, pp. 274, 401, 634.
[8] See above, p. 118, and *Cal. S.P. Dom., 1673–5*, p. 26.
[9] Works 6/1, f. 19ʳ.   [10] *Cal. S.P. Dom., 1673–5, passim.*

acting of Playes before his Majestie', and the following month witnessed the mock re-enactment of the seige of Maestricht in a meadow at the foot of the north terrace.[1]

The king was sufficiently pleased with the delights of the castle to plan further visits to Windsor with the Court but sufficiently dissatisfied with the royal apartments to order their complete reconstruction. A newsletter of 21 July 1674 reported, 'The King . . . has given orders to make several additions and alterations to the Castle and Park, to make it more fit for his summer's residence every year, taking great delight in the situation and pleasant walks about it'.[2]

Letters of Privy Seal of 31 August 1674 authorised the diversion of the Greenwax money 'for the rebuilding the severall Lodgings set apart for the reception of us our dearest Consort the Queene and our deare Brother the Duke of Yorke in our Royall Castle of Windsor', and in May 1675 it was decided to use the remainder of the queen's dowry for the works at Windsor. The declared account for the period 1 April 1674 to 30 September 1675 shows that £10,971 3s. 4½d. of Greenwax money was paid to the Receiver of the Honor and Castle of Windsor, and that over £11,000 was disbursed, largely however in purchasing materials and in repair work, not only in the royal lodgings but on 'the South side the Castle and behind the poore Knights houses' in the Lower Ward.[3] Only after the Court had completed their second stay at Windsor, in the autumn of 1675, could work begin in earnest. In September and October warrants were issued to Prince Rupert, the Constable, and to Sir Thomas Chicheley, Master General of the Ordnance, to permit Officers of the Works to begin demolition of parts of the castle; and when in November 1676 a warrant was issued to pay Hugh May the generous gratuity of £500 per annum 'for his care and pains in the rebuilding and repairing' of the castle, the payments were backdated only to 1 September 1675, 'at or about which time the said work began'.[4]

The reconstruction was carried through in two clearly defined phases. Between September 1675 and the late summer of 1678 new apartments for the king and queen were constructed and decorated in the north range of the Upper Ward, and the duke's and duchess's apartments in the south range of the same ward were remodelled. A single account was declared for these three years, showing receipts of £69,782 18s. 3¾d. (including only £10,689 19s. 1¾d. from the Exchequer, as against moneys 'voluntarily charged', which included £13,000 from the Navy Office and £44,000 through William Chiffinch, of which £18,000 came from the king's subsidy from the King of France), and expenditure which amounted to £74,209 4s. 3¼d.[5] At the end of these three years the Court was able to spend August and September of 1678 at Windsor, and thereafter throughout the rest of Charles II's reign the Court spent several months of each year in residence there.

In the second phase the chapel and St. George's Hall were rebuilt, the rest of the east and south ranges remodelled and the terrace walk extended round on the

---

[1] Works 6/1, f. 20ʳ; LC 5/140, p. 509; Evelyn, *Diary* iv, p. 42.
[2] Hist. MSS. Comm., *12th Report*, Appendix Part VII: *Le Fleming MSS.* (1890), p. 112.
[3] AO 1/2478/268 (E 351/3449); *Cal. Treas. Books* iv, p. 308.
[4] *Cal. S.P. Dom. 1675–6*, pp. 300, 361; *Cal. Treas. Books* v, p. 361.
[5] AO1/2478/270 (E 351/3450), largely printed in Hope, pp. 314–18. Hope omits from his total the 'Allowances by special warrants', which include e.g. May's salary.

outer side of these ranges. Structural work was largely complete by 1680: Evelyn on 24 July of that year saw the Upper Ward and assumed it to be 'now neere finished'.[1] The accounts however show that the decoration of St. George's Hall was not completed until the period 1682–4. During the first two years of this second phase the work was largely financed by payments of £1000 per month out of the Irish revenue of £27,000 per annum reserved for the king's use, on the authority of a royal warrant of 8 October 1678. May, as Comptroller of the Windsor Works, constantly pressed the Vice-Treasurer of Ireland, the Earl of Ranelagh, for regular payment, with such success that by 30 September 1680 Ranelagh had transmitted £28,846 for the Windsor works.[2] The sum total of expenditure declared for this second phase, the six years ending 30 September 1684, when work was virtually complete and the king had but a few months to live, was £53,520 9s. 5¾d., together with a further £3500 odd spent on making an avenue from the castle to the Great Park.

Externally May almost completely redesigned the north front of the state apartments, leaving untouched at the west end Henry VII's Tower and Queen Elizabeth's gallery and at the east end the fabric of the Norman Tower, but demolishing the two intermediate towers. In their place the Star Building occupied the western half of the range, an uncompromising three-storeyed block over a semi-basement, its ten bays divided into pairs, the centre pair of windows spaced more widely than the rest to give room for the solitary embellishment, a gilt star 12 feet in diameter (Pl. 46B). In front of the Star Building the North Terrace was widened by means of a bow-ended addition, which helped to emphasise the Star Building in the distant view. The eastern half of the facade, up to the Norman Tower, a fifteen-bay elevation, must have incorporated a good deal of old masonry, for it was not symmetrical. The weak near-central pedimental feature was merely the gable-end of the crosswing behind. Two flights of steps, one from a low forebuilding, led onto the terrace. May's severe skyline of plain parapets was only faintly enlivened by the tall rectangular chimney stacks with cornice mouldings of upright leaves.

The new east facade was visually more forceful, for the four existing tall rectangular towers created their own strong rhythm, and May merely pierced the walls with a single storey of large windows and created a wide double flight of steps up to the centre from the new terrace. But here too he did not achieve an altogether symmetrical arrangement, although the completely rebuilt south-east tower and the almost rebuilt north-east tower were made identical and appreciably broader than the two intermediate towers. In the south range of the Upper Ward May merely pierced the outer walls with his characteristic windows.[3] Within the Upper Ward he seems to have done no more than refenestrate, leaving intact the two fourteenth-century gate-towers, the Spicery Gatehouse, which was the main entrance to the royal apartments, and the Kitchen Gatehouse in the north-east corner.[4]

---

[1] AO 1/2478/271–2479/273 (E 351/3451–3452); Evelyn, *Diary* iv, p. 207.

[2] *Cal. Treas. Books* v, p. 1128; AO 1/2478/271 (E 351/2451); Bodleian, Carte MS. 53, ff. 180–3.

[3] Contrast the views of Hollar and Wren in Ashmole, *Garter* (Hope, pls. xxxiii, xxxiv) with Wyatville's early 19th-century perspectives (Hope, pls. xxxv, xlvi–xlvii).

[4] Contrast Hollar's drawings in the Bodleian (Hope, pl. xxxi) with Sandby's watercolour (Pl. 44B) and vol. vi, Pl. 22. Works 34/349 is an elevation of the south side of the Upper Ward before Wyatville's remodelling.

Throughout the remodelling of the exterior then May showed himself in sympathy with the blocky massiveness of the Norman castle His work had none of the festive character of the late medieval parts. Nor on the other hand did it concede much to the classical taste of May's own day. Sir John Vanbrugh was the first to comment, and comment favourably, on this 'Castle Air'.[1] The only surviving external features of May's work, two windows in the Henry III Tower, at the south-east corner of the Lower Ward, demonstrate eloquently the compromise which May achieved. They are tall, of roughly classical proportions, but roundheaded, and a broad concave surround of Portland ashlar sinks them deep into the wall. Balustrading of a classical form masks the mezzanine floors.[2] Such windows, with or without the balustrading, May used throughout the principal storey. It is probable that from the start the window frames were sashes, not casements.[3]

Of the materials needed for the structural work, oak timber was felled in Windsor Forest, and stone was largely quarried there too, and also at Frimley and Cobham in Surrey. Chalk was extracted from Sir Denis Hampson's quarries at Taplow. Stockpiling of materials had begun in 1674–5, when £2260 was spent on stone from Burford, Purbeck and Portland, but the main purchases were made in 1675–8. During these years stone was bought to the value of £3940 15s. 1d., and bricks costing £4365 6s. The masons' wages on the other hand and the taskwork of Joseph Marshall, and after his death in April 1678, of John Clarke and George Pile, amounted to no less than £10,211 0s. 2½d., more than four times the cost of the brickwork done by Maurice Emmett, the Master Bricklayer, and the other bricklayers, whose bills totalled £2198 9s. 10d.[4] In fact it is doubtful whether there was any external brickwork in the new buildings, in spite of Celia Fiennes's statement that Windsor Castle was 'partly . . . brick plaister'd over in imitation of stone'.[5]

Internally May's handling of the royal apartments and of the approaches to them gave further evidence of his independence of mind. In the first place he planned within the confines of the rather constricted structure a sequence of spaces which exploited variety of size and lighting in a way that had not been attempted before in England. Through the Spicery Gatehouse in the north-west corner of the Upper Ward the way led through wrought-iron gates into a paved one-storey vestibule, in which four pairs of Ionic columns formed aisles, with Ionic pilaster responds against the walls and niches between. Two of these columns, with wreaths dangling from the volutes of the capitals, have been resited at the approach of Salvin's state staircase of 1866, but it is not known whether the vestibule was vaulted. Immediately beyond the vestibule lay the Queen's Great Staircase, a remarkable room. The stairs rose in straight flights round the walls of a square well and lit only from a glazed lantern in the centre of the domed ceiling and by reflected light through an oval opening in the party wall between the great staircase and the Queen's Back Staircase to the north. In the principal storey the Queen's Guard Chamber stood over the

---

[1] *The Complete Works of Sir John Vanbrugh*, ed. B. Dobrée and G. Webb, vi (1928), p. 14.

[2] See K. Downes, *English Baroque Architecture* (1966), pl. 6. P.R.O. MPD 187 is an early 18th-century plan and elevation of King Edward III's tower as remodelled by May.

[3] AO 1/2478/270 (E 351/3450) first year's bills. Payment of £10 16s. to Thomas Turner, joiner, 'for worke done in the yeare 1675 vizt ffor makeing of shashes and fframes for Shash windowes with severall Moddells of Roomes Staires Lanthornes Windowes and one Chimney'.

[4] *Ibid.*; *Cal. S.P. Dom. 1675–6*, p. 542.     [5] C. Fiennes, *Journeys*, ed. Morris, p. 274.

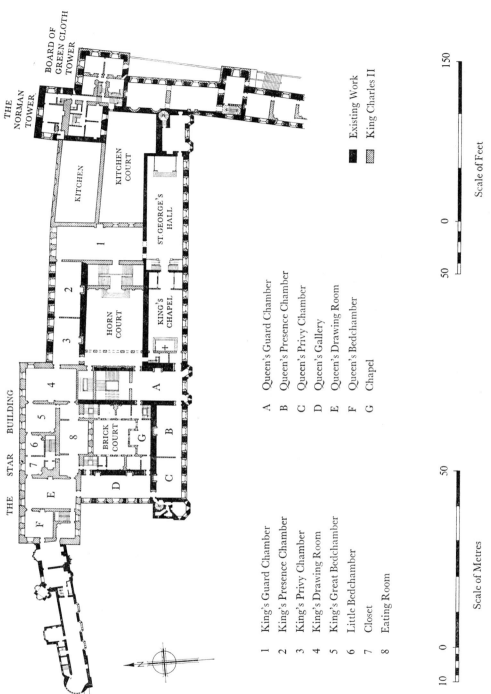

THE NORMAN TOWER

BOARD OF GREEN CLOTH TOWER

THE STAR BUILDING

KITCHEN

KITCHEN COURT

HORN COURT

BRICK COURT

ST. GEORGE'S HALL

KING'S CHAPEL

1    King's Guard Chamber
2    King's Presence Chamber
3    King's Privy Chamber
4    King's Drawing Room
5    King's Great Bedchamber
6    Little Bedchamber
7    Closet
8    Eating Room

A    Queen's Guard Chamber
B    Queen's Presence Chamber
C    Queen's Privy Chamber
D    Queen's Gallery
E    Queen's Drawing Room
F    Queen's Bedchamber
G    Chapel

■   Existing Work
▨   King Charles II

Scale of Feet
150    50    0    50

Scale of Metres
10    0    50

Fig. 27. Windsor Castle: the State Apartments in the reign of Charles II.

vestibule, forming the first in the conventional sequence of state rooms which occupied the south and west ranges of the Brick Court, concluding with the Withdrawing Room and Bedchamber in the western third of the Star Building, in direct communication with the innermost rooms of the king's apartment. Overlooking the Court was a small private chapel for the queen's use.

To reach the king's apartment on the other hand it was necessary to turn right out of the columned vestibule, into an arcaded loggia open to Horn Court ('so called from a pair of stagg horns of a very extraordinary size, taken in the Forest, and set up in that Court'[1]). At the far end of the Court May designed quite a grandiose facade, with giant Corinthian columns carrying a high panelled attic, and in the centre a flight of five broad steps leading up to an arched opening about 24 feet high, lofty enough to open an unimpeded view through to the upper level of the King's Great Staircase, which rose behind the facade in two straight flights and returned in a second pair of flights to the central landing (Pl. 45). From there a doorway opened into the King's Guard Chamber, lying north-south and partly top-lit from a central octagonal lantern.[2] From the north end of the Guard Chamber the rest of the king's apartment extended westwards across the north range. The Presence Chamber and Privy Chamber occupied the north side of Horn Court, so that from the latter it was possible to pass along the marble-lined gallery on the west side of the court into the organ-gallery behind the altar in the King's Chapel. In the north-east angle of the Star Building lay the King's Withdrawing Room, and beyond were Great Bedchamber, Little Bedchamber and Closet, the last being a pair of small rooms flanking the Eating Room, which alone faced south onto Brick Court.[3]

Whether May can take the credit for the novel manner in which the state apartments were decorated is less certain. John Evelyn, who in 1671 first brought Grinling Gibbons's talents as a woodcarver to the general notice, writes of 'having bespoke his Majestie . . . for his Worke at Windsore which my friend Mr. May . . . was going to alter and repair universaly'.[4] In the same year Antonio Verrio, the painter, was brought over to England from Paris by the Duke of Montagu, who is just as likely to have mentioned his protégé first to the king. The gilder who completed the team was René Cousin, a Frenchman. All three artists naturally had assistants. The names of those assistants who were Catholics are known, from the indemnity which was granted to them in 1679, exempting them from the proclamation against Popish Recusants of that year. Gibbons's 'servants' are given as Laurence Vandermulen, Anthony Verhuke and Arnold Quellan; Cousin's son Peter is mentioned and John Caree an apprentice, and Le Mair his servant; and the exemption is extended to Anthony Montingo, flower-painter, Nicholas Lauzellier, painter, and John Vanderstaine, stone carver, and to Vanderstaine's servant, John Oasts.[5]

---

[1] From a MS. description of *c.* 1765 in the Victoria & Albert Museum (86 BB. 14).
[2] The king's backstairs were also top-lit; see the payment in 1677–8 for 'Glasses for the Cupolo of his Majesty's Backe Staires'.
[3] Works 34/292, a plan of the state apartments made *c.* 1780; AO 1/2478/270 (E 351/3450); G. Bickham, *Deliciae Britannicae* (1742), pp. 143, 148; C. Fiennes, *Journeys*, ed. Morris, p. 277.
[4] Evelyn, *Diary*, iii, p. 573.
[5] Privy Council Register P.C. 2/68, printed in *Burlington Magazine* xcix, p. 57. 'Oasts' is presumably John Nost the statuary much employed by William and Mary at Hampton Court.

In the fitting out the rooms were first wainscotted, the state apartments and many other rooms in 1676–7 and the Duke and Duchess of York's apartments and many further rooms the following year, at a total cost of £5066 13s. 7¾d., the lion's share of the work being executed by four joiners, Alexander Fort, John Turner, Thomas Turner and Matthew Williams. Their joinery included moulded cornices, 'arch-work', doors and chimneypieces; but all carved work was the task of Grinling Gibbons and Henry Phillips, the Master Carver, who in these first two years were paid together as if they were in partnership. In 1676–7 they received £625 14s. for 'severall sorts of Carved workes by them performed upon the Chimney peeces Pedestalls and picture frames of the Kings Greate and Little Bedchambers, and Presence, his Majesties Clossett, Musicke roome, Eateing roome, Withdrawing roome, and Backstaires, the Queenes withdrawing roome, Bedchamber and Gallery, and in iiii^e rooms at the Dutches of Portsmouths Lodgings', and the next year their bills amounted to £614 17s. 8d. 'for sundry Carved workes by them performed upon severall Wainscot Chimney-peeces, Doores, Doorecases Pedestalls and Pictures in his Majesty's Greate and Little Bedchambers, Eateing Roome, Musicke roomes and Privy Backstaires, the Queenes Presence, Privy Chambers and Gard-Chamber, the Duke of Yorkes Bedchamber Withdrawing roome and Clossett and in the Dutchesse of Yorkes Presence Chamber Dressing Roome and Withdrawing roome and at the New Tower'. The cornices still surviving in many of the state rooms, carved with upright acanthus leaves, although not specified in the accounts, will have been part of the carvers' task. The virtuoso carving in limewood, of naturalistic fruit, foliage, flowers and other objects in high relief and daringly undercut, characteristic of Gibbons's independent work, which these accounts mainly refer to, has, on the other hand, been largely lost. Only in the King's Eating Room is any of the carving in something like its original setting, but even here Pyne's view of the room as it was *c.* 1800, with Queen Anne's bed in it, shows none of the carving in its present arrangement. Reset carving is in the King's Presence Chamber (now Garter Throne Room). But it seems clear from the accounts and from the carving which survives here and in the Queen's Privy Chamber and Audience Chamber, the former deco-rated by Gibbons in 1678–9, that the carving formed swags and drops enframing paintings over chimneypieces and over doors, and, to a lesser extent, decorative panels entirely of carved wood. Nicholas Largillier and Phillip Delesam were paid £19 9s. 1d. for painting and fitting pictures over doors and chimneys, and Gerrard Vyllenburgh similarly received a gratuity of £50 for 'Enlargeing Painteing fitting and placeing of severall of his Majesty's Pictures sett over all the Chimneys and Doores in the Kings and Queenes Lodgings in Windsor Castle and for severall Journeys to some of the Kings Howses to make Choice of such Pictures as were most fitt to bee sett in the severall places aforesaid according to his Majesty's Directions'.[1]

Less novel, but even more spectacular in their effect, were the ceiling-paintings by Antonio Verrio. The King's Guard Chamber (Pl. 43B) was the first room to be painted, perhaps experimentally to judge of the effect. The ceiling here was complete as early as August 1676, the month in which Maurice Emmett, junior, the master

---

[1] AO 1/2478/270 (E 351/3450), second and third years' bills, printed in Hope, p. 317; W. Pyne, *Royal Residences*, i, facing p. 161.

bricklayer, concluded his measurement of Cousin's gilding for purposes of costing. Emmet's notes, preserved in the Royal Library at Windsor, mention harps, thistles, roses, fleurs-de-lys, crowns, the moulding round the lantern and the circular wreaths to left and right of the lantern.[1] Verrio received £300 for his work on this ceiling, Cousin £29 6s.

By August 1678 Verrio had completed thirteen ceilings, for which he received £2430, including a gift of £200 from the king. Cousin's total of £463 0s. 2d. included, besides the enrichment of these ceilings, £12 for gilding 'the Starr that is Cutt in Stone upon the Wall of the Northside of the Building' and £13 for gilding 'the Ornaments of the Diall over the greate Gate that ffronts to the greate Courte being done of Right Gold Colour, of a Greene Gold Colour, and of a Brasse Colour'. Thus the entire king's apartment was ready decorated in time for the Court's arrival in 1678, but only the inner half of the queen's. Nor were the staircases or Horn Court finished. All these had to wait for the next wave of decorative activity, in 1679–80.[2]

The programmes which Verrio was called upon to realise were fulsomely and unrealistically propagandist in the manner accepted throughout Europe in the seventeenth century. Thus in the four major public rooms in the king's apartment, the ceiling of the Presence Chamber was painted with 'Mercury . . . with the Portrait of King Charles the IId, in his hands, shewing it, with Transport, as it were, to the View of the four Quarters of the World'.[3] In the Privy Chamber the ceiling bore 'a most lively representation of the re-establishment of the Church of England, on the Restoration of Charles 2nd in the Characters of England, Scotland & Ireland, attended by Faith, Hope, and Charity, Religion triumphing over Superstition & Hypocrisy, who are driven by Cupids from before the face of the Church'.[4] In the Withdrawing Room the subject was the Restoration of the Monarchy and in the Great Bedchamber a suppliant figure of France and the four continents bringing their riches to a Charles seated among the clouds. For the rest there were mythologies. The ceiling of the Guard Chamber set a suitably lofty tone at the beginning of the suite, Jupiter, Juno and Mercury appearing on the dome within the central lantern, Iris, Mars and Bellona in the flanking roundels. The Eating Room ceiling, still surviving, is painted appropriately with a banquet of the gods. The ceilings of the private rooms, the Little Bedchamber and Closet, were also appropriate to the king's private life, painted with scenes of Jupiter and Danaë and Jupiter and Leda respectively.

The queen's apartment similarly glorified the queen, starting at once in the Guard Chamber, where she was shown as Britannia, with the Four Continents paying her homage. In the two still surviving ceilings, she appears first in the Presence Chamber in her own person attended by the Virtues, and in the Privy Chamber as Britannia again, in a triumphal car drawn towards the Temple of Virtue. The ceilings of her other rooms were decorated with mythologies; but her Great Staircase had, besides

[1] Royal Library, Windsor Castle, MS: 'The Guilders Account for Windsor Castle 1676 and 1677' etc.
[2] AO 1/2478/270–1 (E 351/3450–1).
[3] G. Bickham, *Deliciae Britannicae* (1742), quoted in Hope, p. 339.
[4] This is the description on an annotated drawing of the room *c.* 1800, in the Royal Library, Windsor Castle.

a ceiling-painting of Apollo permitting Phaeton to drive the chariot of the Sun, monochrome figures on the walls emblematic of the arts.[1] Cousin received £10 15s. 3d. for 'guilding with Copper the Eight figures in the Neaches the two Dolphins over the Doores, the Capitalls and other Ornaments in the Ceiling & walls' of this staircase. There must have been something similar on the ceiling and walls of the upper gallery leading from the king's Presence Chamber to his Chapel, for Cousin's gilding here was of 'the Basrelevres, Statues, the modilion border, the figures. . . '. In the Horn Court itself Cousin gilded 'the seaverall ffigures, Statues & other Ornaments' on the walls.[2]

The lodgings of the Duke and Duchess of York, extending from the duke's Guard Chamber in the north-east corner of the Upper Ward along the east and south ranges as far as the south tower of the latter, were largely reconstructed and wainscotted, if not entirely complete, by August 1678. Also ready for use at that time were the lodgings of the king's mistress, the Duchess of Portsmouth, and her son the Duke of Richmond, situated, it seems, below the king's apartment in the Star Building. Painting by Robert Streater, Sergeant Painter, and Jacob Vanderhoofe paid for in 1677–8 was in these lodgings and in those of the Countess of Suffolk, the Lord Chamberlain, the Privy Purse, Tobias Rustat and 'Mr Price the Serjeant Trumpeter', and in 'the Eateing roomes of the Gentlemen and Groomes of the Chamber'.[3]

Several other tasks were carried out in the first phase of the reconstruction. Nell Gwynn was installed at Windsor in 1678, and a certain Monsieur John Bodevin was paid £100 under contract for repairing her house, later called Burford Lodge, and situated immediately south of the castle walls.[4] Further payments for repairs to Burford Lodge and decoration of the staircase by Verrio appear in the Works declared accounts.[5] Kip's view of 1709, showing the house when it belonged to the Duke of St. Albans, Charles's son by Mrs. Gwynn, suggests that the house had been totally rebuilt since Hollar's view published in 1672; but the Office of Works was not apparently involved in the rebuilding.

Another piece of contract work carried out in 1677–8 was the building by Arthur Michenor, bricklayer, and Nicholas Blackman, carpenter, for £250 of new stables and coach-houses for Prince Rupert at Eton, 150 ft. long, 18 ft. broad and 10 ft high. The stables were timber-framed with brick nogging.[6] During the period of this account the old tennis court, which had been awkwardly situated south-west of the main entrance to the state apartments, was also cleared away and a new brick-built tennis court completed below the castle walls to the south.[7]

A further and even more essential improvement was the engine set up by Sir

---

[1] The ceilings of the King's Eating Room and the Queen's Presence Chamber and Privy Chamber survive, and those in the King's Presence Chamber, Withdrawing Room and Closet are recorded in engravings by Pierre Vandrebanc. For other evidence see E. Croft-Murray, *Decorative Painting in England* i (1962) pp. 240–2.

[2] Royal Library, Windsor Castle, MS: 'The Guilders Account for Windsor Castle 1676 and 1677'.

[3] AO 1/2478/270 (E 351/3450), third year's bills, printed in Hope, p. 316.

[4] AO 1/2478/270 (E 351/3450), third year's bills, printed in Hope, p. 318, where Bodevin's name is wrongly transcribed.

[5] AO 1/2479/272.

[6] AO 1/2478/270 (E 351/3450), third year's bills.

[7] The Tennis Court appears in Kip's view of Burford Lodge (Hope, pl. xxvii). See also Fig. 29.

Samuel Morland in the castle well. Hugh May's certificate, given when Morland was petitioning for a bill to patent the machinery, is dated 14 March 1677 and declares that Morland's engine 'by the labour of a man at 14d. a day, supplied water for the King's household which before cost £60, while the Court was there, for bringing up the Thames water in carts, and, when worked by 4 men, supplied water for the King's great building there'.[1]

Finally the king made provision in 1677–8 for enhancing the ceremonial and dynastic associations of Windsor Castle. The magnificent throne destined for St. George's Hall was constructed in this year. Lewis Vanupstall was paid £20 for making a model of the throne, and he and John Vanderstaine executed the carved work for it, including the six 'slaves' that supported it, three 'ffames' and figures of Prudence and Justice, for £266 10s.[2]

On 29 January 1678 the House of Commons voted the colossal sum of £70,000 'for a solemn Funeral of his late Majesty King Charles the First, and to erect a Monument for the said Prince of glorious Memory; the said Sum to be raised by a Two Months Tax'. The money was never forthcoming, but a design for the monument was. Although it was decided to erect the monument at Windsor on the site of the Tomb-house at the east end of St. George's Chapel, its design was entrusted not to May but to the Surveyor-General, Wren. Only three days after the resolution in the House of Commons, Robert Hooke noted in his diary 'with Sir Chr. Wren about Kings tomb chappell at Winsor'. Wren's designs are for a martyrium in the manner of Bramante's Tempietto, a circular domed structure ringed by a colonnade of attached Corinthian columns. The interior was to have been exceedingly sumptuous, the eight columns to be each a single stone 28 feet long, brought from the Levant, the capitals of gilt brass, the walls incrusted with marble, the heads of the niches of mosaic work, the cupola frescoed. For the monument itself, showing King Charles I trampling on his enemies, alternative designs were made by Grinling Gibbons, one for execution in marble, one in brass. Further statues, including a gilded figure of Fame on the top of the cupola, were to enrich the exterior of the building. Wren's estimate was £43,663.[3]

The next phase was initiated by the royal warrant of 31 October 1678. This authorised the finishing touches to the royal apartments, further painting in the queen's apartments, but mainly the completion of the approach routes. The wrought iron gates for the Spicery Gatehouse were ordered, the paving of 'the large court and the court before the Queen's lodgings', and Verrio's painting of the staircases. Work was also to continue on extending the terraces, with steps from the east terrace to the park, and for Princess Anne, daughter of the Duke of York, the north-east tower was to be reconstructed. The repair of the Greencloth towers was authorised, and the south wall of St. George's Hall was to be taken down 'to the stoole of the windows and [built] up again with a new roof and windows uniform to the rest of the building'.[4] So work began on what was to be the climax of the king's reconstructions, the glorious redecoration of St. George's Hall and the King's Chapel.

[1] *Cal. S.P. Dom. 1677–8*, p. 74.
[2] AO 1/2478/260 (E 351/3450), foreign artists' bills, August 1678.
[3] S. Wren, *Parentalia* (1750), pp. 331–2.  [4] *Cal. Treas. Books* v, p. 1152–3.

During the year ending 30 September 1679 the sum of £408 19s. 1½d. was spent on demolitions and John Clarke and George Pile, master masons, received £1202 11s. 3d. for commencing the new work ordered by the king: 'at the South Tarras wal, the wall under his Majesty's Chappell, St George's Hall, the Green cloth office, the South east Tower, the additional Tarras wall before his Majesty's buildinge, the Draw-bridge Wall at the East end of the North Tarras, the blacke Tarras Wall, and the Middle Tower on the south side of the Castle'. The following year they largely finished these works and 'the New Tower at the North-East corner of the Castle, [and] the new Greencloth Tower' at a cost of £1861 2s. 11d. The joiners and painters were also able to get to work in these areas. Nine marble chimneypieces were supplied for £38 3s., seven of them destined for the new south-east tower. At that price they cannot have been anything special, and indeed the Windsor Office spent almost nothing on special items of decoration in the apartments of the Duke of York and his family. The one striking exception, late in 1684, was the payment of £28 6s. 8d. to Jasper Bream for inlaying the step under the Duchess of York's bed 'with severall coloured Woods in resemblance of fflowers Leaves etc.'.[1] Furthermore the sundial, for which in the previous year Henry Wynne had supplied the brass 'double Horizontall dyall' and John Vanderstaine made the support in the form of stone eagles, was set up on the south-east terrace walk. A second sundial, made in 1679–80, still survives on the north terrace, where it was originally placed. Wynne made, and signed, the dial, the Portland stone pedestal was carved by Gibbons. As for the brass equestrian statue of Charles II set up in 1680 in the centre of the Upper Ward, that was paid for by a gift of Tobias Rustat, the king's personal yeoman of the robes, expressly for the purpose.[2] Rustat's gift did not however include money for the pedestal, for which the Works account for 1678–9 records a payment to John Vanderstaine 'for drawing and making of severall designes, Modells, and figures in Clay' and another, of £2, to James Cottree 'for altering and Painting the forme of the Pedistall'. In the account for 'sundry extraordinary works' during this period Grinling Gibbons received £400 for 'Carving and Cutting the iiii white Marble pannells of the Pedestall of his Majesty's statue on horse backe', and a further small sum for 17 feet of white marble for the two end panels of the pedestal, the masonry of which appears in the task of Clarke and Pile for that year. The carved panels, of swags of fruit and trophies of arms and regalia, survive much weather-worn and reset in the reconstructed pedestal.[3]

The royal apartments meanwhile continued to be enriched. There was first of all the major scheme of decoration to be completed. In 1678–9 Gibbons, whose name from this time onwards appears no longer in partnership with Phillips but alone, received £63 5s. for 'ii° Chimny peices carved with flowers and fruites' for the queen's Privy Chamber and king's Drawing Room, and £60 for 'sixty pannells Carved with fflowers, ffruites, shells, and severall other Ornaments' to go over the corner fireplaces in the king's Great and Little Bedchambers and Closet. Verrio and Cousin were in these years employed first in painting and gilding the ceilings

[1] AO 1/2478/271 (E 351/3451), many entries printed in Hope, pp. 319–323, and AO 1/2479/275 (E 351/3452).
[2] AO 1/2478/271 (E 351/3451); B.M. Lansdowne MS. 989. f. 79ʳ.
[3] AO 1/2478/271 (E 351/3451), entries printed in Hope, pp. 319–20.

of the king's Great Staircase and the queen's Privy Chamber and Presence Chamber, then on the queen's Guard Chamber and Great Staircase and on the decoration of the Horn Court. For the three royal bedchambers Alexander Fort made, for £37 16s., screens of cedar and brass wire to set round the beds.[1] In the account for 1680–2 payment of £17 10s. is made to Isaac Thompson, Engineer, for two close stools, both with pulleys of iron and brass, one having a pair of ivory handles; this was set up in the king's stool room, the other in 'his Majesties upper Lodgings'.[2] Finally the queen's lodgings were given a rooftop vantage point to allow the queen to enjoy the view. This was a 'Wainscott turning Seate . . . sett upon the Plattforme over the Queene's Gallary', for which George Trenhale, joiner, was paid during 1682–4.[3]

But these were trivial works compared with the decoration of the King's Chapel, executed during the period 1680–2. Here Verrio's paintings were not confined to the ceiling, but extended to the altar-piece and the upper parts of the north and south walls as well. Gibbons's carving both covered the lower parts of the side walls, between a series of niches, and also enriched the seating. Altogether the chapel had a decorative unity lacking in the other state apartments. The framework of the painted parts was an order of twisted columns carried round the north, south and west (ritual east) walls, the order being imitated from Raphael's cartoon for 'St. Peter healing the lame man at the Beautiful Gate', in the royal collection. Furthermore the north wall was painted with a related subject, the healing miracles not of St. Peter but of Christ. For the rest, the programme was concerned with the events of Easter week. The altarpiece showed the Last Supper, the ceiling the Resurrection, with the empty tomb in the cove above the altarpiece, the sleeping soldiers round the rest of the cove of the ceiling, and the risen Christ in the centre of the ceiling itself surrounded by a host of angels. Gibbons's wall decoration ('all white natural wood without varnish') took up the theme symbolically, in its sprays of palms and laurels, and the pelican in her piety placed over each niche. In the accounts this decoration is specified as being 'laid upon XXVIII^t Seates and Stalls'. For this and for the twenty feet of framing to each seat and the five feet of 'Cornice that has two members inrich'd with Leaves between each Seate', Gibbons received £518, and a further £498 5½d. for carving 'the Six Vasses with Thistles, Roses and two Boyes Laurels and Palmes and other Ornaments in the ffront and upon the Topp of the Kings Seate', in the royal pew at the east (ritual west) end of the chapel, and for 'Drapery ffruite, fflowers, Crootesses Starres, Roses and severall other Ornaments of Carveing about the Altar, Pews and other places in and about the Kings Chappell'. For painting 'the Ceilings, Side Walls, End Walls, and in the square and round Windowes' Verrio received £1050, and Cousin's gilding there cost £113 2s. 6d. Bernard Smith's alterations to the organ cost £100, as ordered by a Treasury warrant of 9 February 1681/2. John Evelyn 'liked exceedingly the Contrivance of the unseene Organs behind the Altar', for nothing was visible except a group of pipes revealed through the fictive semi-dome above the altarpiece, and flanked by balconies which Celia Fiennes noted to be 'gallerys for the musick'.

The total cost of decorating the chapel therefore amounted to about £2700,

---

[1] AO 1/2478/271 (E 351/3451).
[2] AO 1/2479/272.
[3] AO 1/2479/273.

including the payments made to the joiners, Matthew Williams and John Turner, for wainscotting and furniture.[1]

As soon as the foreign artists had completed their work in the state apartments they were directed to embellish the settings for the Garter ceremonies. The reconstruction of the fabric of St. George's Hall was completed about 1680. The master masons, John Clarke and George Pile, were paid for stonework there and in 'Henry VIII's Chapel'[2] in the account for 1680–2, but in the same account not only did the plasterers, John Martin and John Grove, complete the preparation of the hall for painting, and Martin execute plasterer's work in the chapel, but Verrio did the first instalment of painting, for £1000, in the hall. Verrio received his second £1000 in the following account, having agreed to complete the decoration of the hall by midsummer 1683, and a further £250 for 'extraordinary painting' in the hall over and above his first contract. The decorative scheme introduced St. George and the Dragon on the west wall, above the throne, but its main theme was the glorification of the Garter, with Charles himself in the place of greatest glory, enthroned among clouds in the central oval of the ceiling. In the two octagonal fields which occupied the remainder of the ceiling the Muses were depicted surrounding the Garter Star with other allegorical figures round the Garter Collar. In the cove of the ceiling pairs of putti held up Garter mantles, and the Garter motto was inscribed round each of the six circular upper windows in the south wall. The walls were divided into bays, as in the king's chapel, by feigned columns, here Corinthian columns in pairs. On the north wall the subject was the reception of the Black Prince in triumph by Edward III. Here, in contrast to the king's chapel, Verrio's paintings completely dominated the room. The floor was paved with 'Swedland Marble and Purbeck Mitchells laid togeather' and there were 'Stone and whit Marble Stepps . . . goeing to his Majesties Throne'; and the wall-dado below the painted area was similarly subdued. Gibbons was paid the relatively modest sum of £328 16s. 11¼d. for his carving in St. George's Hall, carving specified in unusual detail in the declared accounts. The specification mentions the enriched mouldings of the wainscot and door surrounds visible in Pyne's print (Pl. 43A), mouldings and some ornaments for the throne, which had itself been executed in 1678, but nothing else in the way of independent carving except 'the Pannell in the front of the Staires, the Garter and ffestoones about the twoe Compass Doores, the twoe Georges'. These last must have been small panels of St George fighting the dragon, one of which still survives, reset in the present Garter Throne Room. The unifying element in the Hall must have been the gilding. Cousin was paid the unusually large amount of £416 6s. 6d., and for that (besides gilding some alterations in the king's chapel and the royal arms in 'Henry VIII's Chapel') he gilded both 'severall Ornaments of painting [in] the Ceiling & Windowes' (i.e. the coffered window reveals), and Gibbons's 'carved framing round the Waynescott', and also applied copious gilding to the throne and the rail round it. The 'Guilders Account' dates this work to June 1684. The 'foure great ffigures' mentioned in the declared account are probably the '4 figures at

[1] AO 1/1479/272; W. Pyne, *Royal Residences* i, plate facing p. 179; Evelyn, *Diary* iv, p. 316; C. Fiennes, *Journeys*, ed. Morris, p. 278; Royal Library, Windsor Castle MS. *cit.* Fragments of Gibbons's carved woodwork survive in the Waterloo Chamber.
[2] I.e. the 'Tomb House', now the Albert Memorial Chapel.

the Kings Chappel stairs' between the hall and the chapel, which Celia Fiennes called 'four Brass Gyants or else painted like brass', and remembered to have seen supporting the royal pew. Oddly, there is no reference in the accounts to the construction of these figures.[1]

From St. George's Hall Verrio moved on to 'Henry VIII's Chapel', where he painted the 'Ceiling, Side Walls and End Walls' for £1000. By the end of September 1684 he had executed painting there valued at £700. The final £300 however was not earned until the period of the account for 1686–8, when he executed the chapel ceiling, in which the new monarch, James II, appeared enthroned among allegorical figures.[2]

So by the time of Charles II's death his great programme had been almost completed. The only works later specified as not done during the time of May's comptrollership were repairs to the wardrobe lodgings and Blackrod Tower, for which an estimate for £500 was submitted in 1695.[3] The two artists, Verrio and Gibbons, who contributed so much to the splendour of the interiors, were treated as specially attached to the Windsor works. From January 1680 Verrio received £200 per annum as a reward for his pains at Windsor. This pension was paid until Christmas 1684, but does not seem to have been continued by James II, for in June 1684 Verrio succeeded Sir Peter Lely as the king's 'first and chief painter', a post to which a salary of £200 per annum was attached. Gibbons's Windsor salary of £100 per annum was first paid in 1682 and was specifically a remuneration 'for repairing cleansing and preserving the carved work in Windsor Castle'. He succeeded in drawing this salary at least until 1713. It may be noted that the payment of £150 to Gibbons for the 'Extraordinary fine peece of Carved worke' sent by Charles II to Cosimo, Grand Duke of Tuscany, and now preserved in the Bargello in Florence, was charged to the Windsor account.[4]

For the castle's water supply the well with Sir Samuel Morland's pump in it soon proved inadequate. In 1681 Morland designed a new pumping engine to bring water up from the Thames at Under Ore (Romney Island) half a mile north of the Castle, where the site of the old town mill was rented from the Corporation of New Windsor for £70 per annum starting in January 1681/2. Morland's first estimate was for £800, but he received between June 1681 and September 1682, besides 68 loads of timber from Windsor Forest, a total of £1500 for the engine and for lead pipes. In 1685 however he presented a petition to the Treasury claiming that because of unforeseen circumstances his total charge had been £2990 4s. 5½d.: 'it was proposed at first only to raise the water out of the mill river, but the King finding tanners' skins and other nastiness in that river petitioner was forced to make a water house and a new engine and be at many unforeseen expenses about sinking the river, the mill, well etc. and being in a hurry and for want of ready money [had] to make bad bargains all which trebled the first estimate, although nothing was done without his Majesty's privity and approbation'. Payment was made in the account for 1682–4 to Maurice Emmett, for brickwork 'done round the conduit and Engine

[1] AO 1/2479/273; Windsor MS. 'Guilders Account'; C. Fiennes, *Journeys*, ed. Morris, p. 278.
[2] AO 1/2479/273 and AO 1/2479/276 (E 351/3453); Croft-Murray, *op. cit.*, p. 241.
[3] T 1/98/1, f. 54.
[4] The pensions are entered in the declared accounts. For the Cosimo panel see AO 1/2479/272.

with paveing bricks'. In 1685 Wren, who had been appointed Comptroller of the Windsor Office on the death of Hugh May in 1684, was ordered to put into effect his designs for a wharf by the engine. Once in operation the engine was serviced by John Taylor, who received £40 per annum for his pains. At Taylor's death in 1709 the task and salary fell to Joseph Roberts, Master Plumber in the Windsor Office.[1]

In the garden and parks Charles II ordered considerably less. In 1676 substantial levelling was carried out in the Little Park, under the direction of George Moore, gardener. This area was planted up *c.* 1680, when £2 4s. was expended on forty-four sacks of hay seeds 'to sow the New levell'd ground in the Parke', and fencing was placed round 600 elm trees there, presumably newly planted. In the same account there is also reference to 'digging down and levelling the brest work in Mastrike', the site of the Duke of Monmouth's mock military displays on the north side of the castle.[2]

In 1680, however, the king decided to enlarge his property at Windsor. A warrant dated 12 May authorised William Harbord, Surveyor General of Crown Lands, and others to treat with the owners of land on the north side of the castle, between the Terrace Walk and the river, and also with owners south of the castle, where the king was 'disposed to have an avenue 240 feet broad made in a direct line between our Castle of Windsor and our Great Park there', a line represented by the present Long Walk.[3] During Charles's reign nothing came of the first proposal, but in spite of certain disputes over the availability of land and the terms offered for its purchase, enough land had been acquired by 1683 to allow work to begin on the avenue. In November 1682 the Treasury authorised the expenditure of not more than £4000, to cover purchase of the land and construction of the avenue.[4] The special account declared shows that between 1 January 1682/3 and 30 June 1685 a total of £3645 16s. 11½d. was spent, of which £1260 12s. 9d. went on the purchase of land. But, as notwithstanding the terms of the warrant the Treasury grant had been only £2500, the account registered a substantial debt, which was added to the general debt on the Windsor account. In all, 1864 elm trees were planted, forming four rows over three miles long. Moses Cooke and George London dug a ditch and bank on either side of the avenue and planted whitethorn quicksets there. Adrian Prat received 4s. a day for supervising the whole operation.[5]

The last construction authorised during the reign was a new guardhouse, for which contracts to an estimate for £610 were drawn up on 27 January 1684/5. The account for the completed building was signed by Wren on 11 September 1685. The total cost was £774 14s., of which Bernard Angier received £370 19s. 9d. for carpenter's work and Maurice Emmett, the Master Bricklayer, £323 16s. 1d. for brickwork, the increase over the contract price being accounted for by 'Raysing the Additionall Storey to the Officers Roomes . . . not in the Contract'.[6]

---

[1] *Cal. Treas. Books* vii, pp. 172, 174, 281, 656, viii, pp. 353, 394, 411–12, 2134; AO 1/2479/272 (payment to Morland and rent for mill); AO 1/2479/273 (Emmett's task); *Cal. Treas. Books* xxiii, p. 434.

[2] AO 1/2478/270 (E 351/3450), task of Thomas Greene and others in the first account, payment to Moore in the second account; AO 1/2478/271 (E 351/3451), Richard Samborne for hay seeds, task of Edmund Cox and others in the second account.

[3] *Cal. Treas. Books* vi, pp. 533–4.　　　　[4] *Cal. Treas. Books* vii, p. 642.　　　　[5] AO 1/2479/274.

[6] Works 5/145, ff. 158–9. Two versions of the account are in B.M. Add. 5755, ff. 295–301 and in Works 5/39, of which the latter is printed in *Wren Soc.* viii, pp. 14–15. See Hope, p. 328 and plate xxx.

For James II and his consort no major new works were undertaken. The accounts record the predictable sums on minor alterations to the royal apartments and fitting up of courtiers' lodgings.[1] The most significant refittings were of the various chapels, which apart from those of the Prince and Princess of Denmark had to be converted for Roman Catholic worship. Verrio's painting in 'Henry VIII's Chapel' in the Lower Ward has already been mentioned. In 1686–8 a further payment for painting there appears in the accounts, Robert Streater, the Sergeant Painter, charging for 'Gray Marble Colour done on the Walls and other Stoneworke'. In the account for 1684–6 Grinling Gibbons was paid for 'Altar Peeces in the Kings and Queens Chappels', besides frames over chimneys and picture-frames in the queen's apartments and elsewhere, to a total of £96 19s. 9d.; and the taskwork of John Clarke and George Pile included 'sawing squaring and laying severall ffoot of white and black Marble at the Altar in his Majestys Chappell'. René Cousin received small sums for gilding the degrees of the altars in the king's and queen's chapels, and for 'Guilding of the Sides and Repairing the Ends of the Picture fframe in the front of the Altar in the Queen's Private Chappell and for mending the Tabernacle there'.[2] The following account contains nothing more, except a payment of £2 to Gibbons for carving two foliage panels for the 'Confession Chaire' in the king's chapel.[3]

The secular amusements of the king and queen were for the most part inexpensive. Charles II had kept cage birds at Windsor, at least since June 1678.[4] His brother had a 'Bird called Cockatoo' in a cage in his eating room; during 1686–8 14 guineas were spent on 'meate for the Kings Cornish Chaffs', and an entry in the Windsor account for the period after James's deposition records money spent in 'feeding and keeping the Cornish Dawes 39 weeks' from 30 December 1688.[5] Early in the reign the masons, Clarke and Pile, supplied 'severall foot of white marble laid in the Queens Bird Cage and a white marble Pedestall and Bason for the same'.[6] Of more ephemeral concern to the Windsor Office were the alterations made in August 1688 by Wren on the warrant of the Lord Chamberlain, the Earl of Mulgrave, 'in the playhouse att Windsor as you shall receive directions from the french Comoedians'.[7]

For the queen two new rooms were fitted up, a round banqueting room on the roof, and a bathing room. For the painted decoration of the banqueting room Verrio received £250, although he asked £300, 'her Majestie having changed the 1st Designe for this which is fuller of figures'. The subject of the ceiling painting is unknown. The wall decoration was partly gilt, 'the upper waynscott pannells with flowers in potts, the lower pannells of waynscott with small figures, and some other parts of the waynscott in Imitation of Marble'. There were also in the room a marble chimneypiece with a mirror over it, and a parquet floor.[8] The bathing room

---

[1] See also the list of works in hand sent by Wren to the Lords of the Treasury on 22 March 1686/7 in Works 6/112.

[2] AO 1/2479/275 (E 351/3452).                        [3] AO 1/2479/276 (E 351/3453).

[4] AO 1/2479/272 (payment to Samuel Hull, Purveyor, for expenses in keeping His Majesty's birds from 8 June 1678 to 31 March 1682).

[5] AO 1/2479/276 (E 351/3453), payment to John Davis. AO 1/2479/277 (E 351/3454), payment to William Winckall.

[6] AO 1/2479/275 (E 351/3452).                        [7] Works 6/1, f. 38ᵛ.

[8] AO 1/2479/275 (E 351/3452), payments to Verrio and Cousin; *Wren Soc.* xviii, pp. 63–4; Windsor 'Guilders Account'; AO 1/2479/276 (E 351/3453), payment to William Cleere, joiner.

contained a marble bathing cistern with a wainscot border round it. Water was conveyed to it through copper pipes, for which Gibbons carved a model costing ten shillings.[1]

King William during the lifetime of his consort took no interest in Windsor. When Evelyn visited the castle in 1692 he found it 'furnish'd, & very neately kept as formerly, onely the Armes in the Gard Chambers & Keepe were removed & carried away'.[2] On 13 November 1695 Wren, as Comptroller of the Windsor Office, and John Ball, the Surveyor, sent a memorandum to the Lords of the Treasury pointing out that the Office was in debt to the tune of nearly £6000, while from the revenue of the Honor of Windsor only about £100 per annum was available to pay for running repairs. They submitted a list of necessary repairs estimated at £835, and a further estimate of £990 for works 'fit to be don in time to prevent charge'. Characteristically, the Treasury voted the former sum but not the latter.[3] In the event the Paymaster of the Works paid over only half of this, plus a further £2000 in 1697. The sole Exchequer grant of the reign was made in 1700, of £5000. These sums, together with the revenues of the Honor of Windsor, proved to be just enough to cover the works executed during the reign, which cost less than £1000 per annum. A single account was declared for the whole period 1688–1702.[4] This account did not however include the extensive painting for which Verrio received £1800 between June 1699 and November 1701. This was for repairing several ceilings and for 'new painting' or 'new doeing' the following: the sides and ends of St. George's Hall, the altarpiece and sides of the chapel, the king's privy stairs, the Stone Gallery, the Court and the sides of the Guard Chamber staircase.[5] Whether this extremely costly repainting involved changes in the compositions, or whether the paintwork had become so decayed as to need wholesale refurbishing is not clear.

The king did however in 1698 entertain ideas of the most grandiose kind for the remodelling of the castle. Among the Wren drawings at All Souls College, Oxford, are a block plan and four variant elevations of a scheme for creating a symmetrical south-facing exterior to the Upper Ward.[6] The plan shows that a primary consideration was to formalise the route through the Castle. Thus the houses of the vicars choral were to be swept away to allow an entrance at the west end of the Lower Ward opposite an impressive flight of steps up to St. George's Chapel. The Middle Ward is shown completely replanned, with a pair of entrances to the Upper Ward leading to a complex flight of steps along the east side of the Round Tower mound. The north and south sides of the Upper Ward were to be linked by a colonnaded gallery. The south elevation, especially in the finest version, drawn by Hawksmoor and dated 1698, is an extremely interesting critique of May's buildings, similar to them in details such as the windows, but far more boldly grouped, and symmetrical about an imposing central block which clearly echoes May's Star Building. What practical use the king could have found for such an increase in the castle's accommodation as this scheme would have entailed is hard to imagine, nor was a penny spent on it.

---

[1] AO 1/2479/276 (payments to John [sic] Trenhaile and Grinling Gibbons); Works 121/9 (Wren's report 22 Mar. 1686/7).  [2] Evelyn, *Diary* v, p. 103.
[3] T 98/1, ff. 53–6; *Cal. Treas. Books* x, pp. 1240, 1288.  [4] AO 1/2479/277 (E 351/3454).
[5] T 98/1, ff. 132–3.  [6] *Wren Soc.* viii, pls. xi, xiii and xv.

For gardens at Windsor the king's ambitions at this time were just as high-flown, and here some preliminary practical steps were taken to implement them. The first we hear of new gardens is in a letter to the king from the Earl of Portland in Paris, dated 7–8 March 1698, in which he writes 'Mr. le Nostre me fera un plan pour les jardins, projettez à Windsor'.[1] A plan which, although by an English draughtsman, may record Le Nôtre's designs, is among the Wren drawings at All Souls. It shows elaborate formal gardens and plantations north, east and south of the Castle.[2] A Treasury warrant of 11 May 1698 authorised Samuel Travers, Surveyor General of Crown Lands, to begin negotiations to purchase lands lying north and east of the castle 'between the Terrace Walk and the river and between the Little Park and the river . . . the chief part whereof lies in a place called Mill Mead or Millfield and other part in a place called Datchet Mead . . . and are intended by his Majesty to be laid into the Little Park and the residue to be taken in and converted to gardens and to other accommodation to the Palace'.[3] In early July the king was at Windsor and 'viewed the ground about the castle markt out by Mr. London and the director of the French kings gardens, who came over with the earl of Portland'.[4] Royal warrants were issued during 1699 and 1700 for over £12,000 to be spent on the purchase of the land, it being proposed to sell Crown lands in order to raise the money; and in May 1701 it was reported that £827 7s. was due to the Dean and Canons of Windsor for land taken into the Little Park.[5]

In 1701 Henry Wise began work on the north side of the castle, terracing the steep slope below the terrace-walk, planting trees and digging a canal in the 'great plantation' on the level ground known since 1674 as Maestricht (see above, p. 316) between the castle and the Thames.[6]

At the king's death the work in the gardens and park stopped. In 1708 however the development of Maestricht was continued, by enlarging the new canal there, which yielded sufficient gravel to surface a new road from Windsor to Staines. (It was presumably in connection with this road that payment of £3000 had been authorised in May 1706 for building a bridge over the Thames at Datchet. The bridge, of timber, was completed after Michaelmas 1708 by John Finkell at a total recorded cost of £1719 15s. 8d.)[7] The work was again entrusted to Wise, who late in 1709 was further engaged on the terraces of the north slope, to make a chaise road for the queen from Maestricht to the Bowling Green in the upper part of the park.[8]

A third phase of work in Maestricht began in 1713, when Wise presented an

---

[1] *Correspondentie van Willem III en van Hans Willem Bentinck*, ed. N. Japikse, 's-Gravenhage, i (1927), p. 246.
[2] *Wren Soc.* viii, pl. xii.
[3] *Cal. Treas. Books* xiii, p. 334.
[4] Luttrell, *Brief Histor. Relat.* iv, p. 401.
[5] *Cal. Treas. Books* xiv, p. 253; xv, p. 112, 228, 231, 245, 287; xvi, p. 260.
[6] Works 5/52 (statement of work done by Wise from 12 Sept. 1701 to 8 March 1701/2 in the House Park and on the north side of the Castle); D. Green, *Gardener to Queen Anne* (1956), p. 79. See also *Cal. Treas. Books* xvii, p. 64.
[7] Copies of a letter from the Officers of the Works to Godolphin 6 May 1708, in Works 6/1, f. 53r., 6/14, f. 163 and T 1/107/4. For the bridge see AO 1/2480/278 (E 351/3455) and AO 1/2480/280 (E 351/3457).
[8] Works 6/5, p. 38. This may have been the occasion on which Thomas Archer presented a model 'for a stair to ascend Windsor Terrace with coaches' (Hist. MSS. Comm. *Portland* x, p. 147, Archer to the Earl of Oxford, 16 March 1713). Wise's taskwork is itemised in AO 1/2480/279 (E 351/3456) and AO 1/2480/280 (E 351/3457).

estimate for 'levelling, New-Making and planting a Division of Ground on the North Side of the Castle . . . which Referrs to a Design her Majesty was pleased to Direct, and has Approved of'. Wise's estimate for £6874 1s. 8d. was accepted by the Treasury. The interruption of the series of declared accounts at Michaelmas 1713 leaves us ignorant of Wise's progress, but by 16 July 1714 he had received £3000 towards the work.[1] By this time however the estimate had nearly doubled, to almost £12,800, since the area of terracing and planting had been enlarged and the whole ground was now to be enclosed by a brick wall with railings 7 ft. high and five pairs of iron gates, estimated to cost £4037 12s. 4½d. in all.[2] Two plans for this scheme survive, varying in their arrangement of the enclosing wall and railings.[3]

The death of the queen at the end of the month brought work to a halt. Today no trace of these garden works remains, except the outline of the canal, visible from the air.

Queen Anne was the only Stuart monarch who felt that Windsor was her home. She had even before her accession bought a house of modest size and pretensions which stood below the west end of the south terrace walk opposite the Rubbish Gate, sharing a garden wall with Burford Lodge. This house, which appears in official documents under the name of the Queen's Little, Lower, or most usually Garden House, the princess had purchased from Lord Godolphin and presented to her husband, Prince George.[4] The house had been built not later than the early seventeenth century, but substantial additions were made to it, probably by Anne before her accession.[5] Celia Fiennes, who justly described the house as 'a little box', yet shows that there was room for Prince George's apartment on the ground floor and an, admittedly curtailed, royal apartment above stairs: presence chamber, bedchamber, (with a 'screen round the bed as the manner is to all the Souveraignes beds') dressing room and closets.[6] The Works declared accounts for Anne's reign include only a few specific references to the Garden House and it is clear that little beyond maintenance work was required during that period.[7] But the queen's fondness for the house is emphasised by the fact that between 1706 and 1709 negotiations were in progress to buy messuages which would, if built on, obstruct the view from the Garden House; as it is also by the relative costs of mourning for the house and for the castle at the death of Prince George, estimated at £1993 for the former but less than half that amount (£925) for the latter.[8]

Considerations of state nevertheless made it inevitable that the queen should use the royal apartments in the castle so near her favoured dwelling-place and improve the appearance of its surroundings. Between 1702 and 1707 almost twice

[1] T 98/1, ff. 366–8 and T 27/21, f. 48, Lowndes to Wise, 12 Oct. 1713.

[2] T 98/1, ff. 305–7, and Works 6/5, p. 298.

[3] P.R.O. MPD 122 (with a plan of the ground before work started, showing the canal dug in 1701) and Soane Museum, the latter reproduced in *Wren Soc.* viii, pl. xvi.

[4] C. Fiennes, *Journeys*, ed. Morris, pp. 357–9; *Cal. Treas. Papers* vi, p. 281.

[5] Compare Hollar's view published in 1672 with Kip's engraving of 1709 (reproduced in Hope i, pls. xxii and xxvii). Lord Godolphin lived at Cranborne Lodge in Windsor Great Park, by virtue of his post of Keeper of the Great Park, so he is unlikely to have made the additions visible in Kip's print.

[6] C. Fiennes, *Journeys*, ed. Morris, pp. 357–9; AO 1/2480/279 (E 351/3456), account for 1707–8.

[7] AO 1/2480/279 under painter's and mason's tasks, including four marble chimneypieces, and AO 1/2480/280 (E 351/2457), account for 1708–13, under painter's taskwork. See also T 98/1, ff. 198, 206, 251 for references to unspecified work done in the Garden House in 1703–4.

[8] *Cal. Treas. Books* xxi, p. 110 and xxiii, p. 421; *ibid.* xxiii, p. 100.

as much money was spent on Windsor as had been laid out during the whole of King William's reign, although little in the way of significant new works was undertaken. By the middle of 1713 the total expenditure had reached about £48,500. Annual warrants of £5000 were made, and paid, towards the Windsor works. From the beginning of 1703 the Treasury required the Windsor Office to furnish quarterly abstracts of expenditure on the castle, its gardens and parks, but this attempt to keep the Windsor works under close surveillance lapsed at the end of 1709.[1]

In the first months of the reign Gibbons received small payments for repairs to carved work in the queen's apartment and Peter Cousin for gilding in her private chapel.[2] During the rest of Anne's reign joiners, painters and plasterers all received large sums for refurbishing the interior of the Castle for the court after its years of neglect by William III. Payments for cleaning the equestrian statue of Charles II in the Upper Ward, for repairing the model of the castle and for making a survey plan of Windsor Great Park all speak of renewed care for Windsor. Yet accounts show little in the way of special items. Before Michaelmas 1707 one can only point to Peter Cousin's expensive regilding of the Great Staircase and of the pipes and carved work of the chapel organ, to the white marble 'compasse shelfes' and oval cistern to go under them in the Duke of Marlborough's dining room, and the white and veined marble chimneypiece for the queen's dressing room, all supplied by John Clarke, the mason, and to a small amount of carving done by Grinling Gibbons, costing no more than £39 19s. 10d. in all, comprising a limewood overmantel and a frame for a mirror in the queen's dressing room, and 'a Cocks Head for the Dutchesse of Marlboroughs Side Board, and a Snakes head for the Basin at the Queen's Back Stairs'.[3] For later years there is nothing to report, except the paving of the Horn Court with 'blew and red Sweed's marble' in 1707–8.[4] Meanwhile other parts of the castle were continuing to decay. In June 1703 Wren's estimate for repairing several ruinous walls came to £1617 17s.; in the last six months of the queen's reign estimates were drawn up for altering and making habitable Garter's Tower and the White Tower.[5]

The eighteenth century was not a period of major building activity at Windsor. Until 1778 none of the Hanoverian kings regularly resided there, and it was not until 1800 that George III allowed James Wyatt to begin the Gothicising process that was to be so expensively continued by his successor. Windsor Castle in the eighteenth century remained substantially as Charles II had left it, and the task of the Georgian Office of Works was essentially one of maintenance. In 1716 the independent comptrollership of works at Windsor was suppressed, and the castle was placed on the same footing as the other royal palaces, with a clerk of works directly responsible to the Board in Whitehall.[6] Windsor was too distant for the employment there of the Board's regular London workmen, and local men were normally used. Though no fee now attached to his post, an official mason was still nominated by the Board and was regularly employed on routine maintenance.[7] The gardens came

---

[1] AO 1/2480/278–80 (E 351/3455–7) for totals of money granted and expenditure; T 98/1, ff. 198–402 for quarterly totals.          [2] AO 1/2479/277 (E 351/3454).
[3] AO 1/2480/278 (E 351/3455).          [4] AO 1/2480/279 (E 351/3456).
[5] T 86/38; T 98/1, ff. 331, 390.          [6] Above, pp. 120–1.
[7] For their names see below, pp. 478–9. No successor to Munden is named in the Board's records.

under the jurisdiction of the Board, but were maintained by contract by a succession of master gardeners: Charles Bridgeman (who had taken over from Henry Wise in 1726 and died in 1738), John Kent (appointed 1738, died 1773) and Adam Younger (1773 onwards).[1] Another of the Board's responsibilities was the maintenance of the pumping-engine on Romney Island. By 1717 Sir Samuel Morland's machinery, which had supplied the castle with water for over thirty years, was 'so faulty and worn' that it was deemed incapable of further repair. Vanbrugh, as Surveyor of Gardens and Waters, obtained authority from the Treasury to replace it by 'an entire new engine' which, together with a new engine-house, cost £2912 to build in 1718.[2] The engine-house, which still exists, is a building so much in Vanbrugh's manner as to suggest that it was built under his personal supervision.[3] The new engine proved to be so much more powerful than the old one that it threatened to burst Morland's two-inch pipe, and a new four-inch one had to be substituted.[4] No details of the machinery are given in the Works records, but when the main shaft had to be replaced in 1759, no merchant could be found to supply a piece of timber of the required dimensions (14 feet in length and 3 feet in diameter), and in the end the Board had to beg one from the naval store-yard at Woolwich.[5]

George I was not often at Windsor, but his presence in the summer of 1724 for a Garter Installation led to a number of repairs and alterations. Most of these concerned the gardens and the 'Garden House', and it would appear that George I, like Queen Anne, resided not in the castle itself, but in this small house near the west end of the South Terrace. In July the Board (consisting of Gill, Dubois and Ripley) spent two days at Windsor with the Clerk of the Works in order to 'view and consider the severall works directed by His Majesty's verbal order, delivered by the Rt. Hon^ble. Robert Walpole Esr^r. to His Majesty's Surveyor'. These, as summarised in a formal letter from the Lord Chamberlain, were 'to make a drawbridge over the ditch between the Castle and the garden of the Garden House, a new pair of gates at the road leading to the Parke, and 2 piers; to make a doore into the garden, a staircase from the garden to the Presence Chamber in the Garden House; to take away the steps and make slopes in the garden. To turn the road from the upper to the lower part of the Park by a new fence of pallisadoes and to repair and remove lower the old fence by the Bowling Green'.[6] The Board's estimate for these alterations was £4056, and by 1 August they were able to report to the Treasury 'that according to order, we have made a great progress in the execution of the several works required to be done for His Majesty's service at Windsor, and hope to compleat the same in the time requir'd'.[7] From a letter to the dean and canons dated 29 July it appears that the road that was to be diverted was the one from Windsor to Datchet, which had hitherto run across the House or Little Park, and was now to be taken

---

[1] Bridgeman had a comprehensive contract for all the royal gardens, but Kent's contract was limited to Windsor and Newmarket, and Younger's to Windsor only (Works 6/114, pp. 7–8, 13–14; Works 6/8, pp. 49–53, 259–62).

[2] Works 6/6, pp. 238–40; Works 6/113, p. 4; Works 5/141, year 1718.

[3] The original measurement of the workmanship involved, signed by the Clerk of Works, Thomas Rowland, and his colleague Thomas Fort from Hampton Court, is in the Bodleian Library (Gough Maps 1, f. 23). It is accompanied by a contemporary plan and elevation of the building.

[4] *Cal. Treasury Papers 1720–8*, pp. 49, 138.

[5] Works 1/3, pp. 132–3. See also *Cal. Treasury Books & Papers 1739–41*, pp. 220, 456.

[6] T 1/250, ff. 156–7; Works 6/15, pp. 54–5.                    [7] T 1/250, f. 142; Works 6/15, p. 47.

'along the foot of the slopes to the gates at the end of Datchett Lane', where it would interfere less with the privacy of the park. Considerable progress had already been made with the new road, but 'finding there may be a nearer and better way made from the 100 steps thro' part of your ground in lease to Mr. Lovegrove into the Lower Parke for the conveniency of your selves and other gentlemen who have now keys of the Tarrass', the Board asked the dean and chapter 'to permitt your said tenant to suffer us to make a way thro' the said ground in the best and easiest manner, His Majesty having instructed us to make all things as easy as possible for every body'. At the same time directions were given for 'a new way to be made out of the Duchess of Kendall's appartment in Windsor Castle into the Terrass walk, and a new doore to be hung at the topp of the stairs leading down to the Terrass; likewise a pair of stairs to be made to the great roome in the Devill's Tower . . . which is to be fitted up for the use of the Board of Green Cloth.'[1] In October a further instruction came from the Lord Chamberlain 'to give orders for digging away the earth on the south side of the Tomb House in Windsor Castle, between the buttresses, and to turn arches between them to keep the wett from soaking thro' the walls, and to secure the roof where the lead is wanting'.[2]

While these alterations were in progress bricklayers were at work in the ditch between the Round Tower and the Upper Ward. The vertical counterscarp of this ditch was supported by a series of 35 brick arches, which probably formed part of the military works carried out in 1670.[3] In 1718 the Board had pointed out to the Treasury that these arches were 'in a very ill state and ruinous condition occasioned by the pressure of the great weight of earth upon the wall', but no *fiat* had then been forthcoming, and they had been propped up with wooden shores. Despite these precautions about 50 feet of the wall above collapsed in 1724, and authority was now given for proper repairs to be carried out at an estimated cost of £850.[4]

George II's first visit to Windsor was in the summer of 1728, when he told Lord Hervey that Richmond was an old friend, but Windsor was a 'new acquaintance' that he was anxious to get to know.[5] He returned in the summer of 1730 in order to hunt and to install the Duke of Cumberland as a Knight of the Garter.[6] Meanwhile orders had been given during the king's absence in Hanover for William Kent to restore the decorative paintings on the two great staircases, which by now were in need of attention. For this task, accomplished in the course of the summer of 1729, Kent received £300.[7] As the order was given while the king was abroad it is very likely that it was due to Queen Caroline, who in her capacity as regent was thus able to employ an artist whom she particularly favoured. It was for the queen that in September 1729 Lord Burlington made a design for altering the terrace at Windsor, sketches for which are preserved at Chatsworth.[8] Many of Verrio's paintings in other parts of the castle were equally in need of repair. Already in the reign

---

[1] Works 4/2, 29 July 1724. For plans of the area see Works 34/175, 263 and 264.
[2] Works 6/15, p. 62.    [3] Above, p. 315.
[4] Works 6/7, pp. 50–1; Works 6/15, pp. 20–1; Works 4/2, 8 Jan., 29 April, 6 May, 18 July, 1724; Works 4/3, 16 Dec. 1724. Works 34/326 in a contemporary plan showing the arches shored up.
[5] Hervey, *Memoirs of the Reign of George II*, ed. Croker i (1884), p. 107.
[6] *Cal. Treasury Books & Papers 1729–30*, pp. 258, 392, 406, 455, 465, 479, 596.
[7] *Cal. Treasury Books & Papers 1729–30*, pp. 92, 168.
[8] They are nos. 46 and 50 in a volume labelled *Chiswick & Chatsworth & Miscellaneous Drawings*.

of George I Defoe had noticed that the representation of the Black Prince's triumph in St. George's Hall was being spoiled by the efflorescence of 'the salts in the lime in the wall', and in 1731 the Board of Works pointed out to the Treasury that 'the paintings in the Court leading to the King's Great Staircase and in the open Gallery of Communication from the King's to the Queen's appartment' were 'so decayed and defaced that if they be not soon repaired it will be impossible to restore them'.[1] Kent was accordingly employed to carry out a programme of restoration of which the stages were as follows:

1730 'repairing the cracks and restoring fifteen ceilings and one of the king's staircases from the top to the bottom' £450[2]

1731 'restoring the paintings in the Court leading to the King's Great Staircase, and in the open gallery of communication from the King's to the Queen's appartment' £450[3]

1736 'repairing and making good the paintings decayed and defaced in the Great Chapel at Windsor Castle' £300[4]

1746 repainting on laths and canvas the whole of the decoration on the window side of St. George's Hall £260[5]

1747 repainting the decoration in the cupola of the Guard Chamber, destroyed in the course of structural repairs £180[6]

Meanwhile, in 1729–31, the Office of Works had been engaged in reconstructing the interiors of three of the towers—the Devil's or Maids' of Honour (now Edward III's) Tower at the south-west corner of the Upper Ward, the Winchester Tower in the northern curtain wall, and the adjoining Ordnance or Magazine Tower. These were later said to have been 'all new built except the outside walls', and the outlay amounted to £2393 in the case of the Devil's Tower, £1156 for the Ordnance Tower and £1173 for the Winchester Tower.[7] For what purposes these 'three great towers' were repaired is not recorded in the Works records. Some repairs were also carried out to the stonework of Garter's Tower in the Lower Ward,[8] but in 1733 John Anstis, then Garter King of Arms, complained in vain that the tower ('appropriated to the office of Garter for the preservation of such Books and Papers as shall relate to the most noble Order of the Garter') was ruinous and uninhabitable, and his successor Stephen Leake had no better success when he made a similar complaint in 1755: indeed the tower appears to have remained an empty shell until its restoration by Salvin in 1860.[9] In 1730 some minor repairs were carried out to the Round Tower at the request of the Constable, the Duke of St. Albans;[10] in 1732 its stone stairs were

---

[1] Daniel Defoe, *Tour through England and Wales* (Everyman edition) i, pp. 305–6; T 56/18, p. 352.
[2] Works 4/4, 7 July 1730; *Cal. Treasury Books & Papers 1729–30*, p. 402; AO 1/2453/164.
[3] Works 4/4, 8 April 1731, *Cal. Treasury Books & Papers 1731–4*, pp. 63, 65, 89; AO 1/2453/165.
[4] Works 6/16, p. 44; AO 1/2455/170.
[5] Works 4/9, 29 Aug. 1745; Works 6/17, f. 15ᵛ.
[6] Works 6/17, p. 36; AO 1/2459/182.
[7] Works 4/4, 23, 26 July, 5, 23 Aug., 2 Sept., 7, 21 Oct. 1729, 26 Jan., 14 July 1730; Works 6/17, p. 25; AO 1/2453/164.
[8] Works 4/4, 24 April, 13 and 27 May 1729.
[9] Works 6/16, p. 11; Works 6/17, p. 142; Works 1/3, p. 118; Hope, p. 529. Works 34/308 is a section and elevation which shows the internal arrangements of the tower before it fell into ruin.
[10] Works 4/4, 29 Sept., 15 Oct., 20 Nov. 1730; Works 6/15, pp. 227, 249.

renewed at a cost of £200,[1] and in 1753 several breaches in its outer curtain wall were made good after complaints from the then Constable, Lord Cardigan.[2]

Except on the occasion of Garter Installations, the castle was rarely if ever visited by royalty during the later years of George II. George III made equally little use of it until 1776, when he resumed possession of the Garden House (then occupied by Lord Talbot, the Steward of the Household) and gave it to Queen Charlotte.[3] By now the royal family was too large for Kew, and as the king's projects for a country palace at Richmond had come to nothing, Windsor offered itself as an alternative. Unfortunately the State Apartments in the Star Building were hopelessly inconvenient and old-fashioned: as for the remainder of the Upper Ward, the absence of communicating corridors made it quite impossible as a basis for family life. Plans exist for rebuilding the entire southern side of the Upper Ward so as to provide a series of comfortable apartments, and for linking it to the State Apartments by a new western range.[4] But the cost would have been enormous, and the king was advised that the castle 'could not be made comfortably habitable'.[5] He accordingly decided to alter the Garden House sufficiently to enable himself and the queen to sleep there 'whenever he might hunt in that neighbouroud or make an excursion, and find it too late for them conveniently to return to Kew or the Queen's Palace in the evening'.[6] But what had begun as a sort of country cottage soon grew to be a substantial house which was five years in building and cost in the end over £40,000.

The Queen's Lodge (to give it the name by which it was henceforth to be known) was an old, irregular, unpretentious building of brick with two bay windows projecting from its north front. Several plans of it exist, and it can be recognised in Kip's view of Windsor Castle from the south.[7] It stood rather awkwardly on the edge of the road leading into the Little Park, but had an attractive garden behind. The works began in 1776 with alterations estimated to cost a mere £3000, but no sooner were they finished than the king ordered 'several other works' estimated at £3850. Further estimates for £9450, £9000 and £3469 were obediently passed by the Treasury in November 1777, October 1778 and October 1779.[8] In 1779 the king bought the Duke of St. Albans' house further down the hill and began to remodel that in the same manner in order to provide accommodation for the four younger princesses.[9] Having acquired some adjoining premises from the dean and canons of Windsor he used the site to build the stables and coach-houses which formed the nucleus of the existing Royal Mews.[10] By 1782 he had spent nearly £50,000 on the Queen's Lodge and its satellite Lower Lodge.[11]

The works were supervised by the Office of Works and accounted for by the

[1] Works 6/15, pp. 249–50.          [2] Works 6/17, pp. 94ᵛ, 104.          [3] RA 2434.
[4] Windsor Castle Library, PA 3, nos. 5, 6 and 7. Works 34/164–169 is a set of designs for remodelling Horn Court which probably dates from this period. It is in the style of Sir William Chambers, and was doubtless his work.
[5] Farington's Diary, 8 June 1794.
[6] Farington's Diary, 22 Nov. 1793; *Court & Private Life in the Time of Queen Charlotte, being the Journals of Mrs. Papendiek*, ed. Mrs. V. Delves Broughton i (1887), pp. 91–3.
[7] Windsor Castle Library, Windsor portfolio (NN); P.R.O. Works 34/224, 930 and 931: St. John Hope, p. 347.
[8] Works 6/19, pp. 133, 157, 164, 166, 169, 219, 276.
[9] Works 6/19, p. 261; Works 4/16, 23 March 1779.
[10] Works 6/19, pp. 286, 364.
[11] Works 4/142; Works 4/16, 10 April 1782.

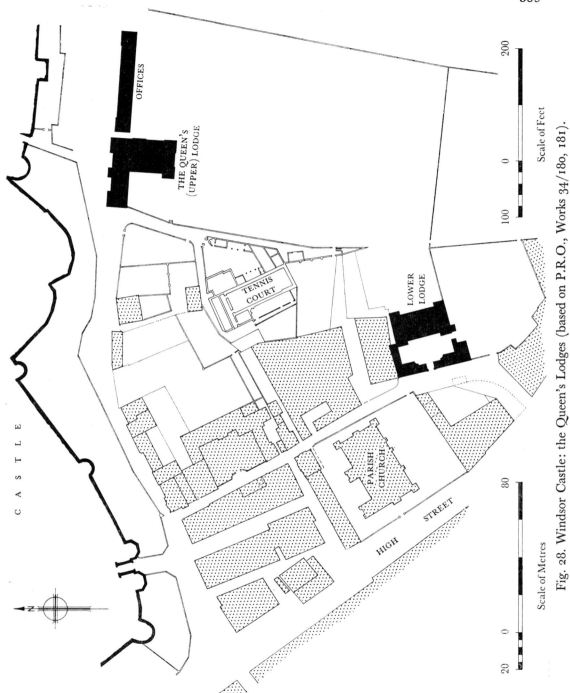

CASTLE

OFFICES

THE QUEEN'S
(UPPER) LODGE

TENNIS
COURT

LOWER
LODGE

PARISH
CHURCH

HIGH STREET

Scale of Metres

20   0                 80

Scale of Feet

100   0                 200

Fig. 28. Windsor Castle: the Queen's Lodges (based on P.R.O., Works 34/180, 181).

Paymaster in the usual way.[1] By the king's order Chambers received £50 each year 'for his extra expence in going to Windsor and giving directions'. It was, however, believed in the early nineteenth century that George III had been his own architect,[2] and it is certainly difficult to believe that Chambers would voluntarily have designed this crudest of all castellated boxes, with its squat towers and its long office-block stretching out to one side like a barracks (Pl. 42). The Gothic porch, decorated with stars and garters carved by Richard Lawrence, was in Portland stone, but the remainder of the building was of brick, covered with grey stucco to match the castle. As the joint effort of a 'virtuoso prince' and his architectural mentor it was a sorry performance, but as a family residence it served its purpose well enough, though Mrs. Papendiek (the wife of a minor member of the royal household) tells us that 'the arrangements in the Windsor Lodge were never altogether favourable to company, for the family began to reside in it before it was completed, and it always had the appearance of a scramble'.[3] In 1823 this expensive but unprepossessing building was pulled down by George IV, and its appearance is known to us only from the original elevation in the castle library, and from one or two contemporary engravings (Pl. 42). The Lower Lodge survived to be remodelled by Wyatville as dwellings for the staff of the Royal Mews, and still exists under the name of 'Burford House'.

Although the king was not resident in the castle his presence at Windsor resulted in certain alterations and repairs to its fabric which would not otherwise have been called for. From his new lodge he looked straight at the southern wall of the Upper Ward—a wall so much out of repair that it had to be shored up during the winter of 1779–80.[4] 'His Majesty', the Board of Works informed the Treasury in May 1780, 'having been pleased to command us to view many defects in the south front of Windsor Castle between the King's Gateway and Wardrobe Tower, we found the same in so dangerous a condition that the outer wall was immediately obliged to be taken down in order to be rebuilt, and to add additional walls for the security thereof; we have made an estimate of the charge of rebuilding the same together with reinstating the inside of the different apartments therto belonging and are of opinion the same will amount to the sum of £1279 11s. od. for which we beg your Lordships' warrant'. In addition they informed the Treasury that 'the walls of the Devil's Tower and the staircase thereunto belonging are very much crackt, but the expence of restoring the defects we cannot as yet ascertain'.[5] In February 1781 they reported that they had made 'considerable progress', but that 'in the course of the work, we found the walls in so bad a state that we were obliged to take down more than we intended, which consequently will encrease the cost considerably'.[6] They were now in a position to submit an estimate for the repair of the Devil's Tower, amounting to £2507. As soon as these repairs were completed, at a total cost of £4126, the king announced that he wanted the Board to take down the ancient curtain wall which encircled the base of the motte, together with the buildings behind it, and build a new wall 'more distant from the Queen's Lodge than the old one'. As the wall was 'very thick, extensive, and lofty, and exceedingly

[1] Works 5/66–69.
[2] A. Poynter in H. Ashton, *Illustrations of Windsor Castle* (1841), p. 16.
[3] *Journals of Mrs. Papendiek*, pp. 163–4.
[4] Works 5/67, Dec. 1779, under 'Queen's Lodge'.
[5] Works, 6/19, p. 291.
[6] Works 6/19, p. 329.

hard', the Board estimated that the cost of demolishing it would amount to at least £291, but in January 1783 Chambers was obliged to tell the Treasury that 'as the old works were much more difficult to destroy than had even at first been apprehended, the foundation very deep, in some places eighteen feet, the wall thick in order to support earth behind it in some places eleven feet high, . . . and the whole built of Heath Stone, with a double facing and coped with Portland, the amount of what has hitherto been done . . . is £1204 2s. 3¾d.'[1] In place of the old wall Chambers built what the antiquary Carter stigmatised as 'a common stone fence', whose line can be seen in Lysons's engraved plan representing the castle in 1805.[2] Another alteration which detracted from the ancient character of the castle (and as such duly incurred Carter's censure) was the filling up of the ditches along the south and east sides of the castle with the rubbish from the old wall and other demolished buildings.

These external changes were as yet matched by little in the way of internal alterations. In 1781 it was decided to give the Prince of Wales quarters of his own in the east range of the Upper Ward, and in May the Clerk of Works attended a Board in Whitehall, bringing with him 'His Majesty's commands relative to fitting up apartments for the Prince of Wales in the Castle'.[3] The resulting alterations do not, however, appear to have been very extensive. Though the remainder of the royal family lived in the two Lodges, the State Apartments were occasionally used for receiving company, and some attempts were made to refurbish the painted decoration, which was once more beginning to deteriorate. In 1776–7 the decayed plasterwork on the walls in Horn Court, which had 'formerly been done with history painting', was stripped off and replaced by new stucco painted a plain colour.[4] In 1778 J. B. Cipriani, 'History Painter', received £75 for 'repairing and new painting a great number of figures in the Queen's Back Stairs and in St. George's Hall', while £179 were paid to John Richards, 'Architect Painter', for 'repairing painting in St. George's Hall and finishing the Queen's Back Stairs, expences excluded'.[5] So far as St. George's Hall was concerned this must have been only a partial restoration, for in 1781 the Board resolved to ask Chambers 'to know His Majesty's pleasure relative to painting St. George's Hall'.[6] Nothing, however, appears to have been done, and it is probable that much of Verrio's painted decoration was in a poor state by the time it was destroyed by Wyatville.

---

[1] Works 6/20, pp. 55, 77.

[2] S. & D. Lysons, *Magna Britannia* i (1805), pp. 420–1. For Carter's strictures see *Gentleman's Magazine* 1805, part 1, pp. 529–30. Plan No. IV (in separate case) shows the Castle before the demolition of the wall, and should consequently (like Hope's plan upon which it is based) be dated 'about 1780' rather than 'about 1790'.

[3] Works 4/16, 4 May 1781.

[4] Works 4/15, 11 Aug. 1775, 28 June 1776.

[5] Works 5/66, Sept. 1778.

[6] Works 4/16, 27 June 1781.

# PART III

## Public Buildings

# THE LONDON CUSTOM HOUSE

THE CUSTOM HOUSE was the only casualty of the Great Fire for whose rebuilding the officers of the Works were corporately responsible. Five months after the catastrophe, orders were given (22 February 1667) for the site to be surveyed by the Surveyor General of Crown Lands (Sir Charles Harbord), the Surveyor General of the Works (Sir John Denham), and the other principal officers of the Works.[1] This survey, if made, does not seem to have survived, but the situation that the Officers of the Works were asked to investigate was a complicated one. The freehold of the site did not belong to the Crown, but to Sir Anthony Cope, and the old Custom House was interlocked with private warehouses whose tenants were, like the Crown, Cope's tenants. The Customs themselves were not directly managed by the Crown, but by farmers. It required a decision of the Fire Court to sort out the tangled rights and responsibilities of the various parties. The outcome was a judgement which enabled the Crown to rebuild the Custom House on a new site immediately in front of the old one, with unimpeded access to the river.[2]

The new building is included in the list of Wren's works compiled by his son and published in *Parentalia*, and he was undoubtedly responsible for its final appearance, though not necessarily for every feature either of its plan or of its elevations. As early as November 1667 he had been involved in the triangular negotiations between the Crown, the farmers and Sir Anthony Cope.[3] This was presumably in his capacity as one of the Commissioners appointed by the king to consider the rebuilding of the City. After this no further reference to Wren occurs for 18 months. During this period plans for the new Custom House appear to have been drawn up by the farmers in consultation with the Officers of the Works. The cost was estimated at £5800, and on 8 February 1669 the Treasury gave orders for a Privy Seal for £6000 to be paid to the Paymaster of the Works out of the Customs revenues for August and September 1670.[4] In March 1669, however, Wren became Surveyor of the Works, and as such took cognisance of the plans. He evidently considered them to be unsatisfactory, and said so at a meeting held at the Treasury on 11 May, and attended by the farmers, the Paymaster (Packer), and the Chief Clerk of the King's Works (Dickinson). Dickinson expressed the view that the alteration proposed by Wren would greatly increase the cost, and Wren was asked to state by the following day

---

[1] SP 29/192, no. 56.
[2] For full details of the site and its proprietors see T. F. Reddaway's valuable article, 'The London Custom House 1666–1740', *London Topographical Record* xxi (1958).
[3] *Cal. Treas. Books* ii, pp. 116–17.
[4] Reddaway, *op. cit.*, pp. 9–10.

what had in mind. His statement is not recorded, but he had his way, for on 25 May 1669 the Treasury Minutes read as follows:

> The Officers of the Workes called in about the additionall charge in building the Custome house its about £3000. The Lords [of the Treasury] agreed to it. That it shalbe placed on the Customes. a Warrant to build it after Mr. Wrenns Modell.[1]

On 23 June 1669 a warrant duly authorised Wren, as Surveyor General, to direct the work, while William Dickinson and a certain Daniel Colwell were, in conjunction with the Comptroller, the Master Mason and the Master Carpenter, to assist 'in the buying, bargaining and contracting and agreeing' for materials and labour, 'according to the directions of the said Dr. Christopher Wren . . . and the Orders and Methods of his Majestie's Works'. The bills were to be passed by three persons—Wren, either Dickinson or Colwell, and one member of the Board of Works.[2]

The plan attached to the warrant has apparently not survived, but the general appearance of the Custom House is known from engravings (Pl. 47B) and from a plan of *circa* 1717.[3] It was a long building of eleven bays, from which wings projected forward at either end. The central part of the ground floor contained a warehouse, but there were spacious entries on either side, and colonnades in the wings stood open for the reception of merchandise. Below ground-level there were cellars. Upstairs, the whole of the body of the building was devoted to one 'Great Room' where the Commissioners of Customs sat for the examination of goods. The principal stairs were at the west end, the 'back stairs' at the east end. In the two wings, or 'pavilions' (as they are called in the accounts), were various offices, including the Council Chamber, the Withdrawing Room, the Treasury Chamber, the Searchers' Room, the King's Waiters' Room, the Secretary's Room, and the Wood-Farm Office. The last was in the east wing, where Sir Anthony Cope had a small counting-house for his own use. He also retained the ownership of a warehouse immediately adjoining the north side of the Custom House. The principal elevation facing the Thames was treated as a classical composition with Tuscan and Ionic Orders defining the two principal storeys. The ends of the two wings formed pedimented temple-fronts, while three more pediments—one triangular, two segmental—accented the long central range. The walls were of brick, but the plinth, columns, pilasters, festoons and other dressings were of stone. The architrave, frieze and cornice, however, were of timber. The eleven round-headed windows lighting the Great Room appear to have been divided by wooden mullions and transoms into five lights—one in the head and four in the rectangular portion of the opening.[4] The eight windows lighting the warehouse beneath are described in the building accounts as having 'scheame heads', that is heads of a segmental shape. Although no specific foreign prototype can be pointed to, the whole building was somewhat in the style of the Dutch architect Van Campen, and would not have looked out of place in Amsterdam or the Hague.

[1] Reddaway, *op. cit.*, p. 11 (*Cal. Treas. Books* iii, p. 74).        [2] T 51/37, pp. 230–2.
[3] T 1/217, f. 120, redrawn by Reddaway, *op. cit.*, Fig. 5, and also in *London Survey* xv, Pl. 65. Works 30/38–9 are ground and first-floor plans made by David Laing in 1811.
[4] Thus the accounts refer to 'eleven circular windows of fower lights apeice besides the circle lights'.

Inside, the Great or Long Room was panelled with deal wainscot and surrounded by benches. The plaster ceiling was divided into square moulded panels. The 'chief seat' was flanked by 'wings' carved with 'cyphers and crownes on top of them', and was surmounted by an achievement of the king's arms three feet wide and four feet high carved by Henry Phillips, the Master Carver to the Works. The Council Chamber and the Withdrawing Rooms were also wainscotted, and most of the rooms were supplied with tables covered with green cloth. The work was measured by Leonard Gammon, the Clerk of the Works at Greenwich. The total cost, as accounted for by the Paymaster, was £10,252 6s. 8¼d.[1]

The principal craftsmen employed, with the sums paid to them, were as follows:

| | | |
|---|---|---|
| Bricklayer | : Richard Boys | £1547 |
| Mason | : Joshua Marshall | £1839 |
| Carpenter | : Edward Kingsley | £3175 |
| Joiner | : Thomas Kinward | £732 |
| Plasterer | : John Grove | £433 |
| Plumber | : Peter Brent | £1522 |
| Glazier | : Thomas Bagley | £51 |
| Smith | : William Wainwright | £288 |
| Carver | : Henry Phillips | £23 |
| Painter | : Robert Streater | £140 |

The new Custom House was finished in 1671. Though no doubt large enough for its purpose at that date, it soon proved too small for the rapidly expanding trade of Stuart London, and in 1698 the Commissioners were obliged to acquire the lease of some adjoining premises in order adequately to perform their duties. An opportunity for further expansion occurred fortuitously in 1715, when gunpowder stored in a house in Thames Street exploded, causing a fire which destroyed much nearby property. Houses were blown up to prevent the fire spreading further, and this so damaged the west end of the Custom House, whose foundations were already regarded as bad, that the building had to be shored up.[2] The Treasury instructed the Office of Works to consult with the Commissioners of Customs about repairing and enlarging the building, and in June 1716 Wren, Vanbrugh, Dartiquenave and Hewett submitted their report.[3] To rebuild the damaged portions—the west wing and two houses to the north—would cost about £13,000. To put an attic storey over the Long Room, thereby providing much-needed extra space, would add £4000, while the east wing was so decayed 'that it must in a few years be rebuilt' at an estimated cost of £2600. Faced with an expenditure of some £20,000, the Commissioners reconsidered the situation. Eleven month later they informed the Treasury that the Works proposal would still not give their officers adequate space, and reported that they had directed Thomas Ripley, their own carpenter and clerk of works, to prepare plans. Ripley's plans were for a new Long Room with a frontage

[1] The detailed 'books' are bound up in Works 5/14, 15 and 17. The enrolled account is AO 1/2492/397.
[2] Reddaway, *op. cit.*, p. 17.
[3] Works 6/6, p. 236; T 1/210, f. 219. There is a discrepancy of £500 between the two copies of the report, the second item (the attic over the Long Room) appearing as £4000 in Works 6/6, but as £4500 in T 1/210.

to Thames Street, estimated to cost no more than £17,000. Difficulties over the acquisition of the site frustrated this scheme, and in the end Wren's Custom House was reconstructed piecemeal by Ripley between 1718 and 1725. First the damaged west wing was rebuilt with the addition of an attic, then the facade of the Long Room, whose 4-inch brickwork was fast decaying, was taken down and rebuilt, minus most of its architectural decoration, but again with the useful addition of an attic, and finally the east wing was reconstructed to match its fellow.[1] The plan was not much altered, but by 1725 little of Wren's facade remained except the Tuscan and Ionic orders and the round-headed windows of the Long Room. In 1814 Ripley's work in its turn perished by fire, with architectural consequences that are described in Volume VI of this *History*.

# THE EXCISE OFFICE

THE EXCISE OFFICE was not a building for whose maintenance the Georgian Office of Works was normally responsible. But in 1768 the erection of a new office was entrusted to the Board of Works as an 'extraordinary' commission. At that time the officers of the Excise occupied a house in the Old Jewry. It was reputed to have been built before the Great Fire, and was, by the reign of George III, quite inadequate for the accommodation of a department which was now responsible for a large part of the public revenue. Not only was it inconveniently small and badly out of repair; but it did not even belong to the Crown, being held on a lease from a private landlord. This lease was due to run out in 1768, and some years previously the Commissioners of Excise had approached the Treasury for permission to look for new premises. They pointed out that they were obliged to conduct the public business 'at a great expence of rent, in a miserable, old, patched building, not the property of the Crown, subject to every circumstance of inconvenience and danger', and in such congested conditions that some of their clerks had to work 'on the staircases and in the passages'. They suggested that they might take a lease of Ely House, Holborn, the ancient but by now unfashionably situated residence of the bishops of Ely. They argued that 'the removal of the office to that place will be very convenient to a great number of traders, who have occasion to attend the Excise Office, as such traders are now spread in great numbers all over Westminster'.[2] Both the Treasury and the bishop were willing to fall in with this proposal, but strong objections were raised by the City merchants, who insisted that the Excise Office should be as near as possible to the Custom House, the Bank and the East India Company's warehouses.

[1] Reddaway, *op. cit.*, pp. 21–3.
[2] H.M. Customs and Excise Library, Customs 48/16, pp. 431, 435, 465; 48/17, pp. 171, 197, 240, 244, 246, 254, 258, 261–2.

The Corporation added its voice in support of the merchants, and offered an alternative building in the heart of the City. This was Gresham College in Old Broad Street, an academic survival from the sixteenth century whose professors seldom had 'above three or four auditors, and those of the most ordinary people'.[1] The Corporation, as joint trustees, with the Mercers' Company, of the Gresham Estate,was in a position to deprive the college of its buildings, compensate the professors, and hand the premises over to the government.[2]

It was at this point that the Officers of the Works were asked by the Treasury to survey both the existing Excise Office and the buildings of Gresham College. The former they pronounced to be 'greatly out of repair and very unsafe from fire, both as to the building and situation, and from the information of the Commissioners and other principal officers of the Excise . . . too small and inconvenient for carrying on that branch of the public revenue'. As for Gresham College, they were 'of opinion that it would not be for His Majesty's service to lay out any money upon the said buildings in fitting them up as a General Excise Office, as they are very inconvenient for that purpose and the walls and roofing are much decayed and the floors quite worn out; and being situated between public stables on the north and south sides of the said premises, would require a considerable expence to secure the buildings from the danger of fire'. They had accordingly 'made a design of a new building for a General Excise Office to be built upon part of the ground of Gresham College, . . . to be built in a plain substantial manner, which we herewith transmit to your Lordships. If this design shall be approved of the expence will be about the sum of £20,920 exclusive of desks, presses and other furniture and ought not to be less than 2 years in building'.[3] The date of this report was 5 May 1767. Nearly a year elapsed before the Treasury authorised the Commissioners of Excise to take possession of Gresham College and to 'call upon the Officers of the Board of Works to begin and proceed upon the erection of a new Office of Excise there'.[4] In obedience to this request the Board directed its Secretary, William Robinson, to wait on the Commissioners, and it was to Robinson that the whole operation of designing, building and accounting for the new Office was deputed. Consultation with the Commissioners showed that his original plans needed modification, and an increased estimate amounting to £21,780 was approved by the Treasury in July.[5] In 1769, after work had already begun, this was increased to £33,250, plus £2150 for fittings, and when the accounts were finally passed by the Board in February 1776 the total expenditure was found to amount to £39,339.[6] The principal workmen were tradesmen regularly employed by the Office of Works: Henry Holland and Son, bricklayers (£10,255), John Phillips, carpenter (£5265), William Jelfe, mason (£4433), John Devall, mason (£863), Jeremiah Devall, plumber (£1855), Messrs. Kelsey and West, joiners (£5173, plus £4382 for presses, desks, etc.), Richard Lawrence, carver (£40).[7] As the Excise Office was 'an Extra Work neither belonging to our

[1] *London & its Environs described* (R. & J. Dodsley, 1761), iii, p. 76.
[2] Customs 48/17, pp. 329–30, 333, 335, 357, 422–3, 442, 445, 454–5; P.R.O., T 29/38, pp. 155, 158–9, 178, 213, 316, 320, 331–2, 357–8, 372, 380, 400.
[3] Works 4/14, 1 May 1767; Works 6/18, p. 157.
[4] Works 4/14, 29 April 1768; Works 6/18, p. 174.     [5] Works 6/18, pp. 177–8.
[6] Works 6/18, pp. 223, 225; Works 6/19, pp. 86, 97; Works 5/64 (Analysis of Expenditure 1769–75).
[7] Works 4/14, 22 July; Works 6/117 (the detailed accounts kept by Robinson).

department nor paid out of the Civil List', Robinson was allowed to remunerate himself by deducting $2\frac{1}{2}$ per cent from the workmen's bills. He died suddenly in October 1775, and the final accounts were submitted by Thomas Robinson, his brother and executor.[1]

Robinson's Excise Office was pulled down in 1854. No complete plan of it is known to exist,[2] and the only effective records of its architecture are Ackermann's view of the interior of the court-room,[3] and an engraving of the main elevation, published in 1771 with the inscription 'W. Robinson *Architecto*, T. Robinson *delineavit*' (Pl. 47A).[4] The four-storey facade with its high rusticated base derived from villa-designs by Scamozzi.[5] Historically it is chiefly of interest as evidence of the ability of the man who, but for his premature death, would have been the architect of Somerset House.[6] In that context it is bound to be dismissed as a last unadventurous essay in a Palladian style still unenlivened by neo-classical influence: but the anonymous regularity of its fenestration was not, perhaps, altogether out of keeping with the functions of the fiscal department which it sheltered.

# THE FLEET AND
# KING'S BENCH PRISONS

LIKE OTHER prisons in the unreformed England of the sixteenth, seventeenth and eighteenth centuries, the Fleet and the King's Bench were public institutions run for private profit. Their principal inmates were debtors condemned in the courts at Westminster, but the upkeep of their buildings was the responsibility of their respective gaolers, who remunerated themselves by the fees which they exacted from those in their custody for supplying them with the necessities of life. Architecturally, they were more like lodging-houses than the penal institutions of today. Externally only the surrounding wall and the barred windows marked them out as places of confinement: internally only the chapel and the begging-box distinguished them from some particularly squalid 'rents'.

The Prison of the Fleet occupied a site on the east side of the Fleet Market, a thoroughfare now represented by Farringdon Street: the Marshalsea of the Court

---

[1] Works 6/18, p. 220; Works 6/19, pp. 86, 97.

[2] P.R.O. MPD 68 is a plan of part of the building, showing alterations proposed in 1829.

[3] *Microcosm of London* iii (1809), p. 268.

[4] Maitland, *History of London*, ed. Entick ii (1775), pl. 125. For a view showing its situation in the street see Burlington Fine Arts Club, *Catalogue of a Collection of Early Drawings and Pictures of London* (1920), pl. xiv, and B.M., King's Maps XXIV, 3b.

[5] Notably the Villa Verlato at Villaverla (Scamozzi, *L'Idea della Architettura*, 1615, Pt. 1, Book 3, p. 287).

[6] Below, p. 366.

of King's Bench (to give it its full title) stood on the east side of Borough High Street in Southwark. The Fleet had been burned down in the Great Fire and afterwards rebuilt by its Warden Sir Jeremy Witchcott. But no beneficient calamity had overtaken the ancient and decrepit buildings of the King's Bench Prison, and by the middle of the eighteenth century hard usage and neglect had already left their mark on the Fleet. Both prisons were, in fact, in a deplorable state. Their respective gaolers were hard-headed men whose expenditure on their upkeep was minimal. As for their inmates, what the Warden of the Fleet called 'an uninterrupted fluctuating Inhabitancy of prisoners (chiefly regardless of preserving any part of their prison but rather doing mischief to it)' had so worn both of them out that nothing short of total rebuilding was likely to be of any avail.[1]

Neither prison came under the jurisdiction of the Board of Works, nor do the judges of the royal courts appear to have concerned themselves with the state of the places to which their judgements annually consigned so many victims. It was in fact those directly affected, the prisoners and the gaolers, who eventually succeeded in getting both of them rebuilt, though their motives were different, the former being concerned exclusively to ameliorate their own unhappy lot, the latter chiefly to ensure the safe custody of those in their charge. It was in 1752 that the prisoners in the King's Bench, perhaps encouraged by a humanitarian Member of Parliament, submitted a petition to the House of Commons

> 'setting forth, That the Prison in which they are confined is an old ruinous Structure, exposed to all the Inclemencies of Weather, equally during the Heats of Summer, and the Rigours of Winter; and at the same time so narrow and inconvenient, that the Petitioners are sometimes crowded to the Number of Seventeen in a Room; by which many Prisoners have died, for want of Attendance and Necessaries during their Sickness; which they cannot obtain, be their Distresses ever so great, or their Diseases ever so violent, in their present miserable Situation'.

The prison, they concluded, had become 'utterly unfit for the purpose of a Gaol, and fatal to the Constitutions and Lives of the unhappy Prisoners'. A Committee, after due investigation, reported to the House 'that the prison of the Marshalsea of the Court of King's Bench is, in its present Condition, unsafe for the Custody, and dangerous to the Health, of the Prisoners; which inconveniences cannot be remedied unless the Prison be rebuilt'. An address was accordingly passed asking for estimates for rebuilding the prison to be laid before the House. In December 1753 the Treasury requested the Board of Works to survey the building, and in January 1754 the Surveyor personally submitted to the House an estimate amounting to £7800 for a new prison designed 'in a strong substantial manner'. By 6 April an Act of Parliament allocating that sum of money had passed through all its stages.[2] Less concerned about the plight of the prisoners than the House of Commons, the Treasury needed the reminder of a further petition, this time from the Marshal of the prison, before taking any action, and it was not until August 1754 that Isaac Ware 'laid before the Board exact plans, elevations and sections of the intended new prison'. Another

[1] Works 6/17, p. 108; Works 6/18, pp. 26–32.
[2] *Commons' Jnls.*, vol. 26, pp. 457, 505–13, 539, 680–2, 764, 921.

long delay followed the submission of these plans to the Treasury, and in the end they were set aside in favour of alternative proposals submitted by the Marshal himself in conjunction with a builder named Soame or Soan, who was prepared to execute them by contract for only £7300. Instead of being erected on some vacant ground adjoining the old prison in Borough High Street, the prison was now to be built half a mile away in St. George's Fields, and the balance of the money voted by Parliament was to be used to purchase the land.

This scheme no doubt appealed to the Treasury because it seemed to ensure that the new prison would be built for no more than the sum voted by Parliament. Asked whether they saw any objection, the Board of Works merely observed that 'as the contractor offers to give your Lordships ample security that the Building shall be erected in a strong & substantial manner; we have no objection that occurs to us against its being carryed into execution'. Neither the plans nor the contract appear, however, to have been submitted to their scrutiny, and it was not until 1758 that, on the completion of the prison, they were asked to survey the building and report whether it conformed to the terms of the contract. Though the structure proved only to be 'performed in the common stile of the Building of the Town, and not . . . in that strong substantial and workmanlike manner as is customary in His Majesty's Works', the Board's report was, nevertheless, that by and large the contract had been satisfactorily performed. It appeared, however, that a number of items, such as the chapel furniture and some improvements to the Marshal's house, had not been included in the agreement, so that Soan had a claim of £380 for extra works, reduced by the Board to £270. Then it was discovered that no arrangements had been made for the supply of water, that the windows were innocent of bars and the fireplaces of grates, and that the provision of these and other necessities would cost a further £720. The Board was instructed to make these deficiencies good, but took no further action on discovering that most of them had already been put in hand by the Marshal without official sanction. The attitude of the Board was, in fact, to dissociate itself as far as possible from a building for whose erection it had had no responsibility, and when, only two years later, extensive dry rot was discovered in the floors and the window bars proved to be 'so weak and insubstantial that they present no obstacle to prisoners', the Board had the satisfaction of representing to the Treasury that these and other defects were

> in a great measure owing to the removal of the said prison from its antient situation, and the not having the Design proposed by the Board of Works executed, which would have render'd it a place of security and accommodation for two hundred prisoners . . . which the Board signified might have been erected for the sum of £7800. . . .

The subsequent proceedings, they continued, were 'not approved of by the Board of Works', and the dry rot appeared to be 'in a great measure owing to the removal of the prison . . . into an open Field, and set too low upon moorish ground, which is in our opinion the cause of so quick a decay of the lower part of the building, as well as rendering it a place of insecurity for the Prisoners'. As for the extra expense, they ventured to wonder 'whether the erecting a large house with its appurtenances for the Marshal has not been a great reason why the other parts more necessary for the security of the prisoners were not sufficiently attended to'. The Treasury refrained from retorting that if the building had been erected by the Board it was most unlikely that the estimates would not have been exceeded by a considerably larger figure, and contented itself with bringing an action against Soan for bad workmanship. But the Treasury had learned its lesson, and no further work on the royal prisons was to be undertaken without duly consulting the Officers of the King's Works.[1]

There can be little doubt that it was the rebuilding of the King's Bench that in 1763 stimulated the Warden of the Fleet to petition the Treasury about the dilapidated state of his prison. This time the Treasury had no truck with contractors, but prudently referred everything to the Board. At first it was thought that the building could be repaired for £2400. But no immediate action was authorised, and by 1768 the prison had so far deteriorated that in the opinion of Messrs. Robinson, Couse and Phillips, 'it is not adviseable to lay out any money in repairing it'. Serious consideration was given to a proposal by the City of London that the Fleet, like the King's Bench, should be removed to St. George's Fields. This was bound up with a scheme of the City's for moving the Fleet Market to the site vacated by the prison. Having, however, ascertained that the cost of building a new prison in Southwark would be nearly twice that of rebuilding it in its old situation, the Treasury asked the City for a contribution of £5000. When the City demurred, the Treasury observed 'that the first proposal for removing the Fleet Prison moved from the City of London, and was represented to be for the accommodation of the Public and the ornament of the City with a view of placing the Market on the ground whereon the Prison now stands. But it now appearing . . . that the City have no longer any such intentions, Direct the Board of Works to proceed with all possible expedition to rebuild the Fleet Prison upon the scite whereon it now stands.' The work was carried out between 1770 and 1773 at a cost of £11,962. This did not, however, include the warden's office and some other administrative buildings which were erected in 1774 at an additional cost of £1480. The brickwork was performed by Henry Holland, the carpentry by John Phillips, the masonry by William Jelfe and Messrs. Life and Saunders, the joinery by Messrs. Kelsey and West.[2] The result was a single barrack-like block containing four storeys and a basement. John Howard visited it in 1777, and described it as follows:

> There are four floors, they call them *Galleries*, besides the cellar-floor, called *Bartholomew-Fair*. Each Gallery consists of a passage in the middle, the whole length of the Prison, i.e. 66 yards; and rooms on each side of it about 14 feet and a half by 12 and a half, and 9 and a half high. A chimney and window in every room. The passages are narrow (not seven feet wide) and darkish, having only a window at each end. On the first floor, the *Hall-Gallery*, to which you ascend eight steps, are, a

---

[1] Works 6/17, pp. 108, 117, 122$^v$, 129, 136, 165, 166, 175–180, 199$^v$, 200, 204$^v$, 207$^v$, 208$^v$; Works 6/18, pp. 81–3; T 1/381 (memorial of W. Sone); Works 4/11, 17 and 23 July, 6 and 13 Aug. 1754; 4 March, 24 June 1755.

[2] T 29/40, pp. 185, 246, 252, 335–6, 348, 352–3; Works 6/18, pp. 26–32, 33–5, 188–90, 192, 287; Works 4/14, 5 and 19 June, 28 Aug. 1772, 24 Dec. 1773, 14 and 25 Jan., 25 March 1774. The detailed accounts have found their way to the Hereford County Record Office (E 1/14–15).

Chapel, a Tap-room, a Coffee-room (lately made out of two rooms for Debtors), a room for the Turnkey, another for the Watchman, and eighteen rooms for Prisoners. . . . The cellar-floor is 16 steps below the hall-gallery. It consists of two rooms [one for the Turnkey, the other for the confinement of disorderly prisoners], the Tapster's kitchen, his four large beer and wine cellars, and fifteen rooms for Prisoners. . . . On the first Gallery are twenty-five rooms for Prisoners. On the second Gallery, twenty-seven rooms. . . . A room at one end is an Infirmary. . . . On the highest story are twenty-seven rooms.

All the rooms I have mentioned are for Master's side Debtors. The weekly rent is one shilling and three-pence unfurnished. . . . When the Prison was built the Warden gave each Prisoner his choice of a room according to his seniority as a Prisoner. If all the rooms be occupied, a new comer must hire of some tenant a part of his room; or shift as he can.

The apartments for Common-side Debtors are only part of the right wing of the Prison. Besides the cellar (which was intended for their kitchen, but is occupied with lumber, and shut up) there are four floors. On each floor is a room about 24 or 25 feet square, with a fire-place; and on the sides seven closets or cabins to sleep in.[1]

Meanwhile the new King's Bench Prison continued to give cause for dissatisfaction. Not only was it badly built: it also proved to be too small to accommodate the increasingly large numbers of debtors sentenced by the Court. In the 1750s the prison had been thought very full if more than 80 prisoners were under confinement. But in 1768 there were 338, in 1769, 413, and in 1773, 213. As the building contained only 132 rooms, most of which were only nine feet square, the overcrowding was deplorable, and in 1773 the Marshal addressed a petition to the House of Commons in which he represented

That the said Prison is much too small for the Number of Prisoners generally confined therein; and that the Number of Prisoners always exceeding the Number of rooms, the Petitioner has been obliged to permit many of them to lie in the Chapel, which renders the same both offensive and dangerous for Divine Worship; others lie under Stair Cases, and other improper Places, and by that Means contract Disorders, which often prove fatal, not only to themselves, but the Prisoners in general; and that it has been the usage of the said Prison for Prisoners to take their Rooms in Seniority, by which means a new Prisoner is under the Necessity of waiting many Months before he can be entitled to a Room, during which time he is obliged to contract with some old indigent Prisoner for a Lodging, at an exorbitant price; and that there are no Rooms or Apartments to which sick Prisoners can be removed, nor any proper Place where riotous or disorderly Prisoners, or such attempting to make their escapes, may occasionally be confined, as there are in other large Prisons, nor for Prisoners committed for capital or high Crimes and Offences, who are sent in Irons, separate from other Prisoners; and that the walls of the said Prison not being of a sufficient heighth and strength, it frequently occasions Prisoners to form schemes for escaping and many have escaped, through and over the walls, charged with large Debts, to the Danger of the Suitors of the Court, and Damage to the Petitioner, who sometimes has prisoners in Custody to the amount of £200,000.

[1] J. Howard, *The State of the Prisons in England and Wales* (1777), pp. 157–9.

The result was a humble address asking for the prison to be enlarged, the House promising to make good the expenditure incurred. The responsibility for taking action rested with the Treasury, who, after consultation with the Board of Works, decided to treat the job as a special commission, for which the Board as such would have no responsibility, but for which their Secretary, William Robinson, would be personally accountable. It was under his supervision that the work was put in hand, and by him that the first account was prepared for declaration at the Exchequer. Owing to his death in October 1775 subsequent accounts were presented by his successor, Kenton Couse, who, like him, received 2½ per cent as remuneration for his services. The work was completed in 1780 and the total cost of building the additional rooms, the lodge and the massive 'fence wall' amounted to £22,028.[1]

Scarcely had the workmen departed before, in June 1780, the enlarged prison was set on fire by the Gordon Rioters, and so burned that nothing remained undamaged except the new wall, which merely suffered the loss of its *chevaux-de-frize*. This was part of a concerted attack on the London prisons, in the course of which the Fleet was also reduced to a burnt-out shell. In this emergency it was the Privy Council from which the Officers of the King's Works received their instructions, first of all to survey the damage (which they estimated at £31,000—£18,000 at the King's Bench, £13,000 at the Fleet) and then to reinstate the two prisons as soon as possible. At first it was thought that at least two years would be needed for the operation, but at the 'pressing instance' of the judges of the royal courts both prisons were in fact ready for reoccupation by the summer of 1781. This was a considerable achievement, for when scaffolding was erected the walls were found to be in a worse state than had been feared, and most of them had in the end to be demolished almost to the foundations. The work at both prisons was supervised by Kenton Couse, who made the drawings and directed the workmen. In plan and elevation the new buildings must have deviated little from the old ones. Some improvements were, however, introduced on the advice of the judges. For the sake of security against fire the lower storeys of both prisons were arched in brick, and the floors and staircases were constructed in stone instead of timber. At the King's Bench, moreover, the Board had not at first estimated for the replacement of twelve 'State Rooms' reserved for the accommodation of prisoners of superior social status. The Court, however, insisted that in the new, as in the old, prison, there should be apartments 'fitted up for, and appropriated to, the Reception of Criminals of Rank', in order to save aristocratic debtors from the indignity of 'associating with the common Prisoners, contrary to the usage of the Prison and the intention of the Court'. These afterthoughts inevitably added to the expense, which was further increased by the urgency with which the work was pressed forward, so that in the end the cost amounted to nearly £40,000. As this was an 'extraordinary' commission, outside the Board's normal responsibility, the money advanced by the Exchequer did not pass through the hands of the Paymaster, but was separately banked in the name of Robert Taylor, the Deputy Surveyor. A deduction of 3 per cent was made from the workmen's bills, 2½ per cent to remunerate Couse for his trouble, the remaining ½ per cent for the benefit of the

---

[1] *Commons' Jnls.*, vol. 34, pp. 104, 123, 221, 224; T 29/43, pp. 58, 311; T 29/45, p. 233; AO 1/2494/408, 409, 410.

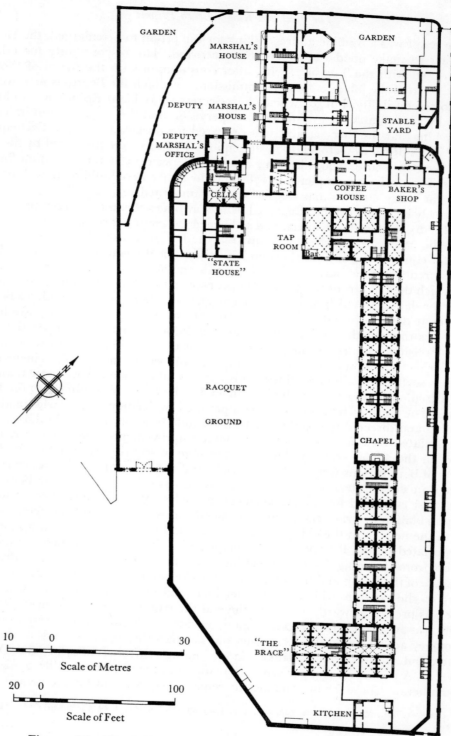

GARDEN

MARSHAL'S HOUSE

GARDEN

DEPUTY MARSHAL'S HOUSE

DEPUTY MARSHAL'S OFFICE

STABLE YARD

CELLS

COFFEE HOUSE

BAKER'S SHOP

"STATE HOUSE"

TAP ROOM

Bar

RACQUET

GROUND

CHAPEL

10   0                    30
Scale of Metres

"THE BRACE"

20   0                    100
Scale of Feet

KITCHEN

Fig. 29. The King's Bench Prison (based on P.R.O., Works 38/16).

clerks employed in keeping the accounts. At the King's Bench the principal workmen were: bricklayers, Henry and Richard Holland, Edward Gray; carpenter, Charles Cole; joiners, Messrs. Kelsey and West; mason, John Devall; plumber, Jeremiah Devall. At the Fleet they were: bricklayer, John Groves; carpenter, William Jaques; joiner, William Clarke; mason, John Gilliam; plumber, Jeremiah Devall.[1]

Within fifty years both prisons were obsolete. In 1842 the Fleet was united with the King's Bench (now renamed 'the Queen's Prison') and was soon afterwards demolished.[2] Imprisonment for debt having been abolished by subsequent legislation, the Queen's Prison became redundant in its turn, and, after a period of use as a military prison, was sold for demolition in 1879. Figure 29 shows its plan in about 1845. No detailed plan of either prison has been found of a date prior to 1780, but a small-scale plan of the King's Bench published by Thomas Manson in 1760 shows that the main block occupied the same site as it did in 1845, and that its basic plan was identical. The building, however, extended only two staircases to the east of the central chapel, and the additions of 1774–80 evidently included the erection of the remaining two staircases and of the cross-wing at the end. The same plan was of course followed in the rebuilding of 1780–1, as the foundations and lower walls were reused as far as possible.

# THE ROLLS HOUSE

FROM THE reign of Edward III to that of Victoria the office of Master of the Rolls carried with it the keepership of the house for converted Jews built by Henry III in what is now Chancery Lane. As the number of converts dwindled, their quarters were appropriated by the Master of the Rolls for his own purposes, and by the sixteenth century they were used partly as a residence, partly as a law-court, and partly as a repository for the Chancery records.[3] It was the Chapel which housed the records, in presses decorated by columns and pilasters of the Ionic and Composite Orders.[4]

Early in the eighteenth century John Strype, in his edition of Stow's *Survey of London*, mentions the 'old and decayed house' of the Rolls as 'much wanting new

[1] Works 4/16, 13, 14, 16, 20 June, 17 Nov., 22 Dec. 1780, 2 Feb., 2, 16 March, 11 May, 6, 13 July, 13 August, 21, 28 Sept., 4, 5 Oct. 1781, 7 March, 1783; Works 6/19, pp. 297–8, 304, 309, 321, 332, 338, 344–5, 346, 347, 348; Works 6/20, pp. 79, 97; AO 1/2494/411; AO 3/1243/7. By order of the Treasury the accounts were subjected to an independent scrutiny by George Dance and John Goreham.

[2] There is a copy of the sale catalogue in the Guildhall Library (Pam. 3393), which also possesses a copy of the set of lithographic views of the prison by Rotaldé which was published in 1845 (A 3.6 (70)). Another view will be found in Ackermann's *Microcosm of London* ii (1808), p. 44. See also the references given in vol. vi of this *History*, p. 628, n. 13.

[3] W. J. Hardy, 'A History of the Rolls House and Chapel', *Middlesex & Herts. Notes & Queries*, ii (1896), pp. 49–68.

[4] E. Hatton, *New View of London*, ii (1708), p. 535. For the history and architecture of the Chapel see H. C. Maxwell Lyte's article in *Deputy Keeper's 57th Report* (1896), pp. 19–47.

building', and after the death in May 1717 of Sir John Trevor, who had held the Mastership of the Rolls since the reign of James II, his successor Sir Joseph Jekyll was able to get the Treasury to agree to spend £5000 on rebuilding the house. As Jekyll was a prominent Whig and had recently played an important part in the prosecution of those concerned in the rebellion of 1715, he was in a strong position to demand this favour of the government.[1]

The work was not entrusted to the Office of Works, but to the architect Colen Campbell, who did not at that time hold any official position. He had, however, had a legal training in Scotland, and may consequently have been personally known to Jekyll. On 29 July 1717 the Treasury authorised the issue to 'Colin Campbell, Dr. of Laws', of £5000 for the purpose of rebuilding the house, and when in due course Campbell accounted for this sum he was described in his declaration as 'the Architect appointed by the Treasury to pull down the House of Converted Jews in Chancery Lane and build a new Edifice there for the use of the Master of the Rolls and likewise to Repair and improve the Chappel of the Rolls and other appurtenances of the said house'.[2] The old house was pulled down forthwith, and the new one with its Palladian elevation (Pl. 48) was erected between 1717 and 1724.[3] It was built of grey stock brick with Portland stone dressings, and included a spacious 'cause-room' two storeys high entered from the hall through a columned screen. The principal craftsmen employed were John Evans, bricklayer, James Paget, mason, Robert Barker, carpenter, William Baverstock and John Lane, joiners, John Hughes, plasterer, and Philip Rudsby, plumber. The carver's work was performed by James Richards. The total cost accounted for by Campbell was £5922 14s. 3¼d. This included his own fee of £300, calculated at the rate of 6 per cent on £5000. It is not clear whether the balance of £922 (less £35 for the sale of old materials) was defrayed by the government or by Jekyll himself. Jekyll subsequently took advantage of an Act of Parliament of 1660 empowering the Master of the Rolls to lay out the Rolls Estate for building. In 1719 nine houses were built under Colen Campbell's direction, and soon afterwards thirty more under that of a surveyor named Biggs.[4]

So far the Rolls House had been no concern of the Office of Works. But in 1749 the Board received instructions from the Treasury to make a survey of the house. This was the result of a petition from William Fortescue, the then Master of the Rolls, who complained that when the house was rebuilt in 1718, 'the Builders and Workmen who contracted for, and were employed in, the said Buildings so ill executed the same in several parts thereof, that notwithstanding your Memorialist and his predecessors have since been every year at a great Expence in repairing the same; your Memorialist is informed by persons (who have lately viewed it) that the Roof of the said House (which is very large) and the Vaults under it and under the Terras walk in the Garden for near an hundred feet, are in so bad a condition that the whole Roof must be taken down and new done, and the greatest part of the said

---

[1] For Jekyll's career see *D.N.B.* and Foss, *Judges of England* (1870), pp. 374-5.
[2] *Cal. Treas. Books*, xxxi, p. 475; AO 1/2494/407, printed in *Cal. Treas. Books* xxxii, Part 1, pp. ccii–ccvi.
[3] *Historical Register* ii (1717), 'Chronological Register', p. 39. The foundation stone was laid by Campbell on 18 Sept. and bore the following inscription: *Georgius Rex fundavit, A.D. 1717. Josephus Jekyl Eques, Sacrorum Scriniorum Magister.* The plan and elevation of the building are given in Campbell's *Vitruvius Britannicus* iii (1725), pls. 44-5. For the chimneypieces see *Architectural Review* 48 (1920), pp. 23, 76.
[4] *Commons' Jnls.*, vol. 25, pp. 355-6, 377-8.

Vaults be new Arch'd, and that several of the Chimneys are in danger of falling unless they are rebuilt. . . .' In its report the Board of Works fully confirmed what the Master of the Rolls alleged, and the house was accordingly reroofed under its direction at a cost of £1311.[1]

Fortescue was at pains to declare that he accepted full responsibility for the routine maintenance of the building, but the success of his petition opened the way for similar applications by his successors, and in 1754 more repairs were carried out by the Office of Works for an incoming Master of the Rolls.[2] In 1764–5 there was further expenditure, partly on certain old buildings left untouched in 1717, and partly for the benefit of a new Master who wanted 'to make the House convenient for a Family' after a long period of bachelor occupation by his predecessor.[3]

In 1772 a Committee of the House of Commons expressed concern about the conditions under which the records were stored in the Rolls Chapel. Some were stated to be 'in danger of destruction' by being placed too close to damp walls, while others, kept in a room above the chapel, were 'continually receiving injuries' by alternate exposure to rain and heat. As a result the fabric of the Chapel was repaired, new presses were installed to contain the records, and a house in Chancery Lane was leased and fitted up by the Office of Works for the accommodation of the Clerk of the Records. The lease of this house expired in 1783, and in the following year the Board of Works was authorised to build a new house for the Clerk of the Records on a vacant site immediately to the south of the Chapel.[4]

# THE SAVOY

FOUNDED BY Henry VII, dissolved by Edward VI, but revived by Queen Mary, the Savoy Hospital was still in theory a corporate body until its final extinction in 1702. In the seventeenth century, however, the offices held by the master and the four chaplains were in practice sinecures, and the buildings were used partly as barracks, partly as dwellings and partly as places of worship for foreign Protestant congregations.[5] The Savoy, wrote Defoe in 1725, 'may be said to be, not a House, but a little Town, being parted into innumerable Tenements and Apartments'.[6] For the maintenance of this complex of buildings, sacred and profane (the one often in

---

[1] Works 6/17, ff. 52–3, 64ᵛ; Works 4/10, 14 March, 4, 11, 20 April, 6 June, 1749, 15 June, 5 July 1750.
[2] Works 6/17, ff. 119ᵛ–120ᵛ; Works 4/11, 23 July 1754.
[3] Works 6/18, pp. 59–60, 65, 69–70, 89–91. Another £600 were spent in 1774–5 (Works 6/19, ff. 29, 56; Works 4/14, 20 May, 1 July 1774).
[4] *Commons' Jnls.*, vols. 33, p. 791, 40, pp. 388, 419, 427; T 1/490; T 29/43, f. 169; Works 6/20, pp. 216–22, 253, 261, 275, 309. The house, known as No. 1, Rolls Yard, was demolished in 1889.
[5] For the vicissitudes of the Hospital see R. Somerville, *The Savoy* (1960).
[6] *A Tour through England and Wales* (Everyman ed. 1948) i, pp. 326–7.

awkward and vexatious proximity to the other), the Office of Works had a responsibility at first somewhat ill-defined. In 1670, after part of the Strand frontage had been gutted by fire, the master, Dr. Killigrew, complained to the Privy Council that one of the tenants was proceeding 'with great irregularities' in pulling down 'the auncient Frontispiece' and its 'noble' entrance-vault. Wren, as Surveyor-General, was accordingly instructed to 'take notice thereof and give direction for the future progress of that worke that no more be taken down than he shall judge requisite for the re-edifying of what was consumed by the Fire'.[1] It is not known whether it was Wren who in 1679 supervised the conversion of the 'great dormitory' of the hospital into barracks for the Foot Guards,[2] but in 1695 he made plans and estimates for cutting off the western end of the same building in order to make it into a military prison, complete with lodgings for the deputy marshal and the guards.[3] The Office of Works was also called on in 1692 to supervise repairs to the buildings in the southern part of the hospital that had recently been vacated by the Jesuits introduced by James II and were now to be occupied by sick and wounded seamen.[4] In 1713 £2406 were spent on converting a further portion of the building into barracks in order to house an additional 500 soldiers.[5]

These were all *ad hoc* commissions, but when the Office of Works was reorganised in 1715, the Board obtained authority from the Treasury to treat the maintenance of the Savoy barracks as a regular part of their duties.[6] A clerk of works and a labourer in trust were appointed,[7] and repairs were carried out from time to time, the most extensive being in 1723, when £884 were spent on providing accommodation for two additional companies of Guards.[8] This arrangement was, however, brought to an end in 1724, when the Office of Works handed over responsibility for all barracks and guard-houses to the Board of Ordnance.[9]

Though it was the military buildings alone for which the Officers of the Works were (from 1715 to 1724) formally responsible, they were also called upon from

---

[1] *Wren Society*, xviii, p. 26.      [2] Somerville, *op. cit.*, p. 74.

[3] T 1/34, ff. 215–22 with drawings; *Wren Society* xviii, p. 121; Somerville, *op. cit.*, pp. 92–3.

[4] *Wren Soc.* xviii, pp. 89, 90, 108; Somerville, *op. cit.*, pp. 79–80, 92.

[5] *Cal. Treasury Papers 1708–14*, pp. 462, 468, 525; *Cal. Treasury Books* xxvii, p. 102, etc.; Works 5/56, under Dec. 1713.

[6] Works 6/6, pp. 65, 90; Works 4/1, 2 Sept. 1715; T 1/193, f. 74 (No. 17A).

[7] There is some confusion in the Office records about their appointments. The Abstracts of the Works accounts (Works 5/56) indicate that Leonard Wooddeson was Clerk of the Works at the Savoy in 1715–16, and in July 1715 Thomas Ripley was appointed 'Labourer in Trust to the Clerk of the Savoy' (Works 4/1, 12 July 1715). But in February 1715/16 the Board asked the Treasury for permission to appoint a Labourer in Trust, the Savoy 'being under the Inspection of none of the Clerks of His Majesty's Works' (Works 6/6, f. 150). Thereafter Ripley was given the title of Clerk of the Works. In 1721 he was succeeded by Thomas Bridge. Bridge's tenure of the office terminated early in 1725, following the transfer of the barracks to the Board of Ordnance.

[8] Works 4/2, 11 Dec. 1722, 14 May, 24 Sept. 1723; Works 6/7, pp. 278–9; Works 5/141, year 1723.

[9] Works 4/3, 20 Jan. 1724/5. The Savoy barracks were destroyed by fire in March 1776. By then the re-development of the whole site was under discussion, and Chambers had already been commissioned to design a new building for the military. Drawings in Sir John Soane's Museum (Drawer 43, Set 1) show a project as monumental as his adjoining Somerset House, with accommodation for 3000 officers and men arranged round three sides of a large square whose fourth side, facing the river, was to be occupied by an open screen. But the barracks took second place to Somerset House, and the project was first postponed and then abandoned (Somerville, *op. cit.*, pp. 106–8; B.M. Add MS. 38447, ff. 246–8). In 1795, when Chambers was on the point of retirement, he wrote to the Treasury about these plans, which had, he said, been approved by the king, the principal officers of the Guards and the Duke of Gloucester. He was requested to transmit them to the Secretary at War, and was authorised to charge £420 for them in the Somerset House accounts (T 29/68, p. 221; AO 3/1244).

time to time to inspect the premises occupied by the various religious communities which by royal favour or tolerance were permitted to worship there. In 1661 Charles II gave the French Protestants leave to use the eastern limit of the former hospital as their chapel. When, in 1686, they obtained permission to rebuild it on a larger scale, it was to Wren that they applied for a plan and elevation, and it was Wren, in his official capacity, who certified that it was 'a charitable and pious designe' to which royal approval might fittingly be given.[1] By the reign of George II the chapel was beginning to need major repairs, for which the resources of the congregation were inadequate. In 1740 they informed the Treasury that they had been obliged to discontinue their services on account of the ruinous state of the roof, and were 'inclined to deliver up the said church to His Majesty, of whose royal bounty they hold it.' Having at their own expense enlarged and maintained it in the past, they optimistically asked to be compensated for their outlay on the king's property. When this request was referred to the Officers of the Works, they reported that the enlargement of the chapel in the reign of Charles II might have cost some £1300. But as the materials were now 'of very little value', and as the French Congregation had had the use of the building for so long, and were 'proposing to leave it at their own desire', they not surprisingly expressed the view that no compensation was called for.[2] The congregation moved to Soho and the remains of its chapel were eventually taken over by the German Calvinists.

The German Lutheran Church occupied a site between the barracks and the river (Pl. 49). It was established there in the reign of William and Mary, and a plan in the Pepys Collection at Magdalene College, Cambridge, shows it as a square building with a roof supported on four columns or posts.[3] In 1721 the Office of Works was consulted before leave was given to the congregation to make a passageway through the barracks 'for the convenience of coaches and chairs passing and repassing to and from the said chapel'. A plan attached to the licence shows that this was the diagonal passage which bisected the nave of the former hospital to the north of the church.[4] When the congregation decided to rebuild their church in 1766 they obtained the services of the Surveyor-General of the day as architect. The exterior (which may have incorporated some of the old walls) was plain, but Chambers provided the Lutherans with an elegant interior in a style suggestive of St. Martin's-in-the-Fields.[5]

Immediately to the south of the Lutheran Church was the smaller and more austere place of worship occupied since the reign of Queen Anne by the Calvinist sect known as the German Reformed Congregation. In 1724, when George I gave them part of the former Master's house as a dwelling for their minister, both the Office of Works and the Surveyor of Land Revenues were called in to survey the

---

[1] The licence, accompanied by a unique engraving of Wren's design, is P.R.O., MPA. 41. The design is reproduced by Somerville, *op. cit.*, p. 66. A survey plan of the chapel, made in 1733, is in Crest 2/914.

[2] Works 6/16, p. 121.

[3] London & Westminster, vol. i, ff. 178–9.

[4] Westminster Public Library, Records of the Lutheran Church, 90/13/1A; Works 6/12, p. 16. Ripley's report on the request was sold at Sotheby's on 27 Oct. 1959, as part of lot 309.

[5] His plans are tipped in at the end of the subscription-book, now Westminster Public Library 90/7. There are also drawings for the building in the Victoria & Albert Museum, two of which are reproduced by J. Harris, *Sir William Chambers* (1970), pls. 142–3. It was demolished in or soon after 1875. For an outline plan of the church before 1766 see T 1/255, f. 167.

H K W—BB

building and give effect to the royal bounty.[1] The remainder of the house was occupied by the minister of the Anglican Savoy Chapel, who proved to be an awkward neighbour, and in 1769 this and other difficulties drove the Calvinists to purchase the derelict French Protestant Church from its trustees and repair it for their own purposes.[2] This time royal favour took the form of a gift of £500 from the king.[3] Even the Quakers, who had been meeting in the Savoy since the seventeenth century, were given official help when, in 1746, their meeting house was damaged by the collapse of some adjacent houses. The damage was, with the approval of the Treasury, made good by the Office of Works at a cost of £13 11s. 6¼d.[4]

The Chapel of the Savoy itself, which, of all the buildings familiar to the Georgian Officers of the Works, alone survives today, was administered by the chapel-wardens and overseers of the Savoy Precinct. Though not a Chapel Royal in the technical sense, it was, after the dissolution of the Hospital, under the jurisdiction of the Treasury, and the Treasury continued to be its effective patron until 1772, when the responsibility was transferred to the Duchy of Lancaster. From 1702 to 1772, therefore, the Board of Works was from time to time called upon to carry out repairs both to the chapel and to the minister's house. In 1721, as a result of a petition by the chapel-wardens, the Treasury authorised repairs costing over £400. These were carried out under the direction of the Clerk of Works, whose report stated that it would be necessary to renew the leading of the roof, to remove the bell from a decayed turret that stood in the middle of the roof and threatened to fall through it, and to rebuild the churchyard wall in order to prevent boys playing in the yard and damaging the windows.[5] In 1741 the then minister, a somewhat dubious character who made a profitable living by celebrating illegal marriages at the chapel, himself carried out repairs and improvements costing £811 and then presented the bill to the Treasury. When his letter was referred to the Board of Works they replied 'that no officer of the Crown was applied to previously to the making any of these repairs or alterations, several of which (especially the organ amounting to £210) were not at least immediately necessary'.[6] In the end authority was given for £513 to be paid to the minister on the Works account.[7] A request for further repairs in 1762 appears to have received no response,[8] and subsequent repairs (including the reconstruction of the chapel after the fire of 1864) have been carried out by the Duchy of Lancaster.[9]

[1] Works 6/12, p. 26; Somerville, *op. cit.*, p. 82.
[2] Somerville, *op. cit.*, pp. 82–3; T 1/6459B/17967, C, no. 122.
[3] Bodleian Library, MS. North c. 70, under 'Bounties'.
[4] Works 6/7, pp. 14ᵛ, 15; Works 5/141 under 'Extra Works'.
[5] Works 4/1, 10 Dec. 1719; Works 4/2, 3 Jan. 1721; Works 6/7, pp. 143–6, 312–13; Works 5/141, year 1722.
[6] Works 6/16, pp. 128, 131.
[7] AO 1/2457/176.
[8] Works 6/18, p. 3.
[9] Somerville, *op. cit.*, chapter xi.

# SOMERSET HOUSE

THE ERECTION of Somerset House was the largest building operation carried out at public expense during the Georgian era. Not since the completion of Greenwich Hospital had any public building of comparable size been in process of erection, nor would another be undertaken before the 'metropolitan improvements' of the early nineteenth century. At a time when both king and parliament made do with old and inconvenient buildings, their readiness to spend large sums of money on erecting a palace of bureaucracy is unexpected, and requires explanation. It is all the more surprising when it is remembered how little tradition there was of parliamentary concern for the civil service, and how ready members of the lower House were to censure any extravagance in public expenditure. The person who was most concerned was Lord North, and the genesis of Somerset House is unfortunately concealed from us by the loss of his papers. All that is possible is to chronicle those decisions that were recorded in the minutes of the Treasury, the Board of Works, and other bodies concerned, and to try to understand the circumstances which brought them about. One point that needs to be emphasised is that in gathering a number of offices together in a single building the Government had no obvious foreign exemplar to emulate. In the Grand Duchy of Florence, it is true, the Uffizi had long fulfilled precisely the same functions on the banks of the Arno as Somerset House was to do on those of the Thames. But the example of Florence would seem too remote both in time and in space to have inspired a Hanoverian government to a major building enterprise. Elsewhere in Europe government departments were often more handsomely housed than was the case in England, but still were not concentrated into a single monumental building designed for the purpose. In these circumstances it is tempting to look for some enlightened individual who first envisaged the idea of what today would be called a 'government centre' and then persuaded the politicians to carry it out. Some such rôle has in fact been attributed to Edmund Burke.[1] It is true that he consistently championed the project against its critics, so much so that in an undated letter to Burke Sir William Chambers was to refer to Somerset House as 'a child of your own'.[2] But on the evidence available the credit for the idea of Somerset House cannot be given to any one person: for the project seems to have developed empirically out of a particular conjunction of circumstances —the urgent need of certain departments for better accommodation, and the decrepit condition of the old palace in the Strand.

It would be difficult to name every government office that existed in the reign of George III. Before the era of reform the English civil service was cluttered with outmoded activities and sinecure functionaries. But there were more than a dozen

[1] E.g. by Sir John Summerson, *Georgian London* (1945), p. 123.
[2] Sheffield University Library, Fitzwilliam MSS., Bk 2/543 +. I owe this reference to Mr. John Harris.

departments that were useful to the state as well as profitable to their titularies. First of all there were the revenue departments known as the Salt, Stamp, Excise, Land-Tax, Hawkers and Pedlars, Hackney Coach and Lottery Offices. Then there were the Surveyor-General of Crown Lands and the Duchies of Cornwall and Lancaster; the Ordnance Office, the Office of Works, the office of the Secretary at War; and the various departments concerned with the administration of the Navy, including the Navy Office itself, the Navy Pay Office, the Victualling Office, and the Office for Sick and Wounded Seamen. In addition there were the officials of the Exchequer, that venerable and seemingly immortal institution which was still permitted to subject a large part of the public revenues to its own esoteric routine of declaration, audit and enrolment. The accommodation provided for these departments was various and scattered. The Salt Office was in York Buildings on the south side of the Strand. The Stamp Office occupied chambers on the west side of Lincoln's Inn. Hawkers and pedlars obtained their licences in Holborn Court, Gray's Inn, hackney coach drivers sought theirs in Surrey Street off the Strand. Lottery tickets were prepared for sale in New Palace Yard, Westminster. The office of the Surveyor-General of Crown Lands was in a house in Berkeley Square, that of the Duchy of Lancaster in the Savoy. As for the Duchy of Cornwall, it had had no official home since 1751, but meetings of its Council were held in the private house of the Deputy Auditor in Marsham Street, Westminster. The Navy Office was still in occupation of the premises off Seething Lane designed for its use by Sir Christopher Wren in 1683: but the Victualling Office was on Tower Hill, the Pay Office in Old Broad Street, and the business of the Office for Sick and Wounded Seamen was conducted from the private house of its secretary.[1]

The dispersal of offices, though in some cases inconvenient, was not in itself a major obstacle to efficiency. But the accommodation was often unsuitable or inadequate, and rents had to be paid for the use of those buildings that were not Crown property. Wren's Navy Office, in particular, was now quite inadequate for the purposes for which it had been built in the reign of Charles II, while several of the adjoining houses into which it had spread were in so bad a state as to be declared unsafe. The Navy Board was, in fact, engaged in enlisting the support of the Admiralty for an expenditure of £30,000 on a 'plain building' designed to accommodate all its scattered dependencies under one roof, if possible on a site somewhat nearer to their Lordships' own office in Whitehall.[2] Already in 1768 the Excise Office, upon whose effectiveness much of the public revenue depended, had succeeded in getting Treasury sanction for the erection of new and better premises in Old Broad Street. An alternative site considered at the time was the Bishop of Ely's old mansion on the north side of Holborn. But this was strongly opposed by the City merchants owing to its distance from their warehouses, and the idea was abandoned in favour of a new office on the site of Gresham College in Old Broad Street.[3] The idea of taking over

---

[1] For the premises occupied by the various departments see Dodsley's *London and its Environs* (1761) and various memoranda among Chambers's plans for Somerset House in Sir John Soane's Museum, Drawer 41, Set 5. For the Navy Office see T. F. Reddaway, 'Sir Christopher Wren's Navy Office', *Bulletin of the Institute of Historical Research*, xxx (1957).

[2] Adm. 106/2202, pp. 285–7.

[3] Above, p. 349.

Ely House was, however, revived in 1771, when the bishop offered to sell the house to the Crown 'if it should be thought proper for any Public Service'. The Treasury immediately thought of the Salt, Stamp, Hackney Coach and Hawkers and Pedlars Offices, and asked for information about the rents they were paying. William Robinson of the Board of Works, who had surveyed the premises for the Excise Office in 1767, was again sent for, and after some negotiation the bishop agreed to accept £6500 and an annuity of £200 secured on 'the revenues of some of the Public Offices to which the premises may be appropriated'. On 26 November the commissioners of the departments concerned were informed that their offices were to be removed to Ely House 'as soon as proper provision can be made for them', but nothing could be done until an Act of Parliament had been obtained to enable the bishop to dispose of the property of his see, and meanwhile Robinson was authorised to negotiate for nine houses in Holborn which were needed to round off the purchase. The intention must have been to build new offices on the site rather than merely to adapt the old buildings which Robinson had condemned in 1767 as 'much decayed and unfit to be alter'd or repair'd'.[1]

The Act became law in 1772, and Ely House duly passed into the possession of the Crown. But for some reason the development of the site was not immediately proceeded with, and no decision as to the architectural form of the new building had yet been taken when, early in 1774, a new and more eligible site suggested itself. This was the old palace of Somerset House, upon whose parlous state the Board of Works submitted a memorandum in May 1774. Nearly all of it was out of repair, parts of it had actually collapsed, and others were only prevented from falling by timber shoring.[2] This report was not drawn up in response to any formal request from the Treasury, but it may perhaps have been prompted by some unofficial intimation that the state of Somerset House was of interest to the Government. However this may be, the Treasury made prompt use of the information thus placed at its disposal. The report was dated 6 May. On 10 May it was resolved that Lord North should discuss the future of Somerset House with the king, and on 17 May he was able to report that it was His Majesty's pleasure that the palace should be demolished 'and that the ground shou'd be employed for the purpose of building such offices as may be necessary and convenient for the public . . . and also that a Bill shou'd be brought into Parliament for divesting those Premises out of the Trustees in whom they are vested for Her Majesty and for settling in lieu thereof, Buckingham House and its appurtenances'.[3] The outcome was the Act of 1775 which substituted Buckingham House for Somerset House as the queen's official dower house, and reimbursed the king for the cost of purchasing the former and adapting it as a royal residence. From figures furnished by the Board of Works it was ascertained that the king's expenditure had amounted to upwards of £100,000, and for that sum Somerset House accordingly passed into public ownership. Provision was also made for the sale of Ely House, and for the proceeds to be devoted to the building of the new public offices. Further sums applicable to the same purpose were also expected to be derived from the

---

[1] T 29/41, pp. 62, 112, 263–4, 288, 296–7, 342, 355, 440, 471–2; Works 6/18, p. 158.
[2] Works 6/19, p. 27. Above, p. 261.
[3] T 29/43, pp. 380, 385–6.

leasing of such parts of the grounds of Somerset House as might not be required for public purposes. Should the total be insufficient, the Treasury was authorised to issue further supplies out of the general revenue, or out of the revenues of any of the departments to be accommodated on the site.[1]

The Act did not specify any particular architectural layout: but it did envisage the embanking of the foreshore in front of both Somerset House and the Savoy. This was the result of a conference held on 24 May 1774. It was presided over by Lord North, and was attended by John Robinson, joint secretary to the Treasury, and William Masterman, clerk of the council to the Duchy of Lancaster. Two surveyors were present: one, William Robinson, nominated by the Treasury, the other, John Norris, by the Duchy. By an Act of 1772 a long legal dispute over the Savoy had been settled by dividing its ownership between the Duchy and the Crown, and it was for this reason that both were represented at the conference. Meeting at John Robinson's house, they resolved to seek powers to embank the river in the manner eventually embodied in the Act. So far as the Savoy was concerned this was a further step in a scheme to lay out the site of the dissolved Hospital for building that had been under negotiation between the Duchy and the Exchequer for some years past. At one time, indeed, there had been a proposal to erect buildings for the Salt, Stamp, Land Tax, Hackney Coach and Hawkers and Pedlars Offices on the waterfront at the Savoy, and William Robinson had made a plan for the purpose which is now in Sir John Soane's Museum.[2]

It was Robinson who was now commissioned to prepare designs for the larger building on the site of Somerset House which was to accommodate not only the revenue departments but the naval offices, the Ordnance Department, the Duchies of Lancaster and Cornwall and the Royal Academy. The inclusion of the Navy Office and its satellites was the result of a timely memorandum from the Admiralty, drawing the Treasury's attention to the urgent need for better offices for the Board's staff, and expressing the hope that part of the Somerset House site would be made available for the purpose.[3] The Royal Academy's claim was based on the fact that since 1771 it had, by royal permission, occupied a suite of rooms in Old Somerset House, and therefore had a prescriptive right to accommodation in the new one. Some energetic lobbying by the Society of Antiquaries and the Royal Society was later to secure for them a similar privilege, but in 1775 the Academy was the only outside body for whom the architect was required to provide quarters. Indeed, when in April 1775 the President of the Society of Antiquaries consulted Worsley as Surveyor of the King's Works, he was told that 'the numerous publick offices intended by Government to be erected thereon, would, according to the present Survey and Plan, occupy the whole of the Ground, and leave no Room for other Uses'.[4] No drawing is known to survive that represents Robinson's proposed layout, but from

---

[1] *Commons' Journals*, vol. 35, pp. 299, 316, 319, 335, 340; *Statutes at Large*, vol. 12 (1776), pp. 307–14 (15 George III, cap. XXXIII). £10,000 were also derived from the sale of the old Navy Offices and £5764 from that of the old Stamp Office in Lincoln's Inn (T 29/58, ff. 43, 101; 59, f. 155; 61, f. 208).

[2] For the whole story see R. Somerville, *The Savoy* (1960), chapter ix. There is a copy of the minutes of the conference in Sir John Soane's Museum, Drawer 41, Set 5. Robinson's plan is in Drawer 43, Set 1. It is undated, but was presumably made in 1773 or 1774.

[3] Adm. 2/548, pp. 493–4; T 29/43, pp. 417–18.

[4] Joan Evans, *A History of the Society of Antiquaries* (1956), p. 170.

the estimate submitted to Parliament in April 1775 it may be inferred that it consisted of two parallel ranges of buildings facing one another across a central courtyard:

| *West Building* | *East Building* |
|---|---|
| Navy Office | Stamp Office |
| Victualling Office | Salt Office |
| King's Barge-Master's House | Land Tax Office |
| Barge Houses | Hawkers and Pedlars Office |
| | Hackney Coach Office |
| | Lottery Office |
| | Navy Pay Office |
| | Ordnance Office |
| | Duchy of Lancaster |
| | Duchy of Cornwall |
| | Royal Academy |

Some difference in size or architectural treatment is indicated by the fact that while the estimate for the West Building was £66,500, that for the East Building was only £62,000. The embankment was to cost an additional £7200, making a total of £135,700.[1]

According to Baretti, whose *Guide through the Royal Academy* was published in 1781, the building envisaged by Robinson was designed 'in a plain manner, rather with a view to convenience than ornament'. But in the course of the debate on the Act of 1775 Burke had 'pressed for Splendour',[2] and he and other 'men of taste in Parliament' were successful in persuading the government to treat the project as an occasion for architectural display. Robinson was accordingly instructed to think in terms of a structure that would be 'an ornament to the Metropolis and a monument of the taste and elegance of His Majesty's Reign', but died before any such designs had been completed. The 'men of taste' had, however, made their point, and it was accepted that the new building was to be 'an object of national splendour' as well as one of public utility.[3]

Robinson's sudden death in October 1775 was a personal tragedy, but from an architectural point of view it was providential, for nothing suggests that he was an architect capable of rising to the opportunity which was offered him and of giving London a building equal in merit to the one that was condemned to destruction. Though Robinson was an official of the Board of Works, it was the Treasury, not the Board, to which he was responsible as architect designate of Somerset House. Once the old palace ceased to be royal property it ceased to be the Board's concern, and any money allocated for the new building would have to be separately accounted for. Robinson's responsibility for Somerset House was therefore a personal one, and the

[1] *Commons' Journals*, vol. 35, p. 321.
[2] *The Correspondence of George III*, ed. J. Fortescue iii (1928), p. 208.
[3] G. Baretti, *A Guide through the Royal Academy* (1781) pp. 3–4. Robinson's drawings were subsequently handed over to Chambers, and on the recommendation of the Board of Works his heirs were paid £315 for his trouble in surveying and drawing (Works 6/19, pp. 85–6, 94).

same was true of his successor, William Chambers, who on 24 November received a royal warrant authorising him to carry out the provisions of the Act.[1] The responsibility thus placed upon him was heavy: he alone was to design a great public building and supervise its execution without the assistance of his colleagues at the Board of Works, and he alone was to choose the craftsmen and authorise the payment to them of the money advanced by the Treasury. With so many different departments to accommodate, his task was bound to be an exacting one, demanding all his considerable powers of diplomacy and persuasion. And if anything went wrong it was himself who would have to bear the blame. On the other hand, in a country in which so many projects for palaces and parliament houses had come to naught, it was an opportunity to achieve at last one of those monumental schemes of which every Georgian architect dreamed. Chambers had had his share of disappointments in connection with George III's proposed palace at Richmond, and this was to be his compensation. He must have been glad, too, that after all it was he and not Robinson who was to be the architect of Somerset House. For he had esteemed the latter neither as a colleague nor as an artist. 'Is it not strange', he had written to Worsley in June 1774, 'that such an undertaking should be trusted to a Clerk in our office; ill-qualified, as appears by what he has done at the Excise and the Fleet; while the King has six Architects in his service ready and able to obey his commands. Methinks it should be otherwise in the reign of a Vertuoso prince'. In the same letter he lamented the destruction of old Somerset House—'no mercy for Inigo Jones's fine front, nor for a great part of that extensive palace almost new', and declared that he could easily save both 'and many thousand pounds' as well.[2] Now it was too late to save the old palace, and his regrets (however genuine they may have been) must have been tempered by satisfaction that in designing his new layout there was no need to compromise with the past.

The site at his disposal was large, amounting to some six acres, but the frontage to the Strand was restricted by private properties which were outside his brief. Otherwise there were no obvious limitations on his freedom of invention. At first his thoughts went back to Inigo Jones, and he worked out a plan with several courts —one of them oval—connected by elaborately conceived vestibules in a manner which recalls some of Jones's projects for Whitehall, though the treatment was in several respects different.[3] In the end he decided on a relatively simple layout which suggests a London square rather than a palace (Fig. 31). What was needed for most of the government departments was, after all, a set of rooms with a separate entrance, and for this purpose a quadrangular layout dignified by uniform architectural treatment was both handsome and practical. The Strand block, however, called for special treatment, not only because it necessarily contained the main entrance, but because it was destined to accommodate the Academy and the two learned societies. The facade, with its arcaded podium of channelled masonry supporting a

---

[1] T 52/64, pp. 126–7; cf. T 29/44, p. 267; T 29/45, pp. 26, 135, 143, 226, 246; T 29/46, pp. 210–12 (3 July 1777).

[2] B.M., Add. MS. 41135, f. 28ᵛ. For his unhappy relations with Robinson see *ibid.* ff. 29–30 and above, p. 139.

[3] Sir John Soane's Museum, Drawer 41, Set 1, no. 1, reproduced by J. Harris, *Sir William Chambers* (1970) pl. 155. Serlio, *Architettura* (1619), book 7, p. 231 is a possible source for the oval courtyard.

Corinthian order, was evidently designed to pay a graceful tribute to the river front-age of the old palace, reputedly designed by Inigo Jones. But the composition un-doubtedly owed something to a building of more recent erection, and one which, like Somerset House itself, was intended for government purposes. This was the Hôtel des Monnaies, designed by J. D. Antoine, which Chambers would have seen when he visited Paris in the summer of 1774. It was from its facade that he must have derived the central attic decorated with statuary, and probably also the triple-arched entry into a vaulted loggia, although in designing the latter he was, no doubt, thinking also of Sangallo's Palazzo Farnese in Rome. The importance of the Strand front was further emphasised by the introduction of 'enriched windows, balustrades, statues, masks, medallions and various other ornamental works', which helped to indicate that the apartments within were (to quote Chambers himself) 'intended for the reception of useful learning and polite arts'.[1] To polite arts, in the shape of the Royal Academy, were allocated the whole of the ground and upper floors to the west of the entrance, together with a top-lit exhibition gallery which extended over the northern half of the entrance itself (Fig. 30). On the other side the representa-tives of 'useful learning' had to divide the same volume of accommodation between their two societies in a manner which was not entirely satisfactory, as it involved the common use of the entrance hall and staircase, and led to some contention over the delimitation of territory in the basement. The scientists were, moreover, obliged to part with their 'Repository' or museum because Chambers could not provide space for its display. However, each society had its own meeting-room and its own library, and, however inconvenient it might be to share the same staircase, the elegance of the interiors was the subject of appreciative comment when, in 1780, the two bodies took possession of their new quarters.[2]

Among the administrative departments it was the Navy Board to which architec-tural priority was given. Two-thirds of the block overlooking the river were reserved for its offices, and it was to have the exclusive use of the spacious entrance-hall which now belongs to the Principal Probate Registry.[3] The three allied departments, the Naval Pay Office, the Victualling Office and the Sick and Hurt Office, occupied nearly all the western range, and it was for Commissioners of the Navy that most of the parallel terrace of houses was reserved, as the exigencies of the service might require their presence at any time of the day or night.[4] The disposition of the remain-ing offices can be seen from the plan (Fig. 31). It was not determined without a great deal of discussion and correspondence between the architect and the depart-ments concerned, each of which had its particular requirements. Surveys had in several cases to be made of their existing premises in order to ascertain their needs, and plans went backwards and forwards between their secretaries and Chambers's office. Sometimes there were snags which even the most intelligent architect could hardly be expected to foresee. The proposed Naval Pay Office, for instance, might

[1] *Commons' Journals*, vol. 37, p. 819.
[2] C. W. Weld, *History of the Royal Society*, ii (1848), pp. 119–22; Joan Evans, *A History of the Society of Antiquaries* (1956), pp. 170–6. Both societies elected Chambers to membership in 1776.
[3] Originally as the plan (Fig. 31) shows there was no communication between this hall and the central corridor to the east, which served a different department.
[4] Memorandum in Sir John Soane's Museum, Drawer 41, Set 5.

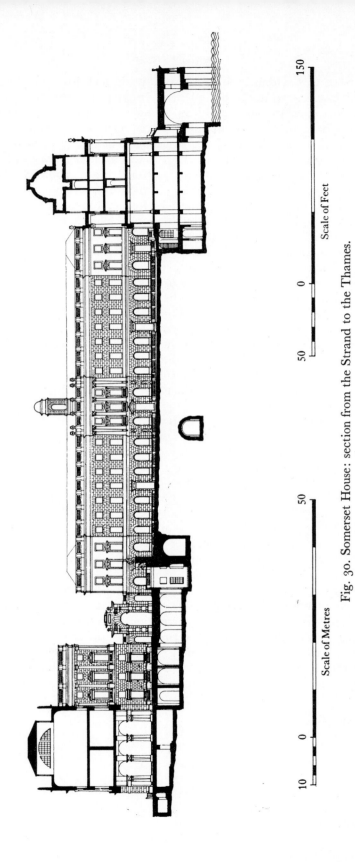

Fig. 30. Somerset House: section from the Strand to the Thames.

Scale of Feet

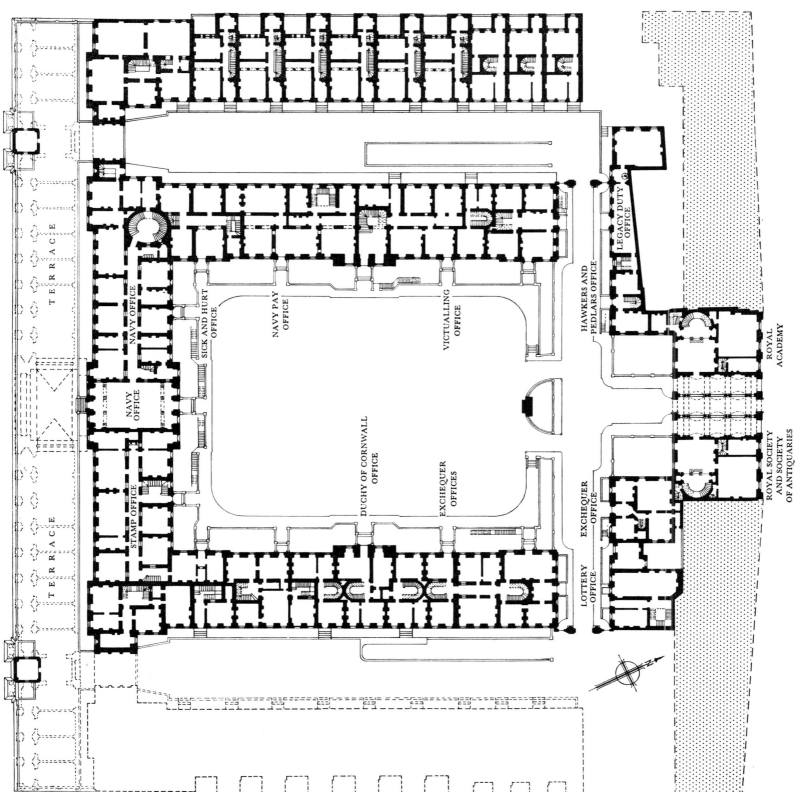

RIVER THAMES

TERRACE

TERRACE

TERRACE

NAVY OFFICE

NAVY OFFICE

NAVY OFFICE

STAMP OFFICE

SICK AND HURT OFFICE

NAVY PAY OFFICE

VICTUALLING OFFICE

DUCHY OF CORNWALL OFFICE

EXCHEQUER OFFICES

LOTTERY OFFICE

EXCHEQUER OFFICE

HAWKERS AND PEDLARS OFFICE

LEGACY DUTY OFFICE

ROYAL ACADEMY

ROYAL SOCIETY AND SOCIETY OF ANTIQUARIES

THE STRAND

Fig. 31. Somerset House: ground-plan

seem admirably designed for its purpose, with a central hall flanked on one side by the Pay Room and on the other by the Short Allowance Room. Through openings in the walls the clerks of these two departments were to issue money to the sailors in the hall. But this simple and apparently foolproof arrangement filled the officials concerned with alarm. 'Those', they wrote, 'who are acquainted with the nature of carrying on the payments of seamen's wages know that the admission of seamen into the hall to receive their pay will be attended with many inconveniences. It will frequently cause so great a croud there as to be an obstruction to those who have business to transact in other parts of the Office, but this is the least objection. Sailors, collected in a body, are very apt to become riotous, and we have experienced times when the tumult has been so great as not only to interrupt the public business, but to make it absolutely necessary to send for a party of the Guards from the Tower for the protection of the Office. Should the like happen in the new office, a few sailors in the hall would easily find means to let in their companions from the street, and then the consequences may be dreaded'.[1]

A factor which added enormously to the difficulty of Chambers's task was the length of time which elapsed between the passing of the Act in 1775 and the completion of the individual offices, amounting in most cases to eleven, twelve or thirteen years. Few departments, even in the eighteenth century, remained quite unchanged over so long a period, and in the case of the revenue departments the tendency was for both their business and their staff to increase. In 1786, for instance, the Commissioners of Taxes, still in their old quarters in New Palace Yard, represented to the Treasury that 'in consequence of the new regulations that have taken place in their office and the additional number of clerks and other officers employed, they conceive the apartments at present allotted for their use at Somerset House are much too small for the purposes intended, and they fear will be found totally insufficient to carry on the business of their department unless some alterations can be made therein'. Confronted with this awkward request, Chambers replied that the Tax Office itself was incapable of enlargement, but that 'whatever more room is wanted to carry on the business must either be taken from the secretary's house contiguous to the office, or from the commissioners' apartments situated within the office itself'. The solution adopted was to absorb the rooms intended for the Senior Commissioner, who was given a housing allowance instead. At the same time the Stamp Office came forward with a similar request, which was met only by sacrificing the accommodation intended for the King's Barge-Master, which happened to be adjacent. Not only did departments provided for in 1775 expand in this inconvenient manner, but others came forward with requests for premises in the new building. Though the Exchequer had not been included in Robinson's original brief, it was added to the list soon after Chambers took charge. But when the rooms were nearly ready it was found that the Foreign Apposer (the official responsible for scrutinising the sheriffs' accounts) had been forgotten, and after some correspondence between Chambers and Horace Walpole, who enjoyed the profits of the offices of Comptroller of the Pipe and Clerk of the Estreats, he was fitted into the quarters allotted to those officials. In 1791, however, a belated request for accommodation from the Stationery Office could not

[1] Sir John Soane's Museum, Drawer 41, Set 5, and cf. Set 3, nos. 116 and 123.

in the end be met, and in 1792 another application of this sort from the Commissioners of Greenwich Hospital was rejected by the Treasury after Chambers had reported that if granted it would 'entirely disunite' the office designed for the Surveyor-General of Crown Lands.[1]

The Strand block was the first to be erected. Whatever practical considerations may have determined its priority, the fact that it was architecturally the show-piece of the whole building must have been a strong inducement to the architect to get it under way as soon as possible, and as Treasurer of the Royal Academy he was no doubt anxious to see that body rehoused at an early date. The foundations were laid in 1776 (apparently without any formal ceremony), and by November 1778 the walls were sufficiently far advanced for the fence to be taken down, revealing the new front to public view. Several London journals marked the occasion by publishing an account of the building which, as it appeared simultaneously in several different papers, may have been supplied by the architect himself.[2] A fuller version of this was printed by Baretti in 1781 in his *Guide through the Royal Academy*. It is valuable as an authoritative description of the elaborate sculptural decoration with which the building was embellished.

The theme of the Strand front was England's connection with the sea. The nine keystones of the basement were carved with masks symbolising Ocean surrounded by the eight great rivers of England. Those representing Ocean, Thames, Humber, Mersey, Medway and Tweed were executed by Joseph Wilton; those of Tyne, Severn and Dee by Agostino Carlini. The central mask represents *Ocean* by the head of a venerable man with a flowing beard resembling waves. On his head is placed a crescent, 'to denote the influence the Moon has on its waters, and round his temples is bound a tiara, adorned with crowns, tridents, and other marks of royalty'. To the right of Ocean is *Thames*, a head crowned with billing swans and garlands of fruits and flowers. The hair and beard are 'dressed and plaited in the nicest order', and the features are intended to express good-humour and urbanity. Next to Thames is *Humber*, a striking contrast, exhibiting 'an athletick hardy countenance', with beard and hair disordered by tempests. The cheeks and eyes are swelled with rage in order to suggest 'the boisterous intractable character of that river'. Next to Humber are *Mersey* and *Dee*, the one crowned with garlands of oak, the other with reeds and other aquatic plants. On the other side of Ocean the first mask is *Medway*, a head similar to that of Thames, but 'more negligently dressed, and bearing for emblems the prow of a ship of war', with festoons of hops, and other Kentish fruits. Next to Medway is *Tweed*, 'represented by a rustick, with lank hair, a rough beard, and other marks of rural simplicity'. This head is crowned with a garland of roses and thistles. The two remaining masks on the left hand represent *Tyne*, with head-dress composed of salmon, intermixed with kelp and other sea-weeds, and *Severn*, crowned with sedges and cornucopias, whence flow streams of water abounding with lamphreys and other fish. On the inner side the five corresponding keystones were carved by Joseph Nollekens, and represent 'lares, or tutelar deities of the place'.

[1] T 29/57, pp. 43, 85, 105, 194, 248, 348, 357, 398, 428, 430, 435, 549; T 29/59, pp. 361, 468; T 29/63, p. 271; T 29/64, pp. 62, 142, 160.
[2] E.g. *London Chronicle*, 19–21 Nov. 1778, *Lloyd's Evening Post*, 18–20 Nov. 1778, *Public Advertiser*, 19 Nov. 1778, *Whitehall Evening Post*, 19–21 Nov. 1778.

Returning to the Strand front, Baretti tells us that the four figures fronting the attic symbolise Justice, Prudence, Valour and Moderation, 'qualities by which dominion can alone be maintained'. The two outer figures were the work of the Italian sculptor Giuseppe Ceracchi, the two inner ones of his compatriot Carlini. The corresponding figures on the courtyard side represent the Continents, 'America armed and breathing defiance', the rest 'loaded with tributary fruits and treasures'. These were all by Wilton. The armorial decorations surmounting the attic on both fronts were by John Bacon.

Baretti's attributions are supported by the accounts, which show that Joseph Wilton received £21 for each of six colossal heads cut in Portland stone, while Agostino Carlini was paid a similar sum for the remaining three. The masks carved by Nollekens also cost £21 each. For his two armorial groups Bacon charged a total of £735. Wilton's statues of Europe, Asia, Africa and America were priced at £120 each, as were Carlini's of Justice and Prudence, but Ceracchi received only £100 each for his companion figures of Temperance and Fortitude (as they are described in the accounts). Inside the courtyard the main doorways were flanked by sculptures symbolising the activities of the Navy Office (tritons with sea-tackle), the Victualling Office (tritons with axes and the heads of slaughtered cattle) and the Duchy of Cornwall ('deities of the woods, with sheaves of corn and rustic emblems'). These spirited groups, which must rank among the best decorative sculpture of their age, were the work of Wilton, who also carved busts of Newton and Michelangelo to mark the entrances to the rooms of the Royal Society and the Royal Academy. It was Bacon who was responsible for the rather insipid bronze statue of George III leaning on a rudder which stands in the main quadrangle.[1] All this expensive sculpture was commissioned by Chambers without formal reference to the Treasury, but not, perhaps, without informal consultation with Lord North. Inside the Royal Academy there was a complementary (though not quite so expensive) patronage of the decorative painter. Reynolds himself received £31 10s. for painting a picture for the library ceiling: it represented 'The Theory of Art', symbolised by 'an elegant and majestick Female' holding a scroll with the legend 'Theory is knowledge of what is truly Nature'. The supporting paintings of Nature, History, Allegory and Fable in the coves of the same ceiling were the work of Cipriani, who also decorated the staircase with two friezes in grisaille—a large one of Minerva visiting the Muses on Mount Parnassus, and a small one of the same goddess accompanied by the geniuses of Painting, Sculpture, Architecture and other arts. Angelica Kauffmann, Benjamin West and Biagio Rebecca shared the decoration of the lecture room or council chamber, while J. F. Rigaud was responsible for that of the ante-room to the exhibition room. Altogether £597 were spent on decorative painting in the Royal Academy's apartments. On the other side of the main entrance the Royal Society was indulged with the comparatively modest outlay of £63 on 'four Chiaro Scuro Paintings representing the four Elements' and 'twelve medallions representing the signs of the Zodiac' (both by Rebecca), while the Antiquaries had to be content with some elegant plasterwork (by James Clarke) unadorned by the painter's art. The

---

[1] This was made in 1787–8 and cost £2270. For a more detailed account of the sculpture based on the accounts see J. B. Papworth in *R.I.B.A. Journal*, N.S., ix (1892–3), pp. 106–10, 119–22.

Academy's first exhibition in its new rooms was held in the spring of 1780, and later in the same year the Royal Society and the Society of Antiquaries received the keys of their respective rooms.

Meanwhile a start had been made with the embankment which formed the lower part of the great river facade, designed to be 550 feet in length and nearly 40 feet in height from water-level to the top of the balustraded parapet. Seen from the south, the main building was to be linked by what were, in effect, huge Palladian bridges to terminal blocks forming the ends of the two flanking terraces of houses for public officials. The eastern terrace was, however, never built (King's College eventually took its place), and in 1776 the supporting embankment was begun on a more restricted frontage of 438 feet. Parts of its foundations stood on piles driven ('with various expensive but necessary precautions') into the river-bed, while others had to be sunk through loose ground, full of pits and holes, to a depth of 10, 12 or even 16 feet.[1] Above water-level it was carried up in the form of an arcaded wall interrupted by a central arch and two flanking 'water-gates' corresponding to the two bridges above. The arch, designed to admit boats to an entrance under the Navy Office used by the King's Barge-Master, was dramatic in a manner suggestive of Piranesi, whose influence has also been detected in the giant swags, suspended beneath labels, which decorate the attics of the two 'water-gates'.[2] The front of the embankment was built of Aberdeen granite. Behind it were the great brick piers which supported the Navy Office block and raised it nearly to the same level as the Strand front (Fig. 30). This massive substructure was necessitated by the steep slope of the river-bank, and its design and execution demanded technical ability of a high order. If a single one of the many piers proved to be ill-founded, settlement of the superincumbent masonry would occur, with effects at best unsightly and at worst catastrophic. One such accident did indeed occur on 26 December 1789, when five of the central piers supporting one of the streets gave way. Chambers at once reported the failure to the Treasury, who asked James Wyatt to inspect the damage in company with the surveyors John Johnson and John White. They reported that it was due to the failure of some of the bricks, but declared themselves 'perfectly satisfied that it has not been due to any bad construction of the plan or to any neglect in the execution', and added that such was the magnitude of the piers and the 'apparent goodness of the materials' that they 'could not have conceived it possible that any accident could have happened'. Harder bricks were obtained, and the damage was made good at a cost of £800. Fortunately none of the buildings was affected, and no lives were lost, although Chambers and his staff had exposed themselves to some danger by ineffectual attempts to shore up the crumbling arches.[3] With this one exception, the substructure stood firm, and in view of the difficulty of establishing satisfactory foundations in the treacherous and much-disturbed soil of the old river-bank, the subsequent stability of his vast and complex building must be regarded as one of Chambers's greatest achievements.

The Navy Office block was ready for occupation in 1786, and the east and west

[1] *Commons' Journals*, vol. 37, p. 819.
[2] J. Summerson, *Architecture in Britain 1530–1830* (1963), p. 357, n. 7.
[3] T 29/60, ff. 121, 124, 137, 235, 255; T 1/666, ff. 86–93, 171–2.

ranges were sufficiently complete for most of the other departments to be in possession by 1788. The first of the western terrace of houses was ready for its destined occupant —the Treasurer of the Navy—early in 1790,[1] but it was some years before the whole range was complete. Some difficulty was caused by the proximity of these houses to the Savoy, whose site was covered with dilapidated buildings and squalid apartments. For years every scheme to redevelop the Savoy had been frustrated by lack of cooperation between its two landlords, the Exchequer and the Duchy of Lancaster, and nothing had so far come of an ambitious plan by Chambers to replace the old Guards' barracks (burned out in March 1776) by a magnificent new structure forming a large three-sided square, closed towards the river by an arcaded screen.[2] Now the building of the new commissioners' houses was being held up because of a 'cluster of wretched old houses' standing within three feet of the site of the new terrace, and 'in constant danger of falling'. Any accident, as Chambers pointed out to the Chancellor of the Duchy, might result in heavy loss of life as well as serious damage to the new houses.[3] The offending tenements were duly pulled down, and the last of the 'Navy Houses' was eventually finished in 1801, but it was not until Waterloo Bridge had been completed in 1817 that the Savoy as a whole was redeveloped in accordance with the designs, not of Sir William Chambers, but of Sir Robert Smirke.

In building Somerset House Chambers followed the usual Office of Works practice of paying the workmen by measure at agreed rates. He entered into no contracts 'by the great', preferring the close supervision which measured work required. The names of the principal master workmen will be found in Appendix C. Several of them were Patent Artisans, and nearly all of them were men regularly employed by the Office of Works elsewhere. They were the leading members of their respective crafts, and Somerset House remains an outstanding exhibit of Georgian building craftsmanship. Immense care was taken by Chambers over the decorative details, many of which were first modelled in wood or wax, and some of which were tried out by full-scale 'mock-ups' before final approval. According to his own statement, 'the Ionic, Composite and Corinthian capitals, to be seen in various parts of Somerset Place, were copied from models executed under my direction at Rome, and imitated, both in point of forms and manner of workmanship, from the choicest antique originals'.[4] Nowhere, in fact, can the exacting standards of the *Treatise on Civil Architecture* have been more meticulously applied than in its author's principal public work.

An office on the site was an obvious necessity, and one of the architect's first steps was to have one fitted up in part of the old palace, whose demolition proceeded gradually as the new building rose in its place. The staff with whom he shared this office consisted of four persons, whose employment was authorised by the Treasury after the Board of Works had given their opinion that 'not less than

[1] T 29/61, p. 258.

[2] Above, p. 360, n. 9. The idea of building new barracks in the Savoy was not finally abandoned until 1804 (R. Somerville, *The Savoy*, 1960, p. 109).

[3] B.M., Add. MS. 38447, f. 129.

[4] *A Treatise on the Decorative Part of Civil Architecture* (1791), pp. 58–9. A quantity of the original working drawings are in Sir John Soane's Museum, and there are other drawings for various parts of the building in the R.I.B.A. Drawings Collection and the Victoria & Albert Museum (for a list see John Harris, *Sir William Chambers*, 1970, pp. 229–32). But many more drawings must have been made than can now be accounted for.

four experienced and able Clerks' were 'absolutely necessary' for the conduct of works of such magnitude.[1] John Yenn and Robert Browne were appointed joint clerks of works at £100 a year each. Thomas Clark was 'superintendant of works' at £84 (later £100) a year, and Francis Symmons acted as office-boy or 'Assistant Clerk' at a guinea a week. Yenn, Browne and Clark remained with Chambers throughout, and the two former in due course graduated to posts in the Office of Works. Symmons, however, did not long remain in his poorly-paid post, and was followed by a succession of young men who were for the most part students at the Royal Academy Schools and were no doubt glad to obtain practical experience under Chambers as well as a modest income. Their names were Samuel Saxon (December 1777–June 1781), Willey Reveley (July 1781–December 1782), Nathaniel Lindegren (January 1783–December 1791) and William Rose (January 1792 onwards). Chambers himself was at first offered the same remuneration as William Robinson had received for building the Excise Office, namely 2½ per cent of the workmen's bills. This percentage was, in accordance with a common eighteenth-century practice, deducted from the bills before they were paid, and therefore cost the government nothing. But it was only half the remuneration usual in private architectural practice, and in 1777 Chambers asked for a total of 5 per cent on the ground that he was obliged to devote his whole attention to Somerset House, 'very much to the prejudice of my own income, which, by having been under the necessity of relinquishing all other employment, is lessened by at least 1,800 pounds a year'. This request was rather belatedly granted three years later, after it had been pronounced by Chambers's colleagues at the Board of Works to be 'exceeding reasonable'.[2] Thereafter he received from the Exchequer an additional 2½ per cent of the total outlay, together with a lump sum representing the same percentage of the expenditure incurred since 1776.

The passing of the accounts was a matter which gave rise to some difficulty. At first they were referred to the Board of Works, who priced the workmanship according to the rates currently paid to their own workmen, but did not consider themselves responsible for checking either its quantity or its quality. The Board justified this on the ground that the building was not their responsibility, and that all they could be expected to do was to see that the accounts were correct. This did not, however, satisfy the the Treasury, who in August 1781 insisted that the Board should themselves 'survey, examine and measure' the works 'so as to enable them correctly to examine, state and certify Sir William Chambers's accounts'. But when, in accordance with this directive, the Board appointed C. A. Craig (then an assistant in the office of Robert Taylor) as 'measuring clerk at Somerset House', Chambers at once protested at what he regarded as an unwarrantable interference. 'The works must, I apprehend', he wrote to the Board, 'be managed by me, as they have hitherto been, and be conducted, under my Direction, by the Clerks, whose Attendance from the first makes them Masters of the Whole Business. I certainly, however, have no Objection to the Attendance of one or more proper Persons, appointed agreeable to the Order

[1] *Copies of the Several Reports made by the Board of Works respecting the work done under the Direction of Sir William Chambers at Somerset House*, 1788 (House of Lords Record Office, Abbott papers, 564), pp. 5–6.
[2] *Copies of the Several Reports*, pp. 4–6.

of the Treasury, at the Measurement of the Works, for the Satisfaction of their Lordships: Such an Appointment would even be very satisfactory to me, both as an additional Guard against Mistakes, and as an unbiassed Testimony of the Order and Accuracy with which that Part of the Business at Somerset House is conducted.' The Treasury consented to respect Chambers's susceptibilities by themselves appointing 'an architect of credit' to examine the accounts, compare them with the vouchers, and 'certify that the money has been properly expended'. The architect in question was James Paine, who thereafter made an annual report to the effect that 'the Money has been properly expended; that the Workmanship and Materials used are very good in their different Kinds; that the Measurements have been taken, and the Accounts kept, in a very clear and exact Manner; and that in all respects the Works at Somerset Place . . . have been carefully and ably conducted, and with every due Attention to the interest and Advantage of the Public'. The accounts were then passed to the Exchequer for audit and enrolment in the usual way. When Paine retired from practice in 1788 his place was taken by George Dance, who continued to certify the accounts until the last one was rendered in 1801.[1]

The insistence of the Treasury on independent verification of the accounts was well-advised in view of the public criticism to which so heavy and prolonged an expenditure was inevitably liable. In 1775 Robinson's estimate for a 'plain substantial' structure had amounted to £135,700.[2] When Chambers obtained the Treasury's approval for his much more elaborate and sophisticated design, no estimate appears to have been either asked for or submitted, but it must have been obvious that the cost would be substantially larger.[3] By the end of 1779 he had already received £90,000, but only the Strand block was in sight of completion, the remainder of the quadrangle being raised no more than two storeys high. Enquiries in the House of Commons elicited from Chambers a statement to the effect that it was impossible to give an accurate estimate of the eventual cost of a building so 'unusually extensive, intricately complicated, and attended with many and great difficulties in the execution', but that so far as 'his Judgment and Experience in Business can guide him, he thinks it will certainly not exceed the Sum of £250,000'. In terms of time, he estimated that 'it will require about six years and a half to complete the whole Design, at an average Expence *per Ann.* of £25,000.'[4] This went far beyond the expenditure envisaged in the original Act, and as the *carte-blanche* then given to the Treasury was found to be 'contrary to the Usage of Parliament, with respect to Grants for other Public Services, which is by Sums voted annually, founded upon proper Estimates', a new Act was passed in June 1780 obliging the

---

[1] For the negotiations between The Treasury, the Board of Works and Chambers see *Copies of the Several Reports* cited above, and *Copies of the Minutes and Proceedings of the Board of Treasury, respecting the Issue of Money for carrying on the Buildings at Somerset House, and the Mode adopted for examining and accounting for the Expenditure thereof*, 1788 (House of Lords Record Office, Abbott Papers 562). Two copies of the accounts submitted to the Exchequer exist, one in the P.R.O. (AO 1/1244), the other in the Library of the Royal Institute of British Architects, to which they were presented in 1892 by W. W. Pocock, who had been given them by a nephew of Robert Browne, one of the two clerks employed at Somerset House by Chambers (*R.I.B.A. Journal*, N.S. ix, 1893, p. 106). The enrolled summaries are AO 1/2495-2499/412-433. The drastic manner in which Dance reduced the bills of the plasterer Thomas Clark was bitterly complained of by his partner Charles Clarke in a pamphlet entitled *The Plaisterer's Bill for Works done at the New Buildings, Somerset House*, 1783 (B.M., 8768. bbb. 21(2)). [2] Above, p. 367.
[3] See the minute of 3 July 1777, printed in *Copies of the Minutes and Proceedings*, p. 4.
[4] *Commons' Journals*, vol. 37, pp. 789, 819.

Treasury to make an annual application for supplies.[1] On this basis the works continued from year to year at a cost which by 1788 had mounted to over £306,000. This was £56,000 more than the sum which Chambers had mentioned in 1780, yet the building was still incomplete, and it was rumoured that another £100,000 would be needed before it was finished. On a previous occasion when doubts had been expressed in the House they had been answered by Burke, who, 'giving way to the liberal impulse of his mind', declared that 'no man who looked at the . . . works going on there would think that the money had been wasted, or lavishly employed; the structure already erected, answering for every pound that had been voted so satisfactorily, that a doubt could not remain in any spectator's mind as to the honesty and care of the application of the sums that parliament had granted'. Such a building, he continued, 'did honour to the present age, and would render the metropolis of Great Britain famous throughout Europe'.[2] Now 'loud complaints' were once more voiced, notably by Sir John Miller, an Irish baronet, and by William Harvey, 'a man of coarse, simple and homely manners', 'exceedingly tenacious of the national purse', who never spoke 'except on pecuniary topics'. Miller, moving for a committee of inquiry, complained of the vagueness of the estimates provided by Chambers and asserted with some justice that no private gentleman would allow his architect to proceed in such a manner. Harvey declared that but for the fact that a right honourable gentleman (Dundas, the Treasurer of the Navy, to whom one of the houses had been allocated) would be enveloped in the conflagration, he could wish the building burned to the ground. Pitt, for the government, reminded the House that the plans had more than once been submitted to its scrutiny, and that Chambers was obliged to account for every penny that he spent, while George Rose, the Secretary to the Treasury, pointed out that 'Mr. Paine, one of the first surveyors of the kingdom', was employed to watch the works in the public interest. Wraxall thought the defence unconvincing, 'but the question not being connected with party, none of the Opposition members attended in their places', and the motion was lost by 76 votes to 21. It was, however, ordered that the plans should once more be laid before the House, and that copies of the Treasury minutes relating to Somerset House should be printed for the benefit of Members. On 27 May Chambers duly appeared with his plans at the bar of the House, an ordeal to which he was again subjected in March 1790.[3] By the latter date the total expenditure amounted to nearly £353,000, and it was ultimately to reach £462,000 before the final account was closed in 1801.[4]

Though Members might complain of extravagance, the Treasury seems on the whole to have been satisfied by the meticulous way in which Chambers kept the

---

[1] *Statutes at Large*, vol. 13 (1780), pp. 562–3 (20 George III, cap. XL).

[2] Hansard, *Parliamentary History* xxii, pp. 297–8 (debate of 21 May 1781).

[3] *Commons' Journals*, vol. 41, p. 786; vol. 42 pp. 724, 734: vol. 43, pp. 489, 509; vol. 45, pp. 75, 116–18, 202, 238, 289; vol. 46, p. 407; Hansard, *Parliamentary History*, vol. 27, p. 395; *Memoirs of Sir N. W. Wraxall*, ed. H. B. Wheatley, 5 (1884), pp. 121–5.

[4] Most of this money was paid out of the Exchequer, but just over £100,000 came direct from the Salt and Stamp Duties in accordance with a provision of the original Act of 1775 which empowered the Treasury to finance the building out of the revenues of the Offices to be accommodated on the site. A further £11,925 was derived from the sale of Ely House to a speculative builder named Cole, and the freeholds of the old Navy Office and Stamp Office contributed £11,500 and £5764 respectively. In 1787 the Treasury ruled that the cost of the fixtures provided for the various departments, valued at nearly £30,000, should be defrayed by the

accounts and by the promptitude with which he attended to matters of detail. In 1788, after Daniel Pulteney had pointed out in the House that 'as Sir William Chambers had 5 per cent on all the money expended, it was his interest to find as many ways of adding to the expense as possible', the Treasury went so far as to express the opinion that it might be 'for the benefit of the public' to put his remuneration on a different footing, but nothing in fact was done to alter the existing arrangement.[1] Further embarrassment was caused in December 1790 by the partial failure of one of the main bearers supporting the floor of the Royal Academy's Exhibition Room. The occasion was the last of Sir Joshua Reynolds's celebrated discourses, and a large and distinguished company was present. Reynolds had just concluded his address, and was in the act of presenting the gold medal for historical painting when a loud crack was heard, and the floor subsided slightly at a point where the audience was concentrated. Chambers was not present, but Yenn was in the room, and was able to reassure the company as to the essential stability of a floor that had, as he pointed out, 'been sufficiently tested by twelve Exhibitions, when more than a thousand persons had been upon the floor at the same time'. The damage was, indeed, found not to be serious, and was easily remedied, but much was made of the incident in the press, and questions were once more asked in the Commons. This time the government took the precaution of consulting virtually every architect of repute in London, and among the Treasury records there is a series of reassuring reports signed, among others, by Robert Adam, Robert Brettingham, James and Samuel Wyatt, John Soane and S. P. Cockerell. Only Robert Mylne expressed some doubt about the use of fir instead of 'good oak timber', and criticised the construction of the Exhibition Room floor, which was complicated by its elevated position at the top of the building. Fortunately the cost of making good the damage was slight, and in due course the incident was forgotten.[2]

For four more years Chambers continued to supervise the building which had become the great preoccupation of his life. But he did not live to see his masterpiece complete. When, in November 1775, he received the royal warrant which made him sole architect of the greatest public building of the reign, he was already fifty-two years old. Nearly twenty years later, feeling his infirmities 'crouding on very fast', he offered his resignation to George III. Having, he wrote, 'relinquished all other business, but such of the Crown as appeared compatible with the said great work', he had hoped to complete it in his lifetime, 'but unfortunately, from a variety of unexpected delays, from age and infirmities incident to old age, which of late have come fast and severely upon me, I am now rendered totally unable to manage such a work, and am constrained to entreat your Majesty's permission to resign its future conduct into hands now more able to bring it to a proper conclusion'. The hands

---

departments concerned, most of whom reluctantly complied in the course of the next few years (*An Account of the Several Sums which have been issued to Sir William Chambers for the Buildings at Somerset House*, 1788, House of Lords Record Office, Abbott Papers, 563; *Commons' Journals*, vol 37, pp. 788–9, vol. 45, pp. 117–18; T 29/58, p. 101; T 29/61, p. 208; T 29/62, pp. 215–17).

[1] Hansard, *Parliamentary History*, xxvii, p. 395; T 29/59, p. 362.

[2] W. T. Whitley, *Artists and their Friends in England 1700–1799*, ii, pp. 134–5; T 1/412, 476, 689, 956; T 27/41, pp. 373, 375, 381, 387, 408, 494; T 27/42, p. 213; T 29/62, pp. 444, 469; T 29/63, pp. 31, 195, 196, 222.

best qualified to accomplish this were, he suggested, those of his faithful adjutants Yenn and Browne, who alone were 'thoroughly conversant' with the complicated affairs of Somerset House.[1] The king thought otherwise, for it was he who prevailed on Pitt to appoint James Wyatt as Chambers's successor. His object, so Farington was told, 'was to prevent the building from being spoilt'.[2] Wyatt took over at Midsummer 1795, and finally brought the works to completion in 1801, just twenty-five years after their commencement in 1775. So far as architecture was concerned, the king's confidence was justified, for Wyatt appears faithfully to have respected his predecessor's intentions: but his accounts displayed a characteristic want of regularity, and when, in 1809, they were finally audited with the professional aid of George Saunders, they were subjected to numerous deductions 'for want of receipts' and other actuarial shortcomings. The only record of Wyatt's expenditure on Somerset House is the enrolled declaration, a summary document from which little can be gleaned about the final phase of work under his direction except its cost. This amounted to £18,055, bringing the total expenditure on Somerset House between 1775 and 1801 to £462,323.[3]

# THE TOWER OF LONDON

MUCH OF the architectural history of the Tower in the seventeenth and eighteenth centuries falls outside the scope of this *History*: for under the later Stuart and Hanoverian kings it was the Office of Ordnance, rather than the Office of Works, which was responsible for all the major works that were carried out in the ancient fortress. The period of the Dutch and French wars saw a great increase in the activities of the officers of the Ordnance, and in about 1680 they removed their quarters from the vicinity of the Chapel of St. Peter ad Vincula to a more commodious site near the Lanthorn Tower. This was within the precincts of the ancient royal palace, the whole of which was demolished within the next few years to make way for various Ordnance buildings.[4] The stone gateway at the entrance to the palace, known as Coldharbour, had already been partially demolished by the Office of Works in 1669–70 after a fall of masonry. With it went 'the Nun's Bower', a prison occupying

[1] Windsor Castle, RA 7791. The letter bears the date 12 March 1795.
[2] Farington Diary, 27 Aug. 1797. For Yenn's disappointment see Farington, 11 Nov. 1797.
[3] AO 1/2499/432–3. Like Chambers, Wyatt received a commission of 5% for supervising the works. The salary of £200 a year which he received from 1801 onwards as 'Surveyor of Somerset Place' was for maintaining the buildings after they were complete.
[4] J. Bayley, *History and Antiquities of the Tower of London*, i (1830), pp. 104, 217; *Cal. S.P. Dom. 1683* (2), p. 317. For plans of the Ordnance Office &c. made in 1731 see Works 31/182–3. Works 31/187 is a plan of the new Ordnance Office built later in the century (probably in 1778), part of whose facade can be seen in Malton's view of 1799.

the rooms over the gateway.[1] The view of the Tower made for Lord Dartmouth, Master General of the Ordnance, shows that by the accession of William III nothing remained of the former royal lodgings, whose place had been taken by the Ordnance Office, the Mortar Piece Storehouse and the Great New Storehouse (now the Horse Armoury). In 1688 the Ordnance Office took most of the ground to the north of the White Tower in order to erect a new Great Storehouse 350 feet long and nearly 70 feet high. It was built by contract by Sir Thomas and John Fitch, and it was presumably their workmen, not those of the Office of Works, who, wearing white aprons and gloves, waited on the guests when the king and queen held a state banquet in the newly-completed building.[2] In 1717 the reconstruction of the Middle Tower (then known as 'Martin's Tower') was likewise carried out by the Ordnance, and later in the century the same department rebuilt the Flint and Bowyer Towers.[3]

In the eighteenth century the Officers of the Works were, in fact, normally concerned only with the residences of the Deputy Lieutenant, the Major and the yeomen warders, together with the Record Office, the Jewel House in the Martin Tower, the lions' dens in the bulwark, and the Chapel of St. Peter ad Vincula. In addition they repaired the roofs of most of the towers and looked after the paving of the Parade, the area between the Lieutenant's Lodgings and the Chapel of St. Peter.[4] Expenditure on these tasks rarely exceeded £1000 in any one year, and the works recorded in the annual accounts under 'Tower of London' were for the most part trivial.

## 1. THE LIEUTENANT'S AND OTHER LODGINGS

For a few years after the Restoration there was some expenditure on the royal lodgings to the south of the White Tower, but after their demolition in the 1680s the principal residence within the Tower was the Lieutenant's Lodging, an ancient and unpretentious timber-framed building which occupied the south-west corner of the inner ward in the vicinity of the Bell Tower.[5] In 1663–4 this was enlarged: two new timber-framed rooms were built, one 21 × 19 feet for the Lieutenant, and the other 15 × 9 feet for his secretary.[6] Subsequently a cantilevered balcony 20 feet long was added 'at the end of the greate roome goinge out on the leades'.[7] In 1679–80 there

---

[1] Works 5/13 ('taking down the stone walls of the Tower going into Coldharbour where it was ready to fall' &c.).

[2] Noel Blakiston, 'The Storehouse in the Tower', *Architectural Review*, June 1957, p. 453; Maitland, *History of London*, i (1775), p. 168. There is no evidence that Wren designed the building.

[3] J. Britton and E. W. Brayley, *Memoirs of the Tower of London* (1830), pp. 328–9. For the rebuilding of the Middle Tower see WO 47/29, p. 58 and WO 51/102, ff. 103–4.

[4] Works 6/14, f. 111, a list of buildings maintained by the Office of Works drawn up in March 1705/6. According to this the Office of Works was responsible for the Jewel, Beauchamp, Bell, Byward, Bloody, Broad Arrow, Salt, 'Queen Elizabeth's' and Water Towers.

[5] Its extent is clearly shown on a plan of *c.* 1690 from the Dartmouth Collection now in the Library of the Department of the Environment.        [6] Works 5/4.

[7] Works 5/13 and 15. The description does not seem quite to fit the cantilevered balcony projecting from the wall of the Lieutenant's Lodging overlooking the Thames, which is visible in the plate of The Tower in Kip's *Britannia Illustrata* (1708).

were further alterations and improvements for a newly-appointed Lieutenant (Capt. Thomas Cheeke), and in 1687–8 the existing staircase was added for his successor Sir Edward Hales. At the same time an old house was 'converted into a Chappell for the Lieutenant'.[1]

The Lieutenant's house was again repaired in 1736, after several complaints as to its bad state of repair, and in 1775 on the appointment of a new Lieutenant-Governor. But its timber-framed structure remained basically unaltered, and in 1776 the Constable, Lord Cornwallis, perhaps incited by his new deputy, tried unsuccessfully to persuade the Board to pull it down and build two new houses on the site, one for the Lieutenant, the other for the Major.[2] For some years the Board also declined to carry out any repairs at all to the warders' houses, on the ground that they were excluded by the 28th article of their instructions, which forbad any expenditure on the lodgings of royal officials that was not essential for the bare maintenance of the structure. As these houses were used for the accommodation of prisoners as well as of the warders, their state of disrepair was highly inconvenient, and in 1722 the Constable protested to the Treasury. The Treasury referred the matter to the Board who, after a personal inspection, reported that the houses were too decrepit to be worth repairing, and submitted an estimate for rebuilding them at a cost of £3286. This was refused by the Treasury, but some minor repairs to two warders' houses were apparently carried out by the Board in 1726, and in 1771 it had Treasury authority to rebuild another warder's house that was beyond repair.[3]

Close to the Lanthorn Tower there were apartments described on the view of *c.* 1685 as 'Constable's Lodging', but on a plan of 1726 as 'Major's Apartments'.[4] Though formerly the official residence of the Constable, they were in fact occupied by the Major.[5] This was Ordnance territory, and it appears that the Major's rooms were on the third floor of a building otherwise occupied by the Ordnance. When this was found to be ruinous in 1741 the lower part was rebuilt by the Ordnance, the upper by the Office of Works.[6] This awkward division of responsibility was resolved in 1776 after a fire had damaged both the Ordnance Office and the adjoining residence. The Major's apartments were surrendered to the Ordnance, who in return handed over the house hitherto occupied by the Treasurer of the Ordnance.[7]

## 2. THE RECORD OFFICE

In the seventeenth and eighteenth centuries the Tower of London provided accommodation for those records of Chancery for which there was no room at the Rolls House in Chancery Lane or in the office of the Six Clerks in Lincoln's Inn. These

---

[1] Works 5/32 and 41; *Cal. Treas. Books*, viii, pp. 1594, 1634.
[2] Works 4/1, 10 July 1718; Works 4/3, 4 Nov. 1724, 22 June 1726, 8 Aug. 1728; Works 5/141, year 1736; Works 6/19, pp. 176, 178, 180, 185, 199.
[3] Works 4/1, 10 June 1718; Works 4/3, 22 June 1726; Works 6/7, pp. 306–8; Works 6/18, pp. 263–4.
[4] Works 31/32.          [5] Works 6/17, p. 151.          [6] Works 4/8, 23 Sept. 1741.
[7] Works 6/19, pp. 87–88, 113; For the fire see *Gent's Mag.*, 1774, p. 45.

documents were preserved partly in 'Caesar's Chapel' in the White Tower and partly in the Wakefield Tower, then often referred to as the 'Record Tower'. In the latter they were kept in wooden presses arranged round the walls, but in 1704 a Committee of the House of Lords found the records in the Chapel lying 'in a confused heap' on the broken floor. As a result of its representations steps were taken by the Office of Works to provide proper shelves and presses, and when the Committee paid a visit of inspection in 1707 it was able to report to the House that 'this Chapel is now made a great and noble Repository, fit to receive many of the Records which now lie crowded in the Chapel at the Rolls'.[1]

Every term more documents accumulated in the Six Clerks' office, and from time to time a fresh consignment of records was brought over to the Tower from Lincoln's Inn. One such transfer took place in 1671. Another was planned in 1712, but was frustrated by lack of space. Wren, asked by the Lord Chancellor to report on the situation, recommended that the keeper of the records should be authorised to take over a large room on the third floor of the White Tower adjoining the Chapel.[2] This room belonged to the Board of Ordnance, who were not willing to relinquish it, and nothing more happened until 1716, when the Six Clerks once more asked for additional space. The Board of Works again insisted that the room in the White Tower was the best for the purpose, an opinion in which they were supported by another Lords' Committee, appointed in 1718 to investigate the state of the Public Records. Authority to dispossess the officers of the Ordnance was, however, still lacking, and it was not until 1737 that, after twenty-five years of intermittent negotiation, the Six Clerks were at last able to secure the room and remove to it the great mass of documents under whose weight their office was literally collapsing. The necessary alterations were carried out by the Office of Works at a cost of £314.[3]

## 3. THE CHAPEL OF ST. PETER AD VINCULA

The chapel underwent a general repair in the reign of Charles II. In 1670–1 repairs were carried out to the masonry, and the diminutive west tower was rebuilt.[4] In 1675–6 the interior was refitted with new paving, wainscoting, pulpit, reading-desk and pedimented reredos. The joinery was performed by Thomas Kinward, the Master Joiner, for £78, and Henry Phillips, the Master Carver, was responsible for the decorative carving, including a shield with the king's arms, Garter and crown.[5] All this work was removed in 1876–7, but the reredos and other fittings are shown in an illustration in Bell's book on the chapel.[6]

[1] *Lords' Journals*, xvii, pp. 555–6, 637–8, xviii, p. 318; *Cal. Treas. Books* xix, pp. 228, 350, 528, xx, p. 403; *Cal. Treas. Papers 1702–7*, pp. 292–3, 509; Works 6/14, pp. 69, 82, 99–102.

[2] *Cal. Treas. Papers 1708–14*, p. 599; Works 6/5, p. 282.

[3] Works 6/7, pp. 60–2, 6/16, pp. 54–6; *Lords' Journals*, xxi, p. 134; *Cal. Treas. Papers 1714–19*, pp. 395, 437, 446–7. The arrangement of the record repository in the White Tower is shown on two plans made by the Ordnance Office but now Works 31/97–8.

[4] Works 5/15.     [5] Works 5/25.

[6] D. C. Bell, *The Chapel of St. Peter ad Vincula* (1877), p. 12.

In 1749 the chaplain's house was rebuilt and the chapel itself was repaired, at a combined cost of £740.[1] In 1755 a gallery was constructed for the officers and men of the battalion on duty.[2] Apart from this nothing more was done until 1779, when £123 were spent on the building after the chaplain had complained that it had got into a condition 'entirely inconsistent with the decency requisite for a place dedicated to divine worship'.[3]

## 4. THE JEWEL HOUSE

The unsatisfactory state of the Jewel House in the north-east corner of the Inner Ward was the subject of several complaints in the early eighteenth century. Some of the offices attached to the building had recently been demolished by the Ordnance Office on the grounds that they were 'too near the Grand Armoury', and the external stairs leading up to the entrance were on the point of collapse. In 1721, after the then Keeper of the Crown Jewels, James Brudenell, had asked for 'some conveniency in lieu of the appartment taken away', a new kitchen and wash-house were built for him at a cost of £87. He also claimed the cost of some iron bars which his predecessor had installed at his own expense, and which the latter's executors would have removed 'if I had not engaged they should be satisfied for them at reasonable rates'. The Treasury accepted the Board's estimate of £14 18s. 4d. as their proper value, but the executors had evidently extracted more than this from Brudenell, for in 1724 the Board agreed to carry out some repairs for the benefit of the next occupant of the office on condition that he renounced his claim to any further demand for the value of the ironwork over and above the amount of £14 18s. 4d. allowed by the Treasury. At the same time the Surveyor of the Ordnance expressed his willingness 'to joyn in the reparation of the stair up to the Jewell Tower, when any of the Board of Works shall please to advise with him in it'. What (if anything) was done does not appear from the records of the Office of Works.[4]

[1] Works 6/17, p. 48.
[2] Works 4/11, 23 Sept. 1755. This gallery was removed in 1876–7.
[3] Works 1/4, p. 157; Works 6/19, p. 182; Works 5/142, year 1778–9.
[4] Works 6/7, pp. 80, 232, 333; Works 4/1, 25 June 1719, Works 4/2, 1 July 1724, Works 5/141, years 1722–3, 1723–4.

# WESTMINSTER

## 1. NEW PALACE YARD

DURING THE period covered by this volume New Palace Yard was transformed from what in 1660 was still recognisable as the outer courtyard of a medieval palace into a public thoroughfare lined by Georgian houses. This transformation was largely the work of the Westminster Bridge Commissioners established by Act of Parliament in 1736, and as such falls outside the scope of this *History*. Some of the ancient buildings surrounding the Yard had, however, once been the responsibility of the Office of Works. Chief among these was the fourteenth-century Clock Tower, which then dominated New Palace Yard much as the tower of Big Ben does today. Howell, in his *Londinopolis* (1657), described it as 'a strong Tower of Stone, containing a Clock, which striketh a great Bell every houre, to give notice to the Judges, how the time passeth; when the wind is *west-south-west*, it may be heard into any part of London, and commonly, it presageth wet weather'.[1] This landmark, visible in one of Hollar's engravings (Vol. I, Pl. 36 B), was repaired by the Office in 1663–4, when new wall-plates were inserted into the old roof, which was newly covered with slates.[2] But after this little was done, and with the advent of clocks the great bell became redundant.[3] In the course of time the tower itself became dangerous, and in 1698 William III was induced to present the belfry to the parishioners of St. Margaret's for the benefit of the poor.[4] They demolished the tower and sold the bell to the dean and chapter of St. Paul's.[5] This act of vandalistic generosity was not recommended by the Treasury until Wren had been asked for a report. The tower, he said, 'was always esteemed by our Office as incumbent upon us to repare', but it was now so hemmed in by private houses that in recent years little had been done. He recalled that

> about 18 years past a designe was given to King Charles and seconded by the then Lord Chief Justice and other eminent Lawyers, to new case it with Ashler, and to put a Lanterne upon it, to raise the Bell higher and to make a new Clock, and as I remember the Estimate of this designe was about £1500: It would have been usefull to the Terme and very ornamentall to this part of the Town, but no order was then

---

[1] S. Howell, *Londinopolis* (1657), p. 378.     [2] Works 5/4.

[3] In 1706, however, the Treasury received a petition asking for 'a good large sundial' to take the place of the demolished clock and bell, which were stated to have been 'very necessary to the Parliament, courts in Westminster Hall, officers in the Exchequer, and to all who had business there' (*Cal. Treasury Papers 1702–7*, p. 409).

[4] N. Luttrell, *Brief Historical Relation*, iv, p. 402; *Cal. Treasury Books*, xiii, p.385; Works 6/2.

[5] The demolition is documented by an account book among the St. Margaret's Parish Records in Westminster Public Library (MS. E 2161).

given. As to my opinion what is fitt to be done Your Lordships are the best Judges how the petitioners may be relieved, as deserving your compassion, yet pardon your Surveyour if out of duty he modestly aske whither it be better to pull downe a public building upon so small a consideration, or to repare it with advantage to the Beauty of the Towne, which wou'd most certainly be done in any of our neighbour Countries who are more sensible than wee, that to adorn their Towns is a lasting benefit to the poor . . .[1]

Further demolitions followed, now in the interests of wheeled traffic. Members of Parliament in their coaches experienced 'great stops and inconveniences' when they attempted to pass through the two gateways by which alone the Yard could be entered, and in 1707 the Great Gate was accordingly pulled down, to be followed in 1728 by the smaller gate which led to St. Margaret's Lane and Old Palace Yard. The demolition of the Great Gate was due to a petition from the Justices of the Peace for the City of Westminster, who complained of the 'great inconveniences' it caused 'to the trade and commerce of this City, more especially in terme time, and during the sitting of Parliament'.[2] Like so many buildings connected with the former Palace of Westminster, it was now in private possession, and its demolition was accomplished by an Act of Parliament compensating its owner for pulling it down at his own expense.[3] The lesser gateway was not so easily disposed of, for the room over the arch served as a repository for some of the records of the Exchequer, while the southern side of the gateway itself had been granted away by Charles I and was now in the possession of a man called Doughty. Moreover it was not a free-standing structure, for on the north it abutted against the former Augmentations Office, and on the south it was hemmed in by houses belonging to Doughty. Both the arches had been repaired by the Office of Works in 1663–4, one of them being largely rebuilt.[4] In 1668 the possibility of pulling the gateway down was discussed by the Treasury, the Office of Works and the Commissioners for Streets and Highways, but the Exchequer asked that nothing should be authorised until alternative accommodation had been provided for the records, and in the end all that was done was to raise the arch to give more head-room. This operation was performed, not by the Office of Works, but by the Commissioners for Streets and Highways, and due care was taken to safeguard the records while the workmen were in occupation.[5] Others, however, were less conscious of the importance of preserving public records. In the reign of James II Mr. Doughty rebuilt the house immediately adjoining the gateway, and provided a doorway from which the tenants were able to go out onto the leads immediately over the record-room. This facility they used first to dry their clothes, then to make a garden and a privy on the roof. In order to hang out their washing they stuck 'piked staves' into the leadwork, so that the water came through and spoiled the records. More damage was done by the earth brought up for the garden, and still more by Doughty cutting through the walls of the gateway itself in order to make a 'stinking vault' or cesspit. In March 1688, at the instance of John Lowe and

[1] T 1/54, no. 46.
[2] *Cal. Treas. Books*, xx, pp. 562, 572–3; Crest 6/23, pp. 222, 229–30.
[3] *Statutes of the Realm*, viii, pp. 583–4.                   [4] Works 5/4.
[5] *Cal. Treas. Books*, ii, pp. 412, 416, 417; E 36/253, f. 129.

Peter Le Neve, the two Deputy Chamberlains of the Exchequer, the Treasury instructed Wren to 'take speedy care that Doughty do not go on with the said work'. It remained, however, to make good the damage. This the Office of Works declined to do on the ground that 'it doth not belong to their office to doe it', and in the end the repairs were effected, with the approval of the Treasury, by workmen employed by the Deputy Usher of the Exchequer, 'whose office it is to repair all the Exchequer buildings adjoyning'. They were expected to cost not less than £76.[1]

What eventually made the removal of the gateway possible was the inquiry into the state of the Public Records initiated by the House of Lords in 1718. This resulted in 1728 in the transfer of the records from the gateway to the Chapter House, after which the Lords recommended to the government that 'the said Gateway may be taken down, by which means the public way to this House, now so incommodious and dangerous, may be enlarged, for the use and convenience of His Majesty and His People'.[2] The Office of Works was called in both to remove the records and to effect the demolition, and found itself involved in some tedious negotiations over compensation with the representative of the Doughty family. In the end the latter accepted £320 for his interest in the southern part of the gateway, but retained his ownership of the adjoining property.[3] Though no drawing of the gateway itself appears to survive, the appearance of the south-west corner of New Palace Yard after its removal can be seen from a drawing by Capon made in 1793.[4]

## 2. WESTMINSTER HALL

Soon after the Restoration defects were noticed in the roof of the Great Hall. On 31 March 1663 the House of Commons, 'taking notice, that the roof of Westminster Hall is much out of repair, so as the Passage through the Hall, in rainy Weather, is very bad; and that the Hall will, in a short time, fall to Decay, if the Roof be not repaired', optimistically sent for the Warden of the Fleet (*ex officio* keeper of the Palace of Westminster) 'to give an Account, whether he be not liable to take care for the keeping the said Hall in Repair'.[5] Of course he did not accept responsibility, and it fell to the Office of Works to carry out the necessary work at the king's expense. It was performed during the summer and autumn of 1663 at a cost of some £1700. Several of the principal timbers had to be partly renewed or secured with iron bolts and stirrups, including two of the hammer-beams, three collar-beams, and one of the great timber arches. The lead was stripped off, melted, recast and relaid by Peter Brent, the Sergeant Plumber, He received £881 4s. 5d. for handling 176 tons, 4 cwt., 3 quarters and 15 pounds at the rate of 5s. a pound.[6]

[1] *Cal. Treas. Books*, viii, pp. 1809, 2133; ix, p. 321; E 36/253, ff. 169, 173, 181, 183, 185, 191, 195.
[2] *Lords' Journals*, xxiii, pp. 282, 287.
[3] Works 4/3, 29 June 1728; Works 4/4, 19, 24 Sept., 2 Nov. 1728, 27 May 1729, 10 April, 8 Sept. 1730.
[4] *Views of the Old Palace of Westminster (Architectural History*, vol. 9, 1966), ed. Colvin, fig. 31.
[5] *Commons' Journals*, 8, pp. 461, 467.          [6] Works 5/4; E 351/3277.

The next major repair of the roof took place in the reign of George II. By now the lead covering was once more in need of renewal, and during the winter of 1739–40 the roof over the Courts of Chancery and King's Bench proved to be so defective that tarpaulins had to be used to keep out the wet. During the Long Vacation of 1740 an examination of the roof disclosed that the timbers as well as the lead were 'in a very bad condition': in fact the state of some of the principals was so alarming that the Board ordered shores to be set up immediately without waiting for Treasury sanction. On 15 August they asked for authority to spend £5000 on repairs in the course of the next four years.[1] Immediate steps were taken to make good the part that covered the two courts, but nothing more was authorised by the Treasury, and the Board took no further initiative until 1748, when the Lord Chancellor and the other judges made a polite complaint about the long continued presence of the props, which, they said, constituted 'an indecent sight in a Room where all the Courts of Justice sit, and which is the access to both Houses of Parliament'.[2] The estimate for repairing the roof was now reduced to £2950. Moreover the Treasury were informed that £1500 could be saved by using Westmorland slates instead of lead, as the cost of slating would be covered by the proceeds of the sale of the old lead.[3] Authority for this economical substitution was soon forthcoming, and a master-slater named Richard Hughes was sent for and ordered to get a sufficient quantity of Westmorland slates laid in 'with all possible speed'. The old lead, weighing 139 tons, was duly sold to John Devall, the Sergeant Plumber, for £1468 18s. 7d., but its removal revealed such extensive decay in the purlins and rafters that a great deal of new timber had to be inserted, and in September 1750 an embarrassed Board was called upon by the Treasury to justify nearly twice the expenditure originally authorised.[4]

Until the reign of George III the sides of the hall were lined with the stalls and counters of the 'Book and printsellers, Mathematical Instrument Makers, Sempstresses, Haberdashers and other tradespeople' who for many years had been permitted to carry on their trade there.[5] Their expulsion was a long overdue improvement, but it exposed to full view both 'the disgraceful appearance of the inside of the walls and the very bad state of the paving'. Complaints soon began to reach the Office of Works, and in 1780, 'after a minute investigation', the Board proposed to repair the walls with stone and to raise the floor a foot 'in order to lessen the damp and prevent its being overflowed by high tides to which it is at present subject'. The work was completed early in 1782. The walls were relined with Portland stone up to the level of the horizontal cornice, and pilasters were rather unnecessarily introduced beneath each of the corbels supporting the principals of the roof. A new floor of Yorkshire flagstones was laid on brick arches in order to avoid damp,

[1] Works 6/16, ff. 113ᵛ–114.

[2] B.M. Add. MS. 35590, f. 77 (Hardwicke papers). The props can be seen in place in an engraving showing the scaffolding erected for the trial of Lord Lovat in 1747 (*Gent's Mag.* xvii, 1747, p. 148). The same engraving was reproduced by J. P. Malcolm, *Londonium Redivivum* iv (1807), p. 174.

[3] Works 6/17, p. 46.

[4] Works 4/10, 1748–50, *passim*; Works 6/18, pp. 46, 68; Works 11/28/8.

[5] E. W. Brayley and J. Britton, *The Ancient Palace of Westminster* (1836), p. 462. The stalls are shown in an engraving reproduced in Brayley's *Londiniana* (1829) i, p. 209. They were leased out for his own profit by the Warden of the Fleet in his capacity as Keeper of the Palace (*Commons' Jnls.*, 8, p. 467; *Cal. Treasury Papers 1714–19*, p. 193).

and the stairs on either side of the hall at its northern end were rebuilt.[1] Neat lanterns were fixed to the pilasters to provide illumination. The bill came to £2481— £1100 more than the estimate.[2]

## 3. THE COURTS OF JUSTICE

An anonymous drawing shows the makeshift wooden enclosures which throughout the seventeenth century provided a draughty and uncomfortable home for the twin Courts of Chancery and King's Bench (Pl. 55B). The Court of Common Pleas, in its enclosure at the other end of the Great Hall, was even more inconveniently situated, especially when the wind was blowing from the north and the door to New Palace Yard was open. Soon after the Restoration there was, indeed, a proposal to remove the Court 'through the wall into a back room which they call the Treasury', maintaining communication with the Hall by means of an arch. But this sensible suggestion was vetoed by Lord Chief Justice Bridgeman's absurd insistence that to move the Court a single inch would be to violate that chapter of Magna Carta which lays down that the Common Pleas shall be held *in certo loco*.[3] It was left to a politer age to reconcile the terms of the Charter with a modicum of comfort for the lawyers and their clients. In 1734 James Ralph drew public attention to 'the slovenly appearance of our courts of justice', and expressed the opinion that 'they should be more pompous and magnificent, in order to inforce the respect which should ever attend on justice'. He concluded by urging the 'sages of the law' to take steps to get their courts rebuilt in a more appropriate manner.[4] It was certainly not to be expected that Georgian judges would endure indefinitely the discomfort of these rough and ready enclosures. Nor were the barristers whose practice took them to Westminster Hall content with the surroundings in which they were expected to work. In 1739, after hearing complaints by 'the Gentlemen of the Profession of the Law, not only to have the said courts repaired, but to have them made more commodious and convenient for the Court and for the Bar', Lord Chancellor Hardwicke and Sir William Lee, Chief Justice of the King's Bench, addressed themselves to the Treasury on the subject. The Board of Works reported that the two courts were so decayed that nothing could be done to improve them, and submitted plans and elevations 'of a design for making new and enlarging the said courts as much as the place will admitt of'.[5] The designs were drawn by William Kent, who proposed to substitute for the old boarded enclosures an elegant Gothic screen pierced with ogee windows and adorned with octagonal buttresses rising into pinnacles. Within, the two courts were separated by a central passage-way from which access could be obtained to the

[1] John Carter records the discovery under the old stairs of the mutilated effigy of a figure in armour, which was 'afterwards broken to pieces' (Gent's *Mag.*, lxx(i) 1800, pp. 214–17). It is illustrated in his *Ancient Sculpture and Painting* (1780–94).

[2] Works 1/5, f. 27ᵛ; Works 4/16, 10 April 1782; Works 6/19, pp. 295–6; Works 6/20, pp. 22, 30.

[3] *The Lives of the Norths*, ed. Jessop (1890), i, p. 126.

[4] *Critical Review of the Publick Buildings in London and Westminster* (1734), pp. 58–9.

[5] Works 6/16, pp. 87ᵛ–88.

House of Commons. The estimate amounting to £1050 was approved in March 1739 and the work was carried out in the course of that year.[1] The design was subsequently illustrated by Vardy in his *Designs of Mr. Inigo Jones and Mr. William Kent* of 1744 (Pl. 55A).[2]

The enclosure was, however, without a ceiling, and behind their Gothic joinery the lawyers continued to freeze in the winter gloom of the Great Hall. So cold and draughty was the Court of King's Bench that in 1755 one of its clerks addressed a petition to the Duke of Newcastle as First Lord of the Treasury begging him to have it altered. 'My Lord Chancellor, My Lord Chief Justice Ryder, Sir Thomas Denison my Master and Sir Michael Foster are', he wrote, 'far advanced in years, and Sir John Eardley Wilmot is very subject to disorder by violent colds. They may not have strength to endure the inclemency of very cold, damp air, for five or six hours together every day as they have done, and if the courts are not made warmer and lighter, it is much to be feared that the last illness of these worthy men and many others will begin in Westminster Hall.' The remedy he proposed was the erection of a partition 'to the top of the third arch of the roof at the south end of the Hall with windows in proper parts thereof, and skylights over each court'.[3] What in the end was done was to double the height of the screen and to roof the courts over just below the level of the projecting hammer-beams. The new elevation, drawn by Isaac Ware and William Robinson, adhered faithfully to Kent's Gothick detailing.[4]

Meanwhile Sir John Willes, the Chief Justice of the Court of Common Pleas at the other end of the Hall, had pointed out that his court too was 'not only very much out of repair but very inconvenient and incommodious both for the Judges and for those who attend the Court'. The Board of Works agreed, and, after consultation with the judges, proposed that the court should be demolished and that a new court should be built on the site of the office of its Custos Brevium, which stood outside the Hall immediately to the south of the Court of Exchequer Chamber. A doorway had already been forced through the wall of the Hall to provide a means of communication between the Court and the office, and this was now enlarged and dressed up with an ogee arch to make a suitably dignified entrance to the new court. This was approximately square on plan, but internal projections in the angles for staircases etc. produced a cruciform floor-area. The room was lighted from above by an octagonal lantern, and there was a gallery on the west side. Rowlandson and Pugin's aquatint in Ackermann's *Microcosm of London* shows that the cornice and soffit of the plaster ceiling were treated in a Gothick manner, as was the canopy over the judges' seats (Pl. 56B). The building, which included a new office for the Custos Brevium, was built in 1740–1 at a cost of £1555[5]. It is likely that the design was the work of Kent, but a sectional drawing which survives among the records of the Office of Works appears to be in the hand of Isaac Ware.[6]

[1] The eventual cost was £1120 (A 01/2456/174).
[2] What is evidently Vardy's original drawing for this plate is in the Collection of the G.L.C. at County Hall (Westminster FB 5997).
[3] Works 6/17, pp. 133–4.
[4] Works 4/11, 4 June 1755. Their drawing is now Works 29/3244.
[5] Works 5/141. The estimate was £1345 (Works 5/16, ff. 110ᵛ–111).
[6] Works 29/3245. In the *R.I.B.A. Journal* for 10 Sept. 1932, p. 803, Fiske Kimball wrongly dated the drawing to Feb. 1739 and ascribed it to Kent.

## 4. THE HOUSE OF LORDS

Between 1660, when the peers resumed their sessions, and 1801, when they removed themselves to the former Court of Requests, the interior of their Chamber underwent little alteration. It was a simple apartment, by no means too large for its purpose (its floor measured 70 feet × 24 feet 6 inches), and of slight architectural pretensions. A plastered barrel ceiling concealed the high-pitched medieval roof. Below this a heavy cornice ran round the walls. The original medieval windows had long ago been bricked up, and light was provided by large dormer windows, irregularly placed in the ceiling, heat by a fireplace in the middle of the east wall (Pl. 51). At one end doorways gave access to the waiting room and lobby, at the other to the Prince's Chamber. Only the throne, the woolsack and the red-painted benches made it clear that this was indeed the High Court of Parliament.

Very little in the way of repairs seems to have been found necessary after the Restoration. New furnishings were then supplied, not by the Office of Works, but by the Yeoman of the Wardrobe of Beds, and they cost only £286.[1] The House was again refurnished in 1713, when Wren received a letter from the Lord Great Chamberlain to say that 'there wants an Adornment of wainscot over the Chimney peice in the House of Lords (the manner of which I leave to your judgment) and . . . the Ceiling thereof wants whitewashing, which in my oppinion will be very necessary and commodious, that things may be suitable to the Throne, and the furnishing and Apparelling of the house, which is to be new'.[2] It is therefore to Wren that the fireplace owed the rectangular overmantel and the swan-necked pediment seen in eighteenth-century drawings of the interior (Pl. 50).

The House, though well adapted to intimate debate, was uncomfortably crowded on state occasions such as the Speech from the Throne. In 1704 the 'great inconveniences' which resulted from the presence of Queen Anne's numerous female attendants induced the Lords to direct the Surveyor of Works to erect a gallery at the lower end of the House in order to accommodate them. Some peers appear to have disapproved of the gallery almost as heartily as they did of its occupants, for persistent motions were put for its removal, and in March 1711 the House at last authorised the Lord Great Chamberlain to have it taken down at the end of the session.[3] Wren's drawings for this ephemeral structure survive at All Souls College.[4] The problem of accommodating the royal entourage, however, remained. In 1735 a Committee appointed 'to consider the order and method to be observed in this House when His Majesty comes here' recommended the construction of a demountable gallery which could 'be speedily put up on such days as His Majesty shall come

---

[1] *Lord's Journals*, xi, p. 215.  [2] Works 6/5, f. 226.

[3] *Lords' Journals*, xvii, pp. 572, 579, 608, 696, xix, p. 246; Works 6/14, ff. 77, 81; Works 6/5, f. 107; *Cal. Treasury Books* xxv, p. 94. Narcissus Luttrell noted on 9 Nov. 1704 that 'Yesterday Sir Chr. Wren was ordered by their Lordships to build galleries within their house for accommodation of the ladies when her Majestie comes thither in her robes' (*Brief Historical Relation*, v, p. 484).

[4] *Wren Soc.*, xi, pls. xxxvii–xxxviii, showing two alternative schemes.

to the House, and taken down again the same day'. This proposal, however, was rejected, and in February 1737 it was agreed to direct the Officers of the Works to erect a gallery with four benches 'according to the plan laid before a Committee of Lords in the year 1704'. This was done, but three years later the House ordered the new gallery to be taken down.[1] The idea was revived in 1778, when drawings were made for a large gallery over the lobby or vestibule between the north end of the House and the south side of the Painted Chamber. This would have involved cutting away part of the end wall of the Lords' Chamber and supporting the gable by means of two iron columns, but it had the advantage of not encroaching on the House itself. The order was given on 2 June, but nothing was done during the summer recess, and on 7 December Chambers was summoned to explain his inactivity. His reasons were evidently convincing, for after debate the House decided to rescind its order.[2] Twenty years later George III was still complaining to James Wyatt of the want of a gallery,[3] and the problem was solved only by the removal of the House in 1801 to the more spacious Court of Requests.

The medieval structure of the House of Lords, like its interior, remained basically unchanged throughout the years from 1778 to 1800. From time to time defects were observed and made good by the Officers of the Works in a manner that calls for little comment.[4] But the repairs carried out in the reign of George I demand special notice in this *History* because it was Benson's mishandling of them that led to his dismissal in August 1719.

During the winter of 1718–19 the ceiling of the rectangular lobby in the angle between the House and the Prince's Chamber collapsed, and this gave rise to some apprehension as to the state of the structure generally. On 14 January the Committee that was dealing with the repair of the Parliament Office was accordingly instructed to 'send for the Officers of His Majesty's Works and cause them to inspect the condition of the Roof of this House, and other parts thereof, and . . . also to inquire into the occasion of the falling in of the ceiling of the lobby of the Prince's Chamber, and report to the House'.[5] Meeting on 15 January the Committee directed the Officers of the Works forthwith to inspect the roof of the House and of the adjoining passages, and asked for a report the following morning.[6] On 17 January the Earl of Clarendon reported on behalf of the Committee that the Officers of the Works were not yet ready to give an account of the roof of the House, but that they had ascertained that the roof of the Prince's Chamber was giving way under the weight of a great quantity of documents deposited within it.[7] On 20 January the Committee received a report signed by Colen Campbell as Deputy Surveyor, Benjamin Benson as Secretary to the Board, and Robert Barker as Master Carpenter, reporting that the lobby had been secured by props and shores, and listing a number of defects in

---

[1] *Lords' Journals*, xxiv, pp. 549, 550, 555, xxv, pp. 29, 86, 571.

[2] *Lords' Journals*, xxxv, pp. 511, 530. The original drawings are Works 29/5, 7, 8 and 9.

[3] *The Farington Diary*, ed. J. Greig i, p. 262.

[4] It should perhaps be recorded that in 1778 the lead covering of the roof was taken off and replaced by slate. At the same time the floor was repaired (Works 6/19, pp. 180, 186, 218; Lord Great Chamberlain's Records, Misc. Papers vol. 1, nos. 135, 137, 138).

[5] *Lords' Journals*, xxi, p. 45.					[6] Works 6/7, pp. 100–1.

[7] *Lords' Journals*, xxi, p. 48. The documents were records of the Courts of Wards and Requests placed there in 1711 (*Cal. Treasury Books*, xxv, p. 590, xxvi, p. 205).

the walls and roof of the House of Lords, the Painted Chamber and other adjoining buildings. The Painted Chamber was stated to be in a precarious condition because of cracks and settlements, the leads over nearly all the roofs were reported to be in a very bad state, and in the House of Lords itself a 'great crack' was found 'from top to bottom in the main wall'. In addition Wren's 'gallery of communication' along the east side of the Court of Requests was said to be 'very dangerous', partly because the eastern parapet of the Court threatened to fall on it, and partly because it was itself unsafe.[1] On the following day Benjamin Benson was summoned to the House to submit this report in writing to the full House, and the Lord Chamberlain announced that 'he had received His Majesty's Commands to direct the Officers of His Works forthwith to secure this House, and the Places adjacent, in the best manner they could for the present, and to begin where it was most necessary'.[2] Meanwhile the Committee had asked Benson and his colleagues 'to give an account tomorrow whether the roof of the House and passages adjacent are in such a condition as that there is a present danger of its falling, and whether it can be secured for the remainder of this Session'. They were also to say 'in what time a convenient place can be prepar'd in Westminster Hall for the House to sit in for the remainder of this Session'. The answer which was delivered at the Bar of the House on 22 January was as follows:

The Leads and the Boarding of the Roof of the House of Lords are intirely decayed; but the Principals are very sound.

There is some Danger, by reason that the Stone with which the whole House is built is of so soft a Nature, that it is every where very much decayed, and not fit to bear any Weight; but it may unquestionably be secured, by Props, during the present Sessions.

The adjacent Passages, particularly the Lord Marshal's Rooms, of which the Principals and Wall Plates are quite rotten, are extremely dangerous; but may be sufficiently secured by Props.

And the Roof of the Painted Chamber, which is in the most dangerous Condition, is now securing by Props, both in the Inside and Out.

A convenient Place may be prepared in *Westminster Hall* for the House to sit in; provided they remove the Seats and other Conveniencies from the House of Lords in about Fourteen Days.

The Passage leading from the House of Commons to the Painted Chamber is extreme dangerous, by reason that the Parapet of the Court of Requests hang over; and likewise by reason of a Brick-building, contiguous to the Court of Requests and Passage, that is cracked in several Places from Top to Bottom, leaning very much to One Side, which was secured Yesterday as well as could be with Props.

The Rafters of the Roof of the Court of Requests are in several Places free of the Wall Plate, and the Wall leaning Outwards. The Gable-end next to the House of Lords is much decayed, through the Badness of the Stone, and often falls down in great Fleaks; and the Leading and Boarding of the Roof are past Repair.

[1] Works 6/7, pp. 102–13.
[2] *Lords' Journals*, xxi, p. 51.
H K W—DD

The Rooms at the North-end of the Court of Requests are dangerous; the Leading, Boarding, and Timber, being quite decayed.

Co. Campbell.
Benj. Benson.
Rob't. Barker.[1]

When asked whether they could make the House safe by the end of the following week they said they could, but added 'that the Roof of the House, being a Compass Roof, must be strengthened by plates and girders, which would require two or three days to fix; and that the seating of the House must be removed, and some of the plastering necessarily come down'. The direction they were given was 'to go immediately about securing the passages to this House, and doing what could be done first, without coming into the House; and at the same time to be preparing materials for securing the House itself as soon as might be'.[2] Six days later, having examined the roof more carefully, they again appeared at the Bar, armed with pieces of rotten timber, and answered that 'they had found that all the rafters were rotten, for two foot, more or less, particularly over the Bishops' side, and the wall plates entirely gone'. As the main structure of the roof consisted entirely of rafters—there being no other principals—this was an alarming disclosure, and authority was given for the roof to be supported by props. The Officers of the Works said that this could be accomplished in about three days if their men could work up to one o'clock daily.[3] This was accordingly done, but when asked about the security of the House 'since the propping of it', the Officers of the Works declared 'they could not say it was secure for a minute'. Confronted with this declaration the Lords then sent for the Surveyor-General himself, who confirmed that in view of the state of the roof 'he did not think it possible . . . to make it secure'.[4] Orders were then given for a temporary House to be prepared in Westminster Hall.[5]

Some doubts must, however, have been felt as to the reliability of these alarming reports, for at the same time orders were given for the Master Mason and the Master Carpenter to 'take such other persons as they shall think proper', 'view the walls and timbers', and report *on oath* to the House. It may be that Benson's demeanour did not inspire confidence in the minds of their Lordships. But the Surveyor-General had his enemies (Vanbrugh among them), and it may equally well be that someone hinted to a friendly peer that all that had been said about the state of the House was not to be trusted. Whether Benson was merely incompetent, or whether it was the dream of a great architectural opportunity that led him on, will be discussed on another page.[6] But for William Benson that dream, if it ever existed, was soon to be

---

[1] *Lords' Journals*, xxi, p. 53; Works 6/7, pp. 104–5. This and the subsequent reports are illustrated by an annotated plan signed by William Benson of which there is a copy in Sir John Soane's Museum (see Fig. 32).

[2] *Lords' Journals*, xxi, pp. 53–4.

[3] *Lords' Journals*, xxi p. 59.

[4] *Lords' Journals*, xxi, pp. 62–3.

[5] Works 4/1, 5 Feb. 1719. The Paymaster's Accounts show that Matthew Churchill received £340 for shoring the House of Lords, Painted Chamber and Cotton Library and for building a house for the Lords in Westminster Hall (AO 1/2449/153). There is a plan of the temporary house among Wren's drawings in the library of All Souls College, Oxford, vol. iii, no. 22. The Lords sat in it for the first time on 4 February (*Historical Register*, iv, 1719, p. 123). They returned to their own Chamber on 28 February (p. 130).

[6] Below, p. 417.

replaced by the unpleasant reality of parliamentary censure and public disgrace. What gave Benson away was the Master Mason's report. Jackson was a truculent character, who did not suffer from undue deference to his superiors, and he was evidently as ready to quarrel with the new Surveyor General as he had been with his predecessor. His statement, fortified by the signatures of James Gibbs, John James, Edward Tufnell (Master Mason of Westminster Abbey) and two other experienced building craftsmen, was as follows:

1. That the Walls of your Lordships House, from the Cellars to the Foot of the Roof, are firm and substantial, being near Five Foot thick at the Top; and, in our Judgement, capable of sustaining the Floor and Roof for many Years to come.

2. That, as to the Crack in the Wall over the Door, near the Gentleman Usher of the Black Rod's Seat, it appears to us to be no other than an upright Joint, against the Jamb of some Aperture of former use, and to be no Way dangerous to the Fabrick; nor do we perceive any essential Defect in any Part of the Walls of your Lordships House. We cannot but apprehend, that the Shores set up against the West Wall of your Lordships House have rather done Injury than Service, by reason of the Largeness of the Holes made to receive the Ends of the Timbers, and the Soundness of the Wall cut away for that Purpose.

3. That, as to the Floor of your Lordships House, the principal Timbers thereof do appear to us to be sound, substantial, and well supported in the original Manner of their framing, and in their present State.

4. That, as to the Roof of your Lordships House, the Disposition of the Timbers at the Foot of the same, where they have been formerly defective by reason of the Drips of the Gutters, has been altered from the First Manner of Framing, in a Method which appears to us to be serviceable and substantial, and has been performed in a Workmanlike Manner: And we do not perceive that there has been any considerable Sinking or Settling of the Rafters since the same was repaired; but that the Contexture of the Timbers, upon which the Strength of the Roof chiefly depends, is very firm and entire.

We beg Leave to observe to your Lordships, that, from the Nature of the Framing of the said Roof, in which every Pair of Rafters are Principals, the Props set up within your Lordships House, for the intended Security of the Roof, could be of little or no service to that Purpose.[1]

Robert Barker, the Master Carpenter, who had signed the previous reports, declined to associate himself with Jackson's statement partly because he said he had been too busy 'erecting a place for your Lordships in Westminster Hall', and partly because 'no man can give a right judgement of those walls, till the hangings are taken down; and as for the timbers, I cannot give a true state of them without taking off the lead, which will render the House unfit for your Lordships to sit in'.[2]

[1] *Lords' Journals*, xxi, p. 67. A drawing preserved with the original report among the papers of the House of Lords shows the manner in which the roof had been repaired by inserting vertical ashlar posts to take the weight off the rotten feet of the rafters. These ashlar posts stood on the cornice inside the walls, which, according to an annotation on the drawing, was only of plaster. As it is scarcely credible that any carpenter would rest the weight of a roof merely on a plaster cornice (or that the cornice would long survive if he did), it seems probable that the statement about the nature of the cornice was one of the misrepresentations made by Benson and his colleagues.

[2] *Lords' Journals*, xxi, p. 65. He subsequently submitted an independent report of his own which is preserved among the papers of the House of Lords.

The reactions of their Lordships to these revelations was to appoint a new Committee consisting of the Lord Chamberlain, the Lord Steward, four dukes, eight bishops and 45 other peers, 'to inquire into the matters contained in the before mentioned Reports . . . and report their opinion thereupon to the House'. Nine days later the Committee reported that it was satisfied that the House 'could in a few days be put in sufficient and secure repair for the present, and was also capable of a durable repair'. Orders were accordingly given for the temporary repairs to be put in hand immediately, it being understood that this could be done without recourse to obtrusive props and shores. Benson's determination to represent the building as past repair now got the better of him, for on the following day (20 February) his brother Benjamin, as Secretary of the Board, minuted an order

> that the Carpenters sett up the shores on the outside of the House of Lords, and that shores be set up in the inside, from the floor, to support each side of the Luthern windows, and braced from each other, and three upright and two raking shores from the north east angle to the window on the east side, and the arch over the Bishops' door, to be secured with three shores, and that the men work on Sunday to dispatch the same.[1]

Jackson lost no time in drawing the attention of the Committee to the fact that 'the Workmen are repairing the House above in a different Method than was proposed to the Committe yesterday'. Ayres, the working carpenter, was sent for and confirmed that 'he was directed so to do by the Surveyor General, though he represented there was no occasion for them' (i.e. the props and shores), whereupon he was ordered by the Lord Chancellor to proceed 'according to the method by him proposed to the Committee yesterday; and this without regard to any other or contrary order from the Officers of the Works'.[2] The next day all the Officers of the Works were summoned to the House and told to secure the roof 'without setting up any props or shores except such as may stand so near the walls that the hangings may cover them'.[3]

Meanwhile the Committee had obtained from Jackson, Gibbs, James and fifteen leading master workmen a further report on the Painted Chamber, Court of Requests and other adjoining buildings which showed that, although some considerable repairs were undoubtedly needed, several of the more alarmist statements made by Benson and his colleagues were unjustified. In particular the walls of the Court of Requests were 'in as good condition as they have probably been for many years past', and those of the Painted Chamber were 'firm and substantial from the foundation to the top of the roof'.[4]

By now there could be no doubt that Benson and his colleagues were either incompetent or had deliberately set out to deceive the House. On 16 March its displeasure was expressed in a formal resolution to the king, and before the end of the year Benson had ceased to be Surveyor General and Benjamin Benson, Colen Campbell and Robert Barker had all been deprived of their posts.[5] This was the

---

[1] Works 4/1, 20 Feb. 1718/19.       [2] *Lords' Journals*, xxi, pp. 76–7.
[3] *Lords' Journals*, xxi, p. 79.
[4] House of Lords Record Office, Main Papers 2 Feb. 1718/19.
[5] *Lords' Journals*, xxi, pp. 102, 143–4; above, pp. 64–5.

end of an extraordinary and discreditable episode in the history of the Office of Works, but not of the repairs which the fall of the ceiling in the lobby of the Prince's Chamber had set in motion: indeed, the dismissed officers might almost have felt themselves vindicated if they had known just how great the cost of the permanent repairs was ultimately going to be. In October 1719 the new Board submitted to the Treasury an estimate of £1951 for 'repairing the House of Lords, House of Commons, Painted Chamber, Court of Requests, Westminster Hall, and severall roomes and passages adjacent', which were duly carried out for that sum.[1] But five years later the Treasury was informed that 'there are great repairs still wanting to be done to the House of Lords and rooms and passages adjacent, and allso to the Painted Chamber, Cotton House and Library, which are in so ruinous a condition that wee were obliged to take down part of Cotton House and to shore up and secure the north east side of the Painted Chamber, which will amount to a considerable sum'.[2] Nor did the expenditure of 1719–21 include the reroofing of the Court of Requests and the rebuilding of the 'passage gallery' between the House of Commons and the Painted Chamber, for which a supplementary estimate amounting to £3659 was submitted in February 1722 and approved the following month.[3] The gallery was completely rebuilt to larger dimensions, and with an upper storey containing rooms for the use of the Clerk of the House of Commons.[4] The old Court of Requests had been lighted by windows in the roof, which were found to have been 'a great occasion of the decay'. These were done away with and their place was taken by a row of semi-circular windows placed high up in the walls on either side. Inside, the building was completely remodelled. Cross walls were inserted in the basement to support a stone pavement, while above Joseph Roberts executed the plasterwork of the great coved ceiling (Vol. VI, Pl. 35A).[5] The work was completed just in time for the building to be used in October 1725 for an 'entertainment' for the benefit of the knights of the newly-revived Order of the Bath.[6] In the end the cost of the works on the Court of Requests and the adjoining gallery amounted to no less than £9516, not counting the preparations for the installation.[7]

Meanwhile the north-east corner of the Painted Chamber was still shored up to support it after the demolition in 1725 of most of the adjoining Cotton House, and in May 1730 the Lords drew up a 'humble address' asking for the east end to be rebuilt.[8] On receiving a request from the Treasury for an estimate the Board agreed that the east end and part of the north wall needed to be rebuilt, and optimistically submitted a set of drawings by Flitcroft for remodelling the whole building in the Palladian style, accompanied by an estimate for £2500.[9] But as the season was 'too

[1] Works 6/7, p. 168; Works 5/141.  [2] Works 6/15, p. 73.  [3] Works 6/7, pp. 254–5.
[4] There are plans of the basement level before and after rebuilding in T 1/252, ff. 255–6. For the Clerk's rooms, see below, p. 480.
[5] For the stone pavement see Works 4/2, 6 May 1724. The cross walls are shown on the upper plan in T 1/252, ff. 255–6. For general views of the remodelled building see J. T. Smith, *Antiquities of Westminster* (1837), p. 146; Brayley and Britton, *Ancient Palace of Westminster* (1836), pls. xxxvii, xxxviii (showing the ruins of the gallery); M. Hastings, *Parliament House* (1950), p. 165.  [6] Works 4/3, 1 June 1725.
[7] Works 5/141. The preparations for the installation cost £1476.
[8] *Lords' Journals*, xxiii, p. 565; *Cal. Treasury Books 1729–30*, pp. 375, 382, 384.
[9] Works 4/4, 4 June and 6 Aug. 1730. The minute of 4 June directs Flitcroft to prepare plans, and the drawings, which survive in T 1/273, ff. 258–65, are in his hand, except for the proposed classical frieze, statues &c., which are in Kent's hand. As Fiske Kimball pointed out in *R.I.B.A. Journal* 6 August 1932, where the drawings are illustrated (p. 736), the whole project was probably due to Kent.

WESTMINSTER
HALL

1 Speaker's Chambers
2 Clerks' Closet
3 Speaker's Withdrawing Room
4 Auction Room
5 Coffee House
6 Stairs to House of Commons
7 Stairs to Speaker's Chambers
8 Gallery from House of Commons
　　　to Painted Chamber
9 Stone Lobby
10 Black Rod's Room
11 Robe or Waiting Room
12 Lobby
13 Gallery leading to House of Lords
14 Clerk's Closet
15 Matted Passage
16 Earl Marshal
17 Archbishops' Closet
18 Bishops' Room
19 Bishops' Lobby
20 Lord Treasurer's Room
21 Lord Chancellor
22 Housekeeper
23 Bishops' Stairs
24 King's Stairs

5　COURT　OF
4　　　　　WARDS
6

7
12

HOUSE
OF
COMMONS

COURT
OF
REQUESTS

8

COTTON
HOUSE

PAINTED　CHAMBER

11　12
9　10
12

13

HOUSE
OF
LORDS

14
15　16
17　18
19
12　　20　21

22

23

PRINCE'S
CHAMBER

24

| 10 | 0 | 20 |
Scale of Metres

| 20 | 0 | 80 |
Scale of Feet

**Fig. 32.** Westminster: the Parliamentary Buildings in the early eighteenth century.

far advanced' for any work to be undertaken that year, they 'thought it proper to acquaint your Lordships that it may be made very secure for the next Sessions at a small charge'. As the Treasury showed no disposition to authorise the more expensive alternative, £21 19s. 6d. were spent on building the great brick shore seen in old views of the Painted Chamber.[1]

It would be difficult—and not very profitable—to unravel the history of the various small rooms that clustered round the House of Lords and the Prince's Chamber. The functions of most of them can be identified from a plan of *c.* 1718 of which there is a copy in Sir John Soane's Museum (Fig. 32). The peers' entrance from Old Palace Yard appears to have been through the 'Stone Lobby' outside the south end of the Court of Requests. Over this lobby an office for the Lord Privy Seal was constructed in 1677.[2] Between the Stone Lobby and the Robe or Waiting Room was Black Rod's room. All the other dignitaries connected with the House of Lords— the Earl Marshal, the Lord Treasurer and the Lord Chancellor, were accommodated in an irregular series of rooms attached to the east side of the Chamber. Here in 1695 Wren constructed a retiring room for the bishops,[3] who had their own stairs leading to the landing-place at Parliament Stairs, whence they could take boat for Lambeth or Fulham. When the government acquired Cotton House and its garden in 1706 Wren prepared plans for a new and more commodious block of offices stretching down to the river, and including a new library for the Cottonian Collection.[4] But nothing came of it, and it does not seem ever to have been seriously considered.

No further expansion of the Lords' territory took place until 1762, when the peers decided to appropriate for their own use the Ordnance Office which stood on the west side of their House facing Old Palace Yard. It was a simple pedimented building erected as recently as 1753, and contained one large room which was well calculated to serve as a committee room.[5] The Office of Works was instructed to prepare estimates for converting it into committee rooms, waiting rooms and a stone staircase for the use of their Lordships.[6] A humble address requesting this to be done received a favourable answer, but nothing happened for four years because the Office of Works did not receive the necessary *fiat* from the Treasury. This oversight was eventually remedied in 1766, when the work was carried out at a cost, apparently, of only £296—£234 less than the original estimate.[7]

[1] Works 4/4, 10 Dec. 1730. See illustrations in J. T. Smith, *Antiquities of Westminster* (1837), p. 45 and *Architectural History* vol. 9 (1966), figs. 108, 114.
[2] Works 5/28 and 29.
[3] Works 5/48; *Wren Soc.* xi, p. 48 and Pl. xxx. See also N. Luttrell, *Brief Historical Relation* iii, p. 524.
[4] *Wren Soc.* xi, Pl. xl.
[5] P.R.O. Ordnance Board Minutes, W.O. 47/41, ff. 169, 408.
[6] *Lords' Journals*, xxx, pp. 250–1, 259; Works 1/4, p. 7.
[7] *Lords' Journals*, xxxi, pp. 284, 286, 288; Works 4/13, 12, 22 August, 19 Dec. 1766; Works 6/18, f. 142; Works 5/142, year 1766–7. Works 29/6 is a plan showing the building rearranged for the use of the Lords.

## 5. THE HOUSE OF COMMONS

There is no known view of the interior of the House of Commons that shows the Chamber as it was after the Restoration. But the accounts do not suggest that any notable changes had taken place since the time of Charles I. During the Commonwealth the royal arms had, of course, been removed from above the Speaker's chair, and they were duly replaced in February 1663.[1] But the chair itself appears to have remained unaltered,[2] and so did the Members' seats, which in February 1670 were painted green.[3] At the west end—no doubt over the lobby—there was a gallery. New stairs to reach this gallery were constructed in 1670, following a request from the Lord Chamberlain.[4] The passage of time was measured by a glass sundial set in one of the windows. A new dial was supplied in 1664 by the Master Glazier, but was blown down in 1676–7 and had to be replaced.[5] There was also a mechanical clock, supplied soon after the Restoration by Edward East, the king's clockmaker.[6]

The first major alteration to the Commons' buildings took place in 1678–9. In that year a 'gallery of communication' was constructed between the House of Commons and the Painted Chamber. The Painted Chamber was regularly used for conferences between the two Houses, but it was separated from the Commons by an open courtyard, and in order to reach their destination Members were obliged to adopt a roundabout route through the Court of Requests. The gallery was built by Matthew Banckes, the Master Carpenter, at a total cost of £197.[7] It was a timber structure about 8 feet wide, standing on timber posts, and had a tiled roof.[8] It survived until 1722–5, when it was rebuilt in brick to more generous dimensions.[9]

Outside events were now to have repercussions on the fabric of the House. This was the year of the Popish Plot, and Members of both Houses were apprehensive that the fifth of November 1678 would see a repetition of Gunpowder Treason. When some inhabitants in the neighbourhood of Old Palace Yard reported sounds of 'knocking and digging in the earth, in some cellars near adjoining to' the Houses of

[1] Works 5/3.

[2] Compare the representation of it on the Commonwealth Great Seal (reproduced by Maurice Hastings, *Parliament House*, 1950, p. 131) with the painting of 1793 by Hickel (*ibid.*, p. 135). There is a careful sketch of it by Thornhill in the G.L.C.'s topographical collection (Pl. 54).

[3] Works 5/15. 'To Robt. Streeter Serjeant paynter for paynting green in oyle the end of the seates & a dorecase & some other things at the House of Commons in February last'. Thornhill's sketch (Pl. 54) shows that parts of the Speaker's chair were painted green. In 1663 a French visitor noted that the benches in the House were covered with green serge (*Les Voyages de M. de Monconys*, iii, Paris, 1695, p. 65), and Hatton's *New View of London*, ii (1708), p. 629, also states that they were 'covered with Green'. On the colours traditionally used in the upholstery of the two houses of Parliament see G. Chowdharay-Best in *Notes & Queries*, vol. 214 (1969), p. 89.

[4] LC 5/12, p. 258; Works 5/14. I owe the former reference to Mr. G. Chowdharay-Best.

[5] Works 5/5, 27 and 28.

[6] LC 5/137, p. 381. He supplied a similar clock for the House of Lords. In 1673 new clocks for both Lords and Commons were ordered by the Lord Chamberlain from James East, clockmaker (LC 5/140, pp. 110, 340). The one in the Commons was replaced in 1692 by a clock with 'carved workes and ornaments' supplied by Thomas Herbert (below, p. 403).

[7] Works 5/31. For the Lord Chamberlain's warrant see *Wren Soc.* xi, p. 120.

[8] Plans which show it are *Wren Society* xi, pl. xxxi and T 1/252, ff. 255–6.

[9] Above, p. 397.

Parliament, the House of Lords sent for Sir Christopher Wren, Hugh May and Sir Jonas Moore (the Surveyor-General of the Ordnance) and ordered them to inspect the cellars under the Palace of Westminster. May was away in Hertfordshire building a house for the Earl of Essex, but Wren and Moore reported 'that the vaults and cellars under and near this House are of such a nature, that there can be no assurance of safety; and the only remedy at present is, that the cellars of the houses near this House and the Court of Requests may be cleared, and a passage made out of one into the other, so that soldiers and centinels may walk day and night there, and have a trusty officer over them'.[1] These measures were accordingly taken, and £49 were spent on converting the cellars into a improvised guard-house.[2] In the course of his investigation Wren appears to have examined not only the cellars, but also the roofs, of the Palace, for on 2 November he came to the bar of the House of Lords, and 'gave the House an account of the weakness and craziness of the roof of the House of Commons, of which there might be danger of falling in stormy weather, and likewise that the Roof of this House is bad'. The Lords at once informed the Commons of their danger, and sent a humble address to the king as a result of which they were informed that steps would be taken to have the roofs of both Houses repaired.[3] In the meanwhile the Commons removed to the Court of Requests while the roof of their own Chamber was shored up.[4] In the course of 1679 the stonework of the upper part of St. Stephen's Chapel was overhauled. Considerable portions of the battlemented parapet were taken down and renewed in Portland ashlar, and the roof itself was secured from danger. The work included the rebuilding of the 'penthouse' which ran across the east end above the great east window and taking down the upper part of the stone staircase in one of the western turrets.[5]

The safety of the roof, so old and so high above the floor of the Chamber, was evidently a source of continuing anxiety, for it was again inspected by Wren five years later, and yet again in the summer of 1691, when the gutters were renewed.[6] In December of that year the Commons themselves asked for a report on its condition. Wren took no chances:

> In obedience to an Order of the Honourable House of Commons dated December 12, 1691, Requiring me to view the Ceiling and Roofe of the House of Commons, and report the condition thereof, I humbly report as followeth.
>
> That the Ceiling (according to the manner used in former times) is made of plaister of paris and not (as the modern way is) of Lime and hair, which yielding to the Timbers when they shrink or swell with weather doth not discover cracks, whereas all plaister cielings haveing the firmeness of Stone doe for that Reason allwayes crack, but without danger, because the Lath is preserved in plaister and is more apt to decay in lime. Yet for greater Caution it is fitt there should be a new cieling because this way being out of use is not generally understood to be safe.
>
> About 8 years since upon the like Order, not only the cieling and floor above but the Roofe also was examined very carefully; the Records above were moved to the

[1] *Lords' Journals*, xiii, pp. 331, 335; Hist. MSS. Comm., *MSS. of the House of Lords 1678–1688*, pp. 16–17.
[2] Works 5/31.
[3] *Lords' Journals*, xiii, p. 335; *Commons' Journals*, ix, pp. 531–2.
[4] Works 5/31.  [5] Works 5/31–32.
[6] Works 5/38 (May 1684); Works 5/45 (Oct. 1691).

walls and many things then done rather out of Caution than of apparent necessity, and this very summer I caused the Gutters to be uncovered, the timbers to be layd open and secured, and great part of the Roofe to be new Leaded, in doing of all which no great defect could be undiscovered.

And now again in pursuance of this Order I have viewed the Cieling and Roofe accompanied with their Majesties Master Carpenter, and though no person ought to be confident in soe great a concerne, yet we were of Opinion that all was firme, finding all things as we lately left it.

Notwithstanding though the Roofe were not now in danger yet it is very old, and the Covering hath been much neglected in former times, neither can it be presumed to last many Years longer, and therefore it seemes most Reasonable that ere long a New Roome be thought of where the important affaires of the nation may be transacted without suspition of this sort: or otherwise for the present that the Records be removed; that a new Cieling be layed and some other repaires don as soon as an Intervall of Sessions and the Season of the year shall permitt.[1]

The Commons thereupon appointed a committee of six to view the roof and ceiling of the House.[2] On 9 January 1692 the committee reported 'that they do find the walls and timber so much decayed that they are of opinion, the Building is in a dangerous condition, and not capable of further Repair'. On the strength of this the House drew up a humble address to the king asking him to provide them with some other place in which to meet. On 18 January the Chancellor of the Exchequer told the House 'that his Majestie was pleased to say he doubted it would be difficult to find a convenient place on a suddaine', but had ordered the Surveyor and Comptroller of his Works to wait on the committee 'to see whether this building be substantiall at present' and that as soon as they had reported he would take whatever steps were necessary. Wren and Talman accordingly joined the committee 'and did view the said Building of the house and debateing upon the place the defects that appeared were of opinion that the danger is not iminent, but notwithstanding to remove any apprehensions for the future doe judge it fitt and necessary that the upper part of the walls be taken much lower and that a new Roofe be laid, and a new Ceiling made and some other things performed of lesse consequence for the accommodation of the house'. Their estimate amounted to £2540, £780 of which was for structural work. £300 was allowed for joinery, £100 for 'a closett for the Speaker', £60 for 'a better paire of stairs up to the Committee Roome', and £40 for 'a roome adjoyning to the Anteroome for the Clerkes, with joyners' worke there'.[3]

The detailed accounts for the work have not survived, but the texts of the contracts with the mason (Thomas Hill), the carpenter (John Churchill), the plumber (Charles Atherton) and the two joiners (Alexander Fort and Charles Hopson) have been preserved, and the names of the other craftsmen can be ascertained from the Paymaster's enrolled account.[4] They were William Emmett and Grinling Gibbons, carvers, John Grove, plasterer, and Robert Streater, painter. The main task was the removal of the fourteenth-century clerestorey and roof, and the construction of a

[1] *Wren Soc.*, xviii, p. 84; *Commons' Journals*, x, p. 605.
[2] *Commons' Journals*, x, p. 605. Nicholas Barbon was a member of it.
[3] *Commons' Journals*, x, pp. 618, 631; Works 6/2.
[4] Works 5/145, pp. 213–17; E 351/3304.

new roof at a lower level. The new ceiling was lower still, so that the main body of the former chapel was now divided horizontally into two storeys, with a floor running right across the great Gothic windows. These were blocked up, and sash windows took their place, rectangular ones in the side walls, a range of three round-headed ones in the east wall (Vol. VI, Pl. 36). The interior was wainscoted, and galleries were constructed along the north and south walls. Access to these galleries was obtained by means of a passage built out in front of the east window, and entered by a doorway behind the Speaker's chair. From this passage stairs rose on either side to the upper level. Space for the stairs was contrived by cutting through the octagonal corner turrets. The galleries themselves were later enlarged, but a drawing by Wren (Pl. 57) shows them in their original form, supported by large console brackets without any columns. Only at the west end, where the galleries returned in front of the lobby, were two columns necessary, one on either side of the entry. In Wren's drawing these are shown as conventional Corinthian columns of wood, but in a memorandum describing the works he refers to 'two iron pillars and capitalls in iron of Tijou's work'. Jean Tijou, the celebrated blacksmith, published in 1693 *A Newe Book of Drawing*, plate 13 of which illustrates an iron capital with column and base—the first of its kind in European architecture. No extant view shows these columns *in situ*, but thin iron columns with capitals of almost identical form are seen supporting the widened side galleries as they existed from 1707 to 1834 (Pl. 53), and the accounts make it clear that these additional capitals were carved by Grinling Gibbons.[1] The conclusion must be that in 1692 Tijou provided two prototypes in iron, and that in 1707 Grinling Gibbons copied them in wood. In 1707, as in 1692, Wren's motive in using attenuated iron columns was no doubt to obstruct Members' vision as little as possible; in so doing he made the House of Commons the scene of a structural innovation for which no parallel can be found for at least fifty years.[2]

When, in November 1692, the Commons returned to their House from their temporary quarters in the Court of Requests,[3] they must have had every reason to be pleased with the transformation. But the Treasury was evidently critical of the cost, which in the end amounted to £4598—over £2000 in excess of the estimate. In order to justify himself, Wren drew up a statement which is so informative that it is worth quoting in full:

A particular of workes done at the House of Commons more than was at **first** intended or estimated.

1. The side galleries & greatest part of the wainscott of the House.

2. New Backs to all the Seates.

3. A new passage Gallery & Staires cutt through the old Turretts to goe to the side galleries & the Speaker's Roome.

4. A little Clossett & a flight of staires added to the Speaker's Roome by his owne letter.

5. A new Clock with carved workes & ornaments.[4]

[1] Below, p. 404.
[2] The significance of the iron columns was first pointed out by John Harris in *Architectural Review*, July 1961, pp. 60–1.
[3] N. Luttrell, *A Brief Historical Relation*, ii, p. 607.
[4] 'Thomas Herbert for a long pendulum clock, £20' (E 351/3304).

6. Two Iron Pillars & Capitals in Iron of Tijou's worke.

7. Guilding about the Clocke & the Speaker's Chaire & the Iron Pillars.

8. Deale Wainscott in the Lobby, the Smoking Roome, the Serjeant's Roome and severall conveniences made for the Clarkes, the housekeeper & Doorekeepers by direction.

9. A particular Clossett made for Mr. Joddrell.[1]

10. The damages done to Sir John Cotton's and Mr. Loveing's houses and gardens by takeing downe soe much stone worke & workeing in the Gardens, proved more than could be expected.

11. A more convenient & safe passage by her Majesty's Command was made for the King, from the landing place to the House of Lords, with a paire of new Stone peers & gates, 4 large oaken doores & Doorecases & the passage Roome made out of the Coale house & decently fitted, severall pavements & necessary Draines made.

12. The passage from Westminister Hall to the Parliament Staires made more lightsome.

Chr. Wren Dec. 13, 1692[2]

In 1707 the Act of Union posed a fresh problem—how to accommodate the 45 extra Scottish members. In a report to the Treasury Wren wrote that 'he is of opinion that if the side Galleries be made broader to containe two rowes of seats (whereas now they are but single) it may be sufficient', and that the necessary work could be done for £270.[3] Only three craftsmen were employed: Charles Hopson, the Master Joiner, who widened the galleries, Grinling Gibbons, Master Carver, who carved the eight capitals which decorated the iron pillars, and Thomas Highmore, Sergeant Painter, who gilded the capitals, coloured the pillars to imitate white marble,[4] and painted the Union Arms over the Speaker's chair.[5]

It was therefore in the years 1692 and 1707 that the interior of the House assumed the appearance familiar from the paintings by Hickel and Hayter, and no further changes of any importance were called for until the further increase of membership brought about by the Act of Union with Ireland in 1800. The more comfortable interior created by Wren did, however, suffer from one drawback: it was intolerably stuffy when the House was full. In 1701 a Committee, assisted by Wren, considered methods of improving the ventilation, and adopted the expedient of making openings in the ceiling, through which it was hoped the foul air would escape into the space above.[6] This was only a partial success, and in 1715 the Speaker invited Dr. J. T. Desaguliers, a Fellow of the Royal Society well known for his experimental work in physics, to 'propose a method to evaporate the unhealthful breathing in the House of Commons'. On 28 January he attended a meeting of the Board of Works in order to explain his proposal, and in 1723 he was paid £105 'for remedying the inconveniency arising by the hot steam and want of fresh air in the House of Commons when sitting late and in full house'.[7] The mechanics of this early

---

[1] Paul Joddrell, appointed Clerk to the House in 1688.
[2] Works 6/2.
[3] Works 6/14, ff. 146–7; *Cal. Treasury Books*, xxi, pp. 33, 296.
[4] This detail is derived from the sketch by Thornhill in the G.L.C. Collection, on which he notes 'white marble pillars' (Pl. 54). [5] E 351/3312.
[6] *Commons' Journals*, xiii, pp. 413, 416; cf. N. Luttrell, *Brief Historical Relation*, v, p. 36.
[7] Works 4/1, 26, 28 Jan. 1715; AO 1/2451/157.

air-conditioning plant are described by Desaguliers in his *Course of Experimental Philosophy*, published in 1744.

> At each corner of the House in the Cieling there is a Hole which was the Bottom of a truncated Pyramid going up six or eight Feet into the Room over the House, set up by Sir *Christopher Wren*, to let the Air (made foul by the Breath of so many People, and the Steam of the Candles when used there) go out; but it so happen'd, that when the Tops of the Pyramids were open'd, the Air above being colder, and consequently denser, push'd down with Violence into the House, and became a Nuisance to People that sate under those Holes. I caus'd two Closets to be built at each End of the Room above the House of Commons between two of the Pyramids above-mention'd; and leading a Trunk from those Pyramids to the square Cavities of Iron, that went round a Fire Grate fix'd in the Closets; as soon as a Fire was lighted in those Grates about Twelve o'Clock at Noon, the Air came up from the House of Commons thro those heated Cavities into the Closets, and so went away up their Chimneys.
>
> Mrs. *Smith*, the Housekeeper, who had Possession of the Rooms over the House of Commons, not liking to be disturb'd in her Use of those Rooms, did what she could to defeat the Operation of these Machines; which she at last compass'd by not having the Fire lighted, 'till the House had sate some time, and was very hot: for then the Air in the Closets, that had not been heated, went down into the House to an Air rarer, and less resisting, whereby the House became hotter, instead of being cool'd. But when the Fire had been lighted before the meeting of the Members, the Air went up from the House into the Closets, and out of their Chimneys, and continued to do so the whole Day, keeping the House very cool.[1]

By the reign of George III Desaguliers' apparatus had, it seems, finally ceased to be effective, for in 1769, after complaints by Sir George Savile and other members 'of great inconvenience from the heat of the House of Commons when it is full, and from the cold when it is thin', the Office of Works was called upon to improve both the heating and the ventilation. New stoves were installed below, while above larger vents were formed in the ceiling and a new louver with moveable shutters was inserted in the roof, from which the hot air had previously been unable to escape except through openings low down in the walls.[2]

Between 1692 and 1782 the only structural repair of any importance was one carried out in 1760 after some loose masonry from the north-east stair-turret had fallen through the roof of the Speaker's withdrawing-room below. The turrets, parapets and the upper parts of the buttresses on both sides of the building were then taken down and rebuilt at a cost of £797.[3]

---

[1] *A Course of Experimental Philosophy* (1744), pp. 560–1. In 1719 Desaguliers was asked to give advice about the chimney in the House of Lords, which failed to warm the building satisfactorily, and devised a contrivance which is described in the second edition of his book *Fires Improved* (1736), pp. 149–51 (*Lords' Journals*, xxi, pp. 38, 39, 43; Works 6/7, p. 100).

[2] Works 4/14, 23 June, 27 Oct. 1769; Works 6/18, p. 212. Works 29/34 is a sectional drawing showing the proposed louver. The exterior of it is seen in an engraving in J. T. Smith's *Antiquities of Westminster* (1837), p. 146.

[3] Works 6/17, p. 199; Works 5/142.

# 6. PARLIAMENTARY OFFICES

The early history of the various parliamentary offices is not easy to follow. Until the latter part of the eighteenth century the Speaker, the Clerk of the House, the Clerk of the Journals, the four under-clerks, the Housekeeper and the Sergeant at Arms were all accommodated in odd corners of the old palace above, below or adjoining St. Stephen's Chapel. Owing to frequent removals and alterations the exact location of some of these offices is difficult to establish. So far as it can be ascertained, their architectural history is as follows.[1]

## *The Speaker*

Until 1794 the Speaker had no official residence within the precincts of the palace. He did, however, have a small 'withdrawing room' which occupied the space between the two easternmost buttresses on the north side of the Chamber. The exact date of its erection is not known, but it was already in existence by 1692, when Wren improved it by the addition of 'a little Clossett and a flight of staires',[2] and it is shown on Benson's plan of 1718 (Fig. 32).

The Speaker also enjoyed the use of four chambers over the west cloister walk in St. Stephen's Court. There were two of these on each floor, one above the other. They did not constitute a regular dwelling, though the Speaker may on occasion have eaten or slept in them. They could be entered either directly through a doorway in the north wall of the lobby, or from ground level by means of a staircase outside the west end of the House (Fig. 32). This was the staircase which was the subject of an order of 29 January 1674 that 'the back door into the Speaker's Chamber be locked up every morning and the key laid and left on the Table during the sitting of the House'—a precaution apparently designed to prevent members slipping out unobserved. At the same time a motion was 'made and debated for Mr. Speaker to send his warrant to His Majesty's Surveyor General, to open the door and passage from the middle of the Gallery into the Speaker's Chamber', thus giving direct access from the House to the two upper rooms.[3] The House's interest in the means of access to the Speaker's chambers was due to the fact that they were regularly used by select committees.[4] From time to time they were repaired by the Office of Works,[5] but they remained virtually unaltered until their destruction by fire in 1834.[6]

---

[1] This section owes much to a typescript work by the late O. C. Williams entitled *The Topography of the Old House of Commons* (1953), of which there are two copies, one in the library of the Department of the Environment, the other is that of the House of Commons.

[2] Above p. 403.               [3] *Commons' Journals*, ix, p. 300.

[4] Williams, *op. cit.*, p. 7.

[5] E.g. Works 4/1, 15 Sept. 1718, 4/2, 12 Sept. 1722.

[6] This can be seen by a comparison of Benson's plan of 1718 and the detailed survey of 1834 (Works 29/20).

## *The Clerks of the House of Commons*

On 24 July 1661 the House of Commons resolved 'that it be recommended to Sir John Denham, K.B., His Majesty's Surveyor General of his Works, to take care in this Recess . . . to prepare a place for the Clerk of this House, and his Assistant, to write in, and for the custody of the Books and Records belonging to this House'.[1] No action appears, however, to have been taken as a result of this resolution, for in January 1674 the House deputed three members to request the Lord Great Chamberlain 'to give order for repairing the Court of Wards and particularly that the inner room be forthwith repaired and put into fitting condition for the keeping of the Journals and Records of this House'[2]. Thereafter there are regular references to 'the rooms belonging to the Clerk of the House of Commons, called the Inner Court of Wards'.[3] The Court of Wards was the large rectangular building which occupied the space between the south end of the Great Hall, the north end of the Court of Requests, and the west end of St. Stephen's Chapel (Fig. 32). In 1617 the then Usher of the Court of Wards had obtained for himself and his heirs the possession of premises within the building then occupied by the court, and after its dissolution in 1660 his successors continued to exercise their rights by subletting the building. In the early eighteenth century part of it was in use as an auction room for pictures, and part as a coffee-house. Both are marked on plans made for Wren in 1712.[4] In 1729 a committee 'for the more effectual preventing the disorders committed by footmen' recommended that the Court of Wards should be fitted up as a room for the footmen attending members of the House. The proprietors were bought out at a cost of £1095, and £611 was spent by the Office of Works on making suitable arrangements for the footmen.[5] The use of the principal rooms within the old Court of Wards first for commercial purposes and then by the footmen points to the two rooms projecting from the south side of the Court as those allotted to the Clerk in 1674: indeed it is they alone that are marked 'Court of Wards' on a plan of 1760 (Works 29/31). They were pulled down ten years later, and a coffee-house was built where they had stood.[6] In 1800 an official of the House told a Select Committee that this coffee-house stood on the site of a room called 'The Outer Court of Wards' in which the papers of the House had formerly been kept.[7] For nearly a century, therefore, the

[1] *Commons' Journals*, vol. viii, p. 310.

[2] *Commons' Journals*, vol. ix, p. 295. The repairs in question are presumably those recorded in the Works accounts in 1677–8 (Works 5/28). The Court of Wards was re-roofed and a 'lanthorn of 8 cants' was built 'to give light into the Court of Wards'. The new roof incorporated a 'platt-forme' which was covered with Purbeck paving-stones 3 feet square. By 1685 the roof was sinking under the weight, and the preparations for the Coronation of James II included 'taking the stone paving off the roof of the Courte of Wards, and shoring, screwing and taking downe the roofe which was in danger of falling', 'framing and raising 3 new trusses of oake, . . . and raising the old lanthorne', and 'framing and raising a new roofe over the inner Courte of Wards 16 foot long 12 foot wide that was fallen downe' (Works 5/38). In 1678 the preparations for the trial of the Earl of Pembroke included 'digging out a doorway thorow the stone wall betwixt the Court of Wards and the greate hall 7 foote thicke and 7 foote high' (Works 5/29). This is the doorway marked '1678' on Capon's plans. The other doorway in the S.W. corner of the Great Hall appears to have been forced through in 1668 (Works 5/11).     [3] Williams, *op. cit.*, p. 4.     [4] *Wren Society*, vol. xi, pl. 36.

[5] Works 6/15, pp. 209–20; Works 5/141. The 'Footman's Room' in the western half of the building is shown on a plan made in 1760 (Works 29/31). The adjoining room (which communicated with Westminster Hall) was used by the Lord Chancellor as a retiring-room when rising from the Court of Chancery. Upstairs a room was provided for the housekeeper.     [6] This coffee-house is marked on Soane's plan of 1793.

[7] *First Report of the Select Committee on Public Records* (1800), p. 67. Evidently the 'outer' room was the one next to the Court of Requests (from which they were entered), the 'inner' the one on its west side.

Court of Wards had served as a repository for records in the Clerk's custody, and the association was so strong that when the Clerk moved elsewhere, his new office was referred to by everyone about the House as 'the Court of Wards'. Only in about 1780 was this confusing usage superseded by the more appropriate title of 'Journal Office'.[1] By this time, however, the Journals had for some time been in the keeping of a new official called the Clerk of the Journals, who was accommodated in a small office between two of the buttresses on the south side of St. Stephen's Chapel.[2] Here, in somewhat cramped conditions, the recent Journals could be consulted by members in search of precedents. The older Journals had, however, been moved first to a building under or adjoining the Court of Requests, and then, when the Court of Requests was rebuilt, to a room over the 'gallery of communication' between the House of Commons and the Painted Chamber.[3] This gallery was rebuilt in 1722–5 as part of the reconstruction of the Court of Requests, against which it abutted, and the provision of new presses for the 'Journals and other books and papers' belonging to the Clerk's office is referred to in the Board's records.[4]

In September 1750 the Speaker addressed a request to the Board for 'a small alteration' to be made in the lobby of the House, and for an additional building to be erected 'for the Clerk and Journals'. The Treasury, while sanctioning the alteration to the lobby (estimated at £90), said it was too late in the year to begin the additional building, and that it would be better to defer it until next spring. The Paymaster's account shows that this 'additional building for the clerks and journals of the House of Commons' was duly erected in 1751 at a cost of £467.[5] This was almost certainly the small building, consisting of two rooms, which is shown projecting from the east side of the Long Gallery in a plan of 1760.[6] It was clearly a later addition, for the southern room covered up the northernmost window of the gallery.

In 1759–60 the Office of Works built an official house in Cotton Garden for the Clerk of the House. This was the result of a petition to the Treasury from the then Clerk, Jeremiah Dyson. He stated that he had charge of 'all books and papers belonging to the House of Commons', and was 'obliged in the execution of his office to a very constant personal attendance at or near the House of Commons'. The estimate of £3159 was approved by the Treasury in September 1758, and on 11 March 1760 the Board reported that Dyson's house was finished. Thus the Clerk got his official dwelling, 'a very plain square box' of three storeys with an attic, which was occupied by successive Clerks of the House until it was destroyed by fire in 1834.[7]

Still more accommodation was, however, made necessary by the increasing complexity of parliamentary business. By the reign of George III the four clerks 'out

[1] Williams, *op. cit.*, p. 6, citing J. Hatsell, *Precedents of Proceedings* ii (1781), p. 275.
[2] This appears from the recommendations of a select committee in 1771 (*Commons Journals* xxxiv, pp. 808–9), and the clerk's occupation of this room is carried back to the reign of George II by a complaint made by the Clerk of the House in 1742 about the inconvenience of the room for the consultation of the Journals. It had, he said, recently been made more dark 'by the erection of a chimney against one of the buttresses of the House' (*Commons' Journals* xxiv, p. 263). No fewer than three chimneys can be seen clustered round the buttress in question in an engraving of the south side of the House of Commons in J. T. Smith's *Antiquities of Westminster* (1837), p. 146.
[3] *Commons' Journals*, xxiv, p. 264.          [4] Works 6/15, pp. 56–7.
[5] Works 6/17, p. 67; Works 5/141.
[6] Works 29/31. They do not appear on a plan of 1725 (T 1/252, f. 255.)
[7] Works 6/17, pp. 171–2; Works 4/12, 11 March 1760.

of doors' each had his own deputy in order to attend committees; there was a Clerk of the Fees to collect the ever-increasing dues incidental to legislation, and a Deliverer of Votes to distribute the Votes and other proceedings of the House to members.[1] In 1770 the passing of Grenville's Act concerning disputed elections necessitated an office for the Clerk of Privileges, as well as additional committee rooms for the hearing of election petitions.[2] At this time the larger of the two rooms built in 1725 was occupied by the four chief clerks out of doors, while the smaller one was used by the Clerk of the Fees. The Clerk of the Journals had his office further east, in the position already described, while the Clerk of the Votes had (or was soon to have) a similar room on the north side, over the cloister walk. Both the four clerks out of doors and the Clerk of the Fees needed more space, and in 1774 a select committee recommended, *inter alia*, that the two rooms projecting from the Long Gallery should be enlarged and thrown into one for the exclusive use of the four clerks, that another similar room should be built above in which to hold committees, that the Clerk of the Journals should surrender his office to the Clerk of the Fees, and that a new office should be provided for him in one of the rooms over the gallery.[3]

The cost of these and some other associated alterations was estimated by Robert Taylor as £1200, the Treasury *fiat* was obtained in July, and the principal part of the works—the enlargement of the clerks' office—was duly carried out.[4] Some of the remainder were held over because 'the season of the year was too far advanced to complete the whole against the meeting of Parliament'. Nothing, however, was done the following summer, and it was not until 1779 that a reminder from the Speaker finally obliged the Office of Works to complete their assignment.[5]

Before the end of the century the administrative accommodation at the disposal of the House was to need still further expansion, but the buildings erected between 1725 and 1779 all survived until the fire of October 1834, and are easily recognisable in a detailed survey of the House and its appendages made by Thomas Chawner earlier that year.[6]

## 7. THE PARLIAMENT OFFICE

In April 1660 Henry Scobell, who had been Clerk of the House of Commons under the Commonwealth, was ordered to restore to John Browne, the Clerk of the Parliaments, possession of 'a certain Stone Building, standing within the Dwelling House in the Old Palace at Westminster belonging to the Clerk of the Parliaments who attends as Clerk to the House of Peers, commonly called the Tower, wherein the

---

[1] Williams, p. 8.　　　　　　　　　　　　　　[2] Williams, p. 15.
[3] *Commons' Journals*, xxxiv, pp. 808–9.
[4] The enlarged building is shown in detail in the survey of 1834 (Works 29/20). Each clerk had a separate cubicle, lighted by a window in the rebuilt east wall of the building.
[5] Works 6/19, pp. 39, 267, 279; Works 4/16, 10 July, 6 Aug. 1779.
[6] Works 29/20.

H K W—EE

Records are usually kept'.[1] This was the former Jewel Tower, which since the reign of James I had housed the records of the House of Lords, and which now resumed its former function. During the next fifty years its fabric gave the Office of Works little trouble. But in 1664 the Surveyor was called on to accompany a committee of Lords in inspecting the ancient moat, which they found 'hath of late been stopped up'. Their lordships condemned any further filling in as 'an annoyance' to the Clerk's house (presumably by depriving it of drainage) and as endangering the security of the records 'by making them more liable to the Danger of Fire, and the easier Access of Thieves'. They accordingly requested the Surveyor of Works and the Commissioners for the Sewers of Westminster to ensure that the watercourse was kept open.[2] It is doubtful, however, whether the moat was ever effectually cleared, and in the eighteenth and nineteenth centuries it disappeared completely beneath the new houses facing onto Abingdon Street, to be restored to view only in the present century.[3]

The fabric of the tower remained substantially unaltered until the reign of George I, when a complaint from the Clerk of the Parliaments resulted in an extensive repair from which the building emerged in good order but shorn of its battlements, gargoyles, Gothic mouldings, and other characteristic medieval features. In November 1716 the Clerk, William Cowper, drew the attention of the Board to 'the ill state and ruinous condition' of the Parliament Office, and complained that the adjoining lodgings and garden walls were 'much out of repair'.[4] The Board agreed to mend the windows forthwith, but required higher authority for any more extensive repairs. Cowper accordingly addressed himself to the Lords, who appointed a committee to view the tower and obtain estimates from the Board. In due course the committee reported that it was 'absolutely necessary' that the tower should be repaired for the preservation of the records kept in it, and, finding that the two rooms where the records were kept were 'so full, as not to be capable of containing any more', recommended that two empty rooms at the top of the tower should be repaired in order to accommodate the overflow.[5] An estimate, amounting to £870, was approved by the Treasury in September 1717, and the work was put in hand under the superintendence of Nicholas Hawksmoor as Clerk of Works at Westminster.[6] Brick parapets with Portland Stone copings took the place of the decayed battlements, and the original windows were cut out and replaced by round-headed ones with iron frames and massive Portland Stone surrounds. It was originally intended to vault the upper storey in brick as a protection against fire, but in the end this was not done because Hawksmoor was doubtful whether the 'contreforts and buttments' were strong enough to take the weight. In the spring of 1719 the committee found that the works were 'not near completed, [though] the estimate . . . was very much exceeded', a state of affairs which was attributed to Hawksmoor's dismissal from office 'upon Mr. Benson's being appointed Surveyor General'. The

[1] *Lords' Journals*, xi, p. 3.
[2] *Lords' Journals*, xi, pp. 598, 608. A rough plan of the area in the P.R.O. (MPE 486) may have some connection with this affair. It dates from the reign of Charles II, and shows the moat as 'The Pond in question'.
[3] For a detailed account of the building see A. J. Taylor, *The Jewel Tower, Westminster* (H.M.S.O. 1965).
[4] Works 4/1, 13 Nov. 1716, 31 Jan. 1716/17.
[5] *Lords' Journals*, xx, pp. 420, 435, 455, 486, 527, 529, 540.
[6] *Cal. Treas. Books*, xxxi, pp. 583–4; Works 6/7, pp. 2–5.

committee now gave further orders for 'the speedy fitting up of the little room on the first floor, for keeping the Journals only', and for a fireplace to be made in it for the convenience of those wishing to consult them.[1] But in 1725 another Committee 'found the room in the office where the Acts of Parliament are deposited not at all commodious or convenient for the proper placing and keeping of the said Acts, so as the same may be easily and readily found'. The Officers of the Works were again sent for, and advised that 'the uppermost room, where the said Acts are kept, may be made secure from Fire, by bringing up a brick wall betwixt it and the room where the Clerks write; by making an iron door and iron window shutters, and securing the roof; and then whatever conveniences shall be requisite therein may be made securely'. These recommendations were carried out during 1726 at a cost of £508, and when the Committee visited the tower in 1728 they were at last able to report that the Journals, Acts of Parliament and other books and papers 'are now placed and kept in the greatest order and safety imaginable'.[2]

Meanwhile nothing had been done to improve the Clerk's lodgings immediately to the north of the tower. In 1737 a new apartment costing £701 had been built 'joyning the House of Lords' for the use of the Clerk, but this was evidently in the nature of an office for use when the house was in session, and did not replace his house.[3] In 1753, on receiving a petition from Ashley Cowper, Clerk of the Parliaments, the Lords directed the Officers of the Works to survey the building. A fortnight later Flitcroft attended at the Bar of the House with a report in which the Clerk's house was described as 'an old timber building, and so ruinous that they do not think it adviseable to lay out any money to repair it'. The Lords thereupon submitted a humble address to His Majesty to order such repairs to the Parliament Office as were necessary, 'and to rebuild the House belonging thereto'. This was agreed, but the Board's first estimate of £5950 was rejected by the Treasury as it was thought 'very large', and it was a reduced estimate of £4300 that was accepted on 10 July 1754. The work was completed in 1756 at a cost of £5031.[4] The result was the pedimented building of Portland Stone which still faces north up St. Margaret's Street. It contained two houses, one for the Clerk himself, the other for the Clerk Assistant. Its design has been ascribed to John Vardy, who had until the summer of 1754 been Clerk of Works at Westminster, but the existence of a drawing of the elevation attributed to Isaac Ware, the Secretary of the Board, suggests that it may have been he rather than Vardy who was the official responsible for this well-known example of mid-Georgian architecture.[5]

[1] *Lords' Journals*, xxi, pp. 134–43.
[2] *Lords' Journals*, xxii, p. 526, vol. 23, pp. 281–2; Works 5/141, 1726.
[3] Works 4/6, 13 Sept. 1737; Works 6/16, p. 64; AO 1/2456/173.
[4] *Lords' Journals*, xxviii, pp. 14, 21, 51, 56; Works 6/17, pp. 96, 103ᵛ, 110, 116ᵛ, 145ᵛ, 149; Works 4/11, 17 April, 16 July, 1753; 20 Aug. 1754; Works 5/142, 1755, 1755–6, 1756–7.
[5] J. Harris, *A Catalogue of British Drawings for Architecture &c. in American Collections* (New Jersey, 1971), p. 267 and pl. 211.

# 8. THE EXCHEQUER

During the latter part of the seventeenth century the complex of buildings occupied by the Exchequer was constantly being adapted to changing needs. The detailed topography of these buildings is unfortunately far from clear. They occupied the east side of New Palace Yard, and extended southwards to the former cloisters of St. Stephen's Chapel, now forming part of the house occupied *ex officio* by successive Auditors of the Receipt. But no detailed plan of the area exists, and surviving views are too inadequate to make it possible to reconstruct its architectural history with any degree of confidence.[1] In these circumstances it would be unprofitable to chronicle every alteration recorded in the Works accounts. Only the more important will therefore be described.

The first was the rebuilding in 1671–2 of the 'Treasury House', recorded in the following terms in the Paymaster's enrolled account for that year:

> Morris Emmett for takeing downe the old building of the Treasury house and for all the new Brickworke and Tyleing of the said Treasury house and raiseing of the Stack of Chimneys for the Pix roome and makeing good the Tyleing of the roofe and over the Starr Chamber, and makeing new draines in the Pallace Yard and digging the Celler at the Treasury house and carrying away all the Earth and Rubbish of all the building there . . . by agreement £196. More to him for cutting a way in the Brick wall of the Starre Chamber for raiseing of a chimney for the Porter's Lodge being 18 foot high and cutting way and putting in a window there . . . £8 8s. 4d. . . . and for 40 tunns of Ragstones delivered for the new paveing of the New Pallace Yard £11, in all the summe of £219 17s. 10d.
>
> John Angeir Carpenter for takeing down all the old Timber building of the Treasury house and makeing the Inclosure in the Pallace Yard for the use of the Building and new building the Treasury House . . . and for raising and laying the floores of the passage into St. Stephen's Court and to the offices and making the great doorcases and the timber particions next to the Treasury House by agreement £255.[2]

Various improvements were made to the house of Sir Robert Long, the Auditor of the Receipt. But far more extensive alterations, costing some £2500, were put in hand in 1673 for the benefit of his successor Sir Robert Howard. Several new rooms were built, a new great staircase was erected 'with cartooses under every step', the great dining room was panelled in deal with bolection mouldings, and the principal fireplace was finished off with 'Italian mouldings and picture frames over them'. An old laundry in his garden beside the Thames was converted into a luxurious

---

[1] Apart from the well-known general plans of Capon, Soane, Richardson and others, attention may be drawn to a plan of premises adjoining the Pells Office made in 1696 (T 1/40, no. 49), and to a plan and section of the offices of the Receipt of the Exchequer dating from 1725 (T 1/252, ff. 67–8). Most of the available topographical views will be found in *Views of the Old Palace of Westminster*, ed. Colvin (*Architectural History*, vol. 9, 1966).

[2] E 351/3285. The detailed account is in Works 5/17, ff. 228–30.

'bathing-room' containing an oval 'bathing cistern' surrounded by a white marble pavement and ornamented with carved wainscot, marble chimneypieces and niches with scalloped heads and Portland stone seats. The water was pumped from the river into a stone storage cistern and heated in a copper before being run into the bath. The plumbing was done under the direction of Sir Samuel Morland, and the best craftsmen were employed.[1] At the same time the 'ante-room and lobby belonging to the Star Chamber' was made into a new office for Sir Robert Howard.[2] In 1693 this office was enlarged after Sir Robert had represented that it was 'so straight that it is scarce sufficient to execute his present business', let alone 'the extraordinary businesse now added to his office by a late Act of Parliament for settling a fund for survivorship and annuitys'.[3] 'A part of the Starr Chamber adjoyning to the auditor's roome' was accordingly fitted up for the purpose at a cost of £112 16s. 6d.[4] In 1694 the complicated provisions of an Act of Parliament to raise £1,000,000 by means of a state lottery necessitated the establishment of a new 'Transfer Office'.[5] This was accommodated in premises immediately adjoining the Star Chamber, while the 'Star Chamber Court' itself was made into an office for the Tellers appointed to handle the money. The resultant arrangements cannot be exactly reconstructed, but the Star Chamber appears to have been on the first floor of the long gabled building on the east side of New Palace Yard, lighted by a range of large bay windows, and it may be noted that the estimate includes 'repairing the 3 bow windowes and putting in two new windowes 8 foot high & 5 foot wide'.[6] Further alterations to the Star Chamber were carried out in 1697 in order to provide offices for the trustees of the newly-invented Exchequer Bills.[7] Subsequently the trustees were obliged to surrender one room to the 'Million Adventure' and a second to the paymaster in charge of another money-raising expedient, the sale of annuities.[8] In 1706–7, however, a new office was built specifically to accommodate those responsible for the annuities.[9]

The results of these works—and of others carried out directly by the Exchequer[10]—was a confused mass of offices and lodgings whose outline can be traced on the plans of Capon, Soane and others. After examining these plans it is easy to understand why in 1712 Lord Halifax, then Auditor of the Receipt, wrote that 'the many new offices of late years erected at the Exchequer have taken up all the room there proper for offices'.[11]

[1] Works 5/24 and 25; E 251/3291.
[2] Works 5/22. The contract with Moses Townsend, carpenter, is entered in Works 5/145, p. 87.
[3] Works 6/2, 30 Jan. 1693; *Cal. Treas. Books* x, pp. 30, 57.
[4] Works 5/46.
[5] *Statutes at Large*, vol. 3, pp. 545–6; cf. N. Luttrell, *Brief Historical Relation*, iii, p. 377.
[6] Works 6/2, 5 Sept. 1694.
[7] *Cal. Treas. Books*, xiii, p. 213; E 351/3309. According to Narcissus Luttrell an office was built this year in the Star Chamber for the Malt Lottery Loan (*Brief Historical Relation*, iv, p. 228), but this is not mentioned in the Works accounts.
[8] *Cal. Treas. Books*, xix, pp. 189, 517.
[9] *Cal. Treas. Books*, xxi, pp. 75, 85; xxii, p. 178; E 351/3312.
[10] In 1717 the Board of Works was asked by the Treasury to examine bills for work done for the Receipt of the Exchequer between 1711 and 1716. They amounted to £1774, which the Board reduced to £1629 (*Cal. Treas. Books*, xxxi, p. 663; Works 6/7, pp. 24–5). In 1726–9 the Cofferer's office over the Watergate was similarly repaired 'by the workmen belonging to the Exchequer', but the bills were subsequently submitted to the scrutiny of the Board of Works (Works 6/15, pp. 229–30, 236.)
[11] *Cal. Treas. Papers 1708–14*, p. 422.

## 9. THE CHAPTER HOUSE

After the Restoration the Chapter House continued to be used as the principal repository for the records both of the Exchequer and of the Courts of Law, and the upkeep of its fabric was recognised as one of the responsibilities of the Office of Works.[1] Although from time to time essential repairs were carried out, notably in 1669–72, 1707 and 1725,[2] the building which had once been one of the architectural glories of Westminster was sadly degraded by its adaptation to the utilitarian purpose of a record-office. Windows were bricked up,[3] one of the great buttresses was taken down,[4] others were mutilated,[5] and the whole interior was filled with shelves and presses. Nor was the ancient Chapter House an ideal building in which to keep records. By the end of the seventeenth century the structure was in urgent need of major repairs, and the great windows were broken and letting in the rain.[6] Hemmed in by dwellings, the Chapter House was also vulnerable to the encroachments of neighbouring householders. In 1686 its keeper complained that one of the canons of Westminster had built a brew-house so close to one of the windows that 'all the steame and smoake of the water and wort comes into the Treasury leaving a great damp therein, rotting and spoyling many records'.[7] In 1703 a crisis of accommodation was caused by a large accession of documents. Peter Le Neve, then one of the Deputy Chamberlains of the Exchequer, asked Wren to build a gallery to house them, but met with a firm refusal, 'for' (as he reported to the Treasury) 'without particular direction the officers of the Works will doe nothing but mend the stone work, lead and glass of that place'.[8] On receiving an official request from the Treasury, Wren eventually took action which resulted in a payment to John Churchill of £113 for 'carpenter's work' which presumably included the much-needed gallery.[9] Two years later a Committee of the House of Lords considering the state of the Public Records drew attention to the 'ruinous state' of the Chapter House, which they said was 'in danger of falling'. Wren's estimate of £1447 for structural repairs was accepted by the Treasury, and the work was carried out in 1707 at a cost of £1531. The largest payment was one of £684 to Edward Tufnell, the Master Mason to Westminster Abbey.[10] The appointment in 1718 of a new Committee of Lords to investigate the state of the Public Records resulted in the provision of 50 large chests at a cost of £290. When they were installed the House was told (May

---

[1] For an account of the records preserved here see *Lords' Journals* xxi, pp. 141–2.

[2] For the repairs of 1669–72 see E 351/3283, 3284, 3286. Two contracts with William Moxam, mason, for these repairs are entered in Works 5/145, pp. 38–9, 73. For the later repairs see below.

[3] E.g. in 1663–4: 'filling up one of the great windows of the Convocation House with brick, plastered' (Works 5/4). A seventeenth-century drawing in Bodleian, MS. Rawlinson C.704 shows the windows still intact with their heraldic glass.

[4] See below.

[5] E.g. in 1672–3: 'taking down two great peers on top of the buttresses at the Convocation house' (Works 5/19).

[6] E 36/253, f. 294 (letter from J. Lowe and P. Le Neve to Wren, June 1701).

[7] E 36/253, f. 169.                    [8] E 36/253, ff. 294–6.

[9] AO 1/2446/140; *Cal. Treasury Books*, xviii, pp. 336, 437.

[10] *Lords Journals*, xviii, pp. 135–6; *Cal. Treasury Books*, xx, pp. 196, 599; Works 5/141, f. 3ᵛ.

1728) that 'the Chapter House is now made a common and commodious Repository for Records'.[1]

The minutes of the Office of Works, however, show that even now the state of the structure was far from satisfactory. It appears that the weight of the vault was tending to push out the walls, particularly on the north side, where a buttress had been removed, probably in 1707. The estimate of £1488 which received Treasury approval in August 1725 evidently included the rebuilding of this buttress, for in October the Board of Works received a letter from the Dean of Westminster object-ing to 'their rebuilding a flying arch for the support of His Majesty's Record room . . . which arch was many years since taken down by order of Sir Christopher Wren, and which if rebuilt would be a great inconvenience to them', no doubt because it would obstruct the entrance to the abbey by way of Poet's Corner. The Board obligingly stopped the work and informed the dean that they would 'endeavour to find out some other proper method to secure the building'.[2] In the following year the mason Woodall was allowed for the workmanship of 500 feet of stone at 8s. per foot which he had prepared for the buttress, but which had not been used because the building 'had been secured another way'.[3] Unfortunately the alternative ex-pedient (whose nature is not disclosed by the records) was to prove ineffective, for in 1737, when the building was again surveyed at the request of the record-keeper, the Officers of the Works found that 'from the decay of the buttresses and from the want of one many years ago taken away for the convenience of passage to the abbey the roof, which is an arch of stone, is in great and imminent danger of falling in'. The solution now advanced by the Board was to dismantle the stone vault and sub-stitute a timber roof. The Treasury showed so little concern for the safety either of the records or of their keeper that neither this application nor a repetition of it in 1738 received any answer, and it was not until 1740 that the Board obtained author-ity to shore the roof up in order to prevent its imminent collapse.[4] Though the shoring sufficed to hold up the vault it could not prevent stones falling from the decaying parapets and buttresses, and as time went on this became a sufficiently common occurrence to constitute something of a hazard to those passing underneath. In 1744 the prebendaries, fearful of a serious accident from the 'great stones' which were 'frequently falling down', appealed to the Treasury to take some action. When, however, the Board reported that the cost of taking down the vault would amount to £625, the Treasury once more turned a deaf ear to all entreaties, and it was not until 1751, when part of the building actually 'tumbled in' during a gale, that per-mission was at last given to remove the shattered vault at a cost now estimated at £680.[5] The work was carried out in 1751–2 at a cost of £802, plus £370 for a new door, some additional shelves and presses, and 'a few other conveniences of small expence'. The new doorway was in the north wall, and was designed to enable the record-keeper to enter the building without going through the abbey.[6]

---

[1] *Lords' Journals*, xxi, pp. 141–3, xxiii, pp. 281–2.
[2] Works 6/15, ff. 104–7, 113; *Lords' Journals*, xxii, p. 551.
[3] Works 4/3, 30 Aug. 1726.  [4] Works 6/16, ff. 58, 73ᵛ, 122.
[5] Works 6/16, f. 169; Works 4/10, 19 March 1751; Works 1/3, ff. 65ᵛ, 66; Works 6/17, f. 74.
[6] Works 6/17, f. 143; Works 5/141, 1752. Cf. a plan of the building in Sir John Soane's Museum, Drawer xxxv, Set 5, no. 19.

## 10. PROJECTS FOR A PARLIAMENT HOUSE

Two unfulfilled projects haunt the history of English architecture in the seventeenth and eighteenth centuries—a royal palace and a parliament house. In the seventeenth century it was a palace for the monarch which preoccupied the minds of Stuart architects: in the eighteenth proposals for a new building to house a victorious parliament were closer to political reality, and came nearer to being carried out. Georgian parliaments assembled, as their predecessors had done since the thirteenth century, in what was still officially a royal palace, maintained at the king's expense. But neither House was accommodated in a manner that could be regarded as altogether satisfactory. The Upper House met in a large room intended originally for the court of a medieval queen, the Lower one in a disaffected chapel, whose collegiate arrangement still exercised its influence on the Members' seating.[1] On state occasions there was insufficient room in the House of Lords for all the participants and spectators, and attempts to solve this difficulty by erecting a gallery failed to meet with general approval.[2] As for the Lower House, it was not, perhaps, inappropriate that members of the unreformed Commons should meet in a building whose structure was as medieval as the electoral system which returned them. But even after Wren had made the interior comfortable with joinery and plasterwork, St. Stephen's Chapel was uncomfortably crowded when Members were present in strength, and all the ingenuity of contemporary technology was needed to 'evaporate the unhealthfull breathings' which made the atmosphere so unpleasant when the House was sitting late.[3]

It was in fact the practical inconvenience of the House of Commons which in 1733 induced Walpole's government to ask the Office of Works to submit plans for a new Parliament House. But the idea had already been publicly advocated by those for whom architectural grandeur was an end in itself. In 1721 Bishop Berkeley put a 'parliament house' first among the building projects which he hoped to see carried out.[4] Lord Shaftesbury declared in 1712 that new Houses of Parliament were 'one of the noblest subjects for architecture', and expressed the hope that when Whitehall was rebuilt, 'the neighbouring *lords* and *commons* will at the same time be plac'd in better chambers and apartments, than at present; were it only for majesty's sake, and as a magnificence becoming the person of the prince, who here appears in full solemnity'.[5] In the reign of William III Wren had in fact added a new parliamentary building at Westminster to his great scheme for Whitehall Palace, and linked them by a long processional gallery.[6] With its clerestory from the Roman Baths and its arcaded podium of rusticated masonry it was evidently intended to provide a setting

[1] M. Hastings, *Parliament House* (1950), pp. 79–80.
[2] See above, pp. 391–2.
[3] Above, pp. 404–5.
[4] George Berkeley, *Essay towards preventing the Ruin of Great Britain* (1721), p. 20.
[5] *Letters of the Earl of Shaftesbury* (1746), pp. 107–8.
[6] K. Downes, *English Baroque Architecture* (1966), pl. 78.

of antique grandeur for the English senate. But nothing came either of the baroque palace or of the classical parliament house.

The next projector of parliament houses was, it seems, Wren's successor, William Benson, whose brief and inglorious tenure of the surveyorship might seem to have allowed him little opportunity for anything of the kind. In 1719, after only fifteen months in office, Benson was dismissed for obstinately and erroneously maintaining that the House of Lords was in imminent danger of collapse.[1] No attempt has ever been made to vindicate Benson against the charge of incompetence formally preferred against him by the highest tribunal in the land, and as formally accepted by the king's ministers. There can, indeed, be no doubt that he misled the House of Lords, and that he deserved his fate. Later in his life Benson was to display signs of insanity. But his colleague Campbell was sane enough, and their persistence in error is difficult to explain in terms of mere stupidity. Why was Benson so determined to insist on the dangerous state of the buildings at Westminster? The clue is to be found in a petition which David Lance, the King's Master Plasterer, addressed to the Treasury in 1722. He was acting as executor of Benjamin Jackson, the recently deceased Master Mason, and was claiming certain expenses incurred by Jackson in surveying the House of Lords during Benson's surveyorship. 'William Benson', he wrote, 'in or about the month of February 1718, having formed to himself a scheme for pulling down and rebuilding both Houses of Parliament, . . . for obtaining his ends therein pretended to his Majesty that the House of Peers was in so great danger of falling that he could not warrant it for many hours.'[2] Lance, as one of the Patent Artisans, was in a position to know the truth about what went on in the Board of Works, and his statement accords well with what we know of Benson and Campbell as pioneers of the new Palladian movement, anxious (we may presume) to exploit their position as officers of the King's Works in order to achieve their artistic programme. Campbell shared in Benson's disgrace, and if he made any designs for a new Parliament House they have not been preserved.[3] Benson's clumsy stratagem was of course fatal to the project as well as to his own career, and it was some time before the idea of rebuilding the Houses of Parliament became politically acceptable once more.

Its resuscitation in 1732 was due to the House of Commons, and was connected with the appointment of a Committee to investigate the custody of the Public Records and the state of the Cottonian Library. The housing of the Cottonian Library was an old problem which had come before the House at intervals ever since 1702, when the library had been given to the public in accordance with the wishes of Sir John Cotton. The collection had been formed in the reign of James I by Sir John's grandfather Sir Robert Cotton, a politically minded antiquary who lived actually within the precincts of the Palace of Westminster. His house occupied the space between the House of Commons and the Painted Chamber, and had a pleasant garden stretching down to the Thames. The famous library was housed in a long narrow room

[1] Above, p. 396.
[2] Works 6/7, p. 321. February 1718 was, of course, February 1719 New Style.
[3] In 1794 when Soane asked Chambers to let him see the plans for new Houses of Lords and Commons preserved in the Office of Works, he referred specifically to those made by Benson, but was told that nothing was known of them at the Office (Works 1/5, f. 129).

against the north side of the Painted Chamber.[1] Here, in the past, Members had been able to reinforce their resistance to arbitrary government by direct reference to historical precedent, and it was the intention of the donor that the manuscripts should continue to be kept in the house which bore their collector's name. However, the library was soon found to be so narrow and damp as to be 'improper for preserving the books and papers', and when in 1706 the fourth baronet sold the house and garden to the Crown, an Act of Parliament provided, among other things, that 'a convenient room shall be built on or near part of the said garden ground' for the accommodation of the collection. In 1703 Wren had already submitted proposals either for rebuilding the library or for transferring its contents to a room over the office of the Usher of the Black Rod. In the end neither alternative was authorised by the Treasury, but 27 new wainscot presses were made to contain the books.[2] Meanwhile the building itself was shored up to prevent it from collapsing, and continued to house the library and its keeper until 1721, when the Board of Works reported that it was in 'so ruinous and dangerous a condition that wee conceive it impracticable to be repaired'. The Treasury thereupon instructed the Board to look for some convenient house to which the library might be removed until such time as Cotton House should be made fit to receive it again. After some difficulty the Board secured a lease of Essex House in the Strand, which they said would be 'very convenient for removing the books by water, and by situation agreeable to the lawyers who have frequent recourse to them'. For eight years (1722–30) the Office paid an annual rent of £140 for Essex House, and carried out minor repairs from time to time. In 1730 new quarters were found for the library in Ashburnham House in Little Dean's Yard. But it returned to Westminster only to be seriously damaged by fire on 23 October 1731.[3] This calamity aroused the House of Commons sufficiently to secure the appointment of a Committee to consider the future of the library. The Committee was nominated on 15 February 1731/2, and on 24 February it was further instructed to 'consider of a proper Place, and Plan, for erecting an Edifice that may be made use of for the reception of the Parliament.' When the Committee reported in May, it expressed the view that 'a convenient room may and ought to be built on or near part of the said Ground [where Cotton House, now demolished, had stood] for the reception of the Library, and that the said Room may be part of an Edifice erected for other uses, and particularly for the preservation of such public Records as shall be thought proper to be deposited therein'. 'Your Committee', the report continued, 'have also considered of a proper Place and Plan for erecting an Edifice, that may be made use of for the Reception of the Parliament, and have received several Designs for that purpose. And it appears to your Committee, that the Building before proposed for the Cottonian Library may be so designed, as to have

---

[1] See the survey plans from Wren's office, reproduced in *Wren Society*, xi, plates xxxi, xxxix, and another plan in T 1/100, f. 176.

[2] *Wren Soc.* xi, pp. 50–9 and plate xxx; *Statutes of the Realm*, viii, pp. 625–6; P.R.O. MPD 165 (plan made by Wren for rehousing the Library in 1703).

[3] Works 4/2, 23 May, 4, 25 July 1722; Works 4/3, 13 Sept. 1727; Works 4/4, 23 July, 27 August, 1729, 19 March, 24, 28 Aug., 26 Nov. 1730; Works 4/5, 7 Dec. 1731, 16 May, 6 June 1732; Works 6/7, pp. 180–7; Works 6/15, p. 111. After the fire the Treasury authorised the Board to pay Lord Ashburnham £574 19s. 11d. in compensation (*Cal. Treasury Books & Papers 1731–4*, p. 229). The old library of Cotton House was finally pulled down in 1737 (Works 4/7, 5 Sept. 1737).

Relation to a future structure, in which the Parliament may be assembled.' On the following day the House asked the king to take steps for the better preservation of the library, but said nothing on the subject of a new Parliament House.[1] The matter was, however, again raised the following March, in the course of a prolonged debate on the proposed duty on tobacco. The House, Lord Egmont records, 'was crowded to an insupportable degree, which occasioned Mr. Gibbon to move that his Majesty might be addressed to build a new House, which was agreed to'.[2] In its address the House promised to 'make good the Expence' incurred in erecting a new building, and on 20 March 1733 it was told that the proposal had been favourably received, and that 'His Majesty will direct some proper place to be pitched upon for erecting the same'.[3] No further action is reflected in the minutes either of the Treasury or of the Board of Works, but behind the scenes Lord Burlington was interesting himself in the project. In March 1732 the *Grub Street Journal* had announced that

> The plan for building the new parliament house is the design of Nicholas Hawksmoor Esq., one of the surveyors of his Majesty's Works, which is said to be very grand and beautiful, and is now under the inspection of the right hon. the Earl of Burlington, for his approbation.[4]

But it is not very likely that designs by Hawksmoor would meet with the approbation of so strict a Palladian as Burlington, and 43 'designs for the Parliament House' were among the architect's effects when he died four years later.[5] Burlington's name, however, continued to be associated with the scheme. In March 1733 the *Gentleman's Magazine* reported that

> The Earl of Burlington has projected a Plan for building two new Houses of Parliament, and a Public Library between them, to be finish'd against next Session, and to cost the Public about £30,000,[6]

while the *London Magazine* informed its readers that

> A Survey was order'd to be taken of several old Houses in St. Anne's Lane near the Old-Palace-Yard, Westminster, in order to prosecute the Earl of Burlington's Plan of an Edifice for the Reception of the two Houses of Parliament, pursuant to a late address of the Hon. House of Commons.[7]

Though nothing came of this survey, certain designs made by William Kent, no doubt with Burlington's approval, can be attributed to the year 1733. They form part of a large number of drawings dating from the years 1733–9 which survive in

[1] *Commons' Journals*, xxi, pp. 799, 811, 917, 918, 919; *Reports from Committee of the House of Commons*, i, p. 448.

[2] *Egmont Diary* (Hist. MSS. Comm.) i, p. 343.

[3] *Commons' Journals*, xxii, pp. 89, 96.

[4] *Grub Street Journal*, no. 170 (29 March 1732) p. 2. I owe this reference to Mr. G. W. Beard.

[5] K. Downes, 'Hawksmoor's Sale Catalogue', *Burlington Mag.*, Oct. 1945, p. 334. Among the drawings from the Bute Sale now in the Victoria & Albert Museum there is a sketch by Hawksmoor for an 'Atrium Corinthium' in the angle between Westminster Hall and St. Stephen's Chapel (E 414–1951) which may perhaps be related to the scheme of 1732.

[6] *Gent's Mag.*, vol. 3 (1733), p. 156.    [7] *London Magazine*, 1733, p. 159.

four different collections.[1] They represent a great rectangular building designed to
stand immediately to the south of Westminster Hall, occupying the sites of the House
of Lords, Painted Chamber and other buildings in that area, and taking up much of
Old Palace Yard. The principal facades are to face west and east, towards Westminster Abbey and the river. The centre of the western elevation is recessed seg-
mentally so as to receive a curved colonnade of giant Corinthian columns framing
a great octastyle portico. The eastern elevation is dignified by another portico projecting from a straight colonnade (Pl. 59). The two Houses occupy the centres
of the north and south sides, the Commons to the north, the Lords to the south,
their lobbies connected by a suite of large apartments. In the middle of the eastern
front, behind the portico, is a great basilical hall of which sections are preserved
in the Soane Museum[2] (Pl. 58). Arcaded galleries along its longer sides provide
accommodation for the Cottonian Library, but in later plans the central space
is designated for conferences between the two Houses, and may possibly have been
intended to fulfil this secondary function from the first. It was to be covered by a
great coffered barrel-vault of the most monumental character, and was to be lighted
by mullioned lunettes at either end. Above the vault sits, rather awkwardly, a
saucer-dome whose circular plan bears no relation to that of the longitudinal vault
below. Beneath the *piano nobile* is a basement containing vaulted vestibules for the
entrance of Members, with broad flights of steps rising to the lobbies above. A
central vestibule, with elliptical staircases, gives access to the library, and at one
side there is a columned vestibule for the use of the sovereign on state occasions,
with its own staircase up to the Lords. Though not without some awkward features,
the plan showed a good understanding of the practical and ceremonial functions of
the Georgian parliament, and was to form the basis of the many subsequent variations for which drawings survive. In its combination of elements from ancient Rome,
Palladio and Inigo Jones, its architectural expression was characteristic of the style
developed by Burlington and Kent, and most of its features can be paralleled in
their executed works.

What reception these drawings had we do not know: but there is no indication
that they were ever officially approved. Burlington's share in the project may have
been prejudiced by his breach with Walpole in 1733, but this did not affect the
latter's patronage of Kent, who had been working on the interiors at Houghton
since 1727, and whose elevation to the positions of Master Mason and Deputy
Surveyor took place in 1735. In his *Critical Review of the Publick Buildings in London
and Westminster*, published in 1734 with a dedication to Burlington, James Ralph

[1] The Soane Museum (Drawer 35), Victoria & Albert Museum (93 H.20), Public Record Office (Works
29/29, a single drawing; Works 29/3358, a bound volume) and R.I.B.A. Library (a bound volume and some
loose drawings). There is also a single plan among the papers of Richard Arundell (Surveyor of Works 1726–37)
at Serlby Hall, Notts. The drawings at the Soane and Victoria & Albert Museums were published by Fiske
Kimball in *R.I.B.A. Journal*, 6 August and 10 Sept. 1932. His analysis of them has been followed here, with
some modifications suggested by further research and the discovery of the P.R.O. and R.I.B.A. drawings.
Attention has been concentrated on the principal schemes submitted to the Treasury, and no attempt has
been made to deal here with the various 'intermediate' schemes. Most of these were described by Fiske Kimball,
but more are to be found in Works 29/3358.

[2] Fiske Kimball attributed these drawings to the year 1735, supposing that the inclusion of the Cottonian
Library was a later instruction rather than one basic to the whole project. He gave a similar date to a corresponding elevation (his Fig. 12, really the front to the River Thames), not noticing that it is signed and dated
'1733 WK' on the back. A related drawing (Works 29/3358, f. 22) is also dated 1733.

refers to the scheme in terms which suggest that its future was still undecided. 'I shall', he says, 'be glad to see this noble project put into execution: 'tis certain nothing can be more unworthy of so august a body as the parliament of *Great Britain*, than the present place of their assembly . . . and if it falls into the noble hands to execute, we have long been flatter'd to believe it would, there is no reason to doubt but the grandeur of this appearance will answer the majestick purposes 'tis to be employ'd in.' Interest in it revived in April 1735, when the Treasury wrote to the Board of Works 'for the plan prepared by them of a new House of Commons and Cotton Library, with the estimate of the charges thereof'.[1] The estimate does not seem to have been preserved, but there is a note in Kent's hand accompanying the drawings for the Cottonian Library which shows that that part of the design alone was expected to cost £59,100. Once more no decision was taken, but in Scotland Yard, at least, the rebuilding of the whole palace continued to be regarded as a likely eventuality, for in October 1736, when appointing successors to Thomas Churchill, the recently deceased Master Bricklayer, the Board of Works specified that 'if a House of Parliament, Bridge or any great workes of that kind be built in Westminster under the direction of the Office of Works, Mr. Stenton is to be equally concerned with Mr. Pratt in such works'.[2] Again, in October 1736, the Board explained to the Treasury that the plainness of their design for a new building for the Clerk of the Parliaments was 'because it can be of no use should the Houses of Parliament ever be rebuilt'.[3]

The matter was in fact taken up anew in the House of Commons in 1739. On 7 March 1738/9 the relevant entries in the Journals of 14 and 20 March 1732/3 were read, and it was resolved to address the Crown once more. On 13 March the Comptroller of the Household told the House 'that their Address of Wednesday last that His Majesty would be graciously pleased to give Directions for the building [of] a more spacious and convenient edifice, that may be made use of for the Reception of the Parliament, had been presented to His Majesty, and that His Majesty had commanded him to acquaint this House, that he will give directions accordingly'.[4] More informatively, *Read's Weekly Journal* for 24 March reported as follows:

> We hear that a Plan of Mr. Kent's and Mr. Ripley's for building a magnificent House of Lords and Commons, has been laid before his Majesty, & approv'd; it is said it will cost upwards of £200000 and will be built in Cotton-Garden.
>
> We hear, that the Right Hon. Sir Robert Walpole, the Right Hon. the Speaker of the House of Commons, and the right Hon. Mr. Henry Pelham, with others, will be appointed Commissioners for Building the New Parliament Houses.
>
> And that a Survey will be taken of the Banqueting House at Whitehall, and of Somerset-House Palace, to see which will be the most convenient for the Parliament to meet in, till the new Work is compleated.

Before the end of the month, the Treasury had in fact instructed the Board of Works to make a survey of the site, to prepare drawings, and to submit an estimate

[1] *Cal. Treasury Books & Papers 1735–8*, p. 13.
[2] Works 4/6, 28 Oct. 1736.
[3] Works 6/16, p 64.
[4] *Commons' Journals*, xxiii, pp. 274, 280.

of the probable cost.[1] The Board's reply did not come until 20 August, the intervening months having evidently been needed to revise the project of 1733 and to work out a building programme that would allow the two Houses to continue their work undisturbed until their new buildings were ready.

To the Rt. Hon[ble] the Lords Commiss[rs]
of His majesty's Treasury
    May it please your Lordships—
    In obedience to your Lordships' Commands signified to us by Mr. Scrope the 30th day of March last. We have viewed the ground & houses & caused a plan to be made thereof on which we propose a more spacious & convenient edifice may be erected for the reception of Parlaiment (*sic*), and we have drawn plans & elevations which we propose to be pursued in carrying on the said edifice & likewise a general plan of Westminster Hall & Houses of Parliament as they now are, and an additional plan how we think Courts of Justice should be erected if required. If these designs should be approved, they may be built at three several times, and the present Houses of Parliament remain as they now are, untill the proposed edifice be intirely erected. Vizt.
    First. the House of Commons, Speaker's Apartment, Committee rooms and other conveniences for the officers attending the House, which part may be built on ground now in possession of the Crown for about the sum of forty six thousand Pounds.
    Second. The House of Lords with Vestibule, Conference Room, Portico, Cupola & conveniences for the officers attending the House, the charge of which will be about the sum of seventy five thousand Pounds.
    Third. The arcade & Court of Requests, passages & conveniences for persons & servants attending each House, the charge of which will be about the sum of thirty nine thousand Pounds, the whole amounting to the sum of one hundred & sixty thousand Pounds.
    We have likewise sent your Lordships three other plans for a House of Commons marked A. B. C. either of which (if thought by your Lordships preferable to that marked E, which is what we apprehend to be the most commodious) may be executed on the same ground & at the same expence as that mark'd E, without causing any alteration in the general plan.
    We are not able yett to inform your Lordships what will be the charge of purchasing ground & houses wanting for this undertaking, not having been impowerd to treat with persons for that purpose.
    All which is humbly submitted by

                               H. FOX
                               T. RIPLEY
                               W. KENT
                               W. GILL[2]

    The new plan was a development of the former one, but compressed so as to achieve a greater integration in the internal arrangements. The Cottonian Library has been eliminated (at any rate as a distinctive architectural feature), and the two Houses are brought closer together on either side of a square central hall or *atrium*. The length of the main facade has consequently been reduced from over 400 feet

[1] Works 6/16, f. 69[v].                                        [2] Works 6/16, f. 98.

to 300. The front is still hollowed, but less deeply than before, and the portico is no longer flanked by colonnades. The separate royal entrance has gone, but the main entrance has gained greatly in dignity (Pl. 60).

As the Board's letter indicates, the building was designed to be carried out in three stages, and drawings survive to show how these were phased. The first stage was to comprise 'The House of Commons, Speaker's Apartment, Committee rooms and other conveniences for the officers attending the House', and the plan shows that the north-east corner of the building, in which they were contained, was to stand immediately to the east of the Painted Chamber and the gallery leading to the existing House of Commons. In the second stage the eastern facade to the Thames has been completed, and the new House of Lords has been built, thus enabling the old House of Lords, Painted Chamber and other buildings to be demolished in order to make way for the western facade.

Copies of the alternative plans for the House of Commons have been preserved.[1] The one marked A represents a chamber with the seating disposed in a circle. In B the arrangement of the seats is elliptical. In C the plan resembles a modern football stadium, with straight sides and curved ends. In D and E the arrangement is essentially the same as it was in St. Stephen's Chapel, with diagonal benches on either side of the Speaker's Chair, and cross benches at the lower end of the House on either side of the entrance to the Lobby. The number of seats provided varied from 528 in A to 480 in C, the actual number of Members at the time being 513. In each case there was a gallery supported on consoles and capable of holding at least 112 persons in 'single rank'. For the House of Lords no alternative plans were submitted, and it was no doubt intended to defer detailed consideration of its internal arrangements until the second stage of the building programme was reached. Two drawings by Kent, however, exist which show that he had in mind a rectangular chamber surrounded by an arcaded gallery based on the exterior of Palladio's Basilica at Vicenza. The room was to be lit from above by a clerestory. This implies an internal situation for the House of Lords which does not correspond with any of the surviving plans, in all of which that House has one external wall pierced by a large Palladian window. One of the two drawings bears annotations implying that it was drawn on the occasion of the presentation of the Speaker to the king on 23 January 1734/5, and it may well have had no association with either the earlier plans of 1733 or the later ones of 1739.

In September the Board was instructed by the Treasury to confer with the Speaker and agree with him upon 'the design or plan which shall in your opinion be thought best to be executed, and to let their Lordships know your determination herein to the end necessary orders may be given for providing materials and making contracts for carrying on the said work'.[2] On 11 December the Board reported that they had waited on the Speaker (Arthur Onslow), made such alterations as he desired, 'and prepared the plan marked D together with a new general plan, both of which we herewith send your Lordships'. 'The aforesaid plan marked D', they continued, 'is in the Speaker's opinion (and we likewise agree in the same opinion)

[1] In Works 29/3358, the R.I.B.A. volume and the Soane Museum (D only).
[2] Works 6/16, f. 28ᵛ.

the most convenient. He likewise approves of the chambers and other accommodations adjoyning to the House of Commons as expressed in the general plan, but as to the rest of the general plan or the elevations of any part of it he desires to be excused giving any opinion.' The total estimate now amounted to £171,067.[1]

Two bound sets of the drawings submitted in December 1739 survive, besides a number of others related to them. In both cases the approved plan of the House of Commons is marked D[2], to distinguish it from the original plan D, but a comparison shows that only minor alterations resulted from the conference with the Speaker. The essential difference in the general plan lay in the abandonment of the curved recess in the middle of the west front, and the substitution of a straight facade, behind which lay a new and larger Court of Requests. In addition the whole structure was moved eastwards so as to create a large open space on the site of Old Palace Yard—so much so that the east front would have encroached on the Thames, which would have had to be embanked to support the foundations.[2] The facades were also revised, but the whole effect was changed by the more elevated treatment of the corner domes and by using the central hall as the base for an octagonal tower, with temple porticoes on its cardinal faces, and above them a small cupola crowned by a lantern (Pl. 61A). In monumental effect this new design was not inferior to any of its predecessors, while its picturesque silhouette would have grouped with the Abbey and Westminster Bridge to form an architectural scene that would have delighted the patrons of Canaletto.

Another new feature of the scheme submitted in December 1739 was that it took account of the need for better accommodation for the Courts of Justice, which were to be ranged along the west side of Westminster Hall in a new building of which only a plan was submitted (Pl. 63). The estimated cost of this was £85,000.

That nothing came of projects so carefully worked out and so long deliberated was due to events, not in England, but in Europe. War with Spain, ending the long peace of Walpole's administration, had broken out in 1739, and in 1741 it merged in the costly war of the Austrian Succession. Walpole was driven from office in 1742, and his successors had their hands full of more pressing matters. The years of war, ending with the Peace of Aix-la-Chapelle in 1748—the year of Kent's death—left the country heavily burdened with debt, and it was not until 1753 that the government once more showed any interest in the building projects of the 1730s. At that time the Treasury was considering the erection of a building in St. Margaret's Lane to house the records of the Court of King's Bench, and asked 'to have all the designs laid before them that are in this Office, and have been intended to be built in Westminster'.[3] John Vardy (whose hand can be recognised in several of the later drawings) was accordingly deputed to take to the Treasury not only the design for

---

[1] Works 6/16, f. 103ᵛ.

[2] Mr. Fiske Kimball thought that the purpose of this was to preserve the old buildings. But it is difficult to believe that anyone in 1739 seriously wished to do so, and the effect of leaving them standing within a few feet of the grand facade of the new building would have been ludicrous. It seems more likely that the **real** motive was to enlarge Old Palace Yard sufficiently to accommodate the Members' coaches, lack of space for which was a perennial problem (cg. Works 6/16, f. 135).

[3] Works 4/11, 12 Nov. 1753. By then the drawings in the Office included 32 designs for the Parliament House by Kent which had been acquired after his death from his executor Stephen Wright. A list of them in Works 4/10 (22 Nov. 1749) evidently includes some which survive, but at least one (No. 19, 'Plan and Elevation of the Great Staircase') can no longer be found.

the Record Office, but also 'a General Plan of Westminster, with the new intended Plan of the House of Lords and Commons drawn upon it, and parts that adjoin Palace Yard', together with 'a book containing all the Plans, Elevations & Sections as designed by Mr. Kent (and drawn by him) for a new House of Lords & Commons, being the same as was laid before their Lordships Anno 1739, with the original Memorial thereto annexed'.[1] In the 'new inended plan' we can probably recognise a reference to a modified proposal in which the old Court of Requests and the Painted Chamber are preserved, but are embedded in a new building for the two Houses which externally retains the principal features of the scheme of 1739. This, however, may already have been obsolete, and if so the 'new intended plan' of 1753 could have been one in which nothing of the grand design remains but the arcaded front, some-what reduced in length, and serving, not to give access to a great new structure, but merely to mask the untidy front of the old parliamentary buildings. Even this was not carried out, and at the beginning of the nineteenth century the only legacy of Kent's great scheme was the Palladian facade to St. Margaret's Lane, built after his death by Vardy and Couse to their own designs, and in any case representing only a secondary feature of the proposals of 1739.[2]

## 11. THE NEW STONE BUILDING

When Kent died in 1748 his great design had been shelved for nearly ten years, and the likelihood that it would ever be carried out was becoming more and more remote. Between 1755 and 1770, however, a series of new government buildings was erected on the east side of St. Margaret's Lane whose plan and elevations were in general conformity to what had been envisaged by Kent and his colleagues for the architectural treatment of that part of the palace. In its ultimate form this 'new stone building' is familiar from views by Malton, Capon and Carter (Pl. 64). Though it presented one regular Palladian facade to the street, and another to Old Palace Yard, it was in fact of piecemeal construction, and served a variety of purposes, legal, parliamentary and administrative.

The central part of the building was the first to be erected, and its purpose was to provide a depository for the records of the Court of King's Bench. These had for long been housed in a building known as the Upper Treasury which stood on the south side of Fish Yard near the south-west corner of the Great Hall.[3] As long ago as 1739 Sir William Lee, Chief Justice of the King's Bench, had complained that this room was 'so very old, decay'd and in so ruinous a condition' that it ought to be

---

[1] Works 4/11, 12 Nov. 1753. Works 29/3358 may well be the volume submitted.

[2] For the building in St. Margaret's Lane see below ('The New Stone Building').

[3] It appears on survey-plans prepared by or for Wren and reproduced in *Wren Soc.* xi, pls. 33–5. The character of the fenestration indicated in these plans suggests that it was built in the 15th or 16th centuries, but no record of its erection has been discovered. From a petition to the Privy Council in 1662 it would appear that it was soon after the Restoration that the king's Store of Fish and Salt was ousted from the building to give way to legal records (PC 2/56, f. 73$^v$), but the records were still being abused by the king's Fishmonger in the reign of Queen Anne (*Cal. Treasury Books* xxv, p. 444).

rebuilt. The Office of Works had concurred, but its estimate of £2775 for erecting a new building on the same site 'in a substantial good manner' had not received Treasury approval, and in 1749 Lee had renewed his petition.[1] The Board, to whom the document was referred, again estimated the cost of rebuilding at £2775, but added that 'if your Lordships should be of opinion, that a Record Office of the King's Bench should be built, where it will be part of a general Design for all the Courts of Justice (the Court of Common Pleas being already built upon that general design a plan of which is hereunto annext)' the cost would be about £4452.[2] This report was accompanied by a site-plan, half of which has unfortunately been lost. Enough, however, survives to show that what was envisaged was a building facing onto St. Margaret's Lane approximately in the position ultimately selected. The Treasury realised that the decision they were called upon to make was one of some importance, for it involved the acceptance in principle of the 'general design' for the area to the west of Westminster Hall referred to by the Board. The planning of this area had recently been given a new significance by the activities of the Commissioners established in 1736 to build Westminster Bridge. Their function was not only to get the bridge built, but also to widen and improve the streets leading up to it, and giving access to the Courts of Justice and to the Houses of Parliament, for which purpose they had power to acquire land.[3] New Palace Yard had already been much altered by the building of the bridge. The Great Gate in its north-west corner had been pulled down in 1707, and in 1728 the lesser gateway at the top of St. Margaret's Lane had likewise been removed by the Office of Works in the interests of wheeled traffic.[4] Further to the south the Commissioners had purchased the Bertie estate and were laying out Abingdon Street as a formal southern approach to the palace.[5] The old Westminster of courtyards and gateways was giving way to the new Westminster of paved streets lined by regularly built houses. In this context the narrow lane between St. Margaret's Church and the irregular conglomeration of buildings on the west side of Westminster Hall was an anomaly which could no longer be tolerated. Several of the buildings in question were, moreover, known to be old, inconvenient and in bad repair. After due deliberation the Lords of the Treasury accordingly instructed the Board in June 1751 to prepare plans not only for a new building to house the King's Bench records, but also to contain the records of the Exchequer, Remembrancer's, Pipe, Augmentations and Tally Offices, and to accommodate the Auditors of the Imprests and the Usher and Clerks of the Exchequer. After conferring with the Chief Justice and the Chief Baron of the Exchequer, the Board submitted a comprehensive plan with an explanatory letter, part of which must be quoted at length:

> We therefore humbly lay before your Lordships the said design as was shewed to them; the middle part we think should be first built, which will contain the records of the King's Bench on the first floor, and will be contiguous to the Chambers of the

---

[1] Works 6/16, ff. 99, 103; Works 6/17, ff. 60ᵛ–61; Works 12/58/7.
[2] Works 12/58/7; Works 6/17, ff. 60ᵛ–61.
[3] *Statutes at Large*, vol. 6 (1764), p. 376.    [4] Above, p. 386.
[5] Works 6/16, f. 135ᵛ. The activities of the Commissioners are fully documented in their own minutes, now Works 6/28–62.

Lord Chief Justice and other judges of the King's Bench; the basement story of the building will contain the Tally and other Offices on the ground floor, between the new middle building and Exchequer Court. The attick story of this building and story above will contain all the offices, papers and records that are one pair of stairs and upwards between the Exchequer Court and new middle building. The charge of this will be about the sum of £4452, and will take two years to complete it.

The building between the middle part and Court of Exchequer will cost about the sum of £4000, and will contain the greatest part of records and offices now in another part of the old building: when that is done the third part of the building at the end of the Exchequer Court which we propose to build in the same stile as the north end of Westminster Hall, which building will cost about the sum of £3500, and will contain all the rest of the papers, records and offices.

We have likewise examined and considered what ground or buildings is in the way of the new buildings proposed, and find that there is on the ground where the middle part will stand a publick house, which is the king's and an old ruinous house and some ground which has been purchased by the Commissioners of the Bridge. We have treated with the said Commissioners and they agree to let the Crown have all the ground they purchased between St. Margaret's Lane and Westminster Hall in consideration of the ground on which the building stands that is between the two Palace Yards, which they desire to be taken down.

There is likewise a small piece of ground and a little old building upon it, which we are told is freehold, belonging to Mr. Walker, Usher of the Law Exchequer; he being out of town, we could not treat with him for it; but this can't be wanted in less time than two or three years.

We propose the whole front to be built of Portland Stone and if this plan is approved by your Lordships the expence will be about the sum of £11,952, and will be six years in completing.[1]

The original plan is no longer extant among the Treasury papers, but in Sir John Soane's Museum there are a number of plans, copied from originals then in the Office of Works, but since lost, which show what the Board had in mind.[2] They all envisage a composition of the standard Palladian character, with a central block flanked by lower wings terminating in pavilions. They also show how the awkwardly projecting Augmentation Office building was to be removed at the request of the Bridge Commissioners, and how the end elevation of the old Exchequer Court was to be tactfully made good by a Gothic building with octagonal buttresses at the angles. No elevations have been preserved, but their character can be guessed from Kent's designs for the projected Houses of Parliament, and from the building actually erected. There is nothing in the Board's minutes to indicate by whom the drawings were made, but in 1762 John Vardy exhibited at the Society of Artists 'A Design for the Court of King's Bench Records etc. in St. Margaret's Lane, Westminster, [made] in 1753, when Clerk of the Works at Westminster'. This may have been an alternative design, but as many of the surviving drawings of Kent's projects for the Houses of Parliament are in Vardy's hand, he is very likely to have been the member of the Office entrusted with the new building. In this connection

[1] Works 6/17, ff. 77ᵛ–78; T 29/31, pp. 243, 261, 376.
[2] Drawer 35, Sets 1 and 2.

it may be significant that when, in November 1753, the Treasury asked to see all the drawings connected with the project, it was Vardy who was deputed to deliver them to their Lordships.[1]

Nearly a year elapsed before Treasury approval was received for the construction of the first stage, at an estimated cost of £4452, and three more before the whole of the site was cleared and ready for the foundations to be laid.[2] Though it was entirely in their own interests that the building should go forward, the Westminster Bridge Commissioners took their time over the execution of the necessary conveyances, and in the end, prompted by a new Lord Chief Justice, the Board had to get the Commissioners to agree to allow work to start before the documents had been exchanged.[3] The foundations were laid in the summer of 1755, and thereafter the building rose steadily until the final account was passed in September 1758.[4] It was not, however, until 1760 that the interior was at last fitted up for the reception of the records, whose former home was by now so ruinous that they were suffering from exposure to the weather.[5] Only the main floors were required for the legal records: the basement was allocated to the Paymaster of Exchequer Bills, who also enjoyed the use of one of the rooms on the second storey.[6] Later, in 1771, the Auditors of Imprests obtained a room in the upper storey for their records, but the two remaining rooms were supposed to be reserved for the records of the Augmentation Office, whose premises were destined for demolition in accordance with the terms of the agreement with the Commissioners of Westminster Bridge.[7]

Meanwhile the new building stood alone in Palladian dignity amid the decayed relics of the ancient palace. Immediately to the north there was a vacant space upon which, in 1773, the Board erected some 'temporary' sheds to protect the judges' coaches.[8] To the south there was another empty space, and beyond that a coffee-house and various old houses, including one occupied by Sir Henry Cheere, the sculptor. According to the programme accepted by the Treasury in 1752 the 'centre building' was to be extended northwards in two stages in order to house the various Exchequer records. No reference was made to the southern extension shown on the plans, although symmetry clearly demanded that it should ultimately be built. In the event the southern extension took priority, and the northern one was postponed until 1821, when the whole Exchequer area was rebuilt to the designs of John Soane.

The initiative for extending the building southwards came from a department that was connected with neither the Law nor the Exchequer. This was the Board of Ordnance, which had once had an office in Old Palace Yard adjoining the Jewel Tower. In 1753 it had been obliged to move in order to allow for the expansion of the Parliament Office, and had built for itself another office on the east side of the Yard close to the House of Lords. In 1766 it was again given notice to move as the Lords wanted to convert its office into committee rooms.[9] On 27 May of that year the Board of Ordnance addressed a letter to the Treasury rehearsing these facts and

---

[1] Works 4/11, 12 Nov. 1753. In the P.R.O. there is a site-plan made by Vardy in 1753 (MPE 489).
[2] Treasury approval was received on 13 May 1752 (Works 6/17, f. 78ᵛ).
[3] Works 6/17, ff. 97, 102ᵛ; Works 4/11, 23 Jan., 6 Feb. 1753; Works 1/3, ff. 108–9.
[4] Works 4/11, 13 May, 12 Aug. 1755, 30 March, 28 Sept. 1756; Works 4/12, 28 June 1757, 5 Sept. 1758.
[5] Works 4/12, 15 Jan. 1760.                               [6] Works 4/12, 29 April 1760.
[7] Works 4/14, 6 April 1770; Works 6/18, p. 267.
[8] Works 6/18, pp. 312–13.                                 [9] Above, p. 399.

asking for a lease of 37 feet of the 'ground next adjoining to Sir Henry Cheere's' in order to erect another office. The Treasury consented, on the understanding that the new building should form part of the general scheme already accepted in principle.[1] On any other site the Ordnance Board would no doubt have erected the building itself. But in this case it was agreed that the work should be carried out on its behalf by the Board of Works. On 11 June 1766 the Board of Works was able to inform the Treasury that the plan had been seen and approved by Sir Charles Frederick, the Surveyor of the Ordnance, and that the estimate for its construction was £2650. Work began almost immediately and the key of the completed building was handed over to a representative of the Ordnance in February 1769. The total cost, defrayed by the Ordnance, was £3068.[2] The new building had a facade of five bays corresponding in style to that of the centre block already erected (Pl. 64). The mason employed was William Jelfe. Joseph Pratt was the bricklayer and John Phillips the carpenter.[3]

The next step in this slow-moving programme of architectural improvement was obviously to build the south-west corner pavilion and the return eastwards to the Court of Requests. This would bring the new building into the territory of the House of Commons, and it was in fact in response to the needs of the Commons that this extension was built in 1768–70. In November 1766 a committee had been appointed to 'consider the passages leading to and from this House', and had, in consultation with Kenton Couse, the new Clerk of Works at Westminster, considered various plans for a new building containing 'a staircase, rooms and passages for the accommodation of this House . . . conformable to the Building now carrying on for the Office of Ordnance'. The intention was to provide a new entrance to the House from Old Palace Yard, a series of new committee rooms, and, in the attic, temporary accommodation for the records of the Augmentation Office while that building was being pulled down and rebuilt in accordance with the general scheme. The committee recommended the adoption of plans and elevations marked B, C and D. These were ordered to be preserved with the report, but were destroyed in the fire of 1834. The estimate for their execution was £4150.[4] The result was an Act 'for rendering the ways and passages to the House of Commons more open, safe and commodious', which received the royal assent on 29 June 1767. The purpose of this Act was to enable the Commissioners of Westminster Bridge to acquire the premises still in private hands and to spend up to £2000 on 'carrying on an additional building for a more commodious passage to the House of Commons'.[5] It is not clear why the House chose to employ the Bridge Commissioners rather than the Office of Works, which had already erected the northern part of the building in question, and which had actually provided the plans which were now to be executed by another body. But Kenton Couse, who had prepared the drawings as Clerk of the Works at Westminster, was authorised by the Commissioners to act as their 'Agent and

---

[1] P.R.O. Ordnance Board Minutes, W.O. 47/67, pp. 381, 454–5; Works 6/18, f. 137.
[2] Works 6/18, ff. 137–8; Works 4/14, 6 Feb., 13 March, 29 May 1768; Works 1/4, p. 75. Works 29/4 is a drawing of the elevation made a few years later by K. Couse.
[3] Works 1/4, p. 63.
[4] *Commons' Journals*, xxxi, pp. 29–30, 113–14. Drawings of the elevations by Couse are among the Works records (Works 29/1 and 2).
[5] *Statutes of the Realm*, vol. 10 (1771), p. 303.

Surveyor' in implementing the Act, so the actual supervision of the work was in the same hands whichever expedient was adopted. From Couse's point of view the arrangement adopted had one great advantage: as surveyor to the Commissioners he received 5 per cent on all the bills, whereas as an official of the Office of Works he could at best have expected some sort of honorarium in recognition of his extra trouble.[1]

By 1768 Cheere and the other private occupants had been bought out, while the proprietor of Alice's Coffee House had agreed to surrender his premises in return for the promise of accommodation in the new building equivalent to what he had given up.[2] The building appears to have been substantially completed by March 1770, when the House of Commons appointed a select committee to inspect the new approach to the House.[3] In the end the outlay amounted to some £12,000, and two further Acts had to be passed in 1768 and 1769 to cover the expenditure. The cost of the building itself was about £7300, the balance being accounted for chiefly by the purchase of property to clear the site. William Jelfe and John Phillips were again employed as mason and carpenter respectively, the bricklayer being Thomas Churchill.[4] The undertaking to Peter Wells, the proprietor of Alice's Coffee House, was rather belatedly honoured in 1770–1 by the erection of a three-storey brick building in the north-east angle of Old Palace Yard, where the new building abutted on the Court of Requests. This coffee house is clearly seen in an engraving of 1796 (Vol. VI, Pl. 37A). Its southern elevation was later obscured by Soane's additions to the House of Lords, and, with them, it perished in the fire of 1834. Its first floor had by then been turned into a committee room for the House of Commons.[5]

By 1770, therefore, the new building in St. Margaret's Street was complete to the extent shown in the plan of 1793 (Vol. VI, Fig. 19). It comprised, from north to south, the King's Bench Records and Exchequer Bill Offices, the Ordnance Office, and the new extension to the House of Commons, consisting of an entrance arcade on the ground floor with committee rooms above. Architecturally, the 'general design' of 1752 had still to be completed by the demolition of the old Augmentations Office building and the erection of the balancing northern wing. Despite the inconvenience to traffic, and frequent reminders from the Westminster Bridge Commissioners,[6] it was not until 1793 that the Augmentations Office was removed, and another thirty years elapsed before Soane at last completed the facade first envisaged by Kent in 1739.

Meanwhile the Commons' insatiable demand for committee rooms had once more led to the Ordnance Office being given notice to quit. In 1774 a select com-

---

[1] Works 6/35, p. 588. In 1787 it was stated that 'Mr. Couse was employed as Architect by the House of Commons under the direction of the Commissioners' (Works 6/36, f. 523 *et seq*). The relations between Commons, Couse and the Commissioners are discussed by O. Williams, *The Topography of the Old House of Commons* (typescript 1953), pp. 13–14.

[2] Williams, *op. cit.*

[3] *Commons' Journals*, xxxii, p. 839. The recommendations of this committee, which resulted in various internal alterations, are best understood by reference to the plans and sections made in 1834, just before the fire (Works 29/20). By then the attics, originally reserved for the temporary accommodation of the Augmentation Office records, had been converted into a flat for the Commons' housekeeper.

[4] Works 6/210 (the account of expenditure by the Commissioners under the Act); Works 6/36, pp. 54, 110, 119.

[5] Williams, *op. cit.*, p. 14.

[6] Works 6/35, pp. 175, 303, 321, 414, 514, 548; Works 6/36, p. 94.

mittee, looking for further space for expansion, observed that 'it would tend further to the accommodation of Committees if the Building at present occupied by the Office of Ordnance was appropriated to the use of this House'.[1] Four years later the Board of Ordnance accordingly purchased a site on the other side of the road immediately to the east of St. Margaret's Church, and erected yet another office, designed this time by its own surveyor, William Tyler, R.A.[2] To this they removed in the spring of 1780, leaving their former building to be used by the House of Commons partly as committee rooms and partly as the residence of John Ley, the Clerk Assistant to the House.[3]

# WHITEHALL

## 1. THE TREASURY

IN 1732 the state of the buildings occupied by the Treasury gave cause for alarm. Having had the structure viewed by 'His Majesty's most experienced workmen', the Board reported on 3 August that 'in our opinion as well as theirs [it] is in so very ruinous & dangerous a condition that we don't think it safe for your Lordships to continue in it'.[4] They suggested that the Lottery Office on the south side of the Banqueting House might be fitted up as a temporary Treasury while the old one was being rebuilt. Their lordships agreed to this suggestion, and resolved meanwhile to meet in Walpole's house in Arlington Street until the Lottery Office was ready for their reception.[5]

Steps were at once taken for the erection of a new building. These included the buying in of certain adjoining premises in the occupation of Mrs. Edith College, which would 'very much obstruct the conveniences and carrying up of the said offices'.[6] The purchase was completed in the course of the summer of 1733, and on 2 August the Board submitted plans and elevations for the new building. They

---

[1] *Commons' Journals*, xxxiv, p. 809.

[2] This building was in turn swept away by the Westminster Improvement Commissioners in 1805, whereupon the Ordnance Office moved to premises in Pall Mall.

[3] Williams, *op. cit.*, pp. 14–15.

[4] Works 6/15, p. 257; T 56/18, p. 399.

[5] *London Survey*, vol. xiv, pp. 29–30. The Lottery Office was evidently ready by December, when the Board passed the bills 'for making a new Treasury at the end of the Banqueting House' (Works 4/5, 19 Dec. 1732). When the new Treasury was completed the Lottery Office was fitted up as an office for the Secretary of State (Works 4/8, 9 March 1742). It remained in use for this purpose until 1771, and was demolished in 1782 (*London Survey*, vol. xiii, p. 222).

[6] *Cal. Treasury Books & Papers 1731–4*, p. 377.

estimated that 'the expence of carrying up and covering in the carcase of the building' would be about £8000, 'the two fronts to the Park being wholly stone'. Walpole reported that the plans had been approved by the king, and on 14 August the Board received authority to proceed.[1] John Mist had already undertaken to pull down the old Treasury and clear away the materials for £456.[2] Flitcroft, as Clerk of Works at Whitehall, was officially responsible for supervising the operation,[3] but in October the Board, 'thinking it necessary that a person should allways be upon the spot, to take the dementions of timber, stone, and other materials as they are laid, and considering the Clerk of the Works' business cannot permit him to be always there; and the Labourer in Trust being advanced in years, and incapable of his business, do order and appoint Robert Newton to assist the Clerk of the Works to be always on the spot, and give an account every night to the said Clerk of the Works, what dementions hee has taken'.[4]

The foundations were probably dug during the autumn of 1733, and the walls were evidently complete by the end of 1735. During the intervening months the surface of Horse Guards Parade had been broken up by the 'frequent passage of carts, loaden with stone and other heavy materials', but by January 1736 a Treasury minute could call for the restoration of the park 'to its Beauty and Convenience' now that the building 'is so far compleated as no longer to require passage for materials of those heavy kinds'.[5] On 10 May 1737 the Board of Works 'past the bills for works done at the new Treasury except the carver's bill', and a week later the carver's bill was also passed.[6] The accounts themselves have not been preserved, but the total cost, as recorded in the Paymaster's books, was just over £20,000.[7] The principal craftsmen concerned were Thomas Churchill (bricklayer), Andrews Jelfe (mason), Thomas Phillips (carpenter), George Worrall (plasterer), John Smallwell (joiner), James Richards (carver) and George Devall (plumber).[8]

Though the Board's minutes are silent as to the authorship of the design, there can be no doubt that it was the work of William Kent, then Master Carpenter and soon to be Deputy Surveyor. In December 1734 Sir Thomas Robinson praised Kent's design in a letter to Lord Carlisle, and sent him 'the upright of it'.[9] This was probably a copy of an engraving by Fourdrinier showing the north facade of 'His Majesty's New Building near Whitehall intended for the Treasury &c. As designed by W. Kent 1734'.[10] This shows a facade of 15 bays, of which only the central portion, seven bays in width, was actually built. With this important difference, the engraving corresponds almost exactly to the existing building (Pl. 66).[11] No doubt Kent hoped that at some later date the building might be extended to the full length shown in the engraving, but the treatment of the western return is sufficiently elaborate to

[1] *Cal. Treasury Books & Papers 1731–4*, pp. 394, 397; Works 6/16, p. 8.
[2] Works 4/5, 27 March 1733.
[3] In July 1733 '4 plans and 2 elevations of the new Treasury' were delivered to him (Works 4/5, 27 July 1733).
[4] Works 4/6, 2 Oct. 1733.                          [5] *London Survey*, vol. xiv, p. 30 (note).
[6] Works 4/7, 10 and 17 May 1737.                   [7] Works 5/141, years 1732–8.
[8] Works 5/58 (1732–4), Works 5/59 (1734–6, 1738, June and Dec.).
[9] Hist. MSS. Comm., *Carlisle*, p. 144.
[10] Reproduced in *London Survey*, vol. xiv, pl. 11.
[11] For measured drawings &c. see *London Survey*, vol. xiv, pls. 12–35, 82–5. There are 18th-century plans of the building in Bodleian Library, Gough Maps 22, ff. 26ᵛ–27.

indicate that this eventuality must have been regarded as remote. The three-storey composition is related to designs by Inigo Jones for Whitehall Palace and Somerset House, and the extensive use of rusticated masonry (intended, no doubt, to express the security of a royal treasury) had Palladian precedent.

No details of the expenditure on the interior decoration are forthcoming from the Paymaster's accounts, but the original design for the chimneypiece in the Board Room is preserved in the Victoria & Albert Museum. The upper part, showing the overmantel, is in Kent's hand, and is endorsed 'For the Treasury W K 1737'. The lower part, showing the fireplace, is in a different hand, believed to be that of John Vardy.[1] The furnishing of the new rooms was not the responsibility of the Office of Works, and if any of the chairs and tables attributed to William Kent were in fact designed by him, the evidence must be sought elsewhere than in the Works accounts.[2] The iron railings which protect the windows of the basement storey were made in 1740 at a cost of £60 17s.[3]

## 2. THE HORSE GUARDS

The history of the English standing army begins after the Restoration of Charles II, when a regiment of Foot Guards and two troops of Horse Guards were created for the king's personal protection. It was for the accommodation of these Life Guards—both mounted and unmounted—that the building now known as the Horse Guards was erected. Though the palace over which they watch has long disappeared, the two sentries on duty still perpetuate the measures taken for the security of the sovereign in the time of Charles II.

The original Horse Guards Building was erected in 1663–4 on a site formerly occupied by the Tilt Yard. The ground floor consisted largely of stabling for the horses, and on the first floor there were rooms for the officers and for the Judge Advocate-General. The way through to St. James's Park was dignified by a gateway in the form of a pavilion whose hipped roof carried a clock-turret surmounted by a leaded lantern (Pl. 35). The building cost just over £4000, and was accounted for by Sir Stephen Fox as Paymaster-General of the Forces.[4] Most of the master-craftsmen employed were, however, Patent Artisans or men regularly employed on the king's works.[5] Moreover it was the Master Carpenter and the Clerk of the Works

---

[1] Harold Barkley, 'A Kent-Vardy Collaboration', *Country Life*, 13 Oct. 1960. The drawing is numbered 3436.199.

[2] On the dating and authorship of the furniture, see W. A. Thorpe, 'Tradition in Treasury Furniture', *Country Life*, 5–12 Jan., 1951.

[3] Works 5/141, year 1740.

[4] AO 1/48/11. One copy of the accounts is in Works 5/4. Another passed into the possession of George Clarke, Secretary at War 1692–1704, and is now MS. 68 in the Library of Worcester College, Oxford. Guardhouses were erected at the same time in the Old Granary in Scotland Yard and by the Jewel House in Whitehall. There is a sectional drawing of the Old Granary Guard-house in Westminster Public Library, Box 11, no. 6 B.

[5] The bricklayer was Maurice Emmett, the carpenter John Angier. Joshua Marshall was the mason, Peter Brent the plumber, Robert Streater the painter and Thomas Kinward the joiner.

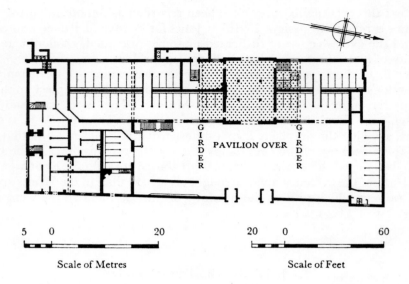

GIRDER  PAVILION OVER  GIRDER

5   0        20        20   0        60

Scale of Metres          Scale of Feet

Fig. 33. Whitehall: plan of the old Horse Guards Building (based on P.R.O., Works 30/168, 169).

KEY TO FIGURE 34

| | | | |
|---|---|---|---|
| 1 | Commissary General | 14 | Quarter Master |
| 2 | Secretary at War | 15 | Orderly Rooms |
| 3 | Court Martial Room | 16 | Foot Guard Rooms |
| 4 | Judge Advocate General | 17 | Magazine |
| 5 | Paymaster General | 18 | Offices of Secretary at War |
| 6 | Chapel | 19 | Judge Advocate's Offices |
| 7 | Surveyor's Apartment | 20 | Horse Guards |
| 8 | Comptroller of the Army Accounts | 21 | Stables |
| 9 | Waiting Room | 22 | Barber |
| 10 | Horseguards | 23 | Gunsmith |
| 11 | Coffee House | 24 | Foot Sutlers |
| 12 | Arms Gallery | 25 | Coffee House |
| 13 | Horse Officers | 26 | Horse Sutlers |

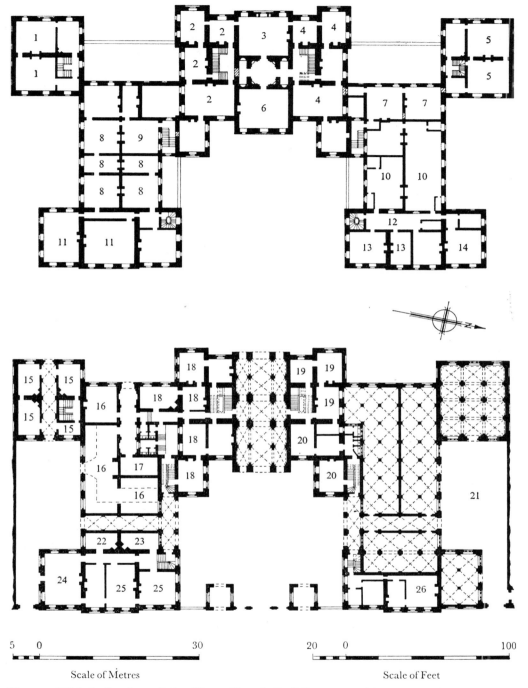

Fig. 34. Whitehall: plan of the Horse Guards Building erected in 1750–9 (from *Vitruvius Britannicus* v, 1771, plates 3–4).

Scale of Metres

Scale of Feet

at Whitehall who measured their workmanship, and their bills were certified by Sir John Denham and the other Officers of the Works.

Though the building was thus not erected without recourse to the Officers of the Works, it did not pass under their jurisdiction, but remained the responsibility of the Secretary at War, who appointed a surveyor of his own to look after it.[1] Whether the Office of Works was in any way responsible for its design it is impossible to say, for the accounts include no payment for any 'draught' or 'model'. In the course of time, however, it became apparent that the building suffered from an inherent weakness. The north and south walls of the central pavilion were not carried down to the ground, but stood on timber girders spanning the walls of the stables below (Fig. 33). Owing to the great weight of superincumbent brickwork these girders eventually failed, and by the reign of George II the brickwork above was described as 'entirely disjointed'. Only by means of props and shores was the whole building prevented from collapsing onto the stables below. Externally the decay of the structure was 'so obvious that it wants no Description to shew its weakness'. Internally the principals of the roof were decayed, and the cupola was in danger of falling.[2]

It was the colonels of the two troops of Horse Guards, Lords Delawarr and Cadogan, who took the first steps which resulted in the erection of a new building. Early in 1745 they joined with the Judge Advocate-General to represent to Sir William Yonge, the Secretary at War, that the whole building was in 'a very rotten and decayed condition and having been supported many years by props . . . is now become so dangerous that it is not safe for the Coaches of his Majesty and the Royal Family to pass under the Gateway, and the Men and Horses doing duty there, are in perpetual danger of loosing their lives by the falling down of the Buildings'. Yonge passed the petition on to the Treasury, who referred it to the Board of Works. The Board had no difficulty in confirming that the building was both 'dangerous and incapable of being repaired', and on 11 July received an order from the Treasury 'to consider of and prepare a plan for the rebuilding of the same . . . and to lay the same before them, with an Estimate of the Expense thereof'.[3] At this time the Board consisted of Henry Finch (Surveyor), Thomas Ripley (Comptroller), William Kent and Westby Gill, and it was evidently to Kent that the task of making the design was entrusted. No formal minute to this effect can be cited, but one early design for the building by Kent has been preserved (Pl. 65A), and in 1752 John Vardy inscribed 'Wm. Kent Invt.' below the plate of the west front which he dedicated to the Surveyor-General.[4] Kent was undoubtedly the most able designer in the Office at the time, and as the architect of the adjoining Treasury Building he was the obvious person to draw up plans for any new government building on that side of Whitehall. Owing no doubt to the Scottish rising and the War of the Austrian Succession his designs were not submitted to the Treasury before his death in April 1748, and some

---

[1] The earlier holders of this office, who combined it with the surveyorship of Chelsea Hospital, were Roger Hewitt (to 1698), Charles Hopson (d. 1710), Hugh Warren (d. 1728) and John Lane (d. 1753). It was the last-named who in 1732–3 was responsible for building the new Paymaster-General's Office on the northern side of the Horse Guards adjoining the Amiralty (*Survey of London*, xvi, pp. 17–18).

[2] Works 4/17, f. 4; Works 6/17, ff. 4ᵛ, 6.

[3] Works 4/9, 11, 20 and 27 June, 1745; Works 6/17, ff. 4ᵛ, 6.

[4] Reproduced in *Survey of London*, vol. xvi, pl. 3, from Bodleian, Gough Maps 22, f. 24.

of them remained in the hands of his assistant Stephen Wright until the following year, when a complete set of plans and elevations for the Horse Guards was among a number of Kent's drawings sold by Wright to the Office of Works.[1] In the summer of 1749, however, following the Peace of Aix-la-Chapelle, the Board was once more called upon by the Treasury 'to lay before their Lordships a Plan for rebuilding the Horse Guards, together with an Estimate'.[2] Henry Fox, now Secretary at War, attended a Board meeting on 11 July, 'look'd over the plans and elevations in this office intended for Building the Horse Guards', and asked for a plan to be made of the old building 'as it now is that the same may be laid with the new Designs before Mr. Pelham'.[3] On 9 August 1749 the Board 'considered and made several alterations to the Plan intended for the New Horse Guards', and on 5 September they transmitted a set of drawings to the Treasury with an explanatory letter. The building which they envisaged was much more than a mere guard-house; in fact it was really a new War Office, for the plan provided for the accommodation on the site not only of the Horse and Foot Guards, but also of the Secretary at War, the Judge Advocate-General and the Commissioners of Chelsea Hospital, together with a chapel and a room for holding courts martial. The chapel was to be on the first floor of the central building on the side facing Whitehall, the Court Martial Room on the same floor overlooking the park. On either side a suite of rooms was planned, that on the south being allocated to the Secretary at War, that on the north to the Judge Advocate-General. The Guards' quarters were to be in the wings, nearly the whole of the ground floor of the north wing being occupied by the vaulted stables of the Horse Guards, while the Foot Guards were accommodated in the south wing (Fig. 34). 'As', the Board concluded, 'this will be a Publick Building, and fronts the one way to the King's Park, and the other way to the great passage leading to the two Houses of Parliament, we propose it to be built in a very substantial Manner, and the whole faced with Portland Stone.' They estimated that it would take four years to build and that the total cost would be £31,748.[4]

Meanwhile temporary stables for the Horse Guards were being erected by the War Office in the neighbourhood of Buckingham House.[5] By March 1750 the Guards were in their new quarters, but no official order to proceed with the new building had been received. In April the Board of Works accordingly addressed a memorial to the Treasury on the subject:

> If the Designs for the Horse Guards meets with your Lordships' approbation we humbly think it will be necessary that Orders be given to proceed, and we think in the following manner
>
> First that two able Clerks be appointed with a Labourer in Trust . . . to keep Accompts of Stores and Deliver them out as the Clerks on duty shall direct, at such an Allowance as shall be thought proper.

[1] Works 4/10, 22 Nov. 1749.　　　　　　　　[2] Works 6/63, 4 July 1749.
[3] Works 4/10, 11 July 1749. The drawings in question are evidently Works 30/168–170, which form the basis of Fig. 33.
[4] Works 6/17, f. 57. For plans see Works 30/171–182 (reproduced in *Survey of London*, vol. xvi, pls. 5–11), and Woolfe & Gandon, *Vitruvius Britannicus*, vol. v (1771), pls. 3–4. For some criticism of the accommodation provided for the Guards, see a memorial submitted to Lord Barrington by Lords Delawarr and Cadogan some time after Barrington had succeeded Henry Fox as Secretary at War in November 1755 (T 1/339/42A).
[5] *Survey of London*, vol. xvi, p. 11.

We propose that two of the Clerks of His Majesty's Works should be the Clerks appointed who are to make all Drawings for the Workmen as they are directed, see the Works carefully sett out, Measure all the Works, and make up the severall Accompts. . . .

We think that the center Building should be first begun on, that it may be got up two Storeys high, before November next, that a proper Passage may be made for His Majesty &c. to pass through; the Stables may be going on at the same time.

We believe that all the new Building between the present Foot Guards & Pay Office may be covered in before November 1751; And completely finished before Xmas 1752. That the Foot Guards may then be moved to over the new Stables, and the Officers into the center building, and remain there till the Building for the Foot Guards is finished; which we think may be done before Xmas 1754. Provided Moneys be Advanced as the Works go on, clear of all Charges.[1]

On the following day the Board was summoned to attend at the Treasury in order to discuss the plans with the Chancellor of the Exchequer (Henry Pelham) and his colleagues. The result was a minute expressing their lordships' opinion 'that as the pulling down and rebuilding the Horse Guards is a matter of great Consequence to the Public and will be a considerable Expence, it should be put under the care, management and Inspection of the Board of Works'. The plans were then submitted to the king, whose approval having been obtained, the Board was authorised (24 April) 'to proceed forthwith, in causing the present Building to be pulled down, and erecting the new Building with all Expedition'. In the course of the next fortnight the Board appointed John Vardy and William Robinson as joint clerks of works and considered which craftsmen to employ. The method of selection is not clear from the minutes, but most of those chosen were men well-known to the Board, and some of them were Patent Artisans. The principal names were those of Andrews and William Jelfe, who were to share the masonry with John Carr;[2] Ralph Crutcher, bricklayer; Kemble Whatley, Strickland Holden and John Richardson, carpenters; John Devall, plumber; and Richard Minns, glazier. John Lane, the surveyor to the former building, was to be employed as a joiner, but died in 1753 before doing any work on the new one. Joseph Pickford, a mason recently employed by Henry Pelham to build his house in Arlington Street, was subsequently added to the list at Pelham's request, and built the north wing.[3] The Board also received and approved a petition from the Master Carver, James Richards, to perform the carver's work in conjunction with his grandson James Ware.[4] The workmen's remuneration was calculated by measure at the standard Office of Works rates, and there were no contracts for work by the great. The money advanced for the purpose by the Exchequer was not accounted for by Denzil Onslow as Paymaster of the Works, but was handled by a specially appointed Paymaster. This was John Calcraft, a protégé of Henry Fox, the Secretary at War, who made a fortune for himself by military contracts and pay-

---

[1] Works 6/17, f. 62ᵛ.

[2] Works 6/63, 29 June 1751. Carr's name duly appears in the records up to 1757, when Joseph Carr took his place.

[3] Works 6/63, 26 April, 1 and 8 May 1750.

[4] Works 6/63, 7 Aug. 1750. Richards's assistant George Murray subsequently took his place as Richards became incapable owing to age.

mastership.[1] In this case he was allowed, with Pelham's approval, to make a levy of 5 per cent. on all the tradesmen's bills in order 'to pay fees of Office'.[2] As the expenditure on the Horse Guards eventually exceeded £65,000, the appointment must have been worth at least £3000 to Calcraft.

Although the practical arrangements were thus settled, it still remained to determine many features of the design. Unfortunately only one of Kent's own drawings is known to have survived (Pl. 65A), and this, an elevation to the Park, does not necessarily represent his final proposal: indeed, it is likely that it is an early sketch rather than one of the numbered drawings which the Board acquired from Stephen Wright in 1749. It is therefore impossible to say how fully Kent's proposals had been worked out before his death, or how far they were subsequently modified. But even after it had been submitted to the king, the approved design was not regarded as unalterable. Thus on 12 June the minutes of the Board record that it 'Examin'd and Corrected the General Plan of the Horse Guards and Section from East to West', and on 5 July that it 'Settled the Design of the Rustick Basement of the Park Front and figured the Dimentions of the Rusticks'. In October the Chancellor of the Exchequer and the Secretary at War 'were waited on . . . with the elevation facing Whitehall, which they approved, and ordered it to be built according to the said Elevation, which is drawn with brown ink and Mark'd letter A'.[3] It was not until 1752 that the form of the turret or lantern (a feature suggested by the old building) was settled with the aid of a model in chalk, and in 1753 it was still possible for Vardy to volunteer a design of his own for an archway to Whitehall.[4] All the official drawings were, however, made by Isaac Ware, who received £100 a year for acting as draughtsman. This was strictly his function, for every feature of the building from the scantlings of the timber to the details of the Ionic Order of the Venetian windows was settled by the Board in committee. Altogether it met 181 times on Horse Guards business between April 1750 and May 1759, and paid 34 corporate visits to the building to inspect progress and give directions to the two clerks of the works. In its final form, therefore, the Horse Guards represents Kent's design as interpreted by the Board of Works, that is by Henry Finch and his colleagues Flitcroft, Ripley and Oram, all of whom attended virtually every meeting. Clearly the building was one to which the Board attached great importance, and, whatever criticisms may be made of the general composition,[5] the excellence of the detailing must be attributed to the solicitude of the Surveyor and his colleagues.

The central building was the first to be erected. Its foundations were laid in the summer of 1750, and the clock-turret was built in 1753.[6] The north wing was

---

[1] For his career see L. Namier and J. Brooke, *The House of Commons 1754–90*, ii (1964), pp. 170–4.

[2] Works 6/64, 7 April 1756.

[3] See the two volumes of minutes relating to the Horse Guards (Works 6/63–4).

[4] Victoria & Albert Museum, Box Q. 1 a, no. 3314. It was not adopted. See also the alternative treatments of the guard-boxes shown in a drawing (no doubt by Vardy) reproduced in *Survey of London*, vol. xvi, pl. 7 from Works 30/171. The idea that 'the western front is more particularly attributed to Kent, and the buildings and facade treatment on the Whitehall side to Vardy' (*Survey of London*, p. 13) must be treated with caution as two elevations for the Whitehall front were among the drawings left by Kent.

[5] Those of a subsequent Surveyor-General, Sir William Chambers, will be found in his *Treatise on the Decorative Part of Civil Architecture* (1759), p. 60.

[6] The old clock was reinstalled after it had been rebuilt by a clockmaker named John Seddon and provided with an additional movement for a minute hand. It long enjoyed the reputation of being the most accurate clock in Westminster (Wheatley & Cunningham, *London Past and Present*, ii, 1891, p. 233).

finished about the same time, but the south wing, containing the Foot Guards' quarters, was not begun until 1754, and the building as a whole was not complete until 1759.[1] The Board's forecast that the work could be done in four years was, therefore, somewhat optimistic, and its original estimate of £31,748 proved to be quite unrealistic. As Calcraft's accounts as Paymaster were apparently never declared, the total expenditure cannot be precisely ascertained. But from the minutes of the Board and the detailed (but imperfect) accounts preserved in the library of the Royal Institute of British Architects, it is clear that the total cost was not less than £65,000.[2]

On its completion responsibility for the maintenance of the building reverted to the Secretary at War, who continued to appoint a surveyor to look after it. When John Lane died holding the office in 1753, John Vardy obtained the appointment, which was worth 2s. 6d. a day. His successors William and Thomas Rice (died 1789 and 1810 respectively) both combined the surveyorship of the Horse Guards with the Clerkship of the Works at Hampton Court, so the maintenance of the buildings remained in the hands of men associated with the Office of Works. In 1777 Sir William Chambers was consulted before some minor alterations were carried out, and in 1779 the Board was asked by the War Office to examine a number of workmen's bills submitted by William Rice, but declined to do so on the ground that too long an interval had elapsed since the performance of the work.[3] Finally in 1817 the separate surveyorship was abolished on the recommendation of a Select Committee on Finance, and the Office of Works assumed full responsibility for the maintenance of the building.[4]

# 3. NO. 10, DOWNING STREET

The house now known as No. 10, Downing Street, was formed between 1732 and 1735 from two houses, one to the north facing the park and the other to the south facing the street. The former and more important house dated from the reign of Charles II, when it had been rebuilt by the Earl and Countess of Lichfield. In 1690 it had passed into the possession of Lord and Lady Overkirk, and on the death of the latter in 1720 it was resumed by the Crown and appointed for the residence of Count Bothmar, the Hanoverian Envoy in London.[5] In May 1720 the Office of Works received instructions 'for repairing and fitting it up in the best and most substantiall

---

[1] This is the date carved on the frieze inside the base of the lantern.

[2] A statement sent to the Treasury in Nov. 1753 shows that over £31,000 had already been spent by June of that year (Works 6/64, 6 Nov. 1753). No figures appear to be available for the period June 1753 to March 1754, but £14,005 were spent between March and Dec. 1754 (Works 6/64, 1 March 1757), nearly £11,100 between Dec. 1754 and March 1757 (Works 6/64, 24 April 1759), some £4890 between March 1757 and March 1758 (accounts at R.I.B.A.), and a sum variously calculated as £3883 or £4073 in 1758–60 (R.I.B.A. accounts and Works 6/64, 26 June 1760).

[3] Letter from Chambers to Col. Jones in R.I.B.A. Library; Works 6/19, p. 258; Works 4/16, 1 April 1779; Works 1/5, p. 17ᵛ.

[4] Works 4/22, p. 411.

[5] For the early history of the house, see *Survey of London*, vol. xiv, pp. 113–16.

manner', and in the course of the next year £2447 were spent on 'the buildings, alteracions and repairs in the house in St. James's Park appointed for Count Bothmar'.[1] In 1723 a further £420 were spent on 'Baron Bothmar's new building', and £69 on repairing a crack in the staircase in his 'old building'.[2] In 1730 the count claimed that the house was 'in so bad a condition that it wants a general and thorough repair without which it cannot stand much longer'. But his account of its condition seems to have been somewhat exaggerated, for the Board's estimate for the necessary work amounted only to £280.[3]

Bothmar died in 1732, and according to Horace Walpole George II then offered the house to Sir Robert Walpole. However, Sir Robert 'would only accept it for his Office of First Lord of the Treasury, to which Post he got it annexed for ever'.[4] In 1732 Walpole's name duly appears in the rate-books in place of Bothmar's and on 22 September 1735 he removed from St. James's Square to his new house, where he entertained the queen to breakfast a few days later.[5]

During the intervening period (1732–5) the house was extensively altered and combined with the smaller house in Downing Street, one of several built as a speculation by Sir George Downing in 1682–3.[6] The enlarged house, hitherto entered from Horse Guards Parade, now had its main entrance from Downing Street, and a small walled garden was formed on its north side. The north front was altered so as to give it a regular elevation topped by a pediment,[7] and the interior was almost completely remodelled. The new interiors are shown in a series of elevational drawings now in the Metropolitan Museum of Art at New York.[8] These drawings are attributed to Isaac Ware, who in 1733 became Clerk Itinerant and Draughtsman to the Board of Works. They would appear, however, to be survey drawings rather than designs, and it does not necessarily follow that Ware was the architect employed. The decorative features are in the style of William Kent, and as the adjoining Treasury was being rebuilt to his designs at the same time, it is possible that he was also responsible for the remodelling of No. 10. The work does not, however, appear to have been accounted for by the Office of Works, and it may have been paid for by Walpole himself. The only other possibility is that it was included in the total of £20,000 spent on the Treasury between 1732 and 1735—a sum so much in excess of the initial estimate (£8000 for the structure only) as to require some explanation. Walpole's insistence on the official status of the house would appear less as an act of self-denial if by this means he got it reconstructed at the expense of the Crown. The formation of the new garden, at least, was paid for out of the Civil List, for the warrant placing the garden-keeper on the establishment of the Board of Works states that the garden had been 'made and fitted up at the charge and expence of the Crown', and that the house and garden were 'meant to be annexed and united to the

---

[1] T 56/18, p. 97; Works 6/7, pp. 171, 174–5; Works 5/141, year 1721.
[2] Works 5/141, year 1723.          [3] Works 6/15, pp. 195–6.
[4] Horace Walpole, *Aedes Walpolianae* (1747), p. 76.
[5] *Survey of London*, vol. xiv, p. 129.
[6] *Survey of London*, vol. xiv, pp. 110–11, 129.
[7] Cf. the engravings reproduced in *Survey of London*, vol. xiv, pp. 115 and 118. The pediment was removed later, probably in 1781–3.
[8] They are reproduced in *Survey of London*, vol. xiv, pls. 147–54, and described by John Harris, *A Catalogue of British Drawings for Architecture &c. in American Collections* (1971), p. 271.

office of His Majesty's Treasury and to be and remain for the use and habitation of the first Commissioner of His Majesty's Treasury for the time being'.[1]

In practice, however, the enlarged house was generally occupied by the Commissioner who was Chancellor of the Exchequer, and those First Lords who did live at No. 10 (e.g. George Grenville, Lord North and William Pitt) were almost invariably Chancellors of the Exchequer as well as Prime Ministers.[2] This arrangement continued until 1828, when the Chancellor moved to No. 11, and No. 10 was once more put at the disposal of the Prime Minister.

In 1766 it was at the request of a newly-appointed Chancellor of the Exchequer, Charles Townshend, that the Board surveyed No. 10, finding 'the walls of the old part of the . . . house next the street to be much decayed, the floors and chimneys much sunk from a levell, and no party wall between the house and the house adjoyning on the west side'. It was therefore decided to take down 'the front next the street and also the east flank wall of the Hall, to build a party wall on the west side to prevent the danger of fire, to repair the remaining part of the old building and to erect an additional building adjoyning thereto'.[3] The estimate amounted to £950. Work costing £668 was carried out in 1766–7, but nothing more was done until 1774, when 'Mr. Couse acquainted the Board that Lord North desired to have the front part of the Chancellor of the Exchequer's house in Downing Street finished which was begun by a warrant from the Treasury dated 9 August 1766', and it was 'ordered that the same be done with all speed'.[4] The expenditure amounted to £502.[5] It was therefore in 1774–5 that the street frontage of No. 10 assumed the appearance which it retained until it was extended eastwards in 1959–60.

Further extensive alterations were carried out in 1781–3. In June 1781 the Board called the attention of the Treasury to 'the dangerous state of the old part of the house occupied by the Chancellor of the Exchequer', and expressed the opinion that 'no time should be lost in taking down the said buildings'. The cost was estimated at £5500.[6] A plan evidently made at this time shows that it was the office area that was affected, and that the new building was designed to include a kitchen, a laundry, a wardrobe and a porter's room.[7] Owing to the nature of the soil considerable difficulty was experienced in laying the foundations, and on three occasions in the summer of 1781 the members of the Board went over to Downing Street and gave directions in person about the method of construction to be followed.[8] In 1782 they were obliged to inform the Treasury that 'from the badness of the foundation,

---

[1] Works 6/8, p. 12.

[2] For a list of the occupants of the house see *Survey of London*, vol. xiv, p. 126. In 1783 Lord North referred to it as 'the house allotted for the residence of the Chancellor of the Exchequer' (*Parliamentary History*, vol. xxiii, 1814, pp. 955–6), but in 1823 Lord Liverpool stated that the first Lord had first claim to it, and that 'if he declines it, the Chancellor of the Exchequer occupies it, not as Chancellor of the Exchequer, but as second in the Commission of the Treasury' (letter quoted in *Survey of London*, p. 127.).

[3] Works 6/18, pp. 141–2.

[4] Works 5/142, year 1766–7; Works 4/15, 30 Sept. 1774. The actual date of the 1766 warrant was 19 August.

[5] Works 5/142, year 1774–5.

[6] Works 6/19, p. 362.

[7] Works 30/310, reproduced in *Survey of London*, vol. xiv, pl. 111.

[8] Works 4/16, 29 June, 6 July, 3 August, 1781. The minute of 6 July is accompanied by a sectional drawing of the foundation of 'the East wall next the Stable Yard'. As money to pay the workmen was imprested to Sir Robert Taylor he was perhaps the member of the Board most closely involved (*Survey of London*, xiv, p. 122).

other alteration(s) and unforeseen defects, the total of the bills will considerably exceed the original estimate sent to your Lordships'. In the end it amounted to £11,078—over twice the original estimate.[1] In the following year much was said about this expenditure in the debate on Pitt's bill for the reform of abuses in the public offices. Pitt, himself a recent Chancellor of the Exchequer, 'mentioned the expense of repairing the house in Downing Street, in which he had the honour to be lodged for a few months. The repairs of that house only, had, he said, . . . cost the public £10,000 and upwards; and for the seven years preceding that repair, the annual expense had been little less than £500. The alterations that had cost £10,000 he stated to consist of a new kitchen and offices, extremely convenient, and with several comfortable lodging-rooms; and he observed, that a great part of the cost, he had understood, was occasioned by the foundation of the house proving bad.' Lord North said that the work had caused considerable inconvenience to himself as the occupant of the house at the time, and that he had agreed to it 'only because the report of the Board of Works declared that the house could not stand long if it was not repaired'. As for the Officers of the Works, he pointed out that they 'could not be benefited by recommending new buildings or repairs, for they had fixed salaries and received no other emolument'.[2] The *Morning Herald* was less restrained in its language: 'Five hundred pounds per annum preceding the great repair, and eleven thousand pounds the great repair itself! So much has this extraordinary edifice cost the country!—For one moiety of which sum a much better dwelling might have been purchased, even supposing government to have been the purchaser'.[3] Stung by these criticisms, the Treasury held up payment until the accounts had been submitted to the scrutiny of James Wyatt. Wyatt's verdict was that he 'had not been able to discover any exceptionable charge', and that in his opinion the total claimed was 'proper and ought to be allowed'.[4]

## 4. SCOTLAND YARD

In the seventeenth and eighteenth centuries Scotland Yard was one of the humbler parts of that vast, ill-planned complex of buildings known as the Palace of Whitehall. It contained a large number of offices and official residences, irregularly grouped round three courts known as Great Scotland Yard, Middle Scotland Yard and Little Scotland Yard. Many of these buildings were at one time or another leased to private persons, and for few of them did the Office of Works accept any regular responsibility.[5] A large part of Great Scotland Yard was, however, occupied by the Office of Works itself, and as such demands special treatment in this *History*. The general disposition of the Office in the reign of Charles II can be seen from

[1] Works 6/20, pp. 15, 20; Works 4/16, 10 April 1782.
[2] *Parliamentary History*, vol. xxiii (1814), pp. 952, 956.
[3] *Morning Herald*, 21 June 1783, quoted in *Survey of London*, xiv, p. 121.
[4] T 29/52, pp. 420–1; 54, p. 50; 55, p. 66.
[5] A detailed account of these buildings will be found in *Survey of London*, vol. xvi.

444

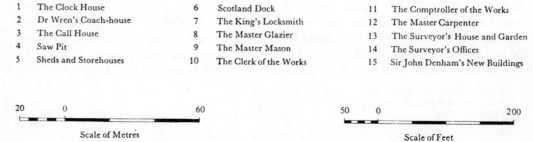

| | | | | | | |
|---|---|---|---|---|---|---|
| 1 | The Clock House | 6 | Scotland Dock | 11 | The Comptroller of the Works |
| 2 | Dr Wren's Coach-house | 7 | The King's Locksmith | 12 | The Master Carpenter |
| 3 | The Call House | 8 | The Master Glazier | 13 | The Surveyor's House and Garden |
| 4 | Saw Pit | 9 | The Master Mason | 14 | The Surveyor's Offices |
| 5 | Sheds and Storehouses | 10 | The Clerk of the Works | 15 | Sir John Denham's New Buildings |

Fig. 35. Whitehall: Scotland Yard in 1670 (based on the plan of Whitehall published by George Vertue in 1747).

the survey of *c.* 1670 (Fig. 35). The Surveyor, the Comptroller, the Master Mason, the Master Carpenter and the Clerk of the Works for Whitehall occupied a row of irregularly built houses along the south side of the Yard. On the north side were the Surveyor's coach-house, while on the east a number of sheds and store-houses ran down to the wharf where materials were landed. The only building with any claim to regularity was the range of lodgings on the west side of the Yard, facing towards Whitehall, which had recently been built by Sir John Denham on ground granted to him by the king in March 1661. These lodgings were 'built in different Apartments, with several Stair Cases, after the same manner as the Inns of Court', and represented a profitable investment for their landlord, for the ground rent was only £5 a year, whereas the income from letting the twenty sets of chambers amounted to over £600. When the Great Fire of London was raging in 1666, steps were taken to dismantle the buildings on the north side of Scotland Yard in order to protect the palace in case the flames spread so far west, and Denham's Buildings were among those 'uncovered and defaced'. The cost of repairing them, amounting to £527, was met by the Crown, and timber and tiles from the old hall and gate-house of Greenwich Palace, then being pulled down, were used for the purpose. The king subsequently entered into negotiations to purchase these buildings, but they were still in Denham's possession at the time of his death.[1]

In 1666 the timber-framed store-rooms of the Office of Works were also sacrificed to the security of the palace and afterwards a new store-house had to be built at a cost of £70 8s. 6d.[2] This store-house was a long shed built up against the west wall of the gardens of Northumberland House, and formed a strictly utilitarian termination to the view through the entry in Denham's Buildings. In 1689 a certain William Killigrew (not the dramatist of the same name) came forward with a proposal to take most of Great Scotland Yard on a 99-year lease in order to build 'stately houses, which will beautifye that yard, and make a handsome square'. His purpose was in fact to create a square of which Denham's Buildings would form one side, the houses of the Officers of the Works the second, and his speculation the other two sides. Although he offered 'to build conveniences for the workmen in the new worke yard as good at least as those sheds they now make use off', Wren was absolutely opposed to the scheme, telling the Treasury that it would 'be much to their Majesty's damage, to the valew of £1000 per annum'. He insisted that the whole of the existing ground and store-houses were needed by the Office of Works and recalled that 'when the late Building was erected near the Privye Garden, not only Scotland Yard but the Peble-Court was then filled with the Timber and floores that were framed and had that roome been wanting the worke must have been longer in performance and much dearer'. Killigrew's proposal was accordingly rejected.[3] In 1706 Wren was equally firm in advising the Treasury to refuse an application from someone who

---

[1] *Cal. S.P. Dom. 1660–1*, p. 458; *1661–2*, p. 130; *1666–7*, p. 140; *1667*, pp. 417–18; *1667–8*, pp. 128, 345; *1668–9*, p. 137; *1670*, p. 706; Works 5/13, ff. 203–5 ('Charges expended in reedifying Sr Charles Dinhams' new buildings in Scotland Yard'). For the subsequent history of the property, see *London Survey*, vol xvi, pp. 210–12, 220–1. The southern part was leased by the government in 1745 to house the Comptrollers of the Army Accounts: the northern part was for many years occupied by the Commissioners for Chelsea Hospital.
[2] E 351/3280.
[3] *Cal. Treas. Books*, ix, pp. 387, 559, 594, 713, T 1/7, ff. 254–7; MPD 47 (a plan showing 'Scotland Yard as it now lyes' and 'as it would be, if built').

asked for a lease of 'a peice of Waste Ground adjoyning to his Dwelling house in Scotland Yard on which stands an old Clockhouse that is of no use to her Majesty'. On the contrary, Wren pointed out, it was 'of manifold & necessary use for the Officers of the Workes, in the discharge of their Dutys'.[1]

Further sheds, and a house for a watchman, were built in 1705 against the wall at the end of the garden of Northumberland House, much to the annoyance of its owner, the Duke of Somerset, who complained of the injury to his trees and view. Wren assured the Treasury that the house was on the queen's ground and that it was 'very much wanted for the safe custody of the yard in winter-nights, to preserve the stores from pilfering'. The duke could not, however, be placated, and continued to write furious letters until the Treasury instructed Wren to reduce the height of the building so that it was no longer visible above the walls of the garden.[2] This affair was to have a regrettable sequel. During his ill-fated surveyorship in 1718–19 William Benson succeeded in acquiring for himself premises in Middle Scotland Yard which included the wharf which had hitherto been used by the Office of Works for landing building materials. Having built some houses between the wharf and the lodgings of the sub-dean of the Chapels Royal (incidentally depriving the latter of light to his kitchen and study, and of access to his stable),[3] Benson promptly sold the estate to the Duke of Chandos, from whose son it was purchased in about 1753 by the Earl of Northumberland.[4] Only a small salient separated the end of the earl's garden from his new acquisition. Like his ancestor, the earl took exception to the sheds whose roofs he could see from the windows of Northumberland House, and lost no time in applying to the Treasury for permission to acquire the ground in order to remove these unsightly objects. The Board pointed out that this was 'part of the ancient storeyard belonging to H.M. Office of Works; and since the grant of His Majesty's wharf to Mr. Benson in the late king's time, is now the only place remaining for depositing the stores and materials necessary for carrying on the . . . works'. As for the buildings complained of 'as interrupting his Lordship's view of the Thames', most of them were below the level of the garden wall of Northumberland House, and the rest could be lowered. Despite the Board's protests, the Treasury were in 1755 prevailed upon to accede to the earl's request.[5] The result was that the Office no longer had any proper store-yard, and was obliged to lay out its materials in various 'open places about Whitehall and Scotland Yard', where it was 'much wasted' in consequence. Thus the territory that Wren had so jealously guarded was lost through the corrupt self-interest of his successor.

The first opportunity to acquire a site for a new store-yard occurred in 1767, when a 'ruinous building' fell vacant on the south side of the passage from Whitehall to Middle Scotland Yard. The Board submitted to the Treasury a scheme for a double improvement. By pulling down this building the passage-way could be widened and sufficient space would remain to allow the erection of a new store-

[1] *Cal. Treas. Papers 1702–7*, p. 433; Works 6/14, f. 115.
[2] *Cal. Treas. Books*, xx, pp. 165, 195, 376, 439, 592; T 1/95/38 and 78; T 1/98/83.
[3] Works 6/7, p. 161.
[4] C. H. and M. I. Collins Baker, *James Brydges, first Duke of Chandos* (1949), pp. 373–5; *London Survey*, xvi, pp. 205–6. The duke paid Benson £7000 for the property.
[5] Works 6/17, pp. 102, 146; Works 4/11, 13 Jan. 1756; T 1/100, pp. 312, 363, 369. MPD 79, MPE 1087 and Works 30/385 are plans made in connection with the earl's request. Cf. *London Survey*, vol. xvi, pp. 206–7.

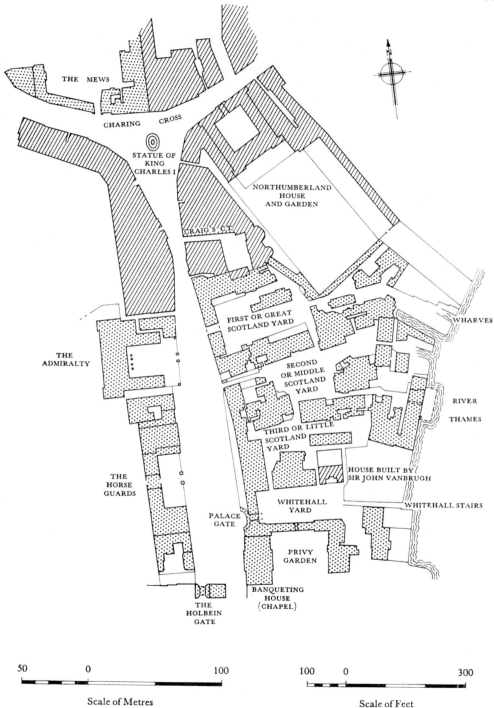

THE MEWS

CHARING CROSS

STATUE OF KING CHARLES I

CRAIG'S CT.

NORTHUMBERLAND HOUSE AND GARDEN

THE ADMIRALTY

FIRST OR GREAT SCOTLAND YARD

SECOND OR MIDDLE SCOTLAND YARD

THIRD OR LITTLE SCOTLAND YARD

WHARVES

RIVER

THAMES

THE HORSE GUARDS

HOUSE BUILT BY SIR JOHN VANBRUGH

WHITEHALL YARD

WHITEHALL STAIRS

PALACE GATE

PRIVY GARDEN

THE HOLBEIN GATE

BANQUETING HOUSE (CHAPEL)

| 50 | 0 | | 100 |
| 100 | 0 | | 300 |

Scale of Metres

Scale of Feet

Fig. 36. Whitehall: Scotland Yard in the eighteenth century (based on P.R.O., Works 30/363–7, 376, 385, 391). Crown property is stippled.

house 107 feet long from east to west and 12 feet 8 inches in width from north to south. This proposal was accepted by the Treasury, but the Board subsequently came to the conclusion that it would be 'of greater utility to H.M. Offices and the public' to utilise the whole space for a widened carriage and footway, and this was accordingly done.[1] In the following year, however, another possible site presented itself. This was a house belonging to Sir Alexander Gilmour, one of the clerks of the Board of Green Cloth, which adjoined the Queen's Treasury at the bottom of Middle Scotland Yard. By partly demolishing the house (which was in bad repair), and by building a wall about 30 feet out into the river and making up the intervening ground, the Office at last created for itself a new store-yard that was partly covered and partly open (Fig. 37).[2] Unfortunately the advantages to be gained by winning ground from the foreshore had occurred to others besides the Office of Works. In 1763 the Board had opposed an application from the tenant of the house immediately to the south of the one occupied by Sir Alexander Gilmour to form a terrace on the foreshore on the ground that it would 'be a great hindrance to the publick stairs at Whitehall' (which the Board continued to repair from time to time), and 'be the means of obstructing the common sewers which empty themselves near that place'.[3] The tenant had nevertheless persisted in his encroachment, and this was continued by his successor, the Earl of Fife, who eventually succeeded in pushing out his garden so far as 'greatly to incommode' the terrace built by the Officers of the Works, and even to encroach on their territory.[4]

The house and office of the Surveyor of Works are marked on the plan of 1670 (Fig. 35). Simon Basil and Inigo Jones had lived in another part of Scotland Yard, and it was only since the Restoration that the house in question had formed the Surveyor's residence.[5] Indeed, in his account of Sir John Denham, John Aubrey states that Denham himself built 'the house of his office'.[6] It appears to have undergone no major alteration between 1660 and 1782. Some minor repairs were carried out in 1660–1[7] and Wren's appointment in 1669 was marked by a payment of £10 6s. 3d. to the Master Joiner 'for wainscotting with deal a lower Room at the Surveyor of the Works his lodgings and for putting a moulding about the dores'.[8] Wren's 'neat new furnished roomes' were remarked on by Robert Hooke in 1672.[9] From a survey of 1689 we learn that Wren's house contained 16 rooms and a cellar.[10] When Wren vacated it in 1718 'several chimney-pieces, casements & sundry other materialls were demolished and taken away', and the Board instructed their Secretary to write to Wren 'to know if they were taken away by his directions, or by whome, and to desire the said materialls may be restored, the Board beleiving the said furnishings were put up at the expence of the Crown'.[11] The outcome is not recorded. On its east side the Surveyor's house interlocked with an old timber-framed house which was out on lease. In the 1760s this house was 'frequently let

[1] Works 6/18, pp. 153–4, 162. Works 30/376 is a plan to illustrate the proposal.
[2] Works 6/18, pp. 179–80. The Yard is shown on plan Works 30/391. It covered an area of about 3850 square feet.					[3] Works 6/18, p. 21.
[4] Works 6/18, pp. 21–5 (with plan), 47–50, 245, 297–302.
[5] *London Survey*, xvi, p. 194.					[6] *Brief Lives*, ed. Clark i (1898), p. 219.
[7] Works 5/2.					[8] E 351/3283.
[9] *The Diary of Robert Hooke*, ed. Robinson and Adams (1935), p. 10.
[10] BM., Lansdowne MS. 736, f. 17.					[11] Works 4/1, 18 June 1718.

to disorderly persons' and the Board was apprehensive of the danger of fire, which might easily spread to the Office itself. In 1770 they were able to set their minds at rest by buying in the end of the lease for £800.[1]

The adjoining office was an old building apparently of no architectural distinction. In 1669 (the year of Wren's appointment as Surveyor) some alterations were carried out which included furnishing the 'Great' or 'Office' Room with a new Portland stone chimneypiece over which Thomas Kinward the Master Joiner set up a 'picture frame' flanked by pilasters and topped by a cornice. He also supplied deal wainscoting with bolection mouldings, architraves for the doors, and a wainscot table 8 feet 6 inches long and 3 feet broad, 'with a strong waynescott frame & turned leggs'. The adjoining Clerks' room was fitted with cupboards, shelves and presses. The Great Room, which was at first floor level, was lighted by sash windows whose sills were set 6 inches above the floor in order 'to stand levell with' the adjoining lodgings of the Master of the Household.[2]

The office was largely rebuilt in 1716–17. In September 1715 the Board 'laid before the Treasury the decaied condition of the House called the Office of Works, and craved for the repairs thereof the summ of 100 pounds'. It was, they said, 'in so ruinous a condition that 'twas a great hazard it had not fallen down and crush'd whoever might have had the misfortune to be under it'. The expenditure was authorised in October, and in March 1716 'Mr. Secretary Hawksmoor' was directed to 'make an estimate for repairing the Office Room, vizt. the front to be of new brick; the stairs to be altered; a new stack of chimneys to be raised. But the same floors and roof to be kept'.[3] However, when the work was put in hand, the building 'which at first was slightly and ill performed' was found to be 'in so ruinous a condition' that it had to be 'taken down to the ground and wholy to be rebuilt with the like conveniencys it had before, vizt.

1st An Office roome and roome of attendance together with the necessary furniture for the same.

2nd An apartment over it belonging to one of the Commissioners.

3 Conveniencys for the Clerks and Officekeeper, together with Closetts, Presses &c. for repositing the Books, Drawings & Designs belonging to the severall Palaces.

4 Strengthening the foundation and adding party walls for duration and security from fire.'

These 'unforseen and unavoidable works' cost £799, and a Treasury warrant to cover the additional expenditure was obtained in July 1717.[4] The new office was pulled down in 1796, and no view of it appears to be extant, but Georgian plans of the ground floor show that the main room was lighted by a tripartite window.[5] The Surveyor's house behind was not rebuilt, but Wren consented to allow a closet 'by the side of the chimney in the Little Parlour belonging to his lodgings' to be added to the Office Room below stairs for the office keeper to set his bed in, that the

---

[1] Works 6/18, pp. 226, 233, 240.  [2] Works 5/13 (at the end).
[3] Works 6/6, p. 104; Works 4/1, 7 March 1716.  [4] Works 6/7, pp. 1–2.
[5] The best plan of the building is Works 30/379, the date of which is probably 1770.

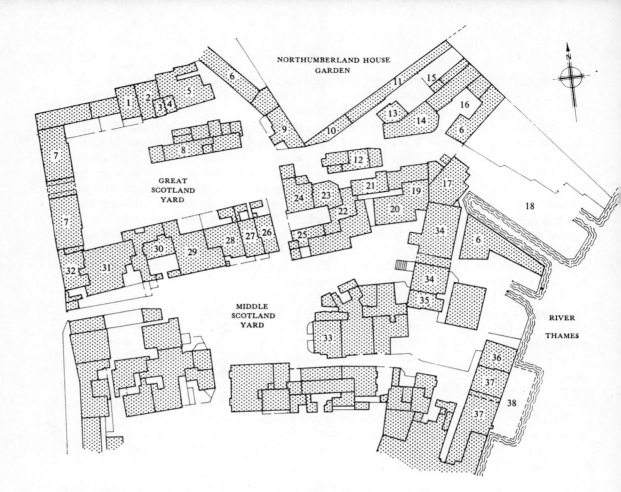

NORTHUMBERLAND HOUSE
GARDEN

GREAT
SCOTLAND
YARD

MIDDLE
SCOTLAND
YARD

RIVER
THAMES

| 1 | Secretary to the Board | 20 | Suttling House |
| 2 | Surveyor General's Stables | 21 | Surveyor General |
| 3 | Clock House | 22 | Chief Clerk of the Works |
| 4 | Comptroller's Stable | 23 | Plumbery |
| 5 | Mr Ripley's Stables | 24 | Sergeant Plumber |
| 6 | Stables | 25 | Locksmith |
| 7 | Denham's Buildings | 26 | Master Glazier |
| 8 | Glazier's Shop and Sheds used by Officers of the Works | 27 | Master Mason |
| | | 28 | Clerk of the Works at Whitehall |
| 9 | Mr Flitcroft's House | 29 | Comptroller |
| 10 | Mr Flitcroft | 30 | Butter and Egg Office |
| 11 | Works Storehouses | 31 | Surveyor General's House |
| 12 | Sheds | 32 | Office of Works |
| 13 | Workshop | 33 | Mr Ripley |
| 14 | Timber and Coal Sheds | 34 | The Foot Guards |
| 15 | Cistern | 35 | Sub-Dean of Chapels Royal |
| 16 | Timber Yard | 36 | Queen's Treasury |
| 17 | Lime House | 37 | Board of Green Cloth |
| 18 | Wharfs belonging to Duke of Chandos | 38 | Terrace built by the Office of Works in 1767 |
| 19 | Officers of the Guards | | |

Scale of Metres

Scale of Feet

Office Common may be more commodious'.[1] Soon after Benson's appointment in 1718 orders were given for the opening of an 'old doorway from the Surveyor's house into the office roome', and for 'the press for Books which now stands against the doore to be sett up in the ante-room'.[2] In 1724 the Board, 'finding an ill conveniency in not having a clock in their office roome', purchased 'a very good clock' from Charles Clay and installed it in 'a plain black varnished case'.[3] In 1738 the adjacent Paymaster's lodgings were 'taken for the use of the office', and the Board Room was moved upstairs to the second floor.[4]

[1] Works 4/1, 14 August 1716.
[2] Works 4/1, 30 June 1718.
[3] Works 4/2, 19 Feb. 1724; 4/13, 14 Sept. 1725.
[4] Works 4/7, 7 Feb. and 28 March 1738.

Fig. 37 (opposite). Whitehall: the Office of Works in the mid-eighteenth century (based on the same sources as Fig. 36).

# CEREMONIAL OCCASIONS

THOUGH WESTMINSTER had long ceased to be the residence of royalty, it continued throughout the seventeenth and eighteenth centuries to be the stage for those traditional ceremonies in which the Stuart and Georgian kings appeared in all the trappings of medieval monarchy. Seven times between 1660 and 1782 the Great Hall and the Abbey were arranged for the magnificent ceremonial of an English coronation. During the same period numerous royal funerals took place in the Abbey, while on seventeen occasions the Great Hall was fitted up for the solemn trial of a lord by his peers.[1]

On all these great occasions it was the Office of Works that was called upon to prepare the appropriate setting for the ceremonial, from the boxes and galleries provided for privileged spectators to the double or even triple coffins in which royalty made their final appearance on earth. Temporary kitchens in Cotton Garden, tin sconces complete with 'deaths' heads and bats' wings' in Westminister Abbey, a stable for the Champion's horse, a box 'for the use of the Gentlemen Pensioners to put their Battle Axes in with their Hats and Cloaks', all these had to be provided by the Office, which was besides responsible for inspecting all privately erected scaffolds and for condemning any that were insufficiently secure.

These great occasions were, of course, expensive. The scaffolding for the trial of a peer cost the king up to £400 in the reign of Charles II, well over £1000 in the eighteenth century. In 1776 the trial of the Duchess of Kingston for bigamy entailed works costing £1741.[2] The most expensive funerals were those of Queen Mary II and Queen Caroline. The former cost £3263 in works alone, the latter £3104.[3] By contrast the interment of William III, which, by his own desire, was carried out privately, at night, is marked in the Works accounts by an outlay of little over £100,[4] while that of George II cost £1768.[5] The cost of coronations

---

[1] To which must be added the trial of Dr. Sacheverell in 1710, which was attended by both Houses. A number of plans and drawings of seating &c. connected with these occasions will be found in the Public Record Office, the British Museum (King's Maps and Crace Collection), Westminster Public Library, the G.L.C. Record Office, and among Wren's drawings at All Souls College, Oxford. An engraved plan showing the arrangements for the trial of Lord Lovat in 1747 was published in *Gent's Mag.*, xvii (1747), p. 149.

[2] Works 5/142. See *Cal. Treasury Books*, xiii, p. 71 for complaints about the cost of scaffolding for Lord Mohun's trial in 1698, and *ibid.* xxiv, p. 169 for the Treasury's refusal to sanction an expenditure of £388 for seats for ladies and other spectators at Dr. Sacheverell's trial in 1710.

[3] E 351/3306; Works 5/141. According to Evelyn the total cost of Queen Mary's elaborate obsequies was 'above £50000' (*Diary*, ed. de Beer, 1959, p. 992). As the expenditure by the Wardrobe amounted to £42884 (*Cal. Treas. Books*, ix (i), pp. cccxii–cccxiii) this was not far out. For an amusing account of the inordinate profits made by the workmen at the expense of the Wardrobe on this occasion see Hist. MSS. Comm. *Downshire*, i (i), pp. 456–8.

[4] Works 5/53; AO 1/2446/139. This did not include the cost of the two 'strong elm coffins . . . covered with purple velvet and finished with plates and handles guilt . . . with crowns and cyphers at each corner' etc., for which Alexander Fort, the Master Joiner, charged £329 10s. (*Wren Soc.*, iv, p. 64).

[5] Works 5/142.

rose fairly steadily. In 1661 the Paymaster accounted for an expenditure of £1558 on the coronation of Charles II.[1] Though James II's coronation was not lacking in splendour the works involved cost only £1181.[2] But in 1689 the joint coronation of William and Mary involved an expenditure on the Works account of £2240,[3] and in 1702 the cost of crowning Queen Anne rose to £4677.[4] Though in no way remarkable, the works for the coronation of George I cost £7287.[5] The coronation of George II, on the other hand, was performed 'with all the pomp and magnificence that could be contrived: the present king differing so much from the last, that all the pageantry and splendour, badges and trappings of royalty, were as pleasing to the son as they were irksome to the father'.[6] In the records of the Office of Works this desire for magnificence is marked by an increased expenditure (£8720), accounted for by a 'large addition of scaffolding' in the Abbey in order to accommodate foreigners, by the 'very great increase in the number of seats' in Westminster Hall, and by superior illuminations in the Hall, which alone cost £815 more than they had done in 1714.[7] But from the point of view of the Office of Works the most striking of the decorations was the Triumphal Arch which stood against the north wall immediately inside the entrance to the Hall. It was designed by William Kent, and was painted on wood and canvas. Two preliminary drawings exist, but Fourdrinier's engraving shows it as finally set up, with four symbolical caryatids supporting a pedimented entablature crowned by figures of Fame, Neptune and Britannia (Pl. 67). The design was personally approved by the king, and the Office considered it to have been carried out 'in a far superior manner than was ever done on the like occasion'.[8]

The arrangements for George III's coronation followed closely the precedents established in 1727,[9] and the fact that the cost mounted to £9430 was due to the rise of prices in the interval rather than to any decorative innovation. This time the triumphal arch was designed by William Oram, the Master Carpenter. Based on the Arch of Titus, it was more classically correct than Kent's lively and almost baroque composition (Pl. 68).[10]

Of the numerous royal funerals conducted by the Office of Works between 1660 and 1782, few demand individual mention. When Charles II died in 1685 a new vault was made for his coffin in the south aisle of Henry VII's Chapel. It cost only £68 to construct,[11] and afforded accommodation for only four more coffins—those

---

[1] Works 5/2; see also *Cal. S.P. Dom. 1663–4*, p. 238.

[2] Works 5/39; Works 3/1, pp. 1, 8–9. The triumphal arch at the north end of Westminster Hall seen in one of the plates in F. Sandford's *History of the Coronation of James II (1687)* was painted by Robert Streater in *trompe l'oeil* for only £15 2s. 8d. (Works 5/39). In 1689 he charged a similar sum 'for the ornaments about the arch' (Works 5/43).

[3] Works 5/43. For the detailed estimate see *Wren Soc.*, xviii, pp. 148–9.

[4] AO 1/2446/139: or £4701 according to a report to the Treasury dated 20 May 1702 (*Wren Soc.*, iv, p. 64). The cost on the Wardrobe account was £7439 (*Cal. Treas. Papers 1702–7*, pp. 15–16).

[5] E 351/3319; cf. Works 6/6, p. 29.

[6] *Memoirs of John, Lord Hervey*, Ed. Croker i, p. 88.

[7] The chandeliers were supplied by the sculptor J. B. Guelfi (AO 1/2452/161).

[8] Works 21/1 (containing a comparison between the expenditure on the coronations of George I and George II); Works 21/13/7(1–2) (detailed bills); Works 4/3, 5 Sept. 1727; Works 6/15, p. 161.

[9] Works 21/1, no. 8.

[10] Oram, like Kent, published a print of which there are copies in B.M. Crowle Collection iii, 172, Bodleian, Gough Maps 23, f. 49 and P.R.O. Works 36/68/25.

[11] E 351/3298; Works 5/38.

of William III, Mary II, Queen Anne and Prince George of Denmark. Queen Mary's funeral was one of the most elaborate ever held at Westminster. The body was conveyed from Whitehall to the Abbey on a funeral car or 'chariot', and lay in state beneath an elaborate catafalque or 'mausoleum' made by the carpenter John Churchill, with embellishments carved by Grinling Gibbons. Both this and the 'chariot' were evidently designed by Wren, for the former is included in the list of Wren's works compiled by his son, and the Works accounts show that Hawksmoor was paid £5 'for his extraordinary paines in copying designes by the direction of Sir Christopher Wren for the Mausoleum in the Abbey and for the Chariot of state'.[1] George I was buried in Hanover, and the first member of his family to be buried in England was Queen Caroline. As Charles II's vault was full, a new vault was made beneath Henry VII's Chapel which, together with the funeral itself, cost over £3000.[2] Within it was placed the black and yellow marble coffin made by Andrews Jelfe and carved by James Richards with 'crowns, palm branches and sceptres'.[3] When the vault was again opened in 1751 for the funeral of Frederick, Prince of Wales, the Surveyor General and his colleagues found it 'very dry and in good order'.[4] It subsequently received the bodies of George II, the Duke of Cumberland, the Duke of York, the Dowager Princess of Wales, and several other children of George II and George III. These were the last royal burials in the Abbey, George III having chosen to transfer his own place of burial to Windsor.

To none of the Stuart or Georgian kings was a monument erected, though several attempts were made to remedy this deficiency, all the more surprising in an age when lesser mortals were so lavishly commemorated in marble. In 1678 there was a proposal before parliament to vote some £70,000 for 'a more decent and solemn interment of his late Sacred Majesty King Charles the First, of blessed memory . . . and for erecting him a monument'. The Bill was read for the first time on 12 February, but relations between Charles II and the Commons were deteriorating, and it never achieved a second reading.[5] Wren's designs for a domed mausoleum at Windsor[6] had perforce to be laid aside, and the only public memorial to the martyred king continued to be the bronze statue set up at Charing Cross in 1675.[7] A project for an equestrian monument to William III, discussed by the Privy Council after his death,[8] had no better fate, nor did anything come of the sketches

[1] S. Wren, *Parentalia* (1750), p. 327; Works 5/47. An engraving of the 'mausoleum' is reproduced in *Wren Soc.* v, p. 12. The design, consisting of pyramids supporting a canopy, was evidently derived from the Roman monument known as the Tomb of Porsenna, engravings of which were known to Wren.

[2] Works 6/16, p. 68; AO 1/2456/172. There is an engraved plan of it (Bodleian, Gough Maps 23, ff. 20ᵛ, 21; B.M., King's Maps xxiv, 4—ff. 2).

[3] Works 4/7, 29 Nov. 1737.

[4] Works 4/10, 11 April 1751.

[5] *Commons' Jnls.*, vol. ix, pp. 428–9, 437, 459, 460–1. The proposal was first made by Lord O'Brien on 30 January, 1677/8, the anniversary of Charles's execution (S. Wren, *Parentalia*, 1750, p. 331).

[6] Reproduced in *Wren Soc.*, vol. v, pls. xli, xlii, together with an estimate amounting to £43,000. See also p. 324 above.

[7] Above, p. 284. In 1678 a white marble monument to the 'Princes in the Tower' (Edward V and Richard, Duke of York) was set up in Westminster Abbey at Charles II's expense. It was made by Joshua Marshall under Wren's direction (S. Wren, *Parentalia*, 1750, p. 333; payment to Marshall in Works 5/30, f. 187; letters etc. relating to the inscription advertised in catalogue of J. F. T. Rodgers & Co. of 34 Bruton Place, 1971, no. 57). The monument is illustrated by F. Sandford, *Genealogical History of the Kings of England*, 1677, p. 403.

[8] PC 2/79, pp. 36–7. Hawksmoor made drawings for this monument which are discussed by Downes, *Hawksmoor* (1959), pp. 66, 284. What the Privy Council envisaged was 'a Statue on Horseback of His late Maᵗʸ to be placed in some most Publick Part about London': cf. Luttrell, *Brief Historical Relation*, v, p. 154.

made by Grinling Gibbons for a grandiose monument in Henry VII's Chapel to William and Mary.[1] In 1719 Stanhope, then Secretary of State, proposed to glorify the Hanoverian succession by erecting a triumphal arch in Hyde Park 'to the Honour and immortal memory of George I'. The Italian architect Leoni was commissioned to make the design, but there is no evidence that the idea was ever seriously considered by the government, and after Stanhope's death in 1721 no more was heard of it.[2]

[1] Reproduced by David Green, *Grinling Gibbons* (1964), pls. 92–3. See also *Wren Soc.*, vol. v, p. 13.
[2] Leoni published the plans in *Some Designs for Buildings both Publick & Private* (1726).

# THE ROYAL GARDENS

DURING THE period covered by this volume extensive works were carried out in the royal gardens. St. James's Park was laid out afresh by Charles II; at Hampton Court William and Mary formed the river terrace and the *patte d'oie* of radiating avenues; at Windsor Queen Anne planted on a grand scale; at Kensington Queen Caroline extended the gardens into Hyde Park, and at Richmond she began those experiments in the picturesque that were to be continued by George III and Queen Charlotte.[1]

Over none of these gardens did the Office of Works exercise the same degree of control that it did over the fabric of the royal palaces. For the superintendence of the gardens was in theory the responsibility of an independent Keeper or Surveyor, and in practice the master-gardeners who came under his jurisdiction were men of high professional standing who required little direction either from their nominal superior or from a Board of architects. Their remuneration, it is true, was the responsibility of the Office in so far as it was recorded in the Paymaster's accounts, but as much of their work was done on the basis of an annual contract with the Treasury, no day-to-day supervision was required and it was only occasionally that matters concerning the royal gardens required the Board's attention.[2]

Under the later Stuarts the Surveyorship of the Royal Gardens carried with it a salary of £200 a year, paid out of the Privy Purse. The first man to enjoy the post was Adrian May, an elder brother of Hugh May, Paymaster and later Comptroller of the Works. He was appointed soon after the Restoration.[3] When he died suddenly in April 1670 his place was taken by his brother,[4] but when Hugh May died in 1684 no successor was appointed—an indication, if it were necessary, that the post was already something of a sinecure. Five years later William III revived it by making the Earl of Portland 'Superintendent of all the King's Gardens' with an establishment consisting of a Deputy Superintendent (£200 p.a.), a Comptroller (£140 p.a.), a Paymaster (£100 p.a.) and a Clerk of Works.[5] This was the organisation that in the course of the next few years created the new gardens at Hampton Court at a cost of some £45,000. It was quite independent of the Office of Works, and accounted

---

[1] Above, pp. 170–4, 203, 221–4, 332–3.

[2] In 1770 'Capability' Brown, the master-gardener at Hampton Court, was indignant when the Board ventured to criticise his management of the gardens in his care. 'I believe' (he wrote) 'I am the first King's Gardiner that the Board of Works ever interfered with. . .' (Works 1/4, pp. 86–7).

[3] *Cal. S.P. Dom. 1663–4*, p. 57.

[4] *Cal. S.P. Dom. 1670*, pp. 186, 294.

[5] *Cal. Treas. Books*, ix, pp. 102, 1095–6. His patent was dated 8 June 1689. According to his first account, covering the years 1689–96 (E 351/3465) George London was Deputy Superintendent, William Talman Comptroller, C. F. Henning Paymaster, and William Deeplove Clerk of the Works. But in other contemporary records it is Talman and not London who consistently figures as Portland's effective deputy (e.g. *Cal. Treas. Books*, ix, pp. 396, 705, 1534, x, pp. 200, 732; Works 6/14, f. 85; T 1/98, f. 446).

direct to the Exchequer.[1] Portland's special status as Superintendent came to an end in 1699, when he resigned all his offices at Court, but in 1696 he had contracted to maintain the principal royal gardens for £4800 a year, and this arrangement continued in a modified form until the end of the reign.[2] On William III's death in 1702 Portland disappeared from the scene, and Queen Anne's government contracted directly (and on more favourable terms) with the master-gardeners, first with Henry Wise (retired 1726) and his partner Joseph Carpenter, and then with Charles Bridgeman.[3] After Bridgeman's death in 1738 his empire was split up, each garden being entrusted to a different gardener.[4]

Meanwhile the office formerly held by Hugh May had in 1715 been revived in favour of Sir John Vanbrugh, who, like May, was also Comptroller of the Works. It was, however, extended in scope to cover 'waters' as well as 'gardens', with an enhanced salary of £400.[5] This salary was charged to the Works account, and thus for the first time brought the Surveyorship of Gardens within the orbit of the Office of Works. For Vanbrugh it was primarily a welcome addition to his income as Comptroller, but he did from time to time give his attention to matters relating to the gardens.[6] For his successor Charles Dartiquenave, however, the Surveyorship of Gardens and Waters was an undemanding place to which he gratefully retired after twenty years as Paymaster, and thereafter the office was to be held by one absentee placeman after another until its abolition in 1782.[7]

[1] Portland's two accounts as Superintendent of the King's Gardens (E 351/3465 and 3469) are printed in *Wren Soc.*, iv, pp. 29–38, from the Audit Office duplicates. A book containing his accounts for the royal gardens from 1696 to 1702 is among C. F. Henning's papers in the Worcestershire Record Office.
[2] The original contract covered the gardens at St. James's, Kensington, Hampton Court, Windsor, Richmond and Whitehall (the Terrace Walk only), but when it expired in December 1700 a new contract was made with Portland for the maintenance of Kensington and Hampton Court only for £2600 p.a. (*Cal. Treas. Books*, xi, p. 116; xii, pp. 188, 217; xvi, pp. 30, 207).
[3] *Cal. Treas. Books*, xvii, pp. 64–6; Hist. MSS. Comm. 12th Report, *MSS. of Earl Cowper*, iii, pp. 118–20; Works 6/114, ff. 7–15. For Wise see David Green, *Gardener to Queen Anne* (1956), for Bridgeman Peter Willis, *Charles Bridgeman and the English Landscape Garden* (1973).
[4] Samuel Milward took over at St. James's and Kensington, George Lowe at Hampton Court, and John Kent at Windsor (Works 4/7, 25 July and 24 August 1738). For a complete list of royal master-gardeners see below, p. 477.
[5] *Cal. Treas. Books*, xxix, pp. 550, 691–2. The 'waters' in question were not only ornamental. Vanbrugh was responsible for 'the several Rivers, Conduits, Pipes and Engines relating to the supply of water to our palaces'.
[6] See Works 6/113, a minute-book dealing with the garden side of Vanbrugh's duties and covering the years 1716–25.
[7] Above, pp. 82–3.

# THE KING'S PRIVATE ROADS

FOR THE use of himself and his servants the king maintained a system of private roads which radiated from London to the various royal palaces in the Home Counties. By the early eighteenth century the only one of these roads that survived was the one that connected Hampton Court, Richmond and Kew with Whitehall and St. James's. The most important portion was the five-mile stretch from Buckingham House to Fulham which still bears the name 'the King's Road' today.[1] Under the Stuart kings the roads were maintained by an independent official who received a salary of £95 from the Exchequer as 'Surveyor of the King's Private Roads' and £82 from the Master of the Horse as 'Guide and Conductor to the King'.[2] In 1717, however, at the suggestion of the then Surveyor, Brigadier William Watkins, the post was attached to the Office of Works, of whose Board the Surveyor became a member, with a salary of £200 per annum.[3]

In this way what had once been an effective office became one of the more profitable sinecures in the Office of Works. For the Surveyor habitually employed a deputy,[4] and the roads themselves were regarded as one of the least important of the department's responsibilities. They were in fact fast becoming an anachronism. There were two reasons for this state of affairs. One was the granting of building leases and way-leaves, which progressively eroded the privacy of the royal highways.[5] The other was the issuing of special passes—and their duplication in the shape of counterfeit tickets—which soon created a situation in which only a tiny minority of those who used the King's Roads were actually engaged upon royal business.[6] The result was a mounting expenditure upon a diminishing asset. Under George I the expenditure on upkeep (excluding officers' and gatekeepers' salaries) seldom reached £300 per annum. But under George II the average was more than twice this sum. And under George III, despite the protests of the Treasury, annual totals of over £1400 were by no means uncommon during the first twenty years of the reign.[7] It should have been obvious that the maintenance of a private road system on the outskirts of an expanding metropolis was no longer a realistic policy. But

[1] P.R.O. MPE 482 is an eighteenth-century survey of it.

[2] T 1/206, ff. 233-5. Since the Restoration, the post had been held by Andrew Lawrence (1660-?1690) and Capt. Michael Studholm (1703-16).

[3] *Ibid.*; *Cal. Treas. Books*, xxxi, p. 263.

[4] Thus Henry Fane appointed Samuel Warren as his deputy in 1772 (Works 1/4, f. 101).

[5] E.g. George III's grant of permission in 1778 to Charles Lord Cadogan and Hans Stanley, both of whom owned land bordering the Fulham Road, to open up a new road across the royal highway, i.e. Sloane Street and Lower Sloane Street, crossing the King's Road at Sloane Square (Works 6/99, ff. 190-1, 20 June 1778, with plan).

[6] For vain attempts to prevent the sale of counterfeit tickets see, e.g. Works 6/16, f. 65 (6 Sept. 1737) and T 29/43, ff. 43-7 (30 April 1773).

[7] Works 5/141. For a warning from the Treasury in 1775 see Works 1/4, f. 113.

throughout the reign of George III the roads continued to be repaired at the king's expense, and it was not until 1815 that the Office of Works was relieved of the responsibility for their upkeep.[1]

[1] See vol. vi, p. 653.

# Appendix A

## THE RECORDS OF THE OFFICE
## OF WORKS 1660–1782

A complete list of Works records will be found in two typescript volumes in the Public Record Office. The following are the principal sources for the history of the Royal Works during the period covered by this volume.

| | | |
|---|---|---|
| Minutes of the Board | 1715 onwards | Works 4/1–16 |
| Correspondence with Treasury | 1685–1702 | Works 6/2 |
| | 1702–9 | Works 6/14 |
| | 1709–14 | Works 6/5 |
| | 1714–17 | Works 6/6 |
| | 1717–23 | Works 6/7 |
| | 1723 onwards | Works 6/15–20 |
| Letter-Books | 1730 onwards | Works 1/1–5 |
| Windsor Castle Warrants | 1668–1710 | Works 6/1 |
| Lord Chamberlain's Warrants | 1701–9 | Works 6/3 |
| Patents | 1715 onwards | Works 6/11–13 |
| Surveyor-General's appointments | 1733–80 | Works 6/9 |
| Treasury Instructions | 1662 onwards | Works 6/368 |
| Royal Letters | 1733–80 | Works 6/8 |
| Contract Book | 1668–1724 | Works 5/145 |
| Royal Gardens | 1706–32 | Works 6/113–114 |
| Maps and Plans | | Works 29–38 |

### Accounts

| Year | Works 5 | British Museum |
|---|---|---|
| 1660–1 | 1 | Harleian MS. 1656 |
| 1661–2 | 2 | |
| 1662–3 | 3 | Harleian MS. 1657 |
| 1663–4 | 4 | Harleian MS. 1618 |
| 1664–5 | 5 & 6 | |
| 1665–6 | 7 & 8 | |
| 1666–7 | 9 | Harleian MS. 1658 |
| 1667–8 | 10 | |
| 1668–9 | 11 & 12 | |
| 1669–70 | 13 & 14 | |

| *Year* | *Works 5* | *British Museum* |
|---|---|---|
| 1670–1 | 15 & 16 | |
| 1671–2 | 17 & 18 | |
| 1672–3 | 19 & 20 | |
| 1673–4 | 21 & 22 | |
| 1674–5 | 23 & 24 | |
| 1675–6 | 25 & 26 | |
| 1676–7 | 27 & 28 | |
| 1677–8 | 29 | |
| 1678–9 | 30 & 31 | |
| 1679–80 | 32 | |
| 1680–1 | *Missing* | |
| 1681–2 | 33 & 34 (33 is wrongly labelled 1680–1) | |
| 1682–3 | 35 & 36 | |
| 1683–4 | 37 | |
| 1684–5 | 38 | |
| 1685–6 | 39 | |
| 1686–7 | 40 | |
| 1687–8 | 41 | |
| 1688–9 | 42 | |
| 1689–90 | 43 | |
| 1690–1 | 44 | |
| 1691–2 | 45 | |
| 1692–3 | *Missing* | |
| 1693–4 | 46 | |
| 1694–5 | 47 | |
| 1695–6 | 48 | |
| 1696–7 | *Missing* | |
| 1697–8 | 49 | |
| 1698–9 | *Missing* | |
| 1699–1700 | 50 | |
| 1700–1 | 51 | |
| 1701–2 | 52 | |
| 1702–3 | 53 | |

End of the series

When there are two volumes to a year they normally contain duplicate copies of the 'Ordinary' accounts. The 'Extraordinary' accounts are bound up in the same volumes, but do not always correspond exactly with their chronology.

After 1703 it is necessary to refer to Works 5/141–2, the Paymaster's annual accounts (1706–82), Works 5/56–65, Abstracts of Accounts (1709–88), and AO 1/2433/85–2471/217, the enrolled Paymasters' Accounts (1660–1782), partially duplicated by E 351/3274–3320 (1660–1715). The enrolled accounts from 1660 to 1718 are summarised, not always accurately, in the *Calendar of Treasury Books*, vols. ii–xxxii.

# *Appendix B*

## EXPENDITURE BY THE OFFICE OF WORKS FROM JANUARY 1761 TO JANUARY 1777

Based on Works 5/64, 1 March 1774 and 10 Jan. 1777

| | Board Officers, Office Clerks, Office Keeper and Messenger | Clerk of Works and Labourers in Trust | Artisans by Patent and Treasury warrant | Surveyor of Private Roads, Deputy and Gatekeepers | Supplying palaces and gardens with water | Slopes and Terrace at Windsor | Ranger of St. James's Park |
|---|---|---|---|---|---|---|---|
| | £ s. d. | £ s. d. | £ s. d. | £ s. d. | £ s. d. | £ s. d. | £ s. d. |
| 1761 | 3391 2 1 | 2215 17 6 | 258 4 6 | 1031 0 10 | 444 18 4 | 140 0 0 | 80 0 0 |
| 1762 | 3882 3 5 | 2182 8 8¼ | 270 7 6 | 1031 0 10 | 440 14 0 | 140 0 0 | 80 0 0 |
| 1763 | 3883 2 3 | 2084 14 8 | 270 7 6 | 1031 0 10 | 427 14 0 | 140 0 0 | 72 11 8¼ |
| 1764 | 3884 5 10 | 2129 8 6 | 270 13 0 | 1031 3 0 | 434 4 0 | 140 0 0 | 80 0 0 |
| 1765 | 3881 16 3 | 2094 19 4 | 264 5 6 | 4031 0 10 | 434 4 0 | 140 0 0 | 80 0 0 |
| 1766 | 3881 16 3 | 2044 1 10 | 233 17 6 | 1031 0 10 | 408 4 0 | 140 0 0 | 80 0 0 |
| 1767 | 3881 10 11 | 2001 6 4 | 229 2 10¼ | 1031 0 10 | 460 4 0 | 140 0 0 | 80 0 0 |
| 1768 | 3885 15 2 | 1988 14 6¼ | 234 1 0 | 1031 3 0 | 434 4 0 | 140 0 0 | 80 0 0 |
| 1769 | 3868 12 6½ | 2781 17 10 | 233 17 6 | 1031 0 10 | 434 4 0 | 140 0 0 | 80 0 0 |
| 1770 | 3881 0 3 | 2159 13 4 | 233 17 6 | 1031 0 10 | 434 4 0 | 140 0 0 | 80 0 0 |
| 1771 | 3881 0 3 | 2432 15 4 | 193 17 6 | 1031 0 10 | 434 4 0 | 140 0 0 | 80 0 0 |
| 1772 | 3885 4 2 | 2269 5 10 | 194 1 0 | 1031 3 0 | 440 0 0 | 140 0 0 | 80 0 0 |
| 1773 | 3881 0 3 | 2675 14 0 | 193 17 6 | 1031 0 10 | 440 0 0 | 4 10 3¾ | 80 0 0 |
| 1774 | 3881 0 3 | 2436 14 8½ | 193 17 6 | 1031 0 10 | 440 0 0 | — | 80 0 0 |
| 1775 | 3933 16 11 | 2338 13 0¼ | 194 17 6 | 1031 0 10 | 440 0 0 | — | 80 0 0 |
| 1776 | 3958 11 2 | 2287 0 5 | 194 1 0 | 1031 0 10 | 416 5 0 | — | 80 0 0 |

| | Auditors of Imprests | Removing Wardrobe | Tradesmen's bills and other continuing expenses on the Ordinary | Ditto on the Extraordinary | Extra Payments to H.M.'s Gardeners | Paymaster's 3d. in £ | Totals |
|---|---|---|---|---|---|---|---|
| | £ s. d. | £ s. d. | £ s. d. | £ s. d. | £ s. d. | £ s. d. | £ s. d. |
| 1761 | 140 0 0 | 12 0 0 | 20034 9 6 | 662 17 9¼ | 5305 13 5 | 547 1 6½ | 34263 5 5¾ |
| 1762 | 140 0 0 | 12 0 0 | 20349 1 2¾ | 12383 10 2¾ | 6588 15 6 | 442 19 3½ | 47943 0 8¼ |
| 1763 | 140 0 0 | 12 0 0 | 17696 6 5¾ | 13363 15 7½ | 6322 19 2 | 525 12 5¾ | 45970 4 8¼ |
| 1764 | 140 0 0 | 12 0 0 | 16088 11 0¼ | 12560 4 4½ | 8873 9 11 | 501 4 4¼ | 46145 4 0 |
| 1765 | 140 0 0 | 12 0 0 | 13578 3 1½ | 16246 0 11½ | 7332 2 7¼ | 493 12 10 | 45728 5 5¼ |
| 1766 | 140 0 0 | 12 0 0 | 15129 14 7¾ | 12100 18 5¼ | 5964 1 4 | 610 16 2 | 41776 11 0 |
| 1767 | 140 0 0 | 12 0 0 | 16450 19 11¾ | 8852 6 3 | 6858 14 3½ | 508 10 5 | 40645 15 10½ |
| 1768 | 140 0 0 | 12 0 0 | 14262 14 11¾ | 8236 17 1½ | 9557 11 5 | 478 13 1½ | 40481 14 4 |
| 1769 | 140 0 0 | 12 0 0 | 17262 11 0½ | 2374 16 3¾ | 7713 16 5½ | 525 16 11½ | 36598 13 5¾ |
| 1770 | 140 0 0 | 12 0 0 | 18852 5 8¾ | 3035 9 6½ | 7347 4 1¼ | 467 19 0½ | 37814 14 4 |
| 1771 | 140 0 0 | 12 0 0 | 21028 5 4¾ | 5891 7 1 | 6932 15 7 | 507 2 8 | 42704 8 7¾ |
| 1772 | 140 0 0 | 12 0 0 | 24439 10 2¾ | 21527 3 6¾ | 7783 16 8½ | 654 0 10½ | 62596 5 4½ |
| 1773 | 140 0 0 | 12 0 0 | 31783 7 2¼ | 11656 5 2¼ | 6637 3 0 | 819 4 8¾ | 59354 3 0 |
| 1774 | 140 0 0 | 12 0 0 | 23145 6 11¼ | 11831 10 0 | 6552 16 5½ | 622 14 3 | 50367 0 11¼ |
| 1775 | 140 0 0 | 12 0 0 | 20880 9 3¾ | 3722 15 5 | 9134 6 9¾ | 492 8 11¾ | 42399 18 9½ |
| 1776 | 140 0 0 | 12 0 0 | 23952 12 0 | 6856 0 8½ | 7261 15 8½ | 591 16 7 | 46781 5 7 |

# Appendix C

## PRINCIPAL CRAFTSMEN AND OTHERS EMPLOYED AT SOMERSET HOUSE 1776–95

The figure given is the total payment recorded in the accounts (R.I.B.A. Library and P.R.O. AO 3/1244)

**BRICKLAYERS**

| | | |
|---|---|---|
| Gray, Edward | £39,198 9 | 0 |
| Grove, John | £27,777 18 | 6 |
|     John & Son (from 1788) | £1,058 11 | 10 |
| Holland, Henry & Richard | £24,011 0 | 6 |
|     Richard & Richard (from 1785) | £10,211 11 | 8 |
|     Richard (from 1789) | £2,933 6 | 9 |

**CARPENTERS**

| | | |
|---|---|---|
| Cole, Charles | £284 14 | 9 |
|     Charles & Martin (from 1784) | £1,999 2 | 3 |
|     Martin (from 1794) | £15 15 | 1 |
| Filewood, James | £14,426 19 | 4 |
| Wyatt, Samuel | £24,334 6 | 1 |

**CLOCKMAKER**

| | | |
|---|---|---|
| Vulliamy, Justin | £363 6 | 9 |

**DECORATIVE PAINTERS**

| | | |
|---|---|---|
| Cipriani, John Baptist | £273 0 | 0 |
| Kauffman, Angelica | £100 0 | 0 |
| Rebecca, Biagio | £73 0 | 0 |
| Reynolds, Sir Joshua | £31 10 | 0 |
| Rigaud, J. F. | £57 15 | 0 |
| West, Benjamin | £125 0 | 0 |

**GLAZIERS**

| | | |
|---|---|---|
| Cobbett, Richard & John | £3,699 8 | 1 |
|     John (from 1793) | £353 3 | 4 |

JOINERS

| | | | |
|---|---|---|---|
| Arrow, James | £2,787 | 17 | 10 |
| Clarke, William | £5,500 | 10 | 10 |
| William & Warren, George (from 1794) | £13 | 5 | 7 |
| Goldsmith, Nathaniel | £145 | 10 | 6 |
| Greenell, William | £2,812 | 2 | 4 |
| Kelsey, William (from 1791) | £736 | 0 | 4 |
| Neale, George | £11,278 | 18 | 4 |
| Russell, John & Thomas | £138 | 14 | 5 |
| Smith, William | £919 | 1 | 5 |
| Warren, George, *see* Clarke | | | |
| West, John, & Kelsey, William | £6,011 | 18 | 1 |

MASONS

| | | | |
|---|---|---|---|
| Devall, John | £36,428 | 14 | 0 |
| John & Son (from 1790) | £1,756 | 11 | 2 |
| Gilliam, John | £47,841 | 1 | 9 |
| John, & Wood, Thomas (from 1792) | £3,298 | 1 | 1 |
| Smith, Robert (junior) & Co. (supplying and working Aberdeen granite) | £1,631 | 10 | 11 |
| Wood, Thomas, *see* Gilliam | | | |

PLASTERERS

| | | | |
|---|---|---|---|
| Clark, Thomas | £1,176 | 8 | 6 |
| Collins, Thomas | £1,990 | 2 | 0 |
| Thomas & Papworth, John (from 1784) | £7,915 | 2 | 8 |
| Palmer, Thomas | £1,148 | 13 | 4 |
| Rose, Joseph | £1,188 | 4 | 8 |
| Thorpe, James (maker of composition ornaments) | £61 | 9 | 10 |

PLUMBERS

| | | | |
|---|---|---|---|
| Devall, Jeremiah & Holroyd, George | £5,022 | 13 | 10 |
| Holroyd, George (from 1783) | £12,144 | 9 | 1 |
| John (from 1789) | £4,152 | 6 | 4 |

SCULPTORS AND CARVERS[1]

| | | | |
|---|---|---|---|
| Alken, Samuel (from 1782) | £468 | 5 | 9 |
| Sefferin (died 1780) | £457 | 13 | 9 |
| Bacon, John | £2,760 | 0 | 0 |
| Banks, Thomas | £289 | 10 | 0 |
| Carlini, Agostino | £303 | 0 | 0 |
| Ceracchi, Joseph | £203 | 3 | 0 |

[1] For details of the works performed by these sculptors and carvers see J. B. Papworth in *Journal of the R.I.B.A.* N.S. ix (1893), pp. 119–22 and R. Gunnis, *Dictionary of British Sculptors* (1953), *passim.*

| | | | |
|---|---:|---:|---:|
| Cheere, John (metal sphinxes) | £126 | 16 | 0 |
| Coade, Eleanor (vases) | £191 | 4 | 6 |
| Greenwood, John | £116 | 15 | 0 |
| Hayward, Richard | £835 | 0 | 3 |
| Lawrence, Richard | £1,479 | 14 | 7 |
| Locatelli, George B. | £64 | 12 | 0 |
| Nollekens, Joseph | £105 | 0 | 0 |
| Rathbone, Richard | £669 | 11 | 0 |
| Rossi, Charles | £200 | 0 | 0 |
| Wilton, Joseph | £5,657 | 10 | 10 |

SMITHS

| | | | |
|---|---:|---:|---:|
| Clarke, William | £829 | 8 | 1 |
| Mackell, John | £2,419 | 14 | 2 |
| Palmer, Martha (from 1794) | £423 | 3 | 2 |
| Palmer, William (d. 1779) & his Executors | £8,922 | 15 | 8 |

*Appendix D*

# PRINCIPAL OFFICE-HOLDERS 1660-1782

|  | *From* |  | *To* |  |
|---|---|---|---|---|
| **SURVEYOR-GENERAL** | | | | |
| Sir John Denham | 13 June | 1660 | March 1669 | (d.) |
| Sir Christopher Wren | 29 March 1669 | | 26 April 1718 | (dismissed) |
| William Benson | 26 April 1718 | | 17 July 1719 | (dismissed) |
| Sir Thomas Hewett | 24 Aug. 1719 | | 9 April 1726 | (d.) |
| Hon. Richard Arundell, M.P. | 4 May 1726 | | 1737 | (resigned) |
| Hon. Henry Fox, M.P. | 23 June 1737 | | 1743 | (resigned) |
| Hon. Henry Finch, M.P. | 30 June 1743 | | 1760 | (retired) |
| Thomas Worsley, M.P. | 15 Dec. 1760 | | 13 Dec. 1778 | (d.) |
| Col. James Whitshed Keene, M.P. | 21 Jan. 1779 | | 1782 | |
| **COMPTROLLER** | | | | |
| Francis Wethered | May 1660 | | 1668 | (d.) |
| Hugh May | 23 June 1668 | | 21 Feb 1684 | (d.) |
| *Vacant 1684–9* | | | | |
| William Talman | 2 May 1689 | | May 1702 | (dismissed) |
| Sir John Vanbrugh | 8 June 1702 | | 26 March 1726 | (d.)[1] |
| Thomas Ripley | 4 May 1726 | | 10 Feb. 1758 | (d.) |
| Henry Flitcroft | 10 March 1758 | | 25 Feb. 1769 | (d.) |
| Sir William Chambers | 9 March 1769 | | 1782 | (promoted) |
| **PAYMASTER** | | | | |
| Hugh May | 29 June 1660 | | 1668 | (promoted) |
| Philip Packer | 6 Aug. 1668 | | 24 Dec. 1686 | (d.) |
| Thomas Lloyd | Jan. 1687 | | 1706 | (d.) |
| Charles Dartiquenave | 27 Nov. 1706 | | 1726 | |
| Hugh Howard | 21 July 1726 | | 1738 | (d.) |
| John Harris, M.P. | 19 May 1738 | | 1741 | (revoked) |
| Sir Robert Brown, Bt., M.P. | 8 May 1741 | | 1742 | (revoked) |
| Sir Charles Gilmour, Bt., M.P. | 12 July 1742 | | 1743 | (revoked) |
| Denzil Onslow, M.P. | 30 Dec. 1743 | | 1756 | (revoked) |
| George Augustus Selwyn, M.P. | 27 Dec. 1756 | | 1782 | |
| **SURVEYOR OF THE ROYAL GARDENS** | | | | |
| Adrian May | *c.* 1660 | | 25 April 1670 | (d.) |
| Hugh May | 24 June 1670 | | 21 Feb. 1684 | (d.) |

[1] Vanbrugh's patent was revoked 16 April 1713, but he was reinstated in January 1715.

|  | From | To |
|---|---|---|
| **Surveyor of Gardens and Waters** | | |
| Sir John Vanbrugh | 15 June 1715 | 26 March 1726 (d.) |
| Charles Dartiquenave | 22 June 1726 | 1737 (d.) |
| Hon. Thomas Hervey, M.P. | 26 May 1738 | 1760 (revoked) |
| Hon. George Onslow, M.P. | 21 March 1761 | 1762 (revoked) |
| Lord Charles Spencer, M.P. | 2 Feb. 1762 | 1763 (revoked) |
| John Marshe Dickinson, M.P. | 14 May 1763 | 1764 (revoked) |
| Hon. Charles Sloane Cadogan, M.P. | 13 May 1764 | 1769 (revoked) |
| William Varey | 14 Oct. 1769 | 1782 |
| | | |
| **Surveyor of the King's Private Roads** | | |
| Brigadier William Watkins | 12 April 1717 | 1731 (d.) |
| Hon. Richard Arundell, M.P. | 15 May 1731 | 1737 |
| Thomas Ripley | 23 June 1737 | 1756 |
| John Offley, M.P. | 14 April 1756 | 1757 (revoked) |
| Sir Henry Erskine, M.P. | 25 July 1757 | 1760 (revoked) |
| Hon. Edward Finch-Hatton, M.P. | 7 Jan. 1761 | 1771 (d.) |
| Thomas Whately, M.P. | 16 Aug. 1771 | 1772 (d.) |
| Hon. Henry Fane, M.P. | 22 June 1772 | 1782 |
| | | |
| **Deputy Surveyor** | | |
| Colen Campbell | 2 Sept. 1718 | July 1719 (dismissed) |
| Westby Gill | 3 Sept. 1719 | July 1735 (promoted) |
| William Kent | 10 July 1735 | 12 April 1748 (d.) |
| Henry Flitcroft | 26 April 1748 | 1758 (promoted) |
| Stephen Wright | 2 May 1758 | 1780 (d.) |
| Robert Taylor | 6 Oct. 1780 | 1782 |
| | | |
| **Deputy Comptroller** | | |
| Thomas Kynaston | 14 Sept. 1718 | 1721 |
| Nicholas Hawksmoor | 5 July 1721 | 1726 |
| | | |
| **Joint Architects of the Works** | | |
| William Chambers | 18 Nov. 1761 | 1769 (promoted) |
| Robert Adam | 18 Nov. 1761 | 1769 (resigned) |
| Robert Taylor | 9 March 1769 | 1777 (promoted) |
| James Adam | 1 Nov. 1769 | 1782 |
| Thomas Sandby | 4 April 1777 | 1780 (promoted) |
| James Paine | 28 Nov. 1780 | 1782 |
| | | |
| **Secretary to the Board** | | |
| Nicholas Hawksmoor | 25 March 1715 | 1718 (dismissed) |
| Benjamin Benson | 1 Sept. 1718 | 1719 (dismissed) |
| John Hallam | Sept. 1719 | 1726 (dismissed) |
| Nicholas Hawksmoor | 4 May 1726 | 1736 (d.) |
| Isaac Ware | 24 May 1736 | 1766 (d.) |

| | From | | To | |
|---|---|---|---|---|
| William Robinson | 10 Jan. | 1766 | 1775 | (d.) |
| Kenton Couse | 10 Oct. | 1775 | 1782 | |

### CHIEF CLERK OF THE KING'S WORKS AND CLERK INGROSSER

| | From | | To | |
|---|---|---|---|---|
| William Dickinson, senr. | 21 July | 1660 | 1702 | (d.) |
| Christopher Wren, jnr. | 5 Dec. | 1702 | 1716 | (dismissed) |
| John Mercer | 2 Oct. | 1716 | 1717 | (dismissed) |
| Edward Wadeson | 8 Aug. | 1717 | 1718 | (dismissed) |
| Colen Campbell | 9 Sept. | 1718 | 1719 | (dismissed) |
| John Showbridge | 24 Feb. | 1720 | 1755 | (d.) |
| Richard Ripley | 8 April | 1756 | 1782 | |

### CLERK ASSISTANT TO THE CHIEF CLERK OF THE KING'S WORKS

| | From | | To | |
|---|---|---|---|---|
| Charles Browne | 1 Feb. | 1684 | 1691 | (d.) |

### CLERK ITINERANT AND DRAUGHTSMAN

| | From | | To | |
|---|---|---|---|---|
| Charles Haughton | Dec. | 1691 | 1715 | (d.) |
| Andrews Jelfe | 13 Aug. | 1715 | 1728 | |
| Isaac Ware | April | 1728 | 1766 | (d.) |
| William Robinson | 10 Jan. | 1766 | 1775 | (d.) |
| Kenton Couse | 10 Oct. | 1775 | 1782 | |

### CLERK TO THE BOARD

| | From | | To | |
|---|---|---|---|---|
| Leonard Wooddeson | 1 Sept. | 1718 | 1733 | (d.) |
| Isaac Ware | ? | 1733 | ? 1766 | (d.) |
| William Robinson | 10 Jan. | 1766 | 1775 | (d.) |
| Kenton Couse | 10 Oct. | 1775 | 1782 | |

### CLERK TO THE COMPTROLLER

| | From | | | To | |
|---|---|---|---|---|---|
| Thomas Kynaston | *c.* 1715 | | 12 July | 1762 | (d.) |
| Kenton Couse | 22 July | 1762 | | 1766 | (promoted) |
| Thomas Fulling | 10 Jan. | 1766 | | | |

### MASTER MASON

| | From | | | To | |
|---|---|---|---|---|---|
| Edward Marshall | 25 June | 1660 | | 1673 | (retired) |
| Joshua Marshall | 2 Oct. | 1673 | April | 1678 | (d.) |
| Thomas Wise | 6 June | 1678 | Dec. | 1685 | (d.) |
| John Oliver | 28 Jan. | 1686 | | 1701 | (d.) |
| Benjamin Jackson | 4 Dec. | 1701 | May | 1719 | (d.) |
| Nicholas Dubois | 11 Nov. | 1719 | July | 1735 | (d.) |
| William Kent | 10 July | 1735 | April | 1748 | (d.) |
| Henry Flitcroft | 10 May | 1748 | | 1758 | (promoted) |
| Stephen Wright | 10 March | 1758 | | 1780 | (d.) |
| Robert Taylor | 28 Nov. | 1780 | | 1782 | |

|                        | *From*          |           | *To*              |
|------------------------|-----------------|-----------|-------------------|

**MASTER CARPENTER**

| John Davenport | 21 July | 1660 | 1668 (d.) |
| Richard Ryder | 27 April | 1668 | 1683 (d.) |
| Matthew Banks, jnr. | 18 May | 1683 | 1706 (d.) |
| John Churchill | 27 May | 1706 | 1715 (d.) |

*The office was abolished after Churchill's death, but was revived in 1718 as a result of the reversion to the establishment of 1705.*

| Robert Barker | 9 Sept. | 1718 | 1719 (dismissed) |
| Grinling Gibbons | 11 Nov. | 1719 | 1721 (d.) |
| Thomas Ripley | 4 Sept. | 1721 | 1726 (promoted) |
| William Kent | 4 May | 1726 | 1735 (promoted) |
| Westby Gill | 10 July | 1735 | 1746 (d.) |
| Henry Flitcroft | 20 Nov. | 1746 | 1748 (promoted) |
| William Oram | 10 May | 1748 | 1777 (d.) |
| Robert Taylor | 4 April | 1777 | 1780 (promoted) |
| Thomas Sandby | 28 Nov. | 1780 | 1782 |

**MASTER BRICKLAYER**

| Isaac Corner | 2 Aug. | 1660 | 6 Feb. | 1677 (d.) |
| Maurice Emmett, jnr. | 7 April | 1677 | Nov. | 1694 (d.) |
| Richard Stacey | 12 March | 1695 | | 1714 (d.) |
| Thomas Hughes | 29 July | 1714 | 22 Nov. | 1725 (d.) |
| Thomas Churchill | 8 Dec. | 1725 | 4 Sept. | 1736 (d.) |
| Thomas Howlett and Joseph Pratt | 27 Sept. | 1736 | | 1759 |
| Joseph Pratt and Thomas Pratt | 2 May | 1759 | | 1768 |

*On Thomas Pratt's death in 1768 the office was abolished.*

**MASTER JOINER**

| Thomas Kinward | 12 Sept. | 1660 | 1682 (d.) |
| Alexander Fort | | 1689[1] | 1706 (d.) |
| Charles Hopson | 1 June | 1706 | 1709 (resigned) |
| John Hopson | 31 March | 1710 | 1718 (d.) |
| John Smallwell | 9 Sept. | 1718 | 1761 (d.) |
| William Greenell | 25 Nov. | 1761 | 1782 |

**MASTER PLASTERER**

| John Grove, snr. | 1 Aug. | 1660 | 1676 (d.) |
| John Grove, jnr. | | 1676 | 1708 (d.) |
| David Lance | 27 May | 1708 | 1724 |
| George Worrall | 17 March | 1725 | 1752 (resigned) |
| Thomas Clark | Jan. | 1752 | 1781 (d.) |

[1] From 1682 to 1689 Fort was suspended from his office, although he had been granted the reversion of it in May 1678 (see p. 27).

|  | | From | | To |
|---|---|---|---|---|
| **MASTER GLAZIER** | | | | |
| Thomas Bagley | | 1660 | | 1676 (d.) |
| John Bagley | 24 June | 1676 | | 1677 (d.) |
| John Ireland | Nov. | 1677 | | 1683 (d.) |
| William Ireland[1] | 15 Nov. | 1683 | | 1709 (resigned) |
| John Ireland[1] | 24 Nov. | 1709 | | 1725 (d.) |
| Charles Corner | 3 June | 1725 | | 1744 (d.) |
| Richard Minns, jnr. | 17 Feb. | 1745 | | 1761 (resigned) |
| Richard Cobbett | 25 Nov. | 1761 | | 1781 ? |
| | | | | |
| **MASTER SCULPTOR AND CARVER IN WOOD** | | | | |
| Henry Phillips | 30 July | 1661 | | 1693 (d.) |
| Grinling Gibbons | 2 Dec. | 1693 | | 1721 (d.) |
| James Richards[2] | 20 Dec. | 1721 | | 1759 (d.) |
| George Murray[2] | 16 Feb. | 1760 | | 1761 (d.) |
| Samuel Norman | 4 Dec. | 1761 | | 1782 |
| | | | | |
| **MASTER BLACKSMITH OR CHIEF SMITH** | | | | |
| Michael Bastian | | 1660 | Dec. | 1666 |
| John Wilkinson | 23 Jan. | 1667 | March | 1680 (d.) |
| William Bache | | 1680 | | 1699 (d.) |
| Josiah Key *or* Kay | | 1700 | July | 1711 (d.) |
| Thomas Robinson | 3 Sept. | 1711 | | 1716 |

*The office was abolished in 1716.*

|  | | From | | To |
|---|---|---|---|---|
| **SERGEANT PAINTER** | | | | |
| Sir Robert Howard | 4 July | 1660 | | 1663 |
| Robert Streater, snr. | 14 April | 1663 | | 1679 (d.) |
| Robert Streater, jnr. | 17 May | 1679 | | 1703 |
| Thomas Highmore | 30 April | 1703 | | 1720 (d.) |
| Sir James Thornhill | 13 April | 1720 | | 1732 (resigned) |
| John Thornhill | 8 Aug. | 1732 | | 1757 (resigned) |
| William Hogarth | 6 June | 1757 | | 1764 (d.) |
| James Stuart | 12 Dec. | 1764 | | 1782 |
| | | | | |
| **SERGEANT PLUMBER** | | | | |
| Peter Brent | 10 May | 1661 | | |
| Charles Atherton | 13 Jan. | 1676 | | 1708 (d.) |
| Joseph Roberts | 4 Oct. | 1710[3] | | 1742 (d.) |
| John Devall | 7 May | 1742 | | 1769 (d.) |
| Daniel Floodman | 14 Dec. | 1769 | | 1781 (d). |

*The office was abolished in 1781.*

[1] Son of his predecessor.

[2] In 1754 the Treasury gave orders that as Richards was 'by Age and Infirmity render'd incapable of performing the Duty of his Office, George Murray who hath been employed as his Assistant, be . . . continued in that Employment' (Works 6/17, p. 128).

[3] The office was vacant throughout the year 1709.

|                              | *From*            | *To*              |
|------------------------------|-------------------|-------------------|

**PURVEYOR**

| Arthur Haughton    | 7 Sept.   1660    | 1683/4  (d.)      |
|--------------------|-------------------|-------------------|
| Joseph Radcliffe   | 12 March 1685/6   | 1694 (d.)         |
| Charles Hopson     | 27 July  1694     | 1709 (resigned)   |
| John Hopson        | 31 March 1710     | 1718 (d.)         |
| James Moore        | 22 Sept.  1718    | 1726              |
| Robert Hardy       | 24 Nov.   1726    | 1728 (d.)         |
| Isaac Ware[1]      | 4 Oct.    1728    | 1746              |
| Thomas Hardy }     | 29 July   1746    | { ?1769           |
| Robert Hardy, jnr. }|                  | { 1777 (d.)       |

*The office was abolished in 1777.*

**CLERK OF THE WORKS AT AUDLEY END**

| John Bennett       | Oct.      1670    | 1678 (d.)         |
|--------------------|-------------------|-------------------|
| Henry Winstanley   | 18 March 1679     | 1701              |

*The office came to an end when the house was reconveyed to the Earl of Suffolk in 1701.*

**CLERK OF THE WORKS AT THE QUEEN'S (BUCKINGHAM) HOUSE**

| William Robinson   | April     1769    | 1775  (d.)        |
|--------------------|-------------------|-------------------|
| Kenton Couse       | 10 Oct.   1775    | 1782              |

**CLERK OF THE WORKS AT CARLTON HOUSE**

| Kenton Couse       | 10 Oct.   1775    |                   |
|--------------------|-------------------|-------------------|

**CLERK OF THE WORKS AT THE MEWS AT CHARING CROSS**

| Thomas Ripley      | 28 Feb.   1716    | 1721              |
|--------------------|-------------------|-------------------|
| Thomas Bridge      | 1721              | 1733              |
| Joseph Phillips    | 23 March 1733     | 1746              |
| James Paine        | 1 Dec.    1746    | 1750 (transferred)|
| Kenton Couse       | 10 July   1750    | 1766 (promoted)   |
| Thomas Fulling     | 10 Jan.   1766    | 1774 (transferred)|
| John Woolfe        | 24 June   1774    | 1775              |
| Henry Holland      | 11 Oct.   1775    | 1782              |

**CLERK OF THE WORKS AT GREENWICH (THE QUEEN'S HOUSE)**

| Leonard Gammon         | occurs 1660–1680 |           |               |
|------------------------|------------------|-----------|---------------|
| Thomas Nevill          | 1 Oct.   1680    | June 1681 |               |
| John Scarborough       | July     1681    |           | 1696 (d.)     |
| William Dickinson, jnr.| 10 Nov.  1696    |           | 1701 *or* 2   |

---

| Leonard Wooddeson  | 24 Feb.   1730    | 1733 (d.)         |
|--------------------|-------------------|-------------------|
| Isaac Ware         | 8 Feb.    1733    | 1736              |
| John Vardy         | 24 May    1736    | 1744 (transferred)|
| James Paine        | 15 Jan.   1745    | 1746 (transferred)|

[1] In trust for Robert Hardy's sons.

| | From | | To | |
|---|---|---|---|---|
| William Robinson | 1 Dec. | 1746 | 1754 | |
| Francis Bickerton | 1 July | 1754 | 1768 | |
| John Robinson | 16 Dec. | 1768 | 1774 | (d.) |
| William Leach | 20 May | 1774 | 1790 | |

### Clerk of the Works at Hampton Court Palace (and Bushy Park)

| | From | | To | |
|---|---|---|---|---|
| Simon Basill | | 1660 | 1663 | (d.) |
| Henry Cooper | July | 1663 | 1687 | (d.) |
| Henry Simmonds | April | 1687 | 1698 | (d.) |
| John Ball, jnr. | | 1698 | 1715 | (dismissed) |
| Thomas Fort | 2 June | 1715 | 1745 | (d.) |
| John Vardy | 15 Jan. | 1745 | 1746 | (promoted) |
| Stephen Wright | 1 Dec. | 1746 | 1758 | (promoted) |
| William Rice | 21 March | 1758 | 1789 | (d.) |

### Clerk of the Works at Kensington Palace

| | From | | To | |
|---|---|---|---|---|
| Nicholas Hawksmoor | | 1689 | 1715 | (promoted) |
| Henry Joynes | 2 June | 1715 | 1754 | (d.) |
| John Vardy | 1 July | 1754 | 1761 | |
| John Smith | 3 March | 1761 | 1782 | |

### Clerk of the Works at Kew and Richmond

| | From | | To | |
|---|---|---|---|---|
| Henry Flitcroft | ? | 1728 | 1746 | |
| Henry Stallard | 1 Dec. | 1746 | 1751 | (d.) |
| William Rice | 29 Jan. | 1751 | 1758 | (promoted) |
| John Smith | 21 March | 1758 | 1761 | (transferred) |
| Joshua Kirby } William Kirby } | 3 March | 1761 | {1774 (d.) {1771 (d.) | |
| Thomas Fulling | 22 June | 1774 | 1790 | (d.) |

### Clerk of the Works at Richmond New Park Lodge

| | From | | To | |
|---|---|---|---|---|
| Roger Morris | 16 March | 1727 | 1749 | (d.) |
| Francis Bickerton | 1 Feb. | 1749 | 1754 | (transferred) |
| Stephen Wright | 1 July | 1754 | 1758 | (promoted) |
| James Paine | 21 March | 1758 | 1780 | |
| John Yenn | 10 Nov. | 1780 | 1782 | |

### Clerk of the Works at Newmarket

| | From | | To | |
|---|---|---|---|---|
| John Bennett | | | 1678 | (d.) |
| Henry Winstanley | | 1679 | 1703 | (d.) |
| Francis Buckle[1] | Jan. | 1704 | 1715 | (dismissed) |
| Andrews Jelfe | 2 June | 1715 | 1718 | |
| Leonard Wooddeson | 1 Sept. | 1718 | 1719 | (dismissed) |
| Thomas Fort | | 1719 | 1745 | (d.) |

[1] The appointment of 'Ralph Buckle' as Clerk of the Works at Newcastle in January 1703/4 is recorded in Works 6/14, f. 55, but in the Paymaster's Account for 1704–5 (AO 1/24416/240) his name is given as 'Thomas Buckle'. In all subsequent accounts it appears as 'Francis Buckle'.

|  | *From* |  | *To* |  |
|---|---|---|---|---|
| Ambrose Paine | 15 Jan. 1745 | | 1750 (d.) | |
| Kenton Couse | 12 June 1750 | | 1750 (transferred) | |
| James Paine | 10 July 1750 | | 1780 (promoted) | |
| Samuel Pepys Cockerell | 17 Nov. 1780 | | 1782 | |

### CLERK OF WORKS AT THE SAVOY

| Leonard Wooddeson | | 1715 | | 1716 |
|---|---|---|---|---|
| Thomas Ripley | | 1716 | | 1721 |
| Thomas Bridge | Sept. | 1721 | | 1725 |

### CLERK OF THE WORKS AT SOMERSET (DENMARK) HOUSE

| Leonard Gammon | June | 1660 | Aug. | 1660 |
|---|---|---|---|---|
| Richard Gammon | Aug. | 1660 | Sept. | 1678 (d). |
| Thomas Rotherham | Oct. | 1678 | | 1714 |
| Richard Neagle | | 1714 | | 1715 |
| Thomas Kynaston | 2 June | 1715 | | 1718 (dismissed) |
| George Sampson | | 1718 | | 1719 (dismissed) |
| Thomas Kynaston | *c.* | 1720 | July | 1762 (d.) |
| William Robinson | | 1762 | | 1775 (d.) |

### CLERK OF THE WORKS AT THE TOWER OF LONDON

| Richard Gammon | | 1660 | Sept. | 1678 (d.) |
|---|---|---|---|---|
| Thomas Rotherham | Oct. | 1678 | | 1715 (dismissed) |
| Thomas Kynaston | | 1715 | | 1718 (dismissed) |
| George Sampson | | 1718 | *c.* 1720 (dismissed) | |
| Thomas Kynaston | *c.* | 1720 | July | 1762 (d.) |
| William Allingham | | 1762 | May | 1766 (d.) |
| John Woolfe | 31 May | 1766 | | 1775 |
| Samuel Pepys Cockerell | | 1775 | | 1782 |

### CLERK OF THE WORKS AT WHITEHALL, WESTMINSTER AND ST. JAMES'S PALACES

| Thomas Rotherham | | 1660 | | 1681 |
|---|---|---|---|---|
| Leonard Gammon | | 1681 | | 1713 (d.) |
| William Dickinson, jnr. | 2 Aug. | 1713 | | 1715 (dismissed) |
| Nicholas Hawksmoor | 2 June | 1715 | | 1718 (dismissed) |
| Benjamin Benson | 1 Sept. | 1718 | | 1719 (dismissed) |
| John Hallam | Sept. | 1719 | | 1726 (dismissed) |
| Henry Flitcroft | 4 May | 1726 | | 1746 (promoted) |
| John Vardy | 1 Dec. | 1746 | | 1754 (transferred) |
| William Robinson | 1 July | 1754 | | 1766 (promoted) |
| Kenton Couse | 10 Jan. | 1766 | | 1775 |
| John Woolfe | 11 Oct. | 1775 | | 1790 |

|  | *From* |  | *To* |  |
|---|---|---|---|---|

### CLERK OF THE WORKS AT WINCHESTER PALACE

| John Scarborough | | *c.* 1685 | | 1696 (d.) |
|---|---|---|---|---|
| Thomas Bateman | 10 Nov. | 1696 | | 1715 (dismissed) |
| Leonard Wooddeson | 2 June | 1715 | | 1718 (transferred) |
| David Toomer | 1 Sept | 1718 | | 1719 (dismissed) |
| Thomas Slightholme | | 1719 | | 1725 |
| Thomas Dubisson | 31 Aug. | 1725 | | 1775 (d.) |

*The post was discontinued in 1775.*

### CLERK OF THE WORKS AT WINDSOR CASTLE

*This post dates from 1715, when Windsor was brought under the central Office of Works.*

| Thomas Rowland | 2 June | 1715 | | 1729 (dismissed) |
|---|---|---|---|---|
| Isaac Ware | 14 Oct. | 1729 | | 1733 |
| Abraham Curtis | 1 April | 1733 | | 1745 (retired) |
| Richard Biggs | 9 May | 1745 | | 1776 |
| Thomas Tildesley | 1 Jan. | 1777 | | 1789 |

### CLERK OF THE WORKS FOR THE KING'S PRIVATE ROADS

| Christopher Buckle | *c.* 1747 | 1760 |
|---|---|---|
| Thomas B. Hooke | 1760 | 1772 |

### MASTER OR CHIEF GARDENER

| | | | | | |
|---|---|---|---|---|---|
| *Hampton Court, Windsor, Newmarket, St. James's and Kensington* | { Henry Wise | | | 1726 (rtrd.) | |
| | { Joseph Carpenter | | | 1726 (d.) | |
| *Hampton Court, Windsor, Newmarket, St. James's, Kensington, Richmond and Kew* | Charles Bridgeman | 18 Oct. 1726 | 19 July | 1738 (d.) | |
| *St. James's and Kensington* | Samuel Milward | 17 Aug. 1738 | | 1751 | |
| *Hampton Court* | George Lowe | 17 Aug. 1738 | | 1758 (d.) | |
| *Windsor and Newmarket* | John Kent | 17 Aug. 1738 | | 1773 (d.) | |
| *Richmond and Kew, St. James's and Kensington* | Thomas Greening { | 1738 | | 1762 | |
| | | 1751 | | | |
| *Hampton Court* | John Greening | 12 Dec. 1758 | | 1764 (rvkd.) | |
| *Hampton Court* | Launcelot Brown | 16 Sept. 1764 | 6 Feb. | 1783 (d.) | |
| *St. James's and Kensington* | John Robinson | Mar. 1763 | | | |
| *Richmond and Kew* | { John Haverfield, snr. | 6 Aug. 1762 { | | 1784 (d.) | |
| | { John Haverfield, jnr. | | | 1795 (rtrd.) | |
| *Windsor* | Adam Younger | 1773 | | | |

## WINDSOR CASTLE

*The separate Works department at Windsor was abolished in 1715–16.*

|  | From |  | To |  |
|---|---|---|---|---|
| **Comptroller of the Works** | | | | |
| Hartgill Baron | 12 Sept. 1660 | 30 Nov. | 1673 | (d). |
| Hugh May | 2 May 1674 | 21 Feb. | 1684 | (d.) |
| Sir Christopher Wren | March 1684 | 3 Feb. | 1716 | |
| **Surveyor of the Works** | | | | |
| William Taylor | June 1660 | | 1669[1] | |
| John Ball | 20 July 1671 | | 1685 | (d.) |
| John Ball, jnr. | Jan. 1686 | | 1716 | |
| **Receiver and Paymaster of the Works** | | | | |
| William Taylor | June 1660 | | 1665 | (suspended) |
| Dudley Rewse | 1665 | | 1669 | |
| Richard Marriott | 22 Nov. 1669 | | 1672 | (dismissed) |
| William Roberts | 13 April 1672 | | 1715 | |
| **Surveyor's Clerk** | | | | |
| Samuel Hull | occurs 1671–c. 1685 | | | |
| Charles Browne | c. 1686 | | 1691 | (d.) |
| John Clark | 1691 | | c. 1700 | |
| James Browne | c. 1700 | | 1714 | (dismissed) |
| Charles Browne, jnr. | 13 Dec. 1714 | | 1715 | |
| **Comptroller's Clerk** | | | | |
| William Rowlandson | July 1668 | | 1671 | |
| Thomas Watkins | 1671 | | 1673 | |
| John Baron | 1673 | | | |
| Thomas Taylor | 1673 | | 1678 | |
| Charles Browne | 1678 | | 1686 | |
| William Dickinson, snr. | 1686 | | 1702 | (d.) |
| William Dickinson, jnr. | 1702 | | 1715 | |
| **Master Mason** | | | | |
| John Stone | Aug. 1660 | Sept. | 1667 | (d.) |
| Joshua Marshall | Sept. 1667 | April | 1678 | (d.) |
| Thomas Wise | 1678 | Dec. | 1685 | (d.) |
| John Clarke | occurs 1704–5 | | | |
| John Woodruff | 13 Nov. 1716 | | 1728 | (d.) |
| Edward Vicars | 18 April 1728 | | | |
| Thomas Windsor | 1 Aug. 1738 | | 1756 | |
| Charles Munden | 1 July 1756 | | | |
| **Master Carpenter** | | | | |
| John Punter | occurs 1668 | | | |
| Richard Ryder | July 1668 | | 1683 | (d.) |
| Matthew Banks | May 1683 | | 1706 | (d.) |
| John Churchill | May 1706 | | ?1715 | |

[1] Taylor was suspended from office from 1665 onwards.

|  | From | To |
|---|---|---|
| *Master Joiner* | | |
| Alexander Fort | | 1706 (d.) |
| Thomas Fort | 23 May 1706 | ?1715 |
| *Master Plumber* | | |
| Alexander White | ?1660 | 1687 (d.) |
| Matthew Roberts | 1687 | |
| Joseph Roberts | 1705 | |
| John Devall | 7 May 1742 | 1769 (d.) |
| Daniel Floodman | 14 Dec. 1769 | |
| *Master Glazier* | | |
| William Ireland | | 1710 (d.) |
| John Ireland | 24 June 1711 | ?1715 |
| *Surveyor and Repairer of Carved Work* | | |
| Grinling Gibbons | 1682 | 1721 (d.) |
| James Richards | 20 May 1724 | 1759 (d.) |
| Richard Lawrence | 24 Jan. 1760 | 1761 |
| Samuel Norman | 30 Oct. 1761 | ?1782 |

## CHESTER CASTLE

| *Surveyor and Master Mason* | | |
|---|---|---|
| John Shaw | Sept. 1660 | |
| William King | | |
| Ralph Whitley | | Oct. 1679 (d.) |
| Edward Morgan | Oct. 1679 | |
| Thomas Whitley ⎫ | | |
| Peter Whitley ⎭ | occur 1689 | |

THE PLATES

*Plate 1*

Sir Christopher Wren in old age, from an ivory relief by David Le Marchand (National Portrait Gallery).

*Plate 2*

Hugh May, Paymaster of the Works 1660–8, Comptroller 1668–84 (Her Majesty the Queen, Windsor Castle).

*Plate 3*

Sir John Vanbrugh, Comptroller of the Works 1702–26, from a portrait by Kneller
(National Portrait Gallery).

*Plate 4*

A. A 'Drawing Room' in the former Council Chamber (from Ackermann's *Microcosm of London* iii, 1808–10).

B. Courtiers passing through the Guard Chamber to attend a 'Drawing Room', by Thomas Rowlandson (The London Museum).

The Court at St. James's Palace in the reign of George III.

*Plate 5*

A. Buckingham House as altered and enlarged by George III, with the Octagon Library on the left: from an engraving dated 1796 (The Royal Library, Windsor Castle).

B. Interior of the Octagon Library built by George III in 1766–7 (from Pyne's *Royal Residences*, 1819).

*Plate 6*

Buckingham House, section through the staircase and the Saloon
(Sir John Soane's Museum, Drawer xxiv, set 5).

*Plate* 7

Buckingham House, the *trompe l'œil* painting at the top of the staircase
(from Pyne's *Royal Residences*, 1819).

*Plate 8*

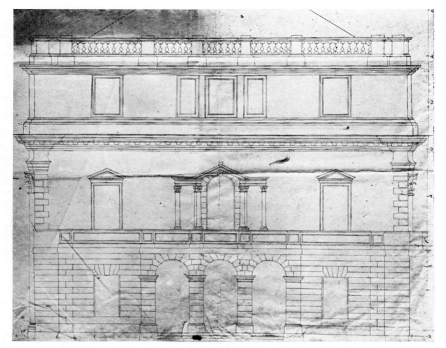

A. Design by John Webb for the south end elevation (R.I.B.A. Drawings Collection, Burlington-Devonshire III/1(9)).

B. The east elevation.
Greenwich Palace: The King Charles Block of 1664–7.

*Plate 9*

A. The Queen's House, Greenwich: ceiling of the east bridge room, 1662 (Royal Commission on Historical Monuments).

B. Greenwich Palace: interior of the central vestibule of the King Charles Block of 1664–7 (Royal Commission on Historical Monuments).

*Plate* 10

Hampton Court: bird's-eye view from the west, *circa* 1705 (from J. Kip, *Britannia Illustrata*, 1708).

*Plate* 11

Hampton Court: aerial view from the south-east.

*Plate 12*

Hampton Court: the south front designed by Sir Christopher Wren (Royal Commission on Historical Monuments).

*Plate 13*

Hampton Court: the Fountain Court designed by Sir Christopher Wren.

*Plate 14*

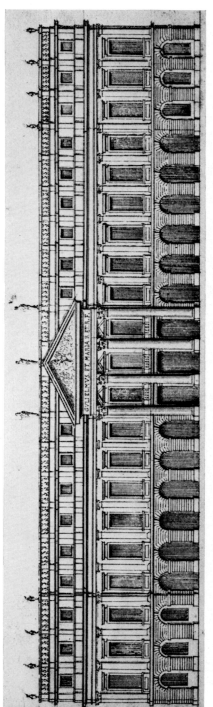

A. Hampton Court: design for the east front by Sir Christopher Wren (Sir John Soane's Museum).

B. Hampton Court: eighteenth-century drawing representing a version of Sir John Vanbrugh's scheme for remodelling the north side of the palace (Department of the Environment).

*Plate 15*

A. Hampton Court: the Bowling Green Pavilions built in 1701, from an engraving of 1744.

B. Hampton Court: the Queen's Guard Chamber (from Pyne's *Royal Residences*, 1819).

*Plate 16*

Hampton Court: interior of the Banqueting House, with decoration by Verrio (Royal Commission on Historical Monuments).

Plate 17

Kensington Palace: the Cube or Cupola Room (from Pyne's *Royal Residences*, 1819).

*Plate 18*

Kensington Palace: the Orangery built in 1704–5 (Royal Commission on Historical Monuments).

*Plate 19*

A. Kensington Palace: the Water Tower designed by Vanbrugh and built in 1722–4 (from *Gentleman's Magazine*, 1821, p. 497).

B. Kensington Palace in about 1690, showing the wings added on the north side in 1689–90 (from an engraving by Sutton Nicholls).

*Plate 20*

Kensington Palace. South-west (A) and south-east (B) views of the palace in 1826 by John Buckler (British Museum, Crace Views, ix, 22–23).

*Plate 21*

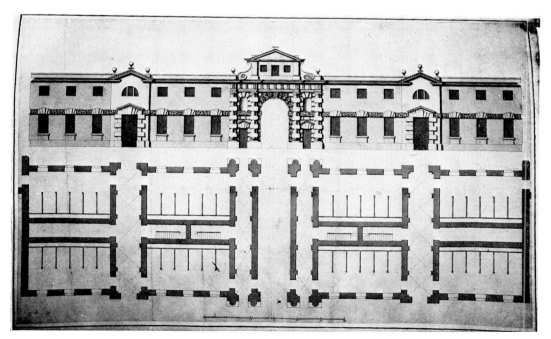

The Royal Mews at Charing Cross. A: engraving from Maitland's *History of London* (1756). B: unexecuted design by William Kent for the southern entrance. C: design for the main building, probably in the hand of Isaac Ware (B and C, Sir John Soane's Museum, Fauntleroy Pennant, vol. ii).

*Plate 22*

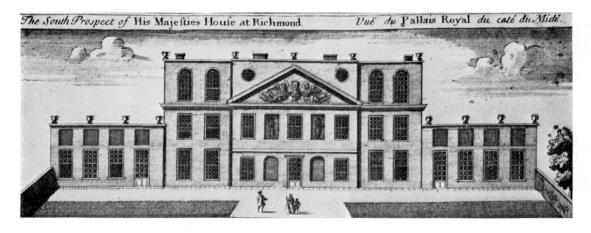

The South Prospect of His Majesties House at Richmond.        Vuë du Pallais Royal du coté du Midi.

Richmond Lodge. A: south front as represented by John Rocque, 1754. B: south front as represented by Paul or Thomas Sandby in the reign of George III (Her Majesty the Queen, Windsor Castle).

*Plate 23*

A. The White Lodge in Richmond Park designed for George I by Roger Morris, with the wings added by Princess Amelia in the reign of George III (from *Vitruvius Britannicus* iv, 1767).

B. North front of Richmond Lodge, from John Rocque's illustrated map of 1754.

C. South front of The White House at Kew, from John Rocque's illustrated map of 1754.

Plate 24

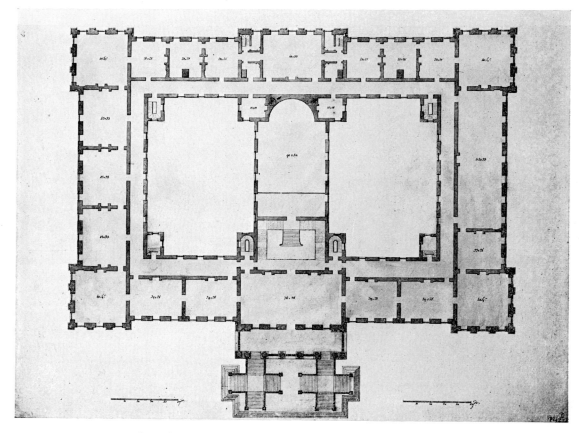

One of the projects for a palace at Richmond for George III.
A. Wooden model, now destroyed.
B. Plan in the Royal Library at Windsor Castle.

Plate 25

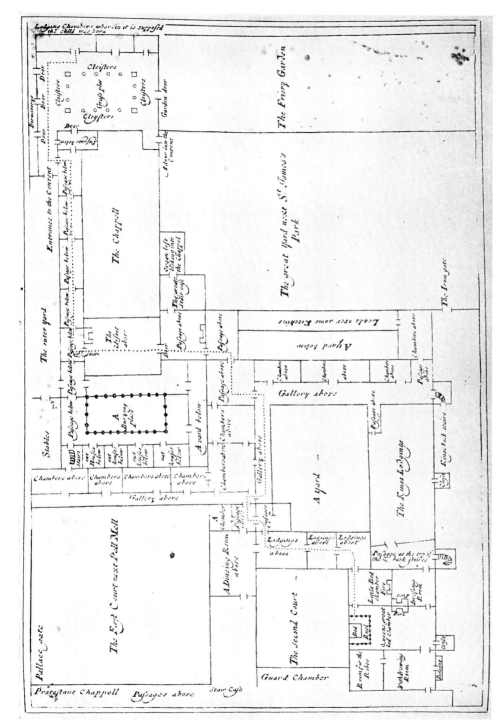

St. James's Palace: outline plan made in 1689, showing the Catholic Chapel and its ancillary buildings (British Museum, Crowle Pennant).

*Plate 26*

St. James's Palace: view from south-west, *circa* 1690 (Her Majesty the Queen, St. James's Palace).

Plate 27

St. James's Palace: view from south-west, *circa* 1705 (from Kip's *Britannia Illustrata*, 1708).

*Plate 28*

St. James's Palace: view of the Queen's Chapel as fitted up for Queen Catherine of Braganza in the reign of Charles II (engraving in Pepysian Library, Magdalene College, Cambridge).

*Plate 29*

A. St. James's Palace, The Queen's Chapel: the arms of Queen Catherine of Braganza over the east window, carved by Grinling Gibbons in 1682–3.

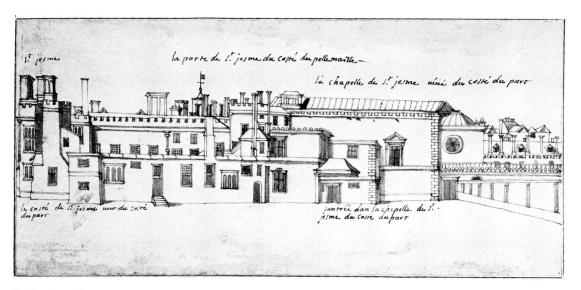

B. St. James's Palace: view of the Queen's Chapel from the south by Gasselin, *circa* 1700, showing the domed addition to the east end designed by Wren for Queen Catherine of Braganza in 1682–3 (British Museum, Crowle Pennant).

*Plate 30*

St. James's Palace: Queen Caroline's Library, designed by William Kent in 1737 and demolished in 1825. A: interior (Westminster City Library). B: an alternative design by Kent (Sir John Soane's Museum, Fauntleroy Pennant, vol. ii).

*Plate 31*

A. St. James's Palace from the north-east, drawn by J. C. Buckler in 1827 (British Museum, Crace Views, Portfolio xi, no. 34).

B. Richmond Park: Queen Caroline's Hermitage  (British Museum, King's MS. 313).

Plate 32

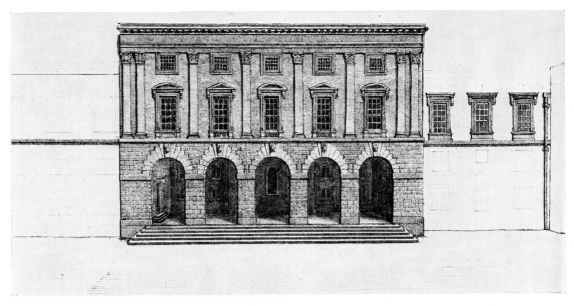

Old Somerset House, the gallery built by Queen Henrietta Maria in 1661–3
A: as represented by James Basire, *circa* 1776 (Society of Antiquaries of London).

B: as represented in a water-colour drawing by Thomas Sandby, *circa* 1770 (The Royal Library, Windsor).

*Plate 33*

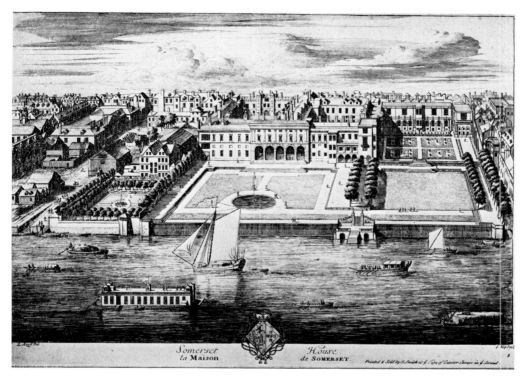

A. Old Somerset House, *circa* 1705 (from J. Kip, *Britannia Illustrata*, 1708).

B. New Somerset House, the Strand Front designed by Sir William Chambers (from Britton & Pugin, *The Public Buildings of London*, 1825).

Plate 34

*The Banqueting House*

*The Cockpit*

*The Queens Lodging*

*The Privey Stairs*

*The Kings Baggage*

*The Landing Place*

Part of WHITE-HALL to the THAMES

Whitehall Palace: two views from the river. A: from a painting of 1683 (Her Majesty the Queen, Kensington Palace). B: from Ogilby & Morgan's map of 1682 (British Museum, Crace Maps, Portfolio ii, 58, sheet 5).

*Plate 35*

WHITEHALL & St JAMES'S PARK. TIME OF CHARLES 2ᵈ BY DANCKER

Whitehall Palace from the park, from a painting of *circa* 1674 attributed to Hendrick Danckerts (the Trustees of the 8th Earl of Berkeley, deceased).

Plate 36

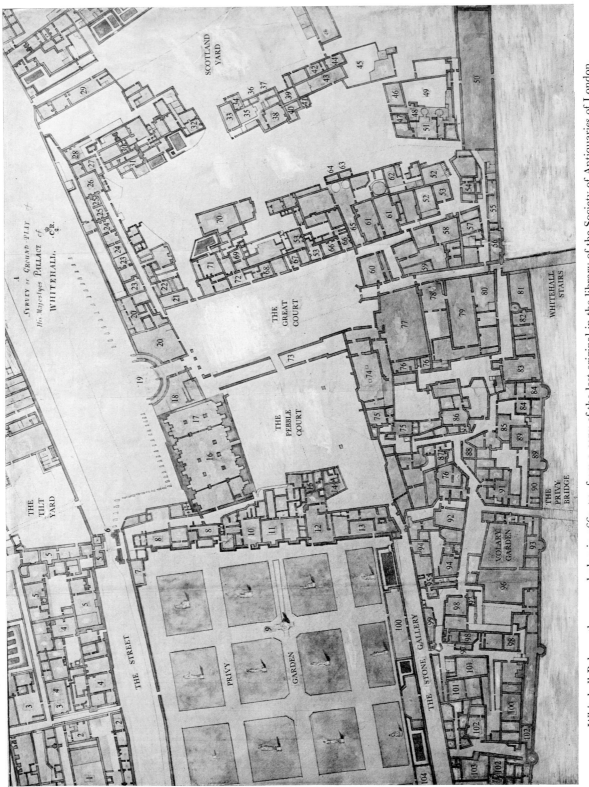

Whitehall Palace: the ground-plan in 1669–70, from a copy of the lost original in the library of the Society of Antiquaries of London.

KEY TO PLATE 36

*Plate 37*

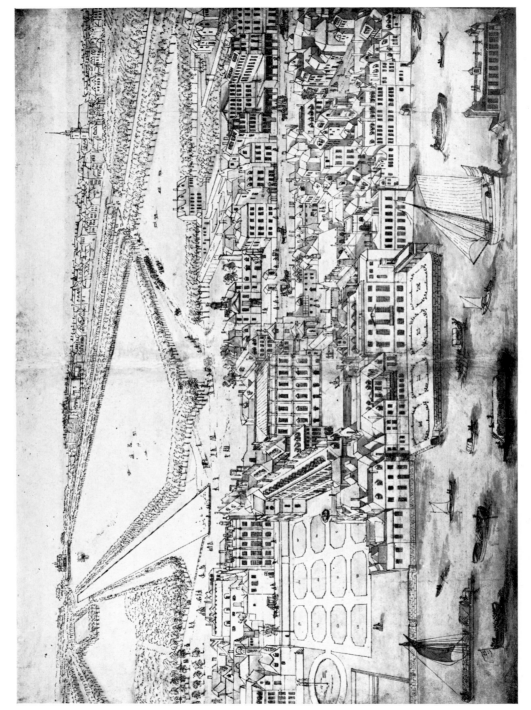

Whitehall Palace: a bird's-eye view from the river, *circa* 1695–7, attributed to Leonard Knyff (Westminster City Library).

Plate 38

His Majesty's Royal Banqueting & House of Whitehal London. 1713.

Whitehall Palace: view of the Banqueting House and gateway, by H. Terasson, 1713 (British Museum, Crace Views, Portfolio xvi, no. 17).

*Plate 39*

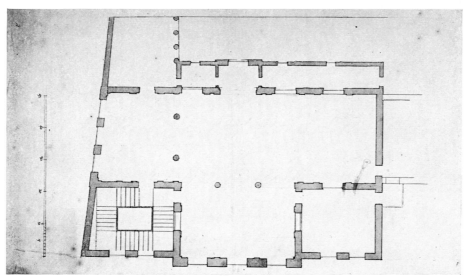

A. Design by Sir Christopher Wren for the altarpiece of the Chapel Royal, Whitehall, 1676 (All Souls College, Oxford, Wren Drawings, ii, 66).
B. Whitehall Palace, Sir Christopher Wren's plan for James II's Catholic Chapel, *circa* 1687 (All Souls College, Oxford, Wren Drawings, ii, 115*).

*Plate 40*

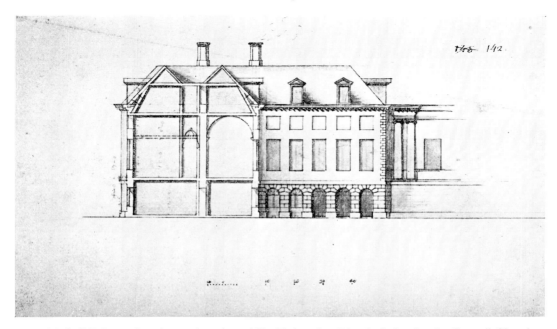

A. Whitehall Palace, elevation and section of Sir Christopher Wren's design for the Council Chamber block, *circa* 1685. (All Souls College, Oxford, Wren Drawings, iv, 142).

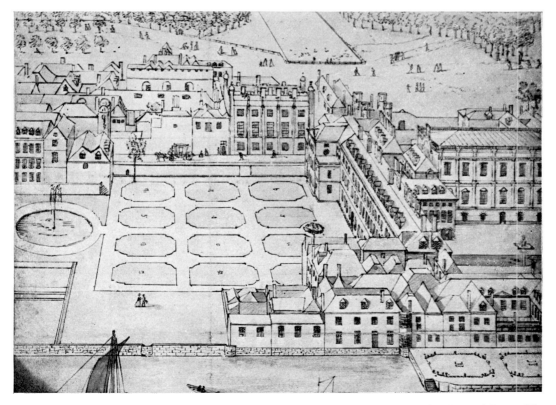

B. Whitehall Palace, detail from Knyff's view of *circa* 1695–7, showing the Privy Garden and James II's buildings (Westminster City Library).

*Plate 41*

Winchester Palace. A: view of Charles II's unfinished palace in the eighteenth century (Bodleian Library, Gough Maps 10). B: engraving in Milner's *History of Winchester* (1798–1801) showing the palace 'as intended to have been finish'd by Sir Christopher Wren'.

*Plate 42*

Windsor Castle, the Queen's Lodge built by George III, from two contemporary engravings in the Royal Library at Windsor. The Lower Lodge is seen in the background of the lower engraving.

*Plate 43*

Windsor Castle as remodelled by Hugh May for Charles II. A: St. George's Hall.
B: the King's Guard Chamber (from Pyne's *Royal Residences*, 1819).

*Plate 44*

Windsor Castle as remodelled by Hugh May for Charles II. A: view from the north by Paul Sandby, showing the Star Building. B: interior of the Upper Ward by Paul Sandby (the Royal Library, Windsor Castle).

Plate 45

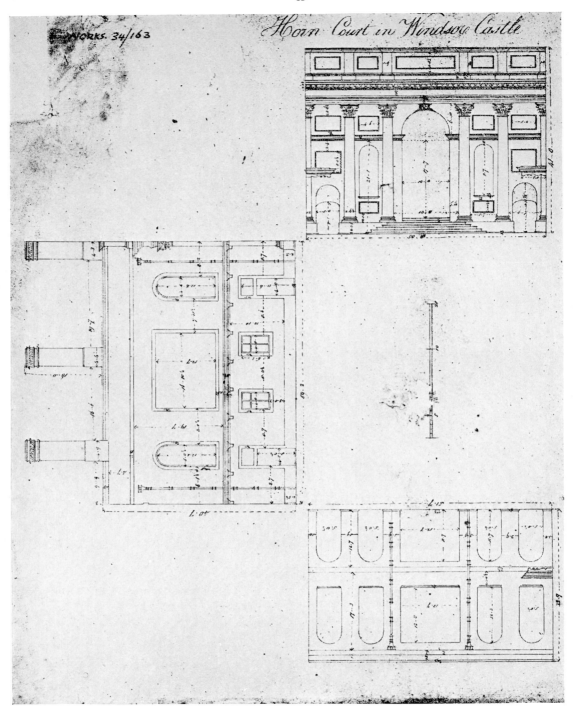

Windsor Castle: elevations of Horn Court as designed by Hugh May (P.R.O., Works 34/163).

*Plate 46*

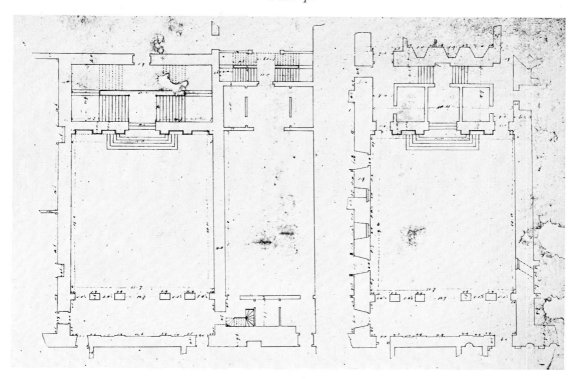

Windsor Castle: A: eighteenth-century plan of Horn Court as designed by Hugh May (P.R.O., Works 34/162). B: eighteenth-century elevation of the Star Building (Works 34/348).

*Plate* 47

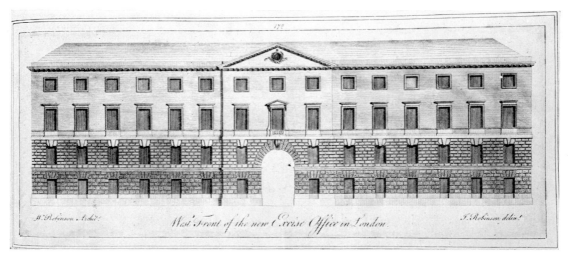

*West Front of the new Excise Office in London*

A. The Excise Office, Old Broad Street, as designed by William Robinson in 1768 (British Museum, Crowle Pennant, xii, f. 172).

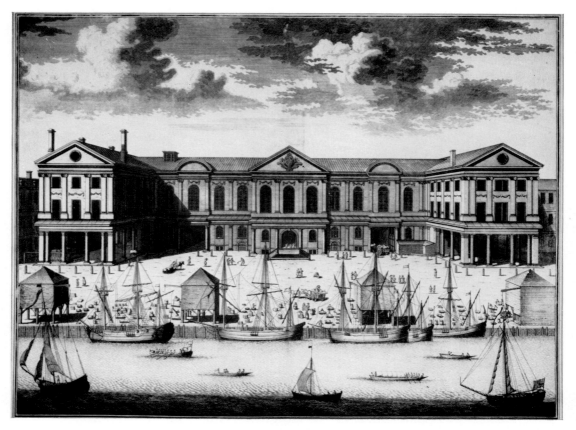

B. The London Custom House built in 1669–71 (British Museum, Crace Views, viii, 16).

Plate 48

The Rolls House in Chancery Lane designed by Colen Campbell and built in 1717–24, with the Chapel in the background (from R. W. Paul, *Vanishing London*, 1894).

*Plate 49*

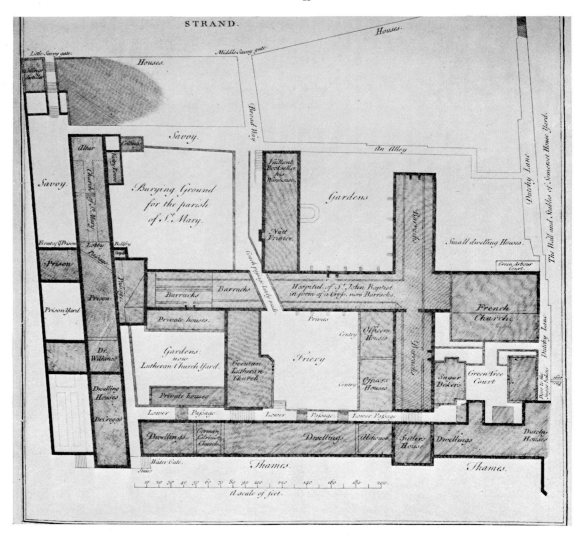

Plan of the former Savoy Hospital made by George Vertue in 1736, showing its division into barracks, dwellings and churches for foreign Protestant congregations (from *Vetusta Monumenta* ii, plate 14). Compare the plan in vol. iii, fig. 2.

*Plate 50*

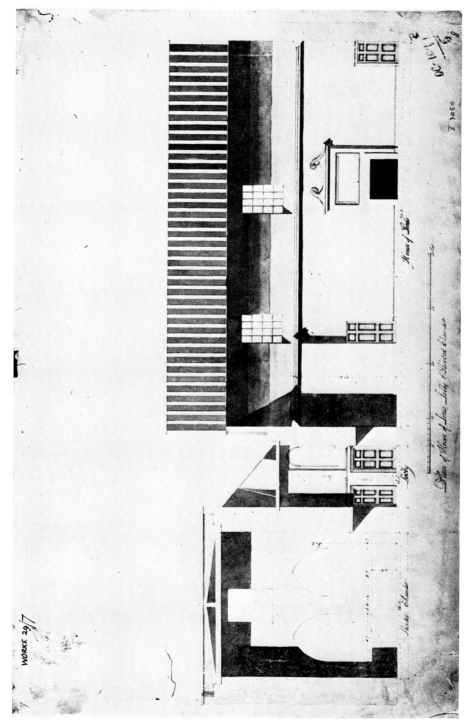

Westminster, a section through the Painted Chamber and the House of Lords in the reign of George III (P.R.O., Works 29/7).

*Plate 51*

ERS, the KING sitting on his Throne, the COMMONS attendin

Westminster, the House of Lords in the eighteenth century (from an engraving by John Pine dated 1742 (Bodleian Library, Gough Maps 23, f. 53).

Plate 52

Westminster, the House of Lords in course of demolition in 1823 (from a water-colour drawing by Sir John Soane, P.R.O., Works 29/17).

*Plate 53*

Westminster, the House of Commons in the eighteenth century (from an engraving by John Pine dated 1742 (Bodleian Library, Gough Maps 23, f. 54).

*Plate 54*

The House of Commons, details of the Speaker's Chair, the galleries, etc., drawn by Sir James Thornhill (G.L.C. Record Office).

*Plate 55*

A. Westminster Hall, the Gothic screen designed by William Kent in 1739 to enclose the Court of King's Bench (from J. Vardy, *Some Designs of Mr. Inigo Jones and Mr. William Kent*, 1744).

B. Westminster Hall, the Courts of Chancery and King's Bench in the seventeenth century (from an anonymous drawing in the British Museum, Department of Prints & Drawings, 1848–9–11–748).

*Plate 56*

A. The interior of the Court of King's Bench, showing the fittings designed by William Kent, and the ceiling inserted in 1755 (from Ackermann's *Microcosm of London*, 1808–10).

B. The interior of the Court of Common Pleas constructed outside the west wall of Westminster Hall in 1740–1 (from Ackermann's *Microcosm of London*, 1808–10).

*Plate 57*

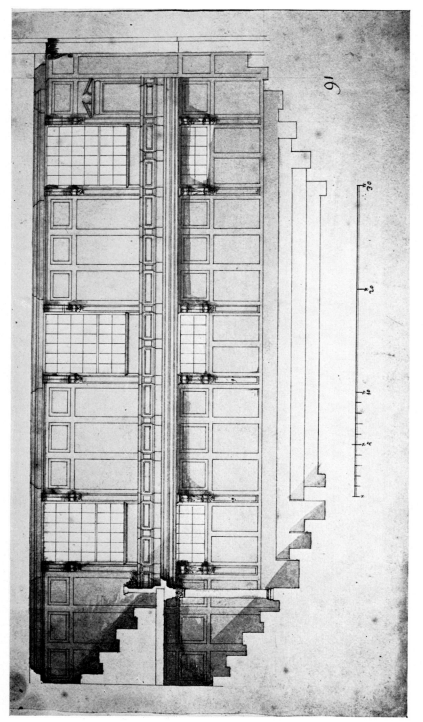

Sir Christopher Wren's design for refitting the House of Commons in 1692
(All Souls College, Oxford, Wren Drawings iv, 91).

*Plate 58*

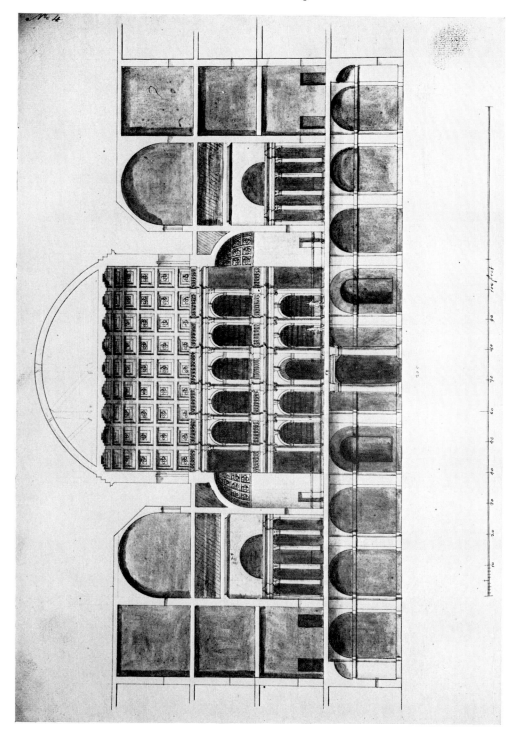

Section of William Kent's design for new Houses of Parliament made in 1733 (Sir John Soane's Museum, Drawer 35). For the plan, see Plate 59.

*Plate 59*

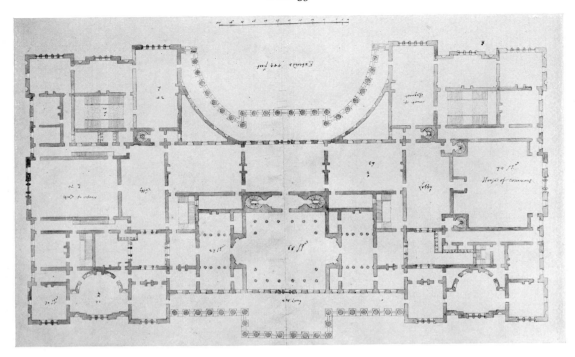

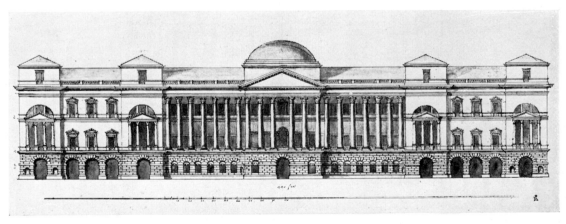

Plan and elevation of William Kent's design for new Houses of Parliament made in 1733 (Victoria & Albert Museum, 93 H.20).

*Plate 60*

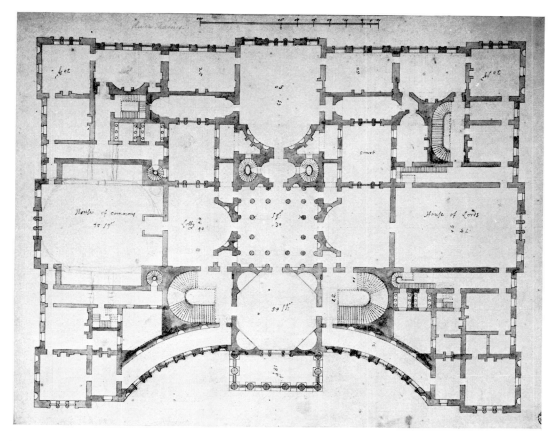

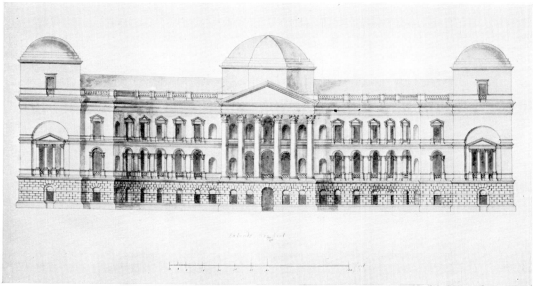

Plan and elevation of William Kent's revised design for new Houses of Parliament, made early in 1739 (Sir John Soane's Museum, Drawer 35).

*Plate 61*

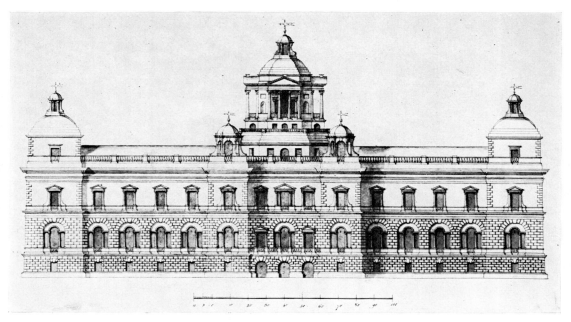

A. Elevation of the design for the new Houses of Parliament submitted in December 1739 (P.R.O., Works 29/3358).

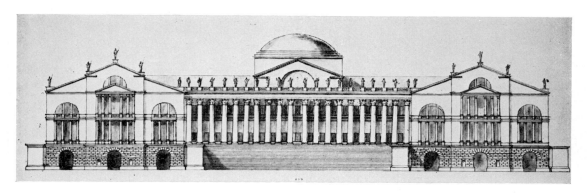

B. Elevation of one of William Kent's designs for the new Houses of Parliament (P.R.O., Works 29/3358).

*Plate 62*

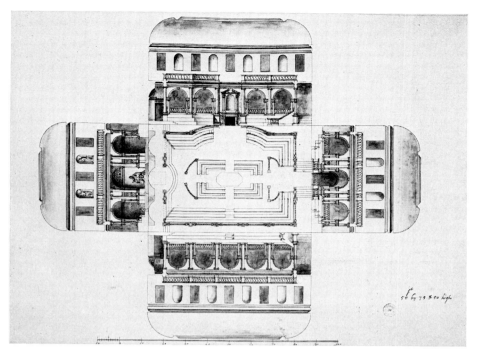

A. Design by William Kent for the House of Lords, 1739 (Sir John Soane's Museum, Drawer 35).

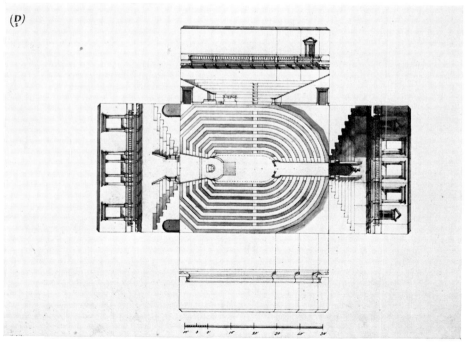

B. The design for the House of Commons approved by the Speaker in December 1739 (P.R.O., Works 29/3358).

*Plate 63*

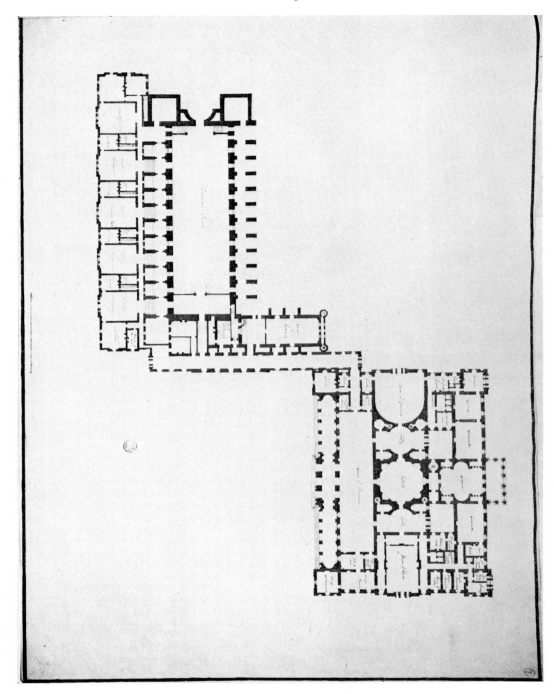

Plan of the new Houses of Parliament and Law Courts on the lines envisaged in December 1739 (Sir John Soane's Museum, Drawer 35).

Plate 64

The 'Stone Building' in St. Margaret's Lane, built between 1755 and 1770 to the designs of John Vardy and Kenton Couse. A: a sketch by William Capon dated 1783 (Westminster City Library). B: an elevation in Sir John Soane's Museum dated 1793 (Drawer xxxv, set 5, no. 5).

*Plate 65*

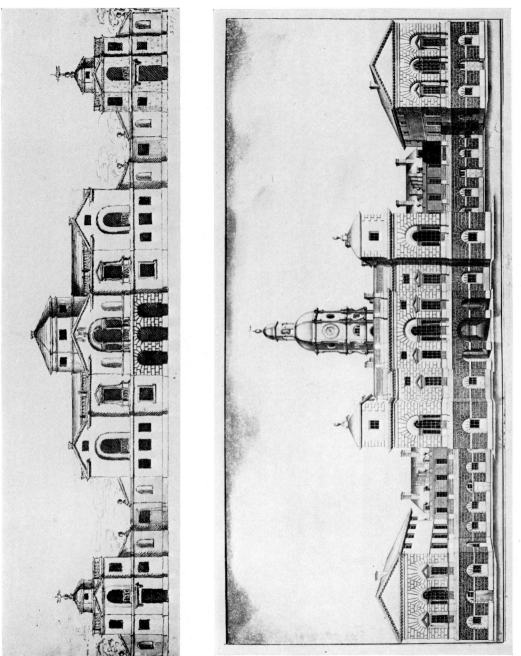

The Horse Guards, Whitehall. A: design made by William Kent before his death in 1748 (Victoria & Albert Museum). B: the building as erected in 1750–9 (British Museum, Crace Views, xii, no. 50).

*Plate 66*

Engraving by John Vardy of the Horse Guards Building and the Treasury,
dated 1752 (British Museum, Crace Views, xii, no. 47).

Plate 67

GEORGIUS II REX ET CAROLINA REGINA

*Triumphal Arch Erected and Painted on the West end of Westminster Hall
for the Coronation of his Maj.ty King George the Second and Queen Caroline.
October the 11.th 1727.
With the Ceremonie of the Kings Champion attended by the Lord High Constable and the Earl Marshal.*

Triumphal Arch in Westminster Hall designed by William Kent for the coronation of George II,
1727 (British Museum, King's Maps, xxiv, 24 n).

*Plate 68*

Design by William Oram for the Triumphal Arch in Westminster Hall for the coronation of George III, 1761 (P.R.O., Works 36/68/32).

Plate 69

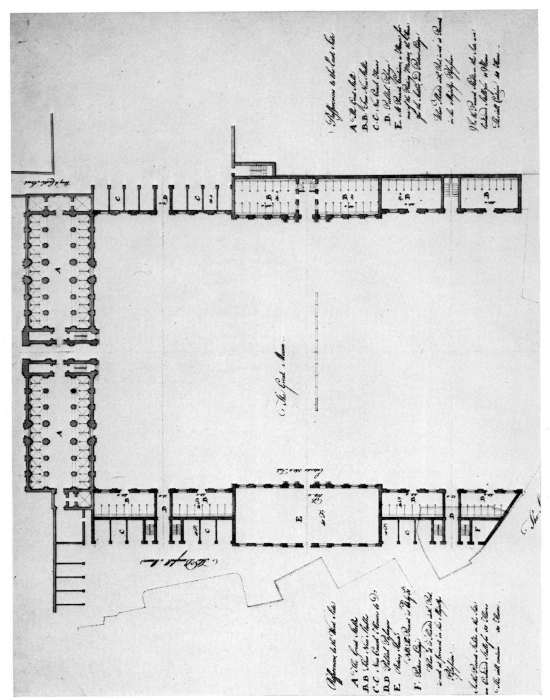

Plan for rebuilding the Royal Mews at Charing Cross (see page 213) (R.I.B.A. Drawings Collection).

# Index

486 *The History of the King's Works*

Printed in England for Her Majesty's Stationery Office by Butler & Tanner Ltd, Frome and London
Dd 503946 K16 3/76